The Standard for Project Management

and

A Guide to the Project Management Body of Knowledge

PMBOK® Guide
Eighth Edition

Project Management Institute

Library of Congress Cataloging-in-Publication Data

Names: Project Management Institute issuing body
Title: The standard for project management and a guide to the project management body of knowledge (PMBOK guide) / Project Management Institute.
Other titles: Guide to the project management body of knowledge (PMBOK guide) | PMBOK guide
Description: Eighth edition. | Newtown Square, Pennsylvania : Project Management Institute, [2025] | Includes bibliographical references and index. | Summary: "A Guide to the Project Management Body of Knowledge (PMBOK® Guide) remains the premier resource for project professionals around the world. The Eighth Edition is the most evidence-based and community-driven revision to date, shaped by nearly 48,000 data points, global practitioner insights, and two rounds of public feedback. Reflecting the evolving needs of the profession, this edition delivers a more accessible, streamlined, and adaptable approach to project management across industries, sectors, and development methods. What's new in the Eighth Edition: Updated definitions of foundational terms and concepts, aligned to current global practice and language accessibility A simplified set of six actionable project management principles The reimagining of Process Groups as five practical Focus Areas Integration of technical ways of working and other core concepts into seven comprehensive Project Performance Domains, including 40 newly evolved processes Key Benefits Bullet Points: With over 5 million copies in circulation, the PMBOK® Guide, issued by Project Management Institute, is the enduring global standard for project management Offers adaptable practices to suit a wide variety of industries, development approaches, and organizational needs Provides globally accessible language and concepts for broader application and easier understanding Equips practitioners to better focus on value delivery, not just output execution"-- Provided by publisher.
Identifiers: LCCN 2025036269 (print) | LCCN 2025036270 (ebook) | ISBN 9781628258295 paperback | ISBN 9781628258301 epub
Subjects: LCSH: Project management
Classification: LCC HD69.P75 G845 2025 (print) | LCC HD69.P75 (ebook) | DDC 658.4/04--dc23/eng/20250828
LC record available at https://lccn.loc.gov/2025036269
LC ebook record available at https://lccn.loc.gov/2025036270

A Guide to the Project Management Body of Knowledge (PMBOK® Guide)—Eighth Edition and The Standard for Project Management

ISBN: 978-1-62825-829-5 (paperback)
ISBN: 978-1-62825-830-1 (ebook)

Published by:
Project Management Institute, Inc.
18 Campus Blvd., Ste. 150
Newtown Square, Pennsylvania 19073-3299 USA
Phone: +1 610 356 4600
PMI.org
Online Support: www.pmi.org/about/contact

The paper used in this book complies with the Permanent Paper Standard issued by the National Information Standards Organization (Z39.48—1992).

This publication has been designed with sustainability in mind, using practices that minimize paper usage and reduce environmental impact.

10 9 8 7 6 5 4 3 2 1

Notice

The Project Management Institute, Inc. (PMI) standards and guideline publications, of which the document contained herein is one, are developed through a voluntary consensus standards development process. This process brings together volunteers and/or seeks out the views of persons who have an interest in the topic covered by this publication. While PMI administers the process and establishes rules to promote fairness in the development of consensus, it does not write the document and it does not independently test, evaluate, or verify the accuracy or completeness of any information or the soundness of any judgments contained in its standards and guideline publications.

PMI disclaims liability for any personal injury, property or other damages of any nature whatsoever, whether special, indirect, consequential or compensatory, directly or indirectly resulting from the publication, use of application, or reliance on this document. PMI disclaims and makes no guaranty or warranty, expressed or implied, as to the accuracy or completeness of any information published herein, and disclaims and makes no warranty that the information in this document will fulfill any of your particular purposes or needs. PMI does not undertake to guarantee the performance of any individual manufacturer or seller's products or services by virtue of this standard or guide.

In publishing and making this document available, PMI is not undertaking to render professional or other services for or on behalf of any person or entity, nor is PMI undertaking to perform any duty owed by any person or entity to someone else. Anyone using this document should rely on his or her own independent judgment or, as appropriate, seek the advice of a competent professional in determining the exercise of reasonable care in any given circumstances. Information and other standards on the topic covered by this publication may be available from other sources, which the user may wish to consult for additional views or information not covered by this publication.

PMI has no power, nor does it undertake to police or enforce compliance with the contents of this document. PMI does not certify, test, or inspect products, designs, or installations for safety or health purposes. Any certification or other statement of compliance with any health or safety-related information in this document shall not be attributable to PMI and is solely the responsibility of the certifier or maker of the statement.

Preface

PMI is committed to representing the voice of the project management community. That commitment drives a pursuit of practitioner input and continuous feedback on how the content of *A Guide to the Project Management Body of Knowledge (PMBOK® Guide)* should evolve.

With the *PMBOK® Guide*—Eighth Edition, PMI delivers the most evidence-based revision to date. Moreover, community input inspired a design that is simultaneously broad in scope and inclusive of all industries and approaches.

Evidence-Based and Globally Represented

To support the creation of this eighth edition, PMI conducted qualitative and quantitative research over the course of 2023 that yielded approximately 48,000 data points.

With this data in hand, a highly selective process was conducted to identify volunteers. That selection process yielded two globally diverse teams of subject matter experts. The development team consisted of 12 subject matter experts with a diverse background from 10 different countries across five continents; the review team featured 12 members from eight different countries, altogether representing dozens of industries and approaches. Over 18 months, the two teams worked independently in a double-blind fashion, iteratively developing and then validating the material in this eighth edition.

That work was validated and refined by two rounds of public community feedback, yielding more than 12,000 comments from project management practitioners around the world.

Summary of Changes

The majority of changes can be grouped into four main categories:

- Key term and concept updates,
- Principle refinement,
- Reintroduction of Process Groups as Focus Areas, and
- Project management performance domain updates.

Update of Key Terms and Concepts

This edition presents updated definitions of key terms and concepts, such as the core definitions for *project*, *project management*, and others. These updates are based on shifts in marketplace expectations encountered by portfolio, program, and project practitioners. While some of these shifts are recent, others accumulated over the last decade or longer. Shifts that motivate these updates include but are not limited to the following:

- **Timeliness.** Some of the key terms and concepts have not been updated in more than 40 years. In that time, the discipline of project management has meaningfully expanded and matured to merit updates.
- **Global accessibility.** The project management community is more global than ever before. The language used in some of the historical definitions has been unfriendly to international translation and nonnative English speakers.
- **Focus on value.** Earlier understandings of project management focused on efficient delivery of work within constraints (e.g., scope, schedule, compliance, quality). However, the current marketplace expects project management to address an expanding set of concepts, including the project's value proposition.

Refined Principles

This edition defines six project management principles that guide effective practice. These six principles are the result of a community-driven simplification of the principles defined in the previous edition's 12 principles. In the eighth edition, principles have been refined to be more actionable, and consolidated to minimize overlap, duplication, and confusion.

Additional details on the refinement of the project management principles can be found in Appendix X5: Evolution of the *PMBOK® Guide*.

Reintroducing Process Groups as Focus Areas

This edition presents five Project Management Focus Areas: Initiating, Planning, Executing, Monitoring and Controlling, and Closing. Most projects feature a life cycle that involves actions and activities related to these Focus Areas.

Historically, these five Focus Areas were presented as logical categories of formal project management processes, known as the Project Management Process Groups. In contrast, today's projects often satisfy these five concepts through the use of multiple approaches. In addition to formal processes, project life cycles are often managed by informal practices and/or flexible policies as well. As such, these historical Process Groups have been reimagined as Focus Areas.

Updated Performance Domains

Community input for the *PMBOK® Guide*—Eighth Edition overwhelmingly recommended updating the project performance domains to include and integrate various project management concepts described in previous editions. The concepts included are as follows:

- Project Management Knowledge Areas are fields or areas of specialization that are commonly employed when managing projects. They are historically defined in prior editions as a set of processes associated with a particular topic. This edition synthesizes those Knowledge Areas with other accepted concepts into seven project management performance domains.
- Project management processes are a formalized series of logically connected activities that manage a project throughout its life cycle. This edition includes a selection of 40 nonprescriptive processes that can be adapted to varied approaches, life cycles, and environments.
- Tailoring considerations and examples are inserted into each performance domain. These considerations and examples illustrate how practitioners can apply context-specific adjustments to individual processes or the overall performance domain.

Table of Contents

The Standard for Project Management

A Guide to the Project Management Body of Knowledge (PMBOK® Guide)

List of Figures and Tables

The Standard for Project Management

Figures

Tables

A Guide to the Project Management Body of Knowledge (PMBOK® Guide)

Figures

Tables

The Standard for Project Management

Approved American National Standard

ANSI

ANSI/PMI 99-001-2025

Section 1

Introduction

1.1 Purpose of *The Standard for Project Management*

The Standard for Project Management provides a basis for understanding project management and how it facilitates intended outcomes. This standard applies to projects across all industries, including business, government, and nonprofit sectors; geographic regions; organizational size; or development approach (e.g., predictive, adaptive, or hybrid). The standard describes the system within which projects operate. This system includes governance, possible functions, the project environment, organizational culture, cross-functional teams, interactions with portfolios and programs, and considerations for the relationships between project management and other management disciplines, including product management.

The standard describes how project management creates value and benefits in organizations as well as how organizational and project leaders can harness the power of project management for success. Effective and efficient project management is a strategic competency within organizations. Projects enable organizations to:

- Align their project deliverables to business strategy and associated goals,
- Compete more effectively,
- Ensure long-term sustainability and growth,
- Drive positive change,
- Respond to the impact of business environment changes, and
- Create a positive impact for society at large.

The project management landscape has undergone significant changes in recent years, shaped by evolving global challenges such as climate change, resource constraints, geopolitical instability, and widening inequalities, alongside advancements in technology like artificial intelligence (AI).

Adaptive project management approaches, including but not limited to agile practices, have become increasingly important. These approaches enable project teams to tailor their strategies to meet the unique challenges and dynamic conditions of each project. While this standard discusses relevant agile practices in project management, it is important to note that the practice of agile extends beyond project management.

Simultaneously, generative AI (GenAI) is contributing to the field of project management by offering advanced tools and capabilities that, when used responsibly and correctly, can potentially improve project outcomes. Artificial intelligence–driven solutions can analyze vast amounts of data to provide actionable insights, predict risks, and recommend optimal courses of action. This technology can enhance decision-making processes, automate routine tasks, and support more accurate forecasting and planning. When applied effectively, AI can help project managers focus on performing strategic activities, managing stakeholder engagement, fostering innovation, and driving continuous improvement within the context of their projects. However, the impact of using AI depends on factors such as the quality of system inputs and human oversight.

In this evolving landscape, the role of a project manager continues to expand beyond traditional organizing skills. Project practitioners should be able to navigate complex environments, leverage emerging technologies, and align project outcomes with organizational strategic objectives. In today's business environment, project managers should be skilled strategists and change managers, capable of driving value to their organization, industry, and situation. While no one person can be an expert in all these things, the expectation in the modern workplace remains the same. Therefore, the practice of project management now requires excellence in an expanding array of disciplines.

The Standard for Project Management serves as a foundational guide for project management practitioners, providing a common language and framework that can be applied across various industries, methodologies, and technological advancements. The standard supports organizations and project professionals in navigating the complexities of modern project management, ensuring consistency and effectiveness in project delivery while allowing for the flexibility needed in today's dynamic business environment. By applying the standard, organizations can better position themselves to achieve strategic objectives, drive innovation, maintain competitiveness, and contribute to societal impact.

1.2 Key Terms and Concepts

The Standard for Project Management reflects the advancement of the profession. Organizations expect projects to deliver outcomes. Project managers are expected to deliver projects that create value for the organization and stakeholders within the organization's system for value delivery. The following terms are defined to provide context for the content in this standard:

- **Artifact.** A document or other item created during a portfolio, program, or project to help manage it and provide information to the project team, stakeholders, and management.

- **Benefit.** A gain or asset realized by the organization and other stakeholders as the result of outcomes delivered.
- **Outcome.** An end result or consequence of a process or project. Outcomes encompass the long-term effects, changes, or value generated by the project's deliverables, which can be either positive or negative. Positive outcomes, often termed "benefits," may include enhancements in performance, efficiency, or customer satisfaction. Conversely, negative outcomes, known as "disbenefits," may involve unintended adverse effects or costs. Evaluating outcomes is essential to determine how effectively a project has achieved its intended objectives and to understand its overall impact.
- **Output.** A product, result, or service generated by a process. May be an input to a successor process.
- **Portfolio.** A collection of programs, projects, and operations managed as a group to maximize overall value delivery and achieve strategic objectives, meet mandatory obligations, or generate income streams. Related activities may include subsidiary portfolios (subportfolios) and operations.
- **Product.** An artifact that is produced, is quantifiable, and can be either an end item in itself or a component item. "Product" is an overarching term that includes tangible (physical goods) and intangible (digital goods and services) items.
- **Program.** A group of related projects and program activities managed in a coordinated manner to obtain benefits not available from managing them individually. These interrelated activities can serve program components to enable the program to deliver the highest value and may include subsidiary programs.
- **Project.** A temporary initiative in a unique context undertaken to create value. The temporary nature of a project indicates a beginning and an end to the project work or a phase of the project work. A project's unique context can be driven by its distinct goals, environmental conditions, approaches, stakeholders, or other dimensions. Projects can be stand-alone efforts or part of a portfolio or program.
- **Project management.** The application of knowledge, skills, tools, and techniques to project activities to meet or exceed the intended value. Meeting or exceeding value in project management does not mean to endorse or accept gold plating or scope creep, but to emphasize a value-driven decision-making process, helping to ensure that the final project outcome satisfies the stakeholders' needs.
- **Project management office (PMO).** Organizational entities, typically established as departments or teams, primarily tasked with centralizing activities related to the management of portfolios, programs, and/or projects. The nature of these activities can vary according to the unique needs of each organization.
- **Project management team.** The members of the project team who are directly involved in project management activities.
- **Project manager.** The person assigned by the performing organization to lead the team that is responsible for achieving the project objectives. Project managers perform a variety of functions such as facilitating the project team's work to achieve the intended outcomes and managing the processes to bring about those outcomes in order to enable value delivery. Additional functions are identified in Section 2.4.

- **Project success.** The consensus view across intended beneficiaries, other stakeholders, and project participants that a project was perceived to have delivered value that was worth the effort and expense.
- **Project team.** A set of individuals performing the work of the project to achieve its objectives.
- **Value.** The excess of financial and nonfinancial benefits over investment that is gained from achieving the goals of a portfolio, program, or project. Different stakeholders perceive value in different ways, which can be explained quantitatively or qualitatively. Thus, organizations may focus on business value as determined by performance metrics or finances, such as return on investment (ROI). Customers may interpret value as the convenience offered by a given product or service. Governments and nongovernmental organizations (NGOs) may prioritize the value of societal impact on groups of people and their communities and environments.
- **Value delivery system.** A collection of strategic business activities aimed at building, sustaining, and/or advancing an organization. Portfolios, programs, projects, products, and operations can all be part of an organization's system for value delivery. This system enables organizations to align their work with their strategic objectives and achieve desired outcomes.

For other terms used in this standard, refer to the glossary and the *PMI Lexicon of Project Management Terms* [1].[1]

1.3 Foundational Elements of Project Management

This section outlines the essential elements required to understand and effectively engage in project management. The section explores key project management perspectives and relationships that are crucial for effective project delivery and organizational success, covering concepts such as the following:

- How projects create value and drive organizational change;
- The link between organizational governance and project governance during project initiation;
- The differences between operations management and project management; and
- The relationships among portfolio, program, and project management, as well as their connections to operations management.

By examining these foundational elements, project management practitioners can gain a comprehensive understanding of how projects fit into the broader organizational context and contribute to value delivery.

1.3.1 Characteristics of a Project

Organizations expect projects to deliver value in addition to outputs and artifacts. Project managers are expected to deliver project outcomes that create value for the organization and stakeholders within the organization's system for value delivery.

[1] The numbers in brackets refer to the numbered list of references at the end of this standard.

Organizational work encompasses both operations and projects. Although both are expected to deliver value beyond outputs and artifacts, they differ in their value-creation processes. The following terms are defined to provide context for these distinctions and the broader content of this standard:

- **Temporary.** Projects are initiated to create value by producing tangible and/or intangible deliverables such as products, services, or other results. Unlike ongoing operations, projects are temporary and have a defined beginning and end. Although projects are temporary, their deliverables often persist beyond the project's conclusion. Usually, a project ends when one or more of the following conditions are met:
    - The project's objectives have been achieved;
    - A governing body, the project sponsor, or the project team has determined that the objectives will not or cannot be met;
    - Resources (funding, human, or physical) are exhausted or no longer available;
    - Due to changes in strategy, priorities, or the external environment, the need for the project no longer exists; or
    - The project is terminated for other reasons such as legal, regulatory, or compliance issues.
- **Unique context.** A unique context in projects refers to the specific conditions and environments that distinguish one project from another, even if they have otherwise similar characteristics. This uniqueness arises from factors such as differences in goals, scope, duration, location, technology, quality, costs, risks, resources, and stakeholders involved in the project. Even if two projects aim for the same value or objectives, each project differs due to the context in which it is carried out. These differences require tailored management approaches to meet the specific needs and challenges of each project. As a result, the unique context of each project requires customized strategies for success.

For example, a large housing development project may involve a single construction vendor in a single government district. However, each of those housing units may involve varying lenders and buyers, distinct customization requests, and unique grading requirements from one plot to another.

- **Value creation through organizational change.** Projects, in pursuit of value, drive change in organizations. From a business perspective, a project's purpose is to move an organization from one state to another to achieve a specific objective (see Figure 1-1). Before the project begins, an organization is in its current state. The desired result of the change driven by the project is described as the future state. For some projects, this shift may involve creating a transition state where several steps are taken in a structured manner to achieve the future state. The successful completion of a project results in the organization moving to the future state and achieving value for the organization, as defined by key stakeholders.

1.3.2 Connecting Organizational Governance and Project Governance

Organizational governance provides direction and control through policies, processes, procedures, and decisions to meet strategic and operational goals. Typically overseen by an executive committee or organizational leaders, organizational governance helps ensure transparency, oversight, compliance, resiliency, and adaptability for its stakeholders. In many organizations, organizational governance is inspired by the country's laws, business domain regulations, industry standards, and

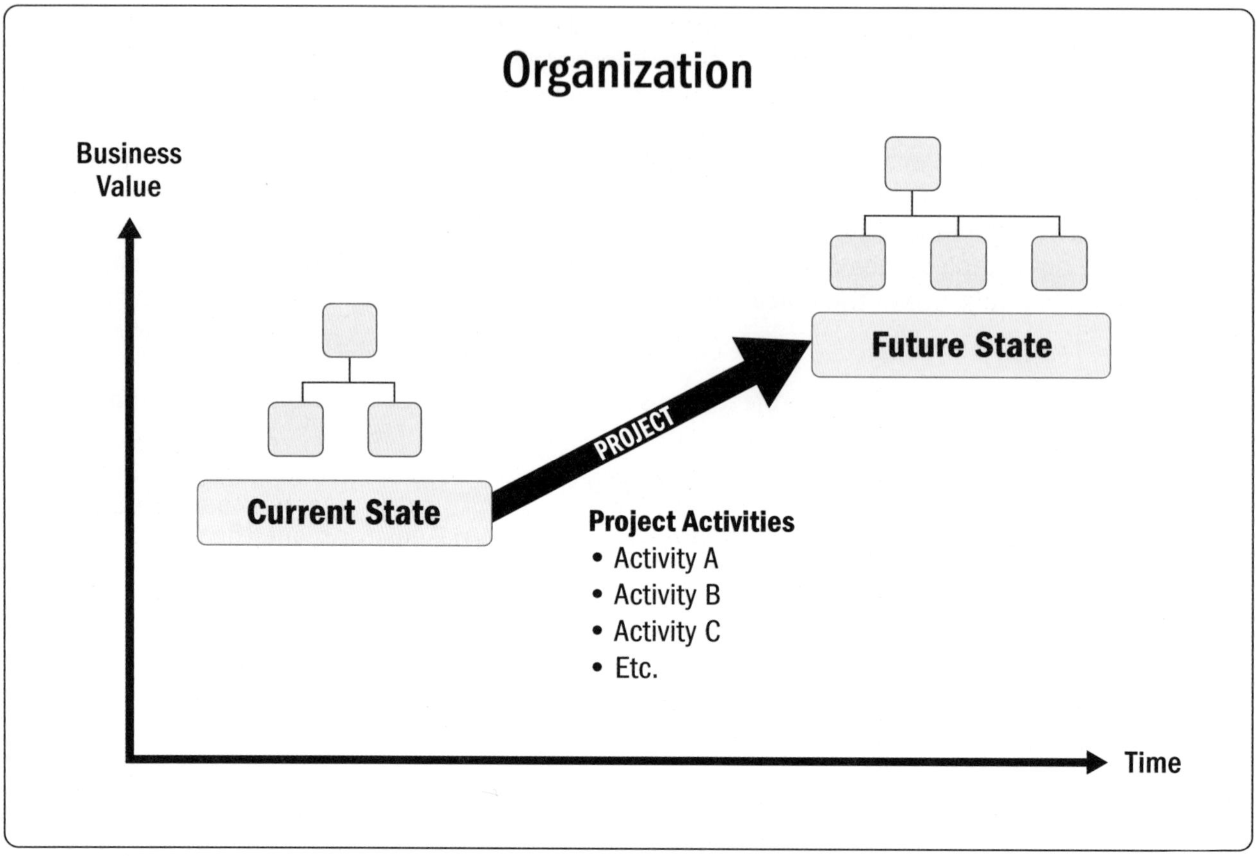

Figure 1-1. Impact of Projects on Organizational States

custom policies that are formed by the organization's unique context. This context can influence the governance of portfolios, programs, and projects in several ways, including the following:

- Enforcing legal, regulatory, and compliance requirements;
- Defining ethical, social, and environmental responsibilities;
- Specifying operational, legal, financial, and risk policies;
- Promoting the alignment of portfolios, programs, and projects with strategic objectives at different hierarchical levels;
- Ensuring that initiatives contribute to the organizational mission and vision: and
- Facilitating decision-making that maximizes delivered value connected to the system for value delivery.

Project governance is the adaptable framework that guides project management activities to create value through a unique product, service, or result aligned with organizational, strategic, and operational goals. Governance provides structure, systems and processes, roles, responsibilities, and decision-making models, such as RACI (responsible, accountable, consulted, informed) matrices or governance boards, to manage projects effectively. Governance frameworks can also ensure alignment with stakeholder expectations by defining accountability and communication protocols.

Additionally, project governance helps prioritize initiatives and allocate resources to support strategic objectives. For instance, a steering committee in a product launch project may oversee milestones, enforce quality standards, and resolve escalated issues. Further details on the Governance performance domain are discussed in the second part of this publication (see Section 2.1 of *A Guide to the Project Management Body of Knowledge [PMBOK® Guide]*) [2].

In summary, while organizational governance provides the overall direction and control for the entire organization, project governance focuses on the specific processes and frameworks that should be implemented to manage individual projects effectively. Both are essential for ensuring that projects contribute to the organization's strategic objectives and are executed successfully.

1.3.2.1 Project Initiation

Organizational leaders authorize projects in response to organizational strategic-objective realization and stakeholder needs. Projects enable organizations to make necessary changes to address these factors. The factors can be categorized into several areas, including the following:

- Meeting regulatory, legal, or social requirements;
- Satisfying stakeholder requests or needs;
- Implementing or changing business or technological strategies; and
- Creating, improving, or fixing products, processes, organizations, or services.

By responding to these factors, leaders can enhance an organization's viability. Projects provide the means to make these changes and should ultimately link to the organization's strategic objectives and business value.

1.3.3 Operations and Project Management

Operations management focuses on the efficient, effective production of products and/or services. Additionally, operations management helps ensure that business operations are conducted efficiently and effectively by utilizing optimal resources to meet customer demands and deliver value. As such, operations management is concerned with managing processes that transform inputs (e.g., materials, components, energy, and labor) into outputs (e.g., products, goods, services, and/or other results). Operations management is distinct from formal project management as outlined in this standard.

Changes in business or organizational operations can be the focus of a project, particularly when significant changes are required due to new products or service delivery offerings. Ongoing operations are outside of the scope of a project. However, there are intersecting points where the two areas cross. For example, projects can intersect with operations at various points during a product life cycle, such as the following:

- When developing new products or services, upgrading offerings, or expanding outputs;
- While improving product or service delivery operations or their development process;
- At the end of the product life cycle; and
- At each closeout phase or iteration.

At determined points, deliverables, human resources, and knowledge are transferred between the project and operations for implementation of the delivered work. These transfers help ensure the seamless integration of project outcomes into the organization's operational framework. This implementation may occur through a transfer of project resources or knowledge to operations or through a transfer of operational resources to the project. Engaging operations teams early in project planning is beneficial and can significantly influence the long-term success and sustainability of a project. This is when the project is typically handed over to operations to sustain and use the results of the project.

1.3.4 Relationship of Portfolio, Program, Project, and Operations Management

By utilizing project management principles, processes, tools, and techniques, organizations can effectively achieve their goals and objectives while delivering value. Portfolios, programs, projects, and operations are integral components of an organization, each serving interconnected roles.

Projects are often managed as stand-alone initiatives but they can also be part of larger portfolios or programs. When projects are grouped together into a program, they are managed in a coordinated manner to obtain benefits not available from managing them individually. Programs drive significant organizational change; they are not merely large projects. Programs aim to achieve organizational change and improvement by connecting resources and aligning projects strategically to create synergies. This integration maximizes generated value, enhances efficiency, and delivers value that individual projects cannot achieve on their own.

Some organizations use a portfolio to manage multiple programs and projects that are underway at any given time. A portfolio is a collection of programs, projects, and operations managed as a group to maximize overall value delivery and achieve strategic objectives, meet mandatory obligations, or generate income streams. Portfolio management involves selecting, prioritizing, managing, and optimizing an organization's programs and projects in line with its strategic goals, obligations (legal or otherwise), or business objectives. This holistic view helps ensure that resources are allocated efficiently and that the portfolio delivers maximum value.

Portfolios, programs, projects, and operations often engage with the same stakeholders and may compete for the same resources. Portfolio, program, and project managers should work together with operations leaders to maintain a balanced approach to resource allocation and stakeholder engagement. Overlap and competition for resources can otherwise threaten the organization's strategic objectives.

Figure 1-2 illustrates a sample portfolio indicating the relationships among the organizational components (i.e., programs, projects, shared resources, and stakeholders). Organizational and portfolio planning impact these components through prioritization based on risks, funding, and other considerations. The portfolio view allows organizations to see how the strategic goals are reflected in the portfolio. This portfolio view also enables the implementation and coordination of appropriate portfolio, program, and project governance. Coordinated governance allows for the authorized allocation of human, financial, and physical resources based on expected performance and benefits.

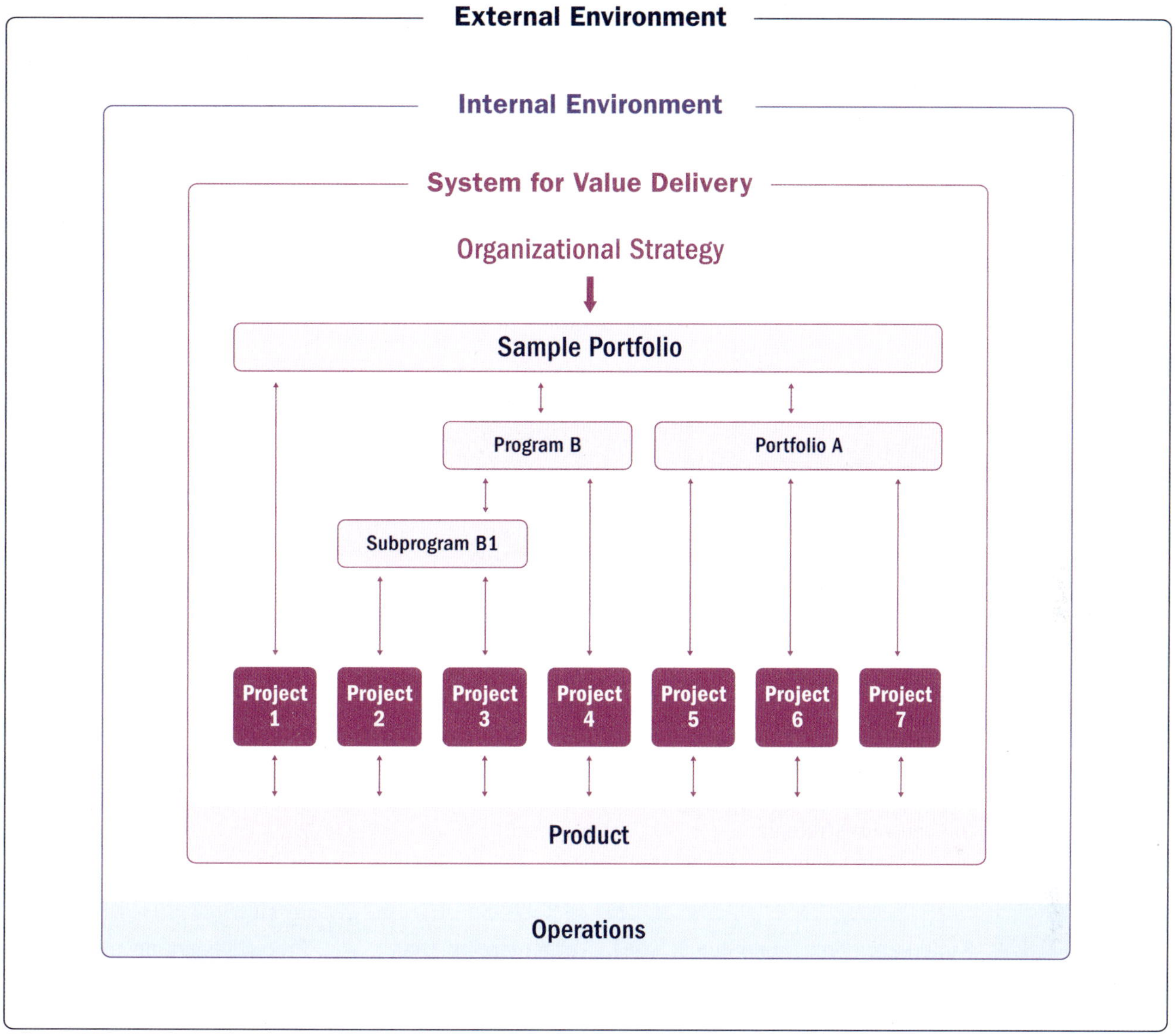

Figure 1-2. A Framework for Managing Portfolios, Programs, Projects, and Operations

Table 1-1 gives a comparative overview of portfolios, programs, and projects from an organizational perspective. The table highlights key differences and similarities in terms of definition, scope, change, planning, monitoring, and success criteria.

Table 1-1. Comparative Overview of Portfolios, Programs, and Projects

Organizational Project Management	Portfolios	Programs	Projects
Definition	A collection of programs, projects, and operations managed as a group to maximize overall value delivery and achieve strategic objectives, meet mandatory obligations, or generate income streams	A group of related projects and program activities managed in a coordinated manner to obtain benefits not available from managing them individually	A temporary initiative in a unique context undertaken to create value
Scope	Organizational scope aligned with strategic objectives	Includes and integrates the scope of its component projects and subprograms	Defined objectives, progressively elaborated
Change	Adaptable to continuous monitoring and adjustment to align with strategic priorities and changes in the environment	Adaptable to optimize value delivery at the program level	Adaptable to enable and maximize value delivery
Planning	Strategic planning, priority definition, and resource allocation between programs and projects	High-level planning that tracks interdependencies and aligns with program objectives	Predictive, adaptive, or hybrid, depending on project requirements and organizational context
Monitoring	Monitors strategic changes and resource allocation	Monitors progress of component projects and benefits realization	Monitoring and controlling outputs and value
Success	Measured by strategic value delivery, overall change management success, and alignment with organizational vision and mission	Measured by the program's ability to collectively deliver benefits and value and achieve strategic objectives	Measured by delivered value that was worth the effort and expense, including quality, timeliness, budget compliance, sustainability, and stakeholder satisfaction

Section 2

A System for Value Delivery

The information in this section provides a context for a value delivery system, the project environment, product management, project functions, and project management roles as follows:

- **Creating Value.** Section 2.1 describes how projects operate within a system to produce value or enhance value production capabilities for organizations and their stakeholders.
- **Project Environment.** Section 2.2 identifies internal and external factors that can influence projects and the delivery of value.
- **Product Management Considerations.** Section 2.3 identifies the ways portfolios, programs, projects, and products relate to one another.
- **Functions Associated With Projects.** Section 2.4 identifies the functions that support project delivery.
- **Project Management Roles.** Section 2.5 describes the various roles of those involved in managing projects and their functions.

2.1 Creating Value

Projects exist in both large and small contexts. These contexts can range from government agencies, enterprises, or contractual arrangements to local nonprofits organizing community events or families organizing their vacations. For brevity, this standard uses the term "organization" broadly to encompass government agencies, enterprises, businesses, contractual arrangements, joint ventures, and other entities. Organizations create value for stakeholders, and the expected value to be created via any project investment should meet or exceed the threshold for targets, both financial and nonfinancial, that have been set. Projects are specifically designed to deliver value or enhance value production capabilities, enabling the organizations involved—and their stakeholders—to maximize value while balancing competing constraints. Additionally, value delivery in today's environment extends beyond organizational objectives to also include societal impact and sustainability goals.

Business value is a net quantifiable benefit in any form of tangible or intangible elements that may contribute to the overall health and well-being of the organization during a project, at the end of the project, or in the long term. Figure 2-1 offers examples of such tangible and intangible elements.

The following are some examples of ways that projects meet or exceed expected value thresholds. Note that such value thresholds should always be considered in their investment context; that is, the expected value should meet or exceed a target threshold of return on project investments, whether that value is financial or nonfinancial or tangible or intangible, such as:

- Creating a new product, service, or result that meets the needs of customers or end users;
- Delivering the project within the performance baseline when the project's constraints baseline represents a high-value outcome;
- Contributing to community development, environmental sustainability, and ethical responsibility;
- Improving efficiency, productivity, effectiveness, responsiveness, or employee well-being;
- Enabling the changes needed to facilitate an organizational transition to its desired future state; and
- Sustaining benefits enabled by previous programs, projects, or business operations, and ensuring continuity of operations.

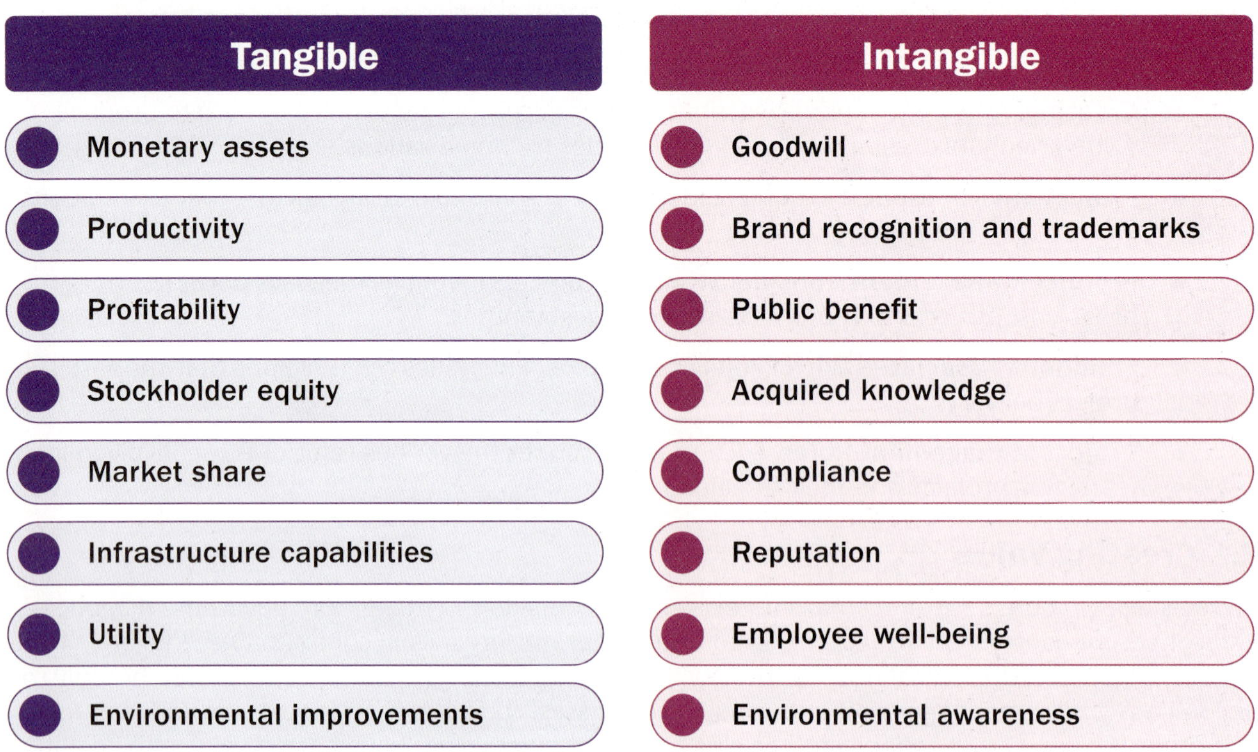

Figure 2-1. Examples of Business Value

2.1.1 Value Delivery Components

Portfolios, programs, projects, products, and operations all generate value, either individually or collectively. Together, these components form an integrated system designed to maximize and sustain value delivery while ensuring alignment with the organization's strategy. Figure 2-2 illustrates this value delivery system.

Portfolio management serves as the central framework that links strategy to execution, optimizing resource utilization to maximize value across programs, projects, products, and operations. Portfolios consist of programs and projects that deliver strategic benefits, including product development and operational improvements. Additionally, programs and projects may encompass product delivery. See Section 2.5 for more details on the relationships among portfolios, programs, projects, and operations.

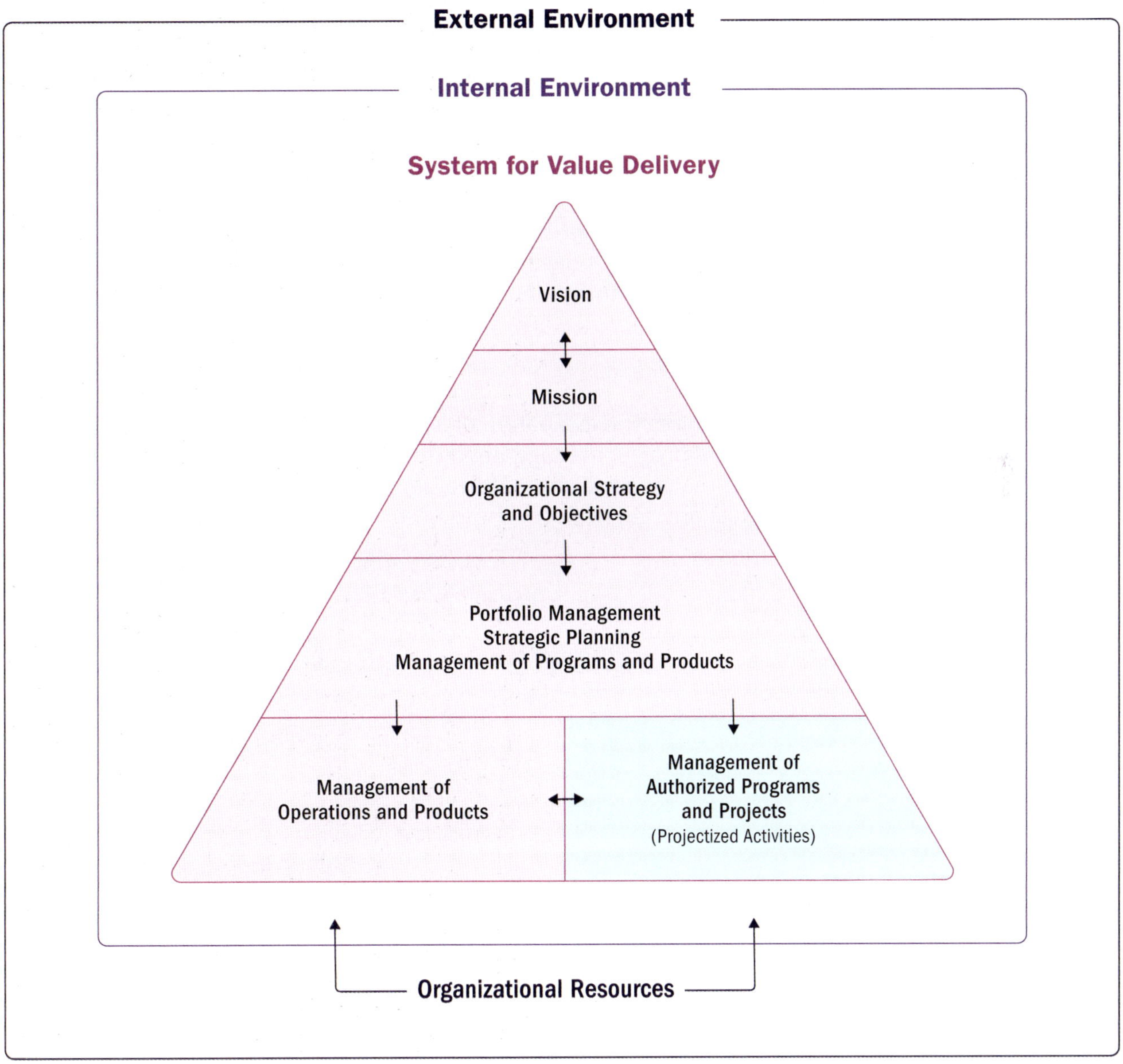

Figure 2-2. Example of a System for Value Delivery

Operations play a critical role in supporting and influencing portfolios, programs, and projects, as well as essential business functions such as payroll and supply chain management. At the same time, portfolios, programs, projects, and products interact dynamically, shaping and influencing one another to drive strategic outcomes.

As shown in Figure 2-2, a system for value delivery is part of an organization's internal environment that is subject to policies, procedures, methodologies, frameworks, governance structures, and so forth. That internal environment exists within the larger external environment, which includes the economy, competitive environment, legislative constraints, etc. Section 2.2 provides more detail on internal and external environments.

The components in a value delivery system create deliverables used to produce outcomes. An outcome is the end result or consequence of a process or project. Focusing on outcomes, possible alternatives, and strategic decisions emphasizes the long-term performance of the project. The outcomes create benefits, which are positive effects realized by the organization, and may also create disbenefits, which are negative consequences or losses. Benefits, in turn, create value, which is something of worth, importance, or usefulness. Because all projects are investments, their expected value—whether financial or nonfinancial—should meet or exceed target thresholds in order to justify the investment in the first place.

A value delivery system works most effectively when information and feedback are shared consistently among all components, keeping the system aligned with strategy and attuned to the environment. Figure 2-3 demonstrates an example of how information flows effectively throughout the system.

2.1.2 Assessing Project Success

The assessment of project success requires the evaluation of two important dimensions: the success of project outcomes and the success of project management processes. The first dimension focuses on the effectiveness of the project in realizing the intended value. The timing of this value realization depends on the nature of the product and the project—it can occur during the project, immediately

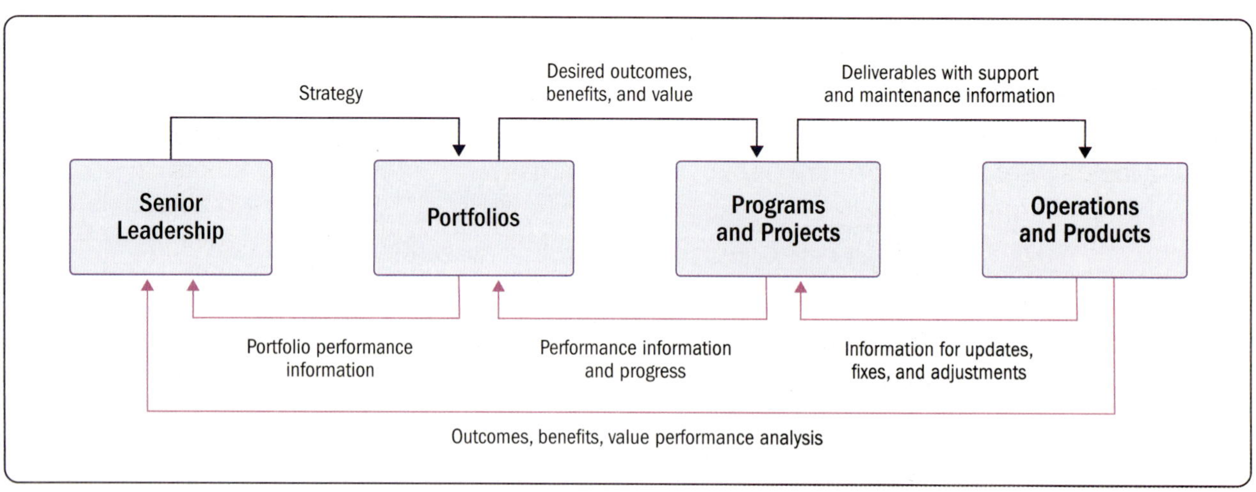

Figure 2-3. Example Information Flow

after its completion, or in the short or long term. This dimension includes achieving strategic objectives, which can be both financial and nonfinancial, such as meeting sales targets, achieving return on investment, acquiring new customers, being first to market, implementing technological or process improvements, complying with new standards and regulations, and meeting social and environmental sustainability goals. These outcomes reflect the project's ability to achieve significant impact and contribute to organizational success.

The second dimension focuses on the efficiency of project management processes, which is measured by how well the project adheres to constraints such as cost, scope, time, and quality. This aspect assesses the project's ability to deliver on time, on budget, and to the required standards, ensuring that resources are used effectively and stakeholder expectations are met.

Focusing on both dimensions is essential for delivering value and success to the organization. While the success of project management helps ensure efficient execution, the success of project outcomes is critical to the targeted business value, regardless of when that value is realized.

For example, in Sydney, Australia, the well-known Sydney Opera House project's initial budget was AUS$7 million and the construction was expected to take 4 years. The final expenditure at completion was AUS$102 million and the construction took 14 years. Today, the monument is a UNESCO World Heritage site—the most known landmark on the continent—and is visited each year by 10.9 million people. The management of this project is generally considered a failure but the project result exceeded the expectations many times over. The successful outcome would have been even stronger had the same scope been delivered years earlier and at a lower investment cost. Conversely, in 2016 in Montreal, Canada, officials discovered that a newly built overpass for Highway 15 did not align with the design plans for the upcoming redevelopment of the adjacent Champlain Bridge. As a result, just a year after a well-managed construction effort, the nearly CA$11 million overpass had to be demolished.

In conclusion, assessing project success requires a balanced focus on both the success of project outcomes and the efficiency of project management processes. Focusing on these two aspects enables companies to not only complete projects effectively, but also to realize their strategic goals, ensuring sustainable growth and competitive advantage.

2.2 Project Environment

Projects exist and operate within the internal and external environments of an organization, and have varying degrees of influence on value delivery. Internal and external environments can influence planning and other project activities. These influences may yield a favorable, unfavorable, or neutral impact on project characteristics, stakeholders, or project teams. Two major categories of influences are enterprise environmental factors (EEFs) and organizational process assets (OPAs).

Enterprise environmental factors may originate from the environment outside of the project and from outside of the enterprise. These EEFs may have an impact at the organizational, portfolio, program, or project level.

Organizational process assets are internal to the organization. These OPAs may arise from the organization itself, a portfolio, a program, another project, or a combination of these. Figure 2-4 shows the breakdown of project influences into EEFs and OPAs.

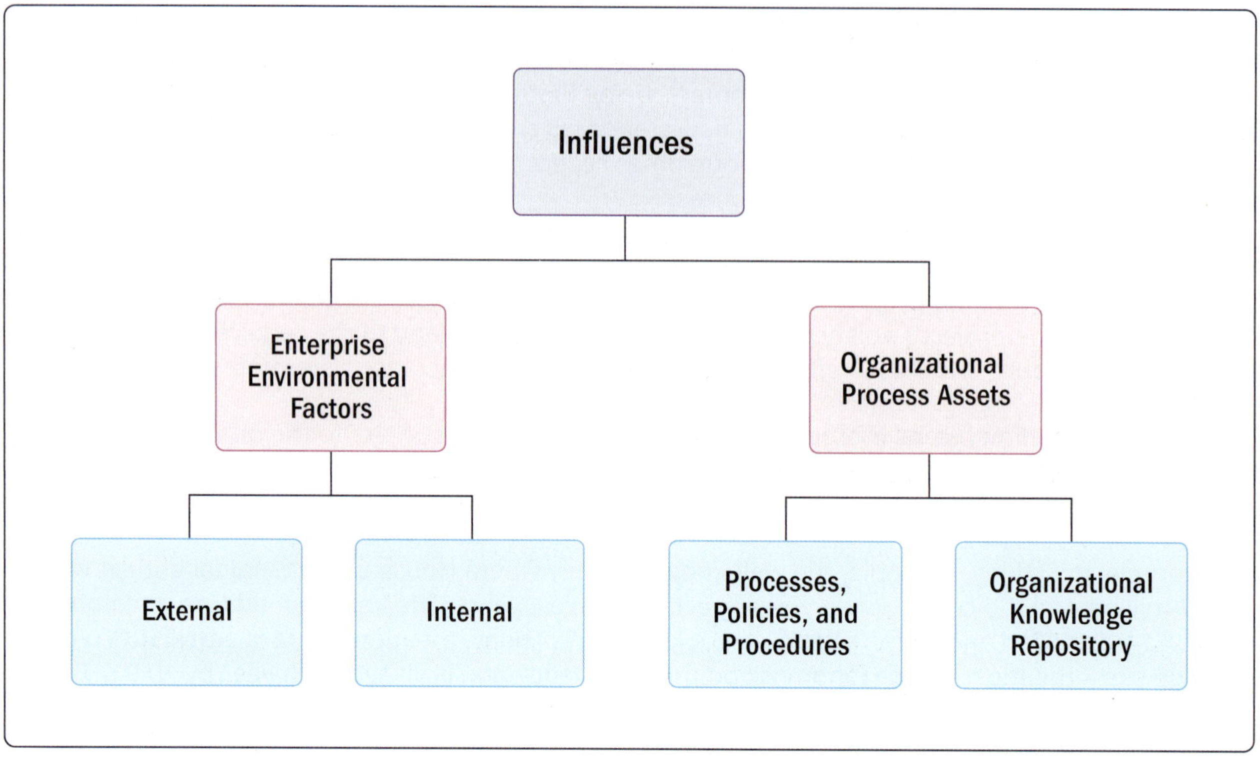

Figure 2-4. Project Influences

2.2.1 Enterprise Environmental Factors

Enterprise environmental factors refer to conditions not directly influenced by the project team that impact, constrain, or direct the project. These conditions can be internal and/or external to the organization. The EEFs are considered as inputs to many project management processes, specifically for most planning processes. These factors can either enhance or constrain project management options as well as influence tailoring needs and project outcomes, positively or negatively.

Enterprise environmental factors vary widely in type or nature and should be considered if the project is to be effective. The EEFs include but are not limited to the factors described in Sections 2.2.1.1 and 2.2.1.2.

2.2.1.1 Enterprise Environmental Factors Internal to the Organization

The following are examples of EEFs that are internal to the organization:

- **Organizational culture, structure, and governance.** Examples include vision, mission, values, beliefs, cultural norms, leadership styles, hierarchy and authority relationships, organizational styles, ethics, and codes of conduct.
- **Geographic distribution of facilities and resources.** Examples include physical locations, corporate offices, research and development centers, customer service hubs, and virtual or hybrid teams.
- **Infrastructure.** Examples include existing facilities, equipment, organizational telecommunications channels, information technology hardware, availability, and capacity.

- **Information technology systems.** Examples include task management tools, cost management tools, scheduling software tools, configuration management systems, web interfaces to other online automated systems, and work authorization systems.
- **Resource availability.** Examples include contracting and purchasing constraints, staffing levels or team capacity, and collaboration agreements.
- **Employee capability.** Examples include existing human resources expertise, skills, competencies, and specialized knowledge.
- **Financial capability of the organization.** Examples include external funding options and additional financial resources that may be required for projects.

2.2.1.2 Enterprise Environmental Factors External to the Organization

The following are examples of EEFs that are external to the organization:

- **Marketplace conditions.** Examples include competitors, customer behavior, market share, brand recognition, and trademarks.
- **Social and cultural influences and issues.** Examples include political climate, codes of conduct, ethics, and perceptions.
- **Legal restrictions.** Examples include country or local laws and regulations related to security, data protection, business conduct, employment, and procurement.
- **Academic research.** Examples include industry studies, publications, benchmarking results, empirical data that can inform decision-making, and emerging trends within the management field that could be insightful for project management.
- **Government or industry standards.** Examples include regulatory agency regulations and standards related to products, production, environment, safety, quality, and workmanship.
- **Financial considerations.** Examples include currency exchange rates, interest rates, inflation rates, tariffs, taxes, and geographic location.
- **Physical environmental elements.** Examples include working conditions, weather, and constraints such as geopolitical issues.
- **Emerging technologies and innovations.** Examples include advancements in artificial intelligence, automation, blockchain, and the Internet of Things (IoT).
- **Public health and safety regulations.** Examples include government-imposed health protocols, travel restrictions, quarantine measures, social distancing guidelines, and public safety mandates.

2.2.2 Organizational Process Assets

Organizational process assets, depending on the industry, organization, and working model, may include the plans, processes, documents, templates, and knowledge repositories specific to and used by the performing organization. These assets influence the management of the project.

Organizational process assets may include any artifact, practice, or knowledge from any or all of the performing organizations involved in the project, which can be used to execute or govern the project. The OPAs also include the organization's lessons learned from previous projects and historical information, as well as lessons from previous work carried out. The OPAs are inputs to many project management processes and may include completed schedules, risk data, and earned value data. Since OPAs are internal to the organization, the project team members may be able to update and add to the OPAs as necessary throughout the project. They may be grouped into two categories:

- **Policies, processes, and procedures.** Generally, these assets are not updated as part of the work required to achieve the outcomes of the project and are usually established by the project management office (PMO) or another function outside of the project (for more details about PMOs, see Appendix X2). These assets can be updated only by following the appropriate organizational policies. Some organizations encourage project teams to tailor templates, life cycles, and checklists for the project. In these cases, the project team should tailor those assets according to the needs of the project.
- **Organizational knowledge repositories.** These assets are updated throughout the project with project information. For example, information on financial performance, lessons learned, performance metrics, and issues and defects are continually updated throughout the project.

2.2.3 Policies, Processes, and Procedures

The organization's policies, processes, and procedures for conducting project work include but are not limited to the following:

- Tailoring guidelines and criteria for the organization's set of standard processes and procedures to satisfy the specific needs of the project;
- Product and project life cycles as well as methods and procedures (e.g., project management methods, estimation metrics, process audits, improvement targets, checklists, and standardized process definitions for use in the organization);
- Templates (e.g., project management plans, project documents, project registers, report formats, contract templates, risk categories, risk statement templates, risk register templates, probability and impact definitions, probability and impact matrices, and stakeholder register templates);
- Preapproved supplier lists, contract templates (e.g., fixed-price, cost-reimbursable, and time and materials [T&M] contracts), and proposal evaluation criteria;
- Progress monitoring processes and procedures to meet or exceed the project's value proposition, reoptimizing the project baseline when advantageous;
- Change control procedures;
- Traceability matrices;
- Issue and defect management processes;
- Resource availability control and assignment management policies;
- Processes for prioritizing, approving, and issuing work authorizations;
- Standardized guidelines, work instructions, and performance measurement procedures and guidelines;

- Verification and validation processes;
- Service-level agreements (SLAs); and
- Project closure guidelines or requirements.

2.2.4 Organizational Knowledge Repositories

The organizational knowledge repositories for storing and retrieving information include but are not limited to the following:

- Configuration management knowledge repositories containing the versions of software and hardware components and baselines of all performing organization standards, policies, procedures, and project documents;
- Financial data repositories containing information such as labor hours, incurred costs, budgets, and any project cost overruns;
- Historical information and lessons learned knowledge repositories such as project records and documents, all project closure information and documentation, information regarding both the results of previous project selection decisions and previous project performance information, and information from risk activities;
- Issue and defect management data repositories containing issue and defect status, control information, issue and defect resolution, and action item results;
- Data repositories for metrics used to collect and make available measurement data on processes and products; and
- Project files from previous projects such as scope, cost, schedules, performance measurement baselines, project calendars, project schedule network diagrams, risk registers, risk reports, and stakeholder registers.

2.2.5 Organizational Structures

Determination of the appropriate organizational structure type is the result of analyzing two key elements. These elements are the organizational structure types available for use and how to optimize them for a given organization. The analysis often involves considerations such as resource allocation efficiency, decision-making speed, communication pathways, and the distribution of authority and responsibility. The optimal structure depends on variables such as the organization's size, industry, geographical spread, strategic objectives, and the complexity of its projects.

There is not a one-size-fits-all structure for any given organization. The final structure for a given organization is unique due to the numerous variables to be considered. Organizational structures take many forms. Table 2-1 compares several types of organizational structures and their influence on projects.

2.3 Product Management Considerations

Product management is the integration of people, data, processes, and business systems to create, develop, and maintain a product or service throughout its life cycle. The product life cycle is a series of phases that represents the evolution of a product, from introduction through growth, maturity, and to retirement.

Table 2-1. Influences of Organizational Structures on Projects

Project Characteristics				
Organizational Structure Type	**Work Group Arrangement**	**Project Manager's Authority**	**Project Manager's Role**	**Resource Availability**
Organic or simple	Flexible; people working side by side	Low	Part-time role; may or may not be a designated job role such as coordinator	Low
Functional (centralized)	Job being done (e.g., engineering, manufacturing)	Low	Part-time role; may or may not be a designated job role such as coordinator	Low
Multidivisional (may replicate functions for each division with little centralization)	One of the following: product; production processes; portfolio; program; geographic region; customer type	Low	Part-time role; may or may not be a designated job role such as coordinator	Low
Matrix—strong	By job function, with project manager as a function	Moderate to high	Full-time, designated job role	Moderate to high
Matrix—weak	Job function	Low	Part-time role; done as part of another job and not a designated job role such as coordinator	Low
Matrix—balanced	Job function	Low to moderate	Part-time role; embedded in the functions as a skill and may not be a designated job role such as coordinator	Low to moderate
Project-oriented (composite, hybrid)	Project	High to almost total	Full-time, designated job role	High to almost total
Virtual/network	Network structure with nodes at points of contact with other people	Low to moderate	Full-time or part-time role	Low to moderate
Hybrid	Mix of other types	Mixed	Mixed	Mixed

The disciplines of portfolio, program, project, and product management are interdependent and operate within a value delivery framework to ensure alignment with organizational strategy. While portfolio, program, and product management are beyond the scope of this standard, understanding each discipline and the relationships among them provides a useful context for projects where the deliverables are products.

Product management may initiate programs or projects at any point in the product life cycle to create or enhance specific components, functions, or capabilities (see Figure 2-5). The initial product may begin as a deliverable of a program or project. Throughout its life cycle, a new program or project may add or improve specific components, attributes, or capabilities that create additional value for customers and the sponsoring organization. In some instances, a program may encompass the full life cycle of a product or service to manage benefits and create value for the organization more directly.

The relationships among portfolio, program, project, and product management can exist in different forms, as shown in Figure 2-5, including but not limited to the following:

- **Program management within a product life cycle.** This approach incorporates related projects, subsidiary programs, and program activities. For very large or long-term products, one or more product life cycle phases may be sufficiently complex to merit a set of programs and projects working together.

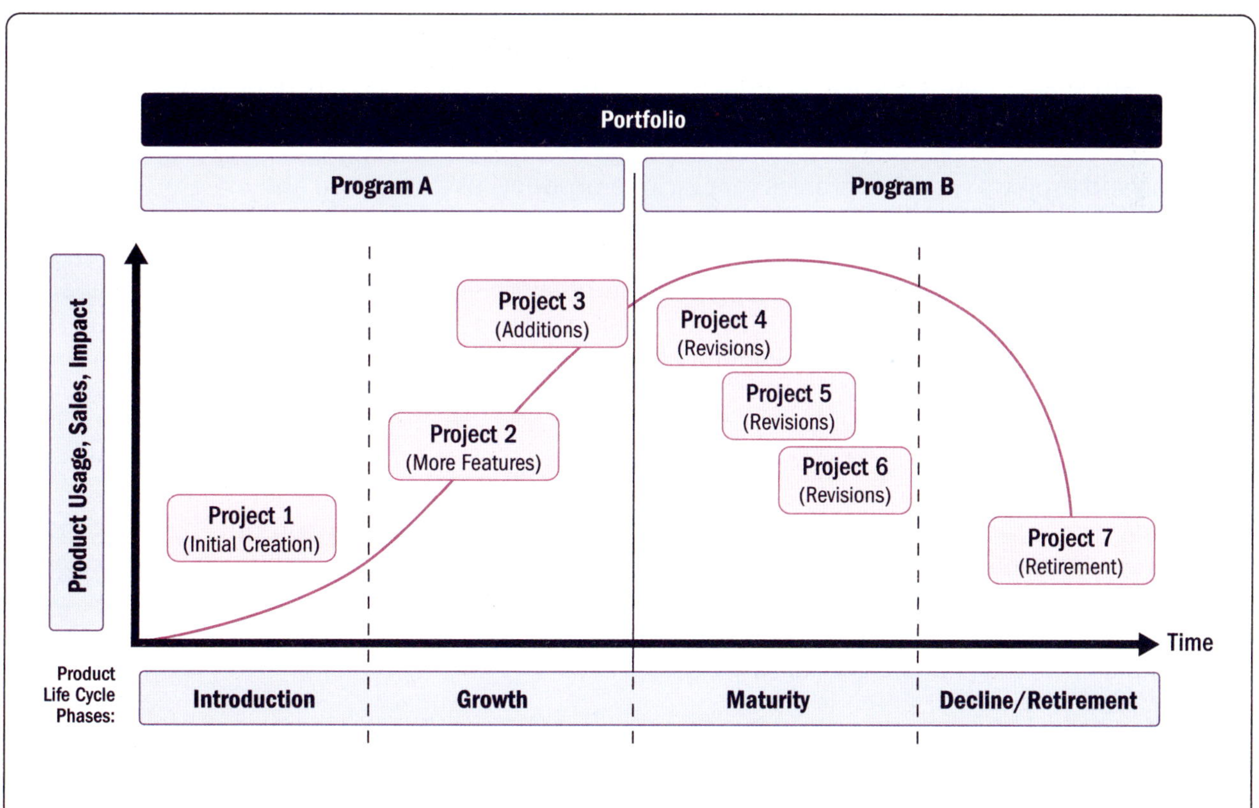

Figure 2-5. Sample Product Life Cycle

- **Project management within a product life cycle.** This approach oversees the development and maturity of product capabilities as an ongoing business activity. Portfolio governance charters individual projects as needed to perform enhancements and improvements or to produce other unique outcomes.
- **Product management within a portfolio.** This approach integrates product management within the structure of a portfolio, where the entire product life cycle is managed within the boundaries of a single portfolio. Portfolio management helps ensure that product-related investments align with business strategy, prioritize high-value initiatives, and allocate resources efficiently across multiple product lines or business units.
- **Product management within a program or project.** This approach applies to the product-related responsibilities that should be performed in a program or project(s) and that are defined as the components of a program or stand-alone projects. This approach focuses on achieving product requirements and scope. While ongoing product, service, or capability support activities may fall within the scope of the program, they typically are operational in nature and are not usually run as programs or projects.
- **Product management across programs and projects.** A product life cycle often spans multiple programs and projects, and thus calls for effective management across those programs and projects.

While product management is a separate discipline with its own body of knowledge, it represents a key integration point within the program management and project management disciplines. Collaboration among these disciplines is essential for delivering cohesive and impactful outcomes. Product management provides the vision and strategy for the product, while program and project management ensure that this vision is brought to life by managing execution, dependencies, and resources.

Programs and projects with deliverables that include products use a tailored and integrated approach that incorporates all of the relevant bodies of knowledge and their related practices, methods, and artifacts. Programs and projects support product management by structuring and guiding the development process, managing risks, and maintaining alignment with organizational objectives. This collaboration helps ensure that the product is delivered efficiently and effectively, with minimal delays and cost overruns, ultimately driving organizational success and customer satisfaction.

Supporting roles, such as product owner and business analyst, can further bridge the gap between project and product management. The product owner should ensure that the development team is focused on delivering valuable features by maintaining and prioritizing the product backlog. The business analyst should gather and document requirements, ensuring that both the project scope and product functionality align with business needs. These roles help to create a seamless flow of communication and understanding among product, project, and development teams, ensuring alignment at every stage of the product life cycle.

2.4 Functions Associated With Projects

People drive project delivery by fulfilling essential functions that ensure projects run effectively and efficiently. These functions can be performed by an individual, a team, or a combination of defined roles.

Coordinating a collective work effort is extremely important to the success of any project. There are different types of coordination suitable for different contexts. Some projects benefit from decentralized coordination, in which project team members self-organize and self-manage (such as agile projects). Other projects benefit from centralized coordination, with the leadership and guidance of a designated project manager or similar role (such as predictive projects). Some projects with centralized coordination can also benefit from hybrid or mixed coordination, including self-organized project teams for portions of the work.

Regardless of how projects are coordinated, the collective effort of the project team delivers outcomes, benefits, and value. The project team may be supported by additional functions depending on the deliverables, industry, organization, and other variables. In addition to these functions, other functions may be necessary to enable project deliverables that produce the desired outcomes. The needs of the project, organization, and environment all influence which functions are used on a project and how those functions are carried out. Sections 2.4.1 through 2.4.7 provide examples of functions commonly found in projects; however, they do not represent an exhaustive list.

2.4.1 Provide Oversight and Coordination

Oversight and coordination enable the project team to deliver value by aligning efforts, removing obstacles, and maintaining team focus. The specifics of how this function is carried out within the project team may vary among organizations but can include all project management activities. In some organizations, this function may involve some evaluation and analysis activities as part of the preliminary project activities. Coordination includes consulting with executives and business unit leaders on ideas for advancing objectives, improving project performance, and meeting customer needs. The coordination activities may also include assisting in business analysis, tendering and contract negotiations, and business case development. Oversight may be involved in follow-on activities related to benefits realization and sustainment after the project deliverables are finalized but before formal closure of the project. Examples of roles responsible for these functions include project managers, who may be formally assigned such activities, and scrum masters (further described in Section 2.5.1), who are asked to lead the project team to perform the activities themselves. Ultimately, the oversight and coordination function is tailored to fit the needs of the organization and its specific portfolio, program, and project requirements.

2.4.2 Solicit and Manage Feedback

Individuals involved in the project contribute perspectives, insights, direction, and expectations. In projects that use adaptive or hybrid approaches, the need for ongoing feedback is greater because the project teams are exploring and developing product elements within specific increments due to ambiguity and complexity. In some project environments, the customer, end user, or product owner engages with the project team for periodic reviews and feedback. In some projects, a representative of the customer or client participates with the project team. Close collaboration can ensure that the customer and end-user input is directly integrated into ongoing development activities. The extent of customer and end-user input depends on factors such as project complexity, product maturity, and level of uncertainty, as well as the guidance or direction that may be required to enable value creation. Feedback can be collected in person or virtually, using both analog and digital techniques. For more information on feedback, please refer to the tools and techniques detailed in Section 5 of *A Guide to the Project Management Body of Knowledge (PMBOK® Guide)* [2].

2.4.3 Facilitate and Support

Facilitation and support within a project involve providing oversight, coordination, and encouragement that are tailored to the needs of the project. The work involves encouraging project team member participation, collaboration, a collective sense of responsibility for the work output, and shared motivation in pursuit of the target outcome. Facilitation helps the project team to create consensus around solutions, resolve conflicts, and make decisions. Facilitation may also be used to coordinate meetings and contribute in an unbiased way to the advancement of project objectives. Supporting people through change and helping to address obstacles that can prevent the team from achieving project success should also be part of this function. Roles such as project managers, scrum masters, team leads, business analysts, and change management specialists are examples of individuals who commonly perform these facilitation and support functions. This support may include evaluating performance and providing individuals and project teams with feedback to help them learn, adapt, and improve.

2.4.4 Perform Work

The people performing this function provide the knowledge, skills, and experience necessary to deliver products and realize the outcomes of projects. Work can be full time or part time for the duration of the project or for a limited period, and the work can be colocated or virtual, depending on the environmental factors. Additionally, projects may harness automation and artificial intelligence to streamline project execution, reduce human error, and enhance productivity. For more information on colocation and virtual collaboration tools, please refer to the tools and techniques detailed within Section 5 of *A Guide to the Project Management Body of Knowledge (PMBOK® Guide)* [2]. Some work may be highly specialized, while other work may be performed by project team members who have broad skill sets.

2.4.5 Apply Expertise

Applying expertise within a project involves contributing specialized knowledge, vision, and skills in a specific subject area. Experts provide advice and support across the organization, enhancing the project team's learning process and improving the accuracy and quality of their work. Experts can also help identify uncertainties and blind spots, and eventually evaluate project progress and ultimate success. These experts can be internal team members or external specialists brought in for the entire project duration or specific timeframes. The unique mix of skills and knowledge provided by experts and other team members often accelerates progress and helps ensure that projects achieve their intended outcomes efficiently.

2.4.6 Provide Organizational Direction and Insight

Guiding and clarifying the direction of the project or product involves prioritizing requirements or scope based on value, dependencies, and technical or operational risks. Those responsible for providing organizational direction help set the course for the next increment or element to be developed or delivered. This role includes engaging with stakeholders, customers, and project teams to collaboratively define the project direction. The primary goal is to maximize the value of project deliverables and ensure a strong return on project investments. In adaptive and hybrid environments, direction and insight may come from regular review cycles or feedback loops. In predictive environments, checkpoints may be established to review progress and provide guidance on project milestones. Roles such as portfolio managers, project sponsors, and product owners are examples of those who typically guide and clarify project direction. These roles can ensure that the project stays aligned with strategic objectives and delivers the intended value, adjusting the course as necessary based on feedback and performance metrics.

2.4.7 Provide Resources

Securing and providing the necessary resources is a crucial activity for project success. Some individuals, such as portfolio managers and project sponsors, are responsible for securing the necessary resources, including funding, physical resources, personnel, and authority, to enable project progress. These individuals champion the project at an organizational level and ensure it receives the necessary support from senior management.

Individuals in resource-related functions, such as functional and resource managers, are responsible for allocating the necessary resources to the project team. These roles assign the right personnel, equipment, and expertise to the project team to meet the project requirements and ensure that resources are allocated efficiently and according to the needs of the project. These people also take care of any resource gaps that may occur during the project life cycle, ensuring smooth execution.

Together, these roles help ensure that the project team is equipped with the necessary resources to achieve the project objectives and overcome any challenges related to resource allocation.

2.5 Project Management Roles

While Section 2.4 describes the functions that drive project delivery, many environments perform those functions through a variety of individuals and/or teams, with some organizations focusing on specific role definitions. Each role within a project setup adds specific value, and the project's outcomes directly depend on those contributions.

This section details some key project roles, such as the project management team, project manager, sponsor, customer, product owner, project team, and end user, which all add value to a project's execution. However, as each enterprise and project is unique, the functions, roles, and responsibilities may differ accordingly.

2.5.1 Project Management Team

The project management team may consist solely of a project manager or may include more individuals who form a team; both structures will be referred to synonymously in this section. The project management team is essential for guiding the assigned team to achieve goals and deliver value to the organization and customers while considering flexibility, adaptability, and tailoring. The critical nature of this role is due to several factors ranging from uncertainty to new ways of working. A project management team performs various functions such as facilitating and mentoring the project team and managing the processes to deliver intended outcomes.

Depending on the organization's policies and processes, it is suggested that the project management team is involved from project initiation through closing and, in some cases, in post-project benefit analysis. Moreover, in some organizations, a project management team may be involved in evaluation and feasibility analysis activities before project initiation and may consult with executives and business unit leaders on ideas for advancing strategic objectives, improving organizational performance, and meeting customer needs. In some organizational settings, the project management team may also be called upon to manage or assist in business analysis, business case development, and aspects of portfolio management for a project. The project management team's role and level of involvement may vary from organization to organization, and hence, the role should be tailored to fit the organizational structure, like tailoring project processes.

The project management team performs numerous functions and roles within its sphere of influence. The project management team is a reflection of the capabilities, value, and contributions of the project management profession. The functions and roles of the project management team in the various spheres of influence are shown in Figure 2-6.

In many organizations, the title of "project manager" or "project management team" may not explicitly denote someone who is managing a project. The governance structure and context of each project often determine the assignment of project management responsibilities. For instance, in some scenarios, a functional manager, such as a finance or human resources manager, may oversee project activities, ensuring that they align with departmental goals and strategies. Also, the function and title for the role may be "project leader" or "project lead" instead of "project manager."

In adaptive development approaches and agile project environments, it is common for a function such as "product owner" or "product manager" to handle some of the project management tasks. The titles and roles of "scrum master," "agile coach," "agile manager," "agile expert," "agile delivery manager," "team lead," "development team," or "project team" may also share some project management responsibilities that are usually performed by project managers. This adaptability reflects an organization's internal regulations and constraints, emphasizing that the essence of

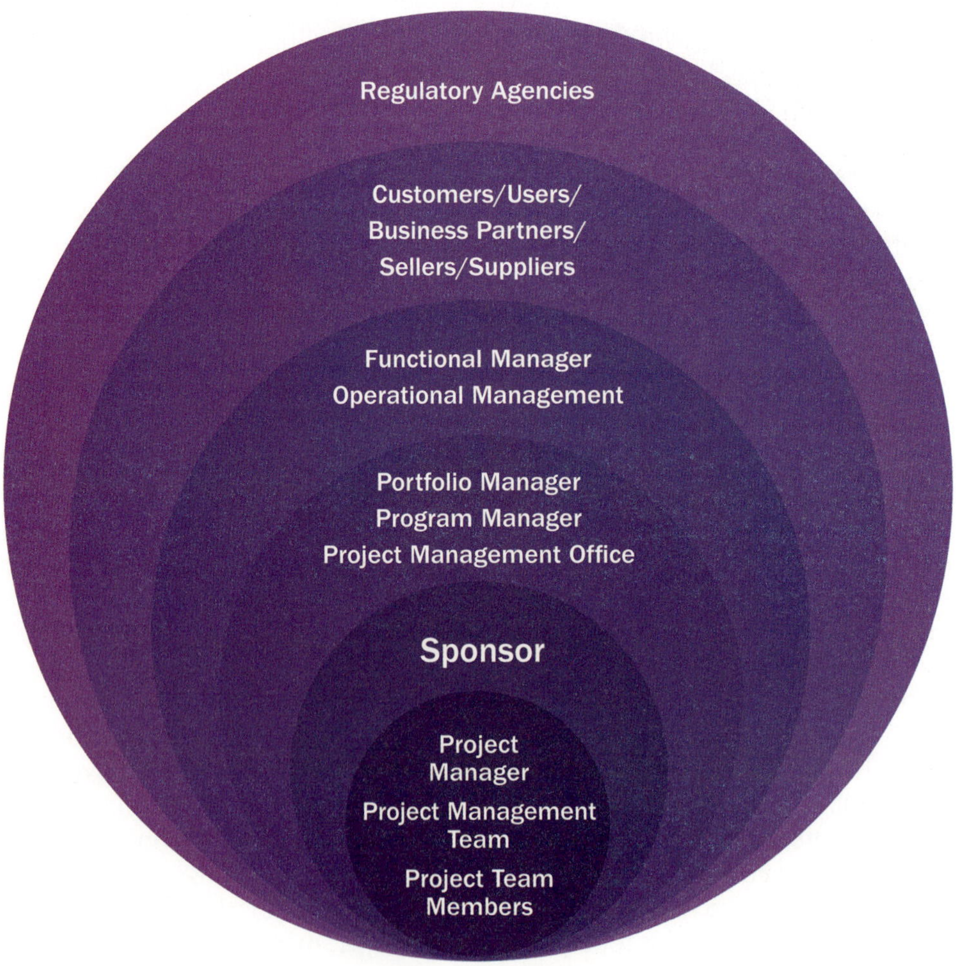

Figure 2-6. Project Management Team Within Various Spheres of Influence

project management lies in the characteristics of the project itself rather than the title of the individual overseeing it. It is crucial for any person fulfilling this function, regardless of their official position, to embrace the core aspects of project management to steer projects toward success. Varying examples of these agile roles are described in the PMI Disciplined Agile® (DA®) tool kit [3].

2.5.1.1 Interaction Between the Project Management Team and Project Aspects

The engagement of a project management team in project tasks is pivotal in bringing focus and clarity to the work. A competent project management team should manage needs and tasks effectively, prioritizing the items that are most urgent and important, and allocating attention accordingly. This prioritization helps ensure that resources are optimized and that critical project milestones are met on schedule. The project management team's presence catalyzes progress and efficiency, maintaining project momentum through strategic oversight, effective communication, and resource management.

There are many leadership styles that members of a project management team can adopt based on the individuals, situations, team structures, stakeholders, and organizational processes and culture. Leaders should be versatile and able to switch between different leadership styles to achieve a better outcome. The project management team proactively interacts and negotiates with other project management teams, portfolio managers, program managers, project managers, and functional managers for demands on critical resources, priorities on project funding, receipt or distribution of deliverables, and in aligning project goals and objectives with those of the organization.

Interacting with others helps to create a positive influence for fulfilling a project's various needs and for sharing experiences and addressing challenges, as a project management team works with and in different areas, departments, industries, and locations. The project management team usually works with the project sponsor, customer, product manager, or product owner to address internal political and strategic issues that may impact the team or the viability or quality of the project or product. The skills of the project management team, due to the complexity of the function and the increasing need for versatility and flexibility, are a mix of different skills such as ways of working, power skills, and business acumen, with a sole aim of accomplishing tasks without compromising their professional and social responsibility to the profession and society at large.

In the context of leadership styles, situational leadership is particularly relevant for project management teams. This approach emphasizes the importance of flexibility and adaptability in leadership based on the evolving demands of the project. A project management team should adjust its leadership style to suit the specific needs of the team, the time sensitivity of tasks, and the complexity of the project. Whether it involves shifting from a more directive approach during critical project phases to a supportive style when team autonomy is beneficial, the ability to adapt one's leadership style is crucial for navigating the diverse challenges that projects typically present. Figure 2-7 represents the competencies that a project management team should have to fulfill the project outcomes in a successful way.

Figure 2-7. Project Management Team Competencies

The competencies that project management team members should possess include the following:

- **Social responsibilities.** This competency refers to the acknowledgment that the project management team makes decisions that are aligned to the common good. The competency includes but is not limited to the following:
  - Giving back to the profession and to society as a responsibility;
  - Adhering to ethical standards by respecting cultural and social norms; and
  - Striving for self-development and continuous improvement.
- **Power skills.** This competency includes all the people skills that a project management team should apply to successfully execute the project (e.g., adaptability and emotional intelligence [EI]). This competency is of significant importance, considering that projects are conceived to add value to society. The competency includes but is not limited to the following aspects:
  - Exercising critical thinking, sound judgment, and decision-making;
  - Implementing team motivation methods; and
  - Using negotiation and conflict resolution skills.

- **Business acumen.** This competency refers to the application of strategic thinking and the alignment of the project management team within the organizational context. Understanding the connections between strategy execution and projects is key to ensuring that the value delivered to organizations and societies is aligned with the overall organizational strategy. The competency includes but is not limited to the following aspects:
  - Setting project selection criteria (cost, feasibility, impact);
  - Applying knowledge of the industry; and
  - Performing strategic thinking, business case development, and financial analysis.
- **Ways of working.** This competency includes the understanding and application of the standards, methodologies, and frameworks that a project management team may use to execute projects and add value to the organization. The competency includes but is not limited to the following aspects:
  - Implementing appropriate project management approaches (predictive, adaptive, hybrid);
  - Using brainstorming techniques; and
  - Applying change management techniques.
- **Results.** This competency refers to the actual work and execution of ideas and projects to add value. The ability to accomplish tasks is a central competency that helps ensure the expected value is delivered. The competency includes but is not limited to the following aspects:
  - Applying problem-solving techniques (e.g., root cause analysis);
  - Acquiring the power and authority to work within organizational policies; and
  - Having the ability to deal with enterprise politics, which involves using skills such as influence, negotiation, autonomy, and power.

2.5.1.2 Competency Development in Project Management

In project management, competency development is crucial to ensure that each team member performs their duties efficiently and grows professionally within the project environment. The project management team plays a pivotal function in this development by fostering a learning culture that blends various competencies across the team. By strategically mixing team members of different seniority levels and expertise, the project management team facilitates an exchange of knowledge and skills that benefits the entire team. This mix of skill levels provides mentorship and coaching opportunities that nurture less-experienced team members, helping them to build their capabilities and confidence through guided learning and hands-on experience.

The project management team's responsibility may extend beyond project deliverables to include the professional growth of the team. This responsibility may also be taken by functional managers, PMOs, line managers of team members, or by each individual team member themself. Nevertheless, this skill development involves identifying individual learning needs and integrating competency development into the project's workflow. Effective project management teams create opportunities for individuals to take on challenges that stretch their skills and provide them with constructive feedback.

Additionally, by promoting a culture of continuous improvement and reflective practice, the project management team helps ensure that lessons learned are captured and shared, enhancing the team's collective expertise. This culture drives project success and prepares individuals for more complex functions in future projects, thereby strengthening the overall project management discipline.

2.5.1.3 Technological Impact on Project Management

Technological advancements significantly boost the efficiency and transparency of project management. For instance, tools that support task scheduling and resource allocation, automate repetitive tasks, create data visualization, assist in brainstorming, optimize schedules, and enhance real-time communication can streamline project phases from planning through execution, ensuring that tasks are effectively tracked and managed. Additionally, the application of artificial intelligence (AI), machine learning (ML), and other emerging technologies can offer predictive insights based on historical data, helping to effectively allocate resources and enhance fact-based decision-making, identify potential risks, report on project progress using leading and lagging indicators, and optimize project trajectories. These technologies provide critical data on team performance and financial management, allowing project managers to make informed decisions promptly.

The advent of cloud computing and fast global internet access has revolutionized data storage and access, facilitating seamless updates and collaboration across global teams. This technology helps ensure that all team members have uniform access to essential project information, enabling quick adjustments to project dynamics and maintaining continuity across dispersed teams. Enhanced agility from cloud-collaboration technologies supports dynamic project execution, accommodating changes swiftly without significant delays.

The project management team's function in leveraging these technologies may involve diligent planning, coordination, testing, or auditing to ensure that the selected technology serves the project's best interests. The project management team should ensure the accuracy of data and the neutrality of outputs, avoiding biases that could skew project results. By selecting appropriate technologies and continuously monitoring their integration and effectiveness, the project management team can safeguard the integrity and success of the project, thereby maintaining high standards of quality and reliability in project outcomes. However, in some organizations, the responsibility for technological impact and tool usage may be handled by the PMO instead of the project management team. As technology advances, the level of information security threats and cybersecurity concerns increases. It is the project management team and project manager's responsibility to be aligned with the organization's IT department to safeguard project information. For further details, see Appendix X2 on PMOs.

2.5.2 Sponsor, Customer, or Product Owner

The project sponsor, customer (either internal or external), and product owner may provide decision leadership outside of the project management team's authority and power. Their active engagement and oversight support the project management team to drive project outcomes efficiently. These roles communicate the organization's vision, goals, or expectations to the project management team and project team, while keeping the project aligned with business objectives, facilitating executive-level decisions, helping to secure resources, advocating for the project team, and addressing issues or removing obstacles that are beyond the project management team's authority. These individuals are also critical for achieving project sustainability, as well as environmental, social, and governance (ESG) goals. The individuals in these roles should continuously monitor project progress and provide advice to the project management team as required so that the project's intended business benefits are realized.

The strategic link that the sponsor, customer, or product owner provides both empowers and enables the project team to optimize its performance by maintaining alignment with the organization's strategy. Thus, their presence and, more importantly, the degree of their involvement, increases the likelihood of achieving the desired project outcome, while their absence might adversely impact the project.

Further details about project teams, functions, roles, responsibilities, and characteristics are elaborated in Section 2.5 (Stakeholders performance domain) in *A Guide to the Project Management Body of Knowledge (PMBOK® Guide)* [2].

2.5.3 Project Team

The project team is a set of individuals who are performing the project's work and are directly responsible for achieving project objectives. The team's size, composition, and skill level depend on the project's type, scale, complexity, and organizational level of maturity. The level of the project team's involvement and the coordination required may vary from project to project and should be tailored according to the project's needs considering factors such as complexity, management approach, and level of changes involved. Some projects benefit from decentralized coordination in which project team members self-organize and self-manage, such as agile teams, while other projects benefit from centralized coordination under the leadership and guidance of a project management team, project manager, or a hybrid governance model. Regardless of how coordination takes place, supportive leadership models and meaningful continuous engagement among project teams and other stakeholders are key to a successful project.

Section 2.6 (Resources performance domain) in *A Guide to the Project Management Body of Knowledge (PMBOK® Guide)* [2] provides further details about project teams, functions, roles, responsibilities, and characteristics of the project team.

2.5.4 End Users and Other Key Stakeholders

To effectively serve a project's target beneficiaries, project management teams and project teams should, when possible, engage in continuous dialogue with end users, influencers, customers, regulators, and other key stakeholders. The goals of doing so are to capture and integrate their feedback throughout the project life cycle, ensure mutual alignment, and build credibility across the project ecosystem. This engagement involves iterative verification and validation processes to help ensure that the project remains aligned with the end users' evolving needs. By prioritizing end-user satisfaction, project management teams can minimize the risks associated with delivering a product or service that does not meet the expected utility. Thus, the integration of end-user feedback refines the project outcome as well as secures its relevance and success by confirming that the deliverables concretely address the needs and expectations of those who will ultimately use them. This strategy helps ensure that the project delivers substantial value, achieving its primary goal of satisfying the end users.

Section 3

Project Management Principles

Principles for a profession serve as foundational guidelines for strategy, decision-making, and problem-solving. Professional standards and methodologies often derive from these principles. In some professions, principles act as prescriptive laws or rules. However, the principles of project management are not prescriptive, but rather are intended to reinforce the mindset and guide the behavior of people involved in projects. This standard is a "principle-based" standard.

By adhering to these principles and aligning them with professional, organizational, and ethical values, project managers can navigate the complexities of their projects and drive meaningful, positive, and sustainable change within their organizations. These principles are broad, allowing for diverse ways through which individuals and organizations can maintain alignment with them, thereby fostering a dynamic and responsive project management environment.

Because the project management principles provide guidance, their application and the manner in which they are applied are influenced by the context of the organization, project, deliverables, project team, stakeholders, and other factors. The principles are complementary and supplement one another, meaning that no principle contradicts another. However, in practice, there may be instances when the principles overlap, reflecting the complex and interconnected nature of project management.

This section defines the six principles of project management:

- Adopt a Holistic View (see Section 3.3);
- Focus on Value (see Section 3.4);
- Embed Quality Into Processes and Deliverables (see Section 3.5);
- Be an Accountable Leader (see Section 3.6);
- Integrate Sustainability Within All Project Areas (see Section 3.7); and
- Build an Empowered Culture (see Section 3.8).

Collectively, these principles describe the mindset of project management, which in turn guides the mechanics of project management. This interplay between mindset and mechanics is discussed in Section 3.1.

3.1 The Project Management Mindset

Project management is much more than a collection of performance domains, processes, and methods; it represents a mindset, sometimes referred to as a "growth mindset," that is fundamental for executing strategy, fostering adaptability, driving change, and generating value. A mindset is a set of beliefs, ways of thinking, and habits that make sense of the behaviors and views of others as well as a way to interpret and deal with various situations. The project management mindset is described by three dimensions and six principles that guide the practice of project management mechanics.

The project management mindset is composed of three dimensions: proactive, ownership, and value-driven. This integrated mindset is essential in today's complex and rapidly changing business environment that should balance diverse customer needs and consider the increasing need for—and importance of—sustainability. Figure 3-1 provides an overview of the relationships among these dimensions and the correlation with the project management principles described in this section.

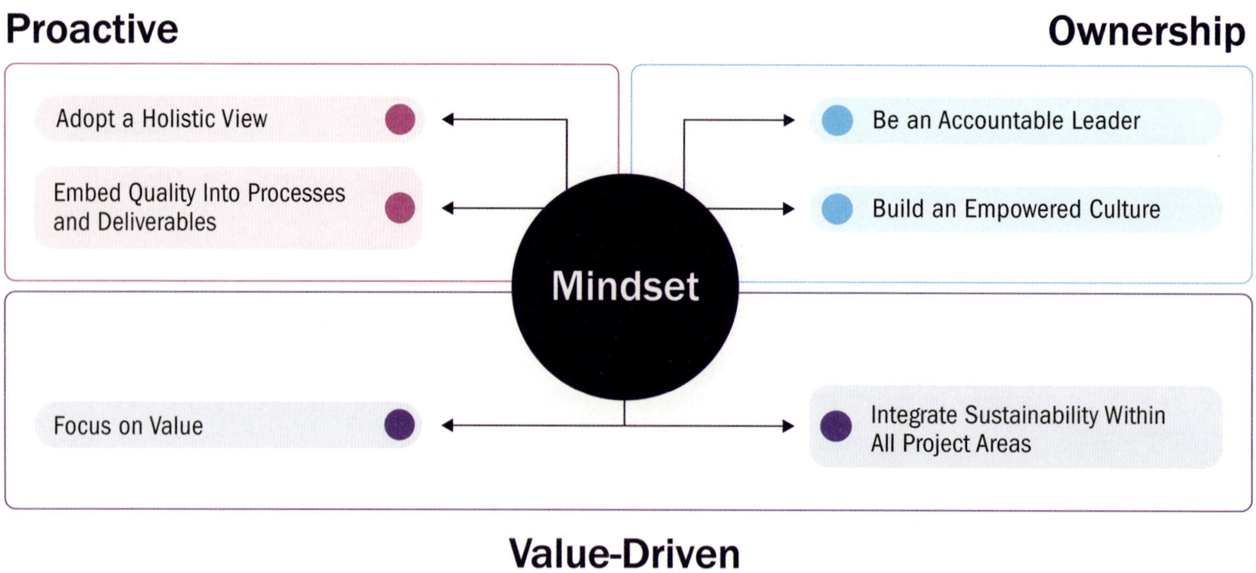

Figure 3-1. The Project Management Mindset

Being proactive is a key habit that shapes effective project management and drives the team toward achieving strategic objectives. The proactive mindset in project management emphasizes systems thinking and appropriate levels of planning to help ensure that target quality thresholds are embedded within every phase of the project. The proactive mindset integrates the project management principles of Adopt a Holistic View and Embed Quality Into Processes and Deliverables, fostering a culture of continuous improvement and forward-thinking action (see Section 3.2 for details on the project management principles). The mindset enables project managers to anticipate challenges, address them promptly, and align processes with evolving project and stakeholder needs, thereby enhancing overall project resilience and success.

The ownership dimension focuses on the accountability of leaders and the development of a high-performance team culture. This dimension integrates the principles of Be an Accountable Leader and Build an Empowered Culture, ensuring that leadership is not just about making decisions but also about fostering a culture of accountability and collaboration. This mindset supports the development of strong, self-reliant teams that drive project success through shared ownership and commitment.

The value-driven dimension emphasizes delivering maximum value by seamlessly integrating sustainability throughout the project life cycle. This dimension incorporates the principles of Focus on Value and Integrate Sustainability Within All Project Areas. By aligning projects with organizational strategic objectives and emphasizing contributions to the broader community and the environment (i.e., achieving the triple bottom line of people, profit, and planet), this dimension helps ensure that project outcomes are both impactful and sustainable. Ultimately, the value-driven dimension promotes a balance between achieving measurable success and advancing broader sustainability goals.

By integrating the proactive, ownership, and value-driven mindset dimensions, organizations can create a solid framework for achieving exceptional project results. This holistic approach helps ensure that projects are planned and executed in a manner intended to meet or exceed target business objectives (proactive), lead with accountability and empowerment (ownership), and drive projects forward with a focus on value and sustainability (value-driven). Together, these dimensions enable organizations to deliver projects that not only drive the execution of an organization's strategy, but are also socially responsible and environmentally sustainable.

3.2 Principles and Performance Domains

Performance domains are designed to enable the practical application of project management principles and ensure this mindset is translated into effective practices and outcomes. These performance domains represent the mechanics of project management, including the knowledge, processes, and methods that are essential for effective project delivery.

The project management performance domains include Governance, Scope (including quality), Schedule, Finance, Stakeholders, Resources, and Risk. These performance domains are described in detail in *A Guide to the Project Management Body of Knowledge (PMBOK® Guide)* [2].

Each performance domain plays an important role in operationalizing project management principles by providing a structured approach to managing various aspects of a project. Conversely, the project management principles serve as the foundation of the performance domains.

While all the principles relate to all performance domains, some are connected more strongly than others. For instance, the Adopt a Holistic View principle is supported by all performance domains, which helps ensure that all project aspects are considered and aligned. The Embed Quality Into Processes and Deliverables and Focus on Value principles are primarily addressed within the Governance, Scope, Risk, Schedule, Finance, and Stakeholders performance domains, ensuring the deliverables genuinely help drive realization of the project's target business objectives. The Be an Accountable Leader principle intersects with the Governance, Stakeholders, and Risk performance domains, highlighting the importance of leadership in project success. Finally, the Integrate Sustainability Within All Project Areas and Build an Empowered Culture principles are relevant across all performance domains.

3.3 Adopt a Holistic View

The Adopt a Holistic View principle involves understanding and managing projects by considering all components and their interdependencies as part of a larger system (see Figure 3-2). This perspective aligns with the concept of systems thinking, which emphasizes the interconnectedness of elements within a project. This principle provides a framework for viewing interrelationships in their full context and for seeing patterns rather than static "snapshots."

Embracing a holistic perspective is crucial for managing project complexity, as it enables project managers to grasp the overall situation and the connections among different project components. This method aids in pinpointing the root causes of challenges and tackling them efficiently. Additionally, aligning with systems thinking, a holistic perspective fosters an in-depth comprehension of the project landscape. Viewing the project as a unified entity makes it simpler to trace problems to their origins, allowing for an interdisciplinary approach that fosters more innovative and effective solutions.

3.3.1 Project Impact

Applying a holistic view to project management results in a more integrated and cohesive approach to achieving project goals. Key characteristics of projects managed with a holistic view include:

- **Alignment with organizational strategy and goals.** Projects are more likely to contribute positively to the strategic objectives of the organization.

Adopt a Holistic View

Adopt a holistic view throughout the project life cycle, from initiation all the way to execution and closing, ensuring seamless integration and alignment at every stage.

- ▶ Viewing a project holistically helps ensure that decisions consider all interconnected elements, optimizing alignment with overarching objectives and enhancing project sustainability.
- ▶ Proactively managing risks across all project domains anticipates challenges and strengthens project resilience, minimizing potential disruptions.
- ▶ Engaging stakeholders throughout the project life cycle fosters collaboration, integrates diverse perspectives, and raises the probability that desired outcomes are achieved.

Figure 3-2. Adopt a Holistic View

- **Integrated decision-making.** Decisions are made considering the disparate perspectives across the entire project ecosystem, ensuring that outputs lead to more sustainable and effective outcomes.
- **Enhanced communication.** Clear and consistent communication across all stakeholders helps ensure that everyone is informed and aligned.
- **Managing uncertainty and complexity.** In projects with high uncertainty, a holistic view helps ensure that planning and execution incorporate techniques to progressively identify and address sources of uncertainty and possible impacts that are likely to harm the project's value proposition. Similarly, for highly complex projects, a holistic approach seeks to understand and simplify the intricate interdependencies within the project, uncovering inherent simplicity.
- **Proactive and pragmatic risk management.** By having a holistic view from the onset, the project management team can have a wider and clearer understanding of the interconnectedness of the project. Hence, the project management team is in a better position for informed and timely decision-making to effectively and efficiently mitigate threats while exploiting opportunities.

Having a holistic approach to sustainability can ensure that all aspects of the project are making a positive contribution (or at least any negative contribution is quantified). This approach can relate to the environmental cost/impact of the project activities as well as the environmental benefits (or negative impacts) delivered by the project. This approach also aligns with the Integrate Sustainability Within All Project Areas principle. By embracing a holistic view, project managers and stakeholders can increase the likelihood of considering all aspects of the project, leading to better decision-making and more effective project execution, which not only aligns with organizational goals but also fosters resilience and adaptability, resulting in a successful project.

3.3.2 Principle in Action

To provide an example of this principle in action, consider a nonprofit, nongovernmental organization (NGO) that is launching a project to promote public health practices in a local community, supported by a dedicated volunteer team. Following a conventional, narrowly focused approach, the focus is on creating educational materials and then organizing events. However, midway through the project, the NGO learns of a local government initiative with similar goals, offering a funding grant for aligned efforts. Recognizing the potential for greater impact, the team adapts their communications to align with the government initiative, qualifying for the grant. While this introduces stricter policy and communication constraints, the project now has more resources and broader reach, enabling the NGO to make a more significant and lasting impact on public health in the community.

3.3.3 Connected Performance Domains

The Adopt a Holistic View principle interacts with and elevates the performance of all domains. By applying this principle, each domain can be managed more effectively, helping to ensure a cohesive and integrated approach to project management. This principle benefits each project management performance domain in the following ways:

- **Governance.** A holistic view promotes transparency and accountability, enabling informed, data-driven decision-making based on a wider scope and impacts that can drive progress in a manner that maximizes the positive impact from project investments for a given portfolio, program, or project.

- **Scope.** The principle of Adopt a Holistic View helps foster alignment of all project activities with the overall project scope, preventing scope creep and misalignment by considering the entire project ecosystem. Also, by promoting clarity on the organizational objectives to be achieved rather than merely the end deliverables, the principle encourages creative solutioning, allowing an equal opportunity to achieve simpler but more effective, sustainable, and long-lasting solutions.
- **Schedule.** A holistic view improves scheduling by considering the interdependencies of all project activities, making timelines more realistic and adaptive to changes and maintaining alignment with project goals. By implementing a holistic view, the project management team can ensure that the most relevant what-if scenarios are drawn out and evaluated, and that candidate baseline changes are evaluated for which one might yield the highest return on investment for that project—and for the project's portfolio and program contexts overall.
- **Finance.** A holistic approach optimizes financial management by aligning budget allocations with project priorities, controlling project costs effectively, and anticipating financial impacts of changes within the broader project context—all aimed at maximizing returns on project investments.
- **Stakeholders.** The Adopt a Holistic View principle enhances the engagement of all relevant stakeholders, from departments to vendors to customers. This engagement is done by ensuring inclusive participation in decision-making processes, leading to improved satisfaction and collaboration as their perspectives are integrated into the project strategy.
- **Resources.** Having a holistic mindset also emphasizes understanding how all project components are intended to integrate in order to maximize the project's value proposition. This view makes it easier to drive the flow of completed work, avoid unnecessary resource conflicts, optimize the use of project resources within a portfolio or program, and equip and empower team members to execute the work, all according to what drives the most value.
- **Risk.** A holistic view facilitates proactive risk management by identifying and managing risks across all project domains, understanding their interdependencies, and developing robust risk management strategies.

3.4 Focus on Value

Value, also referred to as project value, is the ultimate success indicator and driver of projects. Value can be described and assessed using either measurable metrics, such as return on investment, or qualitative observations such as testimonials and societal benefits. Value represents the overall worth of the project outcomes and the net benefits to stakeholders (see Figure 3-3). This value encompasses the deliverables and their related outcomes, particularly from the perspective of key stakeholders. Value can be expressed in various ways, such as financial contributions to the sponsoring or receiving organization, social benefits, or the customer's perceived benefits from the project result. Regardless of their form, all projects exist to pursue target organizational objectives that are worth more than what is invested in pursuit of those objectives—often significantly more than what might be available via alternative investment options.

Project justification and organizational strategy, often detailed in a business case, provide the project team with the necessary information to make decisions that meet or exceed the intended business value. Desired outcomes should be clearly described, iteratively assessed, and updated throughout the project life cycle using quality gates, feedback loops, and regular reviews. The project team should adapt to changes and continuously evaluate alignment with the desired outputs, baselines,

Focus on Value

Continually evaluate and adjust project alignment to business objectives and intended benefits and value.	▶ Value per unit of investment is the ultimate indicator of project success. ▶ Value can be realized throughout the project, at the end of the project, or following project completion. ▶ Value, and the benefits that contribute to it, can be defined in quantitative and/or qualitative terms. ▶ Project teams focus on outcomes that maximize value creation and meet or exceed target business objectives. ▶ Project teams evaluate progress and adapt to maximize the expected value.

Figure 3-3. Focus on Value

business case, and intended outcomes. If misalignment persists or the project is unlikely to deliver the intended value, it may be best to terminate the effort.

A focus on value aims to maximize the return on project investments for the customer, performing organization, and/or other stakeholders. This effort involves delivering the required functionality and quality by optimizing workflows with acceptable risk exposure, using minimal necessary resources, and avoiding unnecessary rework and other types of waste. In adaptive projects without a fixed scope, the project team collaborates with the customer to determine which features are worth the investment in both time and money.

The value contribution of project work can be short term or long term and may be intertwined with operational activities, making it challenging to isolate. When a project is part of a program, evaluating value at the program level is necessary to properly direct the project. The project value provides key data for portfolio management so that decisions can be made on which projects to select or continue based on their value contribution. A reliable evaluation of value should consider the entire context and life cycle of the project as well as its expected payback period, which may extend well beyond project closeout.

3.4.1 Project Impact

Shifting focus from deliverables to intended outcomes allows project teams to deliver on the project's vision or purpose, rather than merely creating a specific deliverable. While a deliverable may support the intended project outcome, it may not fully achieve the project's vision or purpose. For example, customers may want specific software because they believe it will resolve their business need for higher productivity. The software is the output of the project, but it does not enable productivity by itself. Adding a new deliverable, such as training in the use of the software, can enable a higher-value outcome. If the project's output fails to enable the desired productivity, then the value proposition of the project is undermined and may even become more harmful than helpful, given the investment in time and resources. Therefore, project teams, stakeholders, and in particular, team members, should understand both the deliverable and the intended outcome from the deliverable.

3.4.2 Principle in Action

To provide an example of the Focus on Value principle in action, consider a company that is undertaking a project to roll out a new internal technology system. A conventional approach might focus on choosing a product with the most features for the price and then customizing it to meet all of the requested stakeholder requirements. In contrast, a value-focused approach aligns the project with business outcomes like maximizing usage and adoption. A deeper look might reveal a fast-paced organizational culture that values simplicity of experience over complexity of features. By reducing features and customizations, the more simplified solution might better match the culture, and thus increase overall usage and satisfaction.

3.4.3 Connected Performance Domains

The Focus on Value principle interacts with and elevates the practice of all project management performance domains. By applying this principle, each domain can be managed more effectively, ensuring that the project maximizes value for the stakeholders. The relevant connections between this principle and specific project management performance domains include the following:

- **Governance.** A value-focused approach establishes frameworks and processes that help ensure decisions are made in alignment with the project's value objectives. Governance is "right-sized" to focus on value delivery, not bureaucracy.
- **Scope.** A value-focused approach can help to define and control the project scope to ensure that all work contributes to the intended value. This approach involves continuous scope management to prevent scope creep and gold plating and to ensure that the project remains focused on delivering its key outcomes.
- **Schedule.** A focus on value helps to ensure that time is managed effectively to help the project to deliver the expected value by—or earlier than—the target date. This effort includes planning and controlling the project schedule to avoid delays that could diminish the project's value.
- **Finance.** The Focus on Value principle helps ensure that financial resources are allocated efficiently to maximize the project's value. This effort involves continuous assessment of financial performance against the business case to ensure that the project remains viable and delivers the expected financial benefits.
- **Stakeholders.** A value mindset can help when engaging with stakeholders to understand their needs and expectations, ensuring that the project delivers value from their perspective. Effective stakeholder engagement helps align the project's outputs with the desired outcomes and enhances stakeholder satisfaction.
- **Resources.** Keeping a project's value proposition at the center of attention can help inform decisions around physical assets and project team talent. For example, financial constraints may not allow the hiring of specialized team members needed to achieve project goals. In that case, focusing on value can spark alternative solutions such as cross-training existing team members.
- **Risk.** Focusing on value helps ensure that the approach taken to address uncertainty in the project, whether responding to known or emergent threats or responding to opportunities, is pragmatic in the sense of effectiveness, efficiency, and transparency.

3.5 Embed Quality Into Processes and Deliverables

Quality is the degree to which a set of inherent characteristics of a project deliverable or process helps to meet or exceed the project's target objectives. Embedding quality includes the ability to satisfy customers and stakeholders' stated or implied needs as a matter of course, at or above target levels of efficiency (see Figure 3-4). The quality of the deliverable and the processes used to achieve it are measured by conformance to acceptance criteria, the definition of done (DoD), fitness for use, and overall efficiency. While quality thresholds typically address scope specifications, they can also apply to schedule and cost, especially for projects where the value proposition may be highly sensitive to those factors. Adopting a continuous improvement mindset optimizes processes, boosts efficiency, and enhances maturity growth for the whole organization, leading to better project outcomes and overall organizational success for present and future endeavors.

Foundational to embedding target quality thresholds is continuous improvement and waste elimination. These practices enable project teams to refine their processes, optimize resource utilization, and deliver outcomes that meet or exceed target objectives. Continuous improvement allows teams to proactively identify and address areas for enhancement in both deliverables and workflows, while waste elimination streamlines processes, conserving resources and improving performance. Quality spans several dimensions that apply to both deliverables and processes, including but not limited to the following:

- **Performance.** Do the deliverables or processes function as intended by the project team and other stakeholders?
- **Conformity.** Are the deliverables and processes aligned with specifications and fit for use?
- **Reliability.** Do the deliverables and processes maintain the consistency necessary to meet or exceed desired outcomes?

Embed Quality Into Processes and Deliverables

Embed quality into processes and deliverables to maintain a consistent focus on achieving target quality thresholds. This emphasis on quality helps to ensure outcomes that meet project objectives and align with the needs, requirements, and acceptance criteria set by relevant stakeholders.

- ▶ Project quality entails satisfying relevant stakeholders' expectations and fulfilling project and product requirements.
- ▶ Quality focuses on meeting acceptance criteria for deliverables.
- ▶ Project quality entails ensuring project processes are appropriate and as effective as possible.

Figure 3-4. Embed Quality Into Processes and Deliverables

- **Resilience.** Can the deliverables and supporting processes cope with unforeseen failures and recover quickly?
- **Satisfaction.** Do the deliverables and processes elicit valuable feedback from customers and/or end users, including usability and user experience?
- **Uniformity.** Do the deliverables and processes demonstrate parity across similar outputs or workflows?
- **Efficiency.** Are the deliverables and processes optimized to produce the greatest output with the least input?
- **Sustainability.** Do the deliverables and processes contribute positively to economic, social, and environmental outcomes?
- **Compliance.** Do the deliverables and processes comply with regulatory requirements and relevant industry standards, as well as organizational standards?

Project teams measure quality using metrics and acceptance criteria based on project specifications. A specification is an attribute that is necessary to be present in a project deliverable to help meet or exceed a target objective. Quality is linked to the product acceptance criteria, as described in the project charter, statement of work (SOW), or other key documents. In some projects, as the project evolves through experimentation, these criteria should be regularly updated and refined. Ensuring these criteria are validated during the acceptance process is essential to meeting project objectives and delivering a successful product.

Quality is also relevant to the project approaches and activities used to produce the project's deliverables. Project teams can pursue the target quality thresholds of both the project and the product by providing training, conducting inspections, and performing testing. Additionally, project activities and processes are evaluated through reviews and audits. Both approaches aim to identify and prevent errors and defects, thereby maintaining an accelerated flow of completed work while pursuing target quality thresholds.

3.5.1 Project Impact

The objective of quality activities is to help ensure that what is delivered meets the objectives of the customer and other relevant stakeholders. The intention is to minimize the waste of resources and maximize the probability of attaining the desired outcome. This effort results in the following:

- Moving the deliverables to the point of delivery without unnecessary delays, and
- Minimizing the need for rework and/or reducing material waste through the early detection and prevention of defects.

The objective of quality activities is the same whether dealing with an up-front, well-defined set of requirements or a set of requirements that is progressively elaborated and incrementally delivered.

Quality management processes and practices help produce deliverables and outcomes that meet project objectives and align to the expectations, requirements, and acceptance criteria expressed by the organization and relevant stakeholders. Close attention to quality in project processes and deliverables creates positive outcomes, including the following:

- Project deliverables that are fit for purpose and that meet acceptance criteria, stakeholder expectations, and organizational objectives;

- Timely delivery, enhanced cost control, and attainment of the level of product quality associated with meeting or exceeding target objectives;
- Reduced rework, scrap, customer complaints, and other types of waste;
- Effective supply chain integration, increased productivity, and robust service delivery;
- Higher project team morale and satisfaction;
- Reduced negative impact on the environment, including avoiding the unnecessary consumption of natural resources and emissions due to rework activities, as well as the overhead of managing activities that may require travel; and
- Better decision-making and continuous process improvement.

3.5.2 Principle in Action

To provide an example of the Embed Quality Into Processes and Deliverables principle in action, consider a company that is expanding its wholesale shipping services to support an unfamiliar regional market. A conventional approach would focus on meeting the governmental shipping specifications for each target market and ensuring compliance with regulatory requirements.

In contrast, a quality-driven approach would investigate the expectations of the broader stakeholder system, including target distributors and retailers. This deeper analysis might reveal that high-value customers have stricter standards than regulatory bodies, which could influence packaging, delivery times, or product handling. By addressing these higher standards, the company not only meets legal requirements but also exceeds customer expectations, leading to stronger market entry, enhanced customer satisfaction, and potentially greater market share.

3.5.3 Connected Performance Domains

The Embed Quality Into Processes and Deliverables principle is critical in all project management performance domains because it is essential to ensuring that project outcomes meet stakeholder needs and expectations. This principle should be embedded in the project's design across people, processes, and structure. Different industries, companies, and contexts have different approaches to quality, but commitment to achieving the right level of quality is entrenched in the successful outcomes of all projects, across domain areas. A lack of commitment to the right level of quality in any domain can lead to erosion of the end result and poor project outcomes. This quality-focused principle affects the performance domains in the following ways:

- **Governance.** Embedding quality into governance processes improves transparency and accountability. Governance structures help ensure that quality standards are met and can enable decisions that prioritize quality in all project activities.
- **Scope.** The connection between quality and the Scope performance domain is particularly strong, as scope management inherently involves quality management activities. Ensuring that project deliverables meet the requirements, necessary standards, and specifications is an important aspect of scope management. By embedding the right level of quality into the scope, the project team can ensure that all deliverables are not only completed within the defined boundaries, but also meet quality standards, which prevents rework and ensures stakeholder satisfaction.

- **Schedule.** An emphasis on quality has implications for the project's schedule. Examples include ensuring scheduling practices and artifacts are reviewed for completeness and correctness; integrating product quality reviews as scheduled milestones; and practicing a "shift-left" approach, where quality practices are prioritized as early in the project life cycle as possible.
- **Finance.** Embedding quality into finance helps control costs by preventing rework and reducing waste. Aligning financial management with quality objectives supports cost control while pursuing the project's objectives.
- **Stakeholders.** Quality in this performance domain helps ensure that stakeholder expectations are met. Through continuous communication, stakeholder feedback is integrated into the project aspects, leading to increased satisfaction, collaboration, and credibility.
- **Resources.** In this performance domain, embedding quality can ensure that the right resources are allocated to maintain target quality thresholds. This effort includes using skilled personnel and appropriate tools, helping to ensure that the project is adequately supported to deliver the intended results.
- **Risk.** The Risk performance domain encompasses the proactive management of quality-related risks. By embedding quality into every aspect of the project, potential quality issues can be anticipated and mitigated, reducing the risk of defects and noncompliance.

3.6 Be an Accountable Leader

Projects create a unique need for effective leadership. Unlike general business operations, where roles and responsibilities are often established and consistent, projects may involve multiple organizations, departments, functions, or vendors that do not interact on a regular basis. Moreover, projects may carry higher stakes and expectations than regular operational functions. As a result, a broader array of managers, executives, senior contributors, and other stakeholders may attempt to influence a project. This diversity of influence often creates higher degrees of confusion and conflict. Consequently, effective leadership behaviors are found more frequently—and from more people—on high-performing projects than lower-performing projects. Accountable leadership is about being responsible and taking ownership of the project's target business objectives, as well as the actions taken and the decisions made (see Figure 3-5). When accepting or pulling work, accountability means being responsible for the execution of that work. The key characteristics of an accountable leader include the following:

- **Integrity, honesty, and fairness.** These values are required of all team members, where people demonstrate the moral principles that guide their decisions, particularly in tough situations. The decisions made by a leader with integrity and fairness are focused on the common good, helping to build trust with stakeholders.
- **Self-awareness.** Effective leaders have the capability to make connections among their feelings, thoughts, and actions by understanding their motives, values, and strengths. This self-awareness helps professionals build relationships to accomplish results.
- **Respectfulness, humility, and availability.** Leaders should be open to feedback and should work for the team, supporting their needs and removing barriers when possible. These values form the basis for the concept of servant leadership.
- **Flexibility and adaptability.** Leaders should have the capability to adapt their leadership style to the situation and the audience. Leadership styles should be adapted based on the project's needs without losing the leader's core values.

Be an Accountable Leader

Demonstrate leadership behaviors and be an accountable leader by guiding your team with integrity, making responsible decisions, and fostering a culture of trust and responsibility.	▶ Leaders influence, inspire, and motivate others. ▶ Leaders are accountable for their actions. ▶ Effective leaders lead by example. ▶ Leaders demonstrate responsibility, respect, fairness, and honesty. ▶ Effective leaders adapt their style to the situation. ▶ Leaders foster an environment of psychological safety. ▶ Any project professional, stakeholder, and team member can demonstrate leadership behaviors.

Figure 3-5. Be an Accountable Leader

- **Shared leadership.** Leadership is not exclusive to any specific role; in different moments of the project, a team member, stakeholder, or professional may take the leadership seat. High-performing projects feature multiple people exercising leadership skills. Leadership is different from authority. Authority is the position of control given to individuals within the organization, whereas leadership is about inspiring and motivating others through leading by example.

3.6.1 Project Impact

As leaders, project managers influence—through their behavior—all of the professionals involved in a project. A project manager influences the project and team through a combination of leadership, effective communication, decision-making, emotional intelligence, problem-solving, stakeholder engagement, and strategic thinking. Their leadership style directly shapes team dynamics, motivation, and overall performance. Emotional intelligence enables the project manager to navigate conflicts and stress while strong stakeholder engagement helps secure support and buy-in.

Accountable leaders focus on delivering value beyond the project work. They commit to promoting the growth of other leaders around them and making a positive impact on their area of influence. The implications of this principle are profound and diverse for the project manager and all relevant stakeholders and lead to the following:

- Enhanced team performance,
- Increased trust and morale,
- Improved decision-making,
- Greater stakeholder confidence, and
- Resilience in facing challenges.

3.6.2 Principle in Action

To provide an example of the Be an Accountable Leader principle, consider a government megaproject that involves multiple vendors. In the project, a conflict arises among the vendor teams over previously arranged shift rotations. A conventional approach would focus on enforcing the contractually agreed-upon labor policies and holding each vendor accountable for resolving the discontent among their staff.

In contrast, applying this principle could involve holding a series of cross-vendor discussions to explore the root cause of the issue and identify acceptable adjustments to the shift rotations. This collaborative approach not only resolves the conflict but also removes friction that could undermine quality and productivity, fostering a more cohesive and motivated project team.

3.6.3 Connected Performance Domains

The principle of Be an Accountable Leader supports many project management performance domains and can enhance the effectiveness of the project manager when well applied, such as with the following:

- **Governance.** In the Governance performance domain, accountable leadership can ensure that decisions are made transparently and ethically. Leaders take ownership of the project's direction and outcomes, fostering trust and ensuring that governance structures are upheld.
- **Scope.** Every project faces difficult decisions around what scope to include or exclude. Strong leadership should confront and resolve scope disagreements in a way that unites stakeholders on the project's value proposition.
- **Schedule.** Reliable project schedules are the result of collaborative discussions among the project team, senior management, and other stakeholders. Accountable leadership should ensure that those discussions include the appropriate parties and that there is alignment on schedule activities and artifacts.
- **Finance.** Every project involves financial considerations. Accountable leadership neither ignores nor carelessly addresses such considerations. Instead, this principle encourages practitioners to manage pressures that come when costs are scrutinized, reserves are applied, or other financial challenges arise.
- **Stakeholders.** An effective leader is able to engage and influence stakeholders and sponsors to secure and maintain the support that is needed for the project.
- **Resources.** Self-awareness helps to build relationships and foster human interactions to obtain better results. An effective leader manages resources with responsibility and integrity.
- **Risk.** An effective leader can adapt and be flexible to opportunities or threats that a project team may face. Effective leaders demonstrate integrity and accountability to help ensure that risk is managed in a way that protects and enhances the project's overall value proposition.

3.7 Integrate Sustainability Within All Project Areas

The principle of Integrate Sustainability Within All Project Areas involves meeting present needs without compromising the ability of future generations to meet their own needs (see Figure 3-6). This principle may involve adopting technology responsibly to foster a better future, while systematically identifying and mitigating any adverse impacts on the organization, community, and environment.

Integrate Sustainability Within All Project Areas

Consistently integrate sustainability practices across all project areas, through all phases of the project life cycle, as project managers, teams, and sponsors are all jointly accountable for ensuring this integration.

- Integrating sustainability means considering people, the planet, society, and value while performing project-related activities.
- Sustainability encompasses addressing environmental, social, and economic impacts, considering the well-being of people globally, the effective and wise use of natural resources, and implementing sustainable strategies.
- The sustainability principle can be evident at the tactical, operational, and strategic levels of all projects.

Figure 3-6. Integrate Sustainability Within All Project Areas

This principle involves considering strategies to address any externality that the project may create. Such strategies can be categorized as increasingly impactful, from at least compensating stakeholders for the negative outcomes created, to minimizing them, to avoiding them altogether (see Figure 3-7). This approach addresses environmental impacts, considerations for the well-being of people globally, and the implementation of sustainable strategies.

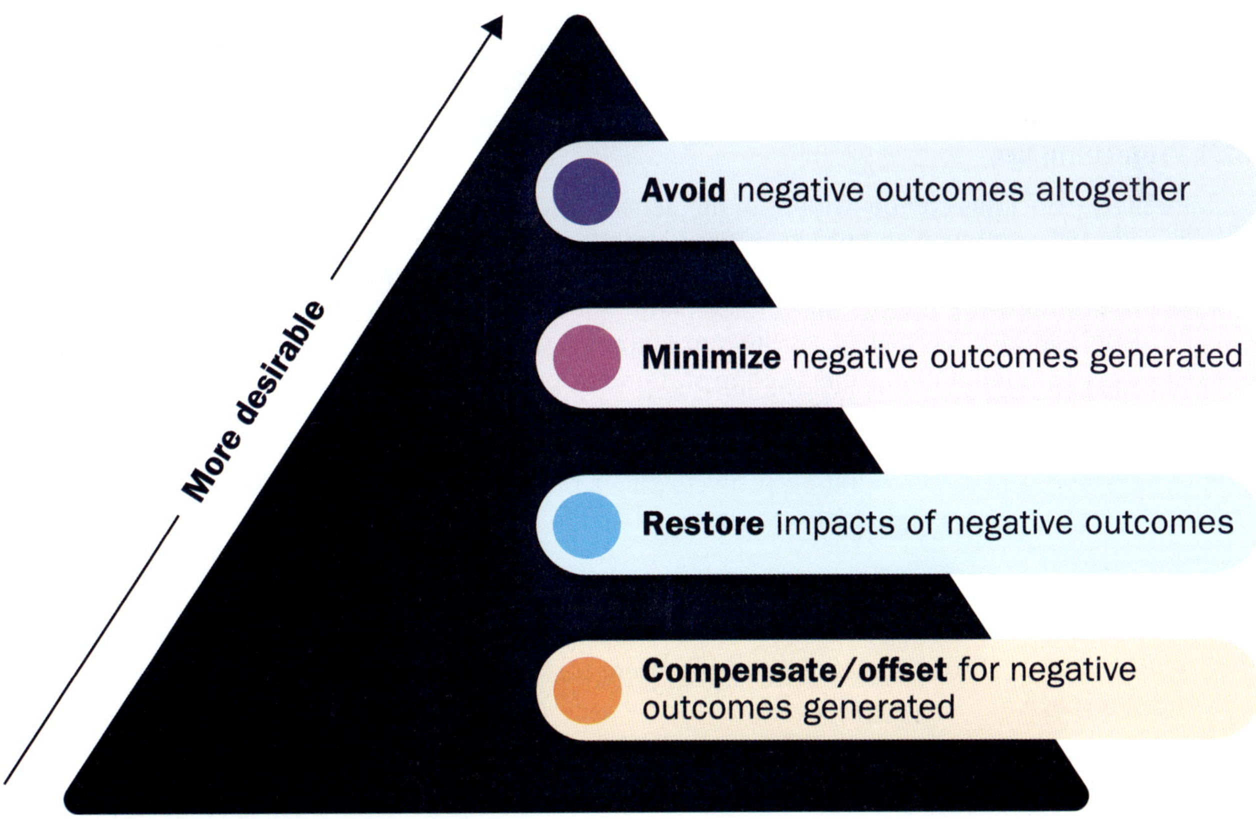

Figure 3-7. The Sustainability Pyramid

Sustainability is essential for addressing global challenges such as climate change, biodiversity loss, pollution, societal inequities, and community well-being. By integrating sustainability into project management, organizations can align with the triple bottom line, balancing social equity, environmental stewardship, and economic prosperity. This dual focus on sustainability and project outcomes not only enhances corporate social responsibility but also fosters innovative and responsible technological practices that contribute to long-term value creation. Other benefits for organizations implementing sustainability broadly include the following:

- **Organizational benefits.** These benefits include employee satisfaction, performance improvements, staff retention, and stronger recruitment. Additional benefits include improved relationships with shareholders and stakeholders, optimized risk responses and impacts, increased resilience and organizational learning, and enhanced decision-making processes. This overall improvement results from resolving ethical dilemmas, enhancing corporate governance, complying with laws and regulations, reducing litigation costs, increasing brand value, and boosting corporate reputation.
- **Operational benefits.** These benefits include innovation in internal processes, productivity improvements due to operational waste minimization, and designing for sustainability.
- **Financial benefits.** These benefits include but are not limited to direct cost savings from reduced material and energy usage, lower operational costs, less waste, decreased capital expenses, increased share value, and more investments from sustainable finance investors.
- **Benefits related to customers and stakeholders.** These benefits include increased satisfaction and innovation driven by active listening and open communication with customers and stakeholders throughout the project life cycle. Additional advantages are market share growth due to the rising demand for sustainable and innovative products globally, a stronger reputation, and new market opportunities.

3.7.1 Project Impact

Sustainability principles can be evident at all tactical, operational, and strategic levels of projects. Indeed, relevant processes and practices may already be integrated into enterprise environmental factors (EEFs). For example, enterprise sustainability or information management strategies may impose requirements on project deliverables and teams. Additionally, these principles can impact projects from initiation to closure. For instance, sustainability-related key performance indicators (KPIs) may be included in the project scope statement, project charter, business case, contracts, or other formal documents authorizing project activities. Compliance can be monitored during project planning, execution, and closure. As sustainability is integrated into strategic goals for most organizations and communities, projects play a pivotal role in realizing sustainable practices and outcomes (see Figure 3-8). Instilling sustainability in project management requires the following:

- Having a societal perspective for projects and their outcomes;
- Maintaining broad stakeholder engagement through a "management for stakeholder" approach;
- Leading the team and stakeholders with responsible (ethical) leadership; and
- Holistically focusing on the value generated by the project from the perspective of the broader stakeholder audience such as value creation and distribution.

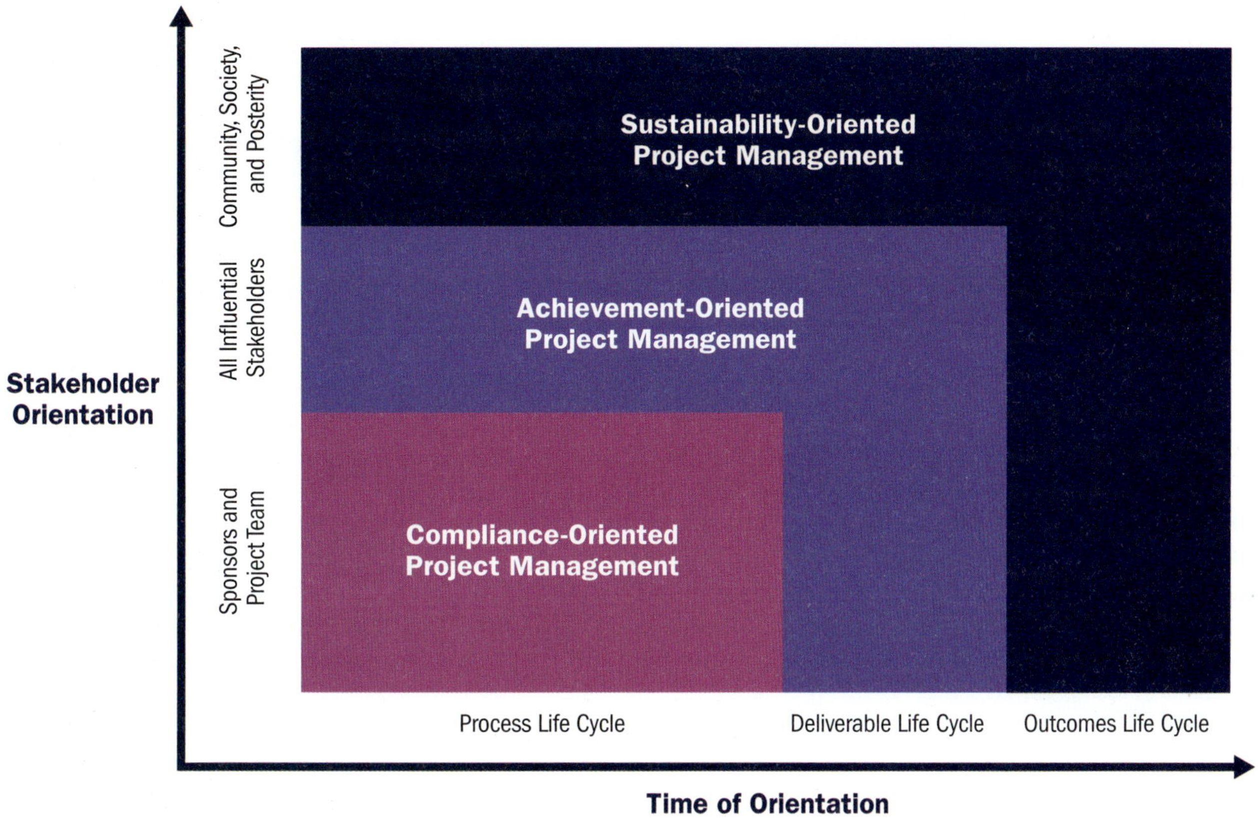

Figure 3-8. Sustainability Broadens the Orientation of Project Management

The inclusion of sustainability goals does generate some challenges, such as the following:

- Integrating sustainability broadens the scope of project management by considering broader time orientations and more stakeholders. This in turn may increase the costs or complexities of managing projects. Sustainability goals should be included in the formal project documents, such as the business case, and confirmed by the project sponsor. If these goals are not included, the project manager should still encourage discussions about their impact during meetings and among stakeholders.
- Sustainability risks arise when project activities fail to balance or integrate societal, economic, and environmental considerations, potentially jeopardizing the overall sustainability of the project. Examples include prioritizing cost over environmental stewardship, failing to account for community impacts, or underestimating regulatory compliance requirements tied to sustainability. Such risks can lead to negative project outcomes, stakeholder dissatisfaction, and long-term harm to the organization's reputation or performance.
- Assessing a project's success is challenging due to the lack of universal sustainability criteria; each project requires a tailored approach. To promote sustainability and reduce waste, the project team should have access to tools that provide the necessary information for them to fully manage the sustainability of their work.

3.7.2 Principle in Action

To provide an example of the principle of Integrate Sustainability Within All Project Areas, consider a construction project. Construction projects often require materials derived from natural resources, which may be sourced externally. If sustainability principles are overlooked, the project team might choose the least expensive materials, potentially harming the environment and human health. By adhering to sustainability principles, the project team not only focuses on the project's value and the internal rate of return, but also demonstrates a commitment to environmental sustainability and the responsible use of materials and natural resources while involving local communities. This effort could involve carefully planning the required materials and selecting sources with the least environmental impact or seeking materials that mimic natural processes and draw inspiration from nature (e.g., constructing urban buildings with wood or using recycled concrete instead of natural stone).

Technology projects can enhance sustainability by integrating eco-friendly practices into project management, emphasizing social responsibility, and maximizing social impact. By adopting appropriate tools and innovative technologies, project teams can reduce resource consumption and waste, streamline processes, and improve efficiency. Projects can also focus on creating positive social impacts such as improving access to education and healthcare through technology. Environmental sustainability is achieved by selecting sustainable materials, minimizing carbon footprints, and implementing eco-friendly technologies. This holistic approach helps foster a more sustainable future.

3.7.3 Connected Performance Domains

The Integrate Sustainability Within All Project Areas principle may impact the Finance performance domain as sustainable practices may require additional funding, but they may also reduce the level of financial threat for the project (and the funding organization). The project team may consider green benefits to be included in the project requirements.

The principle of Integrate Sustainability Within All Project Areas can positively impact the Risk performance domain by enabling proactive identification and mitigation of long-term risks, such as environmental, regulatory, or societal challenges. Sustainability initiatives can also create opportunities for innovation by encouraging project teams to develop resource-efficient solutions and sustainable practices. Embedding societal and environmental values into project management strengthens the Governance, Scope, and Stakeholders performance domains by fostering accountability, aligning scope with organizational goals and societal needs, and enhancing stakeholder trust. This approach benefits the project team during execution and delivers lasting value to the organization, improving its reputation and resilience once the project or product life cycle is complete.

Integrating sustainability can affect many aspects of a project, including but not limited to the following:

- **Governance.** The project team's proactive and collaborative approach with the governance team develops a positive, transparent communication channel with management, helping to ensure alignment with the project objectives and outcomes, with the least deviations and less confusion. This approach includes integrating sustainability goals into governance practices to ensure long-term environmental and social benefits.
- **Scope.** Open-channel communication proactively calibrates to a project's evolving needs to add elements, adjust quality, or remove elements of the scope or project requirements. Sustainability considerations should be embedded into the scope to help ensure that project deliverables meet or exceed the organization's sustainability goals, as well as environmental and social standards.

- **Schedule.** Teams can offer ideas to accelerate, slow down, or stop delivery of key project activities to maximize the available opportunities. Scheduling decisions consider the environmental impacts, aiming to minimize carbon footprints and resource usage.
- **Finance.** Teams help to reduce or eliminate planned expenditures by adding steps, requirements, or restrictions that increase costs or require additional resources. Benefits realization occurs by generating and identifying long-term goals, so the project delivers the intended identified value. Financial planning includes sustainability investments that promote long-term cost savings and environmental benefits.
- **Stakeholders.** Teams establish, influence, or even define the level and character of engagement with stakeholders and the broader organization. Stakeholder engagement strategies include sustainability education and collaboration to ensure all parties are aligned with the project's environmental and social goals.
- **Resources.** Teams restrict or enable access to physical resources in line with project requirements; the same applies for people with the skills, knowledge, and experience needed to deliver the intended outcomes and promote a learning culture. Resource management prioritizes sustainable materials and practices, ensuring minimal environmental impact.
- **Risk.** The team defines the risk thresholds of the project and participates in subsequent risk management activities. Risk management includes identifying and mitigating environmental and social threats to help ensure the project's sustainability objectives are met.

3.8 Build an Empowered Culture

To develop an empowered project culture, the project environment should promote mutual trust among stakeholders and the project team members. There should be full clarity on individual roles, responsibilities, team agreements, and guiding processes. These factors enable individuals to work together and provide synergistic effects from their interactions, which can enable stakeholders to collaborate more effectively and efficiently to drive project success (see Figure 3-9).

Build an Empowered Culture

Build an empowered culture that fosters proactive collaboration and promotes unity in shared objectives efficiently and effectively through stakeholders and teams with diverse skills, knowledge, and experience.

- Stakeholders determine the success of projects.
- Stakeholders and team members on a project are key to its success, and they should be empowered across many dimensions.
- A collaborative project environment enables stakeholders and team members to contribute their ideas and recommendations freely and proactively to meet project outcomes.
- Knowing that key stakeholders can highly influence project performance and outcomes, motivated and empowered project teams actively engage with them to maximize value delivery.

Figure 3-9. Build an Empowered Culture

3.8.1 Project Impact

Project stakeholders are influenced by the cultures of the organizations involved in the project and by the environment in which they operate. Within these influences, project teams often establish their own cultural norms. Project teams have the flexibility to customize their organizational frameworks to optimally achieve the intended project goal within such new cultures.

The principle of Build an Empowered Culture enables successful project execution in the following areas:

- **Diversity.** A diverse project team can enrich the project environment to create a more inclusive space by bringing together different perspectives. In a global economy, the project team may comprise internal organizational staff, contracted contributors, volunteers, or external third parties. Some project team members may also be brought in for a short term to work on a specific deliverable. Incorporating these key members into a project team may present challenges. However, cultivating a team environment that honors diversity and seeks to harness it constructively fosters an atmosphere where conflicts can be managed efficiently.
- **Process definition.** Project teams should define processes that enable the completion of tasks and work assignments. Additionally, project teams should engage other stakeholders to understand, consider, communicate, and respond to their interests, needs, and opinions.
- **Interpersonal skills.** Project team members and stakeholders should develop a set of interpersonal skills such as initiative, integrity, honesty, collaboration, respect, empathy, and confidence. These competencies and perspectives assist teams in adjusting to the tasks and one another. Coupled with an active involvement of stakeholders from inception to completion, these competencies pave the way for success.
- **Knowledge of organizational structures.** Being aware of the various configurations and relationships among the components of project tasks and organizational procedures is important for teams to consider when building an empowered culture. Project teams tailor and employ frameworks that facilitate the synchronization of personal contributions within project tasks.
- **Team agreements.** Team agreements represent a set of behavioral parameters and working norms that are established by the project team and upheld through individual and team commitments. These agreements should be created at the beginning of a project to determine the essential norms and practices that facilitate ongoing collaborative success.

3.8.2 Principle in Action

To provide an example of the principle of Build an Empowered Culture, consider a project team that is facing challenges with stakeholder engagement due to the territorial complexities and diversity of the people involved in the project. Building an empowered culture enables stakeholders to be seen and included from the project's inception. This involvement provides stakeholders with guidelines to add value and actively participate, contributing to the project's success.

Remote and virtual teams face heightened challenges due to varying work styles, time zones, and the absence of in-person interaction, which can hinder collaboration and relationship building. An empowered culture gives all team members and stakeholders the opportunity to build and collaborate in effective and constructive ways, solving differences and managing conflicts proactively.

3.8.3 Connected Performance Domains

Teams and stakeholders can affect many aspects of a project, including but not limited to the following:

- **Governance.** The project team's proactive and collaborative approach with the governance team develops a positive, transparent communication channel with management, helping to ensure alignment with the project objectives and achieve outcomes with the fewest deviations and least amount of confusion.
- **Scope.** Open-channel communication proactively calibrates to a project's evolving needs to add elements, adjust quality, or remove elements of the scope or project and quality requirements.
- **Schedule.** Empowered teams can offer ideas to accelerate, slow down, or stop delivery of key project activities to maximize the available opportunities.
- **Finance.** Empowered teams help to reduce or eliminate unplanned expenditures by performing steps, requirements, or restrictions that increase the focus on value creation. Benefits realization occurs by generating and identifying long-term goals, so the project delivers the intended identified value.
- **Stakeholders.** Teams establish, influence, or even define the level and character of engagement with appropriate stakeholders—both inside and outside the performing organization.
- **Resources.** Teams restrict or enable access to physical resources in line with the project requirements; the same applies for people with the skills, knowledge, and experience needed to deliver the intended outcomes and promote a learning culture.
- **Risk.** The team defines the risk thresholds of the project and participates in subsequent risk management activities.

Section 4

Project Life Cycles

A project life cycle is the series of activities and/or phases that a project passes through from its start to its closure. The project life cycle provides the foundational framework for managing a project. This basic framework applies regardless of the specific project work involved or the adopted project development approach.

This section explores the project life cycle through five factors:

- Project phases,
- Project development approaches (predictive, adaptive, hybrid),
- Considerations for selecting a development approach,
- Delivery cadence, and
- Project Management Focus Areas (formerly known as Process Groups).

4.1 Project Phases

Projects are often decomposed into multiple phases. A project phase is a collection of logically related project activities that culminates in the completion of one or more deliverables and/or outcomes.

The phases may be sequential, transitional, or overlapping. In some projects a combination of these phases may be used, and each phase may include one or more stages of the project life cycle. Project life cycles are independent of product life cycles, which can be part of the outcomes produced by a project. Projects may also generate outputs, which in turn enable outcomes that progressively realize the organization's strategy.

The phases in a life cycle can be described by a variety of attributes. Attributes may be measurable and unique to a specific phase. Attributes may include but are not limited to name, number, duration, resource requirements, entrance criteria for a project to move into that phase, and exit criteria for a project to complete a phase. A phase gate may occur after the end of a phase, before the beginning of the next phase.

Phase gates often include a review—sometimes known as stage gate, gate review, iteration review, or decision point review—to check that the desired outcomes or exit criteria for the phase have been achieved before proceeding to the next phase. Exit criteria may be tied to acceptance criteria for deliverables, contractual obligations, meeting specific performance targets, or other tangible measures. Factors such as resource availability, verification of the project's viability, and current alignment with organizational goals may determine the entry criteria. The project's performance and progress are compared to project and business documents that specify expectations. A decision (e.g., go/no-go decision) is made as a result of this comparison to continue to the next phase, continue to the next phase with modification, end the project or phase, remain in the phase, repeat the phase or elements of it, or park the project temporarily to address another urgent business initiative.

While phase gates are traditionally placed at the end of each phase to review the project's progress, they can also be placed at the start of each phase. These starting phase gates (pre-phase gates) can help ensure that the project is properly aligned, that sufficient resources and planning are in place, and that potential risks are addressed before progressing further. This additional checkpoint enhances the control and success of the project.

Organizations with multiple projects will often adopt a few standard project life cycles. Project managers and project teams may need to advise their management on the most appropriate life cycle to use, or it may be prescribed for them. If there is no standard life cycle, project managers and project teams should determine the best life cycle for each project. The project life cycle should be flexible enough to meet or exceed the project's target objectives in a way that protects and enhances the project's value proposition as much as possible. Life cycle flexibility often includes the following:

- Selecting the development approach or mix of approaches;
- Identifying the types of processes and activities that should be performed; and
- Adjusting the various attributes of an activity, phase, or process (e.g., name, duration, entrance criteria, and exit criteria).

A generic project phase is generally impacted by a series of characteristics. Depending on the project life cycle, these may present a series of scenarios. These characteristics and their scenarios vary greatly but may include the following:

- **Cost and staffing.** In many predictive project scenarios, levels of cost and staffing are low at the start, increase as the work is carried out, and drop rapidly as the project or phase ends.
- **Risk and uncertainty.** Regardless of the project life cycle, these two elements are usually greatest at the start of the project or phase and decrease over the project's life cycle as decisions are reached and deliverables are accepted.

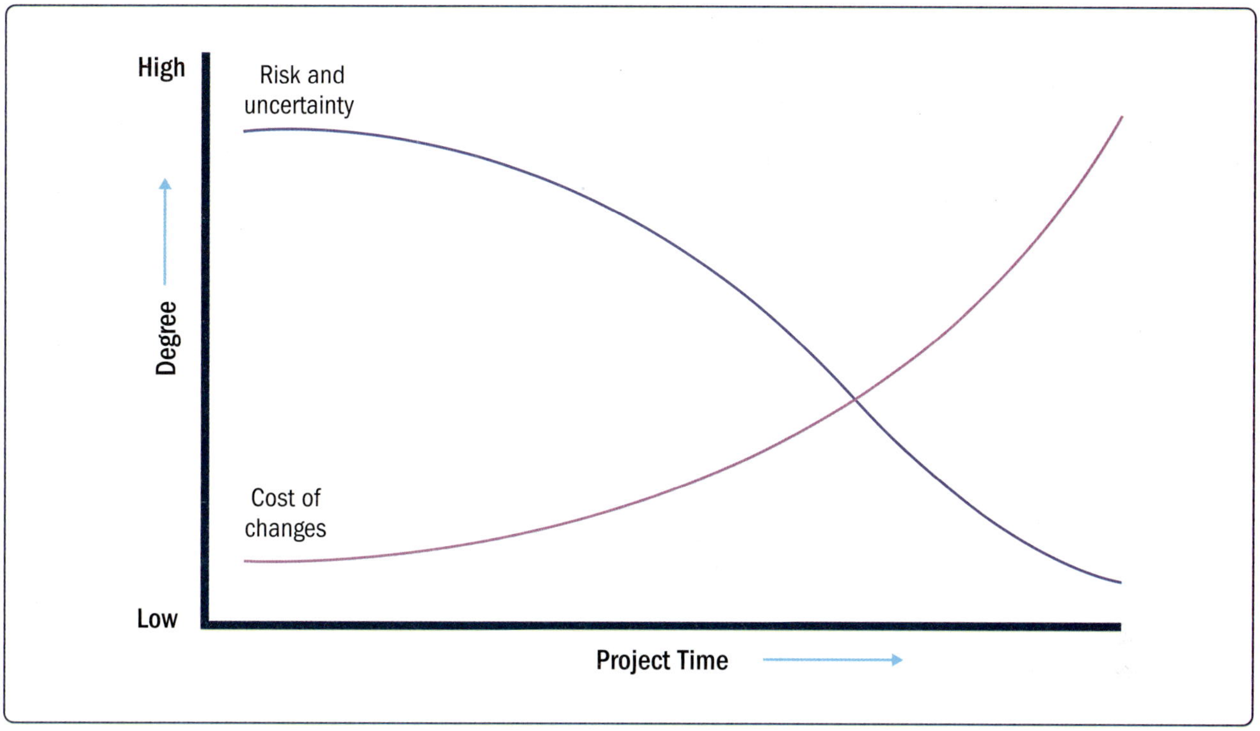

Figure 4-1. Impact of Variables Over Time

- **Stakeholder influence on change.** In some scenarios, the ability of stakeholders to influence the project's scope—increasing value without significantly impacting cost and schedule—is highest at the start of the project or phase and decreases as the project progresses toward completion. In other cases, stakeholders are encouraged to participate actively in the execution process, ensuring that value has been delivered according to their expectations and the organization's best interest. Consistent feedback leads to the possibility of detecting risks and their impacts at an earlier stage (see Figure 4-1).

4.2 Project Development Approaches

A development approach is the means used to create and evolve a product, service, or result during the project life cycle. Note that the term "development approach" is separate from the term "development phase of the project." The development approach refers to the method used to create and evolve the product, service, or result during the project life cycle, such as predictive, adaptive, or hybrid methods. The development approach defines how the project will be managed and executed. Conversely, the development phase of the project is a specific stage within the project life cycle where both the actual creation and testing of deliverables occur. This stage involves detailed work to produce the project's outputs. There are different development approaches, and different industries may use different terms to refer to them.

Three commonly used approaches are predictive, adaptive, and hybrid. These approaches are often viewed as a spectrum, from the predictive approach on one end of the spectrum to the adaptive approach on the other end. The hybrid approach is usually intended as a mix of predictive and adaptive approaches (see Figure 4-2).

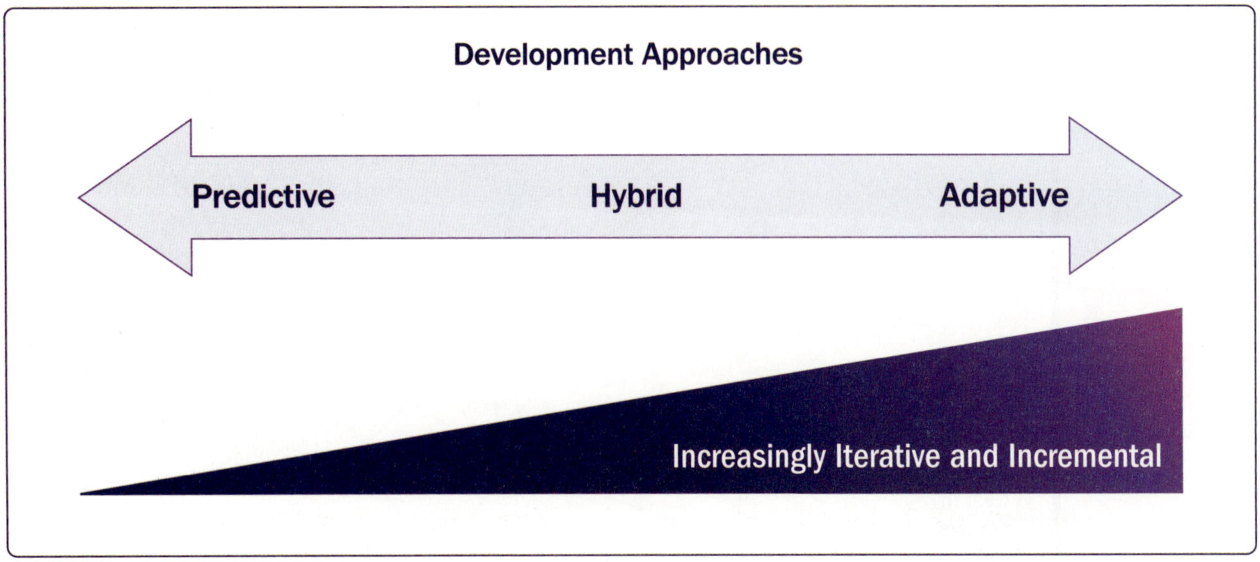

Figure 4-2. The Spectrum of Development Approaches

The choice of the development approach for a project is typically made by the project manager in consultation with the project management team, who, based on the nature of the project, carries out the necessary evaluations for establishing the framework and way of working with the team.

The main factors that play a role in the choice of the approach are related to the requirements, scope, timeline, and goals of the project; the organization's culture and needs; and the level of stakeholder involvement, risk profile, technological considerations, and overall complexity of the broader project context.

When the requirements are sufficiently clear and stable early in the project, a predictive approach may be optimal and, in this setup, the schedule baseline, together with the cost baseline, are determined according to the scope that should be delivered. Taken together, the baselines for schedule, cost, and scope are referred to as the project's integrated baseline.

When the requirements are less clear early in the project, or the project is expected to incur more complexity and uncertainty, then more feedback is needed (e.g., details from the final customer or end user) to ensure project success. In such cases, an adaptive approach may be optimal. In an adaptive approach, work is reviewed periodically, often in a timeboxed cadence, so that feedback can be incorporated as the integrated baseline evolves. At the end of the timebox, the requirements that have been implemented will be reviewed and planning for the next timebox will commence. In this case, based on the timeboxes and the team involved (as well as the budget), the scope will be delivered in an adaptive way.

However, it is important to note that differing possible adaptive approaches may provide different possible sets of project baselines. Projects often need the ability to vary a set of constraints in order to operate with other, more fixed constraints, often called the inverted triangle concept (see Figure 4-3).

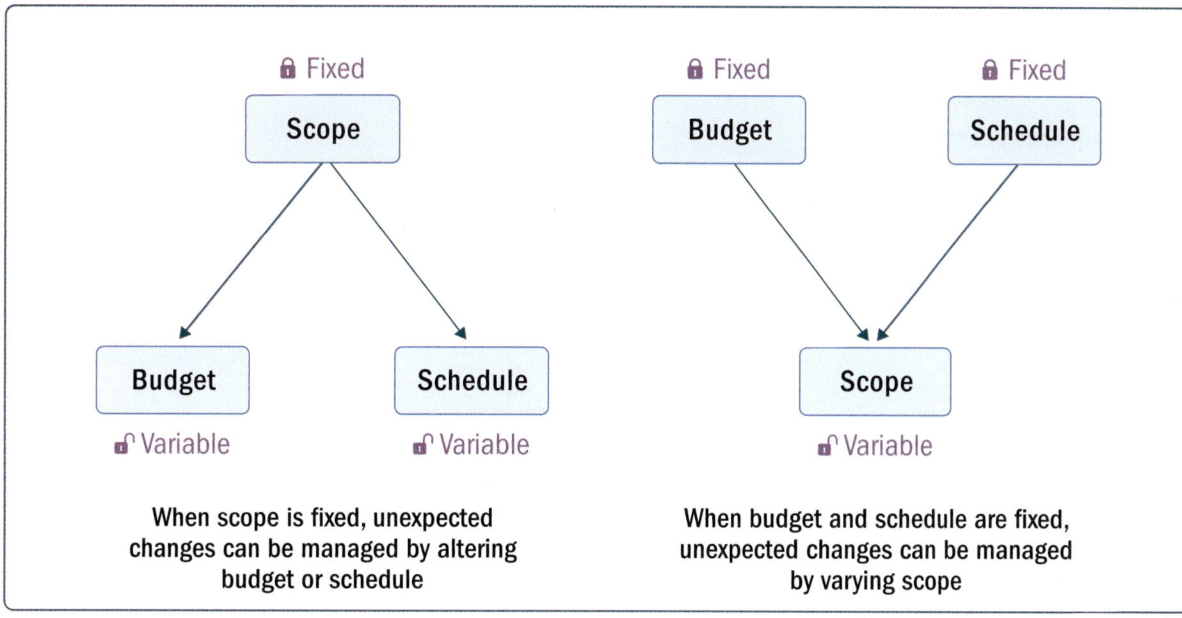

Figure 4-3. Constraint Options for Adaptive Approaches

4.2.1 Predictive Approaches

A predictive approach may be optimal when the project scope can be stabilized early in the project. A predictive approach may also be referred to as a waterfall, plan-driven, or traditional approach. This approach is also suitable for large projects involving significant investment or regulatory oversight. These conditions may require robust change control mechanisms and planned reevaluation between successive phases. The scope, schedule, cost, resource needs, quality requirements, and risks can be well defined in the early phases of the project life cycle and are expected to remain relatively stable. This development approach allows the project team to capture reliable certainty early in the project and to perform much of the planning up front (see Figure 4-4).

For projects or phases in which the cost of iterating far exceeds its value, such as the build phase of many construction projects, a predictive approach may be optimal. Similarly, for projects in heavily regulated environments, such as healthcare, there may be phase gates required in order for regulators to carefully assess whether, for instance, a new drug treatment or medical device has demonstrated sufficient promise to merit further development.

In certain predictive approaches, it may be optimal to deliver the product partially and incrementally, rather than as a single, final release. An incremental approach is used when the overall scope is well understood and planned up front, but phased delivery offers advantages due to the size, complexity, or specific risk factors of the project environment. In this approach, the project is divided into different phases or increments, with each phase or increment delivering a part of the overall product. Each increment builds upon the previous one, progressively adding features and functionality or completing parts of the product (see Figure 4-5). The increments may be sequential or overlap and the phases in each increment may differ, depending on the nature of the work. While stakeholder value is realized earlier through partial delivery, the overall scope and timeline remain largely fixed. This approach allows stakeholders to use and benefit from parts of the product before the entire project is completed and can often enhance the value proposition of the project while still adhering to the predictive framework of structured planning and controlled change management.

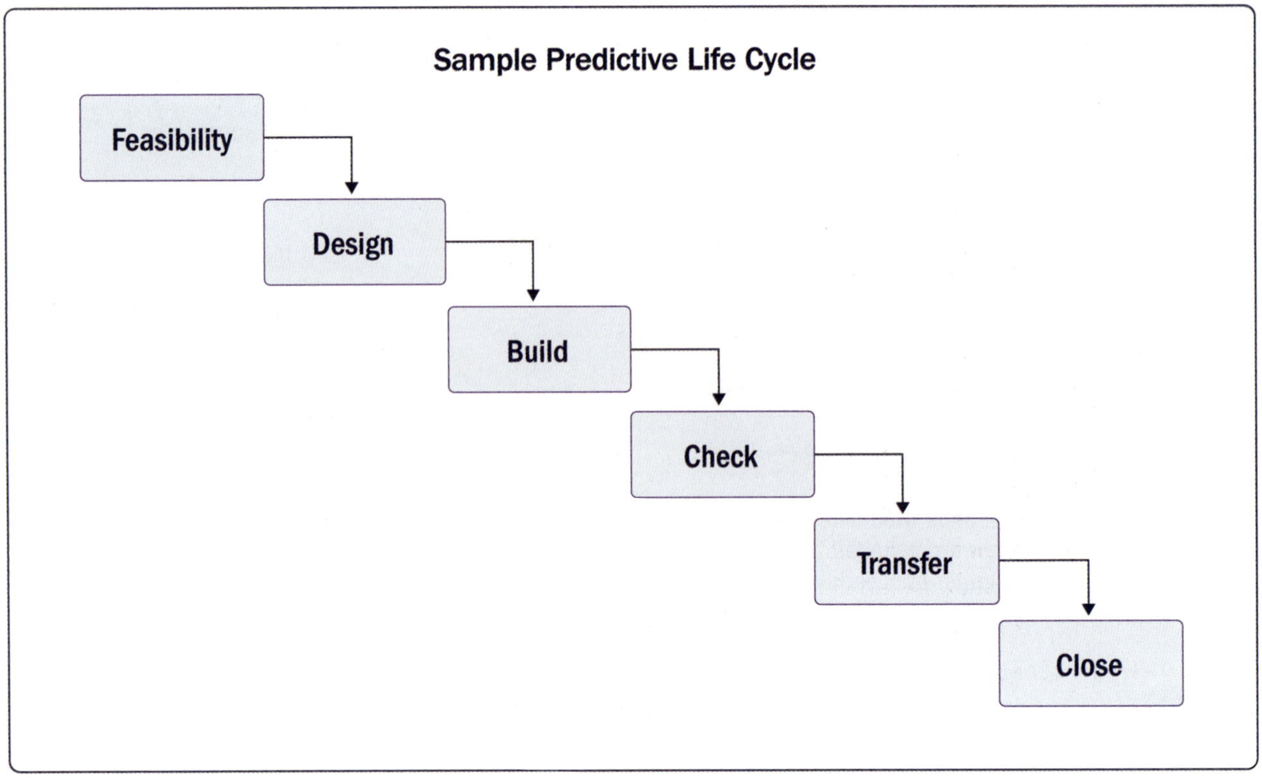

Figure 4-4. Sample Predictive Life Cycle

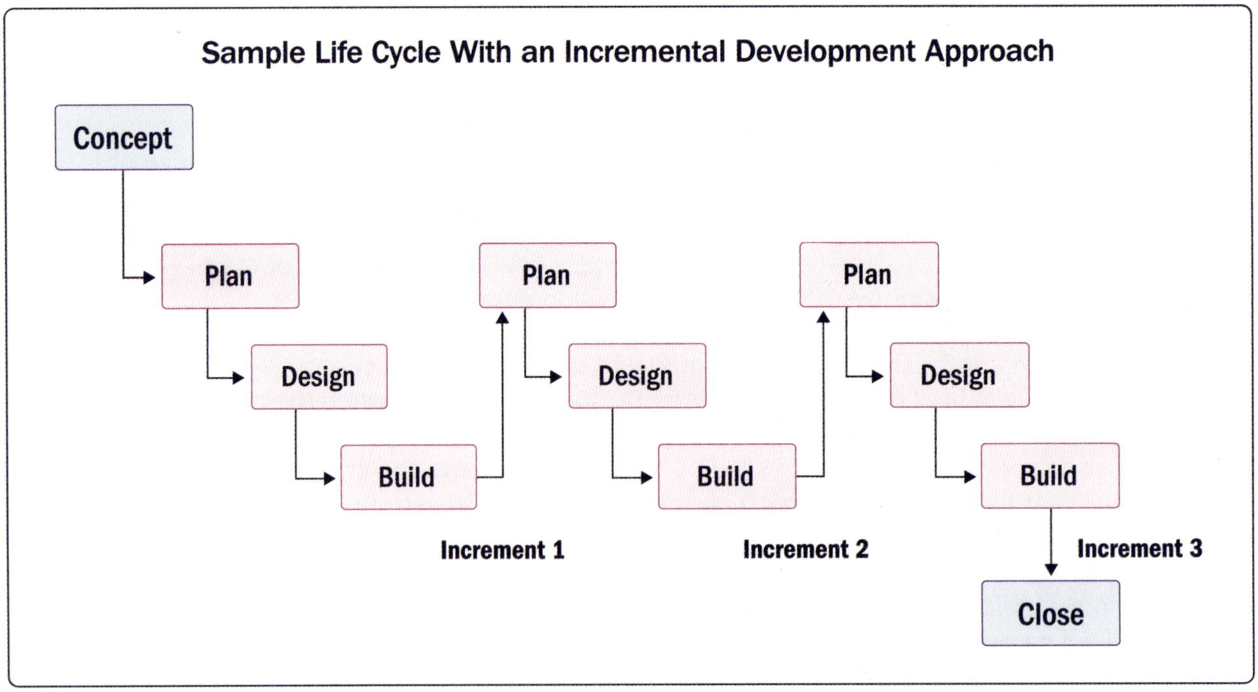

Figure 4-5. Sample Predictive Life Cycle With an Incremental Delivery

4.2.2 Adaptive Approaches

Also referred to as change-driven or agile approaches, adaptive approaches are useful when a project's requirements and technical solution are subject to a high level of uncertainty and volatility and are likely to change significantly throughout the project. A clear vision is established at the start of the project, and the initial known requirements are progressively elaborated, changed, or replaced in accordance with stakeholder feedback, the environment, or unexpected events. Adaptive approaches can be both iterative and incremental. The iterative approach focuses on refining and improving the project through repeated cycles (iterations). The incremental approach delivers the final product in small, usable segments (increments), where the increments each provide value and build on one another until the complete product is delivered.

While agility is a wide mindset that is broader than a development framework, agile approaches can be considered adaptive. Some agile methods entail iterations that are generally 1 to 4 weeks in duration, with a demonstration of the accomplishments at the end of each iteration. The entire project team is heavily involved in the planning at various levels. In the iteration, the team members determine the scope they can achieve based on the prioritized requirements in the form of the product backlog, estimate the amount of work, and work collaboratively to develop the scope during the iteration (see Figure 4-6).

Several adaptive methodologies use flow-based scheduling. Flow-based scheduling is a project management approach that focuses on optimizing the flow of work through a system. One goal is to maximize the flow of deliverables based on resource capacity, materials, and other inputs. A related goal is to minimize time and resource waste and maximize the efficiency of processes and the throughput of deliverables. Projects that use these practices and techniques often adopt them from flow-maximizing approaches such as the Kanban method (a visual workflow management method to limit work in process [WIP] based on lean principles and focusing on continuous delivery without overburdening the team) and the theory of constraints (a management philosophy that focuses on identifying and addressing the most significant limiting factor [constraint] that stands in the way of achieving a goal).

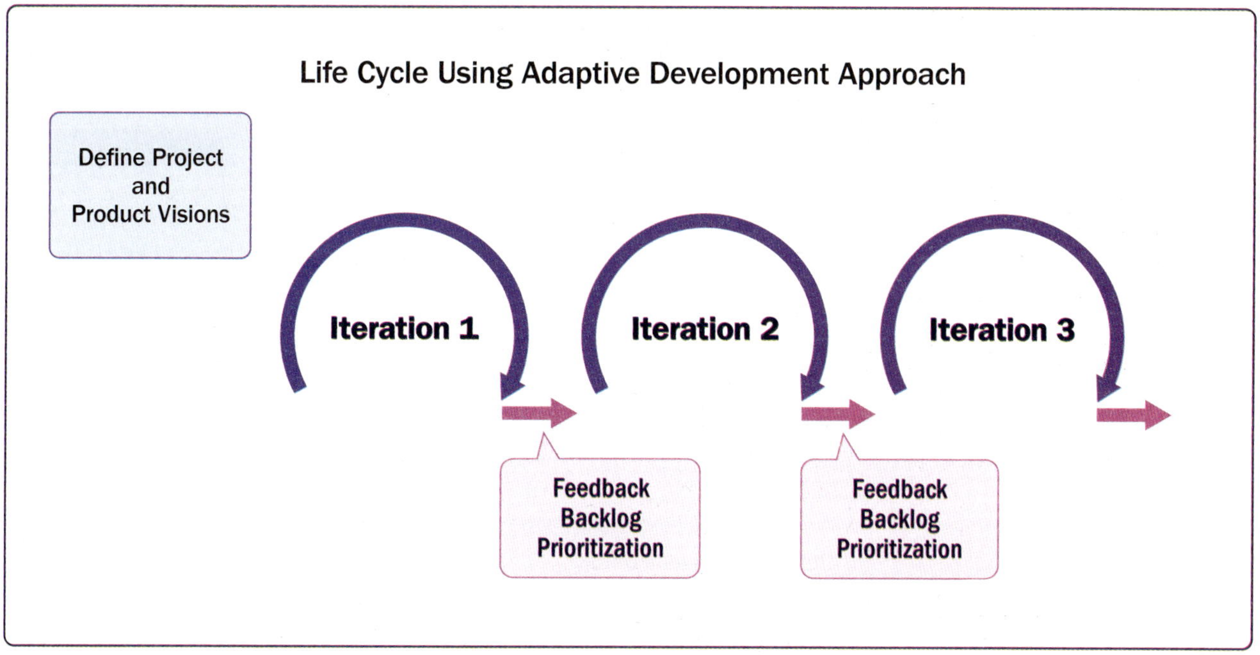

Figure 4-6. Life Cycle With an Adaptive Development Approach

It is useful to distinguish between agile methods designed for a single team versus those designed for larger-scale purposes. Some methods feature more breadth of coverage (how much of the project or product life cycle the approach covers), whereas others feature more depth of coverage (how detailed or prescriptive the guidance is). Figure 4-7 provides examples of agile methods that may be considered.

There is also a meaningful difference between larger-scale methods and larger-scale tool kits. A method is a systematic way of doing something, typically involving a series of steps or procedures designed to achieve a specific outcome. As such, methods provide structured approaches to problem-solving or task completion.

Conversely, a tool kit is a collection of tools, techniques, and resources that can be used to support various methods or approaches. A tool kit provides flexibility and a range of options to choose from based on the context and specific needs of a project or task.

PMI Disciplined Agile® (DA®) [3] is designed to be a tool kit.

Adaptive approaches may be well suited for the following specific types of projects:

- **Design projects.** Adaptive approaches are appropriate for design or new product development projects, where requirements are not fully defined up front and where partial deliveries and changes are expected during the project.

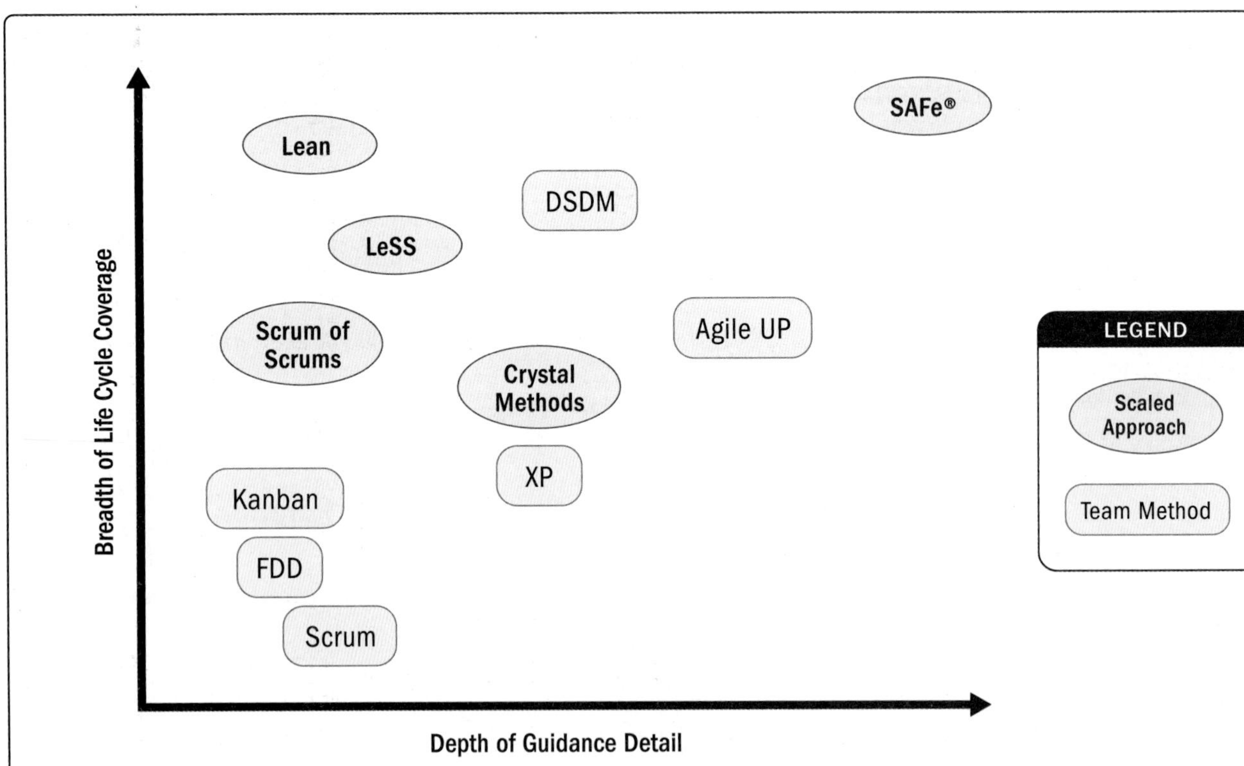

Figure 4-7. Agile Approaches Plotted by Breadth and Depth

- **New product development.** Adaptive approaches are also appropriate for projects where the final features of the product are refined based on market needs such as the development of a new mobile app or web service.
- **Digital projects.** Adaptive approaches are popular with software projects due to their dynamic nature. While not all software development projects require an adaptive approach, those with evolving scope, high uncertainty, and the need for early or incremental delivery are strong candidates for this approach.

4.2.3 Hybrid Approaches

A hybrid development approach is a combination of adaptive and predictive approaches. This development approach incorporates some elements from a predictive approach and some from an adaptive approach. This development approach might be appropriate when there is uncertainty or risk around the requirements such as the design of a custom home. Once the design is complete, it makes sense to iterate no more than once for the build. Hybrid approaches are also useful when deliverables can be modularized or when there are deliverables that can be developed by different project teams.

In practice, most projects can strongly benefit from a hybrid approach that combines adaptive and predictive methodologies. Focusing exclusively on either an adaptive or predictive approach does not fully address the varied challenges and complexities that modern projects present. A hybrid approach provides flexibility to adapt to changing conditions while retaining control over predictable aspects.

Another example is a project with two main deliverables, where one deliverable is developed using an adaptive approach and the other using a predictive approach (e.g., software that will be developed with an adaptive approach but needs to be installed in a new data center that will be built with a predictive approach).

With a hybrid approach, the various phases of the project can be approached differently. Projects can primarily be carried out using one approach while subsidiary streams can use a different way of working—in certain cases, adaptive, and in other cases, predictive.

Hybrid project management methods follow four common patterns, as illustrated in Figures 4-8 through 4-11.

- The early processes use an adaptive development life cycle, which is then followed by a predictive rollout phase.

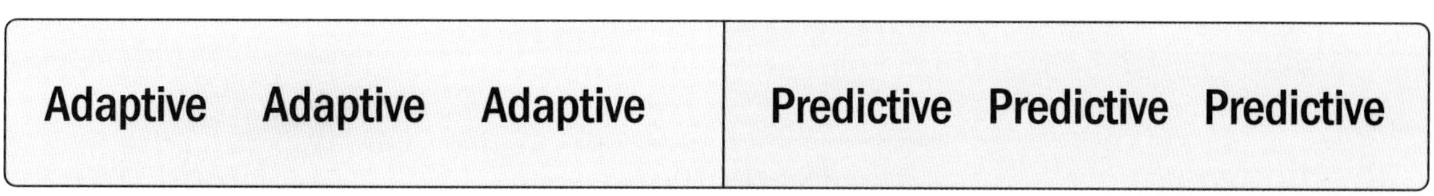

Figure 4-8. Adaptive Development Followed by a Predictive Rollout

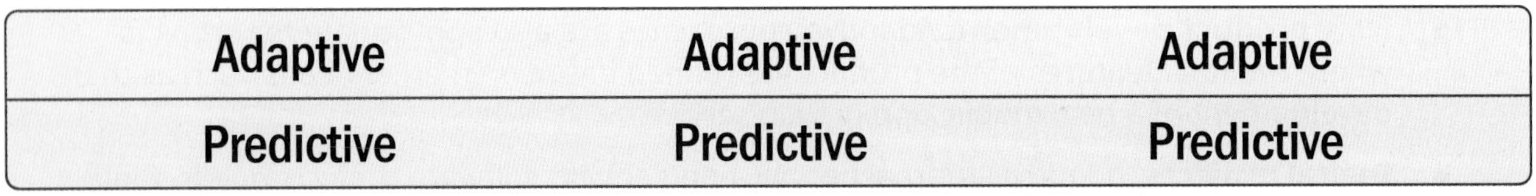

Figure 4-9. A Hybrid of Adaptive and Predictive Approaches Used Simultaneously

- Another approach is to use a combination of adaptive and predictive approaches throughout the life cycle.
- A small adaptive element within a primarily predictive project is used.
- A largely adaptive approach with a predictive component is used.

Some examples where a hybrid approach may be suitable include the following:

- **Construction project with IT integration.** A hybrid approach is appropriate during a construction project (predictive) that involves building a smart building with complex IT systems that need to be flexible during development (adaptive).
- **Healthcare solutions.** A hybrid approach is also appropriate during the implementation of an electronic medical records system in a hospital where certain aspects (infrastructure setup) are predictive but the development and integration of the user interface may benefit from an adaptive approach.

The PMI Disciplined Agile® (DA®) tool kit [4] describes three levels of hybrid approaches commonly found in projects across industries:

- **Hybrid Level 1.** A predictive approach is the dominant contributor to the way of working. Meanwhile, some adaptive elements are leveraged to reduce specific project pain points.
- **Hybrid Level 2.** At this level, both the predictive and adaptive approaches contribute significantly to the success of a project.
- **Hybrid Level 3.** At this point on the spectrum, an adaptive approach becomes the major contributor to the way of working. Some predictive elements are used to satisfy various business constraints.

Today, most projects require a hybrid approach, combining elements of both adaptive and predictive methodologies. Relying solely on one approach—whether adaptive or predictive—is no longer sufficient to address the diverse challenges and complexities that modern projects present. A hybrid approach allows for greater flexibility, enabling project teams to adapt to changing conditions while still maintaining control over predictable aspects of the project.

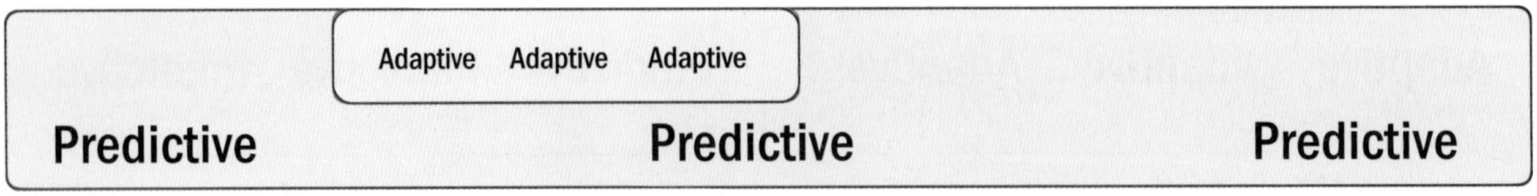

Figure 4-10. A Largely Predictive Approach With an Adaptive Component

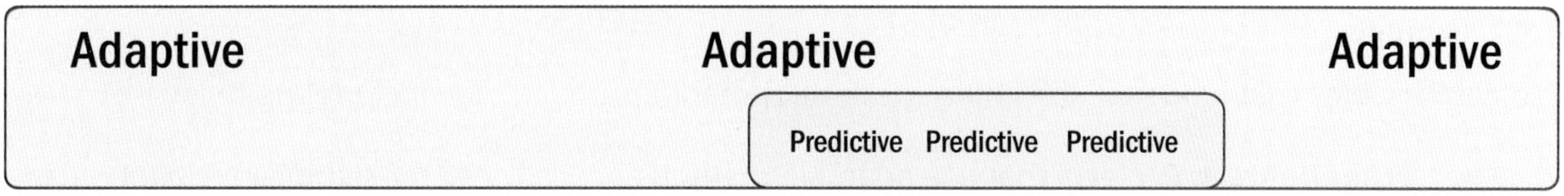

Figure 4-11. A Largely Adaptive Approach With a Predictive Component

4.3 Considerations for a Development Approach Selection

There are several factors that influence the selection of a development approach. The factors can be divided into categories of the deliverables, the project, and the organization. The following subsections describe the variables associated with each category. The diversity of factors often implies that several development approaches may be used within the same projects for different deliverables.

4.3.1 Deliverables

There are many variables associated with project deliverables that can influence the choice of development approach. The following list outlines some of the variables to consider when selecting the development approach:

- **Degree of innovation.** When new or complex technological and/or business model innovation is needed, an adaptive approach may be optimal.
- **Requirements certainty.** When the requirements are well known and straightforward to define, a predictive approach may be optimal.
- **Degree of scope stability.** This variable refers to the degree to which the project scope is stable throughout the project execution. In general, the less stable the scope is, the more optimal it will be to apply an adaptive approach.
- **Ease of change.** If the nature of the deliverable makes it difficult or costly to manage and incorporate changes, then a predictive approach may be optimal.
- **Delivery options.** The nature of the deliverables and whether they can be delivered in components or progressively elaborated can influence the development approach. More details can be found in Section 4.4 on delivery cadence.
- **Risk.** Adaptive approaches may be helpful to manage risk and uncertainty.
- **Safety requirements.** Products that have rigorous safety requirements often use a predictive approach as there is a need for significant up-front planning to ensure safety compliance.
- **Feedback.** If there is significant value likely to be realized from frequent feedback from the end users and stakeholders, an adaptive approach may be optimal.
- **Regulations.** Environments that have significant regulatory oversight may use a predictive approach due to the required processes, documentation, and demonstration needs.

4.3.2 Project

Project variables that influence the choice of development approach may include the following:

- **Stakeholders.** Projects that use adaptive methods typically call for significant stakeholder involvement throughout the process.
- **Schedule constraints.** If there is value to be realized from delivering something early, even if it is not a finished product, an iterative or adaptive approach may be optimal. Meanwhile, when a fixed end date must be met, a predictive approach can help focus planning on delivery timelines.
- **Financing uncertainty.** Projects being executed in an environment of financing uncertainty may generate more value using an adaptive or iterative approach.
- **Project size and complexity.** More flexible approaches are more suitable for larger, complex projects with evolving requirements.
- **Team experience and skills.** Projects managed using an adaptive or agile approach may benefit from teams with strong communication, collaboration, and problem-solving skills.
- **Interdependencies.** A reliance on other projects, departments, or functions for decisions, components, or resources may be a decision factor for the project team to consider for delivering projects with an iterative approach.

4.3.3 Organization

Organizational variables such as the structure, culture, capability, project team size, and location can influence the choice of development approach. The organizational variables to consider may include the following:

- **Organizational structure.** Organizations with a fixed functional structure—and more traditional hierarchical arrangements—are more inclined to select a predictive approach due to preferred lines of authority. Organizations with a network-oriented structure may be more naturally inclined to embrace more adaptive or hybrid approaches.
- **Culture.** A predictive approach may be a better fit in an organization with a culture of managing and directing, where the work is planned out and progress is measured against baselines. Adaptive approaches may fit better in an organizational culture that more easily embraces uncertainty while also emphasizing self-managed teams, flexible thinking, and innovation.
- **Organizational capability.** Organizational policies, ways of working, reporting structures, and attitudes should all be aligned to employ delivery methods successfully. Additionally, the extent to which project management processes are established can influence the reliability and predictability of the chosen project delivery approach.
- **Project team size and location.** Adaptive approaches often work better with smaller project teams. Some adaptive frameworks recommend having between three and nine team members. In predictive and hybrid approaches, this number may depend more on the project's requirements and scope complexity. Team location is relevant to all approaches, though some adaptive methods call for the colocation of team members. For some individuals and teams, remote work may enhance efficiency and focus on the team's execution.

4.4 Delivery Cadence

Based on the selected development approach, projects can have a single delivery, multiple deliveries, periodic deliveries, or continuous deliveries.

- **Single delivery.** Projects that have a single delivery produce all outcomes at the end of the project. For example, a process-reengineering project may not have any deliveries until near the end of the project when the new process is rolled out.
- **Multiple deliveries.** Some projects have multiple deliveries. A project may have multiple components or elaborations delivered at different times throughout the project. For example, a project to develop a new drug may have multiple deliveries, such as preclinical submissions, Phase 1 clinical trial results (safety, side effects, optimal dose, and timing), Phase 2 clinical trial results (effectiveness for 100–300 human volunteers), Phase 3 clinical trial results (tests efficacy against standard treatments), registration and regulatory approval, and then launch. In this example, the deliveries are sequential. Some projects have deliveries that are developed separately rather than sequentially, such as a project to update building security, as many tasks can be performed in parallel. Deliveries may include physical barriers to entry, new badges, new key code pads, and so forth. Each of these is a separate delivery, but few, if any of them, need to follow a specific order. In all cases, however, the deliveries should be concluded in order to meet or exceed the target business objectives.
- **Periodic deliveries.** Commonly used in adaptive approaches, periodic deliveries are like multiple deliveries but are on a regular and fixed delivery schedule such as monthly or semimonthly. A new software application may have internal deliveries every 2 weeks and then periodically release the deliveries into the market.
- **Continuous delivery.** Continuous delivery is the practice of incrementally delivering value to production on an ongoing basis. This approach focuses on delivering tested and validated product increments, ensuring they are production-ready at all times. By leveraging automation and maintaining a continuous flow from backlog prioritization through iterative development and testing, teams can deploy frequently and efficiently while minimizing risks. Continuous delivery fosters responsiveness to customer feedback and evolving market trends, allowing organizations to iterate quickly and provide regular updates without introducing unnecessary deployment overheads.

4.5 Project Management Focus Areas

This standard describes the fundamental actions that take place over the course of any project, regardless of whether the project follows a predictive, adaptive, or hybrid approach. These project management actions are grouped into five Project Management Focus Areas:

- Initiating,
- Planning,
- Executing,
- Monitoring and Controlling, and
- Closing.

These Focus Areas are implemented using formal processes, informal practices, or other policies, procedures, or techniques. The areas can involve iterative, continuous, and/or overlapping actions that are performed when planned or needed during the project and/or in each phase of the project.

While these Focus Areas are presented sequentially, in practice they often overlap and interact dynamically throughout the project life cycle.

The Project Management Focus Areas should not be confused with project phases, although some naming conventions may be the same or a project phase may largely consist of activities that are part of a Focus Area.

Additionally, these Focus Areas intersect with project management performance domains in specific ways. Detailed descriptions of the project management performance domains and their relationships to the Focus Areas are provided in *A Guide to the Project Management Body of Knowledge (PMBOK® Guide)* [2].

4.5.1 Initiating Focus Area

The Initiating Focus Area consists of those processes, practices, or actions performed to define a new project or new phase of an existing project. This area often includes formal authorization to start the project or phase. The purpose of the Initiating Focus Area is to align the stakeholders' expectations and the project's purpose, inform stakeholders of the scope and objectives, align key stakeholders, and discuss how their participation in the project and its associated phases can help to ensure their expectations are met.

Among the various initiating actions, the initial scope is defined and initial financial resources are committed. Stakeholders who will interact and influence the overall outcome of the project are identified and project management roles are assigned. This information is often captured in artifacts such as a project charter or stakeholder register.

The key benefits of this Focus Area are that projects are only authorized when aligned with the organization's strategic objectives and when the business case, benefits, and stakeholders are considered from the start of the project. In some organizations, a project manager is involved in developing the business case and defining the benefits. In other organizations, a broader project management team helps write a formal project charter, while others have the preliminary project work done by the project sponsor, PMO, portfolio steering committee, or another stakeholder group.

Business documents are those documents that generally originate outside of the project but are used as inputs to the project. Examples of business documents include the business case and benefits management plan. Figure 4-12 shows one way a sponsor and related business documents may relate to initiating actions.

In the business documents, the sponsor should provide the minimum information necessary for a project manager to start project activities. Involving the sponsors, customers, and other stakeholders during project initiation creates a shared understanding of success criteria. This involvement also increases alignment on project deliverables as well as stakeholder satisfaction throughout the project.

4.5.2 Planning Focus Area

The Planning Focus Area consists of those processes, practices, or actions that establish the intended scope of the effort, define and refine the objectives, and develop the course of action required to attain those objectives. Such activities may involve developing several artifacts such as a product backlog or a project management plan.

The nature of a project may require the use of repeated feedback loops for additional analysis. As more project information or characteristics are gathered and understood, some additional planning

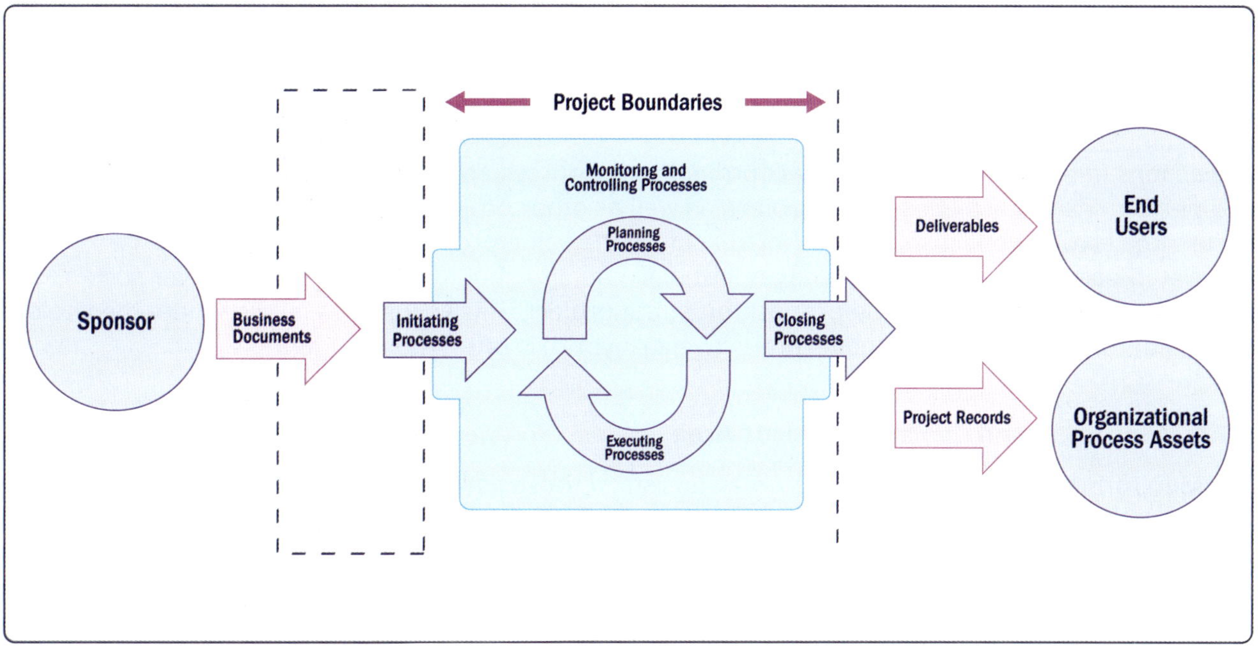

Figure 4-12. Project Boundaries

may be required. In this context, planning can follow a progressive, iterative, or rolling wave approach according to the project phase or life cycle approach.

Moreover, as project changes are encountered, update planning may be required at any appropriate moment of a project phase. This ongoing refinement of the project management plan is called progressive elaboration, indicating that planning is an iterative or ongoing activity. Highly predictive approaches tend to front-load their planning, although plan updates and refinements throughout the project life cycle are not uncommon. In contrast, highly iterative approaches tend to perform some brief, high-level planning up front—sometimes called "roadmapping"—typically followed by a more consistent level of frequent planning and replanning throughout the project life cycle.

The key benefit of this Focus Area is to define the course of action for successfully completing the project or phase.

When the initial planning effort is complete, the collection of knowledge and artifacts describing the course of action is often referred to as the project management plan. In some organizations, that plan is submitted for formal approval and used as the authoritative reference for how the project will be managed.

Once the project management team is oriented to—and confident with—the course of action, they are ready to begin executing.[2]

[2] Note that many project teams consider a simple, high-level roadmapping exercise as sufficient for the initial planning, especially in environments where the scope is expected to change significantly. As a result, the project team may consider a robust analysis of scope/schedule/cost trade-offs to be effectively useless; however, some discussion on how sensitive the project's value proposition is to schedule durations or specific dates can often be crucial, as can any sensitivity to exceeding an investment-cost threshold.

4.5.3 Executing Focus Area

The Executing Focus Area consists of those processes, practices, or actions performed to complete the work in a manner consistent with the currently agreed-upon course of action.

The actions in this Focus Area include coordinating resources, managing stakeholder engagement, and performing the activities of the project, as well as other project tasks. The key benefit of this Focus Area is to drive focused execution to achieve the value proposition represented by the integrated baseline. The project management plan can and should be changed whenever such a change would enhance the value proposition of the project. This Focus Area is also where the choice of development approach (adaptive, predictive, or hybrid) is often most evident.

4.5.4 Monitoring and Controlling Focus Area

The Monitoring and Controlling Focus Area consists of those actions required to track, measure, review, and regulate the progress and performance of the project; identify any areas in which changes to the plan are required; and initiate the corresponding changes.

Monitoring can include comparing project performance data, producing performance measures, comparing actual performance with planned performance, or reporting and disseminating performance information. Controlling can include analyzing variances, assessing trends to affect process improvements, evaluating possible alternatives, and recommending appropriate course corrections as needed.

The key benefit of this Focus Area is to ensure the project is on track to meet expectations. This effort often involves measuring and analyzing project performance at regular intervals, appropriate events, or when exceptional conditions occur. If any variances are found, the project management team identifies what, if any, corrective actions may be needed. Those corrective actions are then negotiated and agreed upon by appropriate stakeholders.

For any project having a stable project management plan, the effort required to perform Monitoring and Controlling will be fairly consistent throughout execution. In contrast, for any project undergoing frequent and significant changes—as is common with adaptive approaches—Monitoring and Controlling efforts are likely to be less consistent.

The Monitoring and Controlling Focus Area monitors and controls the work being done within each life cycle phase and for the project as a whole. The Monitoring and Controlling Focus Area is performed in parallel with the other Focus Areas. It is not a separate, stand-alone area.

4.5.5 Closing Focus Area

The Closing Focus Area consists of the actions performed to formally complete or close a project, phase, contract, or in some cases, to terminate a project before completion. This effort may include the verification that specific actions are completed for other Focus Areas before a given project or phase can be declared as complete.

The key benefit of this Focus Area is that phases, projects, and contracts are closed out appropriately, transitioning to operations in a manner that helps meet or exceed the project's target business objectives. Verifying the achievement of project outputs, outcomes, and benefits as part of this Focus Area is essential to ensuring that the project has met or exceeded the intended value and stakeholders' expectations.

This Focus Area may also address the suspension or early closure of the project (e.g., when canceling the project becomes the best way to maximize the return on that project investment—or perhaps more accurately, to minimize what may have become a negative return).

4.5.6 Focus Areas as a Whole

These five Focus Areas are independent of the application areas (such as marketing, information services, or accounting) or industry focus (such as construction, aerospace, or telecommunications). The Focus Areas are also independent of approach, as all development approaches honor these five in some manner. Individual processes, practices, or actions in the Focus Areas are often iterated prior to completing a phase or a project.

The Project Management Focus Areas are essential for understanding and applying project management principles, regardless of the development approach (predictive, adaptive, or hybrid). Tailoring these areas to each project's specific needs can ensure effective planning, execution, and monitoring and controlling, aligning with organizational goals and stakeholder expectations.

Focus Areas are not project phases. If the project is divided into phases, the actions in the Focus Areas interact within each phase. Moreover, these five Focus Areas are not strictly sequential; they often overlap within a single phase. For example, planning and monitoring can happen simultaneously. This overlap is shown in Figures 4-13 and 4-14, which each illustrate how different aspects of project management may interact throughout the project life cycle.

Figure 4-13 illustrates an example of how Focus Areas can interact during a project or phase using a primarily predictive approach. The level of effort applied to a given Focus Area can vary both within project phases and across the overall project life cycle.

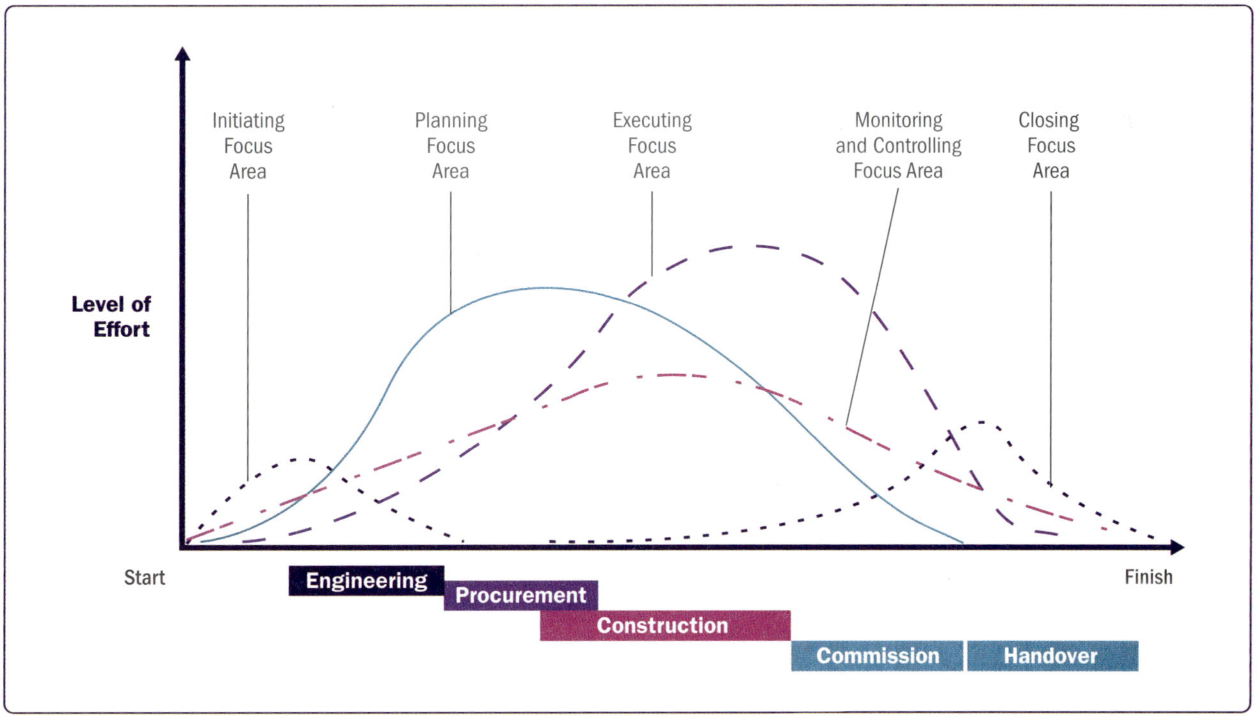

Figure 4-13. Example of Focus Area Interactions Within a Project or Phase Using a Predictive Approach

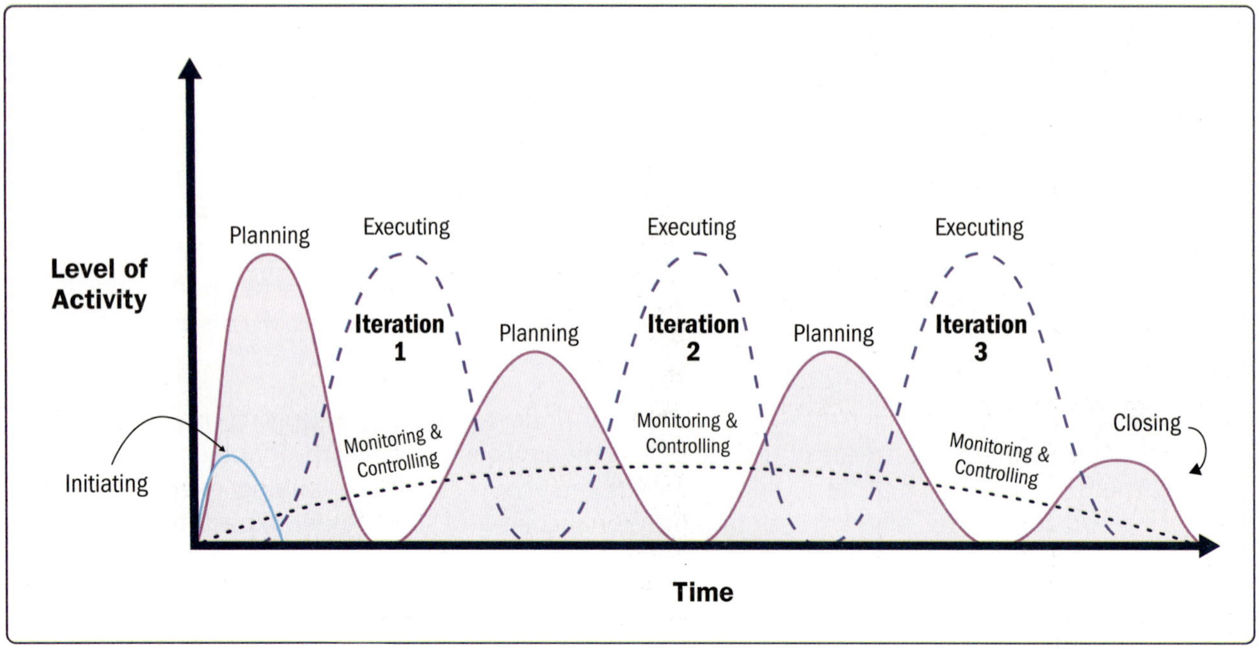

Figure 4-14. Example of Focus Area Interactions Within a Project or Phase Using an Adaptive Approach

Figure 4-14 illustrates an example of how Focus Areas can interact during a project or phase using a primarily adaptive approach. In adaptive development, the Focus Areas—Initiating, Planning, Executing, Monitoring and Controlling, and Closing—are not strictly linear, sequential, or performed all at once. Instead, they interact within short iterations in a flexible and often overlapping manner. Each Focus Area is revisited regularly throughout the project, allowing for continuous refinement and adjustment based on real-time data, feedback, and evolving project needs. This iterative approach enables greater responsiveness to change and helps ensure that the project remains aligned with stakeholder expectations and goals.

References

[1] Project Management Institute (PMI). (2024). *PMI Lexicon of Project Management Terms*—Version 4.0. PMI. https://www.pmi.org/standards/lexicon

[2] Project Management Institute (PMI). (2025). *A Guide to the Project Management Body of Knowledge (PMBOK® Guide)*—Eighth edition. PMI.

[3] Disciplined Agile® (DA®). (n.d.). *Foundation for Business Agility.* Project Management Institute (PMI). https://www.pmi.org/disciplined-agile/

[4] Disciplined Agile® (DA®). (n.d.). *Hybrid Life Cycles.* Project Management Institute (PMI). https://www.pmi.org/disciplined-agile/serial/hybridlifecycles

Index

A

B

C

D

M

N

O

P

Q

R

S

T

U

V

W

A Guide to the Project Management Body of Knowledge

PMBOK® Guide

Eighth Edition

The information contained in the *PMBOK® Guide* is not an American National Standard (ANS) and has not been processed in accordance with ANSI's requirements for an ANS. As such, the information in the *PMBOK® Guide* may contain material that has not been subjected to public review or a consensus process. In addition, it does not contain requirements necessary for conformance to an ANS standard.

Section 1

Introduction

This section describes important information about *A Guide to the Project Management Body of Knowledge (PMBOK® Guide)*—Eighth Edition. The section explains the relationship of the *PMBOK® Guide* to *The Standard for Project Management* [1],[1] details changes to the *PMBOK® Guide*, and provides a brief overview of the content.

1.1 Structure of the *PMBOK® Guide*

In addition to this introduction, this edition of the *PMBOK® Guide* contains four core sections:

- **Project Management Performance Domains.** This section identifies and describes seven project management performance domains that form an integrated system to enable successful delivery of the project and intended outcomes.
- **Tailoring.** This section describes what tailoring is and presents an overview of what to tailor and how to go about tailoring individual projects.
- **Inputs and Outputs.** This section presents a brief description of the assets and artifacts used as either sample inputs to, or sample outputs of, the project management activities and processes presented throughout the project management performance domains. The elements listed in this section are neither intended to be comprehensive, nor required for any given project. Rather, they are commonly used selections from among the countless options that project teams can implement.

[1] The numbers in brackets refer to the numbered list of references at the end of the *PMBOK® Guide*.

- **Tools and Techniques.** This section presents a brief description of the tools and techniques listed for project management activities and the processes presented throughout the project management performance domains. The elements listed in this section are neither intended to be comprehensive, nor required for any given project. Rather, they are offered as commonly used selections from among the countless options that project teams have available.

1.2 Relationship of the *PMBOK® Guide* and *The Standard for Project Management*

Work in the project management performance domains is guided by the principles of project management. As described in *The Standard for Project Management* [1], a principle is a fundamental norm, truth, or value that gives guidance for the project manager and project team. The principles of project management provide guidance for the mindset and behavior of people involved in projects as they influence and shape the performance domains to produce the intended outcomes. While there is conceptual overlap between the principles and the performance domains, the principles guide mindset and behavior, while the performance domains present broad areas of focus in which to demonstrate that mindset and behavior. Figure 1-1 shows how the project management principles create a foundation for the performance domains, providing guidance to processes in each performance domain.

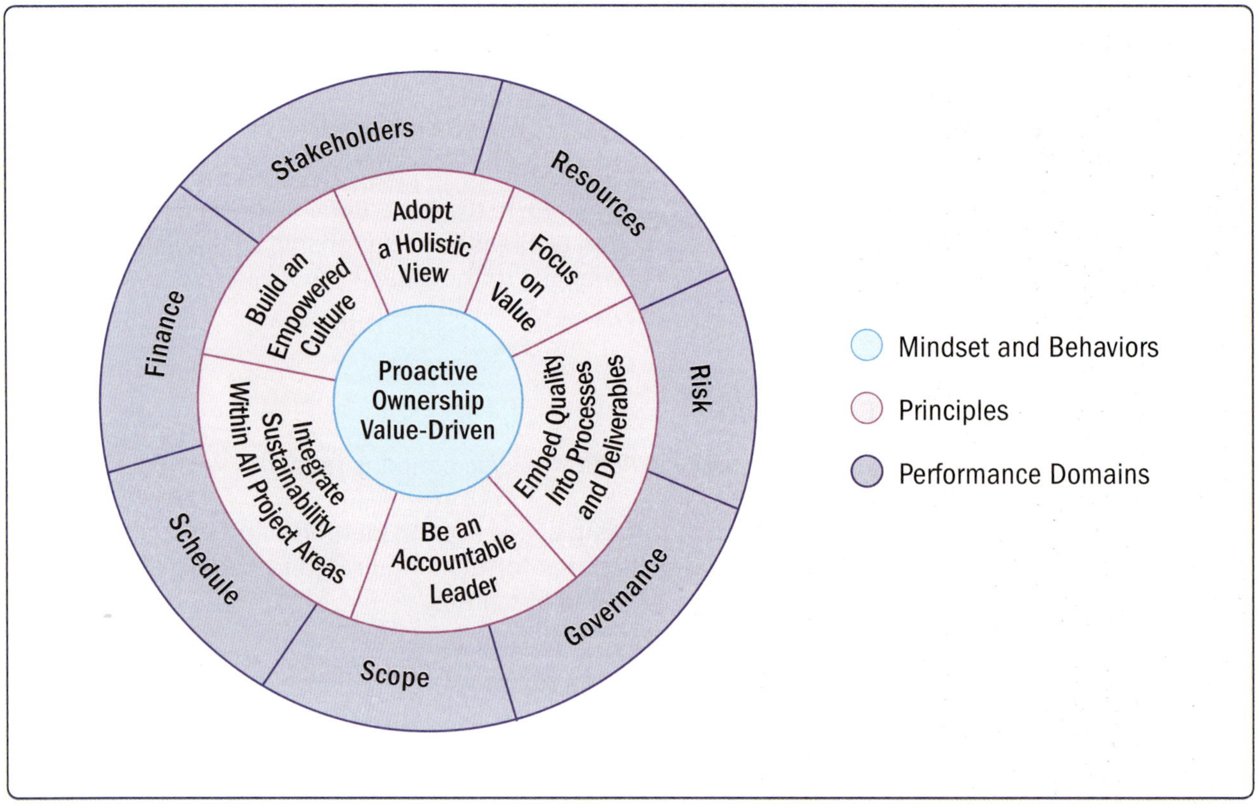

Figure 1-1. Relationship Between Project Management Principles and Project Management Performance Domains

1.3 Changes to the *PMBOK® Guide*

This edition of the *PMBOK® Guide* focuses on delivering outcomes regardless of the approach used by the project team. However, project practitioners using the *PMBOK® Guide* also benefit from some level of understanding of how to deliver projects.

This eighth edition takes the best parts of previous editions of the *PMBOK® Guide* to offer project managers a more practical and complete framework. The detailed, process-oriented approach of the sixth edition (using inputs, tools and techniques, and outputs [ITTOs]) is combined with the seventh edition's valuable concept of performance domains, which emphasizes how different project elements are interconnected. This edition integrates ITTOs and process descriptions directly into the performance domain structure. This combined approach provides both a thorough understanding of individual processes and a broader view of how those processes interact to produce the desired project results. This approach makes the guide more adaptable and useful for project managers using a variety of approaches and working in diverse situations.

Tailoring is the deliberate adaptation of the project management approach, governance, and processes to make them more suitable for a given environment (environmental factors include industry, culture, regulations, etc.) and fit for the purpose of the work at hand. The tailoring process is driven by the guiding project management principles, organizational values, and organizational culture. This guide preserves tailoring guidance from the previous edition while also adding tailoring considerations for each project management performance domain.

In embracing the full spectrum of project management approaches, this edition of the *PMBOK® Guide* recognizes that no publication can capture every tool, technique, process, or practice that project teams might use. Therefore, this edition presents an array of commonly used good practices, activities, and processes that project practitioners can use to accomplish their work. These practices and processes are able to fit most projects most of the time.

Section 2

Project Management Performance Domains

A project management performance domain is a group of related processes that are critical for the effective delivery of project value. These performance domains are interactive, interrelated, and interdependent areas of focus that work in unison to achieve the desired project results. There are seven project management performance domains presented in this guide, without specific weighting or order:

- Governance,
- Scope,
- Schedule,
- Finance,
- Stakeholders,
- Resources, and
- Risk.

The project management performance domains work together as a cohesive whole. In this way, they operate as an integrated system, with each performance domain being interdependent with the others to enable successful delivery of the project and its intended outcomes.

Performance domains run concurrently throughout the project life cycle, regardless of how value is delivered (frequently, periodically, or at the end of the project). For example, project leaders are focused on stakeholders, schedules, and so forth, from the project's outset to its closure. These areas of focus are not addressed as siloed efforts because they overlap and interconnect. The ways in which the performance domains relate are different for each project environment, but they are always present.

Each performance domain is presented with the following primary subsections:

- **Key Concepts**—Performance domains encompass a broad discipline of methods and approaches. This broadness often creates a challenge regarding where project leaders should begin and what they should do next. Each of the performance domains begins with a treatise of the most important ideas, considerations, and concepts for its area. These concepts are often the first discussions for project management efforts and inform the decisions regarding when and how performance domain activities should be practiced.
- **Processes**—The project management activities in each performance domain can be described in various ways such as formal policies and informal procedures. Regardless of how teams and organizations define their project management activities, it is helpful to review the industry's common practices for a given domain.

Accordingly, this guide presents 40 processes to describe the underlying mechanics of performance domain activities. Each process lists a sampling of inputs, tools and techniques, and outputs. Given the diversity of project management practice in today's industry, these processes and their associated lists are illustrative but not comprehensive. Instead, they offer a technical description of project management and are not intended as a prescriptive framework or methodology.

Several artifacts and approaches are used in multiple processes. Therefore, this section focuses on how inputs, tools and techniques, and outputs are leveraged in the context of a given performance domain. Further technical details of those elements are captured in Section 4, Inputs and Outputs, and Section 5, Tools and Techniques.

The performance domain processes are listed in Table 2-1, along with their relationships to the Project Management Focus Areas: Initiating, Planning, Executing, Monitoring and Controlling, and Closing.

- **Tailoring Considerations**—Since all projects are executed in a unique environment, project management activities should be adjusted to fit the characteristics and environment of a given project. In addition to the formal guidance in the project tailoring section, each performance domain offers areas to review. Tailoring considerations should be applied to the corresponding project management activities to ensure alignment with the project objectives, even if those activities are defined per policies, practices, or procedures.
- **Interactions With Other Domains**—While all seven performance domains are interrelated with one another, the specific connections among them are also important. Accordingly, each performance domain highlights overlaps, dependencies, or relationships that practitioners should consider.
- **Check Results**—Project success requires a focus on value delivery, emphasizing meaningful outcomes over just outputs. Project management activities do not provide value by themselves. Rather, they are performed with the intent of delivering and maximizing

Table 2-1. Mapping Project Management Focus Areas to Performance Domains

Performance Domains	Project Management Focus Areas: Initiating Focus Area	Planning Focus Area	Executing Focus Area	Monitoring and Controlling Focus Area	Closing Focus Area
Governance	• Initiate Project or Phase	• Integrate and Align Project Plans • Plan Sourcing Strategy	• Manage Project Execution • Manage Quality Assurance • Manage Project Knowledge	• Monitor and Control Project Performance • Assess and Implement Changes	• Close Project or Phase
Scope		• Plan Scope Management • Elicit and Analyze Requirements • Define Scope • Develop Scope Structure		• Monitor and Control Scope • Validate Scope	
Schedule		• Plan Schedule Management • Develop Schedule		• Monitor and Control Schedule	
Finance		• Plan Financial Management • Estimate Costs • Develop Budget		• Monitor and Control Finances	
Stakeholders	• Identify Stakeholders	• Plan Stakeholder Engagement • Plan Communications Management	• Manage Stakeholder Engagement • Manage Communications	• Monitor Stakeholder Engagement • Monitor Communications	
Resources		• Plan Resource Management • Estimate Resources	• Acquire Resources • Lead the Team	• Monitor and Control Resourcing	
Risk		• Plan Risk Management • Identify Risks • Perform Risk Analysis • Plan Risk Responses	• Implement Risk Responses	• Monitor Risks	

the value of the project investment. To that end, each performance domain concludes with guidance on maintaining a focus on that value. For any process output, there should be a corresponding, higher-order outcome in mind. A project schedule itself does not add value; its true importance lies in fostering stakeholder alignment around the overall timeline for delivering project value.

2.1 Governance Performance Domain

Project governance is applicable across all project management approaches, including predictive, adaptive, and hybrid, with variations based on industry, organizational context, and project specifics. Governance consists of the framework, functions, and processes that guide project management decisions and activities to optimize the project's value delivery. This governance framework is holistic and integrative, considering all other performance domains.

Project governance is shaped by the performing organization's governance model as well as stakeholders such as customers and regulatory bodies. The Governance performance domain includes elements of project integration management related to strategic alignment, decision-making and change, and project success criteria. Additionally, the Governance performance domain integrates risk and opportunity management, helping ensure proactive identification and mitigation of potential issues while leveraging opportunities for added value. This performance domain also helps to ensure project alignment with the portfolio, organizational strategy, and goals. Additionally, the domain involves interrelated activities to identify, define, combine, unify, and coordinate various processes, documents, and project management activities as an integrated system for value delivery. These activities often leverage technology and data-driven tools, enabling real-time tracking, analysis, and reporting to support informed decision-making.

Governance can be tailored to different approaches: lightweight for adaptive methods; moderate or combined for hybrid projects; and comprehensive for large, predictive portfolios, programs, and projects. To help ensure continuous improvement, feedback loops are incorporated into the governance framework, allowing for periodic reviews, lessons learned, and iterative adjustments to governance practices.

2.1.1 Project Value Creation

The fundamental objective of any project is to create positive value that justifies the investment and effort undertaken. Effective governance involves oversight and corrections to help steer a project toward its broader goals.

The Standard for Project Management [1] defines five Focus Areas for the success of any project. The relationship of the Governance performance domain to those Focus Areas is as follows:

- **Initiating.** Successful projects begin with a clear description of the desired end state. A clearly articulated business case enables stakeholder alignment on priorities and constraints, and provides team members with a broader context that informs their work. This alignment can be implemented as part of the Initiate Project or Phase process, via informal governance discussions, and/or other approaches.
- **Planning.** Every part of project planning should be performed with the project's target goals in mind. Explicit deliverables and activities should be identified to enable those goals. This alignment is illustrated in the Integrate and Align Project Plans process.

- **Executing.** Project work can benefit from the shared understanding of its broader goals, such as informing technical decisions or motivating team members. This understanding can be seen in the Manage Project Execution and Manage Project Knowledge processes.
- **Monitoring and Controlling.** As projects proceed, they encounter change. Effective project management requires appropriate adaptations to those changes. The Monitor and Control Project Performance process provides a way to govern effective changes toward value creation.
- **Closing.** All projects and project phases eventually end. They can achieve their desired impact as originally planned, or experience closure earlier or later than expected.

Projects experience any number of governance scenarios during their life cycle. In each case, the overarching value proposition should be the primary factor in project decisions. Table 2-2 illustrates several such scenarios.

Several management disciplines relate to the governance of project value and impact. These include but are not limited to change management, benefits realization, value management, and revenue management. Tools and techniques from these disciplines are often incorporated into the Governance performance domain.

2.1.2 Project Governance Models

Applying the right governance model to a project is an important decision, because too much governance risks wasting resources, while too little may lead to strategic alignment and project performance issues. The need to apply optimum governance varies with the implementation approach and organizational guidelines. The right balance should be made for strategic alignment, compliance, and delivering value. For these reasons, governance models can be applied at the organizational, portfolio, program, or project level, depending upon the approach and complexity (see Figure 2-1).

Table 2-2. Sampling of Common Project Governance Scenarios

Governance Scenario	Description
Project initiation	A new project or phase is deemed to be a worthwhile venture; resources and effort are expended to launch the undertaking
Project replanning	A revision to any element of the project management plan that requires intentional review by the project management team, sponsors, or senior management
Project expansion or contraction	A project or phase undergoes change to its schedule, budget, quality thresholds, compliance, or other constraints as a means to preserve the original value proposition or capture a new one
Early termination for positive cause	A project or phase is closed before exhausting its planned schedule and/or budget because the desired value impact has been achieved
Early termination for negative cause	A project or phase is closed before exhausting its planned schedule and/or budget because the desired value impact is no longer achievable

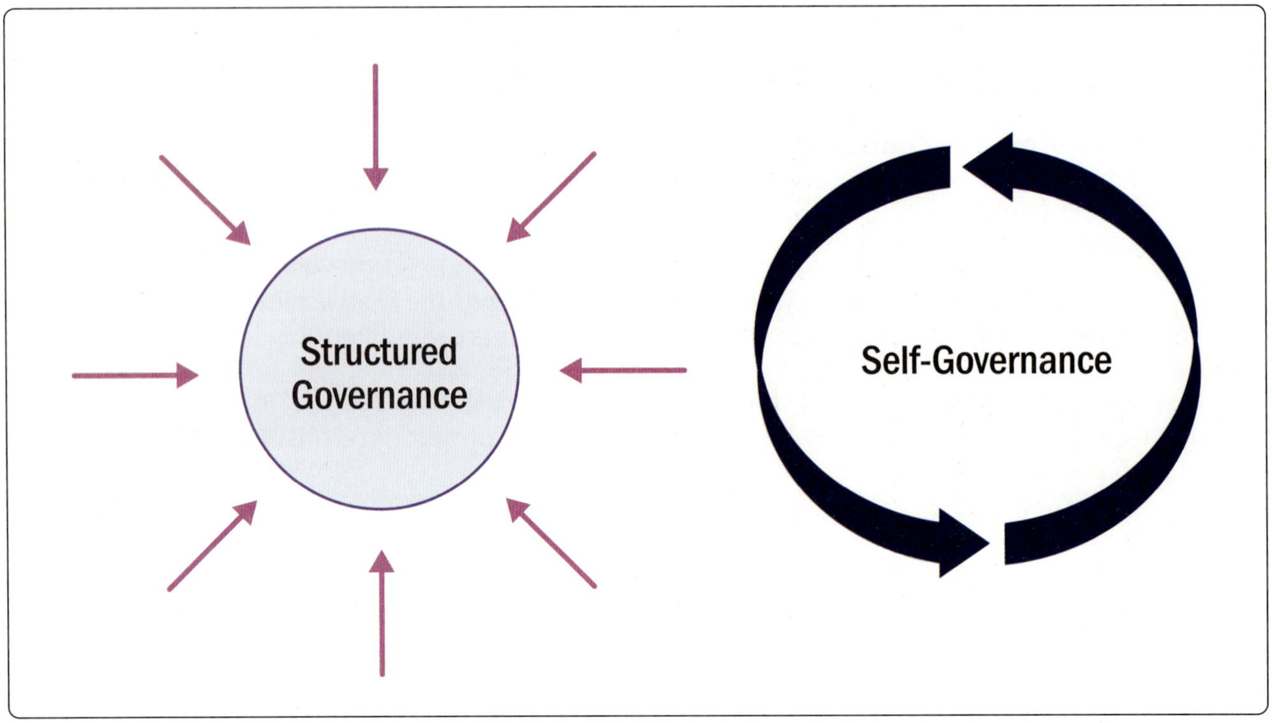

Figure 2-1. Structured Versus Self-Governed Projects

Under a structured governance model, project governance is often composed of an executive project sponsor, project management office (PMO) leader, some type of governance board, and a project manager who can provide project-level oversight while managing the integration of all performance domains for that project. Under a self-governance model, instead of a PMO leader, there may be a group of individual project managers that is collectively accountable for optimizing performance. There are proven and effective self-governance models where project management responsibilities are distributed among the team, rather than assigned to a single individual holding a formal project management title.

A key challenge in self-governance models is the potential for fragmented decision-making, where decision-makers may act in conflicting ways, resulting in a lack of direction or accountability. To address this, it is essential to establish clear, measurable common objectives supported by leading indicators and effective feedback mechanisms. These tools enable self-governed teams to make informed decisions and align their efforts toward shared goals. Notably, structured governance models emphasize similar principles, as detailed in Section 2.1.3.

In a structured governance model, which is often used on more predictive projects, one or more internal or external constituents governs project performance according to organizational requirements. In a self-governing model, which is often used on more adaptive projects, the team ensures the project is delivering value. Governance models should be designed to fit the specific needs of the project within the particular organizational context in which value is being delivered.

2.1.3 Metrics and Mechanisms for Effective Project Governance

Regardless of whether the project governance model is structured or self-governing, or some combination of the two, effective governance typically requires these three core components:

- Target metrics for the project that are clearly aligned and demonstrate meaningful impact to the organization's strategic goals;
- Clear and effective signaling mechanisms or alarm systems for those metrics (typically, leading indicators to give decision-makers and other stakeholders a sense as to whether the current delivery performance is bringing teams closer to the strategic goal); and
- Effective feedback mechanisms that allow decision-makers in governance and integration management to assess the success of their decisions, learn from the feedback, and improve their decision-making effectiveness.

Examples of some key metrics for good project governance may include but are not limited to the following:

- Indicators for how effective the project-prioritization decisions are, such as return on investment (ROI);
- Indicators on whether better decisions are being made to maximize due date performance; and
- Indicators on whether the current integrated project baseline is truly the one carrying the highest possible value proposition.

Each of these example metrics serves as direct or proxy measures for how well projects are achieving their target outcomes, as opposed to input metrics such as utilization of project resources, compliance with a given set of standards, or percentage of team members completing a training class.

2.1.4 Additional Considerations for Predictive Environments

Predictive project environments may call for two additional governance components: escalation and investment control.

- **Escalation** is often useful in hierarchical organizations where decision-making authority includes individuals outside of project team members, or in organizations in which higher-ranking individuals have greater ability to remove persistent obstacles or resolve conflicts to enhance a project's probability of success.
- **Investment control** is often required in environments that call for some type of formal stewardship of project investment funding, such as public corporations, government agencies, and certain financial entities (e.g., retirement funds). Investment control frequently includes a thorough risk evaluation procedure to analyze the possible returns on investment and reduce potential risks. For example, many lender-financed construction projects have defined decision points in the design and build phases of the project to determine whether the next round of investment funding still makes good business sense for the lender and overall project.

2.1.5 Key Concepts

The key concepts detailed in Sections 2.1.5.1 through 2.1.5.4 support effective practices for the Governance performance domain.

2.1.5.1 Leading Indicators

Leading indicators indicate upcoming changes or reveal trends in the project. If the change or trend is unfavorable, the project team should evaluate the root cause of the leading indicator measurement and take corrective actions to address the trend. Used in this way, leading indicators can reduce performance risk on a project by identifying potential performance variances before they cross the tolerance threshold.

Leading indicators may be quantifiable, such as the size of the project or the number of items that are in progress in the backlog. Other leading indicators are more difficult to quantify, but they provide early warning signs of potential problems. The lack of a risk management process, stakeholders who are not available or engaged, or poorly defined project success criteria are all examples of leading indicators that project performance may be at risk.

Using leading indicators is preferable whenever possible because they can be used to prevent future problems that may require rework.

2.1.5.2 Lagging Indicators

Lagging indicators measure project deliverables or events. These indicators provide information after the fact. Lagging indicators reflect past performance or conditions and are easier to measure than leading indicators. Examples include the number of deliverables completed, the schedule or cost variance, and the amount of resources consumed.

Lagging indicators can also be used to find correlations between outcomes and environmental variables. For example, a lagging indicator that reveals a schedule variance may show a correlation with project team member dissatisfaction. This correlation can assist the project team in addressing a root cause that may not have been obvious if the only measurement was the schedule status.

2.1.5.3 SMART Criteria

SMART criteria are guidelines used to set clear, attainable, and meaningful goals. The acronym SMART stands for specific, measurable, achievable, realistic, and time-bound. These criteria help ensure that objectives are well defined and reachable within a certain timeframe, making them more effective and easier to track.

2.1.5.4 Sourcing Strategy

Project resources can be insourced, outsourced, or both. Determining which parts of a project should use which approaches represents a set of governance decisions. A project's sourcing strategy should consider impacts to schedule, scope, finances, resource capacity, risks, and other considerations. These considerations include but are not limited to the following:

- How might the project organization's culture, differentiating skills, and proximity motivate more use of internal resources?
- How might the project's need for specialized skills or supplies, scaled capacity, or variable capacity motivate increased use of outsourcing?

- How might the use of external resources impact the project's overall risk profile?
- How might using internal or external resources benefit the overall value proposition?

The management and oversight of outsourcing efforts can be performed by the project management team and/or a dedicated procurement department within an organization. Procurement management is the discipline of selecting, contracting, and supervising vendors to perform outsourced work. Procurement management is a complementary discipline to project management and is explored in Appendix X4.

2.1.6 Processes

The Governance performance domain encompasses the processes required to make decisions that protect and enhance the value proposition of a project in an integrated and holistic manner, including the authority to cancel a project when necessary.

This performance domain also encompasses the processes and activities to identify, define, combine, unify, and coordinate the various processes and project management activities within the Project Management Focus Areas.

In the project management context, governance includes characteristics of unification, consolidation, communication, and interrelationship. These actions should be applied from the start of the project through completion and integration as appropriate. The Governance performance domain involves making choices about the following:

- Establishing a governance framework that aligns with organizational strategic and operational goals as well as ethical principles;
- Defining roles and responsibilities for decision-making, oversight, and control;
- Ensuring effective communication and coordination among stakeholders;
- Monitoring and managing internal and external dependencies, risks, issues, and escalations;
- Continuously assessing and optimizing the governance framework to improve project outcomes;
- Balancing competing demands;
- Examining any alternative approaches;
- Tailoring the processes to meet the project objectives;
- Managing the interdependencies among the performance domains by encouraging seamless collaboration and transition among various process performances;
- Incorporating feedback mechanisms to adapt governance practices to evolving project needs; and
- Ensuring compliance with regulatory and legal requirements to maintain organizational accountability.

In summary, the Governance performance domain focuses on creating a structured approach to decision-making and oversight, helping to ensure that project activities are aligned with organizational objectives and that the value proposition of the project is protected and enhanced throughout its life cycle.

It should be noted that the processes of the Governance performance domain span across the project life cycle from initiation to closure. Governance is not a one-time activity; it is pervasive throughout the project life cycle. The following processes are included in the Governance performance domain (see Figure 2-2):

- **Initiate Project or Phase.** The process of officially authorizing the start of a project by creating a document that establishes a link between the project and the business objectives.
- **Integrate and Align Project Plans.** The process of consolidating and aligning all of the performance domain's plan components into a unified project management plan that details how the project will be executed, monitored and controlled, and closed.
- **Plan Sourcing Strategy.** The process of deciding whether to use internal or external resources for different parts of a project, considering factors such as organizational culture, specialized skills, resource capacity, risk, and the overall value proposition. Management and oversight of outsourcing efforts can be handled by the project management team or a dedicated procurement department.
- **Manage Project Execution.** The process of leading and performing the work defined in the integrated project plans, including managing resources, addressing issues and risks, and implementing changes to achieve the project objectives.
- **Manage Quality Assurance.** The process of ensuring processes are performed in a manner consistent with stakeholder expectations, involving the implementation of planned and systematic activities defined in the project's quality management plan. This process helps build confidence in future outputs, improves process efficiency and effectiveness, and ensures proper project governance to meet or exceed stakeholder expectations.

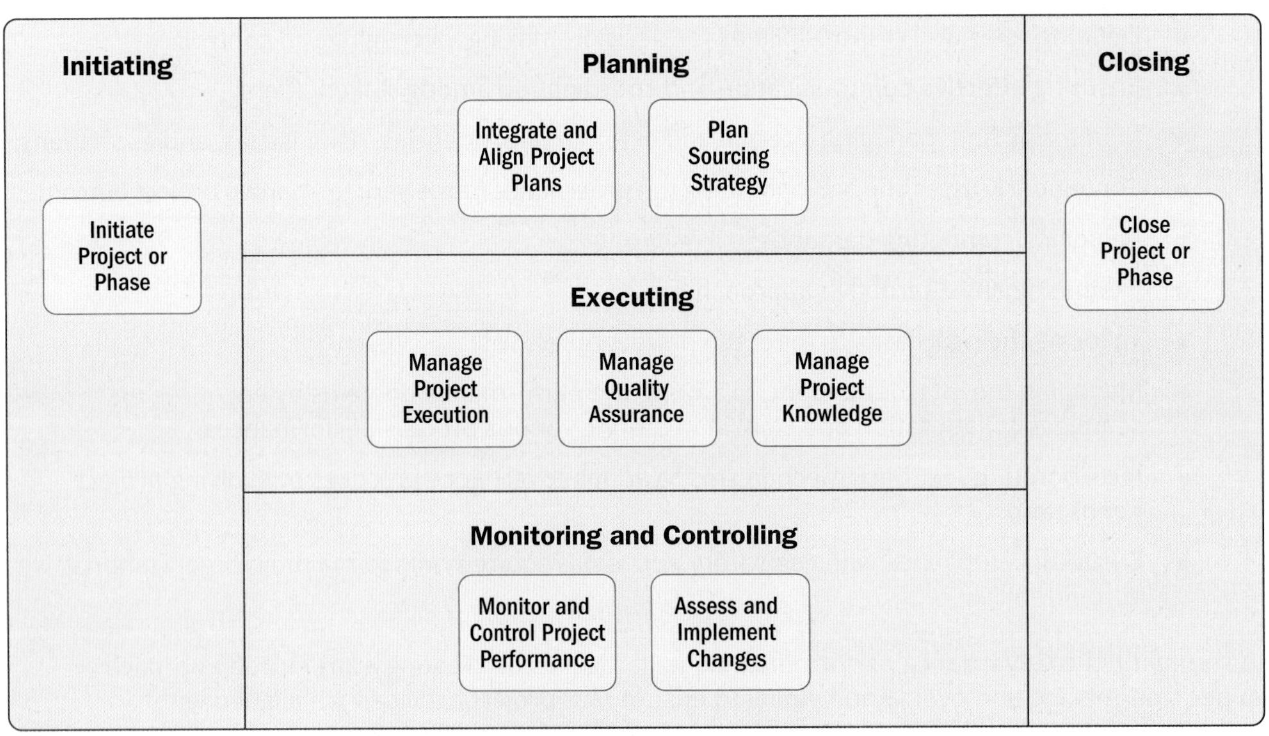

Figure 2-2. Governance Performance Domain Processes Overview

- **Manage Project Knowledge.** The process of utilizing existing knowledge, including lessons learned, and creating new knowledge to achieve project objectives, enhance decision-making, and contribute to organizational learning.
- **Monitor and Control Project Performance.** The process of tracking, reviewing, and reporting overall project progress to meet performance objectives and provide an overview of the status of the project.
- **Assess and Implement Changes.** The process of managing project changes that may impact various aspects of the project and adjusting plans based on stakeholder recommendations throughout the project life cycle.
- **Close Project or Phase.** The process of finalizing all activities related to the project or phase, including archiving knowledge, completing planned work, and releasing resources for new projects or operations.

2.1.6.1 Initiate Project or Phase

The Initiate Project or Phase process officially authorizes the start of a project and grants the project manager the authority to allocate organizational resources to project activities by creating a project charter or similar document. Authorization—typically, but not always, via a charter—establishes a direct link between the project, the business case, and the organization's strategic goals, creating an official record of the project and demonstrating the organization's commitment to the project. This process is usually carried out once or at certain points during the life cycle of a project, depending on the project development approach (see Figure 2-3).

Initiate Project or Phase

Inputs

- Business documents
  - Business case
  - Benefits management plan
- Agreements
- Enterprise environmental factors
- Organizational process assets
- Etc.

Tools & Techniques

- Expert judgment
- Data gathering
  - Brainstorming
  - Focus groups
  - Interviews
- Interpersonal and team skills
  - Conflict management
  - Facilitation
  - Meeting management
- Meetings
- Responsibility assignment matrix
- Project canvas
- Etc.

Outputs

- Project charter
- Assumption log
- Etc.

Figure 2-3. Initiate Project or Phase Inputs, Tools and Techniques, and Outputs

The project charter forms a partnership between the performing and requesting organizations. The approved business case, or similar item, justifies the reason behind initiating the project and the expected value.

For cross-corporate projects with two or more organizations involved, contracts are used to establish an agreement among the organizations. Project charters are then used inside the organizations to create internal agreements to ensure fulfillment of contractual obligations, which are mostly deliveries made by contractors, with payments made by customers. The approved project charter formally initiates the project, identifying and assigning a project manager as early as possible, ideally during the development of the charter and always before planning begins. The project charter can be developed by the sponsor or the project manager in collaboration with the initiating entity, allowing the project manager to gain a better understanding of the project's purpose, objectives, and expected benefits. This understanding facilitates efficient resource allocation to project activities. The project charter grants the project manager the authority to support the project.

In adaptive approaches, project charters are often designed to be more flexible, ranging from minimally impactful worksheets or concise vision statements to moderately detailed documents. These charters are tailored to the iterative and incremental nature of adaptive projects, providing just enough structure to guide the team while allowing for evolving requirements and priorities. An adaptive project charter typically focuses on answering a subset or all of the following key questions:

- Why is the project being undertaken?
- Who will be engaged?
- What is this project about?
- Where will it occur?
- When will it start and end?
- How will it be carried out?
- Who is the customer?

By emphasizing clarity and flexibility, adaptive project charters can ensure alignment among stakeholders while maintaining the ability to adapt to changes throughout the project's life cycle.

2.1.6.2 Integrate and Align Project Plans

The Integrate and Align Project Plans process involves integrating, aligning, and coordinating all plan components and consolidating them into a unified project management plan. The primary benefit of this process is the creation of a thorough document outlining the basis for the various aspects of all project activities and how they will be executed. This process is typically conducted once or at specific intervals during the project.

The project management plan specifies how the project will be executed, monitored and controlled, and closed. Its content varies depending on the project's application context and complexity. The plan can be either high level or detailed, tailored to the project's specific needs. This plan should also be adaptable enough to respond to the dynamic project environment—ideally, by following a progressive elaboration approach—ensuring that more accurate information is available as the project progresses.

The output of this process should be documented and communicated to key project stakeholders.

Integrate and Align Project Plans

Inputs	Tools & Techniques	Outputs
• Project charter • Outputs from other processes • Enterprise environmental factors • Organizational process assets • Etc.	• Expert judgment • Data gathering – Brainstorming – Checklists – Focus groups – Interviews • Interpersonal and team skills – Conflict management – Facilitation – Meeting management • Meetings • Project canvas • Etc.	• Project management plan • Etc.

Figure 2-4. Integrate and Align Project Plans Inputs, Tools and Techniques, and Outputs

This documentation may take the form of a project governance plan, project management plan, project execution plan, project development plan, project implementation plan, or another document that transparently defines—for all team members and stakeholders—the project management framework within which decisions will be made (see Figure 2-4).

At the beginning of the project, this process should establish the overall tailoring considerations and determine the development approach and project life cycle. This information should form part of the project management plan and serve as an input to all performance domains, guiding their planning efforts. Subsequently, all management plans and baselines from the performance domains should be integrated into the project management plan, and their alignments should be verified. Additionally, other management plans, such as the change management plan or configuration management plan, should be included if applicable.

The amount of time spent planning, both up front and throughout the project, should be determined by the circumstances. Therefore, the information gained from planning should be sufficient to move forward in an appropriate manner but not more detailed than necessary. Project teams use planning artifacts to confirm stakeholder expectations and provide stakeholders with the information they need to make decisions, take action, and maintain alignment between the project and its stakeholders.

2.1.6.3 Plan Sourcing Strategy

The Plan Sourcing Strategy process entails documenting project sourcing decisions, specifying the source selection approach, determining the scope of work for external sourcing, and selecting the appropriate contracts and sources for delivering the work (see Figure 2-5).

Plan Sourcing Strategy

Inputs

- Project charter
- Project management plan
  - Scope management plan
  - Quality management plan
  - Scope baseline
  - Schedule management plan
  - Financial management plan
  - Resource management plan
- Project documents
  - Milestone list
  - Requirements documentation
  - Requirements traceability matrix
  - Quality metrics
  - Resource requirements
  - Project team assignments
  - Risk register
  - Stakeholder register
- Enterprise environmental factors
- Organizational process assets
- Etc.

Tools & Techniques

- Expert judgment
- Market research
- Make-or-buy analysis
- Source selection analysis
- Document analysis
- Etc.

Outputs

- Sourcing strategy plan
  - Insourcing or outsourcing decisions
  - Source selection criteria
- Etc.

Figure 2-5. Plan Sourcing Strategy Inputs, Tools and Techniques, and Outputs

This process establishes a clear framework for acquiring project deliverables, either from within the organization or from external sources, defining what to acquire, how to acquire it, and when to acquire it.

The process is used to determine whether work or deliverables can be better accomplished using internal sources or should be purchased from outside sources. Several factors should be considered in the make-or-buy decision (see Table 2-3).

In addition to supporting make-or-buy decisions, the sourcing strategy plan may also include determining the type of contracts to be used for external sources. These contracts should be consistent with the selected sourcing approach, taking into account factors such as project

Table 2-3. Advantages of Insourcing Versus Outsourcing

Advantages of Insourcing/Make	Advantages of Outsourcing/Buy
• Leverages internal expertise when it is available internally • Is often less expensive if substantial new innovation is required • Provides tighter integration with strategic advantage or value proposition • Increases control and oversight of deliverables	• Leverages external expertise when it is missing internally • Is often less expensive if the goods or services are common • Frees up capacity and capital to focus on competitive strengths • Transfers delivery risk to the supplier • Maintains supplier relations

complexity, source performance, and risk exposure. The sourcing strategy plan includes developing a process for managing relationships with external sources, dealing with potential risks, and ensuring clear channels of communication throughout the project life cycle.

A key part of this process is establishing source selection criteria, which help guide the evaluation and selection of vendors. These criteria may include cost, technical capability, past performance, financial stability, compliance with requirements, and alignment with organizational values or sustainability goals. Clearly defining these criteria ensures transparency and consistency in vendor selection and helps ensure that selected partners are capable of delivering the required scope of work effectively and reliably.

The Plan Sourcing Strategy process differs from the Plan Resource Management process (see Section 2.6.2) as it involves the outsourcing of project work and deliverables, taking into account various factors such as determining the scope, time, cost, quality, and resources required to acquire the final work and deliverables from outside the organization.

Participants in this process may include the purchasing or procurement department as well as personnel from the buying organization's legal department. These responsibilities should be documented in the sourcing strategy plan.

The Plan Sourcing Strategy process applies to projects where there is a need to use external sources to complete project work. For more information, see Appendix X4 on Procurement.

2.1.6.4 Manage Project Execution

The Manage Project Execution process involves leading and performing the work defined in the project management plan and implementing approved changes to meet the project's objectives. The primary benefit of this process is the comprehensive management of project work and deliverables, which enhances the likelihood of project success. When leading project teams, the collective team members have more knowledge than any single person. Directing and managing execution provides a way to align the knowledge and skills of all team members toward the project objectives.

This process includes executing the planned project activities to complete deliverables and achieve set objectives. The process also involves allocating resources, managing their efficient use, and making adjustments to project plans based on the analysis of work performance data and

Manage Project Execution

Inputs

- Project management plan
  - Any component
- Project documents
  - Change log
  - Lessons learned register
  - Milestone list
  - Project communications
  - Project schedule
  - Requirements traceability matrix
  - Risk register
  - Risk report
- Approved change requests
- Enterprise environmental factors
- Organizational process assets
- Etc.

Tools & Techniques

- Expert judgment
- Project management information system
- Meetings
  - Daily coordination meetings
- Etc.

Outputs

- Deliverables
- Work performance data
- Issue log
- Change requests
- Project management plan updates
  - Any component
- Project document updates
  - Activity list
  - Assumption log
  - Lessons learned register
  - Requirements documentation
  - Risk register
  - Stakeholder register
- Organizational process asset updates
- Etc.

Figure 2-6. Manage Project Execution Inputs, Tools and Techniques, and Outputs

information. Deliverables are produced as outputs from activities conducted according to the project management plan (see Figure 2-6).

The project manager, along with the project team, manages and enables the execution of planned activities to achieve project objectives, and harmonizes different aspects of both technical and functional activities within the broader project ecosystem. This process also involves reviewing the impact of all project changes and implementing approved changes, including corrective actions, preventive actions, and defect remediation.

During project execution, work performance data is collected and communicated to applicable controlling processes for analysis. This analysis provides information about the completion status of deliverables and other relevant details about project performance. The work performance data is also used as an input to the Monitoring and Controlling Focus Area and serves as feedback for lessons learned to improve the performance of future work packages.

Quality management is relevant during project execution. There are two ways in which quality should be addressed in a project. The first is during the construction of the project management process, which provides process quality assurance and value delivery throughout the project. The second is during deliverable construction and should be addressed through scope management and control.

At this point, quality should be focused on ensuring that deliverables are being produced according to the agreed-upon requirements set in the scope baseline. For adaptative approaches, the scope baseline may be called prioritized requirements or the sprint backlog.

2.1.6.5 Manage Quality Assurance

Manage Quality Assurance is the process of ensuring project processes are performed in a manner consistent with stakeholder expectations. This process involves translating the project management plan into executable activities that incorporate the organization's standards, regulations, and policies. The key benefit of this process is that it increases the probability of meeting the project objectives as well as identifies ineffective processes and causes of poor project performance. This process is performed throughout the project. The inputs, tools and techniques, and outputs are shown in Figure 2-7.

Quality management is sometimes called quality assurance, although quality management has a broader meaning in non-project work. In contrast, project management differentiates quality assurance and quality control as two distinct efforts:

- **Quality assurance** is about using project processes effectively. This effort involves following and meeting standards to assure stakeholders that the project's final results will meet their needs, expectations, and requirements. Related concepts include regulations, compliance, and audits.
- **Quality control** is about creating project deliverables that meet defined specifications and thresholds. This effort involves defining the attributes of the value generated by a project and ensuring project deliverables achieve those attributes. Related concepts include product design, testing, and defects.

Manage Quality Assurance

Inputs

- Project management plan
- Project documents
  - All components
- Organizational process assets
  - Policies
  - Procedures
  - Regulations
- Etc.

Tools & Techniques

- Audits
- Checklists
- Data representation
  - Affinity diagrams
  - Cause-and-effect diagrams
  - Flowcharts
- Decision-making
- Problem-solving
- Process improvement
- Etc.

Outputs

- Quality reports
- Change requests
- Project management plan updates
- Project document updates
- Etc.

Figure 2-7. Manage Quality Assurance Inputs, Tools and Techniques, and Outputs

The Manage Quality Assurance process implements a set of planned and systematic acts and processes defined within the project's quality management plan that can help to achieve the following:

- Build confidence that a future output will be completed in a manner that meets the specified requirements and expectations through quality assurance tools and techniques such as quality audits and failure analysis;
- Improve the efficiency and effectiveness of processes and activities to achieve better results and performance and enhance stakeholder satisfaction; and
- Ensure the project is governed properly, and thus increase the likelihood that it will meet or exceed stakeholder expectations.

In agile or adaptive projects, quality assurance can be performed formally or informally, based on the context. In predictive projects, quality assurance is usually performed in a formal capacity, under the expectation that strong process quality will minimize variances in an otherwise stable project.

Quality assurance tasks may be performed by the project management team, an external entity, or both.

2.1.6.6 Manage Project Knowledge

Manage Project Knowledge is the process of using existing knowledge and creating new knowledge to achieve the project's objectives and contribute to organizational learning (see Figure 2-8). Key benefits of this process include the following:

- Using prior organizational knowledge to produce or improve the project outcome, and
- Collecting new knowledge created by the project to support organizational operations and future projects or phases.

Knowledge management is concerned with managing both explicit and tacit knowledge for two purposes: reusing existing knowledge and creating new knowledge. The key activities that underpin both purposes are knowledge sharing and integration (incorporating knowledge from different domains, contextual knowledge, and project management knowledge).

Managing projects requires both explicit and tacit knowledge:

- **Explicit knowledge.** Explicit knowledge is formal and systematic; it is the type of knowledge that can be readily codified using words, pictures, or numbers. This type of knowledge includes manuals, procedures, and documented processes. Explicit knowledge is easily communicated and shared through information management tools such as databases, registers, and web searches. The following are key characteristics of explicit knowledge:
    - **Codifiable.** Can be documented in words, pictures, or numbers.
    - **Formal and systematic.** Structured and organized in a way that is easy to understand.
    - **Easily communicated.** Can be shared through manuals, procedures, and other documentation.
- **Tacit knowledge.** Tacit knowledge is information that is embedded in a person's mind and is highly personal. Tacit knowledge is difficult to articulate because it consists of technical skills, experiences, insights, and practical knowledge. Tacit knowledge is challenging to

Manage Project Knowledge

Inputs

- Project management plan
  - All components
- Project documents
  - Lessons learned register
  - Project team assignments
  - Resource breakdown structure
  - Stakeholder register
- Deliverables
- Enterprise environmental factors
- Organizational process assets
- Etc.

Tools & Techniques

- Expert judgment
- Knowledge management
- Information management
- After-action reviews
- In-progress postmortems
- Storytelling
- Retrospective meetings
- Interpersonal and team skills
  - Active listening
  - Facilitation
  - Leadership
  - Networking
  - Political awareness
- Etc.

Outputs

- Lessons learned register
- Project management plan updates
  - Any component
- Organizational process asset updates
- Etc.

Figure 2-8. Manage Project Knowledge Inputs, Tools and Techniques, and Outputs

formalize and communicate, making it hard to transfer to others or different projects. The following are key characteristics of tacit knowledge:

- **Personal and embedded.** Resides within an individual's mind.
- **Difficult to articulate.** Challenging to express in words or documentation.
- **Experience-based.** Includes insights, experiences, and practical skills.
- **Challenging to transfer.** Cannot be easily shared or communicated to others.

Managing knowledge involves more than just documenting explicit knowledge for sharing or obtaining lessons learned at the end of the project for use in future projects. Codified explicit knowledge lacks context and is open to different interpretations, so even though it can be more easily shared, it is not always understood or applied in the right way. Tacit knowledge has further context but is difficult to codify.

Tacit knowledge resides in the minds of individual experts or in social groups and situations and is often shared through conversations and interactions between people. Tacit knowledge, often deeply ingrained in experts' experience and intuition, can be shared within a project by fostering a collaborative and trust-filled environment. This effort involves creating opportunities for knowledge transfer through open communication, mentoring relationships, and team-building activities. Encouraging face-to-face interactions and hosting regular brainstorming sessions can help make implicit knowledge more accessible. The latest artificial intelligence (AI) technologies, such as interview bots, add new, strong capabilities in capturing and sharing both tacit and explicit knowledge. An important objective of knowledge management is converting tacit knowledge into explicit knowledge when possible.

Determining how and when lessons learned and retrospectives will be conducted throughout the project helps support knowledge management. Identifying which information should be collected both during the project and at its closure is essential. Additionally, project managers should establish how historical information and lessons learned will be made available to benefit the current project and future projects. When managing project knowledge, AI can be leveraged as a significant source of knowledge. Significant risks are associated with the use of AI, including unintentionally exposing sensitive information and experiencing AI hallucinations. Projects should have responsible AI policies to manage the related knowledge.

Effective knowledge-sharing mechanisms foster a collaborative, evidence-based working environment throughout the project. Through these mechanisms, valuable insights are captured, shared, and utilized to enhance project outcomes and drive continuous improvement.

2.1.6.7 Monitor and Control Project Performance

Monitor and Control Project Performance is the process of tracking, reviewing, and reporting the overall project progress to meet the performance objectives defined in the project management plan. The key benefits of this process are that it allows stakeholders to understand the current state of the project, recognize actions taken to address any performance issues, and gain visibility into the future project status with cost and schedule forecasts (see Figure 2-9).

This process includes evaluating project performance during execution and assessing whether decisions might enhance the project's value proposition. If a decision is likely beneficial and results in a change to the project baseline, integrated change control should be employed.

Monitoring is an ongoing aspect of project management performed throughout the project. Monitoring involves collecting, measuring, and assessing data and trends to drive better project outcomes, maintain project health, and identify areas needing special attention. Controlling involves determining corrective or preventive actions, replanning, and following up on action plans to ensure that performance issues are resolved. The Monitor and Control Project Performance process involves the following:

- Evaluating performance compared to plan;
- Tracking the utilization of resources, work completed, budget expended, etc.;
- Demonstrating accountability;
- Providing information to stakeholders;
- Assessing whether project deliverables are on track to deliver planned benefits;
- Conducting conversations about trade-offs, threats, opportunities, and options;
- Evaluating current risks, identifying new ones, and monitoring responses;
- Ensuring project deliverables will meet the customer acceptance criteria; and
- Updating the sourcing strategy to better meet project goals and constraints.

Monitor and Control Project Performance

Inputs

- Project management plan
  - Any component
- Project documents
  - Assumption log
  - Basis of estimates
  - Cost forecasts
  - Issue log
  - Lessons learned register
  - Milestone list
  - Quality reports
  - Risk register
  - Risk report
  - Schedule forecasts
- Work performance information
- Agreements
- Enterprise environmental factors
- Organizational process assets
- Etc.

Tools & Techniques

- Expert judgment
- Data analysis
  - Alternative analysis
  - Cost-benefit analysis
  - Earned value analysis
  - Root cause analysis
  - Trend analysis
  - Variance analysis
- Decision-making
  - Voting
- Meetings
- Project dashboards
- Visual controls
- Information radiators
- Etc.

Outputs

- Work performance reports
- Change requests
- Project management plan updates
  - Any component
- Project document updates
  - Cost forecasts
  - Issue log
  - Lessons learned register
  - Risk register
  - Schedule forecasts
- Etc.

Figure 2-9. Monitor and Control Project Performance Inputs, Tools and Techniques, and Outputs

The Monitor and Control Project Performance process is linked to measurement, as it relies on the continuous tracking, review, and reporting of project metrics to ensure alignment with the performance objectives set out in the project management plan. Effective measurement provides the necessary data to assess project progress, resource utilization, and the status of the project.

By collecting and analyzing leading and lagging indicators, project practitioners can identify potential problems early, make informed decisions, and take corrective or preventive action to keep the project on track. Measurement also facilitates accountability and transparency, allowing stakeholders to understand the current status of the project and its future development. The Monitor and Control Project Performance process is thus supported by robust measurement techniques that drive process improvements and increase the likelihood of project success.

Measurement requires time and effort that could be allocated to other productive tasks; therefore, project teams should focus on measuring only what is relevant and ensure that the metrics are actionable. Metrics should adhere to the SMART criteria explained in Section 2.1.5.3 to be effective.

2.1.6.7.1 Measurement Pitfalls

Project measurements help the project team meet the project objectives. However, there are some pitfalls associated with measurement. Awareness of these risks can help minimize their negative effects. Project practitioners should be aware of the following risks:

- **Hawthorne effect.** The Hawthorne effect states that the very act of measuring something influences behavior. Therefore, take care in establishing metrics. For example, measuring only a project team's output of deliverables can encourage the project team to focus on creating a large volume of deliverables rather than focusing on deliverables that would provide higher customer satisfaction.
- **Vanity metric.** A vanity metric is a measure that shows data but does not provide useful information for making decisions. Measuring page views of a website is not as useful as measuring the number of new viewers.
- **Demoralization.** If measures and goals are set that are not achievable, project team morale may fall as the team continuously fails to meet targets. Setting stretch goals and aspirational measures is acceptable, but people also want to see their hard work recognized. Unrealistic or unachievable goals can be counterproductive.
- **Misusing the metrics.** Regardless of the metrics used to measure performance, there is the opportunity for people to distort the measurements or focus on the wrong thing. Examples include:
  - Focusing on less-important metrics rather than the metrics that matter most,
  - Focusing on performing well for short-term measures at the expense of long-term metrics, and
  - Working on out-of-sequence activities that are easy to accomplish in order to improve performance indicators.
- **Confirmation bias.** Human beings tend to look for and see information that supports their preexisting points of view. This bias can lead people to make false interpretations of data.
- **Correlation versus causation.** A common mistake in interpreting measurement data is confusing the correlation of two variables with the idea that one causes the other. For example, seeing projects that are behind schedule and over budget might cause one to infer that those projects are over budget because of schedule issues. This assumption may not be true, nor is it always true that projects that are behind schedule cause budget overruns. Instead, there are likely other correlating factors that are not being considered, such as skill in estimating, the ability to manage change, and actively managing risks. Being aware of the pitfalls associated with metrics can help with establishing effective metrics in addition to being vigilant regarding the dangers related to inappropriate measures.

2.1.6.8 Assess and Implement Changes

The Assess and Implement Changes process occurs from the start of a project through its completion, as changes can occur at any stage. Change requests can affect various aspects such as project scope, product scope, project management plan components, and project documents. Such changes can be proposed by any stakeholder and may occur at any point in the project life cycle. The degree of project change request management that is applied depends on the scope of the project, its complexity, the contract requirements, and the development approach being used (see Figure 2-10).

Assess and Implement Changes

Inputs

- Project management plan
  - Change management plan
  - Configuration management plan
  - Scope baseline
  - Schedule baseline
  - Cost baseline
- Project documents
  - Basis of estimates
  - Change log
  - Requirements traceability matrix
  - Risk report
- Work performance reports
- Change requests
- Enterprise environmental factors
- Organizational process assets
- Etc.

Tools & Techniques

- Expert judgment
- Change control tools
- Data analysis
  - Alternative analysis
  - Cost-benefit analysis
- Decision-making
  - Voting
  - Autocratic decision-making
  - Multicriteria decision analysis
- Meetings
- Integrated change control
- Backlog management
- Etc.

Outputs

- Approved change requests
- Project management plan updates
  - Any component
- Project document updates
  - Change log
- Etc.

Figure 2-10. Assess and Implement Changes Inputs, Tools and Techniques, and Outputs

2.1.6.8.1 Predictive Approaches

In predictive project approaches, changes are not formally controlled until baselines are established. However, once the project has a baseline, all changes should go through a formal process to assess and implement changes. The configuration management plan for the project should specify which project artifacts are subject to configuration control. Changes to these artifacts require a formal change request.

Although changes can be initiated verbally, they should be documented in writing and entered into the change or configuration management system. Change requests should typically include information on the estimated schedule and cost impacts before they can be approved. If a change request impacts a project baseline, integrated change control measures should follow a formal process to assess and implement those changes. Each documented change request should be approved, deferred, or rejected by a designated person, such as the project sponsor or project manager, as specified in the project management plan or organizational procedures.

Figure 2-11 shows an example flow of how the Assess and Implement Changes process might be performed.

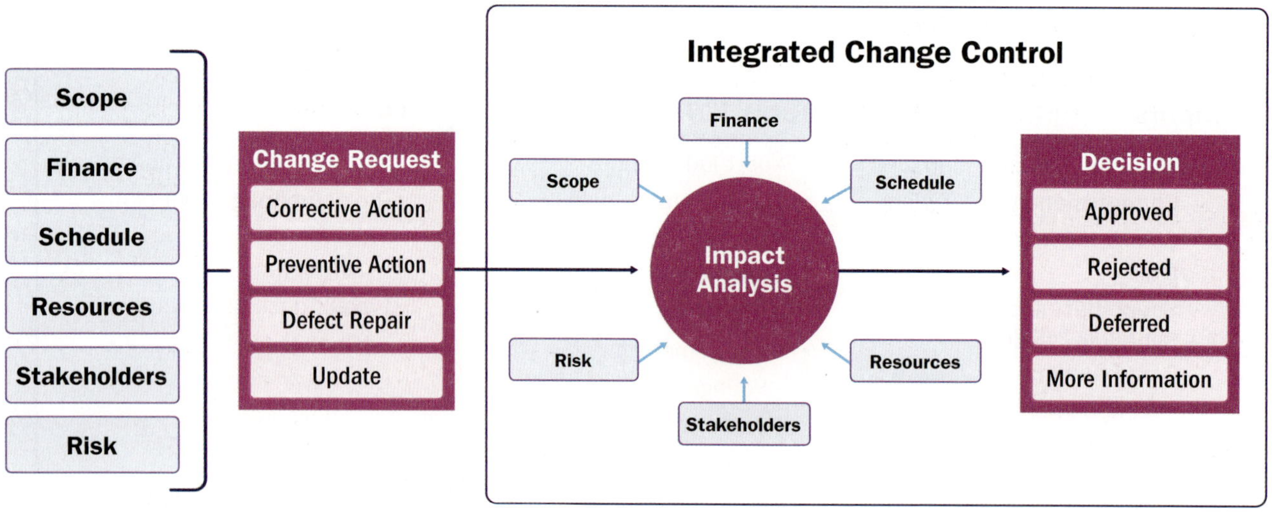

Figure 2-11. Example Flow for Project Changes

When applicable, a change control board (CCB) or project board may be involved. The CCB is a formally established group responsible for reviewing, evaluating, approving, deferring, or rejecting changes—and for documenting and communicating these decisions. While awaiting the decision of the CCB, project managers should continually execute planned tasks while also analyzing the impact and risks related to accepting or rejecting the proposed changes to minimize negative impacts.

Approved change requests may require new or updated cost estimates, schedule adjustments, resource requirements, and risk assessments. These changes may also require updates to the project management plan and other project documents. Depending on the nature of the change, customer or sponsor approval may be required after CCB approval, unless the customer or sponsor is a CCB member.

Changes are made to create improvements to the original plan and baseline, often based on changing conditions. The results of the changes should be monitored to ensure they yield the desired results.

2.1.6.8.2 Adaptive Approaches

In adaptive approaches, managing project changes typically involves backlog management rather than a formal change request process. Changes are continuously assessed and prioritized throughout the iterative development cycle. When a stakeholder proposes a change, it is recorded as a product backlog item and added to the backlog. Although these are not formally termed as change requests, an impact analysis is conducted to evaluate the change's effect and set its priority.

Typically, there is not a formal "approval" process; instead, any proposed change can be added to the backlog. If the proposed change is assigned a lower priority, this essentially means that the change is deferred. Conversely, choosing not to add a change to the backlog, or remove an existing change from the backlog, means that it is rejected.

2.1.6.9 Close Project or Phase

The Close Project or Phase process involves finalizing all activities related to both successful and unsuccessful projects, phases, releases, iterations, or contracts. The primary benefits include archiving project or phase information, completing planned work, and releasing organizational resources for new projects. The process also includes confirming the extent to which value or the capability to deliver value has been achieved (see Figure 2-12).

Close Project or Phase

Inputs

- Project charter
- Project management plan
  - All components
- Project documents
  - Assumption log
  - Basis of estimates
  - Change log
  - Issue log
  - Lessons learned register
  - Milestone list
  - Project communications
  - Quality control measurements
  - Quality reports
  - Requirements documentation
  - Risk register
  - Risk report
- Accepted deliverables
- Business documents
  - Business case
  - Benefits management plan
- Agreements
- Procurement documentation
- Organizational process assets
- Etc.

Tools & Techniques

- Expert judgment
- Data analysis
  - Document analysis
  - Regression analysis
  - Trend analysis
  - Variance analysis
- Meetings
- Etc.

Outputs

- Project document updates
  - Lessons learned register
- Final product, service, or result transition
- Final report
- Organizational process asset updates
- Etc.

Figure 2-12. Close Project or Phase Inputs, Tools and Techniques, and Outputs

2.1.6.9.1 Predictive Approaches

For project closure, the project manager should ensure that all work is completed and that the objectives are met by reviewing the project management plan. Key activities for administrative closure in predictive approaches may include the following:

- **Satisfying completion or exit criteria.** The following steps should be performed when satisfying the exit criteria in the Close Project or Phase process:
  - Ensure all documents and deliverables are updated and all issues are resolved.
  - Ensure that the measurable project value was delivered, and that there is a plan to maintain this value as the project is closed and transitioned to operations.
  - Confirm that deliverables have been delivered and formally accepted by the customer.
  - Verify that all costs have been charged to the project.
  - Close project accounts.
  - Reassign or release project personnel.
  - Address excess project materials.
  - Reallocate or release project facilities, equipment, and other resources.
  - Prepare final project reports as required by organizational policies.
- **Contractual agreement completion.** The following activities should be verified when closing out contractual agreements in the Close Project or Phase process:
  - Confirm formal acceptance of the external source's work.
  - Finalize any open claims, guarantees, and warranties.
  - Update records to reflect the final results.
  - Ensure all invoices due to external sources are paid.
  - Archive relevant information for future use.
  - Resolve any disputes that may arise or refer them to the dispute board.
- **Additional closure activities.** The following additional closure activities should be performed in the Close Project or Phase process:
  - Collect and audit project or phase records.
  - Assess project success or failure.
  - Manage knowledge sharing and transfer.
  - Identify and document lessons learned.
  - Archive project information for future organizational use.
  - Transfer project products, services, or results to the next phase or into production/operations.
  - Collect suggestions for improving or updating organizational policies and procedures and forward them to the appropriate unit.
  - Measure stakeholder satisfaction.
  - Verify that all contractual, regulatory, legal, social, and environmental obligations have been met.

identify outstanding risks that should be accepted or transitioned to operations. The Close Project or Phase process also includes establishing procedures to investigate and document reasons that the project may have been terminated before completion. Engaging relevant stakeholders is crucial to ensure a comprehensive closure process.

2.1.6.9.2 Adaptive Approaches

In adaptative approaches, the Close Project or Phase process centers on wrapping up all activities related to the release or iteration, ensuring the prioritized items are completed and the value is delivered.

Key activities for closing an adaptive project or iteration may include the following:

- **Completion of release or iteration.** The following activities should be performed when completing a release or iteration in an adaptive project:
  - Confirm that prioritized backlog items are finished and that all acceptance criteria are met.
  - Ensure that all deliverables have been reviewed and accepted by stakeholders.
  - Conduct a final review to verify that all project tasks are completed and that no outstanding issues remain.
- **Knowledge transfer and retrospectives.** The following knowledge transfer and retrospectives activities should be performed:
  - Facilitate knowledge-sharing sessions to transfer insights and information among the team.
  - Hold retrospectives to reflect on the iteration and/or release, identifying lessons learned and opportunities for improvement in future work.
  - Discuss outstanding risks that should be accepted or transitioned to subsequent iterations and/or releases, clients, and operations.

2.1.7 Tailoring Considerations

Project governance should be tailored to the context in which the project operates. Governance that brings value relies on deep knowledge of the industry and regulatory considerations, the organization, and the context for a particular project. Additionally, tailoring in this domain may occur based on predictive, adaptive, or hybrid approaches. In fact, agile projects may avoid traditional governance entirely in favor of self-governance that is embedded in project approaches. Customizing governance is typically part of the Initiate Project or Phase process but may occur iteratively throughout the project. Depending on the project approach, outcomes of tailoring decisions may be recorded in the project management plan, another document, or a system of record. In organizations implementing predictive or hybrid approaches, a senior project manager—or in large organizations, a portfolio manager, program manager, or project management office—will likely handle project governance. Considerations for tailoring include but are not limited to the following:

- **Organizational governance.** Governance should be understood from the perspective of other functions and projects within the larger organization. Governance requires the following:
  - Identifying the control boards, committees, and other stakeholders that are part of the project; and
  - Defining the project status reporting requirements.

Additionally, it is essential to assess whether the governance and integration in adaptive projects will lean toward self-governing teams and a total-quality approach. Determining whether and how a project management office should be involved is another critical step. Deciding if the team will establish a governance board and identifying which committees or stakeholders should be involved are further considerations to help tailor the governance approach to fit the specific needs and context of the project.

- **Guided self-governance.** Agile or adaptive projects are designed to be self-governing, meaning that the teams involved have the autonomy to make decisions and manage their work without heavy bureaucracy and oversight. Instead, these teams manage their work with light governance and clear-set boundaries and guardrails. In this way, agile teams are empowered to make decisions about their work processes, priorities, and problem-solving approaches—essentially, self-governance. Additionally, successful agile teams are comfortable with uncertainty and are willing to engage in collaborative decision-making. This collaboration involves facilitating open discussions, exploring differing opinions, and using constructive feedback to navigate through unknowns together. As an example, the practice of daily coordination meetings helps ensure teams maintain focus and alignment and serves as a self-governing mechanism toward that end. Adaptive teams operate with autonomy, leveraging iterative planning, collaborative decision-making, and focused communication to drive continuous improvement, which can lead to successful self-governance.
- **Project life cycle adaptations.** Governance should also be tailored to be appropriate for predictive, adaptive, and hybrid life cycles. This tailoring involves a continuous and iterative process of adapting the approach, governance, and processes to suit the unique objectives, stakeholders, and complexity of the environment. Such deliberate adaptation aims to maximize value, manage constraints, and improve performance by using "just enough" processes, methods, templates, and artifacts to achieve the desired project outcomes. For projects that apply lean/agile approaches, governance may be provided by the project team only in the artifacts and events of the project. Predictive projects may have heavier governance requirements due to internal and external constraints. Project managers should tailor the appropriate framework to enable flexibility and consistently produce positive outcomes within the project's life cycle context. Factors such as the business environment, regulatory requirements, need for innovation, market conditions, team size, degree of uncertainty, and project complexity play a crucial role in how project systems are tailored. Additionally, organizations with established process governance should ensure that tailoring aligns with policy and strategy. The Disciplined Agile® (DA®) tool kit offers further guidance on lean/agile governance.

2.1.7.1 Examples

The following are three examples of how these considerations might be applied:

- **Example 1.** A project may or may not be governed by a project management office (PMO). Thus, project managers should ensure that their governing approach is focused on delivering maximum value. In a small organization, the project manager may make decisions regarding project governance with other key leaders, while a project manager with access to a PMO in a large organization may partner with PMO leadership and/or other portfolio, program, and project managers to help ensure that a project is appropriately governed to achieve strategic alignment and deliver value.

- **Example 2.** A project that requires rapid innovation and approaches may want to adopt a faster feedback cycle that an agile framework may provide. Thus, a self-governing approach may be adopted, where there is no external governance body and the team manages all value delivery, outputs, quality, etc., through typical agile processes.
- **Example 3.** A large, multinational project may require compliance with a variety of regulations across agencies and countries. Thus, project governance should integrate across domains to ensure that work on a project is appropriately monitored and controlled to comply with internal and external standards. Some multinational compliance may have regional variations that should be managed with program- or portfolio-level governance.

2.1.8 Interactions With Other Domains

The Governance performance domain is interrelated with all other project management performance domains. This interrelationship includes ensuring the alignment of project scope, schedule, and financial resources to maximize value delivery while balancing trade-offs. As such, Table 2-4 addresses interactions with the Scope, Schedule, and Finance performance domains, first and foremost.

2.1.9 Check Results

Acknowledging and implementing the appropriate level of project management governance requires a delicate balance that is tailored to the industry, organizational structure, and specific project context. Governance approaches should be contemplated by various stakeholders (from executives to project management office leaders as well as agile practitioners to other project team members) to ensure success. Table 2-5 shows a set of sample target outcomes, along with a potential check to confirm whether those outcomes are met.

2.2 Scope Performance Domain

Scope carries a unique and central place in project management, as the value of a project derives from the outcome delivered in alignment with its scope. The Scope performance domain includes the processes required to ensure that the project encompasses all of the work required to complete the project successfully and that only the required work is mapped and no unnecessary work is performed, thus helping to optimize costs and schedule in order to maximize the project's value.
In addition to defining and managing the scope, the Scope performance domain also focuses on project quality. Quality is defined by meeting stakeholder expectations and fulfilling the project and product requirements. This performance domain helps ensure that deliverables meet the specified acceptance criteria and that the processes used to produce them are effective and efficient. The domain emphasizes continuous process improvement, helping to ensure that both scope and quality are aligned and consistently meet the project's objectives and standards.

2.2.1 Key Concepts

The following key concepts support effective practices for the Scope performance domain:

- **Business case.** The business case is a documented economic feasibility study used to establish validity of the benefits to be delivered by a portfolio component, program, or project. Projects are initiated through a business case that outlines costs, benefits, and how value will be created, together with project success criteria.

Table 2-4. Governance Interactions With Other Performance Domains

Performance Domain	Explanation
Scope	Since project scope is where the project's core value lies, the Governance and Scope performance domains often comprise the most important domain interaction. The Scope–Governance approach can have extensive formal controls or be more informal, but such governance decisions are pivotal.
Schedule	Because most projects involve some form of investment—be it financial, strategic, or otherwise—and because the value proposition is often sensitive to time, the interaction between the Governance and Schedule performance domains can be critical. Well-applied governance may increase a project's speed and effectiveness, while poorly applied governance can slow it down or result in ineffective outcomes.
Finance	All projects are investments, and the value proposition of any investment is sensitive to the amount being invested (i.e., cost). Consequently, the interaction between the Governance and Finance performance domains can impact projects with cost overruns or underruns.
Stakeholders	Well-applied project governance can help ensure that all stakeholders are engaged at the right time in order to achieve project success. Governance considers the vantage points of all players to help ensure individuals are aware of what is happening in a project and can give input, provide advice, or perform work at the appropriate time.
Resources	Since the completion of project work is heavily dependent on how well the right resources are allocated to the right project priorities at the right times, the interaction between the Governance and Resources performance domains requires attention in the context of the specific project, as well as how resources are allocated across the organization.
Risk	All projects are investments with inherent risks, requiring effective interaction between the Governance and Risk performance domains. Risks, encompassing both threats and opportunities, impact project outcomes. Mitigating risks or seizing opportunities should align with strategic objectives and be managed under clear governance to optimize risk-adjusted returns. For example, risk mitigation efforts may incur additional expenditures, but they can be worthwhile if they enhance the overall project outcomes, such as improving safety, regulatory compliance, stakeholder confidence, or the risk-adjusted return on investment.

Table 2-5. Check Outcomes—Governance Performance Domain

Outcome	Check
Projects have an appropriate level of oversight by leadership and third-party stakeholders.	Project teams understand there are agreed-upon processes, protocols, team agreements, or other forms of project governance in tasks in which they are involved. These agreed-upon processes are documented (as appropriate) and aligned with the other organizational governance artifacts (policies, standards, procedures, etc.).
Project governance processes are in place, effective, and continuously improved throughout the project.	Project teams have awareness of—and act appropriately on—governance structure (policies, standards, procedures, guidelines); internal and external auditing/compliance; and customer governance requirements. Project teams ensure that governance of interactions comes from both organizational and third-party governance and is integrated within project governance. The project team may check governance using instruments such as compliance audits or checklists against internal or external standards/benchmarks for predictive approaches. Project teams may ensure that the governance checklist is used regularly, timeboxing is in place, and meetings are held.
Effective signaling mechanisms tied to target project outcomes are in place.	Project teams select and use one or more signaling mechanisms that will align most closely to how the project can maximize its value proposition.
Lessons learned/ retrospectives are managed throughout the project.	Project teams ensure that the project and organizational knowledge and learning are combined to manage project deliverables and value. Lessons learned are incorporated during the ongoing processes, not only at the end of the project.
Key management members are kept apprised of the project.	Project metrics are in place and tracked regularly. Project teams focus efforts on: • Operational status and progress of project components and related activities; • Expected and incurred project resource requirements; • Known project risks, their response plans, and escalation criteria; • Strategic and operational assumptions; • Benefits realized; • Decision criteria, tracking, and communication; • Project change control; • Compliance with corporate and legal policies; • Project information and communications management; • Issues and issue response plans; and • Project funding and financial performance.

- **Project scope.** Project scope encompasses the work performed to deliver a product, service, or result with the specified features and functions. The project scope helps ensure that the expected value is achieved. Scope encapsulates a project's expected value, so it is the most important component of any project's baseline. The delivery of any project's scope should generate expected value that is not only worth the time and resources invested, but also ideally maximized.
- **Requirement.** A requirement is a condition or capability that is necessary to be present in a product, service, or result to satisfy a business need.
- **Scope baseline.** In predictive environments, the scope baseline is the approved version of formal scope documents that can be changed using formal change control procedures and is used as the basis for comparison to actual results. The scope baseline forms part of the performance measurement baseline (PMB), which also includes the schedule baseline and the cost baseline. For adaptive approaches, the baseline is defined at the beginning of each iteration and aligned with the prioritized requirements, based on the value expected from the delivery. In adaptive environments, it is usually a product owner who dynamically approves changes and generates them in a more flexible environment, without a formal change control procedure.
- **Work breakdown structure (WBS).** In a project incorporating aspects of a predictive or hybrid approach, a WBS is a hierarchical decomposition of the total scope of work to be carried out by the project team to accomplish the project objectives and create the required deliverables. In projects using a predictive approach, the WBS, together with the project scope statement and the WBS dictionary, constitutes the scope baseline.
- **Quality as a feature.** Quality is an integral attribute of scope and can include both functional and nonfunctional requirements of the product, service, or result. For example, the scope of a bridge-construction project would include a bridge but should also incorporate some target thresholds for how sturdy, long-lasting, and easy to maintain that bridge should be. These quality features are the same as any consideration of scope, including which cost and schedule trade-offs might yield the highest possible expected lifetime value per unit of investment.
- **Product scope.** The product scope is a description of the features, functions, and characteristics of the product, service, or result the project is intended to deliver. It is what the end result should look like and what it should do. The focus is on the deliverables themselves, including their quality and performance specifications.
- **Value breakdown structure (VBS).** A VBS is a hierarchical structure that connects the project scope and its intended value to the product scope that will generate that value. The top level of the VBS should include the major deliverables that have been discussed and generated among the stakeholders. The value that each deliverable is expected to add should be an input into each item as either a value-based number (e.g., dollars of revenue, students taught to read, or lives saved, depending on the project) or a percentage of the expected total value of the project (100% if the specific deliverable is mandatory). These value-added estimates can then be used to prioritize the deliverables and their work, as well as to estimate the drag cost of each critical path item. Each item at the top of the VBS can then be decomposed into its component subdeliverables, which in turn are decomposed through a work breakdown structure into the project scope and activities to create the valued items in the VBS.
- **Product backlog.** The product backlog is a dynamic, prioritized list of work items and features. The product backlog provides teams in adaptive environments with a framework

for managing scope by focusing on value-driven outcomes, enabling continuous prioritization, and maintaining alignment with stakeholder expectations.

- **Definition of done (DoD).** The DoD is a checklist of all the criteria required to be met so that a deliverable can be considered ready for customer use. In projects using an adaptive approach, a DoD is a shared understanding of the specific criteria that should be met before a piece of work (e.g., a user story, feature, or increment) is considered complete and ready for release to the next stage or the customer.

2.2.2 Processes

The Scope performance domain encompasses the processes necessary to define, develop, monitor, control, and verify the scope of a project, ensuring alignment with stakeholder expectations and project objectives. The following processes are included in this performance domain (see Figure 2-13):

- **Plan Scope Management.** The process of creating a scope management plan that documents how the project and product scope will be defined, validated, and controlled.
- **Elicit and Analyze Requirements.** The process of determining, documenting, and managing stakeholder needs and requirements to meet project objectives.
- **Define Scope.** The process of developing a detailed or high-level description of the project and product. In agile projects, the scope is typically considered at a high level, often represented by the product roadmap with its releases. This process also identifies the quality requirements and standards for the deliverables—and how to demonstrate compliance with them.

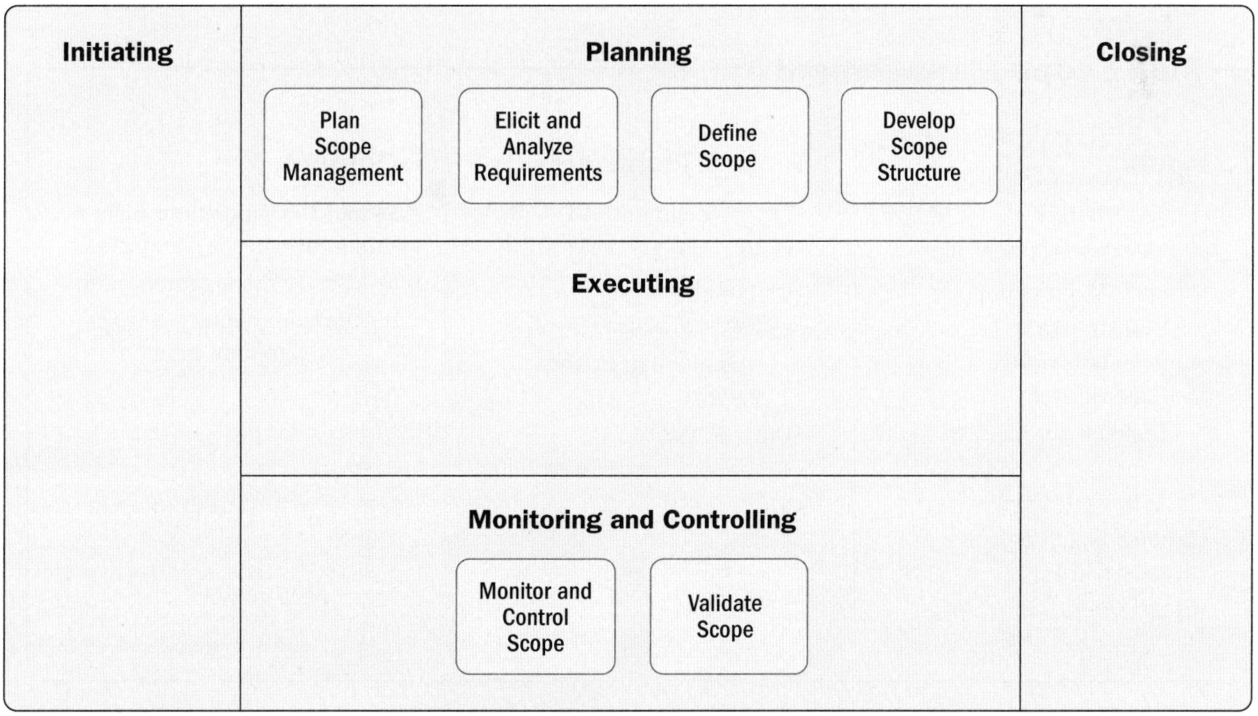

Figure 2-13. Scope Performance Domain Processes Overview

- **Develop Scope Structure.** The process of subdividing project deliverables and project work into smaller, more manageable components. In agile projects, this effort corresponds to the decomposition of the product backlog (product backlog breakdown), where work items can be broken down into epics, features, and user stories.
- **Monitor and Control Scope.** The process of monitoring the status of the project and product scope, managing changes to the scope baseline, measuring the quality of the deliverables, and ensuring fulfillment of the required standards.
- **Validate Scope.** The process of formalizing acceptance of the completed project deliverables.

2.2.2.1 Plan Scope Management

The objective of this process is to create a scope management plan. This process defines how the project will be delivered by establishing all of the work required to complete the project and eliminating or removing unnecessary work that will not add value to the project. The scope management plan should be defined, developed, monitored, validated, and controlled based on the project life cycle. While the objective of scope management—ensuring value delivery—remains the same, the process is approached differently in adaptive projects, if compared to predictive projects, as it is more iterative and collaborative. The key benefit of this process is that guidance on scope management is provided to ensure that value is delivered to stakeholders (see Figure 2-14).

2.2.2.2 Elicit and Analyze Requirements

The objective of this process is to define and document the stakeholders' needs associated with the features and functions required in the product, service, or result to assure quality and value will be

Plan Scope Management

Inputs

- Project charter
- Project management plan
- Project documents
  - Requirements documentation
  - Risk register
  - Stakeholder register
- Enterprise environmental factors
- Organizational process assets
- Etc.

Tools & Techniques

- Expert judgment
- Data gathering
  - Interviews
  - Focus groups
  - Questionnaires and surveys
- Data analysis
- Test and inspection planning
- Etc.

Outputs

- Project management plan updates
  - Scope management plan
  - Requirements management plan
- Etc.

Figure 2-14. Plan Scope Management Inputs, Tools and Techniques, and Outputs

Elicit and Analyze Requirements

Inputs

- Project charter
- Agreements
- Business case
- Project documents
  - Assumption log
  - Lessons learned register
  - Stakeholder register
- Project management plan
  - Requirements management plan
  - Scope management plan
- Enterprise environmental factors
- Organizational process assets
- Etc.

Tools & Techniques

- Expert judgment
- Decision-making
- Data gathering
  - Benchmarking
  - Brainstorming
  - Focus groups
  - Interviews
  - Questionnaires and surveys
- Data analysis
  - Document analysis
- Data representation
- Interpersonal and team skills
  - Nominal group
- Design thinking
- Prioritization/ranking
- Meetings
- Etc.

Outputs

- Requirements documentation
- Etc.

Figure 2-15. Elicit and Analyze Requirements Inputs, Tools and Techniques, and Outputs

delivered to stakeholders. In an adaptive environment, the requirements are collected in the form of user stories that are then prioritized in a backlog. The key benefit of this process is that it provides direction and a starting point to define a product, service, or result that will add value to stakeholders (see Figure 2-15).

2.2.2.3 Define Scope

The objective of this process is to develop a detailed or high-level description of the project, product, and value expected to be delivered, as well as a quality management plan. This description may be done at the beginning of the project for predictive approaches or at the beginning of each iteration for adaptive and hybrid approaches. In predictive approaches, these deliverables should be structured in the WBS, whereas in adaptive approaches, these deliverables are progressively defined through a backlog. This process also identifies the quality requirements and standards for the deliverables, as well as determines how the project will demonstrate that the quality requirements are met. The key benefit of this process is that it helps ensure that the stakeholders and project team understand the value that will be delivered through a product, service, or result (see Figure 2-16).

Define Scope

Inputs	Tools & Techniques	Outputs
• Project charter • Assumption log • Project management plan • Requirements documentation • Enterprise environmental factors • Organizational process assets • Etc.	• Expert judgment • Decision-making • Data analysis • Decomposition • Interpersonal and team skills – Facilitation • Product analysis • Etc.	• Project documents – Project scope statement – Requirements documentation • Etc.

Figure 2-16. Define Scope Inputs, Tools and Techniques, and Outputs

2.2.2.4 Develop Scope Structure

In projects using a predictive approach, the purpose of the WBS is to state the project objectives and define the required deliverables. The WBS represents a structured, hierarchical decomposition of the total scope of work into smaller, manageable work packages that can be easily assigned, tracked, and measured, ensuring that all stakeholders have a clear and shared understanding of the project deliverables. This shared understanding facilitates effective project planning, tracking, and controlling by assigning clear ownership and accountability for each deliverable.

In projects with complex or interdependent deliverables, a WBS dictionary may be developed to provide additional details about each WBS component. The WBS dictionary supports the WBS by elaborating on elements such as scope descriptions, milestones, responsible parties, resource needs, and acceptance criteria. This detailed documentation enhances clarity and alignment across the team.

In agile projects, the WBS corresponds to the product backlog, where work items can be broken down into epics and user stories. The product backlog is a prioritized list of the known features and work the project team will perform. The key benefit of this process is to provide a strategic view of the project's scope and value. This process helps the project team to be aligned and working toward a common goal (see Figure 2-17).

2.2.2.5 Monitor and Control Scope

Monitor and Control Scope is the ongoing process of monitoring and managing changes to the project scope—and measuring the quality and value of the deliverables to fulfill quality standards. This process controls how requests for changes to the detailed project scope statement will be processed while also ensuring the deliverables meet the specified quality requirements and that the scope and quality are aligned to the scope baseline. This process also includes the monitoring and recording of results to assess performance and determine whether the deliverables meet expectations. The primary objective of managing and controlling scope is to ensure the product, service, or result is relevant and delivering value to the stakeholders, as well as fulfilling the requirements specified by the stakeholders (see Figure 2-18).

Develop Scope Structure

Inputs

- Project management plan
- Project documents
  - Project scope statement
  - Requirements documentation
- Approved changes
- Enterprise environmental factors
- Organizational process assets
- Etc.

Tools & Techniques

- Expert judgment
- Brainstorming
- Decomposition
- Etc.

Outputs

- Scope baseline
- Work breakdown structure (WBS)
- WBS dictionary
- User stories
- Product backlog
- Etc.

Figure 2-17. Develop Scope Structure Inputs, Tools and Techniques, and Outputs

Monitor and Control Scope

Inputs

- Project management plan
  - Scope management plan
  - Quality management plan
- Project documents
  - Requirements documentation
  - Performance measurement baseline
  - Quality test and evaluation documents
- Quality metrics
- Approved change requests
- Deliverables
- Enterprise environmental factors
- Organizational process assets
- Etc.

Tools & Techniques

- Data analysis
  - Variance analysis
  - Trend analysis
  - Root cause analysis
- Performance reviews
- Audits and inspections
- Testing/product evaluations
- Data representations
- Process automations
- Etc.

Outputs

- Quality reports
- Verified deliverables
- Change requests
- Quality control measurements
- Project management plan updates
  - Scope management plan
  - Quality management plan
- Project document updates
  - Requirements documentation
  - Lessons learned register
- Work performance information
- Etc.

Figure 2-18. Monitor and Control Scope Inputs, Tools and Techniques, and Outputs

Validate Scope

Inputs	Tools & Techniques	Outputs
• Project documents – Requirements documentation – Scope baseline – Quality reports – Work performance data – Quality control measurements • Verified deliverables • Enterprise environmental factors • Organizational process assets • Etc.	• Data gathering • Data analysis • Inspection • Decision-making • Customer talks and tests • Process analysis • Review meetings • Etc.	• Accepted deliverables • Change requests • Project document updates – Quality reports – Work performance information – Requirements documentation • Lessons learned updates • Etc.

Figure 2-19. Validate Scope Inputs, Tools and Techniques, and Outputs

2.2.2.6 Validate Scope

The Validate Scope process has two main objectives: checking the processes being used to achieve quality standards and formalizing the acceptance of the deliverables. This process helps ensure that deliverables meet established quality standards and that these deliverables gain formal acceptance from stakeholders. The key benefit of this process is that the scope is validated through an objective process to assure value and quality in the product, service, or result delivered. This process also increases the probability of acceptance of the product, service, or result delivered (see Figure 2-19).

2.2.3 Tailoring Considerations

Given the uniqueness of each project, activities and processes within the Scope performance domain should be tailored to align with the project's specific requirements and constraints. Considerations for tailoring include but are not limited to the following:

- **Dependency on external partners.** In projects involving external partnerships, the decision on how to manage scope integration into contractual agreements is critical. This early alignment sets expectations and defines the boundaries within which the project will operate. Furthermore, managing scope in projects that involve third-party suppliers or subcontractors necessitates a harmonization of contractual obligations to ensure all parties' scope-related commitments are synchronized.
- **Environmental dynamics.** In environments characterized by high dynamism—where external factors such as market volatility, technological advancements, and customer preferences evolve rapidly—scope management should be particularly flexible. Projects operating under such conditions should incorporate iterative feedback mechanisms that allow scope

adjustments in response to real-time external inputs. This flexibility enables the project team to continuously refine and realign the project's objectives with the evolving external conditions, thus maintaining relevance and ensuring that the delivered value remains high.

- **Design phase.** Some industries, such as pharmaceutical and construction, rely heavily on the design phase of their projects. In such domains, it is essential to invest considerable effort in the early stages of scope definition to prevent costly changes during the later stages. This strategic rescoping, when done during the design phase, allows for a comprehensive evaluation of the project's direction before substantial resources are committed.
- **Adaptive and hybrid life cycles.** Adaptive ways of working are based on the refinement of the project scope, which takes place throughout several different iterations. Tailoring in a project using a hybrid approach may be even more challenging, as the overall expectations of the project are set with a scope baseline, schedule baseline, and cost baseline, whereas subteams may be working in iterations on the user stories contained in the backlog. In this case, there is an even greater need for a tailored approach to the activities and processes within this performance domain, taking into consideration the variety of ways of working used in the overall project.

2.2.3.1 Examples

The following are three examples of how these considerations might be applied:

- **Example 1.** A project to develop a new product is set up using a backlog with user stories. Rather than delivering all the user stories that are on the backlog, the team focuses on the main product goals to satisfy the customer expectations. The scope of the project is refined through different iterations.
- **Example 2.** A software project to release a mobile app is aimed at a new market where little information is available about customer preferences. Adopting an iterative approach with a clear minimum viable product (MVP), created with the minimum features collected in a backlog, could provide rapid feedback to the team and better support with adaptation to changes.
- **Example 3.** A project for a new city park has been approved with a tight timeline for its execution. With multiple stakeholders providing requirements and feedback, the project manager decides to invest more time in the design phase, creating multiple mock-ups of the park to evaluate before beginning construction.

2.2.4 Interactions With Other Domains

The scope of a project does not exist in isolation; it is deeply interconnected with other performance domains that collectively determine a project's success. While the Schedule and Finance performance domains are the most obvious ones, as they are directly impacted in any scope change, other domains like Risk and Stakeholders are significantly connected as well.

One important aspect is understanding the governance mechanisms within a project, particularly as they relate to the broader organizational context. Changes to the project scope should be navigated within these established governance structures to address potential consequences such as the need for additional budgets or resources. Such changes may be subject to review and approval processes to ensure that relevant scope modifications are justified and aligned with the strategic objectives of both the project and the organization. This adherence to governance is vital because scope fundamentally drives the project's value.

Finally, managing risk is intrinsic to managing scope, as risks can significantly alter a project's trajectory. Comprehensive risk analysis is crucial to understanding potential impacts on the project scope. Rescoping may be employed as a strategy to mitigate, avoid, or transfer risks.

2.2.5 Check Results

Activities within the Scope performance domain should be considered successful only if they contribute to specific outcomes. Table 2-6 shows a set of sample target outcomes, along with a potential check to confirm whether those outcomes are met.

Table 2-6. Check Outcomes—Scope Performance Domain

Outcome	Check
The project employs effective change management.	Projects using a predictive approach have a change log that demonstrates changes, taking into consideration the impact on the Scope, Schedule, Finance, Stakeholders, Resources, and Risk performance domains. Projects employing an adaptive approach use a backlog to manage scope, showing the rate of accomplishing the scope, the rate of adding new scope, and the prioritization and inclusion of stakeholder feedback.
There is a clear understanding of requirements.	In predictive development, fewer changes in the initial requirements may reflect understanding. In projects where requirements are evolving, each iteration provides a clear and well-defined understanding of short-term requirements, enabling a rolling wave approach to uncovering and refining longer-term requirements progressively.
The project is aligned with business objectives and strategy.	The business case and the organization's strategic plan, along with the project-authorizing documents, demonstrate that the project deliverables and business objectives are aligned.
Stakeholders accept and are satisfied with deliverables.	Interviews, observation, and end-user feedback indicate stakeholder satisfaction with the deliverables. Levels of complaints and returns may also be used to indicate satisfaction.
Scope items are clearly defined in the project scope statement in percentages.	The scope definition accuracy is measured as: Scope Definition Accuracy (%) = (Planned Scope Items Correctly Delivered / Total Planned Scope Items) x 100
Scope creep is measured in percentages.	Scope creep, as a percentage, is measured as: Scope Creep (%) = (Total Deliverables / Unplanned Deliverables) x 100
The stability of requirements is measured in percentages.	The stability of requirements, as a percentage, is measured as: Requirements Stability (%) = (Total Requirements / Unchanged Requirements) x 100
Sustainability is considered in the project scope.	The WBS or backlog should include activities to manage sustainability (e.g., assess and manage CO_2 emissions due to project activity, or manage the impact of project execution on local biodiversity in case of a significant impact).

2.3 Schedule Performance Domain

Project scheduling provides a plan that represents how and when the project will deliver the products, services, and results defined in the project scope. The schedule serves as a tool for communication and for managing stakeholder expectations, and provides a basis for performance reporting. The project schedule also facilitates the proactive identification of potential delays and risks, enabling timely corrective actions to keep the project on track.

2.3.1 Key Concepts

Schedule management includes the processes required to oversee the project's timely completion. The detailed project schedule should be flexible throughout the project to adjust for the knowledge gained, increased understanding of the risks and external influences, and value-added activities. Revising and maintaining the project schedule to sustain a realistic schedule should continue throughout the project.

Schedules can be created and defined at various levels. The project team specifies the rules for the relative granularity of the level's schedule activities in the overall schedule model. It should be noted that schedule levels can change depending on the approach (e.g., adaptive or predictive), practitioner, and organizational scheduling requirements.

With project timelines continuously shrinking, there may be insufficient time to analyze the project details (sometimes, the details are also evolving). It may also be impossible to develop a detailed project schedule up front, even in projects using a predictive approach, so a growing number of project management practitioners are preparing detailed schedules progressively as their projects unfold. This effort involves initially outlining the broad milestones and key activities of a project and then refining and expanding upon them as more information becomes available or as the project progresses. This approach allows for flexibility and adjustment as the project evolves and more details become known. A well-known technique that helps with this approach is rolling wave planning.

The following key concepts support effective practices for the Schedule performance domain:

- **Project schedule.** The project schedule is an output of a schedule model that presents linked activities with planned dates, durations, milestones, and resources. The project schedule may include start and finish dates; the total number of work periods required to complete an activity or WBS component, expressed in hours, days, or weeks (known as duration); significant points or events in a portfolio, program, or project (known as milestones); and resources. For further information, see Section 2.6 on the Resources performance domain.
- **Estimate.** An estimate is a quantitative assessment of a variable's likely amount or outcome, such as project effort or duration. Effort is the number of labor units required to complete a schedule activity or WBS component, often expressed in hours, days, or weeks. Duration is the number of work periods needed to complete individual activities with the estimated resources.
- **Schedule baseline.** The schedule baseline is the approved version of a schedule model that can be changed using formal change control procedures and is used as the basis for comparison to actual results. The level of formality on change control procedures tends to be more rigid on projects using predictive approaches and more flexible, or even nonexistent, on projects using adaptive and agile approaches.

- **Schedule flexibility.** Flexibility is essential for adapting to changes, managing risks, and optimizing resource allocations. Flexibility enhances team morale, supports incremental delivery, and helps ensure higher-quality outcomes.
- **Schedule forecasts.** Schedule forecasts are estimates or predictions of conditions and events in the project's future based on information and knowledge available at the time the schedule is calculated. The schedule forecast predicts a timeline based on current progress, performance trends, and other information pertaining to the project. Forecasts are updated and reissued based on work performance obtained as the project is executed.
- **Actual duration.** The actual duration is the time, in calendar units, between the actual start date of the schedule activity and the data date of the project schedule, if the schedule activity is in progress, or the actual finish date if the schedule activity is complete.
- **Project schedule network diagrams.** A project schedule network diagram is a graphical representation of the logical relationships (also called dependencies) among the project schedule activities. Sequencing can be performed by using project management software.

2.3.2 Processes

The Schedule performance domain includes the processes required to manage the timely completion of the project. The following processes are included in the Schedule performance domain (see Figure 2-20):

- **Plan Schedule Management.** The process of establishing policies, procedures, and documentation for designing, developing, managing, performing, and maintaining the schedule.

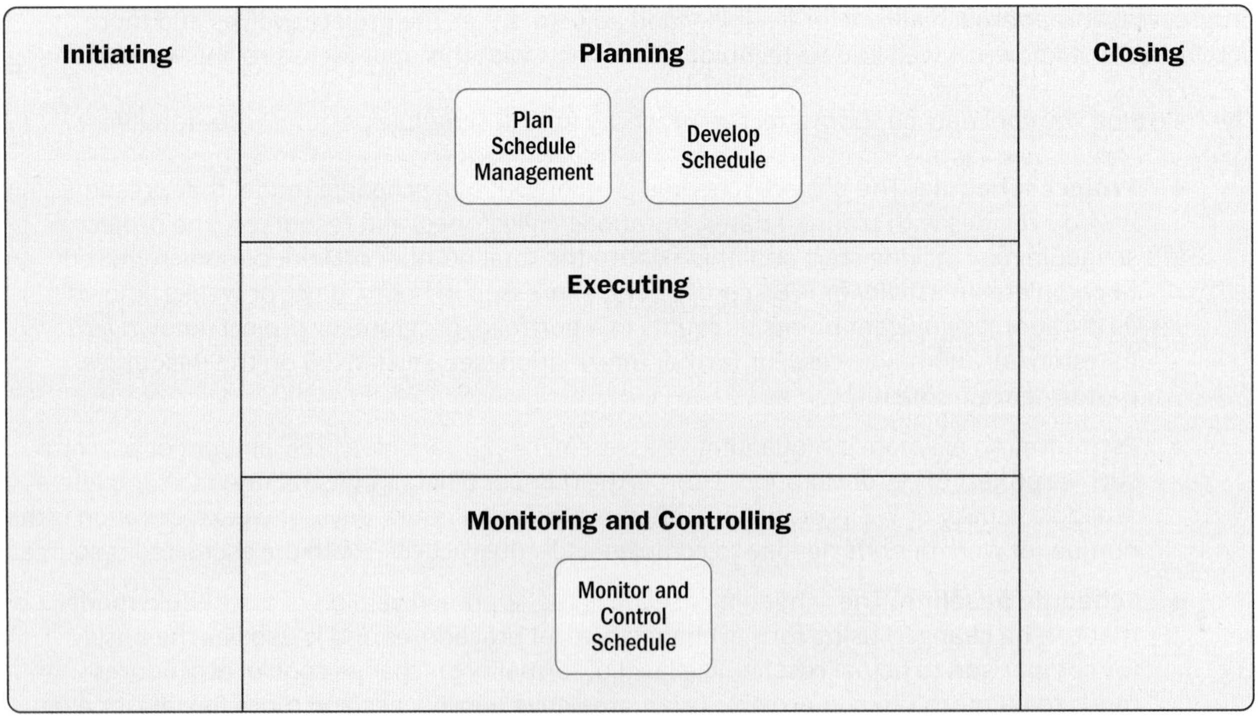

Figure 2-20. Schedule Performance Domain Processes Overview

- **Develop Schedule.** The process of analyzing sequences, durations, resource requirements, and schedule constraints to create a schedule model for project execution and monitoring and controlling.
- **Monitor and Control Schedule.** The process of monitoring the status of the project to update the project schedule, and managing changes to the schedule baseline or agreed-upon schedule.

2.3.2.1 Plan Schedule Management

Plan Schedule Management is the process of establishing policies, procedures, and documentation for designing, developing, managing, performing, and maintaining the schedule. The key benefit of this process is that it provides guidance and direction on how the project schedule will be managed throughout the project (see Figure 2-21).

The specific output of this process is the schedule management plan, including information on project schedule development, release and iteration length, level of accuracy, units of measurement, links to organizational procedures, project schedule maintenance, control thresholds, rules of performance measurement, and reporting formats.

2.3.2.2 Develop Schedule

Develop Schedule is the process of analyzing sequences, durations, resource requirements, and schedule constraints to create a schedule model for project execution and monitoring and controlling. Developing an acceptable project schedule is an iterative process. The schedule model is used to determine the planned start and finish dates for project activities and milestones based on the best available information. Schedule development may require the review and revision of duration estimates, resource estimates, and schedule reserves to establish an approved project schedule that can serve as a baseline to track progress (see Figure 2-22).

Plan Schedule Management

Inputs	Tools & Techniques	Outputs

• Project charter
• Project management plan
  – Scope management plan
• Development approach
• Enterprise environmental factors
• Organizational process assets
• Etc.
	• Expert judgment
	• Data analysis
	  – Alternative analysis
	• Meetings
	• Etc.
		• Project management plan updates
		  – Schedule management plan
		• Etc.

Figure 2-21. Plan Schedule Management Inputs, Tools and Techniques, and Outputs

Develop Schedule

Inputs

- Project charter
- Project management plan
  - Scope management plan
- Development approach
- Project documents
  - Activity attributes
  - Activity list
  - Assumption log
  - Basis of estimates
  - Duration estimates
  - Lessons learned register
  - Milestone list
  - Project schedule network diagrams
  - Project team assignments
  - Resource calendars
  - Resource requirements
  - Risk register
- Agreements
- Enterprise environmental factors
- Organizational process assets
- Etc.

Tools & Techniques

- Expert judgment
- Decomposition
- Rolling wave planning
- Precedence diagramming method
- Logical relationship
- Leads and lags
- Dependency determination and integration
- Estimation techniques
- Reserve analysis
- Data analysis
  - What-if analysis
  - Simulation
  - Alternative analysis
- Voting
- Schedule network analysis
- Schedule compression
- Critical path method
- Critical chain method
- Resource optimization
  - Resource leveling
- Project management information system
- Agile release planning
- Etc.

Outputs

- Schedule baseline
- Project schedule
- Schedule data
- Project calendars
- Change requests
- Project management plan updates
  - Schedule management plan
- Project document updates
  - Activity list
  - Activity attributes
  - Assumption log
  - Basis of estimates
  - Duration estimates
  - Lessons learned register
  - Milestone list
  - Project schedule network diagrams
  - Resource requirements
  - Risk register
- Etc.

Figure 2-22. Develop Schedule Inputs, Tools and Techniques, and Outputs

There are four steps to developing the schedule (see Figure 2-23):

1. Define activities,
2. Determine sequence,
3. Estimate effort and duration, and
4. Adjust.

The work involved in each step is as follows:

- **Step 1: Define activities.** The first step involves identifying and documenting the specific actions to be performed to produce the project deliverables. The key benefit of this process is that it decomposes work packages into schedule activities that provide a

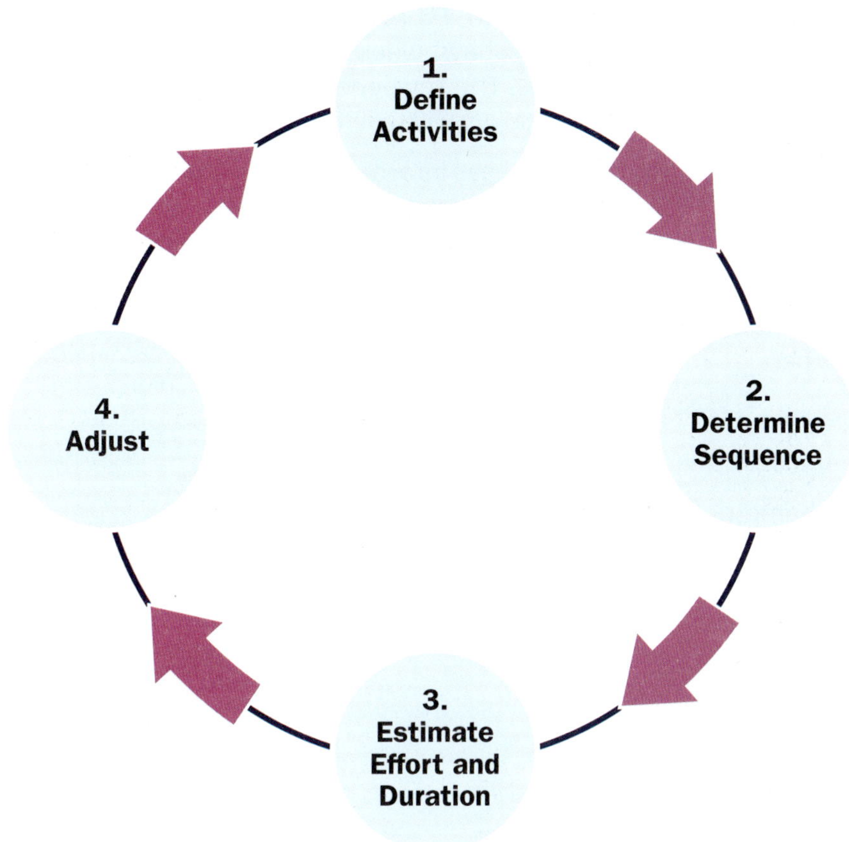

Figure 2-23. Steps for Developing the Schedule

basis for estimating, scheduling, executing, monitoring, and controlling the project work. For more information on work packages, see Section 2.2 on the Scope performance domain.

  - Artifacts for this step include the activity list, activity attributes, and milestones.

- **Step 2: Determine sequence.** Once the activities have been defined, the next step is to determine the logical sequence in which the work will be carried out. This effort involves determining the dependencies and relationships among the schedule elements, or which activities should be completed before others can begin (e.g., start-to-start, finish-to-finish, start-to-finish, finish-to-start). The key benefit of this process is that it defines the logical sequence of work to obtain the greatest efficiency, given all of the project constraints.

  - Every work package and activity, except for the first and last, should be connected to at least one predecessor and at least one successor activity, with an appropriate logical relationship. Logical relationships should be designed to create a realistic project schedule. It may be necessary to use lead or lag time between activities to support a realistic and achievable project schedule.

  - Note: Depending on the degree of decomposition, the sequence can be determined at different levels, including the level of the control account, the work package, or the activity.

- **Step 3: Estimate effort and duration.** Estimating effort and duration is about determining the number of work periods (hours, days, weeks, or other) needed to complete individual activities with estimated resources. The key benefit of this process is that it provides the amount of time and effort each activity will take to complete.
  - Estimating effort and duration uses information from the scope of work, required resource types or skill levels, estimated resource quantities, and resource calendars. (For more information, see the Scope performance domain in Section 2.2 and the Resources performance domain in Section 2.6). The estimates can be based on the following techniques:
    - Expert judgment,
    - Delphi technique,
    - Analogous estimating,
    - Parametric estimating,
    - Program evaluation and review technique (PERT),
    - Bottom-up estimating,
    - Planning poker,
    - Story points,
    - T-shirt sizing, and
    - Many others.
  - Factors that may influence the duration estimates include constraints imposed on the duration, effort involved, or type of resources (e.g., fixed duration, fixed effort or work, fixed number of resources, the experience of the team executing the activity, and the risk involved in the activity), as well as the schedule network analysis technique used. The inputs for the estimates of duration originate from the person or group on the project team that is most familiar with the nature of the work for the specific activity.
  - The duration estimate is progressively elaborated, and the process considers the quality and availability of the input data. For example, as more detailed and precise data are available about the project engineering and design work, the accuracy and quality of the duration estimates may improve.
  - Estimating effort and duration requires an estimation of the amount of work effort required to complete the activity as well as the estimated number of available resources. These estimates are used to approximate the number of work periods (activity duration) needed to complete the activity using the appropriate project and resource calendars.
  - In many cases, the number of resources that are expected to be available to accomplish an activity, along with the skill proficiency levels of those resources, may determine the activity's duration. A change to a driving resource allocated to the activity will usually influence the duration.
  - Sometimes, the intrinsic nature of the work (i.e., constraints imposed on the duration, effort involved, or number of resources) will take a predetermined amount of time to complete, regardless of the resource allocation (e.g., a 24-hour stress test).

Other factors to consider when estimating duration may include:

  - **Law of diminishing returns.** When one factor (e.g., a resource) used to determine the effort required to produce a unit of work is increased while all other factors remain fixed, a point will eventually be reached at which additions of that one factor start to yield progressively smaller or diminishing increases in output.
  - **Number of resources.** Increasing the number of resources to twice the original number of resources does not always reduce the time by half, as it may increase duration due to extra risk. At some point, adding too many resources to the activity may increase duration due to knowledge transfer, learning curves, additional coordination, and other factors involved.
  - **Advances in technology.** Technology advances may also play an important role in determining duration estimates. For example, an increase in the output of a manufacturing plant may be achieved by procuring the latest advances in technology, which may impact duration and resource needs.
  - **Documentation.** All data and assumptions that support duration estimating are documented for each activity duration estimate.
  - **Level of decomposition**. The estimate can be made at distinct levels, at the level of the control account, or at the work package or activity level.
  - **Cognitive bias**. Biases such as planning fallacy and end-of-story illusion, and other phenomena like Hofstadter's law or even the motivation of team members, may also impact the accuracy of the scheduling process.

- **Step 4: Adjust.** This step entails reviewing the draft schedule, based on the sequence, estimates, and resources accumulated in the previous steps. If the draft schedule is unacceptable, various techniques can be applied to adjust those components to find alternative schedule options.
  - Once finalized, the schedule contains a series of unique activities that have varying durations and are linked by defined logical relationships. The schedule provides the project team with information about what work should be done, and in what sequence the project deliverables should be accomplished.
  - After the start and end dates of the activities have been set, it is common for the project team members assigned to the activities to review their assignments. The team members should confirm that the start and end dates do not conflict with resource calendars or assigned activities in other projects or tasks and are therefore still valid. The schedule is then analyzed to identify conflicts with logical relationships and to determine if resource leveling is required before the schedule is approved and used as a baseline.
  - With a draft schedule, it is easier and more accurate to estimate the labor and physical resources required to complete the project objectives. Those resource estimates may influence the decision as to whether the draft schedule is or is not acceptable, and thus may require further adjustment and revision.

2.3.2.3 Monitor and Control Schedule

Monitor and Control Schedule is the process of monitoring the status of the project to update the project schedule and managing changes to the agreed-upon schedule. Updating the schedule requires knowing the actual or forecasted performance to date. The key benefit of this process is maintaining a realistic schedule throughout the duration of the project (see Figure 2-24).

Monitor and Control Schedule

Inputs

- Project management plan
  - Schedule management plan
  - Scope baseline
  - Performance measurement baseline
- Product backlog
- Project documents
  - Lessons learned register
  - Project calendars
  - Project schedule
  - Resource calendars
  - Risk register
  - Schedule data
- Work performance data
- Enterprise environmental factors
- Organizational process assets
- Etc.

Tools & Techniques

- Data analysis
  - Earned value analysis
  - Burnup/burndown chart
  - Performance reviews
  - Trend analysis
  - Variance analysis
  - What-if scenario analysis
- Critical path method
- Critical chain method
- Project management information system
- Resource optimization
- Leads and lags
- Schedule compression
- Branch and bound
- Velocity
- Daily coordination meetings
- Sprint reviews
- Backlog refinement
- Etc.

Outputs

- Work performance information
- Schedule forecasts
- Change requests
- Project management plan updates
  - Schedule management plan
  - Schedule baseline
  - Cost baseline
  - Performance measurement baseline
- Project document updates
  - Assumption log
  - Basis of estimates
  - Lessons learned register
  - Project schedule
  - Resource calendars
  - Risk register
  - Schedule data
- Etc.

Figure 2-24. Monitor and Control Schedule Inputs, Tools and Techniques, and Outputs

When using a predictive approach, any change to the schedule baseline or agreed-upon schedule can only be approved through the Assess and Implement Changes process by applying integrated change control. Monitor and Control Schedule, as part of the Monitoring and Controlling Focus Area, is concerned with the following:

- Determining the status of the project schedule,
- Influencing the factors that create schedule changes,
- Reconsidering necessary schedule reserves,
- Determining if the overall project schedule has changed, and
- Managing the actual changes as they occur.

When an adaptive or agile approach is used, the Monitor and Control Schedule process is concerned with the following:

- Determining the status of the project schedule by comparing the total amount of work delivered and accepted against the estimates of work completed for the elapsed time cycle;

- Conducting retrospectives (scheduled reviews to record lessons learned) for correcting processes and improving them, if required;
- Reprioritizing the remaining work plan (backlog);
- Determining the rate at which the deliverables are produced, validated, and accepted (velocity) in the given time per iteration (agreed-upon work cycle duration, typically 2 weeks or 1 month);
- Determining that the project schedule has changed; and
- Managing the actual changes as they occur.

When work is being contracted, regular and milestone status updates from contractors and suppliers are a means of ensuring that the work is progressing as agreed to ensure that the schedule is under control. Scheduled status reviews and walkthroughs are expected to help ensure that the contractor's reports are accurate and complete.

2.3.3 Tailoring Considerations

Project managers may need to tailor and adapt the way that a project's schedule management processes are applied. Considerations for tailoring include but are not limited to life cycle and development approach selection, product and deliverable attributes, project team attributes, culture, project environments, scheduling approaches and methods, and trends and emerging practices.

2.3.3.1 Life Cycle and Development Approach Selection

The choice of project life cycle and development approach can significantly influence how scheduling processes are tailored and applied throughout the project as follows:

- **Predictive life cycle.** In a predictive life cycle, the schedule is typically defined up front. Detailed planning and sequencing of tasks are done at the beginning, the project baseline is created and approved, and changes are less frequent. Usually, the changes to the project baseline are conducted through formal change management procedures. Tailoring in this context involves setting a comprehensive timeline with clear milestones, dependencies, and critical paths.
- **Adaptive life cycle.** In adaptive projects, schedules are more flexible. The project is divided into sprints or iterations with short-term planning horizons. Tailoring in adaptive projects involves creating timeboxed schedules that can adapt to changes in the project scope and priorities.
- **Hybrid life cycle.** In a hybrid development approach, scheduling combines the flexibility of adaptive methods with the structured planning of a predictive approach. The high-level project schedule is planned to use predictive techniques to outline key milestones and deliverables. Within this framework, the subordinate project streams can use adaptive or predictive methods depending on their characteristics. Adaptive sprints or iterations are used to manage the detailed execution of project components with a high rate of change in requirements, allowing for adaptability and the frequent reassessment of priorities. Other components may use Kanban or the critical path method. This approach can help ensure that the overall project stays on track and that teams can respond quickly to changes and continuously improve the deliverables.

2.3.3.2 Product and Deliverable Attributes

The product and deliverable attributes can influence the tailoring of scheduling processes based on the following factors:

- **Compliance/criticality.** High-criticality projects (i.e., very important projects for the performing organization's strategic goals) may require more detailed and frequent schedule updates to ensure compliance and mitigate risks.
- **Type and technology.** The type of deliverable and the technology involved can dictate the level of detail required in the schedule. New or innovative technologies may require more iterative scheduling due to the uncertainty associated with the project domain.

2.3.3.3 Project Team Attributes

The project team attributes can also influence the tailoring of scheduling processes depending on considerations such as the following:

- **Size and distribution.** The size and geographical distribution of the project team can affect how the schedule is communicated and maintained. Large, dispersed teams may need more sophisticated scheduling tools and regular updates.
- **Experience.** The experience levels of the team members can influence how detailed the schedule should be. Experienced teams may be able to use a less-detailed, high-level schedule, whereas less-experienced teams might require a more detailed, step-by-step plan.

2.3.3.4 Culture

Culture can influence the tailoring of scheduling processes depending on considerations such as the following:

- **Organizational culture.** The culture of the organization, including its tolerance for uncertainty and change, affects how flexible or rigid the schedule should be. An adaptive culture may embrace more fluid schedules, whereas a risk-averse culture may prefer detailed, fixed schedules. Culture can also be driven by industry factors. For example, pharmaceutical companies follow strict processes for product development, whereas technology companies tend to be more aggressive toward assuming risks.
- **Buy-in and trust.** High levels of trust and buy-in from stakeholders can enable more flexible scheduling practices, whereas low levels may require more formal and detailed scheduling.

2.3.3.5 Project Environment

The project environment can influence the tailoring of scheduling processes depending on considerations such as:

- **Project scale and environment.** The scale of the project (e.g., megaprojects versus small projects) and the project environment (e.g., commercial, government, or nonprofit) can influence the level of detail and frequency of schedule updates.
- **Project goals and timeframe.** Projects with aggressive timelines or critical deadlines may require more rigorous scheduling to ensure timely delivery.

2.3.3.6 *Scheduling Approaches and Methods*

As different types of industries and projects require different approaches and methods to scheduling, it is increasingly important to have a contextual framework for effective adoption and tailoring of development practices to respond to the changing demands of the environment. Some approaches for scheduling include the critical path method, critical chain method, location-based scheduling, Last Planner System®, Gantt charts, and Kanban.

- **Location-based scheduling (LBS).** Location-based scheduling allocates quantities to the locations defined in the LBS and takes into consideration the resourcing required to complete this work, including production rates, crew sizing, logic between tasks, and any requirements for splitting or buffering work.
- **Lean scheduling.** Lean scheduling is based on the principles of lean project delivery (on-demand scheduling) and is designed to minimize waste and maximize value. To achieve this goal, deliverables are not assigned to the team. Lean scheduling principles point to the importance of limiting queues by pulling work when there is capacity to place the work into the process. The project team members collaborate in pull-planning sessions where the essential activities, durations, and handoffs between trades to complete milestones are defined. The main steps are master scheduling, phase scheduling, and look-ahead planning.
- **Schedule and deliverable alignment.** Project deliverables and schedules have varying levels of detail. This variation often creates confusion regarding what will be done and when. One approach to increase clarity is to ensure that a given element of the WBS is described by a schedule that has a commensurate level of detail.

2.3.4 Interactions With Other Domains

The Schedule performance domain closely interacts with the Governance, Scope, Finance, Stakeholders, Resources, and Risk performance domains, emphasizing the interdependent nature of project management elements. At the beginning of the project, the expected outcomes are identified, and a high-level schedule is developed to achieve these results. Depending on the selected development approach and life cycle, intensive scheduling may be conducted up front, which is then adjusted or adapted to the actual environment.

Other life cycles encourage just enough scheduling at various points throughout the project, with the expectation that plans will evolve. The duration of the project depends on its scope, cost, resources, and quality. Each of these factors can cause the schedule to become longer or shorter.

The Scope, Schedule, and Finance performance domains are closely linked to one another and changes in any one of them will likely impact the others. While the project outcome is directly dependent on these performance domains, they also are in parallel to, and indirectly connected with, the Stakeholders, Resources, and Risk performance domains in order to maintain a balance and ensure that all of the domains function under the Governance performance domain.

2.3.5 Check Results

Activities related to the Schedule performance domain should be considered successful only if they contribute to specific outcomes. Table 2-7 shows a set of sample target outcomes, along with a potential check to confirm whether those outcomes are met.

Table 2-7. Check Outcomes—Schedule Performance Domain

Outcome	Check
Scheduling approaches are consistent with the project deliverables.	Align the schedule with the development approach for deliverables (predictive, adaptive, or hybrid).
The project life cycle consists of phases that connect the delivery of business and stakeholder value from the beginning to the end of the project.	Represent the project work—from project launch to close—in project phases. Ensure the phases include the appropriate exit criteria.
A holistic approach to delivering the project outcomes is developed.	Select and develop a delivery schedule that demonstrates that the project is planned in a holistic manner with no gaps or areas of misalignment.
Schedule documentation is complete.	Ensure that the schedule documentation includes all essential elements, such as task dependencies, durations, resource allocations, and milestones, based on the development approach selected.
Scheduling tools and techniques are used.	Monitor whether the team employed appropriate scheduling tools (e.g., project management software) and techniques (e.g., critical path method) during the schedule development.
Stakeholders are involved in the schedule development.	Check the level of participation from key stakeholders (e.g., client, team members) during the scheduling process. Low involvement may lead to an unrealistic or poorly developed schedule.
Sufficient buffers are built in for known-unknowns.	Check that major project constraints and known risks are factored into the project schedule by providing sufficient floats, contingency reserves, or alternate activity network strategies such as secondary plans.

2.4 Finance Performance Domain

The Finance performance domain addresses processes and tools related to the use and allocation of monetary resources, both internally and externally, to the performing organization. Financial performance relates to the costs, funding, and, in some cases, the value proposition of the project. Processes described in this performance domain include planning, estimating, budgeting, financing, funding, managing, measuring, and controlling costs so the project can optimize value for the organization.

Having timely and accurate information about project work and performance allows the project team to learn and determine the appropriate actions needed to address current or expected variances from the desired performance. Financial measures are used for multiple reasons, including the following:

- Evaluating performance compared to the plan;
- Tracking the utilization of resources, work completed, budget expended, etc.;
- Demonstrating accountability;

- Providing information to stakeholders;
- Forecasting future trends, including cost overruns, resource shortages, or savings;
- Evaluating return on investment, long-term value, and impacts; and
- Enhancing risk management to help ensure the project's financial health and overall success.

The value of financial measurements is not in the collection and dissemination of the data, but rather in the interactions about how to use the data to make value-adding, well-informed decisions and take appropriate actions. Therefore, while much of this performance domain addresses various types of measurements that can be captured, use of the measurements occurs within the context of activities in other performance domains such as project team and stakeholder discussions, coordinating project work, and so forth.

2.4.1 Key Concepts

The following key concepts support effective practices for the Finance performance domain:

- **Value definition.** Organizations use various strategies to define value, either tangible or intangible, which is often based on financial returns (tangible), with metrics such as return on investment (ROI), internal rate of return (IRR), payback period, or return on assets (ROA) that can be used to measure project success and alignment with organizational goals. The return on average capital employed (ROACE) may also be used. The ROACE method can help calculate the organization's profitability compared to the money that has been invested. Sometimes, other indicators can be used such as compliance with regulations or social impact; therefore, value may be more than just profit (financial) and can also be value for people (social) or the planet (environmental). As an example, sometimes spending more on a given project is acceptable as the value is measured by the outcome of the project being available on a given date. In some cases, projects do not actually bring value by themselves, as they may be a component of a program, where value will be realized in the future. On the other hand, customer satisfaction and innovation are examples of intangible value.
- **Value maximization.** The Finance performance domain focuses not only on cost management but also on ensuring that the project delivers maximum value for the organization. This effort involves aligning with strategy, using clear indicators of project success such as ROI and IRR, and considering other dimensions like social impact, customer satisfaction, and innovation.
- **Funding.** Project management practitioners should have an understanding of how a project acquires its financial resources. Monies can be provided by several means, including but not limited to internal organizational budgets, customer contracts, grants, or customer-driven "crowdfunding." Project practitioners are often called upon to lead or support such funding activities, either before or during a project.
- **Financial constraints.** Budget is generally the primary financial constraint of a project but it is not the only one. Sometimes the project is restricted to the use of a given type of financial resource. Examples may include types of funding like capital expenditures (CapEx) and operational expenditures (OpEx) or internal versus external personnel, which may incur different budget strategies or funding that is allocated for a specific purpose or a specific time period such as a fiscal year. CapEx are intended funds invested by

the performing organization to acquire, upgrade, and maintain physical assets such as property, plants, buildings, technology, or equipment. OpEx are intended funds for the ongoing costs of running the day-to-day business activities or operations. These expenses typically include advertising expenses, administration fees, wages, rent, and utility costs. In some cases, the total amount of OpEx can influence the financial results of the whole organization. In other cases, the budget is allocated annually and therefore has to be used within the year, with no possibility of being transferred to the next year. In projects that implement an agile approach, the budget can be allocated for a quarter and then revised quarterly. This allocation allows more flexibility in terms of budget, based on the amount of work achieved.

- **Project budget.** Project budget buildup depends on organizational process assets (OPAs), policies, governance, portfolio practices, and financial management practices within the organization. The project budget can also be influenced by external regulations, compliance, accounting principles, or industry standards applicable to the organization, leading to significant variations. In one scenario, the initial project budget may contain the sum of approved work package cost estimates, contingency reserve, and management reserve, with reserves managed implicitly. In another scenario, the initial project budget may contain the sum of approved work cost estimates, while contingency reserve and management reserve are managed explicitly. Figure 2-25 illustrates the two possible budget buildup scenarios. However, variations may exist based on organizational preferences or external influences.

- **Cost baseline.** Similar to a project budget, the cost baseline may vary depending on organizational preferences or external factors. The cost baseline is the approved version of the time-phased project budget, excluding any management reserves, which can be changed only through formal change control procedures and is used as a basis for comparison to actual results. Alternatively, the cost baseline may be the approved version of the time-phased initial project budget, excluding both contingency and management reserves, which can be changed only through formal change control procedures and is used as a basis for comparison to actual results. Figure 2-25 presents two possible scenarios: one including contingency reserve in the cost baseline (left side) and one excluding contingency reserve (right side).

- **Reserves.** A reserve is a provision in the project management plan to mitigate cost and/or schedule risks, often used with a modifier (e.g., management reserve, contingency reserve) to provide further detail on what types of risk are meant to be mitigated. Contingency reserves and management reserves are distinct in their purpose and authority of usage and may differ on risk classification (known-unknowns or unknown-unknowns). For more information, see the Risk performance domain in Section 2.7. The contingency reserve is the time or money allocated in the schedule or cost baseline for known risks with active response strategies and is usually allocated in the initial project budget (see Figure 2-25, left side). However, based on different organizational preferences or external factors, it may be outside the initial project budget (see Figure 2-25, right side). The management reserve is time or money that management sets aside in addition to the schedule or cost baseline and releases for unforeseen work that is within the scope of the portfolio, program, or project. This reserve is used for unknown-unknowns rather than specific, identified risks. Typically, management reserves are realized at the discretion of senior leadership or management. However, in some organizations, it may be at the discretion of the project manager or project management team.

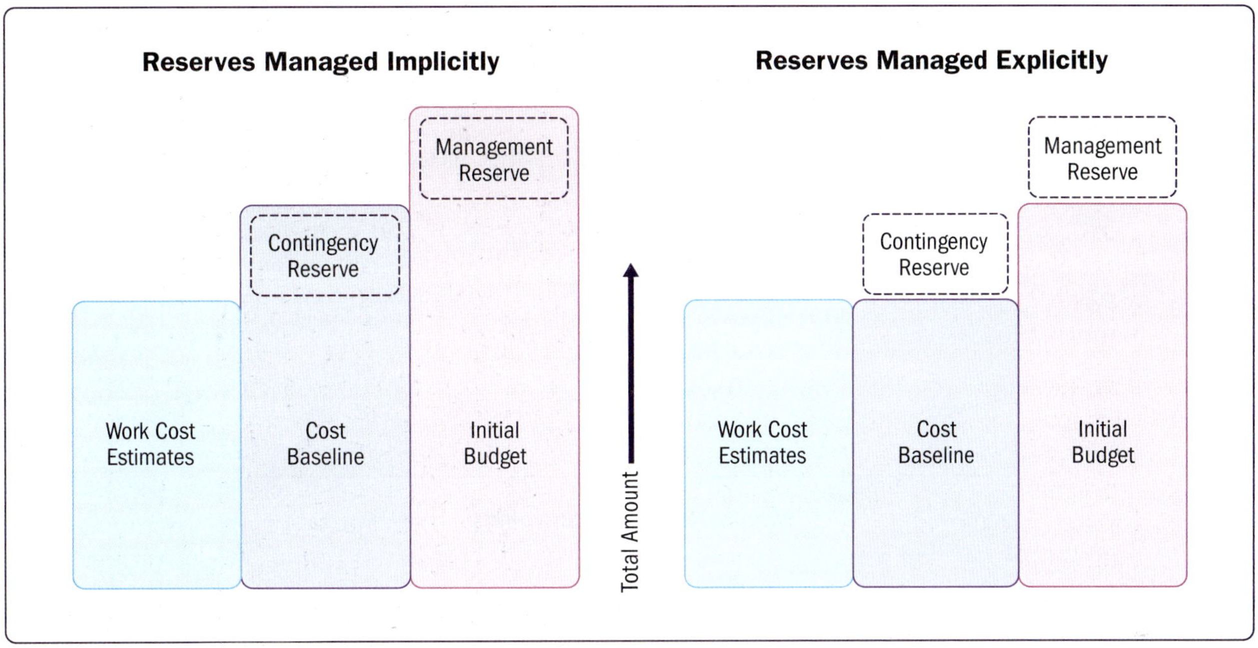

Figure 2-25. Two Scenarios of Budget Buildup

- **Cost management.** The primary source of project costs comes from the resources needed to complete the project activities. Every project decision may incur further costs related to using, maintaining, and supporting the project's purpose to create value, emphasizing the need for life cycle cost and maintenance considerations. For example, limiting the number of design reviews could reduce the cost of the project but increase the resulting product's operating costs.
- **Cost measurement.** Different stakeholders measure project costs in different ways and at different times. For example, the cost of an acquired item may be measured when the acquisition decision is made or committed, the order is placed, the item is delivered, or the actual cost is incurred or recorded for project accounting purposes. In many organizations, predicting and analyzing the prospective financial performance of the project's product is performed outside of the project. In others, such as a capital facilities project, project cost management should include this work.

2.4.2 Processes

The Finance performance domain includes the processes required to determine, manage, and control the finances of the project. The following processes are included in the Finance performance domain (see Figure 2-26):

- **Plan Financial Management.** The process of defining how the project revenues and expenses will be estimated, budgeted, managed, monitored, and controlled, ensuring alignment with project objectives and organizational strategy.
- **Estimate Costs.** The process of developing an approximation of the cost of resources needed to complete project work.

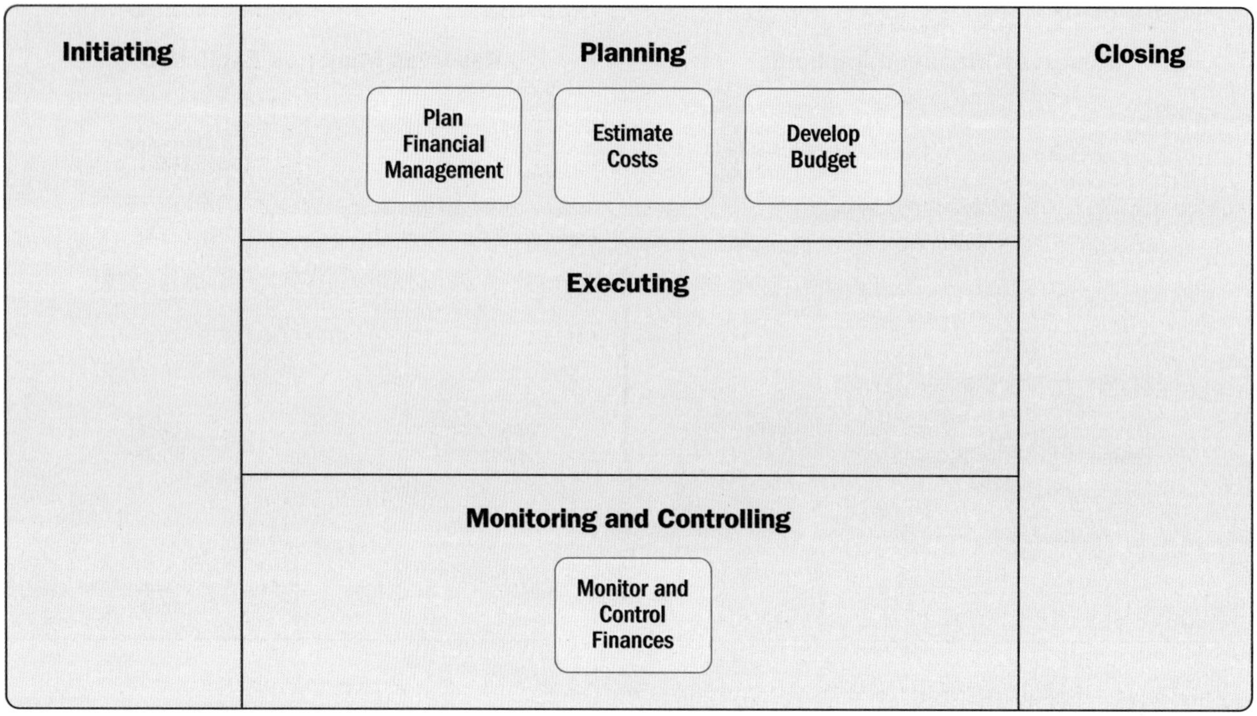

Figure 2-26. Finance Performance Domain Processes Overview

- **Develop Budget.** The process of aggregating the estimated costs of individual activities or work packages to establish an authorized cost baseline.
- **Monitor and Control Finances.** The process of monitoring the project's financial status, updating project finances, managing changes to the cost baseline and revenue forecasts, and ensuring that the project deliverables maintain their financial viability throughout the project life cycle.

2.4.2.1 Plan Financial Management

Plan Financial Management is the process of defining how the project revenues and expenses will be estimated, budgeted, managed, monitored, and controlled. The key benefit of this process is that it provides guidance and direction on how the project finances will be managed throughout the project. This process is performed once up front or at predefined points in the project (see Figure 2-27).

2.4.2.2 Estimate Costs

Estimate Costs is the process of developing an approximation of the cost of resources needed to complete project work. The key benefit of this process is that it determines the monetary resources required for the project. The process is performed periodically throughout the project as needed (see Figure 2-28).

Plan Financial Management

Inputs

- Project charter
- Project management plan
  - Schedule management plan
  - Risk management plan
- Project documents
- Enterprise environmental factors
- Organizational process assets
- Etc.

Tools & Techniques

- Expert judgment
- Data analysis
  - Alternative analysis
- Meetings
- Etc.

Outputs

- Financial management plan
- Funding strategy
- Etc.

Figure 2-27. Plan Financial Management Inputs, Tools and Techniques, and Outputs

Estimate Costs

Inputs

- Project management plan
  - Quality management plan
  - Scope baseline
- Project documents
  - Lessons learned register
  - Project schedule
  - Resource requirements
  - Risk register
- Make-or-buy decisions
- Work package estimation
- Enterprise environmental factors
- Organizational process assets
- Etc.

Tools & Techniques

- Expert judgment
- Analogous estimating
- Parametric estimating
- Bottom-up estimating
- Multipoint estimating
- Data analysis
  - Alternative analysis
  - Reserve analysis
  - Cost of quality
- Project management information system
- Decision-making
  - Voting
- Etc.

Outputs

- Cost estimates
- Basis of estimates
- Project document updates
  - Assumption log
  - Lessons learned register
  - Risk register
- Etc.

Figure 2-28. Estimate Costs Inputs, Tools and Techniques, and Outputs

Develop Budget

Inputs

- Project management plan
  - Financial management plan
  - Resource management plan
  - Scope baseline
- Project documents
  - Basis of estimates
  - Cost estimates
  - Project schedule
  - Risk register
- Business documents
  - Business case
  - Benefits management plan
- Agreements
- Enterprise environmental factors
- Organizational process assets
- Etc.

Tools & Techniques

- Expert judgment
- Cost aggregation
- Data analysis
  - Reserve analysis
- Historical information review
- Funding limit reconciliation
- Financing
- Etc.

Outputs

- Cost baseline
- Project funding requirements
- Project document updates
  - Cost estimates
  - Project schedule
  - Risk register
- Etc.

Figure 2-29. Develop Budget Inputs, Tools and Techniques, and Outputs

2.4.2.3 Develop Budget

Develop Budget is the process of aggregating the estimated costs of individual activities or work packages to establish an authorized cost baseline. The key benefit of this process is that it determines the cost baseline against which project performance can be monitored and controlled. This process is performed once or at predefined points in the project (see Figure 2-29).

2.4.2.4 Monitor and Control Finances

Monitor and Control Finances is the systematic process of overseeing and managing a project's financial health by continuously tracking expenditures, updating financial records, adjusting the cost baseline and revenue forecasts as needed, and implementing corrective actions to address financial risks. This effort ensures that the project remains financially viable and aligned with budgetary goals throughout its entire life cycle. Financial monitoring also includes variance analysis—comparing actual costs against planned costs to identify and address deviations. The key benefit of this process is that the cost baseline is maintained throughout the project, as well as any anticipated revenue or cost savings projections associated with project outcomes. This process enables proactive decision-making

Monitor and Control Finances

Inputs

- Project management plan
  - Financial management plan
  - Cost baseline
  - Performance measurement baseline
- Project documents
  - Lessons learned register
  - Project funding requirements
- Work performance data
- Organizational process assets
- Etc.

Tools & Techniques

- Expert judgment
- Data analysis
  - Earned value analysis
  - Trend analysis
  - Reserve analysis
- To-complete performance index
- Project management information system
- Etc.

Outputs

- Work performance information
- Revenue and cost forecasts
- Change requests
- Funding proposals
- Project management plan updates
  - Financial management plan
  - Cost baseline
  - Performance measurement baseline
- Project document updates
  - Assumption log
  - Basis of estimates
  - Cost estimates
  - Lessons learned register
  - Risk register
- Etc.

Figure 2-30. Monitor and Control Finances Inputs, Tools and Techniques, and Outputs

to address deviations, optimize resource allocations, and ensure alignment with financial goals. The Monitor and Control Finances process is performed throughout the project, ensuring that costs remain under control and that the project is realizing financial benefits, if relevant (see Figure 2-30).

2.4.3 Tailoring Considerations

Because each project is unique, activities and processes in the Finance performance domain should be tailored. Considerations for tailoring include but are not limited to the following:

- **Product.** Heavily regulated industries may require a more formal set of controls related to finance, like compliance with standards such as the Sarbanes-Oxley Act (SOX) or General Data Protection Regulation (GDPR) to ensure financial data integrity and security. Examples include financial or pharmaceutical industries, where multiphase project processes are common and may impact the way finances are planned and tracked along the project life cycle.
- **Development approach.** Iterative approaches impact the project expenditures, flattening the spent curve throughout the project. Both financial planning and controls should be tailored accordingly. For iterative projects, cost management practices, such as time-phased budgeting and continuous funding assessment, are employed to manage evolving project needs.

- **Procurement strategy.** Make-or-buy decisions are connected to the procurement strategy. For buy decisions, procurement tailoring involves selecting the appropriate contract type, such as fixed-price or time and materials (T&M) contracts, based on risk distribution and cost certainty, which may have multiple implications for the financial side of the project. It is important to tailor the financial processes with the procurement strategy to minimize the risk of cost overruns. Sometimes organizations make a buy decision to outsource if they do not have the in-house infrastructure or technologies needed to internally complete the project.
- **Value definition.** The definition of value may vary from one performing organization to another.
- **Resource availability.** Constraints in human resources, as well as physical or virtual resources, may increase a project's actual and forecasted costs due to higher wages or training costs, expedited shipping fees, rental surcharges, additional labor costs, overhead, or penalties for late delivery. See Section 2.6 on the Resources performance domain and enterprise environmental factors (EEFs).

2.4.3.1 Examples

The following are three examples of how these considerations might be applied:

- **Example 1.** A project with an adaptive life cycle may require frequent adjustments to the contract and budget. Thus, contracts should be structured in a way that reflects budget expenditures in alignment with the iterative progress and cadence of the project.
- **Example 2.** A small project may have limited financial flexibility. Thus, a conservative approach to budgeting with contingency and management reserves is crucial to mitigate risks and ensure project stability.
- **Example 3.** A project in the government sector may have a higher demand for fiscal accountability and risk aversion, due to public accountability and regulatory requirements. Thus, budget reserves should be evaluated with a greater buffer to account for potential risks and uncertainties, ensuring that the project can handle any unforeseen financial challenges without compromising its objectives. This effort is influenced by the sponsor and stakeholders, who may prioritize maintaining a higher buffer to mitigate risks.

2.4.4 Interactions With Other Domains

Finance is one of the key pillars of a successful project as it provides access to the resources necessary for its proper execution. In that sense, financial resources and constraints have a direct impact on the Governance, Scope, and Schedule performance domains. The decisions made in those performance domains may affect the Finance performance domain, just as financial activities may affect the other domains. Additionally, the Finance performance domain may be impacted by other performance domains, such as Stakeholders and Risk. On a broader scale, maximizing value delivery should be the primary goal of a project, connecting its results to the performing organization's strategy.

2.4.5 Check Results

Activities related to the Finance performance domain should be considered successful only if they contribute to specific outcomes. Table 2-8 shows a set of sample target outcomes, along with a potential check to confirm whether those outcomes are met.

Table 2-8. Check Outcomes—Finance Performance Domain

Outcome	Check
The project contributes to business objectives and the advancement of strategy (value maximization).	Check parameters such as return on investment (ROI) (metric), net present value (NPV) (metric), internal rate of return (IRR) (metric), cost-benefit analysis, key performance indicators (KPIs), objectives and key results (OKRs), CapEx, and OpEx.
Project completeness is within or below budget.	Check the variance analysis with metrics such as cost variance (CV) and cost performance index (CPI), as well as the accomplishment of financial targets with the vendors based on the signed contract.
Project deliverables are validated according to the plan.	Apply earned value management (EVM) and check other metrics as defined by the organization.
Value is created as an investment or as a different kind of value from the financial perspective.	Use different metrics to be measured as project success based on what is defined in the project success criteria for the project; for instance, the investment or potential value in the future.
Financial visibility is achieved.	Use tools such as trend analysis or graphical analysis and perform forecasting.

2.5 Stakeholders Performance Domain

The Stakeholders performance domain addresses the processes and tools related to stakeholder engagement, starting from the identification of stakeholders through the monitoring of their engagement during the whole life cycle of the project. The project sponsor, team members, and all the people impacted by—or who feel they may be impacted by—the project are considered as stakeholders. This performance domain is closely linked to communications management. Among other abilities, some key skills to develop in this performance domain are negotiation and conflict management.

Internal and external stakeholders include individuals, groups, and organizations (see Figure 2-31). A project can have a small group of stakeholders or potentially millions of stakeholders. There may be different stakeholders in different phases of the project, and the influence, power, or interests of stakeholders may change as the project unfolds.

Effective stakeholder identification, analysis, and engagement includes stakeholders who are either internal or external to the organization, those who are supportive of the project, those who are neutral, and opponents, who are not supportive of the project. The activities of identification, prioritization, and engagement should be reviewed and updated routinely, or at least when the project progresses through phases. While having relevant technical project management skills is an important aspect to delivering successful projects, possessing the interpersonal and leadership skills to work effectively with stakeholders is just as important, if not more so.

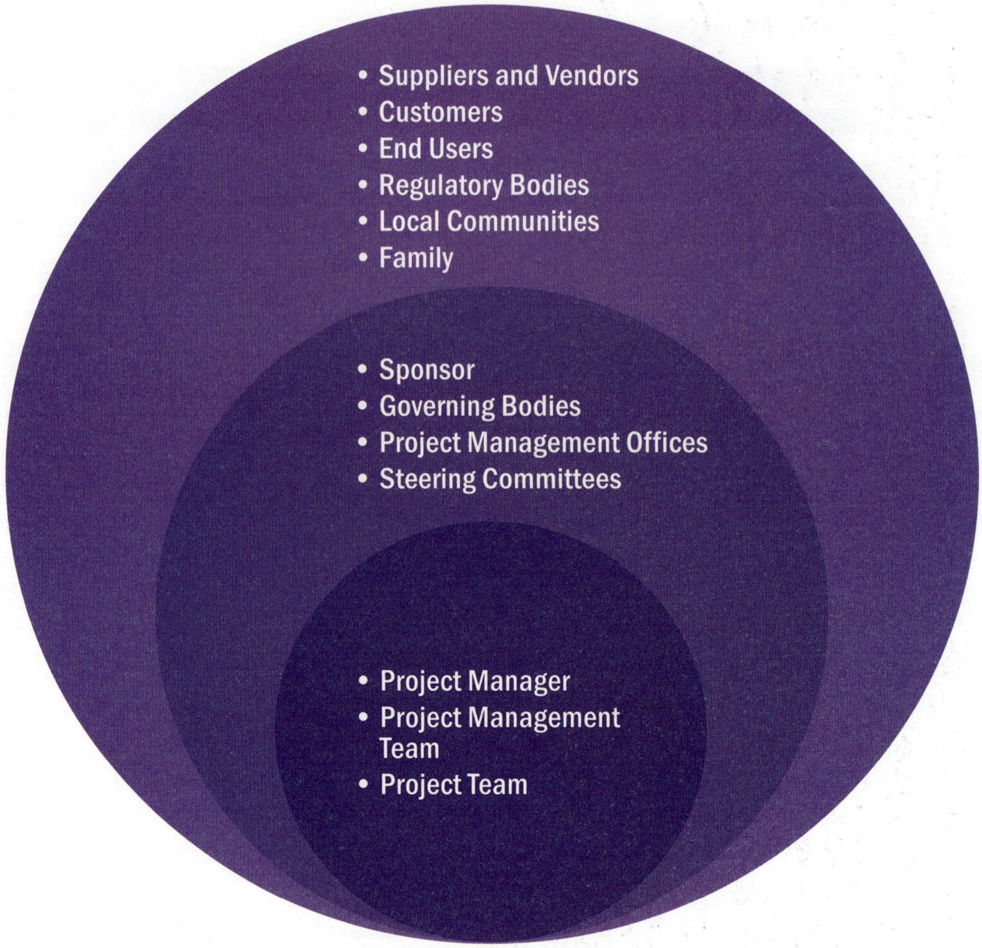

Figure 2-31. Examples of Project Stakeholders

2.5.1 Key Concepts

The following key concepts support effective practices for the Stakeholders performance domain.

- **Stakeholder engagement.** Stakeholder engagement encompasses the activities conducted to identify and analyze stakeholder needs and manage expectations and communications to foster stakeholder support. Stakeholders are a crucial part of project management. Understanding and addressing their different needs, engaging them at the right time, keeping them properly informed, and communicating well are ways to maintain their engagement. Research shows that an active project sponsor is a critical success factor in achieving positive outcomes from projects. Engagement involves the following considerations:
  - **Sponsor engagement.** Sponsors are essential stakeholders who hold decision-making authority; secure human, material, or virtual resources; and ensure alignment with organizational strategy and project objectives. Sponsors are typically involved in activities such as:
    - Initiating the project and defining the project objectives and business case,
    - Approving the project charter and approving any changes to it,

- Assigning and empowering the project manager,
- Initiating a steering committee and being a member of it,
- Approving the project management plan and any changes to it,
- Ensuring the long-term benefits realization of project deliverables,
- Proposing project termination, and
- Authorizing project completion.

In many cases the project sponsor, especially on high-priority projects, may be a member of the executive leadership team. This arrangement requires specific effort in understanding the needs and ways of communication that may better fit this type of stakeholder. Research shows that an active project sponsor is a critical success factor in achieving positive outcomes from projects.

- **Stakeholder satisfaction.** Stakeholder satisfaction should be prioritized and integrated into the project objectives. The key to driving stakeholder satisfaction is maintaining a focus on continuous communication with all stakeholders, including customers, end users, managers, executives, and team members, to understand their needs and expectations, address issues as they occur, manage conflicting interests, and foster appropriate stakeholder engagement in project decisions and activities.
- **Team engagement.** The project team members are also critical stakeholders and should be treated as such. The work done and accomplished during the project comes from the team, as well as the recommendations on the way forward in challenging decisions that are then taken by the sponsor and stakeholders regarding the direction of the project.
- **Communications management.** Communications management is a crucial concept for keeping stakeholders engaged. The way of communicating should be tailored based on the needs and best fit for the stakeholders, so they have all the information they need to make decisions and are aware of the possible risks related to certain actions.
- **Data-driven decision-making**. Effective decision-making is a critical responsibility for project managers, especially when securing timely decisions from stakeholders. This effort requires thorough preparation of supporting materials and the ability to guide the decision-making process. With the increasing volume and complexity of project data, project managers can leverage AI-powered tools to efficiently collect, analyze, and interpret data, generating actionable insights. AI technologies, such as predictive analytics and data visualization, can enhance the project manager's ability to present data-driven recommendations, enabling stakeholders to make informed decisions with greater confidence and speed. Combining AI capabilities with strong leadership skills allows project managers to proactively guide stakeholders toward fact-based, strategic decisions.
- **Vendor and supplier management/procurement**. Even though procurement is not a core part of this performance domain, there are important skills related to vendor management that the project manager should have. Vendors and suppliers are important stakeholders in projects where external resources are involved. In specific industries, such as construction, vendor management and procurement are key elements to the success of the project.

2.5.2 Processes

The Stakeholders performance domain includes the processes required to determine, manage, and control the stakeholder engagement of the project. The following processes are included in the Stakeholders performance domain (see Figure 2-32):

- **Identify Stakeholders.** The process of identifying project stakeholders regularly and analyzing and documenting relevant information regarding their interests, involvement, interdependencies, influence, and potential impact on project success.
- **Plan Stakeholder Engagement.** The process of developing strategies to engage identified project stakeholders based on their needs, expectations, interests, requirements, and potential impact on the project.
- **Plan Communications Management.** The process of planning how to communicate with stakeholders, both inside and outside the team.
- **Manage Stakeholder Engagement.** The process of communicating and working with stakeholders to meet their needs and expectations, address issues, and foster appropriate stakeholder involvement.
- **Manage Communications.** The process of ensuring timely and appropriate collection, creation, distribution, storage, retrieval, management, monitoring, and the ultimate disposition of project information.
- **Monitor Stakeholder Engagement.** The process of monitoring project stakeholder relationships and tailoring strategies for engaging stakeholders through the modification of engagement strategies and plans.
- **Monitor Communications.** The process of ensuring the information needs of the project and its stakeholders are met.

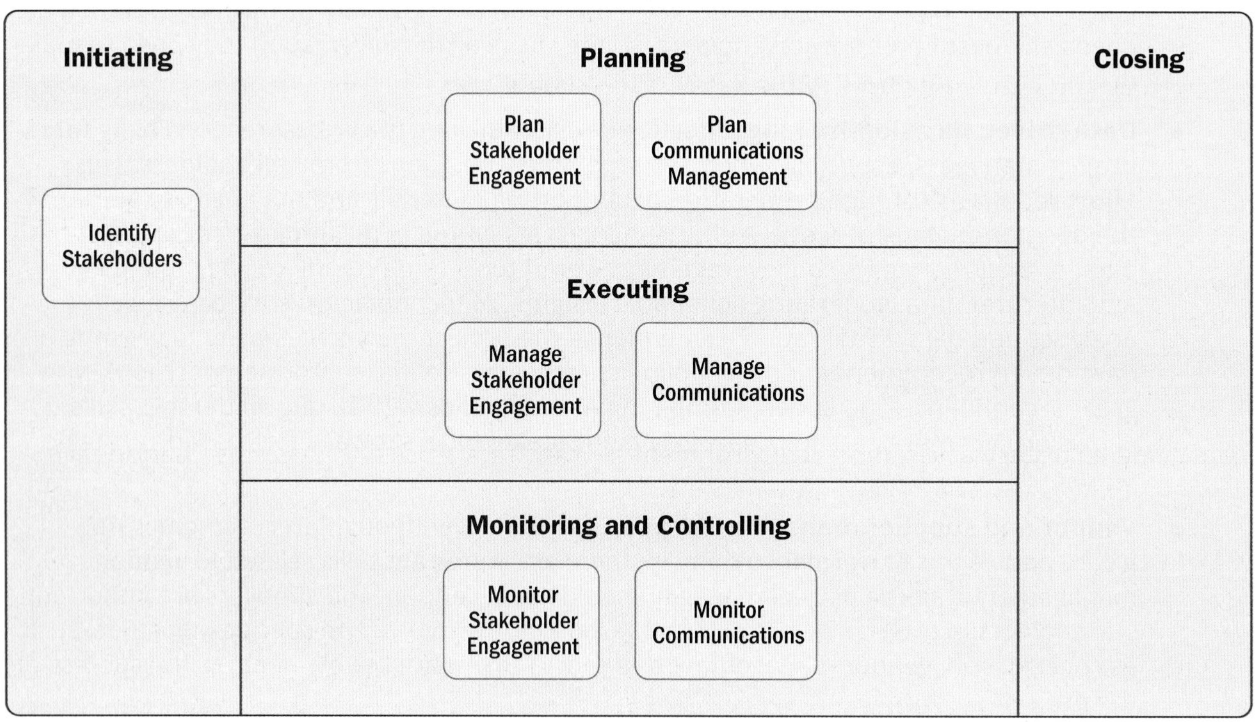

Figure 2-32. Stakeholders Performance Domain Processes Overview

Identify Stakeholders

Inputs

- Project charter
- Business documents
  - Business case
  - Benefits management plan
- Project management plan
  - Communications management plan
  - Stakeholder engagement plan
- Project documents
  - Change log
  - Issue log
  - Requirements documentation
- Agreements
- Enterprise environmental factors
- Organizational process assets
- Etc.

Tools & Techniques

- Expert judgment
- Data gathering
  - Questionnaires and surveys
  - Brainstorming
- Data analysis
  - Stakeholder analysis
  - Document analysis
- Data representation
  - Stakeholder mapping/ representation
- Meetings
- Etc.

Outputs

- Stakeholder register
- Change requests
- Project management plan updates
  - Requirements management plan
  - Communications management plan
  - Risk management plan
  - Stakeholder engagement plan
- Project document updates
  - Assumption log
  - Issue log
  - Risk register
- Etc.

Figure 2-33. Identify Stakeholders Inputs, Tools and Techniques, and Outputs

2.5.2.1 Identify Stakeholders

The Identify Stakeholders process involves selecting the individuals, groups, or organizations that have a stake in the project. The process includes identifying project stakeholders regularly and analyzing and documenting relevant information regarding their interests, involvement, interdependencies, influence, and potential impact on project success. The key benefit of this process is that it enables the project team to identify the appropriate focus for the engagement of each stakeholder or group of stakeholders. Continuous stakeholder identification can work as a risk management strategy as the project environment evolves. This process is performed periodically throughout the project as needed (see Figure 2-33).

2.5.2.2 Plan Stakeholder Engagement

Plan Stakeholder Engagement is the process of developing strategies to engage identified project stakeholders based on their needs, expectations, interests, requirements, and potential impact on the project. The key benefit of this process is that it provides an actionable plan to interact effectively with stakeholders. This process is performed periodically throughout the project as needed (see Figure 2-34).

Plan Stakeholder Engagement

Inputs	Tools & Techniques	Outputs
• Project charter • Project management plan – Resource management plan – Communications management plan – Risk management plan • Project documents – Assumption log – Change log – Issue log – Project schedule – Risk register – Stakeholder register • Agreements • Enterprise environmental factors • Organizational process assets • Etc.	• Expert judgment • Data gathering – Benchmarking • Data analysis – Assumption and constraint analysis – Root cause analysis • Decision-making – Prioritization/ranking • Data representation – Mind mapping – Stakeholder engagement assessment matrix • Meetings • Etc.	• Project management plan updates – Stakeholder engagement plan • Etc.

Figure 2-34. Plan Stakeholder Engagement Inputs, Tools and Techniques, and Outputs

2.5.2.3 Plan Communications Management

The Plan Communications Management process involves the activities to plan how to communicate with the identified stakeholders, both inside and outside the team. Communication planning overlaps with stakeholder identification, analysis, prioritization, and engagement, and is closely aligned with the stakeholder engagement plan, assisting with consistency in communication strategies and alignment with stakeholder expectations. There may be different categories of information, such as internal or external, sensitive or public, and general or detailed. Analyzing the stakeholders, information needs, and categories of information provides the foundation for establishing the communication processes and plans for the project (see Figure 2-35).

2.5.2.4 Manage Stakeholder Engagement

Manage Stakeholder Engagement is the process of communicating and working with stakeholders, which includes collaborating with sponsors to meet their needs and expectations, addressing any issues, and fostering appropriate sponsor involvement. The key benefit of this process is that it allows the project manager to increase support and minimize resistance from stakeholders. This process is performed throughout the project (see Figure 2-36).

Plan Communications Management

Inputs	Tools & Techniques	Outputs
• Project charter • Project management plan – Resource management plan – Stakeholder engagement plan • Project documents – Requirements documentation – Stakeholder register • Enterprise environmental factors • Organizational process assets • Etc.	• Expert judgment • Communication requirements analysis • Communication technology • Communication models • Communication methods • Interpersonal and team skills – Communication styles assessment – Political awareness – Cultural awareness • Data representation – Stakeholder engagement assessment matrix • Meetings • Etc.	• Project management plan updates – Communications management plan – Stakeholder engagement plan • Project document updates – Project schedule – Stakeholder register • Etc.

Figure 2-35. Plan Communications Management Inputs, Tools and Techniques, and Outputs

2.5.2.5 Manage Communications

The Manage Communications process involves setting up and conducting communications with stakeholders (e.g., sponsors, customers, end users, team members, managers, or executives), both inside and outside the team (e.g., external vendors). Manage Communications is the process of ensuring the timely and appropriate collection, creation, distribution, storage, retrieval, management, monitoring, and ultimate disposition of project information. The key benefit of this process is that it enables an efficient and effective information flow between the project team and stakeholders. The Manage Communications process identifies all aspects of effective communication, including the choice of appropriate technologies, methods, and techniques. In addition, the process should foster greater flexibility in the communications activities, allowing for adjustments in the methods and techniques to accommodate the changing needs of stakeholders and the project (see Figure 2-37).

2.5.2.6 Monitor Stakeholder Engagement

The Monitor Stakeholder Engagement process involves assessing the effectiveness of stakeholder engagement efforts, identifying necessary adjustments to improve relationships, and refining strategies or plans to better meet stakeholder participation needs. The key benefit of this process is that it maintains or increases the efficiency and effectiveness of stakeholder engagement activities as the project evolves and its environment changes. This process is performed throughout the project (see Figure 2-38).

Manage Stakeholder Engagement

Inputs

- Project management plan
  - Communications management plan
  - Risk management plan
  - Stakeholder engagement plan
  - Change management plan
- Project documents
  - Change log
  - Issue log
  - Lessons learned register
  - Stakeholder register
  - Risk register
  - Status report
  - Project schedule
- Enterprise environmental factors
- Organizational process assets
- Etc.

Tools & Techniques

- Expert judgment
- Communication skills
  - Feedback
- Interpersonal and team skills
  - Conflict management
  - Cultural awareness
  - Negotiation
  - Observation/conversation
  - Political awareness
- Ground rules
- Meetings
- Etc.

Outputs

- Change requests
- Project management plan updates
  - Communications management plan
  - Stakeholder engagement plan
- Project document updates
  - Change log
  - Issue log
  - Lessons learned register
  - Stakeholder register
- Etc.

Figure 2-36. Manage Stakeholder Engagement Inputs, Tools and Techniques, and Outputs

2.5.2.7 Monitor Communications

Monitor Communications is the process of ensuring the information needs of the project and its stakeholders are met. The key benefit of this process is the optimal information flow as defined in the communications management plan and the stakeholder engagement plan. This process is performed throughout the project (see Figure 2-39).

2.5.3 Tailoring Considerations

Because each project is unique, activities and processes in the Stakeholders performance domain should be tailored. Considerations for tailoring include but are not limited to the following:

- **Organizational culture.** Organizational culture is a key driver for tailoring stakeholder engagement. Flat organizations tend to rely on open communications and foster informal channels, whereas hierarchical organizations use more formal approaches. The entire communication and stakeholder engagement strategy should consider organizational culture in order to properly engage with stakeholders.

Manage Communications

Inputs

- Project management plan
  - Resource management plan
  - Communications management plan
  - Stakeholder engagement plan
- Project documents
  - Change log
  - Issue log
  - Lessons learned register
  - Quality report
  - Risk report
  - Stakeholder register
- Work performance reports
- Enterprise environmental factors
- Organizational process assets
- Etc.

Tools & Techniques

- Communication technology
- Communication methods
- Communication skills
  - Communication competence
  - Feedback
  - Nonverbal communication
  - Presentations
- Project management information system
- Project reporting
- Interpersonal and team skills
  - Active listening
  - Conflict management
  - Cultural awareness
  - Meeting management
  - Networking
  - Political awareness
- Meetings
- Etc.

Outputs

- Project communications
- Project management plan updates
  - Communications management plan
  - Stakeholder engagement plan
- Project document updates
  - Issue log
  - Lessons learned register
  - Project schedule
  - Risk register
  - Stakeholder register
- Organizational process asset updates
- Etc.

Figure 2-37. Manage Communications Inputs, Tools and Techniques, and Outputs

- **Product.** Products that allow or require interactive, incremental, or event-exploratory approaches usually bring a specific framework for stakeholder interactions. For example, the software industry created common events (also known as ceremonies) such as product reviews, planning sessions, and project retrospectives, among others, to update and engage stakeholders.
- **Large language models (LLMs) and artificial intelligence (AI).** The use of AI should be assessed for each project through a decision-making process to determine when AI can assist with tasks or provide more time for other valuable activities. The evaluation should be focused on the use of AI to produce some artifacts for communication with the sponsor, stakeholders, team, and vendors. Proactive security and ethics measures should be considered, such as project managers engaging with the appropriate stakeholders (e.g., the cybersecurity team, if applicable), to understand if the risk of incorporating AI is acceptable for the organization.

Monitor Stakeholder Engagement

Inputs

- Project management plan
  - Resource management plan
  - Communications management plan
  - Stakeholder engagement plan
- Project documents
  - Issue log
  - Lessons learned register
  - Project communications
  - Risk register
  - Stakeholder register
- Work performance data
- Enterprise environmental factors
- Organizational process assets
- Etc.

Tools & Techniques

- Data analysis
  - Alternative analysis
  - Root cause analysis
  - Stakeholder analysis
- Decision-making
  - Multicriteria decision analysis
  - Voting
- Data representation
  - Stakeholder engagement assessment matrix
- Communication skills
  - Feedback
  - Presentations
- Interpersonal and team skills
  - Active listening
  - Cultural awareness
  - Leadership
  - Networking
  - Political awareness
- Meetings
- Etc.

Outputs

- Work performance information
- Change requests
- Project management plan updates
  - Resource management plan
  - Communications management plan
  - Stakeholder engagement plan
- Project document updates
  - Issue log
  - Lessons learned register
  - Risk register
  - Stakeholder register
- Etc.

Figure 2-38. Monitor Stakeholder Engagement Inputs, Tools and Techniques, and Outputs

2.5.3.1 Examples

The following are three examples of how these considerations might be applied:

- **Example 1.** Agile projects require continuous feedback on features and user stories to ensure product alignment with stakeholder needs. To facilitate this, teams often employ daily coordination meetings and utilize dedicated communication platforms for real-time collaboration and information sharing. This approach fosters rapid adjustments, increased stakeholder engagement, and accelerated time to market.
- **Example 2.** A project in the manufacturing industry involves implementing a large-scale enterprise resource planning (ERP) system. Thus, formal project updates are disseminated via biweekly email newsletters and monthly town hall meetings to ensure alignment across hierarchical levels.

Monitor Communications

Inputs

- Project management plan
  - Resource management plan
  - Communications management plan
  - Stakeholder engagement plan
- Project documents
  - Issue log
  - Lessons learned register
  - Project communications
- Work performance data
- Enterprise environmental factors
- Organizational process assets
- Etc.

Tools & Techniques

- Expert judgment
- Project management information system
- Data representation
  - Stakeholder engagement assessment matrix
- Interpersonal and team skills
  - Observation/conversation
- Meetings
- Etc.

Outputs

- Work performance information
- Change requests
- Project management plan updates
  - Communications management plan
  - Stakeholder engagement plan
- Project document updates
  - Issue log
  - Lessons learned register
  - Stakeholder register
- Etc.

Figure 2-39. Monitor Communications Inputs, Tools and Techniques, and Outputs

- **Example 3.** A medium-sized global project requires inclusive communication strategies. Thus, multilingual updates and monthly virtual forums help ensure engagement and feedback from stakeholders across different cultural backgrounds.

Based on stakeholders' varied needs and preferences, there should be different communication methods (e.g., email for formal updates, instant messaging for quick questions, feedback loops, face-to-face meetings, etc.) or adjustments to the level of detail in communications based on each stakeholder's role in the project.

A complex project with numerous stakeholders may require a more sophisticated communications management plan compared to smaller projects, where the communication channels are more limited in number.

2.5.4 Interactions With Other Domains

Stakeholders permeate all aspects of projects. Stakeholders define and prioritize the requirements and scope for the project team, participate in and shape project planning, and determine the acceptance and quality criteria for the project deliverables and outcomes. Much of the project work revolves around engaging and communicating with stakeholders. Throughout a project or at its closure, stakeholders use the project deliverables and influence the realization of project outcomes.

Some stakeholders can assist in lowering the amount of uncertainty present on a project, whereas others may cause an increase in uncertainty. The stakeholders may influence the project risks, especially when the right stakeholders are not identified at the beginning of the project and are not updated and checked throughout the duration of the project. Stakeholders, such as customers, senior management, project management office leads, or program managers, may focus on measures of performance for the project and its deliverables.

The Stakeholders performance domain closely interacts with the Governance performance domain, particularly through the skills needed to engage with project governance bodies and organizational leadership. These interactions demonstrate how the Stakeholders domain connects with other performance domains, although they do not capture all the ways stakeholder interests can influence a project.

The Stakeholders performance domain also aligns with the Finance performance domain, as stakeholders often help define budgets, make funding decisions, and oversee financial controls. These connections highlight the critical role stakeholders play in shaping both the direction and success of a project.

2.5.5 Check Results

Activities related to the Stakeholders performance domain should be considered successful only if they contribute to specific outcomes. Table 2-9 shows a set of sample target outcomes, along with a potential check to confirm whether those outcomes are met.

Table 2-9. Check Outcomes—Stakeholders Performance Domain

Outcome	Check
Stakeholder engagement is maintained.	Collect feedback from stakeholders through interviews or surveys, perform periodic alignment with stakeholders regarding project objectives, and check indicators such as the Net Promoter Score℠ (NPS®).[2]
Risk responses are identified and successfully implemented.	Review the project's issue log, risk register, and stakeholder register for assessment.
Stakeholder agreement with project objectives is achieved.	Review the number of change requests to requirements and collect feedback on increments.
Communications management is performed.	Review the communications management plan periodically and tailor it appropriately based on the needs of stakeholders.
The project plans are integrated with the suppliers' perspectives and work outputs.	Align the project management plan with the vendor's way of working.

[2] Net Promoter®, NPS®, NPS Prism®, and the NPS-related emoticons are registered trademarks of Bain & Company, Inc., NICE Systems, Inc., and Fred Reichheld. Net Promoter Score℠ and Net Promoter System℠ are service marks of Bain & Company, Inc., NICE Systems, Inc., and Fred Reichheld.

2.6 Resources Performance Domain

The Resources performance domain refers to how effectively and efficiently a project team plans for and utilizes its available resources. This performance domain encompasses both human resources (the project team itself) and physical or virtual resources (equipment, materials, supplies, facilities, infrastructure, software, testing environments, licenses, services, information, or documents). The Resources performance domain also covers resource availability, utilization, and maintenance.

2.6.1 Key Concepts

The following key concepts support effective practices in the Resources performance domain. The performance domain delves into the key concepts of effectively and efficiently applying the resources at the project manager's disposal. Different skills and competencies are needed to manage team resources versus physical or virtual resources. This section explores how to oversee human, physical, or virtual resources to foster optimal project outcomes.

- **Project manager.** The project manager, as a leader of the project team, is responsible for team formation and operation as an effective group. Project managers should invest suitable effort in acquiring, managing, motivating, and empowering the project team. Additionally, project managers should be aware of different aspects that influence the team such as team environment, geographical locations of team members, communications among stakeholders, organizational change management, internal and external politics, cultural issues and organizational uniqueness, and other factors that may alter project performance. Proactively developing team skills and competencies while enhancing team satisfaction and motivation also falls under a project manager's responsibility, in addition to awareness of professional and ethical behavior.
- **Resource manager.** The resource manager is an individual with management authority over one or more resources. The project team may or may not have direct control over resource selection because of collective bargaining agreements, use of subcontractor personnel, a matrix environment, internal or external reporting relationships, or other reasons. The resources needed for a project can be internal or external to the project-performing organization. Internal resources are acquired (assigned) from functional or resource managers. External resources are obtained through partnerships, joint ventures, or procurement processes. For further details, see Appendix X4 on Procurement.
- **Human resources (project team members).** Human resources consist of individuals with assigned roles and responsibilities who work collectively to achieve a shared project goal within the project team. The involvement of all team members in project planning and decision-making is also beneficial. Project team members add their expertise to the process, strengthening their commitment to the project. Typically, project team members are guided by the top-down leadership of one or several individuals (see Section 5 on Tools and Techniques—centralized management and leadership). Project team members may also self-organize, and decision-making may be decentralized (see Section 5 on Tools and Techniques—distributed management and leadership).
- **Physical, material, or virtual resources.** These resources refer to any resource that is not a person. These resources may include equipment, materials, supplies, facilities, infrastructure, software, testing environments, licenses, services, and anything else needed for successful and efficient project completion. Organizations should have

sufficient data on resource demands (now and in the future), resource configurations that are required to meet those demands, and the supply of resources. Projects with significant physical or virtual resources, such as engineering and construction, may need to plan for procurement activities to acquire the resources. These activities may be as simple as utilizing a basic ordering agreement or as complicated as managing, coordinating, and integrating several large procurement activities. For further details, see Appendix X4 on Procurement.

2.6.2 Processes

The Resources performance domain includes the processes required to plan, estimate, and acquire the resources needed to successfully complete the project, lead the project team, and control resources. These processes help ensure that the right resources will be available to the project manager and project team at the right time and place.

The following processes are included in the Resources performance domain (see Figure 2-40):

- **Plan Resource Management.** The process of defining how to estimate, acquire, lead, and utilize physical, virtual, or team resources.
- **Estimate Resources.** The process of estimating team resources and the type and quantities of physical or virtual resources necessary to perform project work.
- **Acquire Resources.** The process of obtaining the team, physical, or virtual resources necessary to complete project work, which is based on the activity list.

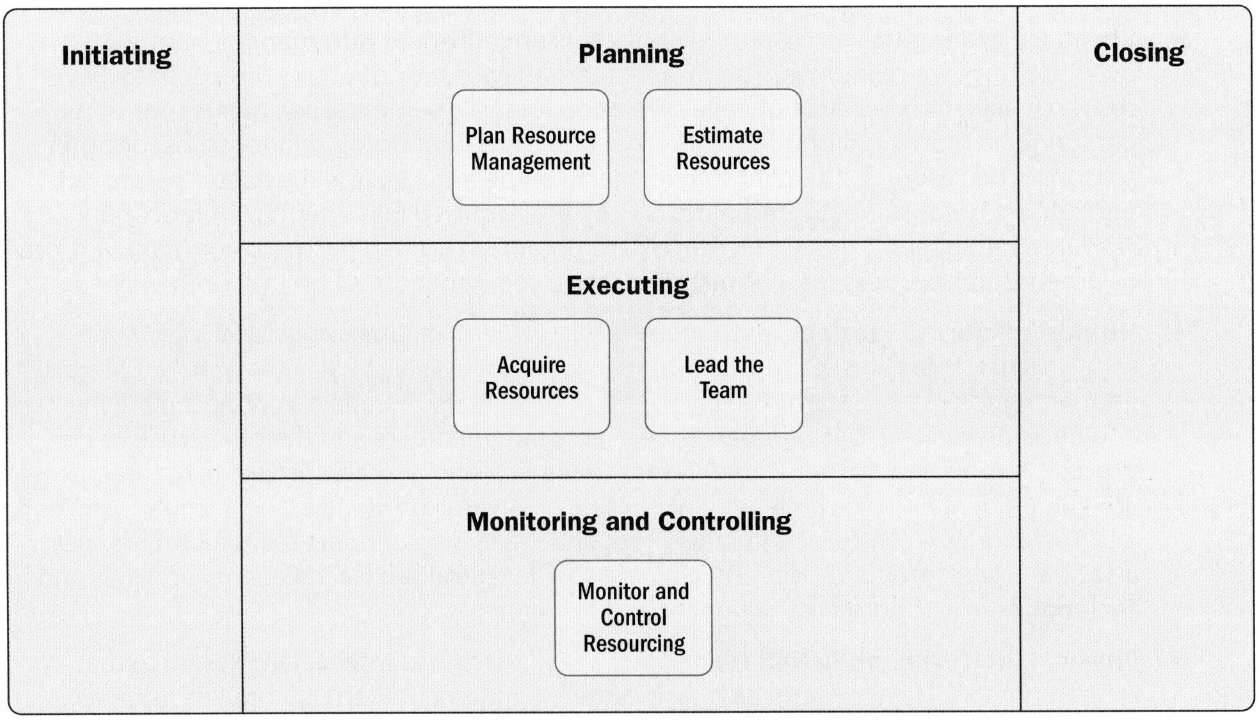

Figure 2-40. Resources Performance Domain Processes Overview

- **Lead the Team.** The process of guiding, developing, and managing the team to enhance performance and achieve project goals through feedback, collaboration, conflict resolution, or escalation.
- **Monitor and Control Resourcing.** The process of ensuring that the physical or virtual resources assigned and allocated to the project are available as planned. This process also monitors the planned versus actual use of resources and performs corrective actions as necessary.

2.6.2.1 Plan Resource Management

The key benefit of this process is that it establishes the approach and level of management effort needed to manage project resources based on the type and complexity of the project (see Figure 2-41).

This process is performed once or at predefined points in the project. Resource planning is used to determine and identify an approach to ensuring that sufficient resources are available for the successful completion of the project. Effective resource planning should consider and plan for the availability of—or competition for—scarce resources.

The specific tools and techniques for the Plan Resource Management process include the responsibility assignment matrix, organizational theory, green human resource management, resource-based view, and SWOT (strengths, weaknesses, opportunities, threats) analysis.

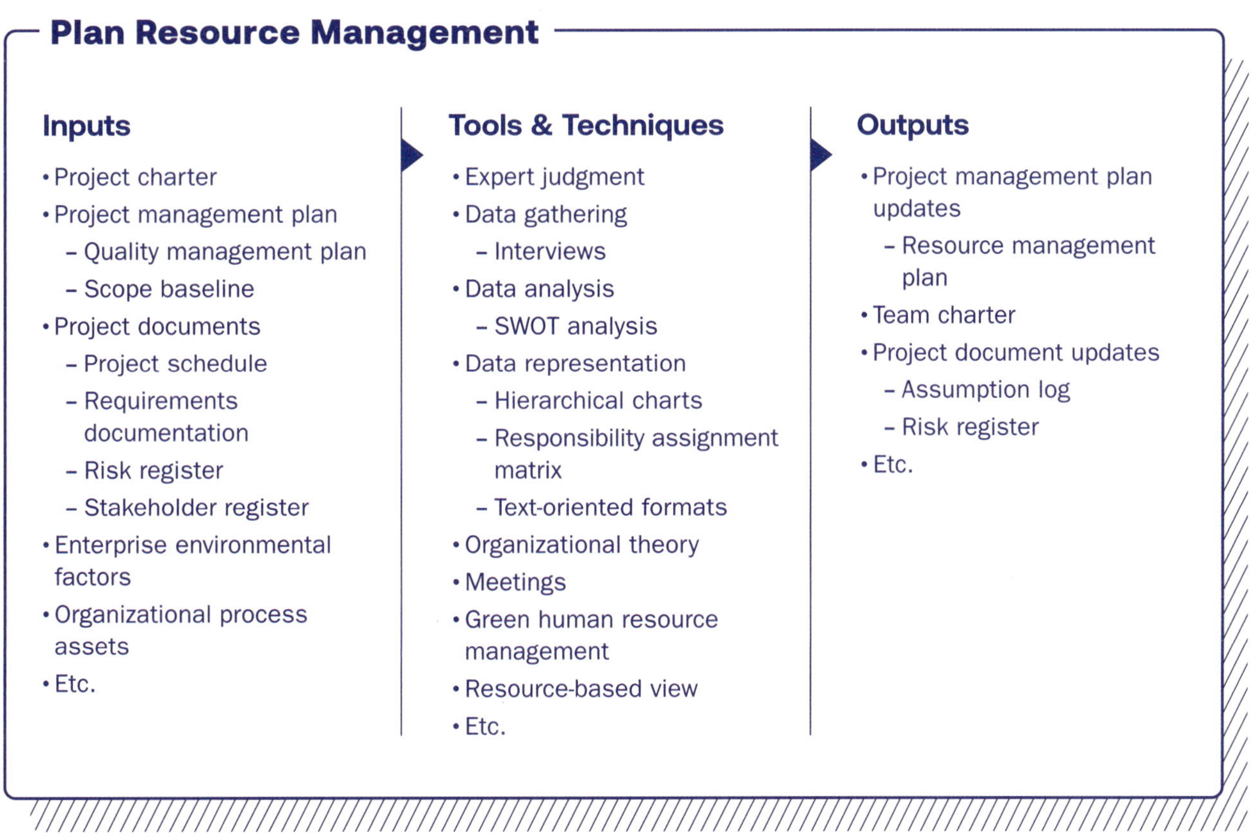

Figure 2-41. Plan Resource Management Inputs, Tools and Techniques, and Outputs

Estimate Resources

Inputs

- Project management plan
  - Resource management plan
  - Schedule management plan
  - Scope baseline
- Project documents
  - Activity attributes
  - Activity list
  - Assumption log
  - Cost estimates
  - Resource calendars
  - Risk register
- Project schedule
- Enterprise environmental factors
- Organizational process assets
- Etc.

Tools & Techniques

- Expert judgment
- Bottom-up estimating
- Analogous estimating
- Parametric estimating
- Data analysis
  - Alternative analysis
- Project management information system
- Meetings
- Data gathering
  - Interviews
- Artificial intelligence
- Predictive analytics
- Virtual reality
- Augmented reality
- Branch and bound
- Genetic algorithms
- Constructive cost model
- Etc.

Outputs

- Resource requirements
- Basis of estimates
- Resource breakdown structure
- Project document updates
  - Activity attributes
  - Assumption log
  - Lessons learned register
  - Risk register
- Etc.

Figure 2-42. Estimate Resources Inputs, Tools and Techniques, and Outputs

2.6.2.2 Estimate Resources

The key benefit of this process is that it identifies the type, quantity, and characteristics of resources required to complete the project. This identification is essential for project managers to plan effectively and ensure that all necessary resources are available. Additionally, this process aids in anticipating potential resource shortages or surpluses, allowing for proactive adjustments. The process also enhances the ability to manage resource allocation and usage risks (see Figure 2-42).

The Estimate Resources process is performed once or at predefined points in the project. The process involves detailed analysis and consideration of all aspects of the project to ensure that the appropriate resources are allocated efficiently. The Estimate Resources process is closely related to the Schedule performance domain (see Section 2.3).

The specific inputs for the Estimate Resources process are the resource management plan and resource calendars.

2.6.2.3 Acquire Resources

The key benefit of this process is that it outlines and guides the selection of resources and assigns them to their respective activities (see Figure 2-43).

Acquire Resources

Inputs	Tools & Techniques	Outputs

• Project management plan
  – Resource management plan
  – Procurement management plan
  – Cost baseline
• Project documents
  – Project schedule
  – Resource calendars
  – Resource requirements
  – Stakeholder register
• Enterprise environmental factors
• Organizational process assets
• Etc.
	• Decision-making
	  – Multicriteria decision analysis
	• Interpersonal and team skills
	  – Negotiation
	  – Problem-solving
	• Preassignment
	• Virtual teams
	• Etc.
		• Physical or virtual resource assignments
		• Project team assignments
		• Resource calendars
		• Change requests
		• Project management plan updates
		  – Resource management plan
		  – Cost baseline
		• Project document updates
		  – Lessons learned register
		  – Project schedule
		  – Resource breakdown structure
		  – Resource requirements
		  – Risk register
		  – Stakeholder register
		• Enterprise environmental factor updates
		• Organizational process asset updates
		• Etc.

Figure 2-43. Acquire Resources Inputs, Tools and Techniques, and Outputs

The Acquire Resources process is performed periodically throughout the project as needed. It is important that the following factors are considered during the process of obtaining the project resources:

- The project manager or project team should collaborate, effectively negotiate, and influence others who are able to provide the required team, physical, or virtual resources for the project.
- Failure to acquire the necessary resources for the project may affect the schedule, budget, customer satisfaction, and quality while increasing risk. Insufficient resources or capabilities decrease the probability of success and, in a worst-case scenario, could result in project cancellation.
- If the team, physical, or virtual resources are not available due to constraints such as economic factors or assignment to other projects, the project manager or project team may be required to assign alternative resources, perhaps with different competencies, features, or costs. Alternative resources are allowed if risks are acknowledged and the legal, regulatory, mandatory, or other specific criteria are not violated.

- These factors and criteria may be considered and addressed during the project planning stage. The project manager or team may need to document the impact of the unavailability of required resources on the project schedule, budget, risks, quality, training plans, and other project management plans.

2.6.2.4 Lead the Team

Lead the Team is the process of applying knowledge, skills, tools, and techniques for managing and leading the team by improving competencies, team member interactions, and the overall team environment to enhance project performance. This process also involves tracking team member performance, providing feedback, resolving and escalating issues, and managing team changes to optimize project performance. The key benefit of this process is that it influences team behavior, manages conflict, and resolves issues among team members (see Figure 2-44).

The Lead the Team process involves both management and leadership activities as follows:

- **Management activities.** Management activities focus on the means of meeting project objectives such as having effective processes, planning, coordinating, measuring, and monitoring work.
- **Leadership activities.** Leadership activities focus on people and encompass influencing, motivating, listening, enabling, and other activities related to leading the project team, all of which are important in delivering the intended project outcomes. A project manager should be sensitive to the willingness and ability of team members to perform their work and should adjust their management and leadership styles to account for these factors as needed.

2.6.2.4.1 Common Aspects of Team Development

Regardless of how management activities are structured, the common aspects of project team development include the following:

- **Vision and objectives.** The vision and objectives are communicated throughout the project and are essential for understanding. This communication includes referencing the intended outcomes when the project team makes decisions and solves problems.
- **Roles and responsibilities.** Project managers should ensure that project team members understand and fulfill their roles and responsibilities. This effort may include identifying gaps in knowledge and skills and developing strategies to address those gaps through training, mentoring, or coaching. For more information, refer to the responsibility assignment matrix information in Section 5, Tools and Techniques.
- **Project team operations.** Facilitating project team communication, problem-solving, and the process of consensus building may include working with the project team to develop a project team charter and a set of operating guidelines or project team norms.
- **Guidance.** Guidance should be directed to the overall project team to keep everyone headed in the right direction. Individual project team members may also provide guidance on a particular task or deliverable.
- **Growth.** Identifying areas where the project team is performing well and pointing out areas where the project team can improve helps everyone grow. Working collaboratively, the project team should identify goals for improvement and take steps to meet those goals. Individuals may want to develop their skills and experience in certain areas, and the project manager can assist with that.

Lead the Team

Inputs	Tools & Techniques	Outputs
• Project management plan – Resource management plan • Project documents – Issue log – Lessons learned register – Project schedule – Resource calendars – Team charter – Work performance reports – Project team assignments • Team performance assessments • Enterprise environmental factors • Organizational process assets • Etc.	• Colocation • Virtual teams • Communication technology • Interpersonal and team skills – Conflict management – Influencing – Motivation – Negotiation – Team building – Decision-making – Critical thinking – Coaching and mentoring – Training • Problem-solving – Six Thinking Hats® • Retrospectives • Recognition and rewards • Individual and team assessments • Data analysis – SWOT analysis • Meetings • Emotional intelligence • Organizational cultural intelligence • Leadership – Distributed management and leadership – Centralized management and leadership – Servant leadership • Tuckman ladder • Project management information system • Virtual collaboration tools • Etc.	• Team performance assessments • Change requests • Project management plan updates – Resource management plan – Schedule baseline – Cost baseline • Project document updates – Issue log – Lessons learned register – Project schedule – Resource calendars – Team charter – Project team assignments • Enterprise environmental factor updates • Organizational process asset updates • Etc.

Six Thinking Hats® is a registered trademark of The de Bono Group.

Figure 2-44. Lead the Team Inputs, Tools and Techniques, and Outputs

2.6.2.4.2 High-Performing Project Teams

The following list is not comprehensive, but identifies some of the factors associated with high-performing project teams, which is a goal of effective leadership:

- **Open communication.** An environment that fosters open and safe communication allows for productive meetings, problem-solving, brainstorming, understanding, trust, and collaboration.
- **Shared understanding.** Shared understanding can be achieved when the purpose of the project and the benefits that it will provide are held in common with the team. Shared understanding is closely related to project alignment, which helps ensure that the project's goals and activities are in line with the organization's mission and strategy. This effort involves developing a shared understanding of the project's purpose and goals—and how to achieve them.
- **Shared ownership.** The more ownership that project team members feel over the outcomes, the more likely they are to perform effectively.
- **Trust.** A project team that is composed of members who trust one another is more willing to perform at a higher level to deliver success. People are less likely to do the extra work it may take to succeed if they do not trust their project team members, project manager, or the organization.
- **Collaboration.** Project team members who work as a team, rather than working in silos or competitively, tend to generate more diverse ideas and deliver better outcomes.
- **Adaptability.** Project teams that can adapt the way they work to their particular environment or situation are more effective.
- **Resilience.** When issues or failures occur, high-performing project teams recover quickly.
- **Empowerment, delegation, and autonomy.** Project team members who feel empowered to make decisions about the way they work and about specific details in the deliverables being produced—even under limited range—perform better and have a higher degree of satisfaction than those who are micromanaged.
- **Recognition.** Project team members who are recognized for the work they put in and the performance that they achieve are more likely to continue to perform well. Even the simple act of showing appreciation reinforces positive team behaviors.

The specific tools and techniques of the Lead the Team process are colocation, virtual teams, recognition and rewards, training, individual and team assessments, emotional intelligence, leadership, distributed management and leadership, centralized management and leadership, servant leadership, coaching and mentoring, organizational cultural intelligence, virtual collaboration tools, retrospectives, critical thinking, and specific problem-solving methods such as Six Thinking Hats®[3] (see Section 5 on Tools and Techniques).

The specific outputs of the Lead the Team process include team performance assessments.

[3] Six Thinking Hats® is a registered trademark of The de Bono Group.

2.6.2.5 *Monitor and Control Resourcing*

The Monitor and Control Resourcing process helps ensure that the physical or virtual resources assigned and allocated to the project are available as planned. The process also monitors the planned versus actual use of physical or virtual resources and performs corrective actions as necessary. The key benefit of this process is ensuring that the assigned physical or virtual resources are available to the project at the right time and in the right place and are released when no longer needed (see Figure 2-45).

The Monitor and Control Resourcing process should be performed continuously in all project phases and throughout the project life cycle. The resources needed for the project should be assigned and released at the right time, right place, and in the right amount for the project to continue without delays. The Monitor and Control Resourcing process is concerned with physical and virtual resources such as equipment, materials, supplies, facilities, infrastructure, software, testing environments, licenses, services, or any other relevant resources. Team members are addressed in the Lead the Team process. Usually, work performance information is intended for assessing resource usage in the project status. However, it is common practice to assess individual performance based on work performance information. For assessing team performance, see the Lead the Team process in Section 2.6.2.4.

Monitor and Control Resourcing

Inputs

- Project management plan
  - Resource management plan
- Project documents
  - Issue log
  - Lessons learned register
  - Physical or virtual resource assignments
  - Project schedule
  - Resource breakdown structure
  - Risk register
- Work performance data
- Agreements
- Organizational process assets
- Etc.

Tools & Techniques

- Data analysis
  - Alternative analysis
  - Cost-benefit analysis
  - Performance reviews
  - Trend analysis
- Problem-solving
- Interpersonal and team skills
  - Negotiation
  - Influencing
- Project management information system
- Value stream mapping
- Continuous improvement
- Theory of constraints
- Control charts
- Branch and bound
- Etc.

Outputs

- Work performance information
- Change requests
- Project management plan updates
  - Resource management plan
  - Schedule baseline
  - Cost baseline
- Project document updates
  - Assumption log
  - Issue log
  - Lessons learned register
  - Physical resource assignments
  - Resource breakdown structure
  - Risk register
- Etc.

Figure 2-45. Monitor and Control Resourcing Inputs, Tools and Techniques, and Outputs

Updating resource allocations requires knowing what actual resources have been used to date and what is still needed. This task is done mainly by reviewing the performance usage to date. The Monitor and Control Resourcing process is concerned with:

- Monitoring resource expenditures,
- Identifying and dealing with resource shortages and surpluses in a timely manner,
- Ensuring that resources are used and released according to the plan and project needs,
- Informing appropriate stakeholders if any issues arise with relevant resources,
- Influencing the factors that can create resource utilization changes, and
- Managing the actual changes as they occur.

The Monitor and Control Resourcing techniques discussed here are those used most frequently on projects implementing a predictive approach. There are many others that may be useful on certain projects or in some application areas. Failing to manage and control resources efficiently is a risk to successful project completion. For example, the following may occur:

- Failing to secure critical equipment or infrastructure on time may result in delays in the manufacture of the final product.
- Ordering low-quality materials may damage the quality of the product, causing a high rate of recalls or rework.
- Keeping too much inventory may result in high operational costs and reduce the organization's profit. Conversely, an unacceptably low inventory level could hinder the ability to satisfy customer demand and, again, reduce the organization's profit.

2.6.3 Tailoring Considerations

Given the uniqueness of each project, activities and processes within the Resources performance domain may be tailored to align with the project's specific requirements, constraints, and stakeholder expectations. Considerations for tailoring include but are not limited to the following:

- **Development approach selection.** Leadership styles are tailored to meet the needs of the project, environment, and stakeholders. Organizations and project teams with experience on a specific type of project may be more self-managing and require less leadership. When a project is new to an organization, the tendency is to provide more oversight and use a more direct leadership style.
    - In a predictive development approach, resource management is typically planned and structured in advance. Tailoring in this context involves defining resource requirements early in the project and allocating them based on the project schedule. This effort includes identifying all necessary skills and resources, creating a detailed resource management plan, and ensuring resource availability throughout the project.
    - In an adaptive development approach, projects with high variability benefit from team structures that maximize focus and collaboration, such as self-organizing teams with generalizing specialists. Collaboration is intended to boost productivity and facilitate innovative problem-solving. Collaborative teams may facilitate accelerated integration of distinct work activities, improve communication, increase knowledge sharing, and provide flexibility of work assignments in addition to other advantages. Although the

benefits of collaboration also apply to other project environments, collaborative teams are often critical to the success of projects with a high degree of variability and rapid changes because there is less time for centralized tasking and decision-making.

- **Maturity of project team culture.** When project teams form across different organizations based on a contract, strategic partnership, or other business relationship, specific roles that perform various functions may be more formalized and less flexible depending on the contract or other terms. Such arrangements often require more up-front work to establish a "one team" mindset; ensure project team members understand how everyone contributes to the project; and establish other enablers that integrate skills, capabilities, and processes. The teams may differ in aspects such as:
  - **Unique culture of the project team.** Each project team develops its own team culture. The project team's culture may be established deliberately by developing project team norms or informally through the behaviors and actions of its project team members. The project team culture operates within the organization's culture but reflects the project team's individual ways of working and interacting.
  - **Transparency on bias.** Human beings have a set of biases, some of them unconscious and some of them conscious. For example, one person may feel that unless a schedule is displayed using a software-generated Gantt chart, it is not a true or valid schedule. Another person may have a contrasting bias that detailed planning further out than 30 days is a waste of time. Being open and transparent about biases up front establishes a culture of openness and trust that can enable consensus and collaboration.
  - **Project manager role.** The project manager role is key in establishing and maintaining a safe, respectful, nonjudgmental environment that allows the project team to communicate openly. One way to accomplish this is by modeling desired behaviors, such as:
    - **Transparency.** Being transparent in how one thinks, makes choices, and processes information helps others identify and share their own processes. This openness can extend to being transparent about biases as well.
    - **Integrity.** Integrity comprises ethical behavior and honesty. Individuals demonstrate honesty by sharing risks, communicating their assumptions and basis of estimates, delivering bad news early, and ensuring that status reports provide an accurate depiction of the project's progress. Ethical behavior can include spotlighting potential defects or negative effects in product design; disclosing potential conflicts of interest; ensuring fairness; and making decisions based on environmental, stakeholder, and financial impacts.
    - **Respect.** Demonstrating respect for each person, how they think, their skills, and the perspective and expertise they bring to the project team sets the stage for all project team members to adopt this behavior.
    - **Positive discourse.** Throughout the project, diverse opinions, different ways of approaching situations, and misunderstandings will occur. These are a normal part of conducting projects. These challenges present an opportunity to have a dialogue rather than a debate. A dialogue entails working with others to resolve divergent opinions. The goal is to arrive at a resolution that all parties can embrace. Conversely, a debate is a win-lose scenario where people are more interested in winning personally than they are in being open to alternative solutions to a problem.

- **Support.** Projects can be challenging from the perspectives of technical challenges, environmental influences, and interpersonal interactions. Supporting project team members through problem-solving and removing impediments builds a supportive culture and leads to a trusting and collaborative environment. Support can also be demonstrated by providing encouragement, showing empathy, and engaging in active listening.
- **Courage.** Recommending a new approach to a problem or a way of working can be intimidating. Likewise, it can be challenging to disagree with a subject matter expert or someone with greater authority. However, demonstrating the courage that it takes to suggest, disagree, or try something new enables a culture of experimentation and communicates to others that it is safe to be courageous and try new approaches.
- **Celebrate success.** Focusing on project goals, challenges, and issues often sidelines the fact that individual project team members and the project team are steadily progressing toward those goals. While work takes priority, project team members may neglect to recognize demonstrations of innovation, adaptation, service to others, and learning. Instantly recognizing and celebrating successes and "quick wins" may offer a sense of accomplishment, keep the team motivated, and highlight the continuous progress made toward project goals.

- **Industry context.** Due to the scarce nature of critical resources, in some industries several trends have become popular in the past few years. There is extensive literature about lean management, just-in-time manufacturing, Kaizen, total productive maintenance, theory of constraints, and other methods. A project manager should determine if the performing organization has adopted one or more resource-related methods, tools, and techniques and adapted them to the project accordingly.
- **Organizational governance structures.** Projects operate within a larger organizational system. There may be the expectation that the organizational leadership style of top management is recognized and reflected in the team's leadership. The organizational structure influences the degree to which authority and accountability are centralized or distributed. For further details, see Section 5 on Tools and Techniques, where centralized management and leadership and distributed management and leadership are explained.
- **Sustainability considerations in decision-making.** Projects should consider the environmental and social impact of every stage in the value chain, from hiring team members to sourcing materials, transportation, and disposal. This effort may involve reducing emissions, using renewable energy sources, minimizing waste, and positively affecting local communities. For further details, please refer to the Integrate Sustainability Within All Project Areas principle in *The Standard for Project Management* [1]. In addition, Section 5 provides further details on tools and techniques such as green human resource management.
- **Maturity of the project team members.** Project team members who are mature in their technical fields may need less oversight and direction than project team members who are new to the organization, team, or technical specialty.
- **Virtual project teams.** A global project workforce is more common today than in the past. Despite the best efforts to connect people virtually, it can be challenging to create the same level of collaboration and relatedness that is achieved when working face to face. To minimize the pitfalls of distributed project teams, technology should be used to increase and improve communication.

- **Emphasis on employee well-being.** Employee burnout has been a major concern in recent years. Quiet quitting is when employees continually put in the minimum amount of effort to keep their jobs but do not go the extra mile for their employer. This lack of engagement could mean a reluctance to speak up in meetings or not volunteering for tasks. Quiet quitting may also result in greater absenteeism. Companies are prioritizing mental health initiatives and creating a work culture that fosters a work-life balance. This effort may include flexible work schedules, stress management programs, and generous time-off policies.

2.6.3.1 Examples

The following are two examples of how these considerations might be applied:

- **Example 1.** A project team working on a large, high-variability project with an adaptive approach may find that resource planning for physical, virtual, or human resources is less predictable, requiring flexible agreements and lean methods to control costs and meet schedule demands.
- **Example 2.** A project with a newly formed virtual team may encounter collaboration issues. Thus, some suggestions that could be provided include:
  - Ensuring there are collaboration sites for working together;
  - Having a project team site to keep all relevant project and project team information available;
  - Using audio, video, and virtual conferencing capabilities for meetings;
  - Using technology to maintain ongoing contact, such as messaging and texting;
  - Scheduling time to get to know remote project team members;
  - Having at least one face-to-face meeting to establish relationships; and
  - Creating a team charter and defining ways of working.

2.6.4 Interactions With Other Domains

The Resources performance domain interacts with all other performance domains. The Stakeholders, Resources, and Risk performance domains significantly impact the project outcome, which is defined by schedule, cost, and scope parameters. Additionally, other projects may compete for the same available resources at the same time and location. This competition for resources may considerably impact project costs, schedules, risks, scope, quality, and other project areas.

The Estimate Resources process is closely coordinated with other processes, such as the Estimate Costs process, to help ensure a comprehensive approach to project planning and execution. This coordination is crucial as it helps to align the resource estimation with the project's overall budget and financial constraints. Doing so helps ensure that the project remains financially viable and that resources are utilized optimally without unnecessary expenditure.

Project managers are responsible for leading the team to work together to focus on what is essential at the project level. This coordination is achieved through the integration of processes, knowledge, and people. So, to integrate all of the performance domains and lead the project work, the project manager's main concern should be to lead the project team to achieve the project objectives.

Table 2-10. Check Outcomes—Resources Performance Domain

Outcome	Check
There is shared ownership of the project.	All project team members know the vision and objectives. The project team owns the deliverables and outcomes of the project.
A high-performing team is in place.	The project team trusts one another and collaborates. The project team adapts to changing situations and is resilient in the face of challenges. Team members feel empowered, and the project manager empowers and recognizes team members while successfully delivering project results.
There is effective resource utilization on the project.	The actual resource usage versus planned resource usage is effectively managed.
There is an acceptable resource-downtime percentage.	The total downtime versus total planned resource time is at an acceptable level.
The team is productive.	The units produced versus the hours worked, or the cost of work performed versus the scheduled time, is at an acceptable level and key performance indicators (KPIs) are regularly reviewed to check team performance.
There is efficient management of physical and/or virtual resources.	The number of materials used, scrap discarded, and amount of rework indicate that resources are being used efficiently.
Resource procurement management is conducted.	The procurement processes, efficiency checks, order, manufacture, and delivery tracking are all successfully managed.

2.6.5 Check Results

Activities related to the Resources performance domain should be considered successful only if they contribute to specific outcomes. Table 2-10 shows a set of sample target outcomes, along with a potential check to confirm whether those outcomes are met.

2.7 Risk Performance Domain

The Risk performance domain represents a comprehensive approach to creating project resilience by managing risk through risk management practices. The Risk performance domain emphasizes the project team's ability to anticipate, prepare for, respond to, and adapt to various risks and disruptions, helping ensure continuity and success under varying uncertainties. The Risk performance domain advocates for a proactive stance in planning for identified project risks and disruptions, coupled with adaptive and flexible response mechanisms in case they occur.

2.7.1 Key Concepts

The following key concepts support the effective practices for the Risk performance domain:

- **Risk.** A risk is an uncertain event or condition that, if it occurs, has a positive or negative effect on one or more portfolio, program, or project objectives. Identified risks may or may not materialize in a portfolio, program, or project. Potentially harmful risks, often called threats, may negatively impact one or more project objectives through project delays, cost overruns, or reputation damage. Positive risks, better known as opportunities, may positively affect one or more project objectives, including a potential increase in market share, cost savings, or a positive environmental impact. A risk may be described in a "cause, event, and consequence" structure (see the risk register in Section 4 on Inputs and Outputs). Risks can also be classified into unknown-known, unknown-unknown, known-known, and known-unknown (see Figure 2-46).

- **Issue.** An issue is a current condition or situation that may have an impact on one or more project objectives. An issue has already occurred and may require immediate action or management attention. Reviewing the project issue log and risk register can identify challenges associated with individual stakeholders. Risks and issues may be closely related as an issue may arise from a poorly managed risk. However, issues also differ from risks as issues have already occurred or are still occurring, whereas risks are potential future problems that have not yet occurred.
- **Overall risk.** Overall risk is the effect of uncertainty on the portfolio, program, or project as a whole. Overall risk may arise from everything that is uncertain or unknown in the project, including individual risks. Responses to overall project risk are the same as for individual threats and opportunities, though responses are applied to the overall project rather than to a specific event. If the overall risk to the project is too high, the organization may choose to cancel the project.

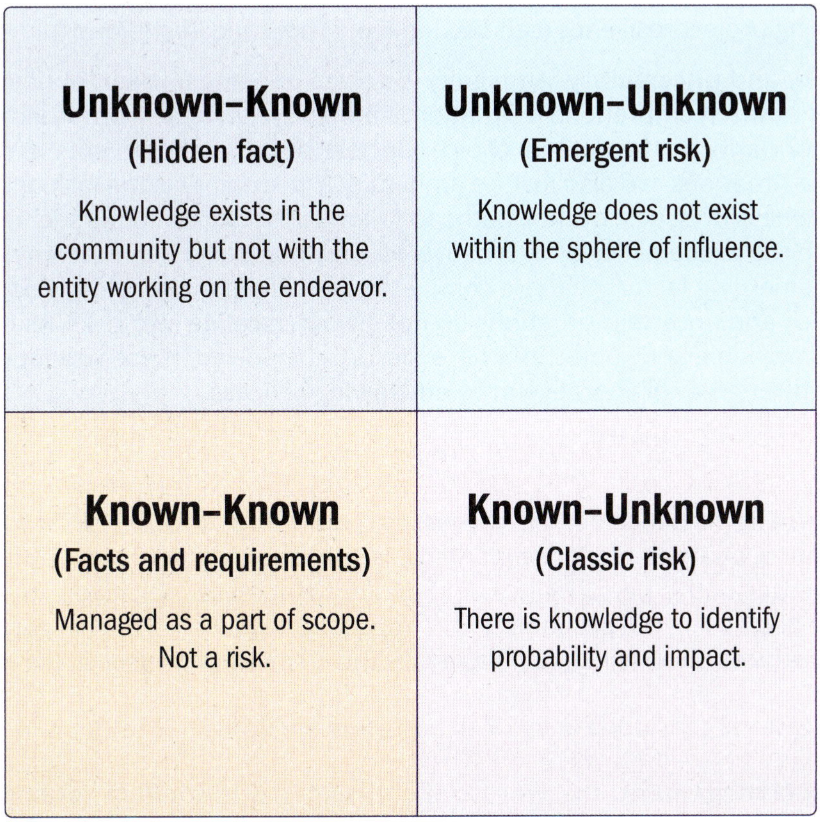

Figure 2-46. Risk Classification

- **Risk appetite.** Risk appetite is the degree of uncertainty an organization or individual is willing to accept in anticipation of a reward. Risk appetite is often quantified through a risk threshold.
- **Risk threshold.** The risk threshold is the measure of acceptable variation around an objective that reflects the risk appetite of the organization and stakeholders (internal and external) (e.g., a risk threshold of ±5% around a cost objective reflects a lower risk appetite than a risk threshold of ±10%).
- **Risk exposure.** Risk exposure is an aggregate measure of the potential impact of all risks at any given point in time in a portfolio, program, or project.
- **Risk response.** A risk response is an action, planned or implemented, to address particular threats and opportunities. Adequate and appropriate risk responses can minimize individual and overall project threats and maximize individual and overall opportunities. Types of risk response strategies include opportunity and threat acceptance or escalation, opportunity enhancement, opportunity exploiting, opportunity sharing, threat mitigation, threat avoidance, and threat transference.
- **Project resilience.** Resiliency consists of the ability to absorb impacts and recover quickly from setbacks or failures. Projects are not immune to unexpected disruptions, effects of high-impact and low-probability events (black swan events), or emergent risks, which are essentially unknowable within the context of portfolio, program, and project management (unknown-unknowns). Incorporating resilience into project management is essential to equip projects with the ability to anticipate, respond to, and recover from unexpected disruptions. Embedding resilience ensures projects are robust enough to maintain continuity and minimize the impact of adverse events. Reserve analysis is often related to establishing project resilience (see Section 5 on Tools and Techniques).
- **Ambiguity and uncertainty.** Ambiguity is a state of being unclear, of not knowing what to expect or how to comprehend a situation. Ambiguity can arise from having many options or a lack of clarity on the optimal choice. Unclear or misleading events, emerging issues, or subjective situations can also lead to ambiguity. Uncertainty is the lack of understanding and awareness of issues, events, paths to follow, or solutions to pursue. Uncertainty deals with the probabilities of alternative actions, reactions, and outcomes. Uncertainty includes emerging factors that are completely outside of existing knowledge or experience. Ambiguous and uncertain situations do not always escalate into risks. As more information becomes available and subject matter experts get involved, these situations can often be resolved through a collaborative problem-solving process.

2.7.2 Processes

The Risk performance domain includes the processes required to conduct risk management planning, identification, analysis, response planning, response implementation, and risk reviews on a project. The objectives of this performance domain are to increase the probability and impact of positive risks while decreasing the probability and impact of negative risks. This approach accelerates project resilience, reduces uncertainty, and increases the chances of project success.

The following processes are included in the Risk performance domain (see Figure 2-47):

- **Plan Risk Management.** The process of outlining how to conduct risk activities early in the project, starting at project conception.

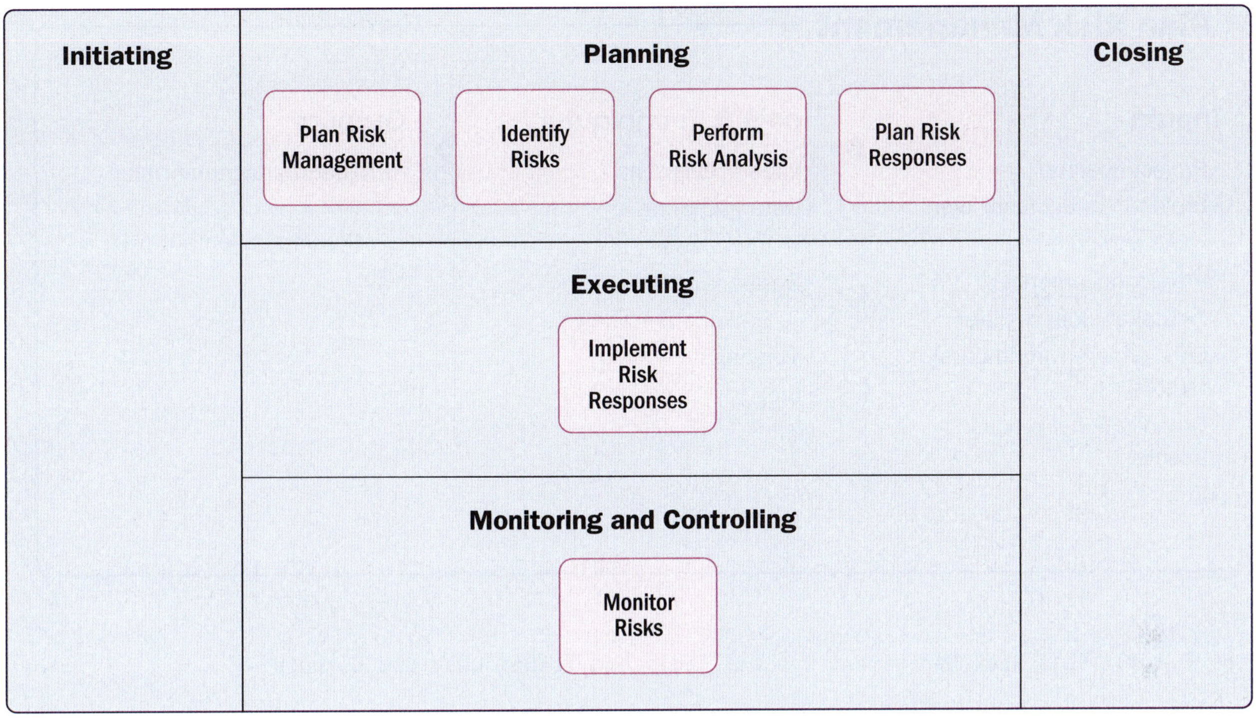

Figure 2-47. Risk Performance Domain Processes Overview

- **Identify Risks.** The process of identifying project threats and opportunities. An important part of the Identify Risks process is separating real risks from concerns, knowing initial identification is incomplete. Iterative identification adapts to new information as the project progresses.
- **Perform Risk Analysis.** The process of analyzing risks using an iterative approach that may combine qualitative and quantitative risk analyses. Qualitative analysis evaluates risks based on their probability and impact throughout the project. Quantitative analysis, when required, assesses the combined effect of risks and uncertainties on project objectives.
- **Plan Risk Responses.** The process of developing suitable and effective responses to manage overall project and individual risks, which is performed throughout the project.
- **Implement Risk Responses.** The process of executing risk plans to address project risks, minimize threats, and maximize opportunities.
- **Monitor Risks.** The process of tracking and analyzing risks, implementing response plans, and evaluating their effectiveness throughout the project, ensuring continuity and effective risk management.

2.7.2.1 Plan Risk Management

Plan Risk Management defines how to conduct risk management activities for a project. The process should begin when a project is conceived and should be completed early in the project. Risk management activities and tools are a key element of this process (see Figure 2-48).

Plan Risk Management

Inputs

- Project charter
- Project management plan
  - All components
- Project documents
  - Stakeholder register
- Enterprise environmental factors
- Organizational process assets
- Etc.

Tools & Techniques

- Expert judgment
- Data gathering
  - Interviews
- Data analysis
  - Stakeholder analysis
- Meetings
- Etc.

Outputs

- Project management plan updates
  - Risk management plan
- Etc.

Figure 2-48. Plan Risk Management Inputs, Tools and Techniques, and Outputs

2.7.2.2 Identify Risks

Identify Risks includes recognizing both negative and positive risks. The process of risk identification focuses on distinguishing genuine risks from nonrisks, such as concerns and issues. It is important to recognize that not all risks can be identified at the outset due to the inherent uncertainties and unknowns present at the beginning of a project. Therefore, risk identification should be an iterative process, allowing for continuous identification and assessment of risks as more information becomes available and the project evolves. This iterative approach helps ensure that the risk management process remains dynamic and responsive, addressing emerging risks effectively and to a practical extent throughout the project life cycle (see Figure 2-49).

2.7.2.3 Perform Risk Analysis

Perform Risk Analysis involves an iterative process that combines both qualitative and quantitative risk analysis actions. Qualitative risk analysis is conducted throughout the project to evaluate individual project risks by assessing their probability of occurrence and impact. Other characteristics of assessment may include the degree of impact on the objectives, manageability, timing of possible impacts, relationships with other risks, and common causes or effects. Quantitative risk analysis, depending on the project, may not always be required, but when it is, it is also conducted throughout the project. This process includes numerically analyzing the combined effect of identified individual project risks and other sources of uncertainty on overall project objectives (see Figure 2-50).

2.7.2.4 Plan Risk Responses

Plan Risk Responses is the process of developing options, selecting strategies, and agreeing on actions to address overall project risk exposure, as well as to treat individual project risks. The key benefit of this process is that it identifies suitable ways to address overall project risk and individual

Identify Risks

Inputs	Tools & Techniques	Outputs
• Project management plan – Requirements management plan – Schedule management plan – Financial management plan – Quality management plan – Resource management plan – Risk management plan – Scope baseline – Schedule baseline – Cost baseline • Project documents – Assumption log – Cost estimates – Duration estimates – Issue log – Lessons learned register – Requirements documentation – Resource requirements – Stakeholder register • Agreements • Enterprise environmental factors • Organizational process assets • Etc.	• Expert judgment • Data gathering – Brainstorming – Checklists – Interviews • Data analysis – Root cause analysis – Assumption and constraint analysis – SWOT analysis – Document analysis • Interpersonal and team skills – Facilitation • Prompt lists • Meetings • Artificial intelligence • Etc.	• Risk register • Risk report • Project document updates – Assumption log – Issue log – Lessons learned register • Etc.

Figure 2-49. Identify Risks Inputs, Tools and Techniques, and Outputs

project risks. This process also allocates resources or includes reserves (see the Finance performance domain in Section 2.4) and inserts activities into project documents and the project management plan as needed. The risk responses for threats and opportunities are listed in Section 5 on Tools and Techniques (see contingent response strategies, strategies for managing threats, strategies for managing opportunities, and strategies for managing overall project risk). This process should be performed throughout the project (see Figure 2-51).

Perform Risk Analysis

Inputs

- Project management plan
  - Risk management plan
  - Scope baseline
  - Schedule baseline
  - Cost baseline
- Project documents
  - Assumption log
  - Cost estimates
  - Duration estimates
  - Resource requirements
  - Risk register
  - Stakeholder register
- Enterprise environmental factors
- Organizational process assets
- Etc.

Tools & Techniques

- Expert judgment
- Data gathering and analysis
  - Interviews
- Interpersonal and team skills
  - Facilitation
- Risk categorization
- Data analysis
  - Risk probability and impact assessment
  - Simulations
  - Sensitivity analysis
  - Decision tree analysis
  - Influence diagrams
- Data representation
  - Probability and impact matrix
- Etc.

Outputs

- Project document updates
  - Assumption log
  - Issue log
  - Risk register
  - Risk report
- Etc.

Figure 2-50. Perform Risk Analysis Inputs, Tools and Techniques, and Outputs

2.7.2.5 Implement Risk Responses

Implement Risk Responses is the process of implementing sufficient risk response plans. The key benefit of this process is that it ensures that agreed-upon risk responses are executed as planned to address overall project risk exposure, minimize individual project threats, and maximize individual project opportunities (see Figure 2-52).

2.7.2.6 Monitor Risks

Monitor Risks is the process of monitoring the implementation of risk response plans, tracking identified risks, identifying and analyzing new risks, planning responses for new risks, and evaluating the effectiveness of risk responses and processes throughout the project. This process helps ensure that risk owners are assigned to maintain continuity and address emerging risks effectively (see Figure 2-53).

2.7.3 Tailoring Considerations

Because each project is unique, activities and processes in the Risk performance domain should be tailored. Considerations for tailoring may include the following:

- **Project size and complexity.** Determine if the project's size or complexity necessitates a more detailed risk management approach or if a simplified process suffices. Constraints

Plan Risk Responses

Inputs	Tools & Techniques	Outputs
• Project management plan – Resource management plan – Risk management plan – Cost baseline • Project documents – Lessons learned register – Project schedule – Project team assignments – Resource calendars – Risk register – Risk report – Stakeholder register • Enterprise environmental factors • Organizational process assets • Etc.	• Expert judgment • Data gathering – Interviews • Interpersonal and team skills – Facilitation • Strategies for threats • Strategies for opportunities • Contingent response strategies • Strategies for overall project risk • Data analysis – Alternative analysis – Cost-benefit analysis • Decision-making – Multicriteria decision analysis • Etc.	• Change requests • Project management plan updates – Schedule management plan – Financial management plan – Quality management plan – Resource management plan – Procurement management plan – Scope baseline – Schedule baseline – Cost baseline • Project document updates – Assumption log – Cost forecasts – Lessons learned register – Project schedule – Project team assignments – Risk register – Risk report • Etc.

Figure 2-51. Plan Risk Responses Inputs, Tools and Techniques, and Outputs

such as urgency and industry or government regulations may impact the way risks are managed in the project.

- **Risk appetite and threshold.** Assess how the organization's risk appetite and threshold guide or limit risk responses, considering historical experiences and risk-aversion levels.
- **Holistic view to project risk management.** Ensure that risk impact and responses are viewed across various project domains like schedule, budget, scope, and stakeholders.
- **Strategic importance.** Evaluate the project's strategic importance and its associated risk level due to breakthrough opportunities, performance blocks, or major innovations.
- **Development approach.** Identify if the project follows a predictive, adaptive, or hybrid approach to appropriately tailor the risk processes.
- **Planning and implementing risk responses with flexibility.** Manage risk responses by allowing for timely adjustments to risk strategies without compromising project goals and maintain open communication with relevant stakeholders.

Implement Risk Responses

Inputs

- Project management plan
  - Risk management plan
- Project documents
  - Lessons learned register
  - Risk register
  - Risk report
- Organizational process assets
- Etc.

Tools & Techniques

- Expert judgment
- Interpersonal and team skills
  - Influencing
- Project management information system
- Etc.

Outputs

- Change requests
- Project document updates
  - Issue log
  - Lessons learned register
  - Project team assignments
  - Risk register
  - Risk report
- Etc.

Figure 2-52. Implement Risk Responses Inputs, Tools and Techniques, and Outputs

Monitor Risks

Inputs

- Project management plan
  - Risk management plan
- Project documents
  - Issue log
  - Lessons learned register
  - Risk register
  - Risk report
- Work performance data
- Work performance reports
- Etc.

Tools & Techniques

- Data analysis
  - Technical performance analysis
  - Reserve analysis
- Audits
- Meetings
- Etc.

Outputs

- Work performance information
- Change requests
- Project management plan updates
  - Any component
- Project document updates
  - Assumption log
  - Issue log
  - Lessons learned register
  - Risk register
  - Risk report
- Organizational process asset updates
- Etc.

Figure 2-53. Monitor Risks Inputs, Tools and Techniques, and Outputs

- **Exploring complementary techniques in risk identification and analysis.** Utilize advanced techniques like generative artificial intelligence (GenAI) and data analytics for comprehensive risk identification and analysis.
- **Necessity for resilience planning.** Prepare for major disruptions with scenario planning and ensure alignment with the organization's business continuity or emergency response plan.

2.7.3.1 Examples

The following are two examples of how these considerations might be applied:

- **Example 1.** A renewable energy project team may focus on large-scale solar power plant construction to meet a company's sustainability objectives. The risk management process should be tailored to include specific actions to significantly advance the organization's green energy initiatives and market position. This customization involves regular meetings with key stakeholders to address their concerns and collect feedback. Additionally, conducting regular risk assessments allows for timely identification of potential threats and opportunities and the formulation of suitable risk responses. Appointing dedicated risk managers who utilize advanced simulation models aids in forecasting and mitigating potential risks.
- **Example 2.** A project with an agile life cycle may involve developing a new software application to meet rapidly changing market demands. Thus, to tailor risk management for this development approach, the project team conducts risk assessments at the beginning of each sprint instead of only during the initial planning phase. This adjustment allows the team to quickly identify and address emerging risks, ensuring flexibility and responsiveness. Additionally, regular risk review meetings are held with stakeholders at the end of each iteration to incorporate their feedback and adjust risk strategies accordingly. The frequent, iterative risk management process and risk-adjusted backlogs help maintain alignment with the project's dynamic requirements and stakeholder expectations.

2.7.4 Interactions With Other Domains

The Risk performance domain is closely interrelated with the Scope, Schedule, Finance, and Stakeholders performance domains.

Stakeholders are critical sources of information regarding risks and uncertainty. They provide insights about potential risks, suggest risk assessment methods, and assist in managing uncertainties. Effective stakeholder engagement and communication can help ensure that risk management processes align with stakeholder expectations and can assist with proactively addressing concerns.

The Scope, Schedule, and Finance performance domains are also crucial areas of interaction. In predictive projects with stable scopes, schedule reserves help manage identified risks and maintain timelines. In adaptive projects with evolving requirements, the team should adjust plans to address new risks and uncertainties. Risks can impact the project scope, either increasing or decreasing it, which in turn affects the schedule and budget. Additionally, the Finance performance domain is directly influenced by risk management, with internal projects experiencing increased or decreased costs, and external projects facing potential revenue generation or loss. Effective risk management requires integrating scope management, schedule planning, financial considerations, stakeholder engagement, and communication to help ensure tailored and comprehensive risk response strategies.

2.7.5 Check Results

Activities in the Risk performance domain are considered successful when they contribute to specific outcomes. Table 2-11 shows a set of sample target outcomes, along with a potential check to confirm whether those outcomes are met.

Table 2-11. Check Outcomes—Risk Performance Domain

Outcome	Check
There is an awareness of the environment in which projects occur, including technical, social, political, market, and economic contexts.	The team incorporates environmental considerations when evaluating uncertainty, risks, and responses.
The project team proactively explores and responds to uncertainty.	Risk responses are aligned with project constraints such as budget, schedule, and performance.
The project team has the capacity to anticipate threats and opportunities and understands the consequences of issues.	A process is in place, and well understood by the project team, for identifying, assessing, documenting, and responding to risks.
Project delivery is achieved with minimal negative impact from unknown events or conditions.	Reserves are in place and utilized, scheduled delivery dates are met, and the budget performance is within the variance threshold.
Opportunities to improve project performance and outcomes are realized.	Project teams use established mechanisms to identify, leverage, and track the realization of opportunities.
Project contingency reserves are used effectively to maintain alignment with project objectives.	Project teams take steps to proactively prevent threats, thereby limiting the use of project contingency reserves.
Resilience and the ability to recover quickly from setbacks are being developed throughout the project.	The project team is aware of the larger organization's business continuity plan or emergency response plan. Where applicable, a project continuity plan is developed. A management reserve is available to cover unknown risks. During times of crisis, the project team can quickly adjust its structure and processes to adapt to new constraints.

Section 3

Tailoring

Tailoring is the deliberate adaptation of the project management approach, governance, and processes to align with the project's environment and objectives. Tailoring considers the development approach, processes, project life cycle, deliverables, and the approach to stakeholder and team involvement, ensuring alignment with project objectives and constraints.

3.1 Overview

The tailoring process is driven by the guiding project management principles in *The Standard for Project Management* [1]. For instance, organizations with a low risk appetite often implement structured processes and oversight mechanisms to minimize uncertainty. In contrast, organizations with higher risk tolerance may prioritize agility and decision-making autonomy, adjusting process rigor based on project needs rather than applying a fixed number of procedures. Tailoring entails the mindful selection and adjustment of multiple project factors to determine which elements are most useful given the project context, goals, operating environment, scale, and complexity in order to better align with and achieve the project outcomes.

Projects operate in unique contexts that should consider and balance potentially competing demands, including but not limited to the following:

- Delivering as quickly as possible,
- Minimizing project costs,
- Optimizing the value delivered,

- Creating high-quality deliverables and outcomes,
- Ensuring compliance with regulatory standards and sustainability considerations,
- Satisfying diverse stakeholder expectations, and
- Adapting to change.

These factors should be understood, evaluated, and balanced to create a practical operating environment for the project. There may be situations that limit the degree to which project teams can tailor their approach (e.g., when organizational policies mandate the use of a specific approach or when a contract specifies a mandated approach).

3.2 Why Tailor?

The structure used to deliver projects can be extensive or minimal, rigorous or lightweight, and comprehensive or streamlined. In short, there is no single approach that can be applied to all projects all of the time. Tailoring is performed to better suit the organization, operating environment, and project needs. Many variables factor into this process, including the criticality of the project, scale, duration, complexity, industry standards, organizational culture, number of stakeholders involved, and level of organizational project management maturity. For example, the rigor, checks and balances, and reporting requirements for a critical nuclear reactor project are much greater than those for building a new office building. Similarly, the communication and coordination needs for a 10-member project team are far less extensive than for a project team of 200 people.

Too few processes can lead to ineffective project management, while employing more processes than required is costly and wasteful. Thus, tailoring leads to optimum and effective project management that can deliver direct and indirect value to organizations, including the following benefits:

- More commitment from the project team members who helped to tailor the approach;
- Customer-oriented focus enhancements, as the needs of the customer are an important influencing factor in its development; and
- More efficient use of project resources.

3.3 What to Tailor

This section discusses three project aspects that can be tailored:

- Life cycle and development approach selection,
- Processes, and
- Engagement.

Sections 3.3.1 through 3.3.3 explore each of these in more detail.

3.3.1 Life Cycle and Development Approach Selection

Deciding on a life cycle and its phases is an example of tailoring; additional tailoring can be done while selecting the development approach for the project. For instance, building a new data center could involve (a) the use of predictive approaches for the physical building construction and finishing and (b) an adaptive approach for understanding and establishing the computing capabilities required. Viewed from a project level, this combination of approaches represents a hybrid approach, but the construction team and the computing team may only experience a predictive or adaptive development approach.

3.3.2 Processes

Process tailoring involves determining which elements should be either:

- **Added**, to address unique conditions or increase rigor;
- **Modified**, to better fit project or team needs, including adjusting inputs, outputs, and tools and techniques;
- **Removed**, to reduce unnecessary cost or effort;
- **Blended**, to combine elements for added value; or
- **Aligned**, to ensure consistency in definition and application.

3.3.3 Engagement

Tailoring engagement for the people involved in the project includes the following:

- **People.** This effort involves assessing the skills and capabilities of the project leadership and team, ensuring they adapt to evolving project needs.
- **Empowerment.** Empowerment involves choosing which responsibilities and forms of local decision-making should be deferred to the project team. The project environment and team member capabilities can lead to high levels of empowerment, while in other cases more supervision and directions may be required.
- **Integration.** Tailoring considers how to create one project team from a diverse collection of contributors (contracted entities, channel partners, and other external entities, in addition to staff from inside the sponsoring organization) to facilitate optimal project team performance and the realization of project outcomes.

3.4 The Tailoring Process

Projects exist in environments that hugely influence how projects are executed and their resulting outcomes. Prior to tailoring, the project environment should be thoroughly analyzed and understood. Tailoring begins by selecting a development approach (e.g., predictive, adaptive, or hybrid), tailoring it for the organization and project, and finally, implementing its ongoing improvement. These steps are shown in Figure 3-1 and described in detail in Sections 3.4.1 through 3.4.4.

3.4.1 Select Initial Development Approach

This step determines the development approach that will be used for the project. Project teams apply their knowledge of the product, delivery cadence, and awareness of the available options to select the most appropriate development approach for the situation.

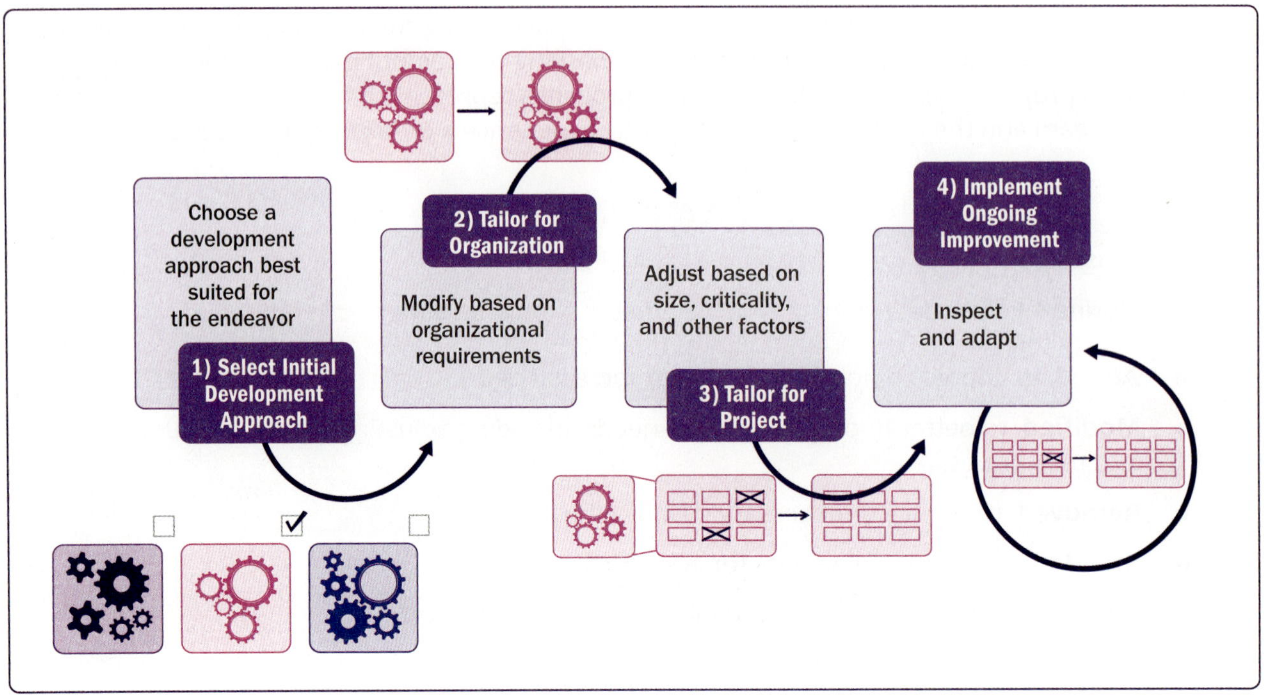

Figure 3-1. Details of the Steps in the Tailoring Process

Tailoring project management approaches requires thoughtful consideration of contextual factors to ensure that the chosen methodology aligns with project needs and organizational goals. One useful concept in this regard is the suitability filter. A suitability filter is not a rigid method or procedure, but rather a decision-making tool that helps project teams evaluate their unique circumstances. A suitability filter assists project teams with analyzing the project's characteristics and determining the best fit among predictive, adaptive, or hybrid approaches. The suitability filter combines its assessment with other data and decision-making activities, so the appropriate tailored approach is decided for each project. By evaluating criteria based on culture, project team dynamics, and project factors, a suitability filter assists discussion and decision on the initial approach.

3.4.2 Tailor for the Organization

Project teams own and improve their processes, but organizations can provide methodologies and development approaches as starting points for projects requiring oversight. These guides can help support repeatable processes, consistent capability measurement, and continuous improvement. Organizations that have established process governance should ensure tailoring is aligned to policy. Tailoring for the organization involves adding, removing, and reconfiguring elements of the approach to make it more suitable for the individual organization. This process is shown in Figure 3-2.

Tailoring within an organization should also consider the context of the program and/or portfolio within which the project operates. Aligning tailoring decisions across related projects can enhance consistency and efficiency, promoting a cohesive approach within the organizational structure.

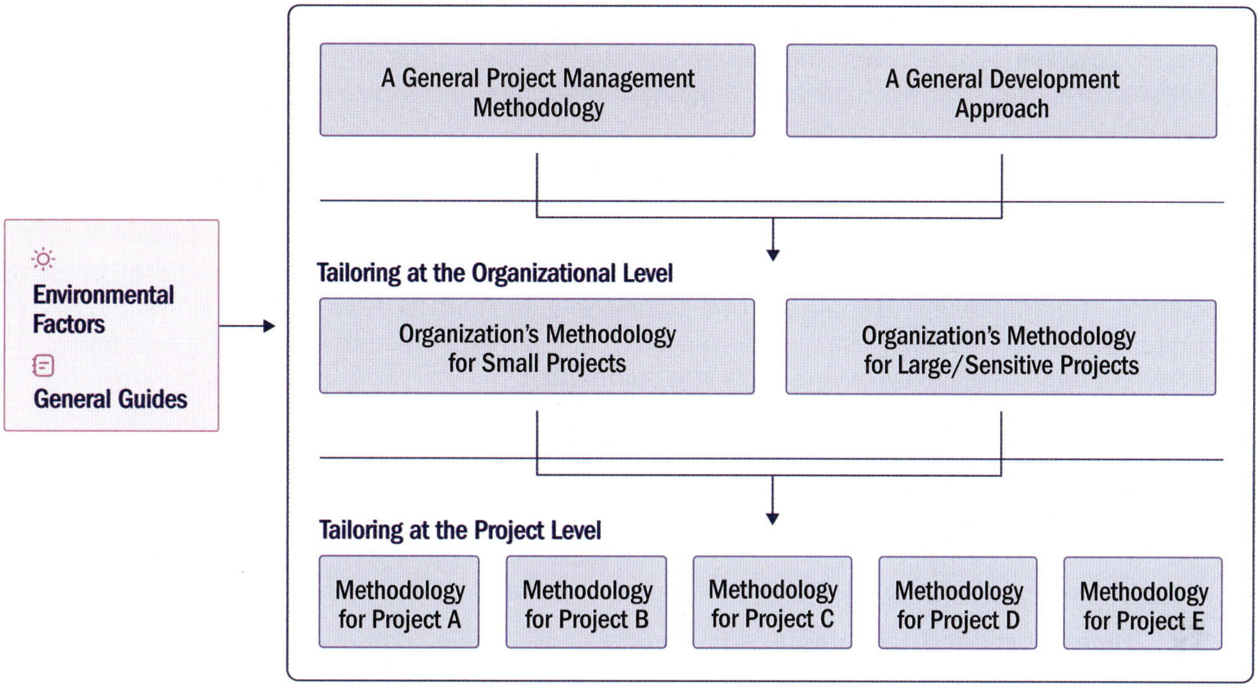

Figure 3-2. Assessing the Organizational and Project Factors When Tailoring

A project management office (PMO), in organizations that have one, can play a vital role in reviewing and approving tailored development approaches, which is well aligned to organizational policy. Tailoring that impacts the project team requires less oversight than tailoring impacting external groups, so project manager approval is usually enough for internal project tailoring. Tailoring that affects external groups may require the approval of PMOs, which may also assist project teams as they tailor their approaches by providing ideas and solutions from other projects.

Project management offices continue to evolve in form, function, and naming, reflecting the unique needs and delivery approaches of each organization. Regardless of structure, what remains consistent is the PMO's alignment to business priorities. The mission of a PMO is often centered on solving critical organizational challenges such as enabling value delivery, ensuring compliance, improving cost control, or enhancing delivery consistency.

Modern PMOs are increasingly expected to go beyond operational support, acting as enablers of strategy execution and contributors to enterprise-wide outcomes. Their ability to adapt services based on what the organization values most—and to evolve in response to changing priorities—determines their long-term relevance and impact. See Appendix X2 on PMOs for more details.

Projects sometimes require the collaboration of multiple organizations, with each bringing its own processes, governance structures, and delivery approaches. In such cases, it is important that tailoring is done using a multiorganization approach to help ensure alignment and cohesion.

Tailoring in multiorganization projects requires careful consideration of how different organizational processes, governance structures, and delivery approaches align. Integration planning should ensure that tailored practices from each participating organization are harmonized to achieve cohesive project outcomes.

3.4.3 Tailor for the Project

The key attributes that influence tailoring for the project are the product or deliverable, project team, and culture. The project team should ask questions about each attribute to help guide them in the tailoring process. Answers to these questions can help identify the need to tailor the processes, development approach, life cycle, and tools and techniques.

3.4.3.1 Product or Deliverable

Key attributes associated with the product or deliverable include the following:

- **Standards compliance.** How much process rigor and quality assurance are appropriate?
- **Type of product/deliverable.** Is the product well known and easy to recognize, like a building, or something intangible like software or the design of a new drug or vaccine?
- **Industry market.** What market does the project, product, or deliverable serve? Is that market highly regulated, fast moving, or slow to evolve? What about competitors and incumbents?
- **Technology.** Is the technology stable and well established or rapidly evolving and at risk of obsolescence?
- **Timeframe.** Is the project timeframe short, in weeks or months, or does it span several years?
- **Stability of requirements.** How likely are there to be changes to core requirements?
- **Security.** Are elements of the product business confidential or classified?
- **Incremental and iterative delivery.** Is this something the project team can develop and get stakeholder feedback on incrementally and iteratively, refining the product through repeated cycles, or is it hard to evaluate until it is near completion?

3.4.3.2 Project Team

Project team considerations include the following:

- **Project team size.** How many full-time and/or part-time people will be working on the project?
- **Project team geography.** Where are the team members predominantly located geographically? Will some or all of the team be remote or colocated?
- **Organizational distribution.** Where are the supporting groups and stakeholders located?

- **Project team experience.** Do the project team members have any experience in the industry, organization, or working with one another? Do they have the skills, tools, and technology required for the project under consideration?
- **Access to customer.** Is it practical to get frequent and timely feedback from customers or customer representatives?
- **Team diversity.** Are there diverse skills, experiences, and perspectives within the team that can enhance problem-solving and innovation?

3.4.3.3 Culture

Evaluating the culture includes the following considerations:

- **Buy-in.** Is there acceptance, support, and enthusiasm for the proposed development approach?
- **Trust.** Are there high levels of trust that the project team is capable of—and committed to—delivering the project outcomes?
- **Empowerment.** Is the project team trusted, supported, and encouraged to own and develop its working environment, agreements, and decisions?
- **Organizational culture.** Do the organizational values and culture align with the project approach? This evaluation includes distinctions between empowering versus specifying and checking, and trusting local decision-making versus requesting external decision-making, etc.

Through the evaluation of these attributes, tailoring decisions around engagement, processes, and tools can be made for the project.

3.4.4 Implement Ongoing Improvement

The process of tailoring is not a single, one-time exercise. During progressive elaboration, issues with how the project team is working, how the product or deliverable is evolving, and other learnings can indicate where further tailoring could bring improvements. Review points, phase gates, and retrospectives all provide opportunities to inspect and adapt the process, development approach, and delivery frequency, as necessary.

Keeping the project team engaged with improving its process can foster pride of ownership and demonstrate a commitment to implementing ongoing improvements and quality. Empowering the project team to find and implement improvements also demonstrates trust in their skills and suggestions. Project team engagement with tailoring demonstrates a mindset of innovation and improvement rather than settling for the status quo.

The way an organization tailors itself can also be tailored. However, most organizations undertake some or all of the four steps described. Organizations can use elements of selecting an initial approach, tailoring for the organization, tailoring for the project, and implementing ongoing improvement, as shown in Figure 3-3.

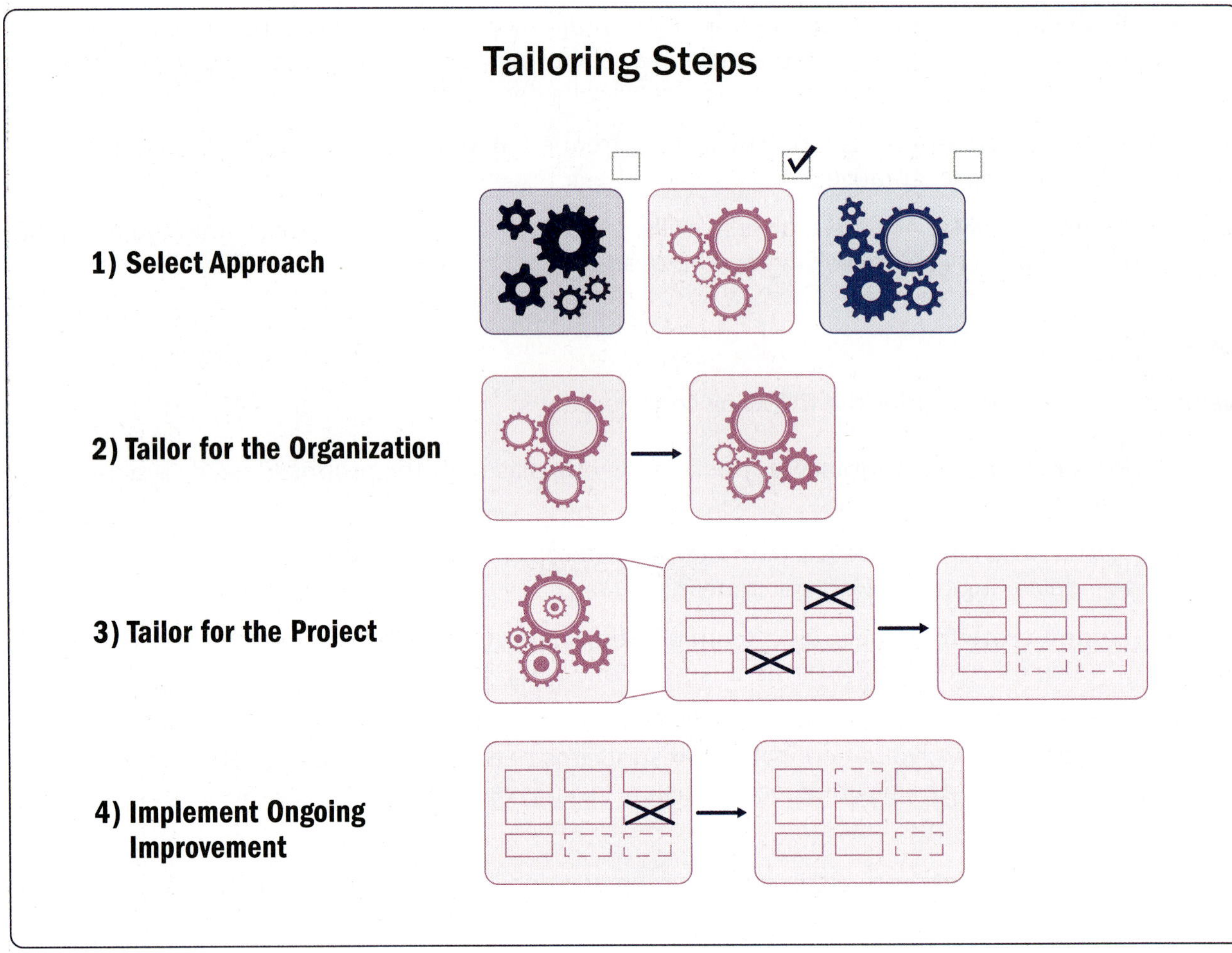

Figure 3-3. The Tailoring Process

3.5 Tailoring the Performance Domains

The work associated with each performance domain can also be tailored, based on the uniqueness of the project. As shown in Figure 3-4, the principles for project management provide guidance for the behavior of project practitioners as they tailor the performance domains to meet the unique needs of the project context and environment. Tailoring consideration examples for each project management performance domain are specifically covered in Section 2 on performance domains.

3.6 Diagnostics

Periodic reviews, such as retrospectives or lessons learned, help assess the effectiveness of current approaches and identify areas for improvement through tailoring. Teams that do not use retrospectives can rely on issues, threats, quality metrics, and stakeholder feedback to determine if further tailoring is needed. Table 3-1 provides common situations and tailoring suggestions.

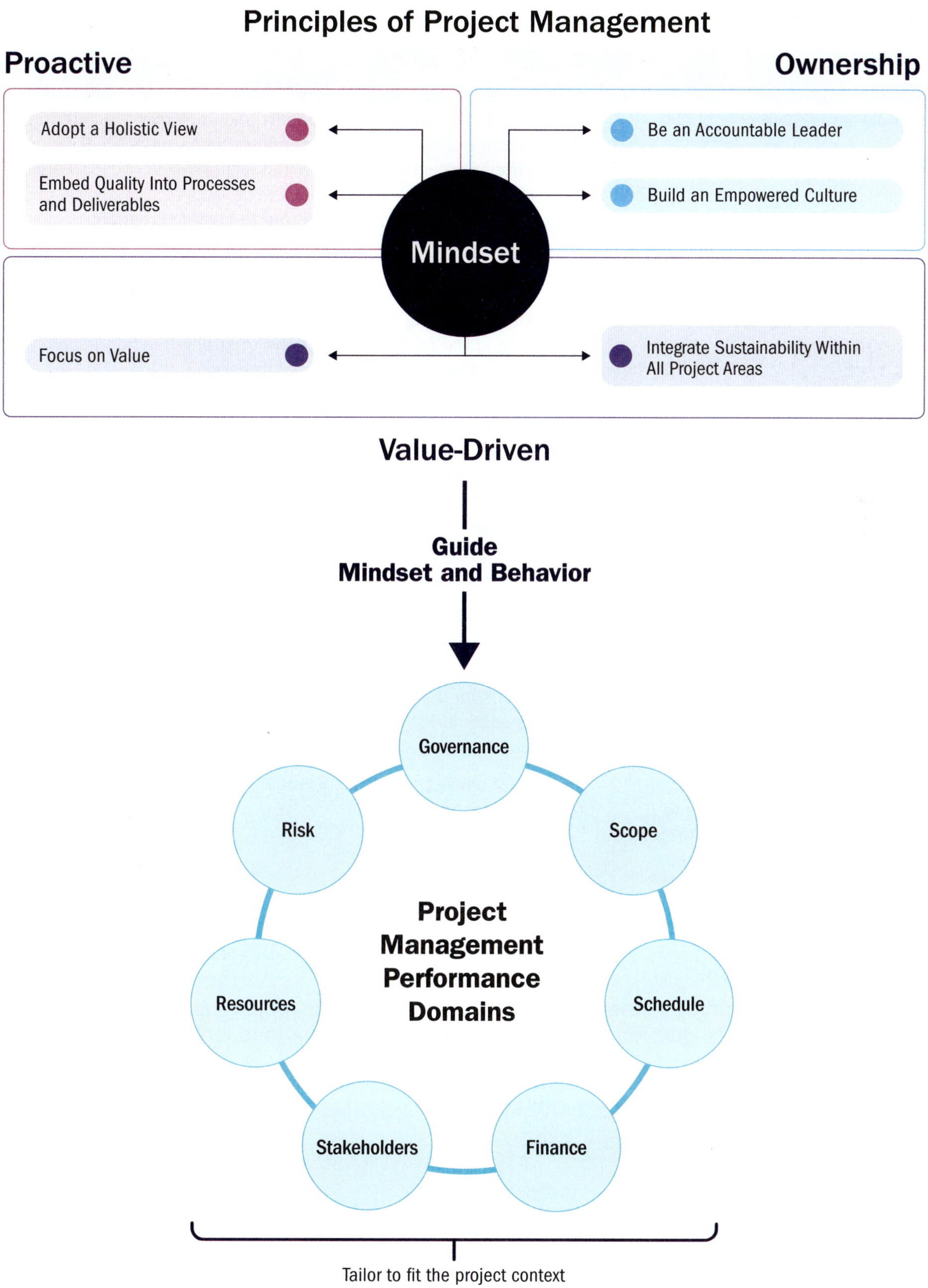

Figure 3-4. Tailoring to Fit the Project Context

Table 3-1. Common Situations and Tailoring Suggestions

Situation	Tailoring Suggestion
The deliverables are poor quality.	Analyze the root causes of poor quality and implement targeted feedback and quality assurance measures where needed. Focus on process improvements rather than just increasing verification steps.
Team members are unsure of how to proceed or undertake their work.	Assess the specific needs of the team to identify the most appropriate support mechanisms, including guidance, mentorship, training, and knowledge-sharing practices.
Team members are not cooperative and are working in silos.	Conduct team-building activities and hold individual meetings to understand the cause. Take actions to strengthen bonds and promote coordination among team members.
There are long delays waiting for approvals.	Streamline the approval process by appointing people who are authorized to make decisions up to certain value thresholds, shortening the time needed for approvals.
There is too much work in progress and/or waste.	Use techniques like value stream mapping and kanban boards to visualize work, identify issues, and find solutions.
Stakeholders are not engaged or they share negative feedback.	Assess whether stakeholders receive timely and relevant information, tailoring communication methods to balance simplicity with the need for deeper engagement.
There is a lack of transparency and understanding about project progress.	Check to ensure that appropriate data is collected, analyzed, shared, and discussed during team and stakeholder meetings. Validate agreement on the measures with the team and stakeholders.
Issues and/or risks for which the team is unprepared continue to surface, requiring the team to react rather than make progress on their work.	Explore root causes to identify whether there are related gaps in project processes or activities.

3.7 Summary

Tailoring adapts the approach, governance, and processes to fit the project's environment and objectives, which involves analyzing and modifying people, processes, and tools. The tailoring process includes four steps:

- Select the initial development approach,
- Tailor for the organization,
- Tailor for the project, and
- Improve continuously.

Tailoring is typically led by project stakeholders, with organizational guidelines and governance ensuring alignment and consistency across teams. Tailoring is not just about making changes, but also about verifying and validating that the tailored approaches are effective and aligned with project outcomes.

Section 4

Inputs and Outputs

All of the inputs and outputs in this section appear in alphabetical order; therefore, no section numbers are assigned.

Accepted deliverables. Accepted deliverables are the products, services, and capabilities that are created through a project and are validated by an appointed individual or a group of individuals against established criteria. When such criteria are met, the deliverables are approved and accepted.

The authorized stakeholder who approves the deliverables should get involved early on in the process and provide feedback regarding the quality of the deliverables so that the team can assess quality and performance and recommend any necessary changes.

Activity attributes. Activity attributes are multiple attributes associated with each schedule activity that can be included within the activity list. Activity attributes extend the description of the activity by identifying multiple components associated with each activity.

The components for each activity evolve over time. During the initial stages of the project, they include the unique activity identifier (ID), work breakdown structure (WBS) ID, deliverables ID, and activity label or name. When completed, they may include activity descriptions, predecessor activities, successor activities, logical relationships, leads and lags, resource requirements, imposed dates, constraints, and assumptions. Activity attributes can be used to identify the place where the work should be performed, the project calendar the activity is assigned to, and the type of effort involved. Activity attributes are used for schedule development and for selecting, ordering, and sorting the planned schedule activities in various ways within reports.

Activity list. An activity list is a documented tabulation of schedule activities that shows the activity description, activity identifier, and a sufficiently detailed scope of work description so project team members understand what work is to be performed.

Agreements. Agreements are any document or communication that defines the initial intentions of a project. These agreements can take the form of a contract, service-level agreement (SLA), memorandum of understanding (MOU), letters of agreement, verbal agreement, purchase order, email, etc.

Agreements can be simple or complex. A complex project may involve multiple contracts simultaneously or in sequence. Agreements should comply with local, national, and international laws regarding contracts.

Approved change requests. Approved change requests are change requests that were processed according to the change management plan by the project manager, change control board (CCB), or another designated person, and are either approved, deferred, or rejected.

Approved change requests are implemented via the Manage Project Execution process. Deferred or rejected change requests are communicated to the person or group requesting the change. The dispositions of all change requests are recorded in the change log as a project document update. See also *change requests*.

Approved changes. Approved changes are changes or modifications that are being implemented—or have been implemented—as part of the project scope. Approved changes result from change requests that have been fully approved through change control review meetings, either by the project manager or change control board (CCB).

Assumption log. An assumption log is a project document used to record all assumptions and constraints throughout the project. New assumptions and constraints may be added, and the status of existing assumptions and constraints may be updated or closed out.

High-level (strategic and operational) constraints are normally identified in the business case before the project is initiated and then flow into the project charter. Lower-level activity and task assumptions are generated throughout the project such as defining technical specifications, estimates, schedule activities, risks, etc. The assumption log is used to record all assumptions and constraints throughout the project life cycle.

Backlog. A backlog is an ordered list of work to be done, often written as user stories, and prioritized by the business to manage and organize an adaptive or agile project's work. The backlog reflects the current project needs, including the product requirements and user stories, and contains a reprioritized plan for the remaining work.

The types of backlogs commonly used in adaptive and agile projects include the following:

- **Product backlog.** Usually prepared by the product owner, the product backlog includes requirements, features, epic user stories, and user stories, representing the overall scope and vision of the product.
- **Iteration backlog.** An iteration backlog is a subset of the product backlog that contains selected user stories and the required tasks to complete the committed work during the current iteration.

- **Release backlog.** A release backlog is a subset of the product backlog that includes items planned for a specific release. The release backlog helps organize the work to be delivered at the end of a release cycle, which may encompass multiple sprints or iterations.

The project team determines the scope they can achieve based on the prioritized backlog, estimates the work involved, and works collaboratively throughout the iteration to develop the scope.

Basis of estimates. The basis of estimates is the supporting documentation that outlines the details used in establishing the project estimates such as assumptions, constraints, levels of detail, ranges, and confidence levels.

Regardless of the level of detail, the basis of estimates should provide a clear and complete understanding of how an estimate was derived. Documentation may include how the basis of estimate was developed, assumptions made, known constraints, range of possible estimates (e.g., ±10%), confidence level of the final estimate, and individual project risks influencing the estimate.

Benefits management plan. The benefits management plan is the documented explanation defining the processes for creating, maximizing, and sustaining the benefits provided by a program or project.

The benefits management plan is the document that describes how and when the benefits of the project will be delivered and the mechanisms that should be in place to measure those benefits. A project benefit is an outcome of actions, behaviors, products, services, or results that provides value to the sponsoring organization as well as to the project's intended beneficiaries. Development of the plan begins early in the project life cycle with the definition of the target benefits. The plan describes key elements of the benefits and may include the following:

- **Target benefits.** The expected tangible and intangible value to be gained by the implementation of the project; financial value may be expressed as net present value (NPV).
- **Strategic alignment.** The alignment of the project to the business strategies of the organization.
- **Timeframe for realizing benefits.** The length of time to realize benefits, for example, short term, long term, ongoing, or by phase.
- **Benefits owner.** The person accountable for monitoring, recording, and reporting realized benefits throughout the timeframe established in the plan.
- **Metrics.** The direct and indirect measures used to determine the benefits realized.
- **Assumptions.** The factors expected to be in place or to be in evidence.
- **Risks.** The risks that pertain to the realization of benefits.

The data and information that are documented in the business case and needs assessment are used to develop the benefits management plan. The benefits management plan and the project management plan include a description of how the business value resulting from the project becomes part of the organization's ongoing operations, including the metrics to be used. The metrics provide verification of the business value and validation of the project's success.

Development and maintenance of the benefits management plan is an iterative activity. The benefits management plan complements the business case, project charter, and project management plan. The project manager works with the sponsor to ensure that the project charter, project management plan, and benefits management plan remain in alignment throughout the life cycle of the project.

Both the business case and the benefits management plan are developed prior to the project being initiated. Additionally, both documents are referenced after the project has been completed. Therefore, they are considered business documents rather than project documents or components of the project management plan. As appropriate, these business documents may be inputs to some of the processes involved in managing the project, such as developing the project charter.

Business case. A business case is a documented economic feasibility study used to establish validity of the benefits to be delivered by a portfolio component, program, or project. The business case helps to define a selected component that is lacking sufficient explanation and that is used as a basis for the authorization of further project management activities.

The business case lists the objectives and reasons for project initiation. The business case helps to measure project success at the end of the project against the project objectives. The business case is a project business document that is used throughout the project life cycle. The business case may be used before project initiation and may result in a go/no-go decision for the project.

Both the business case and the benefits management plan are developed prior to the project being initiated. Additionally, both documents are referenced after the project has been completed. Therefore, they are considered business documents rather than project documents or components of the project management plan. As appropriate, these business documents may be inputs to some of the processes involved in managing the project, such as developing the project charter.

Business documents. Business documents include the business case and the benefits management plan; they contain information about the project's objectives and how the project will contribute to the business goals. Although both documents are developed prior to the project, they are reviewed periodically.

In some organizations, the business case and benefits management plan are maintained at the program level. The project sponsor is generally accountable for the development and maintenance of the project's business case document. The project manager is responsible for providing recommendations and oversight to keep success measures for the project's business case, project management plan, project charter, and benefits management plan in alignment with one another and with the goals and objectives of the organization.

Change log. A change log is a comprehensive list of changes submitted during the project, which includes the current status of the submitted changes. The disposition of all change requests is recorded in the change log as a project document update.

Change management plan. A change management plan is a component of the project management plan that establishes the change control board (CCB), also known as a steering committee; documents the extent of its authority; and describes how the change control system will be implemented.

The change management plan provides the direction for managing the change control process and documents the roles and responsibilities of the CCB.

Change requests. A change request is a formal proposal to modify a document, deliverable, or baseline. Change requests may be initiated internally or externally to the project.

When issues are found while project work is being performed, change requests are submitted to modify project policies or procedures, project or product scope, project cost or budget, project schedule, or the quality of the project or product results. Change requests may include corrective actions, preventive actions, defect repairs, or updates that reflect modified or additional ideas or content. Other change requests cover the needed preventive or corrective actions to eliminate or minimize a negative impact later in the project.

Any stakeholder may request a change. Change requests are processed for review and disposition through the Assess and Implement Changes process.

Communications management plan. The communications management plan is a component of the portfolio, program, or project management plan that describes how, when, and by whom information will be administered and disseminated. The communications management plan describes how project communications will be planned, structured, implemented, and monitored for effectiveness. The plan contains, but is not limited to, the following information:

- Stakeholder communication requirements;
- Information to be communicated, including language, format, content, and level of detail;
- Escalation processes;
- Reason for the distribution of that information;
- Timeframe and frequency for the distribution of required information and receipt of acknowledgment or response, if applicable;
- Person responsible for communicating the information;
- Person responsible for authorizing release of confidential information;
- Person or groups that will receive the information, including information about their needs, requirements, and expectations;
- Methods or technologies used to convey the information, such as memos, emails, press releases, or social media announcements;
- Resources allocated for communication activities, including time and budget;
- Method for updating and refining the communications management plan as the project progresses and develops, such as when the stakeholder community changes as the project moves through different phases;
- Glossary of common terminology;
- Flowcharts of the information flow in the project, workflows with possible sequence of authorization, list of reports, meeting plans, etc.; and
- Constraints derived from specific legislation or regulations, technologies, organizational policies, etc.

The communications management plan may include guidelines and templates for project status meetings, project team meetings, virtual meetings, and email messages. The use of a project website and project management software can be included if these are to be used in the project.

The communications management plan is both an input and an output that plays a crucial role in ensuring the smooth execution and delivery of a project. As an input, it serves as a guideline for the project team on how to disseminate information effectively. The communications management plan outlines:

- Who needs to receive information (stakeholders, team members, etc.);
- What information needs to be communicated (project updates, risks, changes, etc.);

- When and how often communication should occur (daily updates, weekly meetings, etc.); and
- How the information will be delivered (emails, meetings, reports, etc.).

As an output, the communications management plan is a dynamic document that evolves throughout the project life cycle. The communications management plan is regularly updated to reflect changes in project scope, stakeholder requirements, team structure, or the project environment. The plan helps ensure that all parties are kept informed and that the project remains transparent and on track.

Communications management plan updates. Communications management plan updates refer to the process of revising and enhancing the existing communications management plan to reflect the current needs and status of the project. The update is a critical component that helps ensure all stakeholders are kept informed and engaged throughout the project life cycle.

Component. A component is a predetermined element of a portfolio, program, or project that is work related to the achievement of the strategic objectives of the portfolio, program, or project. Various components interrelate with one another during the process of project management.

Configuration management plan. A component of the project management plan, the configuration management plan is a collection of procedures used to track project artifacts and monitor and control changes to these artifacts. The plan describes how to identify and account for project artifacts under configuration control as well as how to record and report changes to them. The configuration management plan describes how the information about the items of the project (and which items) will be recorded and updated so that the product, service, or result of the project remains consistent and/or operative.

Cost baseline. The cost baseline is the approved version of the time-phased project budget, excluding any management reserves, which can be changed only through formal change control procedures and is used as a basis for comparison to actual results.

Cost baseline updates. Cost baseline updates involve revising the approved budget to accommodate changes that impact on the project's financials. These updates are a critical aspect of cost control and help ensure that the project remains financially viable. Updates can occur during inputs and outputs.

Inputs:

- **Approved project budget.** The original cost baseline against which performance is measured.
- **Change requests.** Formal proposals for changes that affect the project's scope, schedule, or cost.
- **Actual costs.** The real expenses incurred during project execution.
- **Project management plan.** The guiding document that includes the financial management plan.

Outputs:

- **Revised cost baseline.** An updated version of the cost baseline that reflects the approved changes.
- **Updated cost estimates.** New cost projections based on changes to the project scope or resources.

- **Budget forecasts.** Predictions of future project expenditures based on current data.
- **Change log.** Documentation of all changes made to the cost baseline.

Cost estimates. A cost estimate is a quantitative assessment of the likely costs for resources required to complete an activity. The cost estimate is a prediction that is based on the information known at a given point in time. Cost estimates include the identification and consideration of costing alternatives to initiate and complete the project. Cost trade-offs and risks should be considered, such as make versus buy, buy versus lease, and the sharing of resources in order to achieve optimal costs for the project.

Cost estimates are generally expressed in units of some currency (e.g., dollars, euros, yen, etc.). In some instances, other units of measure, such as staff hours or staff days, may be used to facilitate comparisons by eliminating the effects of currency fluctuations.

Cost estimates should be reviewed and refined during the course of the project to reflect additional details as they become available and assumptions are tested. The accuracy of a project estimate will increase as the project progresses through the project life cycle.

Costs are estimated for all resources that will be charged to the project. These resources include but are not limited to labor, materials, equipment, services, and facilities, as well as special categories such as an inflation allowance, cost of financing, or contingency costs. Cost estimates may be presented at the activity level or in summary form.

Cost forecasts. Based on the project's past performance, cost forecasts are used to determine if the project is within defined tolerance ranges for the budget and to identify any necessary change requests. A calculated estimate at completion (EAC) value is documented and communicated to stakeholders.

Deliverable. A deliverable is any unique and verifiable product, result, or capability to perform a service that is required to be produced to complete a process, phase, or project. Projects are undertaken to fulfill objectives by producing deliverables. Deliverables may be tangible or intangible.

Development approach. The development approach is the method used to create and evolve the product, service, or result during the project life cycle, such as an adaptive, predictive, or hybrid method.

Duration estimates. Duration estimates are quantitative assessments of the likely number of time periods that are required to complete an activity, phase, or project. Duration estimates do not include any lags. Duration estimates may include some indication of the range of possible results. For example:

- A range of 2 weeks ± 2 days, which indicates that the activity will take at least 8 days and not more than 12 (assuming a 5-day work week); or
- A 15% probability of exceeding 3 weeks, which indicates a high probability—85%—that the activity will take 3 weeks or less.

Enterprise environmental factors (EEFs). Enterprise environmental factors are conditions, not under the immediate control of the team, that influence, constrain, or direct the portfolio, program, or project. These conditions can be internal and/or external to the organization. The EEFs are considered as inputs to many project management processes, specifically for most planning processes. These factors may enhance or constrain project management options. In addition, these factors may have a positive or negative influence on the outcome.

EEFs internal to the organization:

- **Organizational culture, structure, and governance.** Examples include vision, mission, values, beliefs, cultural norms, leadership style, hierarchy and authority relationships, organizational style, ethics, codes of conduct, policies, and procedures.
- **Geographic distribution of facilities and resources.** Examples include factory locations and virtual teams.
- **Infrastructure.** Examples include existing facilities, equipment, organizational telecommunications channels, information technology hardware, availability, and capacity.
- **Information technology software.** Examples include scheduling software tools, configuration management systems, web interfaces to other online automated systems, and work authorization systems.
- **Resource availability.** Examples include contracting and purchasing constraints, approved providers and subcontractors, and collaboration agreements.
- **Employee capability.** Examples include existing human resources expertise, skills, competencies, and specialized knowledge.

EEFs external to the organization:

- **Marketplace conditions.** Examples include competitors, market share, brand recognition, and trademarks.
- **Social and cultural influences and issues.** Examples include political climate, codes of conduct, ethics, and perceptions.
- **Legal restrictions.** Examples include country or local laws and regulations related to security, data protection, business conduct, employment, and procurement.
- **Commercial databases.** Examples include benchmarking results, standardized cost estimating data, industry risk study information, and risk databases.
- **Academic research.** Examples include industry studies, publications, and benchmarking results.
- **Government or industry standards.** Examples include regulatory agency regulations and standards related to products, production, environment, quality, and workmanship.
- **Financial considerations.** Examples include currency exchange rates, interest rates, inflation rates, tariffs, and geographic location.
- **Physical environmental elements.** Examples include working conditions and weather constraints.

Enterprise environmental factor updates. Enterprise environmental factor (EEF) updates refer to modifications or changes made to the conditions that influence, constrain, or direct a project. These factors can be internal or external to the organization and are not under the control of the project team. Updates to EEFs are important as they can enhance or constrain project management options and have a positive or negative influence on the project's outcome. Understanding and updating EEFs is essential for effective project management.

Final product, service, or result transition. A product, service, or result, once delivered by the project, may be handed over to a different group or organization that will operate, maintain, and support it throughout its life cycle. This output refers to the transition of the final product, service, or result that the project was authorized to produce (or in the case of phase closure, the intermediate product, service, or result of that phase) from one team to another.

Final report. A final report is a summary of project performance, which can include information such as:

- Summary-level description of the project or phase;
- Scope objectives, the criteria used to evaluate the scope, and evidence that the completion criteria were met;
- Quality objectives, the criteria used to evaluate the project and product quality, the verification and actual milestone delivery dates, and reasons for variances;
- Cost objectives, including the acceptable cost range, actual costs, and reasons for any variances;
- Summary of the validation information for the final product, service, or result;
- Schedule objectives, including whether the results achieved the benefits that the project was undertaken to address (If the benefits are not met at the close of the project, indicate the degree to which they were achieved and an estimate for future benefits realization.);
- Summary of how the final product, service, or result achieved the business needs identified in the business plan (If the business needs are not met at the close of the project, indicate the degree to which they were achieved and an estimate for when the business needs will be met in the future.); and
- Summary of any risks or issues encountered on the project and how they were addressed.

Financial management plan. A financial management plan is a component of a program or project management plan that describes how costs will be planned, structured, and controlled. The financial management processes, and their associated tools and techniques, are documented in the financial management plan. For example, the financial management plan can establish the following:

- **Units of measure.** Each unit used in measurements (e.g., staff hours, staff days, or weeks for time measures; meters, liters, tons, kilometers, or cubic yards for quantity measures; or lump sum in currency form) is defined for each of the resources.
- **Level of precision.** This is the degree to which cost estimates will be rounded up or down (e.g., US$995.59 to US$1,000) based on the scope of the activities and magnitude of the project.
- **Level of accuracy.** The acceptable range (e.g., ±10%) used in determining realistic cost estimates is specified and may include an amount for contingencies.
- **Organizational procedures links.** The work breakdown structure (WBS) (see Section 5) provides the framework for the financial management plan, allowing for consistency with the estimates, budgets, and control of costs. The WBS component used for project cost accounting is called the control account. Each control account is assigned a unique code or account number(s) that links directly to the performing organization's accounting system.
- **Control thresholds.** Variance thresholds for monitoring cost performance may be specified to indicate an agreed-upon amount of variation to be allowed before some action should be taken. Thresholds are typically expressed as percentage deviations from the baseline plan.

- **Rules of performance measurement.** Earned value management (EVM) rules of performance measurement are set. For example, the financial management plan may:
    - Define the points in the WBS at which measurement of control accounts will be performed;
    - Establish the EVM techniques (e.g., weighted milestones, fixed formula, percent complete, etc.) to be employed; and
    - Specify tracking methodologies and the EVM computation equations for calculating the projected estimate at completion (EAC) forecasts to provide a validity check on the bottom-up EAC.
- **Reporting formats.** The formats and frequency for the various cost reports are defined.
- **Additional details.** Additional details about financial management activities include but are not limited to:
    - Description of strategic funding choices,
    - Procedure to account for fluctuations in currency exchange rates, and
    - Procedure for project cost recording.

Funding proposals. Projects often require dedicated funding efforts either before or after the projects have started. Additionally, certain phases of a given project may require specific funding requests to cover approved budgets associated with that phase. In these cases, estimated costs and reserves are calculated as part of a business value proposition. The value proposition is then used to request the needed funds from the appropriate internal or external funding source.

Funding strategy. Projects require funding to be successful. Funding can come from sources either internal or external to the project's performing organization. Some projects require more than one approach to secure the needed monies. Any single approach, or combination of approaches, can be considered a funding strategy. Approaches range from organizational budget transfers to customer contracts to government or nongovernmental organization (NGO) grants. Common funding strategies include but are not limited to the following:

- **Fixed or reallocated internal budgets.** Internally owned assets and employees are funded by fixed annual departmental budgets and then applied to specific projects as needed. Alternatively, existing budgets within the organization that have surplus funds or lower-priority initiatives can be reallocated to the project.
- **Lump sum.** The entirety of the project's budget and reserves are allocated all at once.
- **Incremental disbursement.** Project funds are secured and allocated in multiple increments, specific to individual phases or key milestones.
- **External investment.** This strategy involves high-net-worth individual or institutional investors who are willing to provide capital to early-stage or innovative projects, often in exchange for interest in long-term ownership or operations.
- **Governmental or nongovernmental organization (NGO) grants.** Projects may be partially or fully funded by relevant grants offered by government agencies, NGOs, or philanthropists that support projects aligning with their specific objectives.
- **Crowdfunding.** This strategy involves the accumulation of small contributions from a large number of individuals who are interested in supporting the project or its mission. This strategy can be particularly effective for projects with strong community appeal.

- **Client contract.** Many projects are the result of a customer procurement effort, where the performing organization serves as a vendor to a sponsor organization. Procurement is a complementary discipline to project management and is further explored in Appendix X4.

Issue log. An issue log is a project document where information about issues is recorded and monitored.

Lessons learned register. A lessons learned register is a project document or repository used to record knowledge gained during a project, phase, or iteration so that it can be used to improve future performance for the team and the organization. Lessons learned from previous projects can be used in the current project and entered into the lessons learned repository.

The lessons learned register may include the category and description of the situation. The register may also include the impacts, recommendations, and proposed actions associated with the situation. The lessons learned register records challenges, problems, realized risks and opportunities, or other content as appropriate.

The lessons learned register is created as an output of the Manage Project Knowledge process early in the project. Thereafter it is used as an input and updated as an output in many processes throughout the project. The persons or teams involved in the work are also involved in capturing the lessons learned. Knowledge can be documented using videos, pictures, audio, or other suitable means that ensure the efficiency of the lessons captured.

At the end of a project or phase, the information is transferred to an organizational process asset called a lessons learned repository.

Lessons learned updates. Lessons learned updates refer to the process of capturing, documenting, and integrating knowledge gained during a project to improve future performance. This effort involves identifying what went well, what did not, and how similar situations can be better managed in future projects.

Make-or-buy analysis and decisions. Make-or-buy analysis is the decision-making process of gathering and organizing data about product requirements and analyzing them against available alternatives, including the purchase or internal manufacture of the product. A make-or-buy analysis results in a make-or-buy decision as to whether particular work can be best accomplished by the project team or if it should be purchased from outside sources.

Milestone list. A milestone list identifies all of the project milestones and indicates whether the milestone is mandatory, such as those required by contract, or optional, such as those based on historical information. Milestones have zero duration because they represent a significant point or event in a project.

Organizational capabilities. Organizational capabilities include all of the organizational policies, ways of working, reporting structures, and attitudes that should be aligned to employ adaptive methods successfully, as organizational capabilities influence the development approach. Transitioning from predictive development approaches to adaptive approaches and then to using agile methods is more than just stating that the organization has now become agile. The transition entails shifting the mindset starting at the executive level and continuing throughout the organization, as well as promoting and sustaining ongoing efforts to stay agile.

Organizational process assets (OPAs). Organizational process assets are plans, processes, policies, procedures, regulations, and knowledge bases specific to and used by the performing organization. These assets influence the management of the project.

The OPAs include any artifact, practice, or knowledge from any or all of the performing organizations involved in the project that can be used to execute or govern the project. The OPAs also include the organization's lessons learned from previous projects and historical information. Additionally, OPAs may include completed schedules, risk data, and earned value data. The OPAs are inputs to many project management processes. Since OPAs are internal to the organization, the project team members may be able to update and add to them as necessary throughout the project. A project's OPAs may be grouped into two categories:

- **Processes, documents, and templates.** Generally, assets in this category are not updated as part of the project work. Processes, documents, and templates are usually established by the project management office (PMO) or another function outside of the project. These assets can be updated only by following the appropriate organizational policies associated with updating them. Some organizations encourage the team to tailor templates, life cycles, and checklists for the project. In these instances, the project management team should tailor those assets to meet the needs of the project.
- **Organizational knowledge repositories.** Assets in this category are updated throughout the project with project information. For example, information on financial performance, lessons learned, performance metrics and issues, and defects are continually updated throughout the project.

Organizational process asset (OPA) updates. Any OPA can be updated as a result of a process. Updates include plans, processes, and knowledge repositories specific to and used by the performing organization.

Outputs from other processes. Outputs from other processes are integrated to create the project management plan. Subsidiary plans and baselines that are outputs from other processes are inputs to this process. In addition, changes to these documents may necessitate updates to the project management plan.

Performance measurement baseline (PMB). The performance measurement baseline includes the integrated scope, schedule, and cost baselines used for comparison to manage, measure, and control project execution.

Physical or virtual resource assignments. The physical and virtual resource assignments document the materials, equipment, supplies, locations, and other physical resources, as well as digital tools, remote team members, and virtual assets that will be utilized during the project. This documentation describes the expected resource utilization and whether the resource is internal to the organization, outsourced, or remotely engaged. Physical and virtual resource assignments are dynamic and subject to change due to availability, project needs, organizational requirements, the environment, or other factors.

Procurement documentation. Procurement documentation includes all of the documents used in signing, executing, and closing an agreement. Procurement documentation may include documents predating the project. This documentation contains the complete supporting records for administration of the procurement processes. Procurement documentation includes the statement of work (SOW), payment information, contractor work performance information, plans, drawings, and other correspondence.

Procurement management plan. The procurement management plan is a component of the program or project management plan that describes how a team will acquire goods and services from outside of the performing organization.

The procurement management plan contains the activities to be undertaken during the procurement process. The plan should document whether international competitive bidding, national competitive bidding, local bidding, etc., should be done. If the project is financed externally, the sources and availability of funding should be aligned with the procurement management plan and the project schedule.

The procurement management plan may include guidance for the following:

- How procurement will be coordinated with other project aspects such as project schedule development and control processes;
- Timetable of key procurement activities;
- Procurement metrics to be used to manage contracts;
- Stakeholder roles and responsibilities related to procurement, including authority and constraints of the project team when the performing organization has a procurement department;
- Constraints and assumptions that could affect planned procurements;
- Legal jurisdiction and the currency in which payments will be made;
- Determination of whether independent estimates will be used and whether they are needed as evaluation criteria;
- Risk management issues, including identifying requirements for performance bonds or insurance contracts to mitigate some forms of project risk; and
- Prequalified sellers, if any, to be used.

A procurement management plan can be formal or informal, highly detailed or broadly framed, and is based upon the needs of each project.

Product. An artifact that is produced, is quantifiable, and can be either an end item in itself or a component item. *Product* is an overarching term that includes both tangible (physical goods) and intangible (digital goods and services) items.

Project calendars. A project calendar is a calendar that identifies working days and shifts that are available for scheduled activities. The project calendar distinguishes time periods in days, or parts of days, that are available to complete scheduled activities from time periods that are not available for work. A schedule model may require more than one project calendar to allow for different work periods for some activities to calculate the project schedule. Project calendars may be updated.

Project charter. A project charter is a document issued by the project initiator or sponsor that formally authorizes the existence of a project and provides the project manager with the authority to apply organizational resources to project activities.

Project communications. Project communications may include but are not limited to performance reports, deliverable status, schedule progress, cost incurred, presentations, and other information required by stakeholders.

Project documents. The project documents include documentation created throughout the five Project Management Focus Areas to initiate, plan, execute, monitor and control, and close the project before delivering it. Examples include the change log, issue log, project schedule, project scope statement, requirements documentation, risk register, and stakeholder register.

Project document updates. The project document updates include updates to the project documents created throughout the five Project Management Focus Areas to initiate, plan, execute, monitor and control, and close the project before delivering it.

Project funding requirements. The project funding requirements are the total funding requirements and periodic funding requirements (e.g., quarterly, annually) that are derived from the cost baseline. The cost baseline includes the projected expenditures plus the contingency reserves. Funding often occurs in incremental amounts and may not be evenly distributed (see Figure 4-1). The total funds required are those included in the cost baseline plus management reserves, if any. Funding requirements may include the source(s) of the funding. The budget at completion (BAC) is the sum of all budgets established for the work to be performed.

Project management plan. The project management plan is the document that describes how the project will be executed, monitored and controlled, and closed. The project management plan defines the basis for all project decisions and is a living document that can be expected to change over time. A project management plan typically consists of the following components: change management plan, communications management plan, financial management plan, iteration plan, procurement management plan, quality management plan, requirements management plan, release plan, resource management plan, risk management plan, schedule management plan, scope management plan, sourcing strategy plan, stakeholder engagement plan, and test plan. However, the project team or the organization may tailor the content of the project management plan to include only those elements that are most relevant to the specific project context, objectives, and organizational requirements.

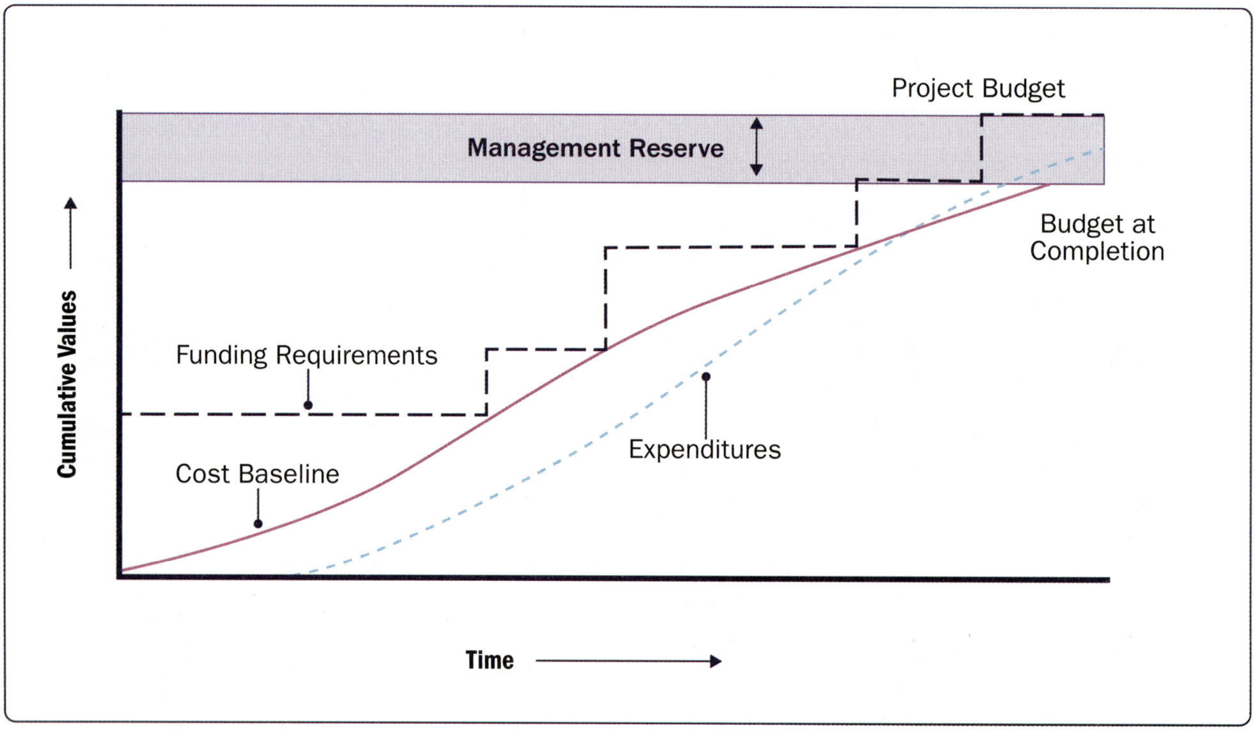

Figure 4-1. Cost Baseline, Expenditures, and Funding Requirements

Project management plan updates. Project management plan updates are updates to the document that describes how the project is being executed, monitored and controlled, and closed.

Project schedule. The project schedule is an output of a schedule model that presents linked activities with planned dates, durations, milestones, and resources. The detailed project schedule should be flexible throughout the project to adjust for the knowledge gained, increased understanding of the risks, and value-added activities.

Project schedule network diagram. The project schedule network diagram is a graphical representation of the logical relationships among the project schedule activities. Logical relationships may also be referred to as dependencies. Figure 4-2 illustrates a project schedule network diagram. A project schedule network diagram is produced manually or by using project management software. The diagram may include full project details or may have one or more summary activities. A summary narrative can accompany the diagram and describe the basic approach used to sequence the activities. Any unusual activity sequences within the network should be fully described within the narrative.

Activities that have multiple predecessor activities indicate a path convergence. Activities that have multiple successor activities indicate a path divergence. Activities with divergence and convergence are at greater risk as they are affected by multiple activities or can affect multiple activities. Activity I is called a path convergence, as it has more than one predecessor, while activity K is called a path divergence, as it has more than one successor.

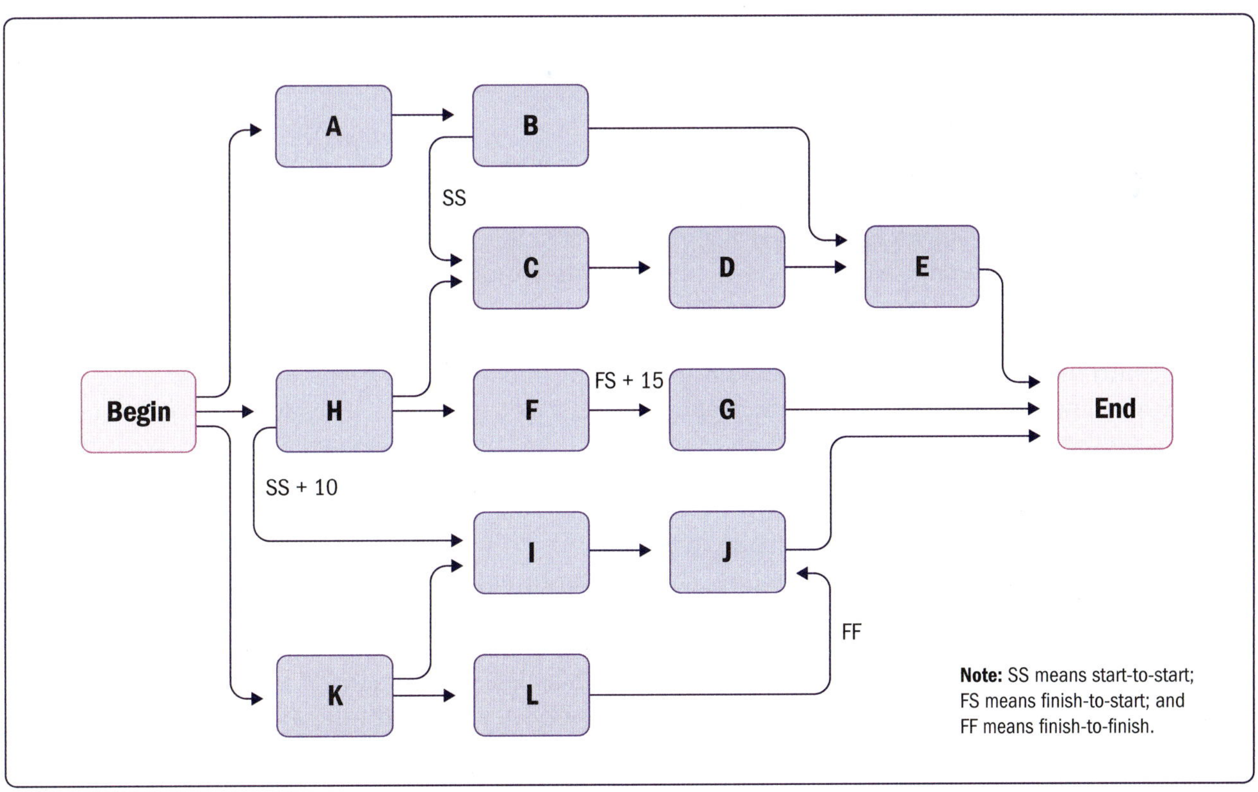

Figure 4-2. Example of a Project Schedule Network Diagram

Project scope statement. The project scope statement is the description of the project scope, major deliverables, assumptions, and constraints. The project scope statement documents the entire scope, including the project and product scope. The statement describes the project's deliverables in detail and provides a common understanding of the project scope among project stakeholders. The document may contain explicit scope exclusions that can assist in managing stakeholder expectations. The project scope statement enables the project team to perform more detailed planning, guides the project team's work during execution, and provides the baseline for evaluating whether requests for changes or additional work are contained within or outside the project's boundaries.

The degree and level of detail to which the project scope statement defines the work that will be performed and the work that is excluded can help determine how well the project management team can control the overall project scope. The detailed project scope statement, either directly or by reference to other documents, includes the following:

- **Project scope description.** The project scope description progressively elaborates the characteristics of the product, service, or result described in the project charter and requirements documentation.
- **Deliverables.** A deliverable is any unique and verifiable product, result, or capability to perform a service that is required to be produced to complete a process, phase, or project. Deliverables also include ancillary results such as project management reports and documentation. These deliverables may be described at a summary level or in great detail.
- **Acceptance criteria.** The acceptance criteria is a set of conditions that are met before deliverables are accepted.
- **Project exclusions.** Project exclusions identify what is excluded from the project. Explicitly stating what is out of scope for the project helps manage stakeholders' expectations and can reduce scope creep.

Although the project charter and the project scope statement are sometimes perceived as containing a certain degree of redundancy, they are different in the level of detail contained in each. The project charter contains high-level information, while the project scope statement contains a detailed description of the scope components. These components are progressively elaborated throughout the project. Table 4-1 describes some of the key elements for each document.

Project team assignments. Project team assignments are recorded in a document containing a list of the team members and their roles and responsibilities for the project. This documentation can include a project team directory and names inserted into the project management plan, such as the project organization charts and schedules.

Quality control measurements. Quality control measurements are the documented results of the Manage Quality Assurance process activities. The measurements should be captured in the format specified in the quality management plan.

Quality management plan. The quality management plan is a component of the program or project management plan that describes how an organization's policies, procedures, and guidelines will be implemented to achieve the quality objectives. The plan describes the activities and resources necessary for the project management team to achieve the quality objectives set for the project. The quality management plan may be formal or informal, detailed or broadly framed. The style and detail of the quality management plan are determined by the requirements of the project. The plan should

Table 4-1. Elements of the Project Charter and Project Scope Statement

Project Charter	Project Scope Statement
• Project purpose • Measurable project objectives and related success criteria • High-level requirements • High-level project description, boundaries, and key deliverables • Overall project risk • Summary milestone schedule • Preapproved financial resources • Key stakeholder list • Project approval requirements (i.e., what constitutes success, who decides the project is successful, who approves the project) • Project exit criteria (i.e., what are the conditions to be met in order to close or cancel the project or phase) • Assigned project manager, responsibility, and authority level • Name and authority of the sponsor or other person(s) authorizing the project charter	• Project scope description (progressively elaborated) • Project deliverables • Acceptance criteria • Project exclusions

be reviewed early in the project to ensure that decisions are based on accurate information. The benefits of this review may include a sharper focus on the project's value proposition, reductions in costs, and less frequent schedule overruns that are caused by rework.

The quality management plan may include but is not limited to the following components:

- Quality standards that will be used by the project;
- Quality objectives of the project;
- Quality roles and responsibilities;
- Project deliverables and processes subject to quality reviews;
- Quality control and quality management activities planned for the project; and
- Quality tools and methodologies to be employed, alongside detailed procedures for handling nonconformance and continuous improvement.

Quality metrics. Quality metrics specifically describe project or product attributes and how the Manage Quality Assurance process will verify compliance with them. Some examples of quality metrics include percentage of tasks completed on time, cost performance measured by a cost performance index (CPI), failure rates, number of defects identified per day, total downtime per month, errors found per line of code, customer satisfaction scores, and percentage of requirements covered by the test plan as a measure of test coverage.

Quality reports. A quality report is a project document that includes quality management issues, recommendations for corrective actions, and a summary of findings from quality control activities.

The quality report may include recommendations for any process, project, and product improvements.

Quality test and evaluation documents. Quality test and evaluation documents are essential components in project management that are designed to ensure a product or service meets the specified quality objectives. These documents outline the activities and processes used to assess whether the deliverables align with the quality standards set in the quality management plan. The quality test and evaluation documents are crucial for identifying errors, defects, or nonconformance issues early in the project life cycle, thereby reducing the cost and effort required to address the issues later.

Regulations. See *organizational process assets (OPAs)*.

Requirements documentation. Requirements documentation is a description of how individual requirements should meet the business needs of the project. Requirements may start out at a high level and become progressively more detailed as more information about the requirements becomes known. Before being baselined, requirements should be unambiguous (measurable and testable), traceable, complete, consistent, and acceptable to key stakeholders. The format of the requirements documentation may range from a simple document listing all of the requirements categorized by stakeholder and priority, to more elaborate forms containing an executive summary, detailed descriptions, and attachments. The documentation may also include static or dynamic graphic information.

Many organizations categorize requirements into different types such as business and technical. Business requirements refer to stakeholder needs and technical requirements determine how those needs will be implemented. Requirements can be grouped into classifications allowing for further refinement and detail as the requirements are elaborated. These classifications may include the following:

- **Business requirements.** These requirements outline the strategic objectives and high-level needs of the organization, ensuring alignment with broader organizational goals.
- **Stakeholder requirements.** These requirements describe the needs of a stakeholder or stakeholder group.
- **Solution requirements.** These requirements describe the features, functions, and characteristics of the product, service, or result that will meet the business and stakeholder needs. Solution requirements are further grouped into functional and nonfunctional requirements:
  - **Functional requirements.** Functional requirements describe the behaviors of the product. Examples include actions, processes, data, and interactions that the product should execute.
  - **Nonfunctional requirements.** Nonfunctional requirements complement functional requirements by specifying performance, security, and operational criteria essential for product effectiveness and user satisfaction. Examples include reliability, security, performance, safety, level of service, supportability, retention/purge, etc.
- **Transition and readiness requirements.** These requirements describe temporary capabilities, such as data conversion and training requirements, needed to transition from the current, as-is state to the desired future state.

- **Project requirements.** These requirements describe the actions, processes, or other conditions the project should meet. Examples include milestone dates, contractual obligations, constraints, etc.
- **Quality requirements.** These requirements capture any condition or criteria required to validate the successful completion of a project deliverable or fulfillment of other project requirements. Examples include tests, certifications, validations, etc.

Requirements management plan. A requirements management plan is a component of the program or project management plan that describes how requirements will be analyzed, documented, and managed. According to *Business Analysis for Practitioners: A Practice Guide* [2], some organizations refer to the requirements management plan as a business analysis plan. Components of the requirements management plan may include but are not limited to the following:

- How requirements activities will be planned, tracked, and reported;
- Configuration management activities such as:
  - How changes will be initiated;
  - How impacts will be analyzed;
  - How changes will be traced, tracked, and reported; and
  - Authorization levels required to approve these changes.
- Requirements prioritization process;
- Metrics that will be used and the rationale for using them; and
- Traceability structure that reflects the requirement attributes captured on the requirements traceability matrix.

Requirements traceability matrix. The requirements traceability matrix is a grid that links product requirements from their origin to the deliverables that satisfy them. The implementation of a requirements traceability matrix helps to ensure that each requirement adds business value by linking it to the business and project objectives. The matrix provides a means to track requirements throughout the project life cycle, helping to ensure that requirements approved in the requirements documentation are delivered at the end of the project. Finally, it provides a structure for managing changes to the product scope.

The requirements traceability matrix includes but is not limited to the following:

- Business needs, opportunities, goals, and objectives;
- Project objectives;
- Project scope and WBS deliverables;
- Product design;
- Product development;
- Test strategy and test scenarios; and
- High-level requirements to more detailed requirements.

Attributes associated with each requirement can be recorded in the requirements traceability matrix. These attributes help to define key information about the requirement. Typical attributes

Requirements Traceability Matrix									
Project Name:									
Cost Center:									
Project Description:									
ID	Associate ID	Requirements Description	Business Needs, Opportunities, Goals, Objectives	Project Objectives	WBS Deliverables	Product Design	Product Development	Test Cases
001	1.0							
	1.1							
	1.2							
	1.2.1							
002	2.0							
	2.1							
	2.1.1							
003	3.0							
	3.1							
	3.2							
004	4.0							
005	5.0							

Figure 4-3. Example of a Requirements Traceability Matrix

used in the requirements traceability matrix may include a unique identifier, a textual description of the requirement, the rationale for inclusion, the owner, source, priority, version, current status (e.g., active, canceled, deferred, added, approved, assigned, completed), and status date. Additional attributes to help ensure that the requirement has met stakeholder satisfaction may include stability, complexity, and acceptance criteria. Figure 4-3 provides an example of a requirements traceability matrix with its associated attributes.

Resource breakdown structure. A resource breakdown structure is a hierarchical representation of resources by category and type. Examples of resource categories include but are not limited to labor, materials, equipment, and supplies. Resource types may include the skill level, grade level, required certifications, or other information as appropriate to the project. See Figure 4-4 for an example.

Resource calendar. A resource calendar is a calendar that identifies the working days and shifts during which each specific resource is available. The calendar should include the start and end of normal business hours, weekends, and public holidays when each specific resource is available. Information on which resources (such as team resources, equipment, and materials) are potentially available during a planned activity period is used for estimating resource utilization. Resource calendars also specify when, and for how long, identified team and physical or virtual resources will be available during the project. This information may be at the activity or project level. This calendar may include consideration of attributes such as resource experience and/or skill level, as well as various geographical locations.

Resource management plan. A resource management plan is a component of the project management plan that describes how project resources are acquired, allocated, monitored, and controlled. The plan

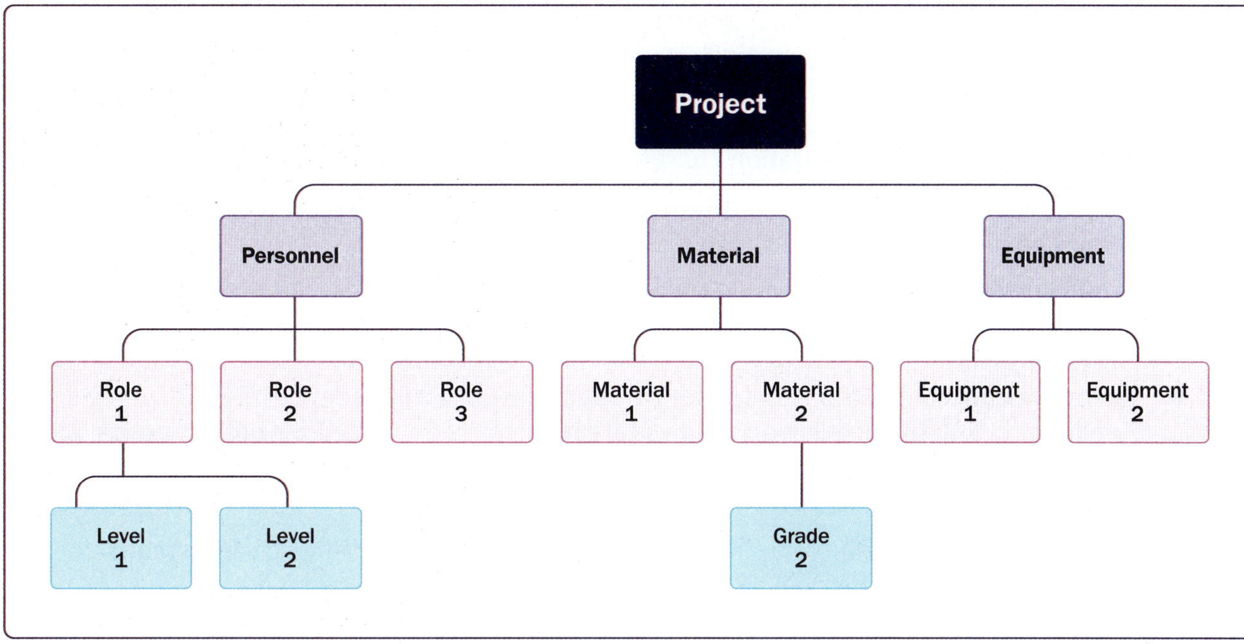

Figure 4-4. Sample Resource Breakdown Structure

may be divided between the team management plan and the physical resource management plan according to the specifics of the project.

The resource management plan may include but is not limited to the following:

- **Identification of resources.** Methods for identifying and quantifying the team and physical resources needed.
- **Acquiring resources.** Guidance on how to acquire the team and physical resources for the project.
- **Roles and responsibilities:**
  - **Role.** The function assumed by, or assigned to, a person in the project. Examples of project roles are civil engineer, business analyst, and testing coordinator.
  - **Authority.** The right to apply project resources, make decisions, sign approvals, accept deliverables, and influence others to carry out the work of the project. Examples of decisions that should have clear authority include the selection of a method for completing an activity, quality acceptance criteria, and how to respond to project variances. Team members operate best when their individual levels of authority match their individual responsibilities.
  - **Responsibility.** The assigned duties and work that a project team member is expected to perform in order to complete the project's activities.
  - **Competence.** The skill and capacity required to complete assigned activities within the project constraints. If project team members do not possess required competencies, performance can be jeopardized. When such mismatches are identified, proactive responses such as training, hiring, schedule changes, or scope changes are initiated.

- **Project organization charts.** A project organization chart is a graphical display of project team members and their reporting relationships. The chart can be formal or informal, highly detailed or broadly framed, based on the needs of the project. For example, the project organization chart for a 3,000-person disaster response team should have greater detail than a project organization chart for an internal, 20-person project.
- **Project team resource management.** Guidance on how the project team resources should be defined, staffed, managed, and eventually released.
- **Training.** Training strategies for team members.
- **Team development.** Methods for developing the project team.
- **Resource control.** Methods for ensuring adequate physical resources are available as needed and that the acquisition of physical resources is optimized for project needs. The resource control includes information on managing inventory, equipment, and supplies throughout the project life cycle.
- **Recognition plan.** A plan for which recognitions and rewards will be given to team members, and when they will be given.

Resource requirements. Resource requirements identify the types and quantities of resources required for each work package or activity in a work package and can be aggregated to determine the estimated resources for each work package, each WBS branch, and the entire project. The amount of detail and the level of specificity of the resource requirement descriptions can vary by application area. The resource requirements documentation may include assumptions made in determining which types of resources should be applied, their availability, and what quantities are needed.

Revenue forecasts. Revenue forecasts are projections of the future financial performance of an organization or project, specifically focusing on the expected income generated from sales or services over a certain period. These forecasts are crucial for strategic planning, budgeting, and decision-making processes as they provide insights into potential financial outcomes and help in managing resources effectively.

Risk management plan. The risk management plan is a component of the project management plan and describes how risk management activities will be structured and performed.

The risk management plan may include some or all of the following elements:

- **Risk strategy.** The risk strategy describes the general approach to managing risk on a project.
- **Methodology.** The methodology defines the specific approaches, tools, and data sources that will be used to perform risk management on a project.
- **Roles and responsibilities.** The roles and responsibilities define the lead, support, and risk management team members for each type of activity described in the risk management plan and help to clarify their responsibilities.
- **Funding.** Funding identifies the funds needed to perform activities related to the management of risk. Funding also establishes protocols for the application of contingency and management reserves.
- **Timing.** Timing defines when and how often the risk processes will be performed throughout the project life cycle and establishes risk management activities for inclusion in the project schedule.

- **Risk categories.** Risk categories provide a means for grouping individual project risks. A common way to structure risk categories is with a risk breakdown structure (RBS), which is a hierarchical representation of potential sources of risk (see an example in Figure 4-5). An RBS helps the project team consider the full range of sources from which individual project risks may arise. This view can be useful when identifying risks or when categorizing identified risks. The organization may have a generic RBS to be used for all projects,

RBS Level 0	RBS Level 1	RBS Level 2
0. All Sources of Project Risk	1. Technical Risk	1.1 Scope definition
		1.2 Requirements definition
		1.3 Estimates, assumptions, and constraints
		1.4 Technical processes
		1.5 Technology
		1.6 Technical interfaces
		Etc.
	2. Management Risk	2.1 Project management
		2.2 Program/portfolio management
		2.3 Operations management
		2.4 Organization
		2.5 Resourcing
		2.6 Communication
		Etc.
	3. Commercial Risk	3.1 Contractual terms and conditions
		3.2 Internal procurement
		3.3 Suppliers and vendors
		3.4 Subcontracts
		3.5 Client/customer stability
		3.6 Partnerships and joint ventures
		Etc.
	4. External Risk	4.1 Legislation
		4.2 Exchange rates
		4.3 Site/facilities
		4.4 Environmental/weather
		4.5 Competition
		4.6 Regulatory
		Etc.

Figure 4-5. Excerpt From a Sample Risk Breakdown Structure

there may be several RBS frameworks for different types of projects, or the project may develop a tailored RBS. Where an RBS is not used, an organization may use a custom risk categorization framework, which may take the form of a simple list of categories or a structure based on project objectives.

- **Stakeholder risk appetite.** The risk appetites of key stakeholders on the project are recorded in the risk management plan, as they inform the details of the Plan Risk Management process. Stakeholder risk appetite should be expressed as measurable risk thresholds around each project objective. These thresholds should determine the acceptable level of overall project risk exposure, and they are also used to inform the definitions of probability and impacts to be used when assessing and prioritizing individual project risks.
- **Definitions of risk probability and impacts.** Definitions of risk probability and impact levels are specific to the project context and reflect the risk appetite and thresholds of the organization and key stakeholders. The project may generate specific definitions of probability and impact levels, or it may start with general definitions provided by the organization. The number of levels reflects the degree of detail required for the risk process, with more levels used for a more detailed risk approach (typically five levels), and fewer for a simple process (usually three levels). Table 4-2 provides an example of definitions of probability and impacts against three project objectives. These scales can be used to evaluate both threats and opportunities by interpreting the impact definitions as negative for threats (delay, additional cost, and performance shortfall) and positive for opportunities (reduced time or cost and performance enhancement). While most risks can be mapped into the probability and impact scales, it is important to be mindful that there may be risks such as ethical risks or those that may impact the organization's reputation, team morale, or other intangible factors.

Table 4-2. Example of Definitions for Probability and Impacts

Scale	Probability	+/– Impact on Project Objectives		
		Time	Cost	Quality
Very high	>70%	>6 months	>US$5M	Very significant impact on overall functionality
High	51%–70%	3–6 months	US$1M–$5M	Significant impact on overall functionality
Medium	31%–50%	1–3 months	US$501K–$1M	Some impact on key functional areas
Low	11%–30%	1–4 weeks	US$100K–$500K	Minor impact on overall functionality
Very low	1%–10%	1 week	<US$100K	Minor impact on secondary functions
Insignificant	<1%	No change	No change	No change in functionality

Risk register. A risk register is a repository in which outputs of risk management processes are recorded. The risk register captures details of identified individual project risks. The results of the following processes are recorded in the risk register as these processes are conducted throughout the project:

- Identify Risks,
- Perform Risk Analysis,
- Plan Risk Responses,
- Implement Risk Responses, and
- Monitor Risks.

The risk register may contain limited or extensive risk information depending on project variables such as size and complexity.

When the Identify Risks process is performed, the content of the risk register may include but is not limited to the following:

- **List of identified risks.** Each individual project risk is given a unique identifier in the risk register. Identified risks are described in as much detail as required to ensure unambiguous understanding. A structured risk statement may be used to distinguish risks from their cause(s) and their effect(s).
- **Potential risk owners.** Where a potential risk owner has been identified during the Identify Risks process, the risk owner is recorded in the risk register. This information will be confirmed during the Perform Risk Analysis process.
- **List of potential risk responses.** Where a potential risk response has been identified during the Identify Risks process, it is recorded in the risk register. This information will be confirmed during the Plan Risk Responses process.

Additional data may be recorded for each identified risk, depending on the risk register format specified in the risk management plan. This may include the following:

- Short risk title,
- Risk category,
- Current risk status,
- One or more causes,
- One or more effects on objectives,
- Risk triggers (events or conditions that indicate that a risk is about to occur),
- WBS reference of affected activities, and
- Timing information (when a risk was identified, when a risk might occur, when a risk may no longer be relevant, and the deadline for taking action).

Risk register updates. The risk register updates refer to the process of revising the risk register to reflect new risks, reassess existing risks, and update response strategies as the project progresses. Risk register updates are a key component of risk management that help to ensure the project's risk documentation remains current and actionable. The process of updating the risk register is iterative and should be performed regularly throughout the project life cycle.

Risk report. The risk report presents information on sources of overall project risk, together with summary information on identified individual project risks. The risk report is developed progressively throughout the risk processes. The risk report may include the results of the following processes as these processes are completed:

- Perform Risk Analysis,
- Plan Risk Responses,
- Implement Risk Responses, and
- Monitor Risks.

When the Identify Risks process is completed, information in the risk report may include but is not limited to the following:

- Sources of overall project risk, indicating which are the most important drivers of overall project risk exposure; and
- Summary information on identified individual project risks, such as number of identified threats and opportunities, distribution of risks across risk categories, metrics and trends, etc.

Additional information may be included in the risk report, depending on the reporting requirements specified in the risk management plan.

Schedule baseline. The schedule baseline is the approved version of a schedule model that can be changed using formal change control procedures and is used as the basis for comparison to actual results. The schedule baseline is accepted and approved by the appropriate stakeholders as the baseline for the schedule, with baseline start dates and baseline finish dates. During monitoring and controlling, the approved baseline dates are compared to the actual start and finish dates to determine if variances have occurred. The schedule baseline is a component of the project management plan.

Schedule baseline updates. The schedule baseline updates refer to the modifications made to the project's original schedule baseline, which is the approved timeline for the project's tasks and milestones. These updates are necessary when significant changes occur that affect the project's timing and should be formally integrated into the plan.

Schedule data. The schedule data for the project schedule model is the collection of information for describing and controlling the schedule. The schedule data includes, at a minimum, the schedule milestones, schedule activities, activity attributes, and documentation of all identified assumptions and constraints. The amount of additional data varies by application area. Information frequently supplied as supporting detail includes but is not limited to the following:

- Resource requirements by time period, often in the form of a resource histogram;
- Alternative schedules, such as best case or worst case, not-resource-leveled or resource-leveled, or with or without imposed dates; and
- Applied schedule reserves.

Schedule data may also include items such as resource histograms, cash flow projections, order and delivery schedules, or other relevant information.

Schedule forecasts. Schedule forecasts are estimates or predictions of conditions and events in the project's future based on information and knowledge available at the time the schedule is calculated.

Forecasts are updated and reissued based on work performance information provided as the project is executed. The information is based on the project's past performance and its expected future performance based on corrective or preventive actions. This information may include earned value (EV) performance indicators as well as schedule reserve information that could impact the project in the future.

Schedule management plan. The schedule management plan is a component of the program or project management plan that establishes the criteria and the activities for developing, monitoring, and controlling the schedule. The schedule management plan may be formal or informal and highly detailed or broadly framed based on the needs of the project. The plan also includes appropriate control thresholds.

The schedule management plan can establish the following:

- **Project schedule model development.** The scheduling methodology and the scheduling tool to be used in the development of the project schedule model are specified.
- **Release and iteration length.** When using an adaptive life cycle, the timeboxed periods for releases, waves, and iterations are specified. Timeboxed periods are durations during which the team works steadily toward completion of a goal. Timeboxing helps to minimize scope creep as it forces the team to process essential features first, then other features when time permits.
- **Level of accuracy.** The level of accuracy specifies the acceptable range used in determining realistic activity duration estimates and may include an amount for contingencies.
- **Units of measure.** Each unit of measurement (e.g., staff hours, days, or weeks for time measures, or meters, liters, tons, kilometers, or cubic yards for quantity measures) is defined for each of the resources.
- **Organizational procedures links.** The work breakdown structure (WBS) provides the framework for the schedule management plan, allowing for consistency with the estimates and resulting schedules.
- **Project schedule model maintenance.** The process used to update the status and record progress of the project in the schedule model during the execution of the project is defined.
- **Control thresholds.** Variance thresholds for monitoring schedule performance may be specified to indicate an agreed-upon amount of variation to be allowed before some action should be taken. Thresholds are typically expressed as percentage deviations from the parameters established in the baseline plan.
- **Rules of performance measurement.** Earned value management (EVM) rules or other physical measurement rules of performance measurement are set. For example, the schedule management plan may specify:
  - Rules for establishing percent complete,
  - Any EVM techniques (e.g., baselines, fixed formula, percent complete, etc.) to be employed (for more specific information, refer to *The Standard for Earned Value Management* [3]), and
  - Schedule performance measurements, such as schedule variance (SV) and schedule performance index (SPI), used to assess the magnitude of variation to the original schedule baseline.
- **Reporting formats.** The formats and frequency for the various schedule reports are defined.

Scope baseline. The scope baseline is the approved version of formal scope documents that can be changed using formal change control procedures and is used as the basis for comparison to actual results. The scope baseline may include the approved version of a scope statement, work breakdown structure (WBS), and its associated WBS dictionary, and is a component of the project management plan.

Components of the scope baseline include the following:

- **Project scope statement.** The project scope statement includes the description of the project scope, major deliverables, and exclusions.
- **WBS.** The WBS is a hierarchical decomposition of the total scope of work to be carried out by the project team to accomplish the project objectives and create the required deliverables. Each descending level of the WBS represents an increasingly detailed definition of the project work:
  - **Work package.** The lowest level of the WBS is a work package with a unique identifier. These identifiers provide a structure for hierarchical summation of costs, schedule, and resource information and form a code of accounts. Each work package is part of a control account. A control account is a management control point where the scope, budget, and schedule are integrated and compared to the earned value for performance measurement. A control account has two or more work packages, though each work package is associated with a single control account.
  - **Planning package.** A control account may include one or more planning packages. A planning package is a WBS component below the control account and above the work package with known work content but without detailed schedule activities.
- **WBS dictionary.** The WBS dictionary is a document that provides detailed deliverable, activity, scheduling, cost, and resource information about each component in the WBS. The WBS dictionary is a document that supports the WBS. Most information included in the WBS dictionary is created by other processes and added to this document at a later stage. Information in the WBS dictionary may include but is not limited to the following:
  - Code of account identifier,
  - Description of work,
  - Assumptions and constraints,
  - Responsible organization,
  - Schedule milestones,
  - Associated schedule activities,
  - Resources required,
  - Cost estimates,
  - Quality requirements,
  - Acceptance criteria,
  - Technical references, and
  - Agreement information.

Scope management plan. A scope management plan is a component of the program or project management plan that describes how the scope will be defined, developed, monitored, controlled, and validated.

The components of a scope management plan include the following:

- Process for preparing a project scope statement,
- Process that enables the creation of the work breakdown structure (WBS) from the detailed project scope statement,
- Process that establishes how the scope baseline will be approved and maintained, and
- Process that specifies how formal acceptance of the completed project deliverables will be obtained.

The scope management plan can be formal or informal and broadly framed or highly detailed, based on the needs of the project.

Skill matrix. The skill matrix is a tool that maps out the skills and competencies required for a team or project and compares them against the skills available within the team. The matrix is used to identify any gaps in skills that should be addressed for the successful completion of a project. Creating and updating a skill matrix is an ongoing process that should be revisited regularly to ensure it reflects the current capabilities of the team and the needs of the project.

Sourcing strategy plan. The sourcing strategy plan is a component of the project management plan that describes which elements of the project will be insourced, outsourced, or both. The sourcing strategy should contain the rationale for a given approach, based on the desired impact to project value, schedule, risk, finances, or other considerations. A sourcing strategy can be formal or informal, highly detailed or broadly framed, and is based upon the needs of each project. The sourcing strategy plan may or may not include the details of how outsourced procurement should be performed. The components of the sourcing strategy plan may include the following:

- Insourcing or outsourcing decisions, and
- Source selection criteria.

Stakeholder engagement plan. The stakeholder engagement plan is a component of the program or project management plan that identifies the strategies and actions required to promote productive involvement of stakeholders in program or project decision-making and execution. The plan can be formal or informal and highly detailed or broadly framed, based on the needs of the project and the expectations of stakeholders. The stakeholder engagement plan may include but is not limited to specific strategies or approaches for engaging with individuals or groups of stakeholders.

Stakeholder register. A stakeholder register is a project document that contains information about project stakeholders, including an assessment and classification of project stakeholders. This document contains information about the identified stakeholders that includes but is not limited to the following:

- **Identification information.** Name, organizational position, location and contact details, and role on the project.

- **Assessment information.** Major requirements, expectations, potential for influencing project outcomes, and the phase of the project life cycle where the stakeholder has the most influence or impact.
- **Stakeholder classification.** Internal/external, impact/influence/power/interest, upward/downward/outward/sideward, or any other classification model chosen by the project manager.

Status report. A status report is a document that provides information on the current status of the project. The report may include information on progress since the last report and forecasts for cost and schedule performance.

Team charter. The team charter is a document that establishes the values, agreements, and operating guidelines for the team. The team charter may include but is not limited to the following:

- Team values,
- Communication guidelines,
- Decision-making criteria and processes,
- Conflict resolution processes,
- Meeting guidelines, and
- Team agreements.

The team charter establishes clear expectations regarding acceptable behavior by project team members. Early commitment to clear guidelines decreases misunderstandings and increases productivity. Discussing areas such as codes of conduct, communication, decision-making, and meeting etiquette allows team members to discover values that are important to one another. The team charter works best when the team develops it or at least has an opportunity to contribute to it. All project team members share responsibility for ensuring the rules documented in the team charter are followed. The team charter can be reviewed and updated periodically to ensure a continued understanding of the team ground rules and to orient and integrate new team members.

Team performance assessments. As project team development efforts such as training, team building, and colocation are implemented, the project management team makes formal or informal assessments of the project team's effectiveness. Effective team development strategies and activities are expected to increase the team's performance, which increases the likelihood of meeting project objectives.

The evaluation of a team's effectiveness may include indicators such as:

- Improvements in skills that allow individuals to perform assignments more effectively,
- Improvements in competencies that help team members perform better as a team,
- Reduced staff turnover rate, and
- Increased team cohesiveness where team members share information and experiences openly and help one another to improve the overall project performance.

As a result of conducting an evaluation of the team's overall performance, the project management team can identify the specific training, coaching, mentoring, assistance, or changes required to improve the team's performance. This effort should also include identifying the appropriate or required resources necessary to achieve and implement the improvements identified in the assessment.

Team performance assignments. The team performance assignments refer to the allocation of tasks and responsibilities to team members based on their skills, roles, and the project's requirements. The assignments are used to ensure that the project progresses efficiently and effectively.

User stories. A user story is a brief, textual description of an outcome from a specific stakeholder perspective, and is a promise for a conversation to clarify details. User stories clarify details or required functionality in a conversational manner, which is a clear and concise representation of a requirement written from the end user's perspective. A typical user story should describe the user or stakeholder's role, who benefits from the feature (role), what the stakeholder needs to accomplish (goal), and the benefit to the stakeholder (motivation). The acceptance criteria in a user story should focus on the specific functionalities and end-user expectations that should be fulfilled.

Verified deliverables. Verified deliverables are completed project deliverables that have been checked and confirmed for correctness through the Monitor and Control Scope process. A goal of the Monitor and Control Scope process is to determine the correctness of deliverables. The results of performing the Monitor and Control Scope process are verified deliverables that become an input to the Validate Scope process for formalized acceptance. If there are any change requests or improvements related to the deliverables, they should be changed, inspected, and reverified.

Virtual resource assignments. Virtual resources include software, testing environments, licenses, and anything else created or seen using computers or the internet that is needed for efficient and effective project completion. Virtual resource assignments are the documentation of the virtual resources that will be used during the project. The virtual resource assignments describe the expected resource utilization and details such as type, amount, location, and whether the resource is internal to the organization or outsourced.

WBS dictionary. See *scope baseline*.

Work breakdown structure (WBS). See *scope baseline*.

Work package estimation. The work package estimation is defined at the lowest level of the work breakdown structure (WBS), for which cost and duration are estimated and managed. For example, simulation can be used to estimate work packages. The simulation involves calculating multiple work package durations and costs with different sets of activity assumptions, constraints, risks, issues, or scenarios using probability distributions and other representations of uncertainty. Throughout the project, work packages are progressively elaborated into activities.

Work performance data. Work performance data includes the raw observations and measurements identified during activities being performed to carry out project work. The data is often viewed as the lowest level of detail from which information is derived by other processes. The data is then gathered through work execution and passed to the controlling processes for further analysis.

Examples of work performance data include work completed, key performance indicators (KPIs), technical performance measures, actual start and finish dates of schedule activities, story points completed, deliverables status, schedule progress, number of change requests, number of defects, actual costs incurred, actual durations, etc.

Work performance information. Work performance information includes the work performance data collected from controlling processes, analyzed in comparison with project management plan components, project documents, and other work performance details. This comparison helps to indicate how the project is performing.

Specific work performance metrics for scope, schedule, budget, and quality are defined at the start of the project as part of the project management plan. Performance data is then collected during the project and compared to the plan and other variables to provide a context for work performance.

For example, work performance data on cost may include funds that have been expended. However, to be useful, that data should be compared to the budget, the work that was performed, the resources used to accomplish the work, and the funding schedule. This additional information provides the context to determine if the project is on budget or if there is a variance. This information also indicates the degree of variance from the plan, and by comparing it to the variance thresholds in the project management plan it can indicate if preventive or corrective action is required. Interpreting work performance data and additional information provides a sound foundation for making project decisions.

Work performance reports. Work performance reports are the physical or electronic representations of work performance information compiled in project documents, which are intended to generate decisions, actions, or awareness. The reports are circulated to project stakeholders through the communication processes as defined in the project's communications management plan.

Examples of work performance reports include status reports and progress reports. Work performance reports may contain status of configuration items, earned value (EV) graphs and information, trend lines and forecasts, iteration burndown charts, defect histograms, contract performance information, and risk summaries. The reports can be presented as dashboards, heat reports, stoplight charts, or other representations useful for promoting awareness and generating decisions and actions.

Section 5

Tools and Techniques

All of the tools and techniques in this section appear in alphabetical order; therefore, no section numbers are assigned.

Active listening. Active listening involves techniques such as acknowledging, clarifying, confirming, understanding, and addressing barriers that hinder effective communication and comprehension. Active listening is used to reduce misunderstandings and other miscommunications with stakeholders. It is particularly critical when working in global or cross-cultural environments, where team members may interpret messages differently due to diverse linguistic and cultural backgrounds.

Affinity diagram. An affinity diagram shows large numbers of ideas classified into groups for review and analysis. Affinity diagrams can also organize potential causes of defects into groups showing the areas that should be focused on the most.

After-action reviews (AARs). After-action reviews are a simple, structured process used to analyze what happened, why it happened, and how it can be done better by the participants and those responsible for the project or activity. Originating from the U.S. Army, AARs are designed to improve team performance by reflecting on actions taken and outcomes achieved. The AARs are typically conducted at the end of a project or after significant milestones to capture lessons learned and inform future activities. The AARs may include the following:

- **Diagnostic process.** The diagnostic process involves diagnosing what went well and what did not, and identifying both strengths and weaknesses.
- **Documentation.** Findings from the AARs are documented and shared with relevant stakeholders to help ensure that valuable lessons are captured and disseminated.

- **Learning and improvement.** The primary goal is to reinforce learning and improve future performance by applying the insights gained from the review.
- **Participant involvement.** All team members involved in the project participate in the review, ensuring a comprehensive understanding of the events and outcomes.
- **Structured reflection.** The AARs follow a structured format, asking four key questions:
  - What was supposed to happen?
  - What actually happened?
  - Why were there differences?
  - What can we learn?

In summary, AARs are a valuable tool for continuous improvement in project management. The reviews provide a structured approach to reflect on project performance, engage team members in the diagnostic process, and capture lessons learned to enhance future projects.

Agile release planning. Agile release planning provides a high-level summary timeline of the release schedule (typically 3–6 months) based on the product roadmap and the product vision for the product's evolution. Agile release planning determines the number of iterations or sprints in the release. This planning empowers the product owner and team to determine the development scope, timelines, and a releasable product, factoring in business goals, dependencies, impediments, and resource availability.

Since features represent expected value to the customer, the timeline provides a more easily understood project schedule as it defines which features will be available at the end of each iteration.

Figure 5-1 shows the typical relationship among product vision, product roadmap, release planning, and iteration planning. While the figure shows tasks estimated in hours, it is important to note that many agile teams use story points instead. Story points reflect the relative effort or complexity rather than absolute time, based on the understanding that teams are typically better at comparing work items than predicting precise durations. This approach simplifies planning while preserving accuracy, as estimating hours can be more time-consuming and less reliable in dynamic environments.

Alternative analysis. Alternative analysis is a method used to evaluate identified options in order to select the options or approaches to use when performing the work of the project. In a project context, two examples include (1) determining what solution might best address a project's business or mission objectives, and (2) determining the best approach for executing and completing project tasks within the defined constraints.

Analogous estimating. Analogous estimating is a technique for estimating the duration, cost, or required resources for an activity or a project using historical data from a similar activity or project. Analogous estimating uses parameters from a previous, similar project, such as duration, budget, size, weight, and complexity, as the basis for estimating the same parameter or measure for a future project. When estimating durations, this technique relies on the actual duration of previous, similar projects as the basis for estimating the duration of the current project. It is a gross value estimating approach, sometimes adjusted for known differences in project complexity. Analogous duration estimating is frequently used to estimate project duration when there is limited detailed information about the project.

Analogous estimating is generally less costly and less time-consuming than other techniques but can also be less accurate. Analogous duration estimates can be applied to a total project or to segments of a project and may be used in conjunction with other estimating methods. Analogous estimating is

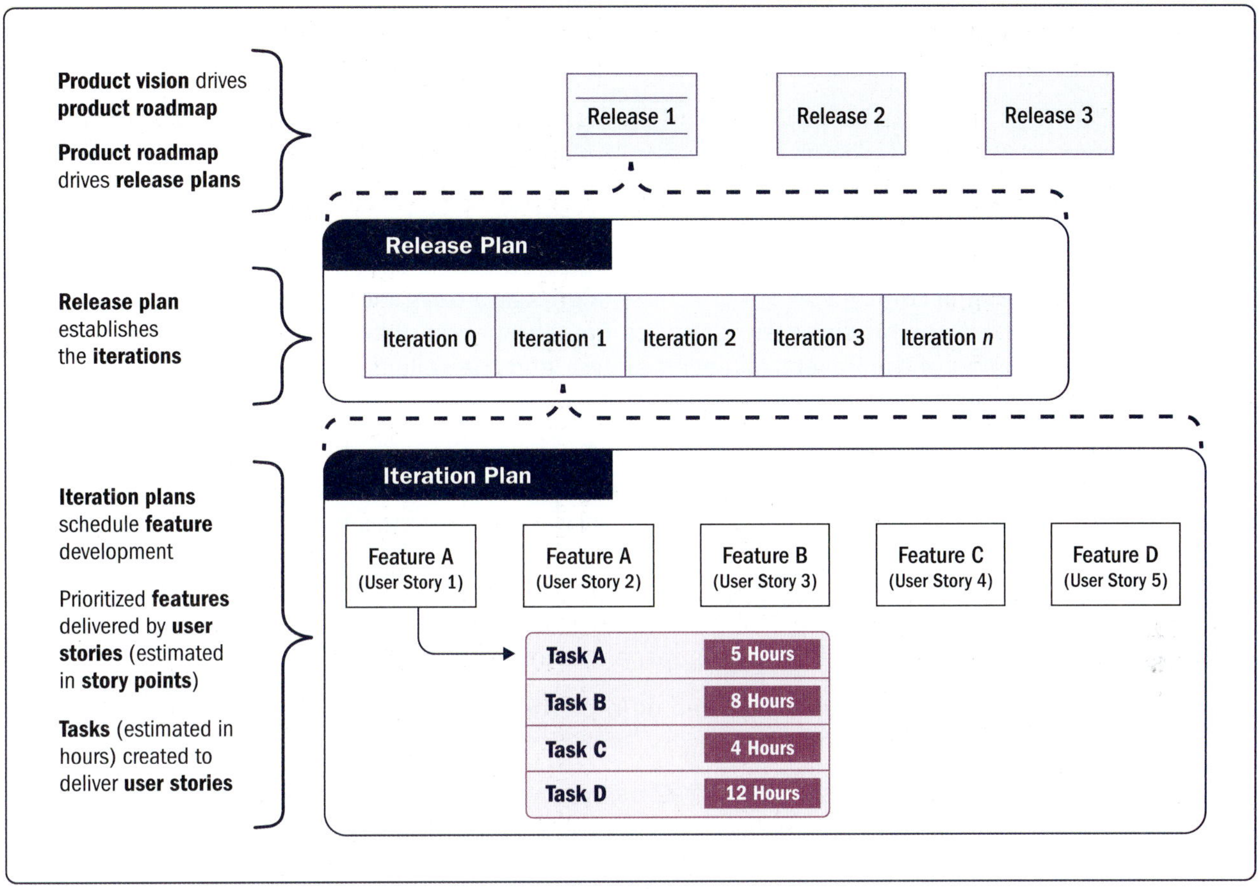

Figure 5-1. Relationship Among Product Vision, Release Planning, and Iteration Planning

most reliable when the previous activities are similar in fact and not just appearance, and when the project team members preparing the estimates have the needed expertise.

Artificial intelligence (AI). AI is the programming of machines with patterns and processes similar to those observed in—and by—humans and human interactions.

- **Machine learning (ML).** Machine learning is a part of AI, and its main goal is to develop software that can learn from past experiences, similar to what humans do. Common fields include recognizing speech and images; predicting weather, stock market behavior, and traffic; operating autonomous cars; filtering email spam; and providing a medical diagnosis.

- **Natural language processing (NLP).** The NLP technique's goal is to build software that can process natural language, like humans. In other words, people communicate with computers in their own natural language. Some NLP examples include chatbots, speech recognition, text extraction and summarization, and sentiment analysis.

Assumption and constraint analysis. Every project is conceived and developed based on a set of assumptions and within a series of constraints. These assumptions and constraints are often already incorporated in the scope baseline and project estimates. Assumption and constraint analysis explores the validity of assumptions and constraints to determine which pose a risk to the project. Threats may be identified from the inaccuracy, instability, inconsistency, or incompleteness of assumptions. Constraints may give rise to opportunities through removing or relaxing a limiting factor that affects the execution of a project or process.

Audits. An audit is a structured, independent process used to determine if project activities comply with organizational and project policies, processes, and procedures.

- **Procurement audit.** A procurement audit is a structured review of the procurement process, which includes the review of contracts and contracting processes for completeness, accuracy, and effectiveness. Rights and obligations related to audits should be described in the procurement contract. Resulting audit observations should be brought to the attention of the buyer's project manager and the seller's project manager for adjustments to the project, when necessary.
- **Quality audit.** A quality audit is usually conducted by a team external to the project, such as the organization's internal audit department, project management office (PMO), or an auditor external to the organization. Quality audit objectives may include but are not limited to the following:
    - Identifying all good practices being implemented;
    - Identifying all nonconformities, gaps, and shortcomings;
    - Sharing good practices introduced or implemented in similar projects in the organization and/or industry;
    - Proactively offering assistance in a positive manner to improve the implementation of processes to help raise team productivity;
    - Highlighting contributions of each audit in the lessons learned repository of the organization;
    - Subsequent efforts to correct any deficiencies should result in a reduced cost of quality and an increase in sponsor or customer acceptance of the project's product;
    - Quality audits may be scheduled or random, and may be conducted by internal or external auditors; and
    - Quality audits can confirm the implementation of approved change requests including updates, corrective actions, defect repairs, and preventive actions.
- **Risk audit.** A risk audit is a type of audit that may be used to consider the effectiveness of the risk management process. The project manager is responsible for ensuring that risk audits are performed at an appropriate frequency, as defined in the project's risk management plan. Risk audits may be included during routine project review meetings, may form part of a risk review meeting, or the team may choose to hold separate risk audit meetings. The format for the risk audit and its objectives should be clearly defined before the audit is conducted.

Augmented reality (AR). Augmented reality is the use of technology to simulate and enhance the actual, physical reality and environment through the overlay of digital information. This technique connects the real and digital worlds through technologies and devices such as smartphones or headsets.

Autocratic decision-making. See *decision-making.*

Backlog management. Backlog management is primarily used in adaptive approaches to maintain the list of backlog items to be worked on during a project and refers to the process by which the owner of the backlog, commonly a product owner, assists in keeping the backlog up to date. To avoid confusion, it is important to distinguish between the product backlog, which contains the complete list of desired features and changes for the product, and the sprint backlog, which includes only the subset of items selected for delivery in a specific iteration.

In adaptive approaches, backlog management is the technique used to manage changes. The list of backlog items is ranked in order of business value or importance to the customer and sized by the development team so that the highest value items are selected and delivered in the next development cycle. Dependencies and constraints are also taken into account, which could impact the order of the new item and changes in the backlog.

Backlog refinement. Backlog refinement is the progressive elaboration of the content in the backlog and reprioritization of it to identify the work that can be accomplished in an upcoming iteration. This technique is used mostly within adaptive development approaches. Backlog refinement involves constantly reviewing, revising, ranking, and editing the product backlog in order to build features that are needed by the business and the customer. During a backlog refinement meeting, the backlog is elaborated and reprioritized to identify the work that can be accomplished during the upcoming iteration.

Benchmarking. Benchmarking is the comparison of actual or planned products, processes, and practices to those of comparable organizations to identify good practices, generate ideas for improvement, and provide a basis for measuring performance. Benchmarked projects may exist within the performing organization or outside of it, or can be within the same application area or other application area. Benchmarking allows analogies to be made for projects in different application areas or industries.

Bottom-up estimating. Bottom-up estimating is a method of estimating the duration, cost, or required resources by aggregating the estimates of the lower-level components of the work breakdown structure (WBS). When an activity's duration cannot be estimated with a reasonable degree of confidence, the work within the activity is decomposed into more detail. The detailed durations are estimated. These estimates are then aggregated into a total quantity for each of the activity's durations. Activities may or may not have dependencies between them that can affect the application and use of resources. If there are dependencies, this pattern of resource usage is reflected and documented in the estimated requirements of the activity.

Brainstorming. The brainstorming technique is used to identify a list of ideas in a short period of time. Brainstorming is conducted in a group environment and is led by a facilitator. The technique comprises two parts: idea generation and analysis. Brainstorming can be used to gather data and solutions or ideas from stakeholders, subject matter experts, and team members.

Brainstorming techniques. There are many brainstorming techniques, including the following:

- **Brain-netting**, or virtual brainstorming, uses a digital collaboration platform, documents stored on a cloud or server, or other online tools in order to generate and prioritize ideas, discussing the advantages and disadvantages of specific topics. Anonymous idea sharing can be included as well.
- **Brainwriting** encourages everyone in the brainstorming session to participate and write their ideas down before sharing them with other team members. Later, the facilitator collects the ideas and shares them or asks others to share and discuss them with the group.
- **Idea napkin** involves documenting ideas in five steps on a napkin. The five steps include such topics as people, offering, customer, value proposition, and core competencies.

- **Individual brainstorming** encourages creative thinking and includes techniques such as:
  - **Free writing.** A time-based writing session when people generate ideas and write until an alarm sounds, ignoring grammar and spelling;
  - **Word association.** Creating a list of words and relating them to a topic, which stimulates the development of numerous creative and unconventional ideas; and
  - **Spiderwebs.** Visual note-taking that diagrams the process of thought, where one idea can stimulate other related ideas.
- **Mind mapping.** See *mind mapping*.
- **Reverse brainstorming** is a brainstorming technique used by teams to create ideas about how to make a problem worse instead of solving it, which may help to identify the root cause of a problem.
- **Round-robin** is a brainstorming technique where everyone within the team takes a turn to generate and develop ideas.
- **Starbursting** is a brainstorming technique with a main goal of creating a list of questions related to an idea or an issue from different angles. The star has six points, each representing a different question: who, what, when, where, why, and how.
- **SWOT (strengths, weaknesses, opportunities, threats) analysis.** See *SWOT analysis*.
- **Five whys analysis** is an iterative brainstorming technique that repeatedly asks "why" in order to get beyond symptoms and get to the root cause of the problem.

Branch and bound. The branch and bound technique is a minimal path to the optimal solution for a given problem. Branch and bound is an optimization problem-solving method that involves breaking down a problem into smaller subproblems and using bounding functions to eliminate any subproblems that do not contain the optimal solution. This technique could be used for project scheduling by systematically exploring and pruning potential schedules to find an optimal sequence of tasks that minimizes project completion time while satisfying all constraints.

Burndown chart. A burndown chart is a graphical representation of the work remaining versus the time left in a timebox. See also *iteration burndown chart*.

Burnup chart. A burnup chart is a graphical representation of the work completed toward a milestone. Burnup charts are used mostly within adaptive development approaches to show project progress over time. The chart tracks the amount of work to be completed as a straight line across the top of the graph. The work completed starts at zero and increases as more work is completed. See also *visual controls*.

Cause-and-effect diagram. A cause-and effect diagram is a visual representation that helps trace an effect back to its root cause. A cause-and-effect diagram may also be known as a fishbone or Ishikawa diagram. This type of diagram breaks down the causes of the problem statement identified into discrete branches, helping to identify the main or root cause of the problem.

Centralized management and leadership. While leadership activities should be practiced by all project team members, management activities may be centralized or distributed. Centralized management and leadership is a management structure that consists of top-down leadership and instructions for decision implementation for other levels of management. As opposed to implementing distributed management and leadership, a centralized management and leadership structure means that the decision-making and authority are centralized within top management and are conducted by a small number of senior leaders. In an environment where management activities are centralized, accountability (being answerable for an outcome) is usually assigned to one individual such as the project manager or similar role. In these situations, a project charter or other authorizing document can provide approval for the project manager to form a project team to achieve the project outcomes. See also *distributed management and leadership*.

Change control tools. To facilitate configuration and change management, both manual and automated tools can be utilized. Configuration control focuses on specifying both deliverables and processes, while change control is concerned with identifying, documenting, and approving or rejecting changes to project documents, deliverables, or baselines. Tool selection should be based on the needs of project stakeholders, considering organizational and environmental constraints.

Configuration management activities supported by these change control tools include identifying configuration items, recording and reporting their status, and performing configuration item verification and audits. These activities can ensure that the product configuration is defined and verified, changes are managed, and accountability is maintained, meeting the functional requirements outlined in the configuration documentation.

Change management activities supported by these change control tools include identifying and selecting change items, documenting changes into proper change requests, and deciding on changes by reviewing, approving, rejecting, or deferring them. Additionally, tools help track changes by verifying that they are registered, assessed, approved, and communicated to stakeholders. Tools also manage change requests and the resulting decisions, with additional considerations for communication to assist the change control board (CCB) in their duties and to distribute decisions to the appropriate stakeholders.

Checklists. A checklist is a list of items, actions, or points to be considered. Checklists are often used as reminders and are developed based on historical information and knowledge accumulated from similar projects and other sources of information. Using checklists is an effective way to capture lessons learned from similar completed projects, listing specific individual project risks that have occurred previously and that may be relevant to the current project.

The organization may maintain checklists based on completed projects or use generic checklists from the industry. While a checklist may be quick and simple to use, it is impossible to build an exhaustive one. The project team should also explore items that do not appear on the checklist. Additionally, the checklist should be reviewed from time to time to update new information as well as remove or archive obsolete information. Checklists can also serve as an effective way to ensure that a project or task is ready to start; such a checklist is also called "definition of ready" or "full kit," and can be particularly useful in minimizing rework.

Coaching and mentoring. Coaching provides guidance and helps people (e.g., a project team member or a stakeholder) to find a solution to a specific problem on their own by asking the right questions. Mentoring is serving as a counselor, guide, or mentor by sharing knowledge, skills, or experience with a person who has to develop their own knowledge or skills. Both coaching and mentoring include one-to-one conversations. However, coaching is more related to achieving specific goals, while mentoring is a more long-term, ongoing relationship-building practice.

Colocation. Colocation is an organizational placement strategy where the project team members are physically located close to one another in order to improve communication, working relationships, and productivity.

Colocation involves placing many or all of the most active project team members in the same physical location to enhance their ability to perform as a team. Colocation can be temporary, such as at strategically important times during the project, or can continue for the entire project. Colocation strategies may include a team meeting room, common places to post schedules, and other conveniences that enhance communication and a sense of community.

Communication competence. Communication competence is a combination of tailored communication skills that considers factors such as clarity of purpose in key messages, effective relationships and information sharing, and leadership behaviors.

Communication methods. A communication method is a systematic procedure, technique, or process used to transfer information among project stakeholders.

There are several communication methods that are used to share information among project stakeholders. These methods are broadly classified as follows:

- **Interactive communication.** Interactive communication occurs between two or more parties performing a multidirectional exchange of information in real time. Interactive communication employs communications artifacts such as meetings, phone calls, instant messaging, some forms of social media, and videoconferencing.
- **Push communication.** Push communications are sent or distributed directly to specific recipients who need to receive the information. This method ensures that the information is distributed but does not ensure that it reaches or is understood by the intended audience. Push communication artifacts include letters, memos, reports, emails, faxes, voicemails, blogs, and press releases.
- **Pull communication.** Pull communications are used for large, complex information sets or for large audiences, and require the recipients to access content at their own discretion subject to security procedures. These methods include web portals, intranet sites, eLearning courses, lessons learned databases, or knowledge repositories.

Different approaches should be applied to meet the needs of the major forms of communication defined in the communications management plan:

- **Interpersonal communication.** Interpersonal communication is information that is exchanged between individuals, typically face-to-face.
- **Small group communication.** Small group communications occur within groups of three to six people.
- **Public communication.** Public communication occurs when a single speaker, or group of speakers, addresses a larger audience.
- **Mass communication.** Mass communication is an approach with minimal connection between the person or group sending the message and the large, sometimes anonymous, groups for whom the information is intended.
- **Networks and social computing communication.** This type of communication approach supports emerging communication trends of many-to-many, which is often supported by social computing technology and the media.

Possible communication artifacts and methods include but are not limited to the following:

- Notice boards;
- Newsletters, in-house magazines, and e-magazines;
- Letters to staff or volunteers;
- Press releases;
- Annual reports;
- Emails and intranets;
- Web portals and other information repositories (for pull communication);
- Phone conversations;
- Presentations;
- Team briefings or group meetings;
- Focus groups;
- Face-to-face formal or informal meetings among various stakeholders;
- Consultation groups or staff forums; and
- Social computing technology and media.

Communication models. A communication model is a description, analogy, or schematic used to represent how the communication process will be performed for the project.

Communication models can represent the communication process in its most basic linear form (sender and receiver), in a more interactive form that encompasses the additional element of feedback (sender, receiver, and feedback), or in a more complex model that incorporates the human elements of the sender(s) or receiver(s) and attempts to show the complexity of any communication that involves people.

- **Sample basic sender/receiver communication model.** This model describes communication as a process and consists of two parties, defined as the sender and receiver. This model is concerned with ensuring that the message is delivered rather than understood. The sequence of steps in a basic communication model is as follows:
  - **Encode.** The message is coded into symbols, such as text, sound, or some other medium, for transmission (sending).
  - **Transmit message.** The message is sent via a communication channel. The transmission of this message may be compromised by various physical factors such as unfamiliar technology or inadequate infrastructure. Noise and other factors may be present and contribute to loss of information in transmission and/or reception of the message.
  - **Decode.** The data received is translated by the receiver back into a form useful to the receiver.
- **Sample interactive communication model.** This model also describes communication as a process consisting of two parties, the sender and receiver, but recognizes the need to ensure that the message has been understood. In this model, noise includes any interference or barriers that might compromise the understanding of the message, such as the distraction

of the receiver, variations in the perceptions of receivers, or lack of appropriate knowledge or interest. The additional steps in an interactive communication model are:

- **Acknowledge.** Upon receipt of a message, the receiver may signal (acknowledge) receipt of the message, but this does not necessarily mean agreement with or comprehension of the message—merely that it has been received.
- **Feedback/response.** When the received message has been decoded and understood, the receiver encodes thoughts and ideas into a message and then transmits this message to the original sender. If the sender perceives that the feedback matches the original message, the communication has been successful. In communication among people, feedback can be achieved through active listening.

As part of the communication process, the sender is responsible for the transmission of the message, ensuring the information being communicated is clear and complete, and confirming the message is correctly interpreted. The receiver is responsible for ensuring that the information is received in its entirety, interpreted correctly, and acknowledged or responded to appropriately. These components take place in an environment where there will likely be noise and other barriers to effective communication.

Cross-cultural communication presents challenges to ensuring that the meaning of the message has been understood. Differences in communication styles can arise from differences in working methods, age, nationality, professional discipline, ethnicity, race, or gender. People from different cultures communicate using different languages (e.g., technical design documents or different styles) and expect different processes and protocols.

The communication model shown in Figure 5-2 incorporates the idea that the message itself, and how it is transmitted, is influenced by the sender's current emotional state, knowledge, background, personality, culture, and biases. Similarly, the receiver's emotional state, knowledge, background, personality, culture, and biases will influence how the message is received and interpreted and will contribute to the barriers or noise.

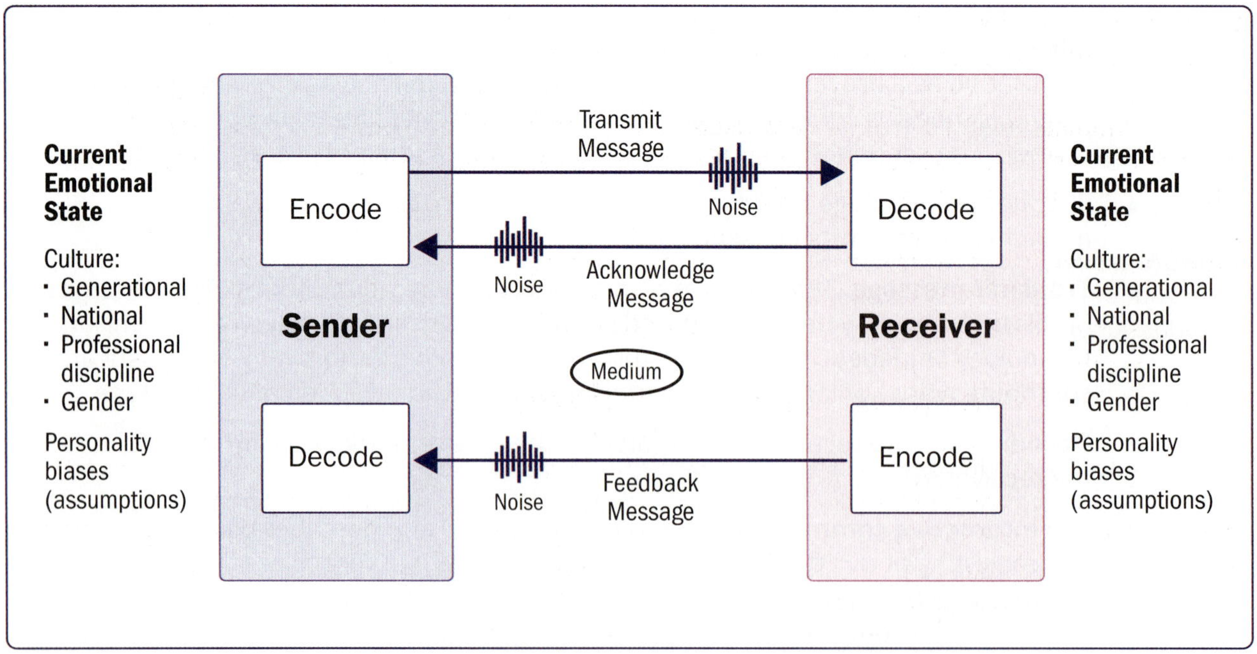

Figure 5-2. Communication Model for Cross-Cultural Communication

This communication model and its enhancements can assist in developing communication strategies and plans for person-to-person or even small-group-to-small-group communications. The model is not useful for other communications artifacts such as emails, broadcast messages, or social media.

Communication requirements analysis. Communication requirements analysis is an analytical technique used to determine the information needs of the project stakeholders through interviews, workshops, the study of lessons learned from previous projects, etc. Analysis of communication requirements determines the information needs of the project stakeholders. These requirements are defined by combining the type and format of information needed with an analysis of the value of that information. Sources of information typically used to identify and define project communication requirements include but are not limited to the following:

- Stakeholder information and communication requirements from within the stakeholder register and stakeholder engagement plan;
- Number of potential communication channels or paths, including one-to-one, one-to-many, and many-to-many communications;
- Organizational charts;
- Project organization and stakeholder responsibilities, relationships, and interdependencies;
- Development approach;
- Disciplines, departments, and specialties involved in the project;
- Logistics of how many persons will be involved with the project and at which locations;
- Internal information needs (e.g., when communicating within organizations);
- External information needs (e.g., when communicating with the media, public, or contractors); and
- Legal requirements.

Communication skills. Communication skills are a collection of skills to provide, receive, and elicit information from various sources. Communication skills can be oral, visual, or electronic. Oral communication skills include interaction, presentation, active listening, and meeting facilitation. Visual communication skills include data visualization and nonverbal communication. Electronic communication skills include electronic tools such as professional writing, crafting emails, texting, chatting, AI prompts, and similar activities.

Communication styles assessment. A communication styles assessment is a technique used to assess communication styles and identify the preferred communication method, format, and content for planned communication activities. Often used with unsupportive stakeholders, this assessment may follow a stakeholder engagement assessment to identify gaps in stakeholder engagement that require additional tailored communication activities and artifacts.

Communication technology. Communication technology includes specific tools, systems, computer programs, etc., used to transfer information among project stakeholders. The methods used to transfer information among project stakeholders may vary significantly. Common methods used for information exchange and collaboration include conversations, meetings, written documents, databases, social media, and websites.

Factors that can affect the choice of communication technology may include the following:

- **Urgency of the need for information.** The urgency, frequency, and format of the information to be communicated may vary from project to project and within different phases of a project.
- **Availability and reliability of technology.** The technology that is required for distribution of project communications artifacts should be compatible, available, and accessible for all stakeholders throughout the project.
- **Ease of use.** The choice of communication technologies should be suitable for project participants, and proper training events should be planned where appropriate.
- **Project environment.** Factors to consider include:
  - Will the team meet and operate on a face-to-face basis or in a virtual environment?
  - Will the team be located in one or multiple time zones?
  - Will the team use multiple languages for communication?
  - Are there any other project environmental factors, such as various aspects of culture, that may constrain the efficiency of communication?
- **Sensitivity and confidentiality of the information.** Some aspects to consider include:
  - Will the information to be communicated be sensitive or confidential? If so, additional security measures may be required.
  - Does the organization have social media policies for employees to ensure appropriate behavior, security, and the protection of proprietary information?

Conflict management. Conflict is inevitable in a project environment. Sources of conflict include scarce resources, scheduling priorities, and personal work styles. Team ground rules, group norms, and solid project management practices, such as communication planning and role definition, can reduce the amount of conflict.

Successful conflict management results in greater productivity and positive working relationships. When managed properly, differences of opinion can lead to increased creativity and better decision-making. If the differences become a negative factor, project team members are initially responsible for their resolution. If conflict escalates, the project manager should help facilitate a satisfactory resolution. Conflict should be addressed early and usually in private, using a direct, collaborative approach. If disruptive conflict continues, formal procedures may be used, including disciplinary actions.

The success of project managers in managing their project teams often depends on their ability to resolve conflicts. Different project managers may use different conflict resolution methods. Factors that influence conflict resolution methods may include:

- Importance and intensity of the conflict,
- Time pressure for resolving the conflict,
- Relative power of the people involved in the conflict,
- Importance of maintaining a good relationship, and
- Motivation to resolve conflict on a long-term or short-term basis.

There are five general techniques for resolving conflict. Each technique has its place and use:

- **Withdraw/avoid.** Retreating from an actual or potential conflict situation; postponing the issue to be better prepared or to be resolved by others.
- **Smooth/accommodate.** Emphasizing areas of agreement rather than areas of difference; conceding one's position to the needs of others to maintain harmony and relationships.
- **Compromise/reconcile.** Searching for solutions that bring some degree of satisfaction to all parties in order to temporarily or partially resolve the conflict. This approach occasionally results in a lose-lose situation.
- **Force/direct.** Pushing one's viewpoint at the expense of others; offering only win-lose solutions, usually enforced through a power position to resolve an emergency. This approach often results in a win-lose situation.
- **Collaborate/problem-solve.** Incorporating multiple viewpoints and insights from differing perspectives; requires a cooperative attitude and open dialogue that typically leads to consensus and commitment. This approach can result in a win-win situation.

Constructive cost model (COCOMO). A constructive cost model is a cost-estimation model for effort, time, and cost, usually associated with software development projects. The source lines of code or function points and adjustment factors are usually used as inputs and help to predict the software development cost.

Contingent response strategies. There are five strategies that may be considered for dealing with opportunities, as follows:

- **Escalate.** This risk response strategy is appropriate when the project team or project sponsor agrees that an opportunity is outside the scope of the project or that the proposed response would exceed the project manager's authority. Escalated opportunities are managed at the portfolio level, program level, or other relevant part of the organization, but not on the project level. The project manager determines who should be notified about the opportunity and communicates the details to that person or part of the organization. It is important that ownership of escalated opportunities is accepted by the relevant party in the organization. Opportunities are usually escalated to the level that matches the objectives that would be affected if the opportunity occurred. Escalated opportunities are not monitored further by the project team after escalation, although they may be recorded in the risk register for information.
- **Exploit.** The exploit strategy may be selected for high-priority opportunities where the organization wants to ensure that the opportunity is realized. This strategy seeks to capture the benefit associated with a particular opportunity by ensuring that it definitely happens, increasing the probability of occurrence to 100%. Examples of exploiting responses may include assigning an organization's most talented resources to the project to reduce the time to completion or using new technologies or technology upgrades to reduce cost and duration.
- **Share.** Sharing involves transferring ownership of an opportunity to a third party so that it shares some of the benefit if the opportunity occurs. It is important to select the new owner of a shared opportunity carefully, so they are best able to capture the opportunity for the benefit of the project. Risk sharing often involves payment of a risk premium to the party taking on the opportunity. Examples of sharing actions include forming risk-sharing partnerships, teams, special-purpose companies, or joint ventures.

- **Enhance.** The enhance strategy is used to increase the probability and/or impact of an opportunity. Early enhancement action is often more effective than trying to improve the benefit after the opportunity has occurred. The probability of occurrence for an opportunity may be increased by focusing attention on its causes. Where it is not possible to increase probability, an enhancement response might increase the impact by targeting factors that drive the size of the potential benefit. Examples of enhancing opportunities include adding more resources to an activity to finish early.
- **Accept.** Accepting an opportunity acknowledges its existence but no proactive action is taken. This strategy may be appropriate for low-priority opportunities. It may also be adopted where it is not possible or cost-effective to address an opportunity in any other way. Acceptance can be either active or passive. The most common active acceptance strategy is to establish a contingency reserve, including amounts of time, money, or resources to take advantage of the opportunity if it occurs. Passive acceptance involves no proactive action apart from a periodic review of the opportunity to ensure that it does not change significantly.

Continuous improvement. Continuous improvement is an ongoing process that focuses on efforts to improve processes, products, systems, or services. It involves identifying, analyzing, and implementing incremental improvements. Continuous improvement can use approaches such as plan-do-check-act (PDCA), Lean, Total Quality Management, Six Sigma, Five Focusing Steps (5FS), and similar methods.

Control charts. Control charts are used to determine whether or not a process is stable or has predictable performance. Upper and lower specification limits are based on the requirements and reflect the maximum and minimum values allowed. Upper and lower control limits are different from specification limits. The control limits are determined using standard statistical calculations and principles to ultimately establish the natural capability for a stable process. The project manager and appropriate stakeholders may use the statistically calculated control limits to identify the points at which corrective action will be taken to prevent performance that remains outside the control limits. Control charts can be used to monitor various types of output variables. Although used most frequently to track repetitive activities required for producing manufactured lots, control charts may also be used to monitor cost and schedule variances, volume, frequency of scope changes, or other management results to help determine if the project management processes are in control.

Cost aggregation. Cost aggregation is a cost estimate that is aggregated by work packages in accordance with the work breakdown structure (WBS). The work package cost estimates are then aggregated for the higher component levels of the WBS (such as control accounts) and, ultimately, for the entire project.

Cost-benefit analysis. Cost-benefit analysis is a financial analysis method used to determine the benefits provided by a project against its costs. The analysis is used to estimate the strengths and weaknesses of alternatives in order to determine the best alternative in terms of benefits provided. A cost-benefit analysis can help the project manager to determine if project activities are cost-effective. A cost-benefit analysis compares the cost of an activity to the expected benefit.

Cost of quality (CoQ). The cost of quality includes all costs incurred over the life of the product by investment in preventing nonconformance to requirements, appraisal of the product or service for conformance to requirements, and failure to meet requirements. The CoQ associated with a

Cost of Conformance

Prevention Costs
(Build a quality product)
- Training
- Document processes
- Equipment
- Time to do it right

Appraisal Costs
(Assess the quality)
- Testing
- Destructive testing loss
- Inspections

Money spent during the project **to avoid failures**

Cost of Nonconformance

Internal Failure Costs
(Failures found by the project)
- Rework
- Scrap

External Failure Costs
(Failures found by the customer)
- Liabilities
- Warranty work
- Lost business

Money spent during and after the project **because of failures**

Figure 5-3. Cost of Quality

project consists of one or more of the following costs (see Figure 5-3, which lists examples for each cost group):

- **Prevention costs.** Costs related to the prevention of poor quality in products, deliverables, or services of the specific project.
- **Appraisal costs.** Costs related to evaluating, measuring, auditing, and testing products, deliverables, or services of a specific project.
- **Failure costs (internal/external).** Costs related to nonconformance of products, deliverables, or services based on the needs or expectations of the stakeholders.

The optimal CoQ is one that reflects the appropriate balance for investing in the cost of prevention and appraisal to avoid failure costs. Models show that there is an optimal quality cost for projects, where investing in additional prevention/appraisal costs is neither beneficial nor cost-effective.

Critical chain method. A schedule method that allows the project team to place buffers on any project schedule path to account for limited resources and project uncertainties. See also *critical chain project management (CCPM).*

Critical chain project management (CCPM). A set of techniques used to promote fast execution and high due-date performance by aggregating task-level (or sprint-level) variability to a project buffer, and then allocating the project buffer only when and where needed in order to protect the project due date. While the concept of a project reserve or contingency is similar, the difference is that a critical chain buffer is *in lieu of* task-level or sprint-level buffers, and not in addition to them. CCPM uses nearly identical scheduling logic as the critical path method (CPM), as both are based on critical path analysis, and both call for a resource-loaded and resource-leveled critical path (RLCP). Indeed, when identifying the longest path or chain of tasks in a project schedule, "the RLCP" is synonymous with "the critical chain."

The only meaningful difference in scheduling logic between CCPM and CPM is that CCPM also calculates the percentage of the project buffer remaining, and then compares it with the percentage of the critical chain remaining, giving all project participants a "thumb on the pulse" signal of project schedule performance. This signal is called the "buffer protection index (BPI)," and differs from the schedule performance index (SPI) from earned value management (EVM) in that BPI is designed to protect the project due date, whereas SPI is designed to gauge how far from the schedule baseline the project may be. Also, a big benefit of BPI is its use in prioritizing day-to-day tasks according to which ones will help protect the due dates of projects most at risk of missing them. (Note that, in addition to the project-level set of techniques briefly described above, CCPM also has portfolio-level techniques.)

Critical path drag. Critical path drag is the amount of time that an activity on the critical path is adding to the project duration. Alternatively, it is the maximum amount of time that one can shorten the activity before it is no longer on the critical path or before its duration becomes zero.

Critical path drag cost. Critical path drag cost is the amount by which a project's expected return on investment (ROI) is reduced due to the critical path drag of a specific critical path activity. In other words, it is the true economic cost of a specific critical path activity, comprised of its resource cost plus the cost of delay (or foregone acceleration premium).

Critical path method (CPM). Critical path method is a method used to estimate the minimum project duration and determine the amount of scheduling flexibility (float) on the logical network paths within the schedule model. The CPM identifies the critical path, which is the sequence of activities that determines the shortest possible duration to complete the project. This method involves schedule network analysis by calculating the early start (ES), early finish (EF), late start (LS), and late finish (LF) dates for each activity, without regard to resource limitations, by performing a forward and backward pass through the schedule network.

- The **forward pass** begins at the project start and calculates the earliest possible start and finish dates for each activity. For example: If Activity A has an early start (ES) of Day 1 and a duration of 3 days, its early finish (EF) is Day 3 (calculated as EF = ES + Duration – 1). This means the activity would start on Day 1 and complete by the end of Day 3.
- The **backward pass** begins at the project end and determines the latest allowable start and finish dates without delaying the project. For example: If an activity must finish no later than Day 10 (LF = 10), and it has a duration of 4 days, its late start (LS) would be Day 7 (calculated as LS = LF – Duration + 1). This means the latest it can start without delaying the project is Day 7.

The difference between late and early dates yields the total float, which indicates how much an activity can be delayed without affecting the project's finish date. Activities with zero total float form the critical path. Figure 5-4 illustrates a sample network. In this example, the longest path includes Activities A, C, and D. Thus, the sequence A–C–D is identified as the critical path.

The resulting early and late start and finish dates do not represent the actual project schedule, but rather define time windows within which each activity may be executed, based on the model inputs such as durations, dependencies, leads, lags, and constraints.

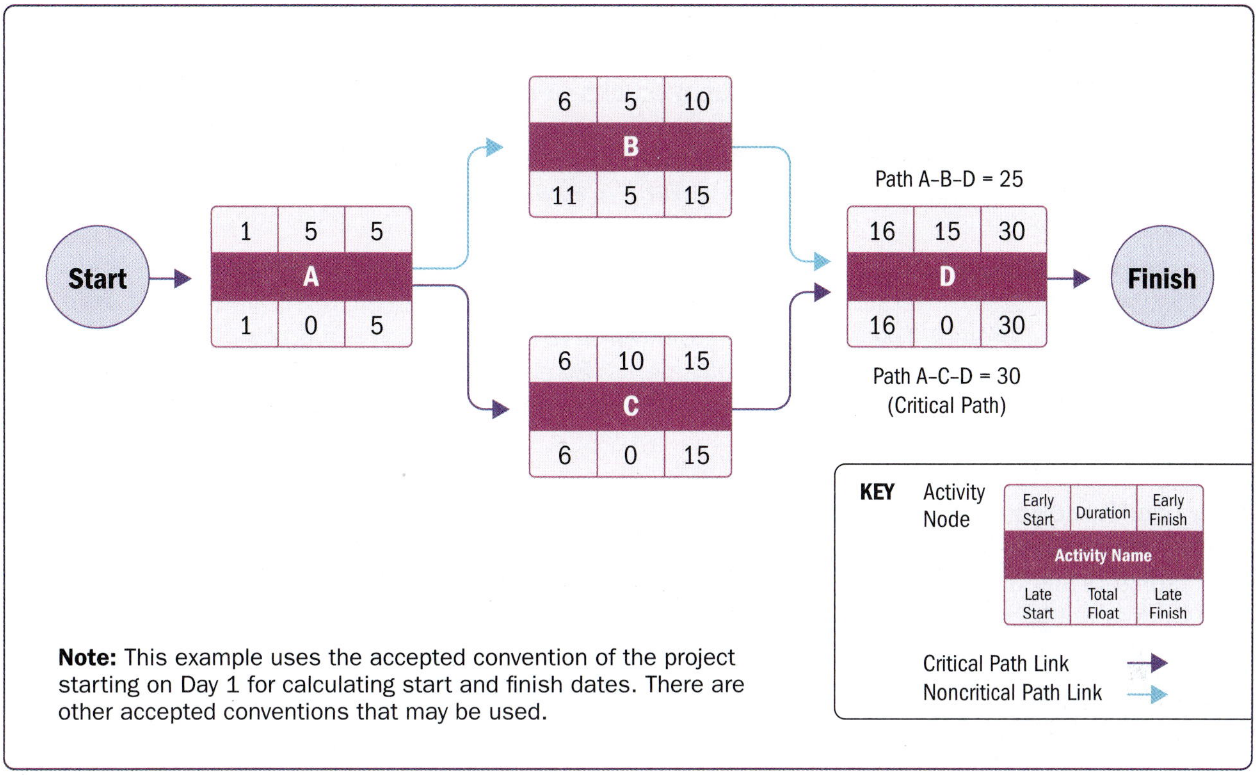

Figure 5-4. Example of Critical Path Method

The critical path method is also used to calculate the total and free float, or scheduling flexibility, for all logical paths in the network. On any network path, total float refers to the amount of time an activity can be delayed without delaying the project finish date or violating a constraint. Free float is the time an activity can be delayed without affecting the early start of its successor; for example, the free float for Activity B in Figure 5-4 is 5 days.

While the critical path is usually characterized by zero total float, positive float may occur if a constraint is placed later than the calculated early finish (from the forward pass). Conversely, negative float occurs when constraints force dates earlier than logic and duration allow. Negative float analysis can be used to explore acceleration strategies.

Some schedule networks may have multiple near-critical paths, and many software tools allow users to define how criticality is measured. Adjustments to activity durations, logical relationships, leads and lags, or constraints may be necessary to bring float values to zero or positive levels.

Critical thinking. Critical thinking is the ability to objectively question, analyze, interpret, evaluate, and judge information to make reasonable decisions. Throughout the various project management performance domains, there is a need to recognize bias, identify the root cause of problems, and consider challenging issues such as ambiguity and complexity. Critical thinking helps to accomplish these activities. Critical thinking includes disciplined, rational, logical, and evidence-based thinking. This approach requires an open mind and the ability to analyze objectively. Critical thinking, especially when applied to discovery, can include conceptual imagination, insight, and intuition; it can also include reflective thinking and metacognition (thinking about thinking and being aware of one's awareness).

Cultural awareness. Cultural awareness is an understanding of the differences among individuals, groups, and organizations and adapting the project's communication strategy in the context of these differences. This awareness and any consequent actions can minimize misunderstandings and miscommunication that may result from cultural differences within the project's stakeholder community. Cultural awareness and cultural sensitivity help the project manager to plan communications based on the cultural differences and requirements of stakeholders and team members.

Customer talks and tests. Customer talks and tests consist of the collaborative processes and activities involving direct interaction and feedback from customers during the development and testing phases of a project. These practices are integral to ensuring that the final product or service aligns with customer expectations and requirements. By engaging customers early and throughout the project life cycle, organizations can enhance transparency, build trust, and improve the overall quality of the deliverables.

Daily coordination meeting. A daily coordination meeting is a brief, daily collaboration meeting in which the team reviews progress from the previous day, declares intentions for the current day, and highlights any obstacles encountered or anticipated. Daily coordination meetings are a key tool used to enable the project team to self-direct and self-manage project work, particularly in agile approaches to project management. The primary goal is to increase visibility, foster collaboration, and ensure that the team is aligned and moving forward effectively.

- **Short and focused.** Daily coordination meetings are typically brief, lasting no more than 15 minutes. This brevity helps ensure that the meeting remains focused and efficient.
- **Progress updates.** Team members share what they accomplished the previous day, what they plan to do today, and any obstacles they are facing. This structure helps to keep everyone informed about the current status of the project.
- **Obstacle identification.** By discussing obstacles or blockers, the team can quickly identify issues that should be addressed, allowing for timely problem-solving and support.
- **Accountability.** Regular updates create a sense of accountability among team members, as they commit to specific tasks and report on their progress daily.
- **Collaboration and communication.** Daily coordination meetings enhance communication within the team, fostering a collaborative environment where team members can support one another and work together more effectively.

Data analysis. Data analysis is a process that involves data preprocessing, cleaning, transforming, analyzing, interpreting, and visualization in order to discover insights for informed and data-driven project decision-making. Data analysis can be done manually by project team members or other dedicated functions or by including business intelligence tools and software.

Data gathering. Data gathering is a process of selecting, collecting, measuring, and analyzing data based on the area of interest or variables (e.g., to answer relevant project-related questions or outcomes).

Data representation. Data representation is the way that data is stored, processed, and transmitted. Data representation can include but is not limited to the following:

- **Pie chart or circle chart for nominal data representation.** Nominal data can be categorized (e.g., it can be a mode of transportation such as a car, train, bus, or bicycle).

- **Bar chart or bar graph for ordinal data.** Ordinal data can be grouped into categories based on natural order or hierarchy (e.g., level of education such as high school diploma, bachelor's degree, master's degree, doctorate degree).
- **Histogram for discrete data.** Discrete data will usually have limited, finite value numbers (e.g., product reviews).
- **Line graph or line chart for continuous data.** Continuous data can take any value (e.g., temperature).

Decision-making. Decision-making techniques include but are not limited to the following:

- **Voting.** Voting is a collective decision-making technique and an assessment process having multiple alternatives with an expected outcome in the form of future actions. These techniques can be used to generate, classify, and prioritize product requirements. Examples of voting techniques include:
    - **Unanimity.** A decision that is reached whereby everyone agrees on a single course of action.
    - **Majority.** A decision that is reached with support obtained from more than 50% of the members of the group. Having a group size with an uneven number of participants can ensure that a decision will be reached rather than resulting in a tie.
    - **Plurality.** A decision that is reached whereby the largest block in a group decides, even if a majority is not achieved. This method is generally used when the number of options nominated is more than two.
- **Autocratic decision-making.** In this method, one individual takes responsibility for making the decision for the group.
- **Multicriteria decision analysis.** A technique that uses a decision matrix to provide a systematic, analytical approach for establishing criteria, such as risk levels, uncertainty, and valuation, to evaluate and rank many ideas.

Decision tree analysis. Decision tree analysis is a diagramming and calculation technique for evaluating the implications of a chain of multiple options in the presence of uncertainty. Decision trees are used to support selection of the best of several alternative courses of action. Alternative paths through the project are shown in the decision tree using branches representing different decisions or events, each of which can have associated costs and related individual project risks (including both threats and opportunities). The end points of branches in the decision tree represent the outcome from following that particular path, which can be negative or positive.

The decision tree is evaluated by calculating the expected monetary value of each branch, allowing the optimal path to be selected. An example decision tree is shown in Figure 5-5.

Decomposition. Decomposition is a technique used for dividing and subdividing the project scope and project deliverables into smaller, more manageable parts. The work package is the work defined at the lowest level of the work breakdown structure (WBS) for which cost and duration can be estimated and managed. The level of decomposition is often guided by the degree of control needed to effectively manage the project. The level of detail for work packages varies depending on the size

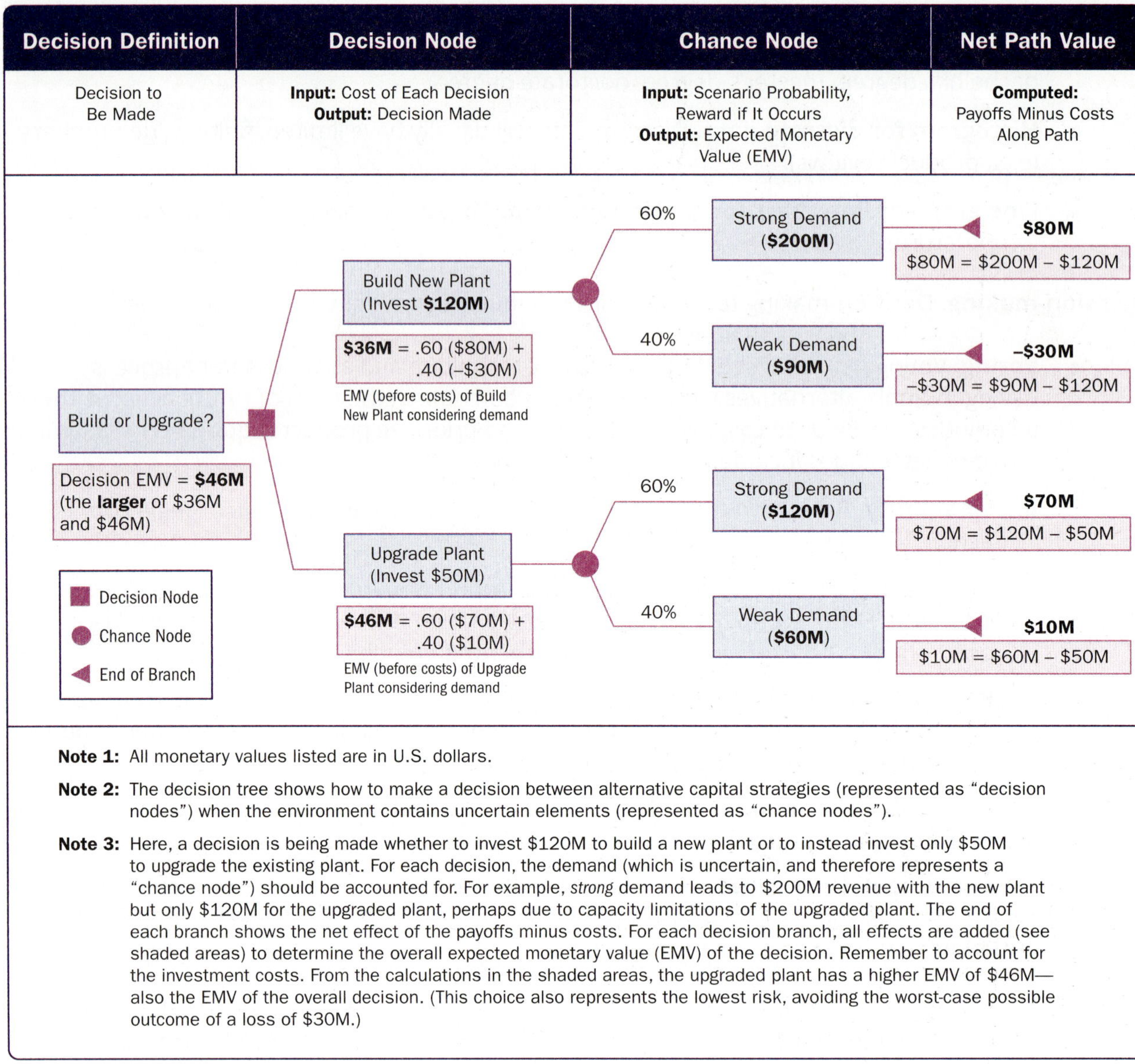

Figure 5-5. Example Decision Tree

and complexity of the project. Decomposition of the total project work into work packages generally involves the following activities:

- Identifying and analyzing the deliverables and related work,
- Structuring and organizing the WBS,
- Decomposing the upper WBS levels into lower-level detailed components,
- Developing and assigning identification codes to the WBS components, and
- Verifying that the degree of decomposition of the deliverables is appropriate.

A portion of a WBS with some branches of the WBS decomposed down through the work package level is shown in Figure 5-6.

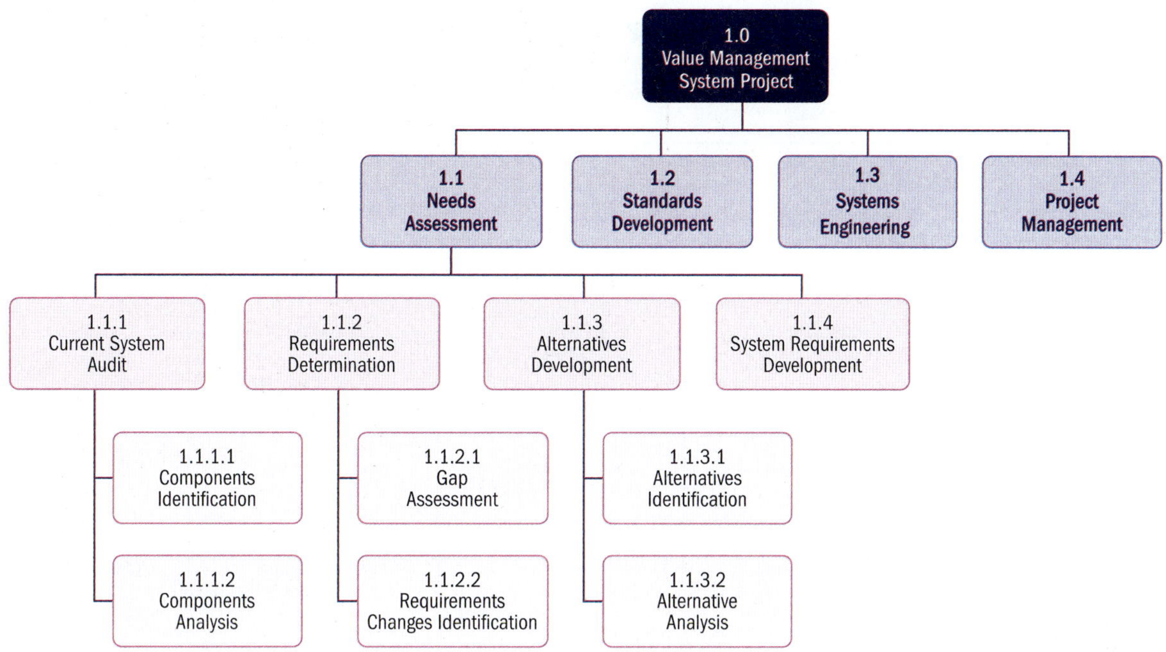

Note: The WBS is illustrative only. It is not intended to represent the full project scope of any specific project, nor to imply that this is the only way to organize a WBS on this type of project.

Figure 5-6. Sample WBS Decomposed Down Through Work Packages

A WBS structure may be created through various approaches. Some of the popular methods include the top-down approach, the use of organization-specific guidelines, and the use of WBS templates. A bottom-up approach can be used to group subcomponents. The WBS structure can be represented in various forms, such as:

- Using phases of the project life cycle as the second level of decomposition, with the product and project deliverables inserted at the third level, as shown in Figure 5-7;
- Using major deliverables as the second level of decomposition, as shown in Figure 5-8; and
- Incorporating subcomponents that may be developed by organizations outside the project team, such as contracted work. The seller then develops the supporting contract WBS as part of the contracted work.

Decomposition of the upper-level WBS components requires subdividing the work for each of the deliverables or subcomponents into its most fundamental components, where the WBS components represent verifiable products, services, or results. If an agile approach is used, epics can be decomposed into user stories. The WBS may be structured as an outline, organizational chart, or other method that identifies a hierarchical breakdown. Verifying the correctness of the decomposition requires determining that the lower-level WBS components are those that are necessary and sufficient for completion of the corresponding higher-level deliverables. Different deliverables can have different levels of decomposition.

To arrive at a work package, the work for some deliverables should be decomposed only to the next level, while others may require additional levels of decomposition. As the work is decomposed

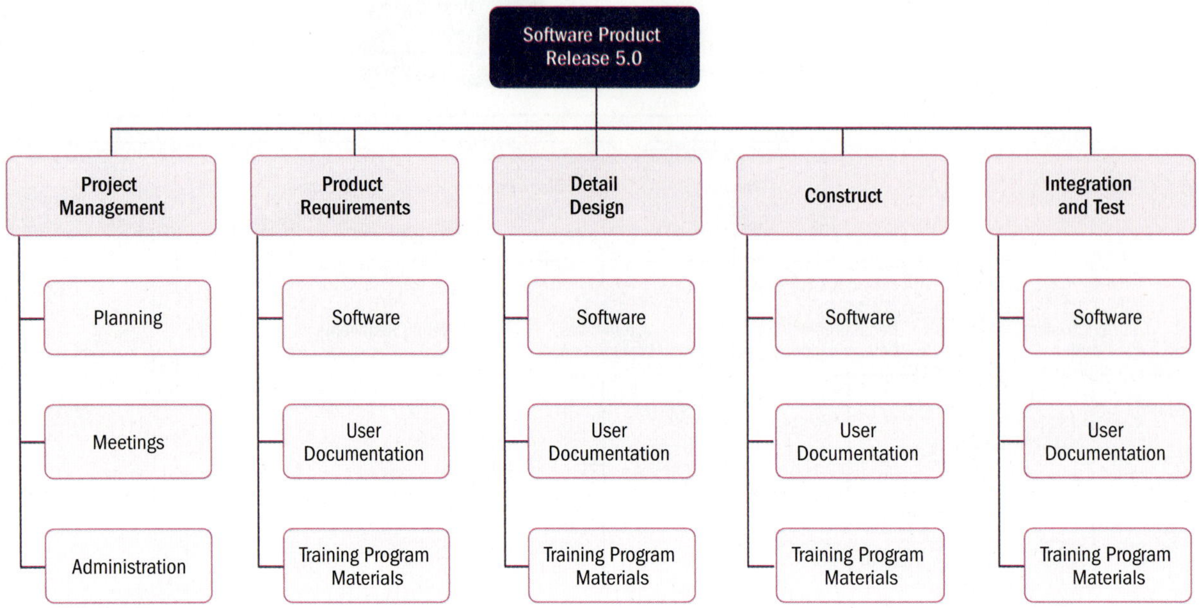

Note: The WBS is illustrative only. It is not intended to represent the full project scope of any specific project, nor to imply that this is the only way to organize a WBS on this type of project.

Figure 5-7. Sample WBS Organized by Phase

to greater levels of detail, the ability to plan, manage, and control the work is enhanced. However, excessive decomposition can lead to a nonproductive management effort, inefficient use of resources, decreased efficiency in performing the work, and difficulty aggregating data over different levels of the WBS.

Decomposition may not be possible for a deliverable or subcomponent that will be accomplished far into the future. The project management team usually waits until the deliverable or subcomponent is agreed on so that the details of the WBS can be developed. This technique is sometimes referred to as rolling wave planning.

The WBS represents all product and project work, including the project management work. The total of the work at the lowest levels should roll up to the higher levels so that nothing is left out and no extra work is performed. This is sometimes called the 100 percent rule.

For specific information regarding the WBS, refer to the *Practice Standard for Work Breakdown Structures* [4]. The practice standard contains industry-specific examples of WBS templates that can be tailored to specific projects in a particular application area.

Dependency determination and integration. Dependencies may be characterized by the following attributes: mandatory or discretionary and internal or external. Dependency has four attributes, but two can be applicable at the same time in the following ways: mandatory external dependencies, mandatory internal dependencies, discretionary external dependencies, or discretionary internal dependencies.

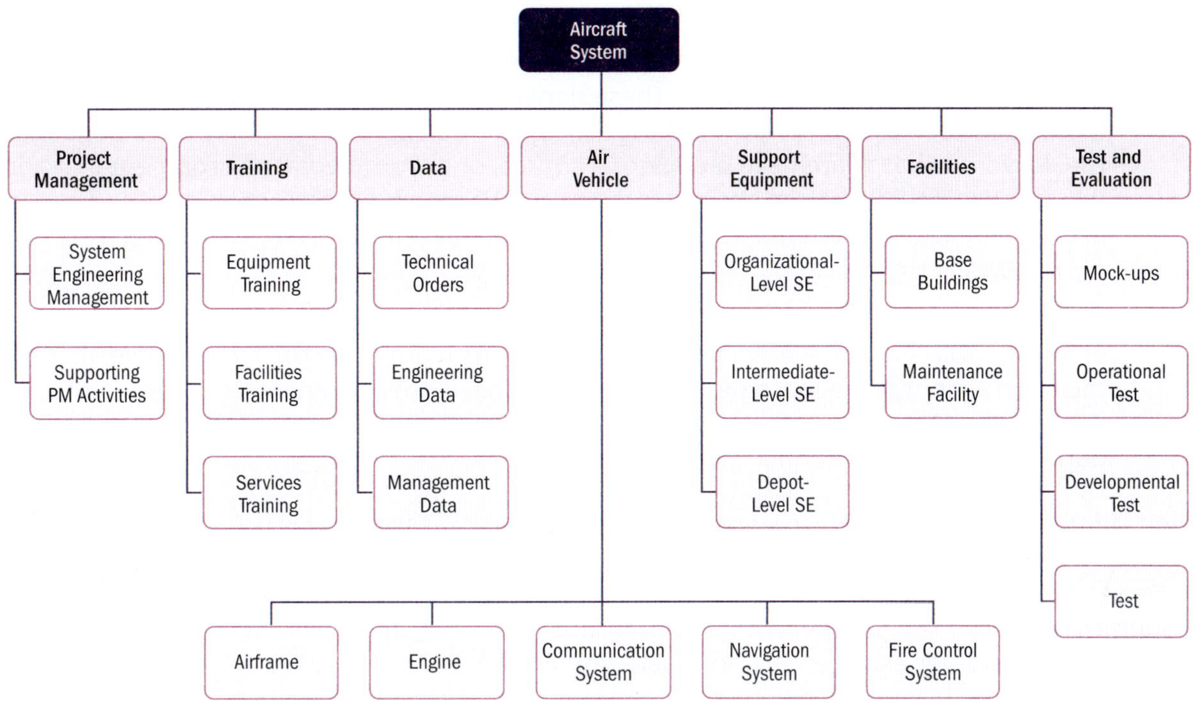

Note: The WBS is illustrative only. It is not intended to represent the full project scope of any specific project, nor to imply that this is the only way to organize a WBS on this type of project.

Figure 5-8. Sample WBS With Major Deliverables

- **Mandatory dependencies.** Mandatory dependencies are those that are legally or contractually required or inherent in the nature of the work. Mandatory dependencies often involve physical limitations, such as on a construction project, where it is impossible to erect the superstructure until after the foundation has been built, or on an electronics project, where a prototype has to be built before it can be tested. Mandatory dependencies are sometimes referred to as hard logic or hard dependencies. Technical dependencies may not be mandatory. The project team determines which dependencies are mandatory during the process of sequencing the activities. Mandatory dependencies should not be confused with assigning schedule constraints in the scheduling tool.
- **Discretionary dependencies.** Discretionary dependencies are sometimes referred to as preferred logic, preferential logic, or soft logic. Discretionary dependencies are established based on knowledge of good practices within a particular application area or some unusual aspect of the project where a specific sequence is desired, even though there may be other acceptable sequences. For example, generally accepted good practices recommend that during construction, the electrical work should start after finishing the plumbing work. This order is not mandatory and both activities may occur at the same time (in parallel); however, performing the activities in sequential order reduces the overall project risk. Discretionary dependencies should be fully documented since they can create arbitrary total float values and can limit later scheduling options. When fast tracking techniques are employed, these discretionary dependencies should be reviewed and considered

for modification or removal. The project team determines which dependencies are discretionary during the process of sequencing the activities.

- **External dependencies.** External dependencies involve a relationship between project activities and non-project activities. These dependencies are usually outside of the project team's control. For example, the testing activity in a software project may be dependent on the delivery of hardware from an external source, or governmental environmental hearings may need to be held before site preparation can begin on a construction project. The project management team determines which dependencies are external during the process of sequencing the activities.
- **Internal dependencies.** Internal dependencies involve a precedence relationship between project activities and are generally inside the project team's control. For example, if the team cannot test a machine until they assemble it, there is an internal mandatory dependency. The project management team determines which dependencies are internal during the process of sequencing the activities.

Design thinking. Design thinking is a nonlinear, iterative process that teams use to understand users, challenge assumptions, redefine problems, and create innovative solutions to prototype and test. Design thinking is a human-centered needs analysis process, popularly used for new product development projects. The process encourages collaboration and the exploration of different ideas with a focus on customer experience, and is performed using several iterative activities such as defining the problem, ideating options, prototyping, and testing.

Distributed management and leadership. This management structure emphasizes teamwork and empowered individuals. As opposed to centralized management and leadership, a distributed management and leadership structure means that decision-making and authority are decentralized and distributed among various individuals and teams. Sometimes project management activities are shared among a project management team, and project team members are responsible for completing the work. There are also situations where a project team may self-organize to complete a project. Rather than having a designated project manager, someone within the project team may serve as facilitator to enable communication, collaboration, and engagement. This role may shift among project team members. See also *centralized management and leadership*.

Document analysis. Document analysis consists of reviewing and assessing any relevant documented information. There is a wide range of documents that may be analyzed. Examples of documents that may be analyzed include but are not limited to the following:

- Agreements and contracts;
- Business plans, processes, or interface documentation;
- Business rules repositories;
- Current process flows;
- Marketing literature;
- Plans, assumptions, constraints, historical files, and technical documentation;
- Problem/issue logs;
- Policies and procedures;

- Quality reports, test reports, performance reports, and variance analysis;
- Regulatory documentation such as laws, codes, or ordinances, etc.;
- Requests for proposal; and
- Use cases.

Earned value (EV) analysis. Earned value analysis compares the performance measurement baseline to the actual schedule and cost performance. Earned value management (EVM) integrates the scope baseline with the cost baseline and schedule baseline to form the performance measurement baseline. EVM develops and monitors three key dimensions for each work package and control account:

- **Planned value (PV).** PV is the authorized budget assigned to scheduled work. It is the authorized budget planned for the work to be accomplished for an activity or work breakdown structure (WBS) component, not including management reserve. This budget is allocated by phase over the life of the project, but at a given point in time. PV defines the physical work that should have been accomplished. The total of the PV is sometimes referred to as the performance measurement baseline (PMB). The total PV for the project is also known as budget at completion (BAC).
- **Earned value (EV).** EV is the measure of work performed expressed in terms of the budget authorized for that work. It is the budget associated with the authorized work that has been completed. The EV being measured should be related to the PMB, and the EV measured cannot be greater than the authorized PV budget for a component. The EV is often used to calculate the percent complete of a project. Progress measurement criteria should be established for each WBS component to measure work in progress. Project managers monitor EV, both incrementally to determine current status and cumulatively to determine the long-term performance trends.
- **Actual cost (AC).** AC is the realized cost incurred for the work performed on an activity during a specific time period. The AC is the total cost incurred in accomplishing the work that the EV measured. The AC should correspond in definition to what was budgeted in the PV and measured in the EV (e.g., direct hours only, direct costs only, or all costs including indirect costs). The AC will have no upper limit; whatever is spent to achieve the EV will be measured.

There are tools and techniques that can be applied to calculate the EVM for projects carried out with an adaptive approach (see *The Standard for Earned Value Management*, p. 91) [3].

In adaptive approaches, effort can be expressed through story points. The result is a calculation of EV and PV for the different iterations that is based on the story points assigned to each user story. The PV is the amount of story points estimated for the user stories planned until a certain date, usually the end of the iteration, and EV represents the story points estimated for the user stories that are considered done at the end of the same iteration. The AC value is related to the costs for the team working on the user stories during the iteration, usually derived from the working hours.

Emotional intelligence. Emotional intelligence is the ability to identify, assess, and manage the personal emotions of oneself and other people, as well as the collective emotions of groups of people. A project team can use emotional intelligence to reduce tension and increase cooperation by identifying, assessing, and controlling the sentiments of project team members, anticipating their actions, acknowledging their concerns, and following up on their issues.

A project manager should invest in their personal emotional intelligence by improving inbound (e.g., self-management and self-awareness) and outbound (e.g., relationship management) competencies. Research suggests that project teams that succeed in developing team emotional intelligence or become an emotionally competent group are more effective. Additionally, there is usually a reduction in staff turnover. See also *leadership*.

Estimation techniques. Estimating is a process of determining the time and resources needed to complete the project. Estimation techniques involve various methods for forecasting variables. Estimating techniques can be qualitative or quantitative. Qualitative estimating techniques involve estimates based on understanding processes, behaviors, and conditions that individuals or groups perceive. Qualitative estimating techniques can be used together with quantitative methods. Quantitative estimating techniques include numerical estimates of effort, duration, or cost. The most common estimation techniques include the following:

- Expert judgment (see *expert judgment*),
- Analogous estimating (see *analogous estimating*),
- Bottom-up estimating (see *bottom-up estimating*),
- Multipoint estimating (see *multipoint estimating*),
- Parametric estimating (see *parametric estimating*), and
- Relative size estimation (see *relative size estimation*).

Expert judgment. Expert judgment is judgment provided based upon expertise in an application area, discipline, industry, etc., as appropriate for the activity being performed. Such expertise may be provided by any group or person with specialized education, knowledge, skill, experience, or training.

Facilitation. Facilitation is the ability to effectively guide a group event to a successful decision, solution, or conclusion. A facilitator helps ensure the following:

- There is effective participation,
- Participants achieve a mutual understanding,
- All contributions are considered,
- Conclusions or results have full buy-in according to the decision process established for the project, and
- Actions and agreements that are achieved are appropriately dealt with afterward.

Feedback. Feedback is information about reactions to communications, a deliverable, or a situation. Feedback supports interactive communication among the project manager, project team, and all other project stakeholders. Examples include coaching, mentoring, and negotiating.

Financing. Financing entails acquiring funding for projects. It is common for long-term infrastructure, industrial, and public services projects to seek external sources of funds. If a project is funded externally, the funding entity may have certain requirements that must be met.

Flowchart. Flowcharts are visual representations that map out the sequence of steps and branching possibilities within a process. They are also known as process maps and are used to transform one or more inputs into one or more outputs. Flowcharts are instrumental in illustrating the activities, decision points, branching loops, parallel paths, and overall order of processing within a horizontal value chain. This visualization helps in understanding the operational details of procedures and can be particularly useful in project management for outlining processes and identifying potential areas for improvement.

Focus groups. Focus groups are an elicitation technique that brings together prequalified stakeholders and subject matter experts to learn about their expectations and attitudes about a proposed product, service, or result. A trained moderator guides the group through an interactive discussion designed to be more conversational than a one-on-one interview.

Funding limit reconciliation. Funding limit reconciliation is the process of reconciling the expenditure of funds with any funding limits on the commitment of funds for the project. A variance between the funding limits and the planned expenditures will sometimes necessitate the rescheduling of work to level out the rate of expenditures. This leveling is accomplished by placing imposed date constraints for work into the project schedule.

Genetic algorithms. Genetic algorithms are an optimization technique and iterative process inspired by natural selection to find solutions to complex problems. Genetic algorithms can be utilized for project optimization, exploring all possible decision combinations without human bias. For example, it can be used in project scheduling and resource management as a tool for developing scheduling strategies, resolving issues related to scheduling conflicts, resource leveling and constraints, and critical path planning. Genetic algorithms are a specific type of metaheuristic method.

Green human resource management. Green human resource management is a set of people management policies and practices that focuses on the sustainable use of resources, preserving the natural environment, and improving environmental performance. For example, green human resource management can involve incorporating green practices while considering project team member recruitment and selection, training and development, performance management, and compensation and rewards, as well as reviewing project team members' involvement with green practices when performing individual and team assessments.

Ground rules. Ground rules are expectations regarding acceptable behavior by project team members. Defined in the team charter, ground rules set the expected behavior for project team members and other stakeholders with regard to stakeholder engagement.

Hierarchical charts. Hierarchical charts are a traditional organizational chart structure that can be used to show positions and relationships in a graphical, top-down format. Other hierarchical charts include the following:

- **Work breakdown structure (WBS).** A WBS is a hierarchical decomposition of the total scope of work to be carried out by the project team to accomplish the project objectives and create the required deliverables. The WBS is designed to show how project deliverables are broken down into work packages and provides a way of showing high-level areas of responsibility.
- **Organizational breakdown structure (OBS).** An OBS is a hierarchical representation of the project organization that illustrates the relationship between project activities and the organizational units that will perform those activities. While the WBS shows a breakdown of project deliverables, an OBS is arranged according to an organization's existing departments, units, or teams, with the project activities or work packages listed under each

department. An operational department, such as information technology or purchasing, can see all of its project responsibilities by looking at its portion of the OBS.

- **Resource breakdown structure.** A resource breakdown structure is a hierarchical representation of resources by category and type. The resource breakdown structure is used for planning, managing, and controlling project work. Each descending (lower) level represents an increasingly detailed description of the resource until the information is small enough to be used in conjunction with the WBS to allow the work to be planned, monitored, and controlled.
- **Value breakdown structure (VBS).** A VBS is a WBS with value estimates assigned to each element. The VBS can be useful in determining whether a given scope element is truly mandatory—that is, equal to the value of the entire project, as removing that scope element would erase the value of the project. When a VBS element is on the critical path, it can be useful to help assess whether a higher-value baseline may exist (e.g., when the value of accelerating or removing a given VBS element might exceed the cost of doing so).

Historical information review. Reviewing historical information can assist in developing parametric estimates or analogous estimates. Historical information may include project characteristics (parameters) to develop mathematical models to predict total project costs. Such models may be simple (e.g., residential home construction is based on a certain cost per square foot of space) or complex (e.g., one model of software development costing uses multiple separate adjustment factors, each of which has numerous points within it).

Both the cost and accuracy of analogous and parametric models can vary widely. They are most likely to be reliable when:

- Historical information used to develop the model is accurate;
- Parameters used in the model are readily quantifiable; and
- Models are scalable, such that they work for large projects, small projects, and phases of a project.

Individual and team assessments. Individual and team assessment tools give the project manager and the project team insight into areas of strengths and weaknesses. These tools help project managers assess team members' preferences and aspirations, as well as how they process and organize information, make decisions, and interact with people. Various tools are available such as attitudinal surveys, specific assessments, structured interviews, ability tests, and focus groups. These tools can provide improved understanding, trust, commitment, and communication among team members and facilitate more productive teams throughout the project.

Influence diagrams. Influence diagrams are graphical representations of situations that can be used when making decisions under uncertainty. They show causal influences, time ordering of events, and other relationships among variables and outcomes. An influence diagram represents a project or situation within the project as a set of entities, outcomes, and influences, together with the relationships and effects among them. Where an element in the influence diagram is uncertain as a result of the existence of individual project risks or other sources of uncertainty, this can be represented in the influence diagram using ranges or probability distributions. The influence diagram is then evaluated using a simulation technique, such as Monte Carlo analysis, to indicate which elements have the greatest influence on key outcomes. Outputs from an influence diagram are similar to other quantitative risk analysis methods, including S-curve diagrams and tornado diagrams.

Influencing. Because project managers often have little or no direct authority over team members in a matrix environment, their ability to influence stakeholders on a timely basis is critical to project success. Key influencing skills include the following:

- Ability to be persuasive;
- Clearly articulating points and positions;
- High levels of active and effective listening skills;
- Awareness of, and consideration for, the various perspectives in any situation; and
- Gathering relevant information to address issues and reach agreements while maintaining mutual trust.

Information management. Information management tools and techniques are used to create and connect people to information. These tools are effective for sharing simple, unambiguous, codified explicit knowledge. The tools include but are not limited to the following:

- Methods for codifying explicit knowledge (e.g., for producing lessons-to-be-learned entries for the lessons learned register);
- Lessons learned register;
- Library services;
- Information gathering (e.g., web searches and reading published articles); and
- Project management information system (PMIS), which often includes document management systems.

Tools and techniques that connect people to information can be enhanced by adding an element of interaction (e.g., including a "contact me" function so users can get in touch with the originators of the lessons and ask for advice specific to their project and context).

Interaction and support also help people to find relevant information. Asking for help is generally quicker and easier than trying to identify search terms. Search terms are often difficult to select because people may not know which keywords or phrases to use to access the information they need.

Knowledge and information management tools and techniques should be connected to project processes and process owners. Communities of practice and subject matter experts, for example, may generate insights that lead to improved control processes (having an internal sponsor can ensure improvements are implemented). Lessons learned entries may be analyzed to identify common issues that can be addressed by changes to project procedures.

Information radiators. An information radiator is a visible, physical display that provides information to the rest of the organization, enabling timely knowledge sharing. Information radiators may also be known as big visible charts. Information radiators are posted in a place where people can see the information easily, rather than having information in a scheduling or reporting tool. The information radiators should be easy to update and should be updated frequently. They are often "low tech and high touch" in that they are manually maintained rather than electronically generated. Figure 5-9 shows an information radiator associated with work completed, work remaining, and risks.

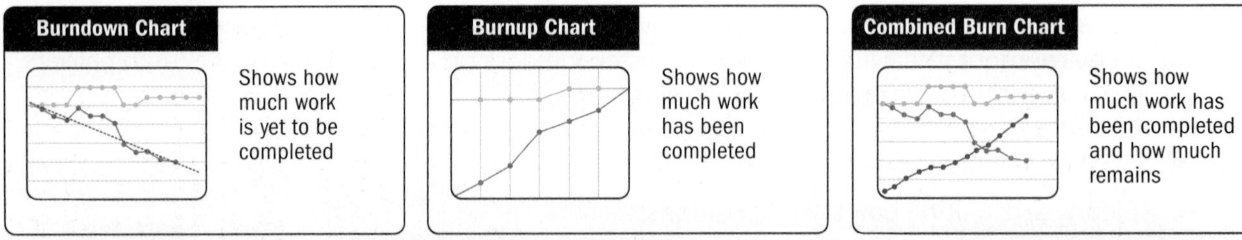

Reference	Risk Description	Date	Likelihood	Impact	Risk Rating	Response	Owner
1	The main supplier cannot deliver on time because of other commercial commitments	03/21	Likely	High	**High**	Include financial penalties in contract; build contingency into the schedule; monitor contractor performance	Annie
2	The lead time for the leased line exceeds 90 days	03/21	Unlikely	Medium	**Medium**	Order leased line earlier than necessary; incur additional rental fees	Jim
3	Release of the new system is delayed because user acceptance testing commences after the planned start	03/21	Very likely	High	**High**	Employ temporary staff to free up resources for testing; revise project schedule	Mark
4	There is insufficient capacity to create additional database instances for data migration and testing	04/18	Very unlikely	Medium	**Low**	Prioritize projects; temporarily remove alternative development instance	Jim

Risk Log

Figure 5-9. Information Radiator

In-progress postmortems. An in-progress postmortem is a structured process conducted at various stages of the project life cycle to analyze current performance, identify issues, and implement improvements. Unlike traditional postmortems held at the end of a project, these reviews are conducted periodically to ensure continuous improvement and timely problem-solving.

Inspections. An inspection is the examination of a work product to determine if it conforms to documented standards. The results of inspections generally include measurements and may be conducted at any level. The results of a single activity can be inspected or the final product of the project can be inspected. Inspections may be called reviews, peer reviews, audits, or walkthroughs. In some application areas, these terms have narrow and specific meanings. Inspections also are used to verify defect repairs.

Integrated change control. Integrated change control helps ensure that changes to the project are managed in a coordinated and controlled manner. By evaluating change requests, conducting impact analyses, making informed decisions, and documenting and communicating changes, the project can maintain alignment with its objectives and constraints, ultimately contributing to project success.

Interpersonal and team skills. Interpersonal skills that are used frequently in projects include emotional intelligence, decision-making, facilitation, and conflict management and resolution, among others. (See *emotional intelligence; decision-making; conflict management.*) As for team management, this effort entails applying knowledge, skills, tools, and techniques for management activities as well as leadership activities. Management activities focus on the means of meeting project objectives, such as having effective processes, planning, coordinating, measuring, and monitoring work, among others. Leadership activities focus on people. Leadership includes influencing, motivating, listening, enabling, and other activities having to do with the project team. Both are important in delivering the intended outcomes. See also *centralized management and leadership* and *distributed management and leadership*.

Interviews. Interviews are a formal or informal approach to elicit information from stakeholders by talking to them directly. Interviews are typically performed by asking prepared and spontaneous questions and recording responses. Interviews are often conducted on an individual basis between an interviewer and an interviewee but may involve multiple interviewers and/or multiple interviewees. Interviewing experienced project participants, sponsors, executives, and subject matter experts can aid in identifying and defining the features and functions of the desired product deliverables. Interviews are also useful for obtaining confidential information.

Iteration burndown chart. An iteration burndown tracks the work that remains to be completed in the iteration backlog. An iteration burndown chart is used to analyze the variance with respect to an ideal burndown based on the work committed from iteration planning. A forecast trend line can be used to predict the likely variance at iteration completion and take appropriate actions during the course of the iteration. A diagonal line representing the ideal burndown and daily actual remaining work is then plotted. A trend line is then calculated to forecast completion based on the remaining work. Figure 5-10 is an example of an iteration burndown chart.

Knowledge management. Knowledge management tools and techniques connect people so they can work together to create new knowledge, share tacit knowledge, and integrate the knowledge of diverse team members. The tools and techniques appropriate in a project depend on the nature of the project, especially the degree of innovation involved, project complexity, and the level of diversity (including diversity of disciplines) among team members.

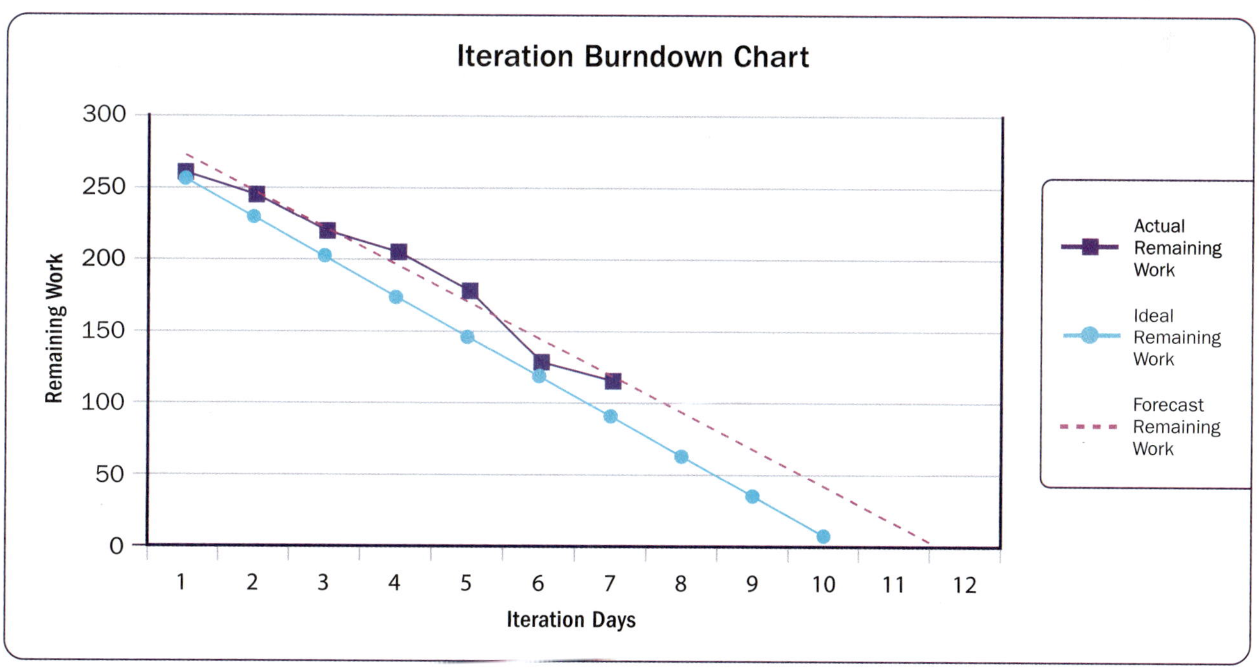

Figure 5-10. Iteration Burndown Chart

Knowledge management tools and techniques include but are not limited to the following:

- Networking, including informal social interaction and online social networking (Online forums where people can ask open questions such as: "What does anyone know about . . .?" are useful for starting knowledge-sharing conversations with specialists.);
- Communities of practice (sometimes called communities of interest or just communities) and special interest groups;
- Work shadowing and reverse shadowing;
- Discussion forums such as focus groups;
- Knowledge-sharing events such as seminars and conferences;
- Workshops, including problem-solving sessions and learning reviews designed to identify lessons learned;
- Creativity and idea management techniques;
- Knowledge fairs and cafés; and
- Training that involves interaction among learners.

Leadership. Leadership encompasses the knowledge, skills, and behaviors needed to guide, motivate, and direct a team to help an organization achieve its business goals. These skills may include demonstrating essential capabilities such as negotiation, resilience, communication, problem-solving, critical thinking, and interpersonal skills. Projects are becoming increasingly more complicated with more and more businesses executing their strategy through projects. Project management is more than just working with numbers, templates, charts, graphs, and computing systems. A common denominator in all projects is people. People can be counted, but they are not numbers.

Leadership skills are useful for all project team members, whether the project team is operating in an environment with a centralized authority or a shared leadership environment. The following sections describe some of the traits and activities associated with leadership:

- **Establishing and maintaining vision.** Every project has a purpose. Understanding that purpose is critical for people to commit their time and energy in the right direction toward achieving the project purpose. The project vision summarizes the project's purpose clearly and succinctly. The vision describes a realistic, attractive view of the future project outcomes. In addition to briefly describing the desired future state, the vision is a powerful motivational tool. It is a way to create passion and meaning for a project's envisioned goal. A common vision helps keep people pulling in the same direction. When immersed in the details of everyday work, a clear understanding of the end goal can help guide local decisions toward the desired project outcome.
  - A vision developed collaboratively between project team members and key stakeholders should answer these questions:
    - What is the project purpose?
    - What defines successful project work?
    - How will the future be better when the project outcomes are delivered?
    - How will the project team know that it is drifting from the vision?

- A good vision is clear, concise, and actionable. It does the following:
  - Summarizes the project with a powerful phrase or short description;
  - Describes the best achievable outcome;
  - Creates a common, cohesive picture in project team members' minds; and
  - Inspires passion for the outcome.

- **Critical thinking.** Critical thinking, especially when applied to discovery, can include conceptual imagination, insight, and intuition. Project team members apply critical thinking to do the following:
  - Research and gather unbiased, well-balanced information;
  - Recognize, analyze, and resolve problems;
  - Identify bias, unstated assumptions, and values;
  - Discern the use of language and its influence on oneself and others;
  - Analyze data and evidence to evaluate arguments and perspectives;
  - Observe events to identify patterns and relationships;
  - Apply inductive, deductive, and abductive reasoning appropriately; and
  - Identify and articulate false premises, false analogy, emotional appeals, and other faulty logic (for more information, see *critical thinking*).

- **Motivation.** Motivating project team members has two aspects: The first is understanding what motivates project team members to perform, and the second is working with project team members in such a way that they remain committed to the project and its outcomes (for more information, see *motivation*).

- **Interpersonal skills.** Interpersonal skills that are used frequently in projects include emotional intelligence, decision-making, and conflict resolution, among others.
  - **Emotional intelligence.** Emotional intelligence is the ability to identify, assess, and manage the personal emotions of oneself and other people, as well as the collective emotions of groups of people. There are multiple models for defining and explaining emotional intelligence. Figure 5-11 shows the key points for each of the four aspects of emotional intelligence and how they relate. The aspects having to do with oneself are on the top, and the social aspects are on the bottom. Awareness is on the left side, and management and skill are on the right side.

  Emotional intelligence models converge on four key areas:
    - *Self-awareness*. Self-awareness is the ability to conduct a realistic self-assessment. This ability includes understanding our own emotions, goals, motivations, strengths, and weaknesses.
    - *Self-management*. Self-management, also known as self-regulation, is the ability to control and redirect disruptive feelings and impulses. It is the ability to think before acting, suspending snap judgments and impulsive decisions.
    - *Social awareness*. Social awareness is about empathy and understanding and considering other people's feelings. This key area includes the ability to read nonverbal cues and body language.

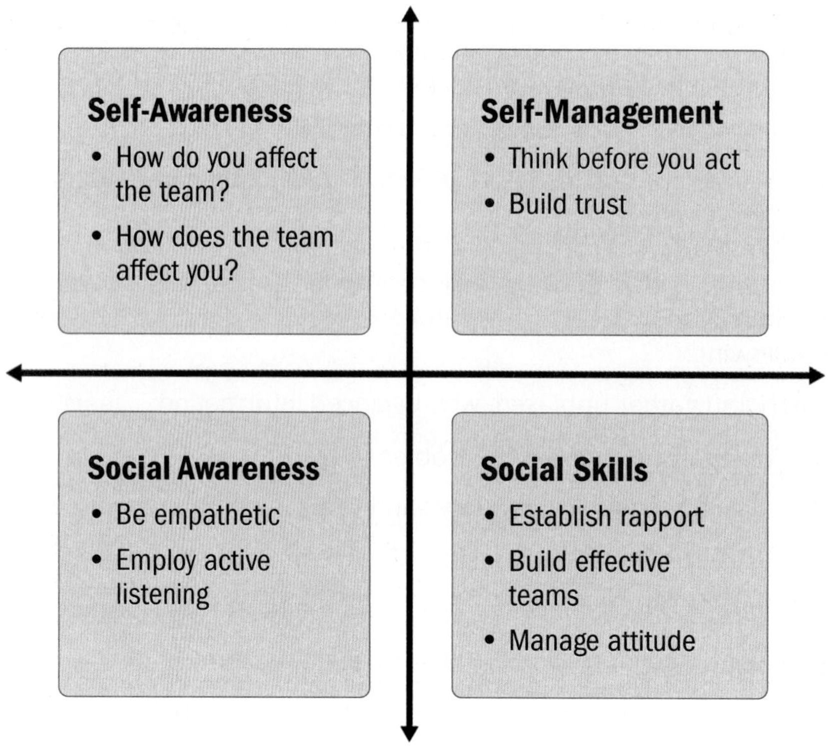

Figure 5-11. Components of Emotional Intelligence

- *Social skills*. Social skills are the culmination of the other dimensions of emotional intelligence. Social skills are concerned with managing groups of people, such as project teams, building social networks, finding common ground with various stakeholders, and building rapport.

Self-awareness and self-management skills are required to remain calm and productive during difficult project circumstances. Social awareness and social skills allow for better bonds with project team members and project stakeholders. Emotional intelligence is a basis of all forms of leadership.

Some models for emotional intelligence include a fifth area for motivation. Motivation in this context is about understanding what drives and inspires people. For more information, see *emotional intelligence*.

- **Decision-making.** Project managers and project teams make many decisions daily. Some decisions may be fairly inconsequential to the project outcome, such as where to go for a team lunch, and others will be very impactful, such as what development approach to use, which tool to use, or what vendor to select.
  - Decisions can be made unilaterally. This has the advantage of being fast but is prone to errors when compared to engaging the wisdom of a diverse set of people. Unilateral decision-making can also demotivate people who are impacted by the decision since they may feel their views and concerns were not considered.
  - Group-based decision-making has the benefit of tapping into the broad knowledge base of a group. Engaging people in the decision-making process also increases buy-in

of the outcome, even if the option selected may not have been everyone's first choice. Generally, inclusion increases commitment to the decision. The downside of group decision-making is the time required and the interruption to the team's work that can occur when members are consulted about a decision.

  - Project team decision-making often follows a diverge/converge pattern. This pattern means that stakeholders are first engaged to generate a broad set of solution alternatives or approaches. This work is often done individually to avoid the effect of senior or charismatic stakeholders unduly influencing other stakeholders. Then, after a broad spectrum of decision alternatives has been generated, the project team converges on a preferred solution.
  - The goal is to make decisions quickly while engaging the diverse knowledge of a group in an inclusive and respectful manner. Some decisions may be made in a different direction than some people prefer, but everyone has an opportunity to explain their position. In the end, the deciding authority, whether an individual or a group, makes a decision based on the presented analysis and with consideration for stakeholder expectations.
  - Careful selection of which decisions should go for group discussion and using voting can limit the interruptions and task switching experienced by the project team. Many approaches such as Roman voting, wideband Delphi estimating, and fist of five voting use the diverge/converge pattern. These approaches aim to engage individual input while voting at the same moment, which minimizes groupthink.
  - For those decisions that are beyond the authority of the project team to decide, the project team can investigate alternatives, consider impacts of each alternative, and escalate the decision to someone with the proper authority. This process aligns with the philosophy of "do not bring me problems, bring me solutions" while remaining aligned with organizational governance regarding decision-making authority.

- **Conflict management.** Addressing conflict before it escalates beyond useful debate leads to better outcomes. The following approaches can help:
  - **Keep communication open and respectful.** Because conflict can cause anxiety, it is important to keep a safe environment to explore the source of the conflict. Without a safe environment, people will stop communicating. Make sure words, tone of voice, and body language remain nonthreatening.
  - **Focus on the issues, not the people.** Conflict is based on people perceiving situations differently. Conflicts should not be personal. The focus is on resolving the situation, not casting blame.
  - **Focus on the present and future, not the past.** Stay focused on the current situation, not past situations. If something similar happened previously, bringing up the past will not resolve the current situation. In fact, it can further intensify the current situation.

  Search for alternatives together. Damage incurred from conflict can be repaired by looking for resolutions and alternatives together. This collaboration can also create more constructive relationships. This effort to resolve the problem moves the conflict into a problem-solving space where people can work together to generate creative alternatives (for more information, see *conflict management*).

Leads and lags. A lead is the amount of time whereby a successor activity can be advanced with respect to a predecessor activity. For example, on a project to construct a new office building, the landscaping could be scheduled to start 2 weeks prior to the scheduled punch list completion. This activity would be shown as a finish-to-start (FS) with a 2-week lead as shown in Figure 5-12. A lead is often represented as a negative value for lag in scheduling software.

A lag is the amount of time whereby a successor activity will be delayed with respect to a predecessor activity. For example, a technical writing team may begin editing the draft of a large document 15 days after they begin writing it. This can be shown as a start-to-start (SS) relationship with a 15-day lag as shown in Figure 5-12.

The project management team determines the dependencies that may require a lead or a lag to accurately define the logical relationship. The use of leads and lags should not replace schedule logic. Also, duration estimates do not include any leads or lags. Activities and their related assumptions should be documented.

Leads and lags can also be represented in project schedule network diagrams. For more details, see the entry for *project schedule network diagrams* in Section 4.

Logical relationship. A logical relationship is a dependency between two activities or between an activity and a milestone. The four most common types of logical relationships are finish-to-start, finish-to-finish, start-to-start, and start-to-finish. See also *precedence diagramming method*.

Make-or-buy analysis and decisions. Make-or-buy analysis is the decision-making process of gathering and organizing data about product requirements and analyzing them against available alternatives, including the purchase or internal manufacture of the product. A make-or-buy analysis results in a make-or-buy decision as to whether particular work can be best accomplished by the project team or if it should be purchased from outside sources.

Market research. Market research is a data-gathering technique that includes examination of industry and specific seller capabilities. Procurement teams may leverage information gained at conferences, online reviews, and a variety of sources to identify market capabilities. The team may also refine specific procurement objectives to leverage maturing technologies while balancing risks associated with the breadth of sellers who can provide the desired materials or services.

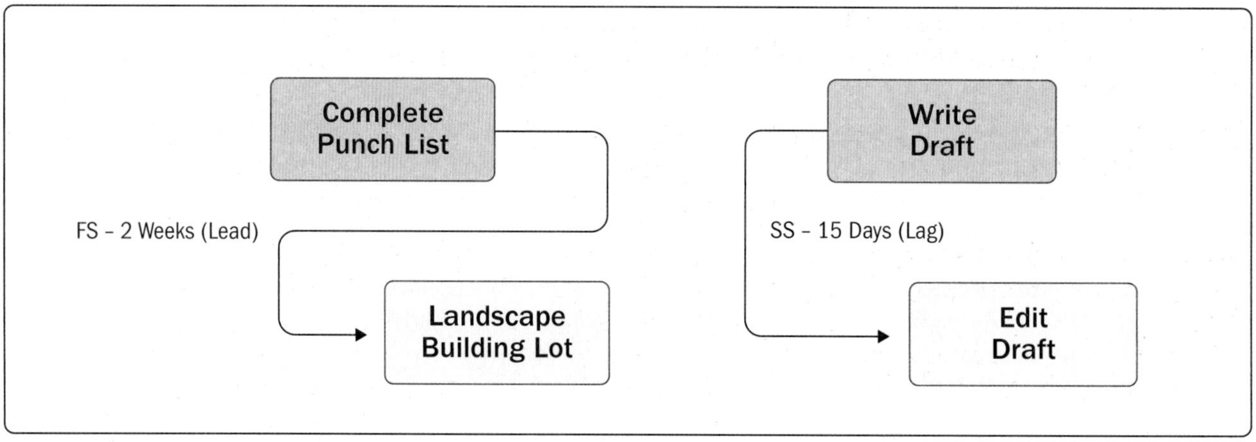

Figure 5-12. Examples of Lead and Lag

Meeting management. Meeting management is an interpersonal and team skill used to ensure meetings meet their intended objectives effectively and efficiently. The following steps should be used for meeting planning:

- Prepare and distribute the agenda stating the objectives of the meeting;
- Ensure that the meeting starts and finishes at the published time;
- Ensure the appropriate participants are invited and attend;
- Stay on topic;
- Manage expectations, issues, and conflicts during the meeting; and
- Record all actions along with the individual who has responsibility for completing the action.

Meetings. Project meetings can include virtual or face-to-face meetings and can be supported with document collaboration technologies such as email messages and project websites. Examples of meetings include but are not limited to the following:

- Decision-making,
- Facilitated workshops,
- Issue resolution,
- Lessons learned and retrospectives,
- Project kickoffs,
- Sprint planning, and
- Status updates.

Mind mapping. Mind mapping is a technique used to consolidate ideas created through individual brainstorming sessions into a single map to reflect commonality and differences in understanding and to generate new ideas. Mind mapping is a diagrammatic method used to visually organize information.

Motivation. Motivation is providing a reason for someone to act. Teams can be motivated by empowering them to participate in decision-making and encouraging them to work independently.

- **Motivation models.** People perform better when they are motivated, and people are motivated by different things. Understanding what motivates project team members and other stakeholders helps to tailor rewards to the individual, thereby eliciting more effective engagement. There are a significant number of models that illustrate how people are motivated. Four models are described, though these are a small representation of available models.
    - **Hygiene and motivational factors.** Frederick Herzberg conducted a study of motivational factors in working life. He believed that job satisfaction and dissatisfaction stem from conditions called motivational factors. Motivational factors include matters that relate to the content of the work, such as achievement, growth, and advancement. Insufficient motivational factors lead to dissatisfaction. Sufficient motivational factors lead to satisfaction. Herzberg also identified hygiene factors related to the work, such as company policies, salary, and the physical environment. If hygiene factors are insufficient, they cause dissatisfaction. However, even if they are sufficient, they do not lead to satisfaction.

- **Intrinsic versus extrinsic motivation.** Daniel Pink published several books about the intrinsic factors that motivate people. He stated that while extrinsic rewards, such as salary, are motivators to a certain extent, once a person is paid fairly for their work, the motivational power of extrinsic rewards ceases to exist. For complicated and challenging work, such as much of the work on projects, intrinsic motivators are far longer lasting and more effective. Pink identifies three types of intrinsic motivators: autonomy, mastery, and purpose:
  - *Autonomy*. Autonomy is the desire to direct one's own life. This desire is aligned with being able to determine how, where, and when to accomplish work. Autonomy includes flexible work hours, working from home, and work on self-selecting and self-managing project teams.
  - *Mastery*. Mastery is about being able to improve and excel. The desire to do excellent work, learn, and achieve goals are aspects of mastery.
  - *Purpose*. Purpose speaks to the need to make a difference. Knowing the project vision and how work contributes to achieving that vision allows people to feel like they are making a difference.
- **Theory of needs.** David McClelland's model states that all people are driven by needs of achievement, power, and affiliation. The relative strength of each need depends on an individual's experiences and culture.
  - *Achievement.* People who are motivated by achievement, such as reaching a goal, are motivated by activities and work that is challenging but reasonable.
  - *Power.* People who are motivated by power like to organize, motivate, and lead others. They are motivated by increased responsibility.
  - *Affiliation.* People who are motivated by affiliation seek acceptance and belonging. They are motivated by being part of a team.
- **Theory X, Theory Y, and Theory Z.** Douglas McGregor devised the Theory X and Theory Y models, which represent a spectrum of employee motivation and corresponding management styles. This spectrum was later expanded to include Theory Z.
  - *Theory X.* The X side of the spectrum assumes individuals work for the sole purpose of income. They are not ambitious or goal oriented. The corresponding management style to motivate these individuals is a hands-on and top-down approach. This management style is often seen in a production or labor-intensive environment, or one with many layers of management.
  - *Theory Y.* The Y side of the spectrum assumes that individuals are intrinsically motivated to do good work. The corresponding management style has a more personal, coaching feel. The manager encourages creativity and discussion. This management style is often seen in creative and knowledge worker environments.
  - *Theory Z.* Abraham Maslow saw Theory Z as a transcendent dimension to work where individuals are motivated by self-realization, values, and a higher calling. The optimal management style in this situation is one that cultivates insight and meaning. William Ouchi's version of Theory Z focuses on motivating employees by creating a job for life, where the focus is on the well-being of employees and their families. This style of management seeks to promote high productivity, morale, and satisfaction.

Multicriteria decision analysis. Multicriteria decision analysis is a technique that utilizes a decision matrix to provide a systematic analytical approach for establishing criteria, such as risk levels, uncertainty, and valuation, to evaluate and rank many ideas. Multicriteria decision analysis tools (e.g., prioritization matrix or analytic hierarchy process [AHP] software) can be used to identify the key issues and suitable alternatives to be prioritized as a set of decisions for implementation. Criteria are prioritized and weighted before being applied to all available alternatives to obtain a mathematical score for each alternative. The alternatives are then ranked by score.

Multipoint estimating. Multipoint estimating is a method used to estimate cost or duration by applying an average or weighted average of optimistic, pessimistic, and most likely estimates when there is uncertainty with the individual activity estimates. The accuracy of single-point duration estimates may be improved by considering estimation uncertainty and risk. Using multipoint estimates helps define an approximate range for an activity's duration:

- **Most likely (*tM*).** This estimate is based on the duration of the activity, given the resources likely to be assigned, their productivity, realistic expectations of availability for the activity, dependencies on other participants, and interruptions.
- **Optimistic (*tO*).** The activity duration based on analysis of the best-case scenario for the activity.
- **Pessimistic (*tP*).** The duration based on analysis of the worst-case scenario for the activity.

Depending on the assumed distribution of values within the range of the estimates, the expected duration, *t*E, can be calculated. One commonly used formula is triangular distribution:

$$tE = (tO + tM + tP) / 3$$

Triangular distribution is used when there is insufficient historical data or when using judgmental data. Duration estimates based on three points with an assumed distribution provide an expected duration and clarify the range of uncertainty around the expected duration.

Negotiation. Negotiation is a discussion aimed at reaching an agreement. Negotiation is used to achieve support or agreement that supports the work of the project or its outcomes and to resolve conflicts within the team or with other stakeholders. Negotiation among team members is used to reach consensus on project needs. Negotiation can build trust and harmony among team members.

Procurement negotiation clarifies the structure, rights, and obligations of the parties and other terms of the purchases so that mutual agreement can be reached prior to signing a contract. Final document language reflects all agreements reached. Negotiation concludes with a signed contract document or other formal agreement that can be executed by both buyer and seller.

The negotiation should be led by a member of the procurement team who has the authority to sign contracts. The project manager and other members of the project management team may be present during negotiation to provide assistance as needed.

Networking. Networking is the establishment of connections and relationships with other people from the same or other organizations for the purpose of exchanging information and developing contacts. Networks provide project managers and their teams with access to informal organizations to solve problems, influence actions of their stakeholders, and increase stakeholder support for the work and outcomes of the project, thus improving performance.

Nominal group. The nominal group technique is a structured method used to facilitate group decision-making by gathering input from participants in a systematic manner. The technique was developed to address the challenges of chaotic and unproductive discussions, particularly in large groups dealing with controversial topics. This technique aims to equalize participation and minimize the dominance of more vocal members, ensuring that all ideas are considered before any discussion takes place.

Nonverbal communication. Examples of nonverbal communication include appropriate body language to transmit meaning through gestures, tone of voice, and facial expressions. Mirroring and eye contact are also important techniques. The team members should be aware of how they are expressing themselves, both through what they say and what they do not say.

Observation/conversation. Observation and conversation provide a direct way of viewing individuals in their environment to see how they perform their jobs or tasks and carry out processes. Observation and conversation are particularly helpful for detailed processes when the people who use the product have difficulty or are reluctant to articulate their requirements. Observation is also known as "job shadowing." The observation is usually done externally by an observer viewing a business expert performing a job. The observation can also be done by a "participant observer" who performs a process or procedure to experience how it is done to uncover hidden requirements.

Organizational cultural intelligence. Organizational cultural intelligence is the capability of the enterprise to perform effectively in culturally diverse, complex situations and a multicultural world. For example, project managers and teams with high organizational cultural intelligence may demonstrate strong cultural skills and recognize that different team members from different cultural regions can think and express themselves differently. However, at the same time, these project managers and teams avoid demonstrating careless cultural stereotyping.

Organizational theory. Organizational theory provides information regarding the way in which people, teams, and organizational units behave. Effective use of common techniques identified in organizational theory can shorten the amount of time, cost, and effort needed to create the Plan Resource Management process outputs and improve planning efficiency. Applicable organizational theories may recommend exercising a flexible leadership style that adapts to the changes in a team's maturity level throughout the project life cycle. It is important to recognize that the organization's structure and culture impact the project's organizational structure.

Parametric estimating. Parametric estimating is an estimating technique in which an algorithm is used to calculate cost or duration based on historical data and project parameters. Parametric estimating uses a statistical relationship between historical data and other variables (e.g., square footage in construction) to calculate an estimate for activity parameters, such as cost, budget, and duration.

Durations can be quantitatively determined by multiplying the quantity of work to be performed by the number of labor hours per unit of work. For example, duration on a design project is estimated by the number of drawings multiplied by the number of labor hours per drawing, or on a cable installation, the meters of cable multiplied by the number of labor hours per meter. If the assigned resource is capable of installing 25 meters of cable per hour, the duration required to install 1,000 meters is 40 hours (1,000 meters divided by 25 meters per hour).

This technique can produce higher levels of accuracy depending on the sophistication and underlying data built into the model. Parametric schedule estimates can be applied to a total project or to segments of a project, in conjunction with other estimating methods.

Performance reviews. Performance reviews measure, compare, and analyze actual performance of work in progress on the project against the schedule baseline, such as actual start and finish dates, percent complete, and remaining duration for work in progress.

Political awareness. Political awareness helps project managers to plan communications based on the project environment as well as their organization's political environment. Political awareness concerns the recognition of formal and informal power relationships and the willingness to operate within these structures. Aspects of political awareness include the following:

- Understanding the strategies of the organization,
- Knowing who wields power and influence in this arena, and
- Developing an ability to communicate with these stakeholders.

Preassignment. When physical or team resources for a project are determined in advance, they are considered preassigned. This situation can occur if the project is the result of specific resources being identified as part of a competitive proposal or if the project is dependent upon the expertise of particular persons. Preassignment might also include the team members who have already been assigned in Initiating or in other processes before the initial resource management plan has been completed.

Precedence diagramming method. Precedence diagramming method is a technique used for constructing a schedule model in which activities are represented by nodes and are graphically linked by one or more logical relationships to show the sequence in which the activities are to be performed.

Precedence diagramming method includes four types of dependencies or logical relationships. A predecessor activity is an activity that logically comes before a dependent activity in a schedule. A successor activity is a dependent activity that logically comes after another activity in a schedule. These relationships are as follows and are illustrated in Figure 5-13:

- **Finish-to-start (FS).** A logical relationship in which a successor activity cannot start until a predecessor activity has finished. For example, installing the operating system on a PC (successor) cannot start until the PC hardware is assembled (predecessor).
- **Finish-to-finish (FF).** A logical relationship in which a successor activity cannot finish until a predecessor activity has finished. For example, writing a document (predecessor) is required to finish before editing the document (successor) can finish.
- **Start-to-start (SS).** A logical relationship in which a successor activity cannot start until a predecessor activity has started. For example, leveling concrete (successor) cannot begin until pouring the foundation (predecessor) begins.
- **Start-to-finish (SF).** A logical relationship in which a predecessor activity cannot finish until a successor activity has started. For example, a new accounts payable system (successor) has to start before the old accounts payable system can be shut down (predecessor).

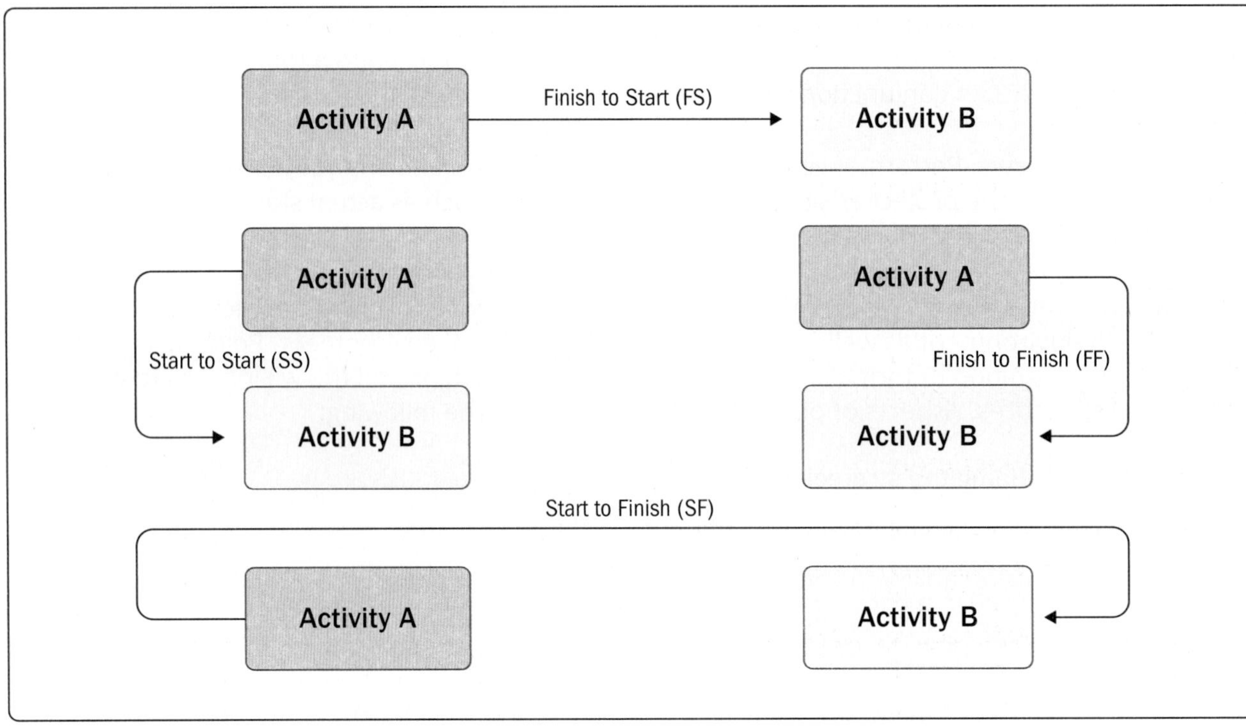

Figure 5-13. Precedence Diagramming Method Relationship Types

In the precedence diagramming method, FS is the most commonly used type of precedence relationship. The SF relationship is very rarely used, but it is included here to present a complete list of the relationship types in the precedence diagramming method.

Two activities can have two logical relationships at the same time (for example, SS and FF). Multiple relationships among the same activities are not recommended, so a decision has to be made to select the relationship with the highest impact. Closed loops are also not recommended in logical relationships.

Predictive analytics. Predictive analytics uses machine learning and current and historical data to discover patterns and to predict and forecast future scenarios, performance, trends, or events. For example, predictive analytics can be used when predicting project risks and suggesting effective mitigation strategies based on historical data.

Presentations. A presentation is the formal delivery of information and/or documentation. Clear and effective presentations of project information to relevant stakeholders can include but are not limited to the following:

- Progress reports and information updates to stakeholders;
- Background information to support decision-making;
- General information about the project and its objectives, for the purposes of raising the profile of the work of the project and the team; and

- Specific information aimed at increasing understanding and support of the work and objectives of the project.

Presentations are successful when the content and delivery take the following into account:

- Expectations and needs of the audience, and
- Needs and objectives of the project and project team.

Prioritization/ranking. Stakeholder requirements should be prioritized and ranked, as should the stakeholders themselves. Stakeholders with the most interest and the highest influence are often prioritized at the top of the list. Commonly used methods include MoSCoW (must have, should have, could have, and will not have), 100-point method, cost of delay, and Kano analysis.

Probability and impact matrix. A probability and impact matrix is a grid for mapping the probability of occurrence of each risk and its impact on project objectives if that risk occurs. Prioritization rules may be specified by the organization in advance of the project and included in organizational process assets, or they may be tailored to the specific project. Opportunities and threats are represented in a common probability and impact matrix using positive definitions of impact for opportunities and negative impact definitions for threats. Descriptive terms (such as very high, high, medium, low, and very low) or numeric values can be used for probability and impact. Where numeric values are used, these can be multiplied to give a probability–impact score for each risk, which allows the relative priority of individual risks to be evaluated within each priority level. An example probability and impact matrix is presented in Figure 5-14, which also shows a possible numeric risk-scoring scheme.

Problem-solving. Problem-solving entails finding solutions for issues or challenges. Problem-solving can include gathering additional information; critical thinking; and creative, quantitative, and/or logical approaches. Effective and systematic problem-solving is a fundamental element in quality

Probability	Threats					Opportunities					Probability
Very High 0.90	0.05	0.09	0.18	0.36	0.72	0.72	0.36	0.18	0.09	0.05	Very High 0.90
High 0.70	0.04	0.07	0.14	0.28	0.56	0.56	0.28	0.14	0.07	0.04	High 0.70
Medium 0.50	0.03	0.05	0.10	0.20	0.40	0.40	0.20	0.10	0.05	0.03	Medium 0.50
Low 0.30	0.02	0.03	0.06	0.12	0.24	0.24	0.12	0.06	0.03	0.02	Low 0.30
Very Low 0.10	0.01	0.01	0.02	0.04	0.08	0.08	0.04	0.02	0.01	0.01	Very Low 0.10
	Very Low 0.05	Low 0.10	Moderate 0.20	High 0.40	Very High 0.80	Very High 0.80	High 0.40	Moderate 0.20	Low 0.10	Very Low 0.05	
	Negative Impact					Positive Impact					

Figure 5-14. Example Probability and Impact Matrix With Scoring Scheme

assurance and quality improvement. Using a structured problem-solving method can help eliminate the problem and develop a long-lasting solution. Problem-solving methods generally include the following actions:

- Define the problem,
- Identify the root cause,
- Generate possible solutions,
- Choose the best solution,
- Implement the solution, and
- Verify solution effectiveness.

Process analysis. Process analysis identifies opportunities for process improvements. The analysis also examines problems, constraints, and non-value-added activities that occur during a process.

Process automations. Process automation, which can also include robotic process automation (RPA), helps speed up business processes. Process automation can reduce manual project work and costs, enhance project team and customer experiences by configuring computer software, or be a software robot that performs tasks by mimicking a human. Process automation can be used for project team meeting scheduling, sending reminders, or other manual project tasks that take a sufficient number of hours and can be described as a set of rules or instructions.

Process improvement. Process improvement refers to the systematic approach of enhancing the efficiency and effectiveness of a process within an organization. This approach involves analyzing current processes, identifying areas for improvement, and implementing changes to achieve better performance, quality, and customer satisfaction. The ultimate goal of process improvement is to optimize operations, reduce waste, and increase value for both the organization and its customers.

Product analysis. Product analysis can be used to define products and services. This analysis includes asking questions about a product or service and forming answers to describe the use, characteristics, and other relevant aspects of what is going to be manufactured or delivered.

Each application area has one or more generally accepted methods for translating high-level product or service descriptions into meaningful deliverables. Requirements are captured at a high level and decomposed to the level of detail needed to design the final product. Examples of product analysis techniques include but are not limited to the following:

- Product breakdown,
- Requirements analysis,
- Systems analysis,
- Systems engineering,
- Value analysis, and
- Value engineering.

Project canvas. A project canvas is a visual tool used to outline and plan the key elements of a project (see Figure 5-15). A project canvas provides a structured framework that helps project

<table>
<tr><td>Purpose
What is the intent of this project?
Why are we doing this project?</td><td>Objective</td><td>Project Approval Requirements
What constitutes project success, who decides if the project is successful, and who approves the project?</td></tr>
<tr><td rowspan="2">Scope/Requirements</td><td>Scope/Deliverables</td><td>Assumptions/Constraints</td></tr>
<tr><td>Scope Exclusion</td><td>Resources
What resources do we need in this project?
• Physical (office, building, server)
• Financial (money)
• Human (time, knowledge)</td></tr>
<tr><td>Milestones</td><td>Stakeholders
Who has an interest in the success of the project?
In what way are they involved in the project?
Users
Who will benefit from the outcome of the project?</td><td>Risks
Which risks may occur during the project?
How do we treat these risks?</td></tr>
<tr><td>Project Phases</td><td>Team
Percentage of who are the participants?
Percentage of who is the project manager?
Percentage of what other roles are present in the team?</td><td>Lessons Learned</td></tr>
</table>

Figure 5-15. Project Canvas Example

managers and teams capture, organize, and communicate essential project information in a clear and concise manner. The project canvas typically includes various sections that cover different aspects of the project such as objectives, stakeholders, deliverables, resources, risks, and timelines.

The project canvas offers a visual representation of the project, making it easier to understand and communicate the project's scope and key components. By presenting information visually, the project canvas allows team members and stakeholders to quickly grasp the overall picture and see how different elements of the project interconnect. This visual approach is particularly useful in complex projects where multiple factors should be considered simultaneously.

One of the main advantages of a project canvas is that it provides a comprehensive overview of the project. The project canvas includes sections for project objectives, stakeholders, deliverables, resources, risks, and timelines, ensuring that all critical aspects of the project are captured in one place. This holistic view helps project managers to identify potential gaps or issues early on and to plan more effectively.

The project canvas also serves as a powerful collaboration tool. By providing a common platform for discussing and aligning on project details, it facilitates communication and collaboration among team members and stakeholders. This collaborative approach helps ensure that everyone involved in the project has a shared understanding of its goals, scope, and key components, which can lead to better decision-making and more successful project outcomes.

Project dashboards. A project dashboard is a set of charts and graphs showing progress or performance against important measures of the project. A common way of showing large quantities of information on metrics is a dashboard. Dashboards generally collect information electronically and generate charts that depict status. Often, dashboards offer high-level summaries of data and allow drill-down analysis into contributing data. Figure 5-16 and Figure 5-17 each provide examples of a dashboard.

Dashboards often include information displayed as stoplight charts (also known as red–amber–green [RAG] charts), bar charts, pie charts, and control charts. A text explanation can be used for any measures that are outside the established thresholds.

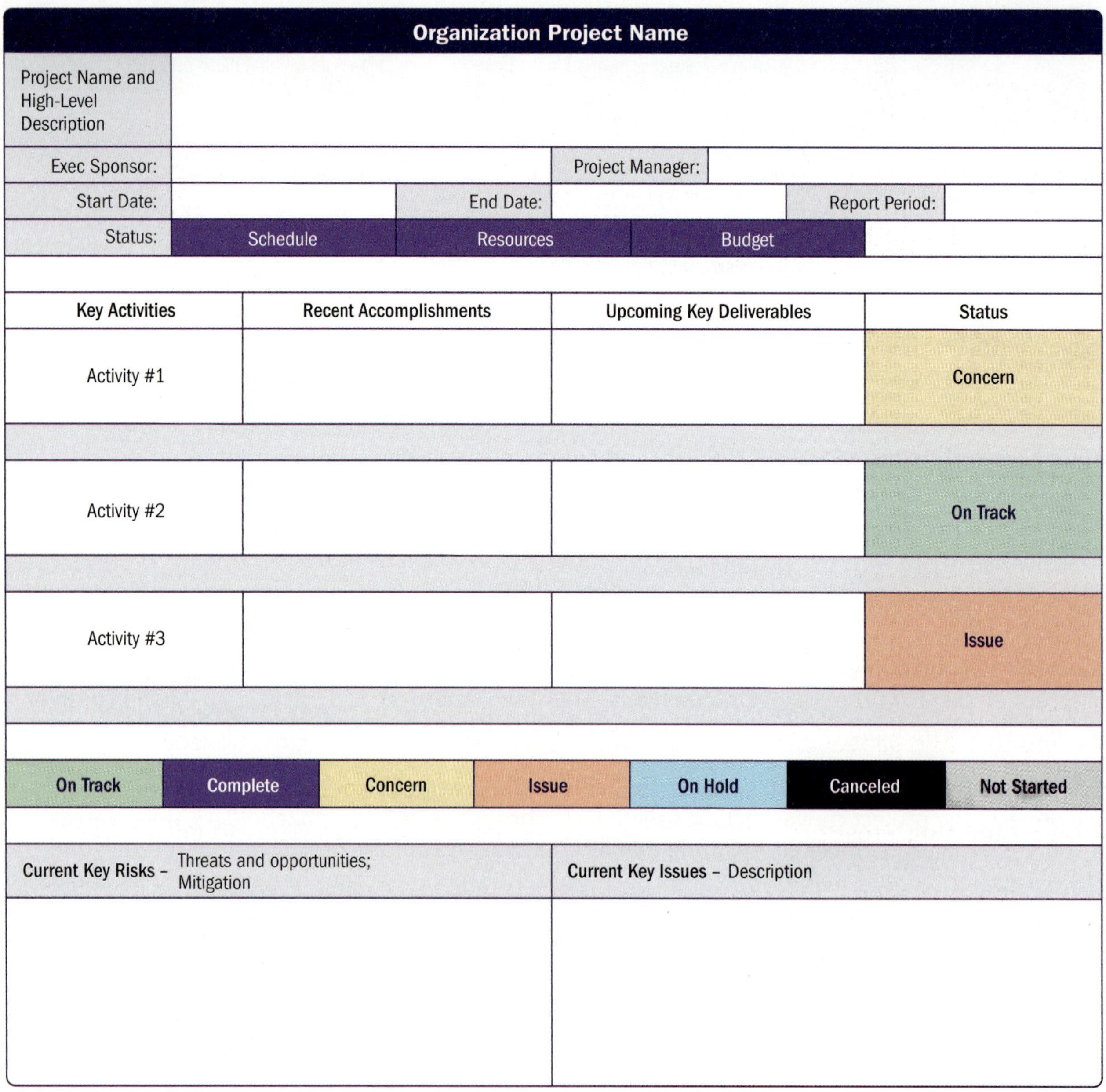

Figure 5-16. Project Dashboard Example 1

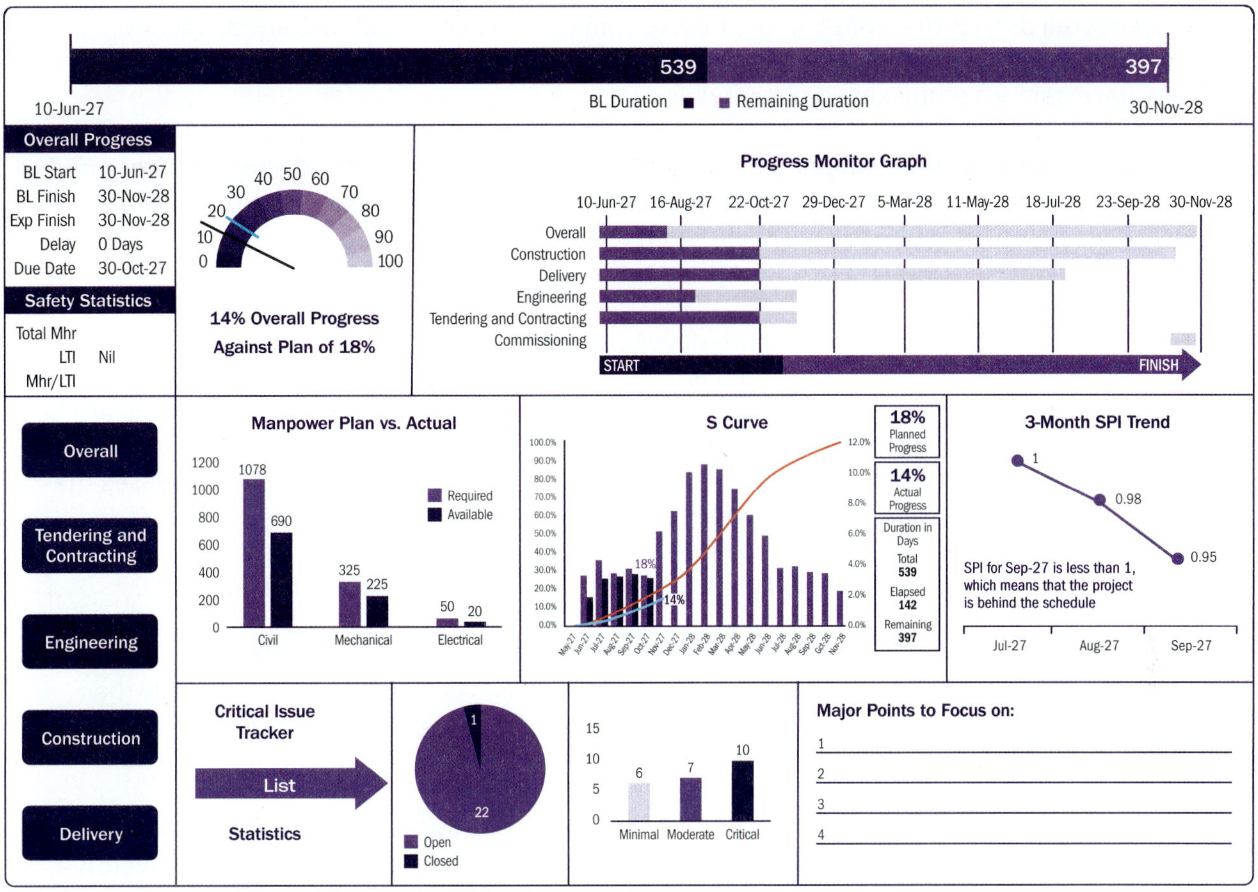

Figure 5-17. Project Dashboard Example 2

Project management information system (PMIS). A PMIS is an information system consisting of the tools and techniques used to gather, integrate, and disseminate the outputs of project management processes. A PMIS provides access to information technology software tools, such as scheduling software tools, work authorization systems, configuration management systems, and information collection and distribution systems, as well as interfaces to other online automated systems such as organizational knowledge repositories. Automated gathering and reporting on key performance indicators (KPIs) can be part of this system.

Project reporting. Project reporting is the act of collecting and distributing project information. Project information is distributed to many groups of stakeholders and should be adapted to provide information at an appropriate level, format, and detail for each type of stakeholder. The format may range from a simple communication to more elaborate custom reports and presentations. Information may be prepared regularly or on an exception basis.

Prompt lists. A prompt list is a predetermined list of risk categories that might give rise to individual project risks and that could also act as sources of overall project risk. The prompt list can be used as a framework to aid the project team in idea generation when using risk identification techniques. The risk categories in the lowest level of the risk breakdown structure can be used as a prompt list for individual project risks. Some common strategic frameworks are more suitable for identifying sources of overall project risk, for example PESTLE (political, economic, sociocultural, technological, legal, environmental), TECOP (technical, environmental, commercial, operational, political), or VUCA (volatility, uncertainty, complexity, ambiguity).

Questionnaires and surveys. Questionnaires and surveys are written sets of questions designed to quickly accumulate information from a large number of respondents. Questionnaires and/or surveys are most appropriate with varied audiences, when a quick turnaround is needed, when respondents are geographically dispersed, and where statistical analysis could be appropriate.

Recognition and rewards. Part of the team development process involves recognizing and rewarding desirable behavior. The original plan for rewarding people is developed during the Plan Resource Management process. Cultural differences influence how recognition and rewards are best delivered, and understanding these differences helps ensure that the rewards program is meaningful and motivating for everyone. Tailoring recognition to align with cultural preferences increases the effectiveness of reward systems and enhances employee satisfaction.

People are motivated when they feel they are valued in the organization, and this value is demonstrated by the rewards given to them. Generally, money is viewed as a tangible aspect of any reward system, but intangible rewards could be equally or even more effective. Most project team members are motivated by an opportunity to grow, accomplish, be appreciated, and apply their professional skills to meet new challenges. A good strategy for project managers is to give the team recognition throughout the project life cycle rather than waiting until the project is complete.

Regression analysis. Regression analysis is an analytical method where a series of input variables are examined in relation to their corresponding output results in order to develop a mathematical or statistical relationship. This technique analyzes the interrelationships between different project variables that contributed to project outcomes in order to improve performance on future projects.

Reserve analysis. Reserve analysis is a method used to evaluate the amount of risk on the project and the amount of schedule and budget reserve to determine whether the reserve is sufficient for the remaining risk. Reserve analysis is used as an analytical technique to determine the essential features and relationships of components in the project management plan in order to establish a reserve for the schedule duration, budget, estimated cost, or funds for a project.

Cost estimates may include contingency reserves (sometimes called contingency allowances) to account for cost uncertainty. Contingency reserves are the budget within the cost baseline that is allocated for identified risks. Contingency reserves are often viewed as the part of the budget intended to address the known-unknowns that can affect a project. For example, rework for some project deliverables could be anticipated, while the amount of this rework is unknown. Contingency reserves may be estimated to account for this unknown amount of rework. Contingency reserves can be provided at any level from the specific activity to the entire project. The contingency reserve may be a percentage of the estimated cost, a fixed number, or may be developed by using quantitative analysis methods. As more precise information about the project becomes available, the contingency reserve may be used, reduced, or eliminated. Contingency should be clearly identified in the cost documentation. Contingency reserves are part of the cost baseline and the overall funding requirements for the project.

Resource leveling. See *resource optimization technique.*

Resource optimization technique. The resource optimization technique is a technique in which activity start and finish dates are adjusted to balance demand for resources with the available supply. Examples of resource optimization techniques that can be used to adjust the schedule model due to the demand and supply of resources include but are not limited to the following:

- **Resource leveling.** A resource optimization technique in which adjustments are made to the project schedule to optimize the allocation of resources and which may affect the critical path. The resource leveling technique adjusts the start and finish dates based on resource constraints with the goal of balancing the demand for resources with the available supply. Resource leveling can be used when shared or critically required resources are available only at certain times or in limited quantities, are overallocated, such as when a resource has been assigned to two or more activities during the same time period (as shown in Figure 5-18), or when there is a need to keep resource usage at a constant level.

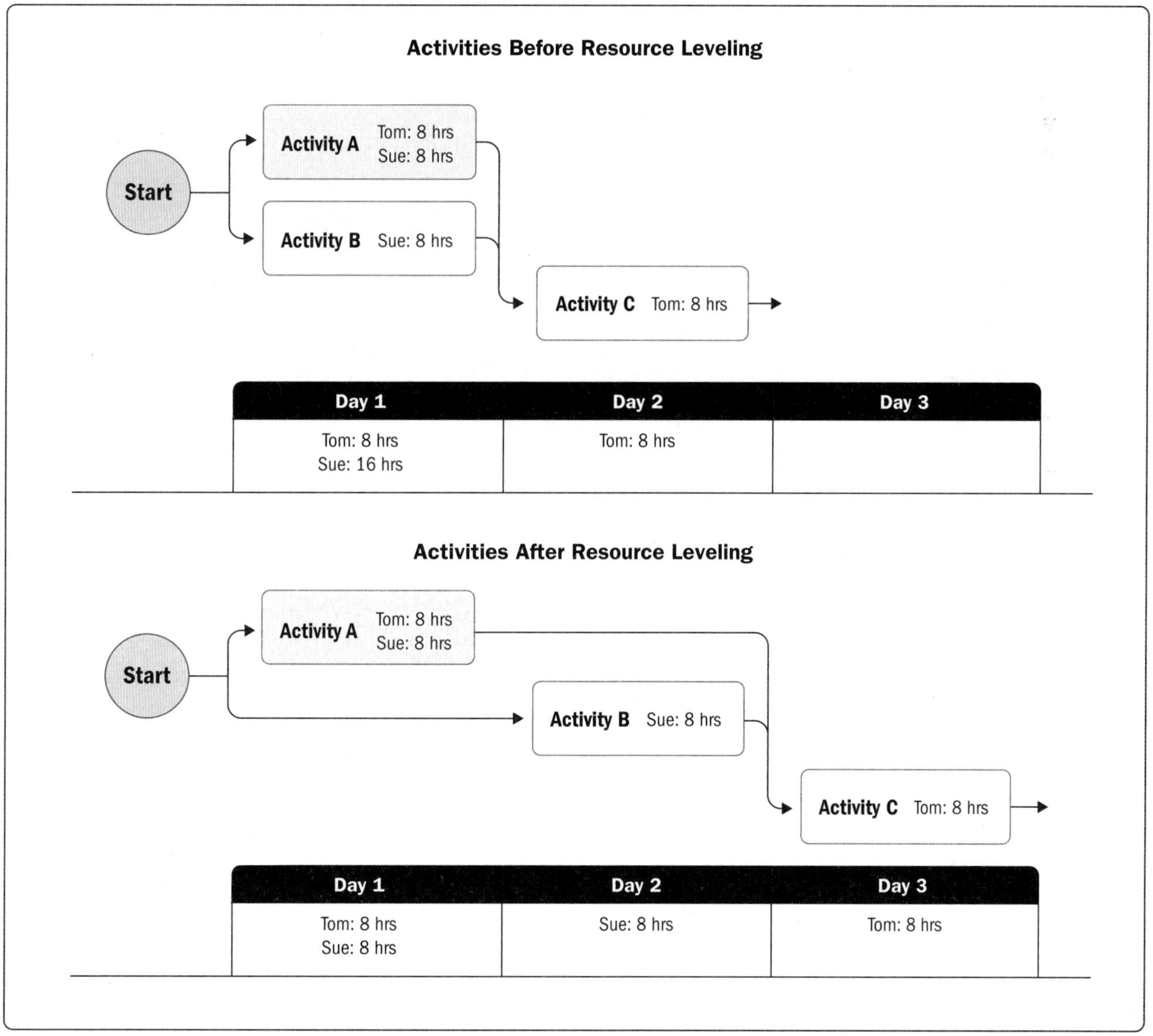

Figure 5-18. Resource Leveling

Available float is used for leveling resources. Consequently, the critical path through the project schedule may change.

- **Resource smoothing.** A resource optimization technique in which free and total float are used without affecting the critical path. Resource smoothing is a technique that adjusts the activities of a schedule model such that the requirements for resources on the project do not exceed certain predefined resource limits. In resource smoothing, as opposed to resource leveling, the project's critical path is not changed and the completion date may not be delayed. In other words, activities may only be delayed within their free and total float. Resource smoothing may not be able to optimize all resources.

Resource-based view. Resource-based view is a managerial framework for identifying strategic resources that can provide an enterprise with a competitive advantage against its competitors. The resource-based view emphasizes evaluating the organizational internal assets, capabilities, and competencies to achieve superior competitive performance or project deliverables. Enterprise strengths and weaknesses of resources and capabilities and their competitive advantage can be evaluated using a framework like VRIO. VRIO stands for value, rarity, imitability, and organization:

- **Value** can include both tangible and intangible resources and capabilities.
- **Rarity** means that resources and capabilities are not available to other enterprises.
- **Imitability** is the extent to which resources and capabilities are difficult to imitate.
- **Organization** means that the enterprise is effectively utilizing its resources and capabilities.

Responsibility assignment matrix. A responsibility assignment matrix is a grid that shows the project resources assigned to each work package. The matrix is used to illustrate the connections between work packages, or activities, and project team members. On larger projects, a responsibility assignment matrix can be developed at various levels. For example, a high-level matrix can define the responsibilities of a project team, group, or unit within each component of the WBS. A lower-level matrix can be used within the group to designate roles, responsibilities, and levels of authority for specific activities. The matrix format shows all activities associated with one person and all people associated with one activity. This format also ensures that there is only one person accountable for any one task to avoid confusion about who is ultimately in charge or has authority for the work. One example of a responsibility assignment matrix is a RACI (responsible, accountable, consulted, informed) matrix, shown in Figure 5-19. The sample chart shows the work to be done in the left column as activities. The assigned resources can be shown as individuals or groups. The project manager can select other options, such as "lead" and "resource" designations, as appropriate for the project. A RACI matrix is a useful tool to ensure the clear assignment of roles and responsibilities when the team consists of internal and external resources.

Retrospectives. A retrospective is a regularly occurring workshop in which participants explore their work and results in order to improve both the process and product. Retrospectives are a form of a lessons learned meeting and are conducted frequently throughout the project (at minimum, at the end of each iteration). Retrospectives usually cover process-based questions such as what worked well and what did not and what are the project team recommendations for future iterations. The term *retrospective* is usually used within adaptive development approaches but can refer to any lessons learned session in any approach.

This frequent reflection helps ensure that the team can quickly address issues and implement improvements, rather than waiting until the end of the project. The entire project team participates in

RACI Matrix	Person				
Activity	Ann	Ben	Carlos	Dina	Ed
Create charter	A	R	I	I	I
Collect requirements	I	A	R	C	C
Submit change request	I	A	R	R	C
Develop test plan	A	C	I	I	R
	R = Responsible A = Accountable C = Consulted I = Informed				

Figure 5-19. Sample RACI Matrix

these meetings, fostering a collaborative environment where everyone can contribute their insights and suggestions. The outcomes of retrospectives are actionable, with specific actions identified and owners assigned to implement the improvements. This immediate impact allows for quick adjustments and continuous enhancement of the project process.

Risk categorization. Risks to the project can be categorized by sources of risk (e.g., using the risk breakdown structure [RBS]); the area of the project affected (e.g., using the work breakdown structure [WBS]); or other useful categories (e.g., project phase, project budget, and roles and responsibilities) to determine the areas of the project most exposed to the effects of uncertainty. Risks can also be categorized by common root causes. Risk categories that may be used for the project are defined in the risk management plan.

Grouping risks into categories can lead to the development of more effective risk responses by focusing attention and effort on the areas of highest risk exposure, or by developing generic risk responses to address groups of related risks.

Risk probability and impact assessment. Risk probability assessments consider the likelihood that a specific risk will occur. Risk impact assessments consider the potential effect on one or more project objectives such as schedule, cost, quality, or performance. Impacts will be negative for threats and positive for opportunities. Probability and impact are assessed for each identified individual project risk. Risks can be assessed in interviews or meetings with participants selected for their familiarity with the types of risk recorded in the risk register. Project team members and knowledgeable persons external to the project are included. The level of probability for each risk and its impact on each objective are evaluated during the interview or meeting. Differences in the levels of probability and impact perceived by stakeholders are to be expected, and such differences should be explored. Explanatory detail, including assumptions justifying the levels assigned, are also recorded. Risk probabilities and impacts are assessed using the definitions given in the risk management plan. Risks with low probability and impact may be included within the risk register as part of a watch list for future monitoring.

Rolling wave planning. Rolling wave planning is an iterative planning technique in which the work to be accomplished in the near term is planned in detail, while the work in the future is planned at a higher level. This progressive elaboration allows work to exist at various levels of detail, depending on the project life cycle stage. During early strategic planning, when information is less defined, work packages are outlined at a high level. As more information becomes available, these packages are decomposed into detailed activities.

Root cause analysis. Root cause analysis is an analytical method used to determine the basic underlying reason that causes a variance, defect, or risk. A root cause may underlie more than one variance, defect, or risk. Root cause analysis may also be used as a technique for identifying the root causes of a problem and solving them. When all root causes for a problem are removed, the problem does not recur.

Schedule compression. Schedule compression is a technique used to shorten the schedule duration without reducing the project scope. Schedule compression techniques are used to meet schedule constraints, imposed dates, or other schedule objectives. A helpful technique is the negative float analysis. The critical path is the one with the least float. Due to violating a constraint or imposed date, the total float can become negative. Schedule compression techniques are compared in Figure 5-20 and include:

- **Crashing.** A schedule compression technique used to shorten the schedule duration for the least incremental cost by adding resources. Examples of crashing include approving overtime, bringing in additional resources, or paying to expedite delivery to activities on

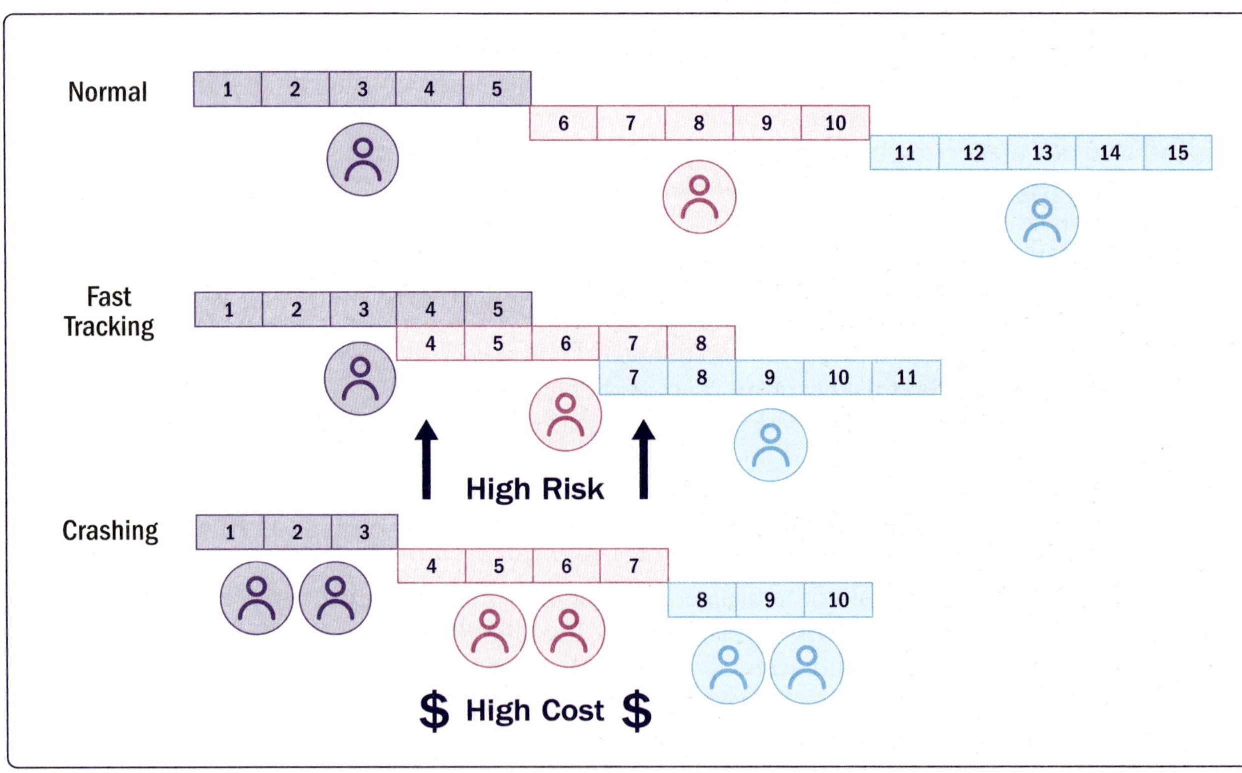

Figure 5-20. Schedule Compression Comparison

the critical path. Crashing works only for activities on the critical path where additional resources will shorten the activity's duration. Crashing does not always produce a viable alternative and may result in increased risk and/or cost.

- **Fast tracking.** A schedule compression technique in which activities or phases normally done in sequence are performed in parallel for at least a portion of their duration. An example is constructing the foundation of a building before completing all of the architectural drawings. Fast tracking may result in rework and increased risk. Fast tracking only works when activities can be overlapped to shorten the project duration on the critical path. Such overlapping requires increased coordination efforts between the activities concerned, potentially resulting in greater quality risk. Fast tracking may also increase project costs.

Schedule network analysis. Schedule network analysis is a technique used to identify early and late start dates, as well as early and late finish dates, for the uncompleted portions of project activities. Schedule network analysis is the overarching technique used to generate the project schedule model. The analysis employs several other techniques such as critical path method, resource optimization techniques, and modeling techniques. Additional analysis includes but is not limited to the following:

- Assessing the need to aggregate schedule reserves to reduce the probability of a schedule slip when multiple paths converge at a single point in time, or when multiple paths diverge from a single point in time, to reduce the probability of a schedule slip.
- Reviewing the network to see if the critical path has high-risk activities or long-lead items that would necessitate use of schedule reserves or the implementation of risk responses to reduce the risk on the critical path.

Schedule network analysis is an iterative process that is employed until a viable schedule model is developed.

Sensitivity analysis. Sensitivity analysis helps to determine which individual project risks or other sources of uncertainty have the most potential impact on project outcomes. The analysis correlates variations in project outcomes with variations in elements of the quantitative risk analysis model.

One typical display of sensitivity analysis is the tornado diagram, which presents the calculated correlation coefficient for each element of the quantitative risk analysis model that can influence the project outcome. This analysis can include individual project risks, project activities with high degrees of variability, or specific sources of ambiguity. Items are ordered by descending strength of correlation, giving the typical tornado appearance. An example tornado diagram is shown in Figure 5-21.

Servant leadership. Servant leadership is the practice of leading the team by focusing on understanding and addressing the needs and development of team members in order to enable the highest possible team performance. Servant leadership is performed in service to the project's business/mission objective(s).

Simulation. Simulation models the combined effects of individual project risks and other sources of uncertainty to evaluate their potential impact on achieving project objectives. The most common simulation technique is Monte Carlo analysis, in which risks and other sources of uncertainty are used to calculate possible schedule outcomes for the total project. Simulation involves calculating multiple work package durations with different sets of activity assumptions, constraints, risks, issues,

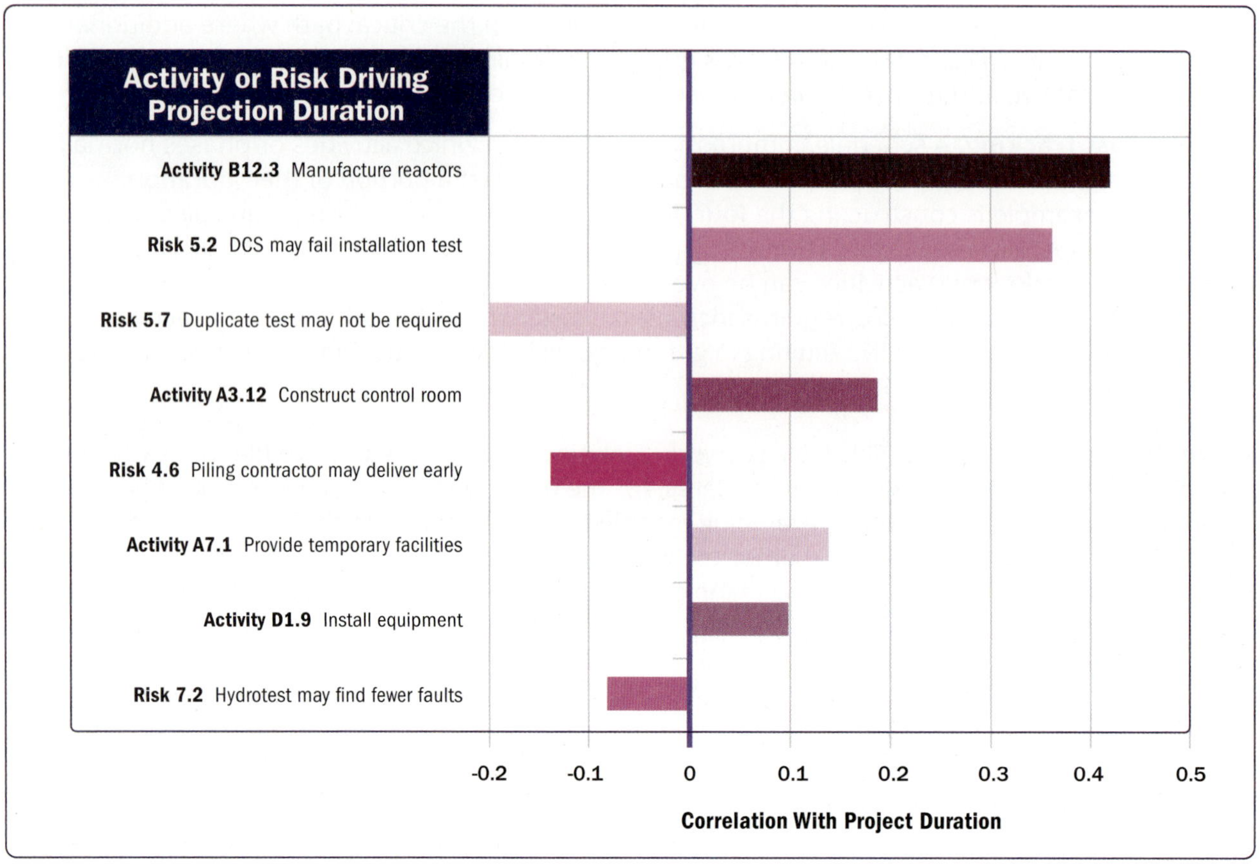

Figure 5-21. Example Tornado Diagram

or scenarios using probability distributions and other representations of uncertainty. Figure 5-22 shows a probability distribution for a project with the probability of achieving a certain target date (i.e., project finish date). In this example, there is a 10% probability that the project will finish on or before the target date of 13 May 2027, while there is a 90% probability of completing the project by 28 May 2027.

For more information on how Monte Carlo simulation is used for schedule models, see the *Practice Standard for Scheduling* [5].

Six Thinking Hats®.[1] Six Thinking Hats® is a group discussion and creative conversation technique that involves six different metaphorical hats that are each a different color to represent different ways of thinking:

- **Blue hat** usually facilitates the meeting and considers the big picture of the idea or issue discussed;
- **White hat** considers facts and information;
- **Red hat** shows feelings and emotions;
- **Black hat** has a negative point of view;

[1] Six Thinking Hats® is a registered trademark of Edward de Bono Limited.

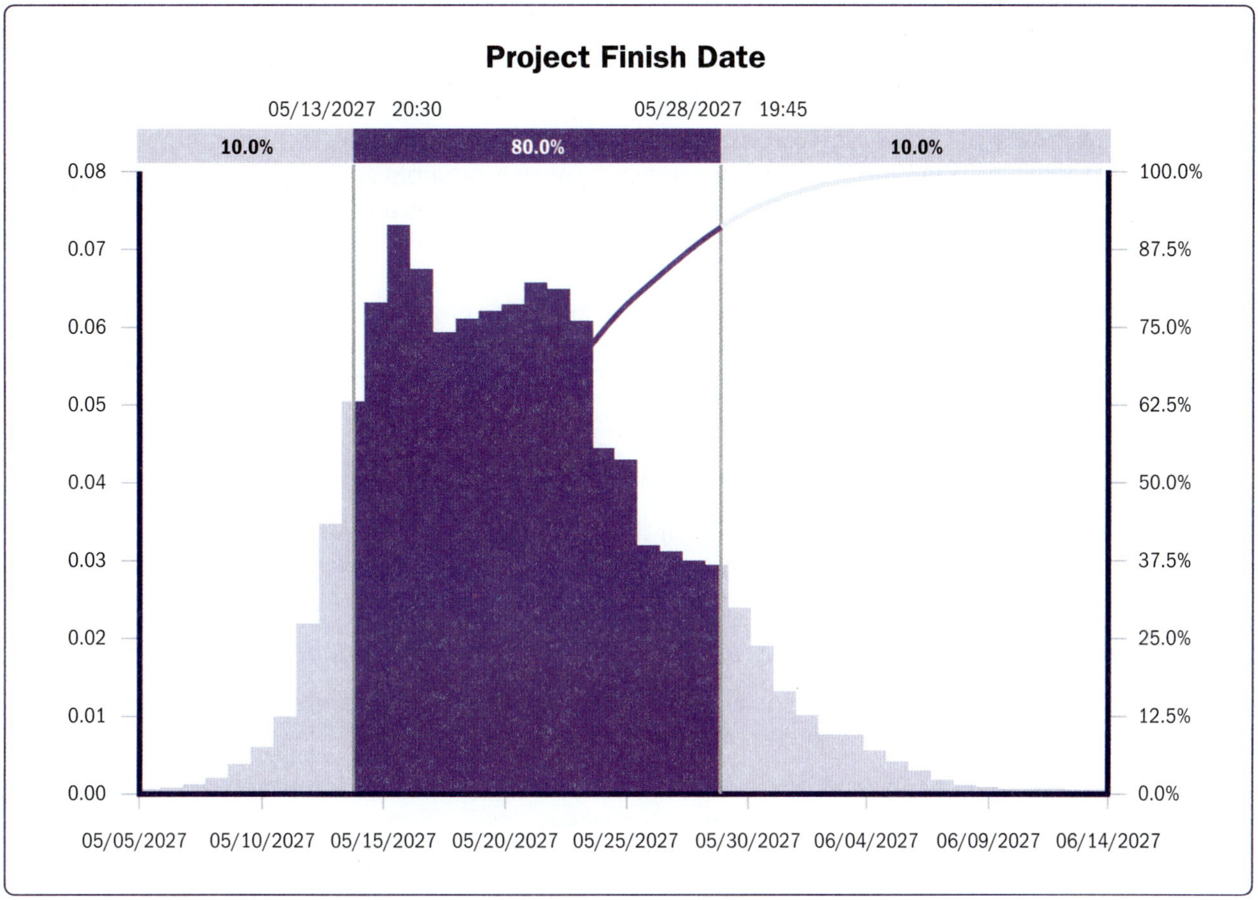

Figure 5-22. Example Probability Distribution of a Target Milestone

- **Yellow hat** focuses on positive aspects; and
- **Green hat** is responsible for generating new ideas.

Sprint review. A sprint review is a collaborative review session where the team demonstrates the work that was completed during the sprint to stakeholders and solicits their feedback. A sprint review or iteration review is held at the end of a sprint or iteration to demonstrate the work that was accomplished during the sprint or iteration.

Stakeholder analysis. Stakeholder analysis results in a list of stakeholders and relevant information such as their positions in the organization, roles on the project, "stakes," expectations, attitudes (their levels of support for the project), and their interest in information about the project. Stakeholders' stakes may include but are not limited to a combination of the following:

- **Interest.** A person or group can be affected by a decision related to the project or its outcomes.
- **Rights (legal or moral rights).** Legal rights, such as occupational health and safety, may be defined in the legislation framework of a country. Moral rights may involve concepts of protection of historical sites or environmental sustainability.
- **Ownership.** Ownership is when a person or group has a legal title to an asset or a property.

- **Knowledge.** The person may have specialist knowledge, which can benefit the project through more effective delivery of project objectives, organizational outcomes, or knowledge of the power structures of the organization.
- **Contribution.** The person may provide funds or other resources, including human resources, or offer support for the project in more intangible ways, such as advocacy in the form of promoting the objectives of the project or acting as a buffer between the project and the power structures of the organization and its politics.

Stakeholder engagement assessment matrix. A stakeholder engagement assessment matrix is a matrix that compares current and desired stakeholder engagement levels. One way to classify the engagement level of stakeholders is shown in Figure 5-23. The engagement level of stakeholders can be classified as follows:

- **Unaware.** The stakeholder is unaware of the project and its potential impacts.
- **Resistant.** The stakeholder is aware of the project and potential impacts but resistant to any changes that may occur as a result of the work or outcomes of the project. These stakeholders will be unsupportive of the work or outcomes of the project.
- **Neutral.** The stakeholder is aware of the project but neither supportive nor unsupportive.
- **Supportive.** The stakeholder is aware of the project and its potential impacts and supportive of the work and its outcomes.
- **Leading.** The stakeholder is aware of the project and its potential impacts and actively engaged in ensuring that the project is a success.

In Figure 5-23, C represents the current engagement level of each stakeholder and D indicates the level that the project team has assessed as essential to ensure project success (desired). The gap between current and desired for each stakeholder will direct the level of communications necessary to effectively engage the stakeholder. The closing of this gap between current and desired is an essential element of monitoring stakeholder engagement.

Stakeholder mapping/representation. Stakeholder mapping and representation is a method of categorizing stakeholders using various methods. Categorizing stakeholders assists the team in building relationships with the identified project stakeholders. Common methods include the following:

- **Power/interest grid, power/influence grid, or impact/influence grid.** Each of these techniques supports a grouping of stakeholders according to their level of authority (power), level of concern about the project's outcomes (interest), ability to influence the outcomes

Stakeholder	Unaware	Resistant	Neutral	Supportive	Leading
Stakeholder 1	C			D	
Stakeholder 2			C	D	
Stakeholder 3				D C	

Figure 5-23. Stakeholder Engagement Assessment Matrix

of the project (influence), or ability to cause changes to the project's planning or execution. These classification models are useful for small projects or projects with simple relationships between stakeholders and the project, or within the stakeholder community itself.

- **Stakeholder cube.** This is a refinement of the grid models previously explained. This model combines the grid elements into a three-dimensional model that can be useful to project managers and teams in identifying and engaging their stakeholder community. It provides a model with multiple dimensions that improves the depiction of the stakeholder community as a multidimensional entity and assists with the development of communication strategies.
- **Salience model.** The salience model describes classes of stakeholders based on assessments of their power (level of authority or ability to influence the outcomes of the project), urgency (need for immediate attention, either time-constrained or relating to the stakeholders' high stakes in the outcome), and legitimacy (their involvement is appropriate). There is an adaptation of the salience model that substitutes proximity (stakeholders' direct involvement in the project activities, such as their physical proximity to the worksite, or their direct contribution to project deliverables) for legitimacy (applying to the team and measuring their level of involvement with the work of the project). The salience model is useful for large, complex communities of stakeholders or where there are complex networks of relationships within the community. It is also useful in determining the relative importance of the identified stakeholders.
- **Directions of influence.** This technique classifies stakeholders according to their influence on the work of the project or the project team itself. Stakeholders can be classified in the following ways:
  - **Upward** (senior management of the performing organization or customer organization, sponsor, and steering committee);
  - **Downward** (the team or specialists contributing knowledge or skills in a temporary capacity);
  - **Outward** (stakeholder groups and their representatives outside the project team, such as suppliers, government departments, the public, end users, and regulators); or
  - **Sideward** (the peers of the project manager, such as other project managers or middle managers who are in competition for scarce project resources or who collaborate with the project manager in sharing resources or information).
- **Prioritization.** Prioritizing stakeholders may be necessary for projects with a large number of stakeholders, where the membership of the stakeholder community is changing frequently, or when the relationships between stakeholders and the project team or within the stakeholder community are complex.

Storytelling. Storytelling in project management is a powerful tool for conveying lessons learned, good practices, and project outcomes through narratives. Unlike traditional reports or data presentations, storytelling engages the audience by making the information more relatable and memorable.

Stories are particularly effective for transferring tacit knowledge, which is often difficult to articulate through formal documentation. By illustrating real-life scenarios and solutions, storytelling helps team members understand complex concepts and apply them in their work. Additionally, storytelling can shape organizational culture by highlighting values, successes, and learning moments, thereby reinforcing desired behaviors and practices.

Effective storytelling enhances communication within the team and across the organization. Storytelling makes complex information more understandable and relatable, which can lead to better decision-making and problem-solving. Moreover, sharing success stories and overcoming challenges can inspire and motivate team members, fostering a positive and collaborative work environment.

Strategies for opportunities. There are five alternative strategies that may be considered for dealing with opportunities, as follows:

- **Escalate.** The escalate risk response strategy is appropriate when the project team or project sponsor agrees that an opportunity is outside the scope of the project or that the proposed response would exceed the project manager's authority. Escalated opportunities are managed at the portfolio level, program level, or other relevant part of the organization, but not at the project level. The project manager determines who should be notified about the opportunity and communicates the details to that person or part of the organization. It is important that ownership of escalated opportunities is accepted by the relevant party in the organization. Opportunities are usually escalated to the level that matches the objectives that would be affected if the opportunity occurred. Escalated opportunities are not monitored further by the project team after escalation, although they may be recorded in the risk register for information.
- **Exploit.** The exploit strategy may be selected for high-priority opportunities where the organization wants to ensure that the opportunity is realized. This strategy seeks to capture the benefit associated with a particular opportunity by ensuring that it definitely happens, increasing the probability of occurrence to 100%. Examples of exploiting responses may include assigning an organization's most talented resources to the project to reduce the time to completion or using new technologies or technology upgrades to reduce cost and duration.
- **Share.** Sharing involves transferring ownership of an opportunity to a third party so that it shares some of the benefit if the opportunity occurs. It is important to select the new owner of a shared opportunity carefully, so they are best able to capture the opportunity for the benefit of the project. Risk sharing often involves payment of a risk premium to the party taking on the opportunity. Examples of sharing actions include forming risk-sharing partnerships, teams, special-purpose companies, or joint ventures.
- **Enhance.** The enhance strategy is used to increase the probability and/or impact of an opportunity. Early enhancement action is often more effective than trying to improve the benefit after the opportunity has occurred. The probability of occurrence for an opportunity may be increased by focusing attention on its causes. Where it is not possible to increase probability, an enhancement response might increase the impact by targeting factors that drive the size of the potential benefit. Examples of enhancing opportunities include adding more resources to an activity to finish early.
- **Accept.** Accepting an opportunity acknowledges its existence but no proactive action is taken. This strategy may be appropriate for low-priority opportunities, and it may also be adopted where it is not possible or cost-effective to address an opportunity in any other way. Acceptance can be either active or passive. The most common active acceptance strategy is to establish a contingency reserve, including amounts of time, money, or resources to take advantage of the opportunity if it occurs. Passive acceptance involves no proactive action apart from periodic review of the opportunity to ensure that it does not change significantly.

Strategies for overall project risk. Risk responses should be planned and implemented not only for individual project risks but also to address overall project risk. The same risk response strategies that are used to deal with individual project risks can also be applied to overall project risk:

- **Avoid.** Where the level of overall project risk is significantly negative and outside the agreed-upon risk thresholds for the project, an avoid strategy may be adopted. This strategy involves taking focused action to reduce the negative effect of uncertainty on the project as a whole and bring the project back within the thresholds. An example of avoidance at the overall project level might include removal of high-risk elements of scope from the project. Where it is not possible to bring the project back within the thresholds, the project may be canceled. This strategy represents the most extreme degree of risk avoidance, and it should be used only if the overall level of threat is, and will remain, unacceptable.
- **Exploit.** Where the level of overall project risk is significantly positive and outside the agreed-upon risk thresholds for the project, an exploit strategy may be adopted. This strategy involves taking focused action to capture the positive effect of uncertainty on the project as a whole. An example of exploiting at the overall project level might include the addition of high-benefit elements of scope to the project to add value or benefits to stakeholders. Alternatively, the risk thresholds for the project may be modified with the agreement of key stakeholders in order to embrace the opportunity.
- **Transfer/share.** If the level of overall project risk is high but the organization is unable to address it effectively, a third party may be involved to manage the risk on behalf of the organization. Where overall project risk is negative, a transfer strategy is required, which may involve payment of a risk premium. In the case of a high positive overall project risk, ownership may be shared in order to reap the associated benefits. Examples of both transfer and share strategies for overall project risk include but are not limited to setting up a collaborative business structure in which the buyer and seller share the overall project risk, launching a joint venture or special-purpose company, or subcontracting key elements of the project.
- **Mitigate/enhance.** These strategies involve changing the level of overall project risk to optimize the chances of achieving the project's objectives. The risk mitigation strategy is used where overall project risk is negative, and risk enhancement applies when it is positive. Examples of mitigation or enhancement strategies include replanning the project, changing the scope and boundaries of the project, modifying project priority, changing resource allocations, adjusting delivery times, etc.
- **Accept.** Where no proactive risk response strategy is possible to address overall project risk, the organization may choose to continue with the project as currently defined, even if overall project risk is outside the agreed-upon thresholds. Risk acceptance can be either active or passive. The most common active acceptance strategy is to establish an overall contingency reserve for the project, including amounts of time, money, or resources to be used if the project exceeds its thresholds. Passive acceptance involves no proactive action apart from periodic review of the level of overall project risk to ensure that it does not change significantly.

Strategies for threats. There are five alternative strategies that may be considered for dealing with threats, as follows:

- **Escalate.** Risk escalation is appropriate when the project team or project sponsor agrees that a threat is outside the scope of the project or that the proposed response would exceed the project manager's authority. Escalated risks are managed at the portfolio level, program level, or other relevant part of the organization, but not at the project level. The project manager determines who should be notified about the threat and communicates the details to that person or part of the organization. It is important that the ownership of escalated threats is accepted by the relevant party in the organization. Threats are usually escalated to the level that matches the objectives that would be affected if the threat occurred. Escalated threats are not monitored further by the project team after escalation, although they may be recorded in the risk register for information.

- **Avoid.** Risk avoidance is when the project team acts to eliminate the threat or protect the project from its impact. Avoidance may be appropriate for high-priority threats with a high probability of occurrence and a large negative impact. Avoidance may involve changing some aspect of the project management plan or changing the objective that is in jeopardy in order to eliminate the threat entirely, reducing its probability of occurrence to zero. The risk owner may also take action to isolate the project objectives from the risk's impact if it were to occur. Examples of avoidance actions may include removing the cause of a threat, extending the schedule, changing the project strategy, or reducing scope. Some risks can be avoided by clarifying requirements, obtaining information, improving communication, or acquiring expertise.
- **Transfer.** Risk transference involves shifting ownership of a threat to a third party to manage the risk and to bear the impact if the threat occurs. Risk transfer often involves the payment of a risk premium to the party taking on the threat. The risk transfer can be achieved by a range of actions, which include but are not limited to the use of insurance, performance bonds, warranties, guarantees, etc. Agreements may be used to transfer ownership and liability for specified risks to another party.
- **Mitigate.** In risk mitigation, action is taken to reduce the probability of occurrence and/or impact of a threat. Early mitigation action is often more effective than trying to repair the damage after the threat has occurred. Adopting less-complex processes, conducting more tests, or choosing a more stable seller are examples of mitigation actions. Mitigation may involve prototype development to reduce the risk of scaling up from a bench-scale model of a process or product. Where it is not possible to reduce probability, a mitigation response might reduce the impact by targeting the factors that drive the severity. For example, designing redundancy into a system may reduce the impact from a failure of the original component.
- **Accept.** Risk acceptance acknowledges the existence of a threat, but no proactive action is taken. This strategy may be appropriate for low-priority threats, and it may also be adopted where it is not possible or cost-effective to address a threat in any other way. Acceptance can be either active or passive. The most common active acceptance strategy is to establish a contingency reserve, including amounts of time, money, or resources to handle the threat if it occurs. Passive acceptance involves no proactive action apart from periodic review of the threat to ensure that it does not change significantly.

SWOT (strengths, weaknesses, opportunities, threats) analysis. SWOT analysis is the analysis of strengths, weaknesses, opportunities, and threats of an organization, project, or option. For risk identification, it is used to increase the breadth of identified risks by including internally generated risks. The technique starts with the identification of strengths and weaknesses of the organization, focusing on either the project, organization, or the business area in general. SWOT analysis then identifies any opportunities for the project that may arise from strengths, and any threats resulting from weaknesses. The analysis also examines the degree to which organizational strengths may offset threats and determines if weaknesses might hinder opportunities.

Team building. Team building is conducting activities that enhance the team's social relationships and build a collaborative and cooperative working environment. Team-building activities can vary from a 5-minute agenda item in a status review meeting to an off-site, professionally facilitated event designed to improve interpersonal relationships. The objective of team-building activities is to help individual team members work together effectively. Team-building strategies are particularly valuable when team members operate from remote locations without the benefit of face-to-face contact. Informal communication and activities can help in building trust and establishing good working relationships. While team building is essential during the initial stages of a project, it should be a continuous process. Changes in a project environment are inevitable, and to manage them effectively, a continuous or renewed team-building effort may be applied. The project manager should continually monitor team functionality and performance to determine if any actions are needed to prevent or correct various team problems.

Technical performance analysis. Technical performance analysis compares technical accomplishments during project execution to the schedule of technical achievement. The analysis requires the definition of objective, quantifiable measures of technical performance, which can be used to compare actual results against targets. Such technical performance measures may include weight, transaction times, number of delivered defects, storage capacity, etc. Deviation can indicate the potential impact of threats or opportunities.

Test and inspection planning. During the planning phase, the project manager and the project team determine how to test or inspect the product, deliverable, or service to meet the stakeholders' needs and expectations, as well as how to meet the goal for the product's performance and reliability. The tests and inspections are industry dependent and can include, for example, alpha and beta tests in software projects, strength tests in construction projects, inspection in manufacturing, and field tests and nondestructive tests in engineering.

Testing/product evaluations. Testing is an organized and constructed investigation conducted to provide objective information about the quality of the product or service under test in accordance with the project requirements. The intent of testing is to find errors, defects, bugs, or other nonconformance problems in the product or service. The type, amount, and extent of tests needed to evaluate each requirement depend on the nature of the project, time, budget, and other constraints. Tests can be performed throughout the project, as different components of the project become available, and at the end of the project on the final deliverables. Early testing helps identify nonconformance problems and helps reduce the cost of fixing the nonconforming components.

Different application areas require different tests. For example, software testing may include unit testing, integration testing, black-box, white-box, interface testing, regression testing, alpha testing, etc. In construction projects, testing may include cement strength, concrete workability tests, nondestructive tests at construction sites for testing the quality of hardened concrete structures, and soil tests. In hardware development, testing may include environmental stress screening, burn-in tests, system testing, and more.

Text-oriented formats. Team member responsibilities that require detailed descriptions can be specified in text-oriented formats. Usually in outline form, these documents provide information such as responsibilities, authority, competencies, and qualifications. The documents are known by various names including position descriptions and role–responsibility–authority forms. These documents can be used as templates for future projects, especially when the information is updated throughout the current project by applying lessons learned.

Theory of constraints (TOC). Theory of constraints is a body of knowledge focused on improving the system-level performance of an organization, end-to-end process, project portfolio, or project. The TOC application to a project or project portfolio is critical chain project management (CCPM). See also *critical chain project management* and *continuous improvement.*

To-complete performance index (TCPI). The to-complete performance index (TCPI) is a measure of the cost performance that should be achieved with the remaining resources in order to meet a specified management goal, expressed as the ratio of the cost to finish the outstanding work to the remaining budget. The TCPI is the calculated cost performance index that is achieved on the remaining work to meet a specified management goal such as the budget at completion (BAC) or estimate at completion (EAC). If it becomes obvious that the BAC is no longer viable, the project manager should consider the forecasted EAC. Once approved, the EAC may replace the BAC in the TCPI calculation. The equation for TCPI is: (BAC − EV) / (BAC − AC) where: BAC = budget at completion, EV = earned value, and AC = actual cost.

The TCPI is conceptually displayed in Figure 5-24. The equation for the TCPI is shown in the lower-left corner as the work remaining (defined as the BAC minus the EV) divided by the funds remaining (which can be either the BAC minus the AC, or the EAC minus the AC).

If the cumulative CPI falls below the baseline (as shown in Figure 5-24), all future work of the project should be performed immediately in the range of the TCPI (BAC) (as reflected in the top line of Figure 5-24) to stay within the authorized BAC. Whether this level of performance is achievable is a judgment call based on several considerations, including risk, time remaining in the project, and technical performance. Such a level of performance is displayed as the TCPI (EAC) line. The equation for the TCPI is based on the EAC: (BAC − EV) / (EAC − AC). The EVM formulas are provided in Table 5-1.

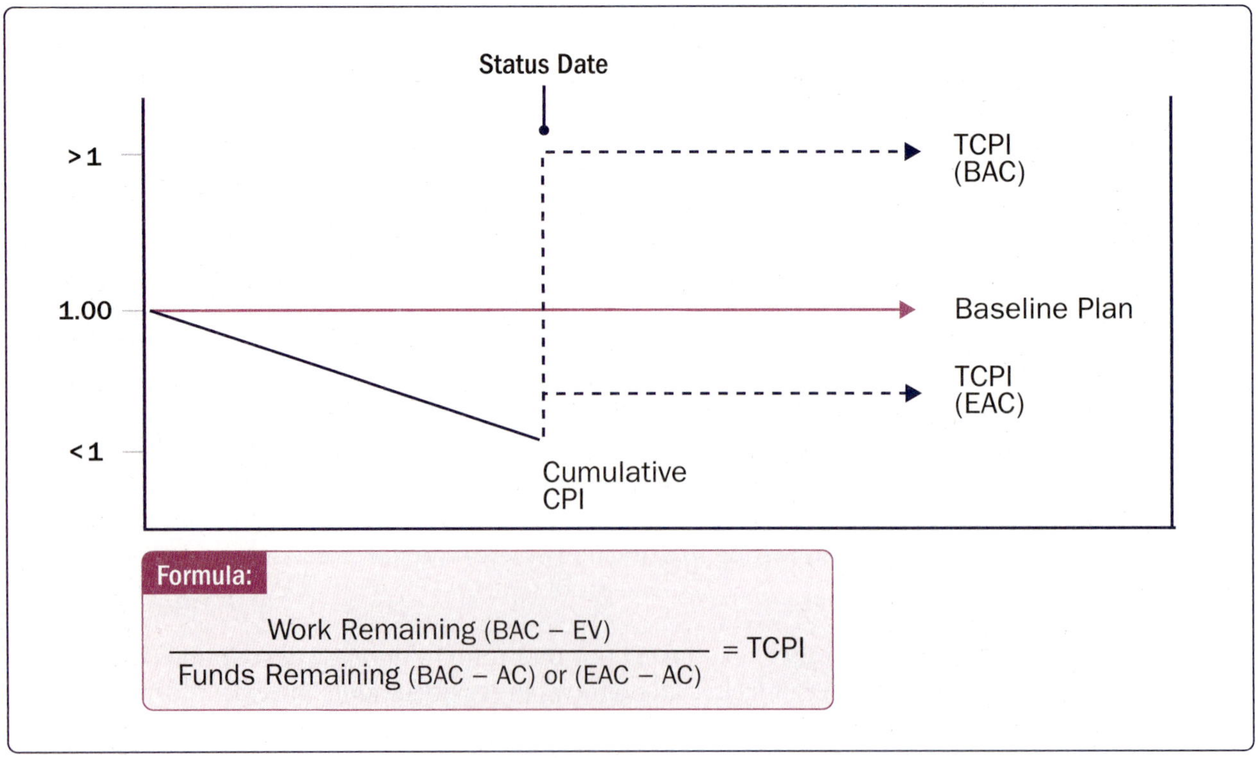

Figure 5-24. To-Complete Performance Index (TCPI)

Table 5-1. Earned Value Calculations Summary

Earned Value Analysis					
Abbreviation	**Name**	**Lexicon Definition**	**How It Is Used**	**Equation**	**Interpretation of Result**
PV	Planned value	The authorized budget assigned to scheduled work	It is the value of the work planned to be completed to a point in time, usually the data date or project completion.		
EV	Earned value	The measure of work performed expressed in terms of the budget authorized for that work	It is the planned value of all the work completed (earned) to a point in time, usually the data date, without reference to actual costs.	EV = Sum of the planned value of completed work	
AC	Actual cost	The realized cost incurred for the work performed on an activity during a specific time period	It is the actual cost of all the work completed to a point in time, usually the data date.		
BAC	Budget at completion	The sum of all budgets established for the work to be performed	It is the value of total planned work: the project cost baseline.		
CV	Cost variance	The amount of budget deficit or surplus at a given point in time, expressed as the difference between the earned value and the actual cost	It is the difference between the value of work completed to a point in time, usually the data date, and the actual cost to the same point in time.	CV = EV − AC	Positive = Under planned cost Neutral = On planned cost Negative = Over planned cost

(continued)

Table 5-1. *(Continued)*

Earned Value Analysis					
Abbreviation	**Name**	**Lexicon Definition**	**How It Is Used**	**Equation**	**Interpretation of Result**
SV	Schedule variance	A measure of schedule performance expressed as the difference between the earned value and the planned value	It is the difference between the work completed to a point in time, usually the data date, and the work planned to be completed to the same point in time.	SV = EV – PV	Positive = Ahead of schedule Neutral = On schedule Negative = Behind schedule
VAC	Variance at completion	A projection of the amount of budget deficit or surplus, expressed as the difference between the budget at completion and the estimate at completion	It is the estimated difference in cost at the completion of the project.	VAC = BAC – EAC	Positive = Under planned cost Neutral = On planned cost Negative = Over planned cost
CPI	Cost performance index	A measure of the cost efficiency of budgeted resources expressed as the ratio of earned value to actual cost	A CPI of 1.0 means the project is exactly on budget; that the work actually done so far is exactly the same as the cost so far. Other values show the percentage of how much costs are over or under the budgeted amount for work accomplished.	CPI = EV / AC	Greater than 1.0 = Under planned cost Exactly 1.0 = On planned cost Less than 1.0 = Over planned cost

Table 5-1. *(Continued)*

Earned Value Analysis					
Abbreviation	**Name**	**Lexicon Definition**	**How It Is Used**	**Equation**	**Interpretation of Result**
SPI	Schedule performance index	A measure of schedule efficiency expressed as the ratio of earned value to planned value	An SPI of 1.0 means that the project is exactly on schedule; that the work actually done so far is exactly the same as the work planned to be done so far. Other values show the percentage of how much the work is ahead or behind schedule based on the projected timeline for work planned.	SPI = EV / PV	Greater than 1.0 = Ahead of schedule Exactly 1.0 = On schedule Less than 1.0 = Behind schedule
EAC	Estimate at completion	The expected total cost of completing all work, expressed as the sum of the actual cost to date and the estimate to complete	If the CPI is expected to be the same for the remainder of the project, EAC can be calculated using:	EAC = BAC / CPI	
			If future work will be accomplished at the planned rate, use:	EAC = AC + BAC – EV	
			If the initial plan is no longer valid, use:	EAC = AC + Bottom-up ETC	
			If both the CPI and SPI influence the remaining work, use:	EAC = AC + [(BAC – EV) / (CPI × SPI)]	
ETC	Estimate to complete	The expected cost to finish all the remaining project work	Assuming work is proceeding as planned, the cost of completing the remaining authorized work can be calculated using:	ETC = EAC – AC	
			Reestimate the remaining work from the bottom up.	ETC = Reestimate	

(continued)

Table 5-1. *(Continued)*

Earned Value Analysis					
Abbreviation	**Name**	**Lexicon Definition**	**How It Is Used**	**Equation**	**Interpretation of Result**
TCPI	To-complete performance index	A measure of the cost performance that should be achieved with the remaining resources in order to meet a specified management goal, expressed as the ratio of the cost to finish the outstanding work to the remaining budget	It is the efficiency that should be maintained in order to complete on plan.	TCPI = (BAC – EV) / (BAC – AC)	Greater than 1.0 = Harder to complete Exactly 1.0 = Same to complete Less than 1.0 = Easier to complete
			It is the efficiency that should be maintained in order to complete the current EAC.	TCPI = (BAC – EV) / (EAC – AC)	Greater than 1.0 = Harder to complete Exactly 1.0 = Same to complete Less than 1.0 = Easier to complete

Training. Training includes all activities designed to enhance the competencies of the project team members. Training can be formal or informal. Examples of training methods include classroom, online, computer-based, on-the-job training from another project team member, mentoring, and coaching. If project team members lack the necessary management or technical skills, such skills can be developed as part of the project work.

Scheduled training takes place as stated in the resource management plan. Unplanned training takes place as a result of observation, conversation, and project performance appraisals conducted during management of the project team. Training costs could be included in the project budget or supported by the performing organization if the added skills may be useful for future projects. Training may be performed by in-house or external trainers.

Trend analysis. Trend analysis is an analytical method that uses mathematical models to forecast future outcomes based on historical results. The analysis looks ahead in the project for expected slippages and warns the project manager in advance that there may be problems later in the schedule if established trends persist. This information is made available early enough in the project timeline to give the project team time to analyze and correct any anomalies. The results of trend analysis can be used to recommend preventive actions if necessary.

Tuckman ladder. One of the models used to describe team development is the Tuckman ladder, which includes five stages of development that teams may go through. Although it is common for these stages to occur in order, it is not uncommon for a team to get stuck in a particular stage or regress to an earlier stage. Projects with team members who worked together in the past may also skip a stage.

- **Forming.** This phase is where the team members meet and learn about the project and their formal roles and responsibilities. Team members tend to be independent and not as open in this phase.
- **Storming.** During this phase, the team begins to address the project work, technical decisions, and the project management approach. If team members are not collaborative or open to differing ideas and perspectives, the environment can become counterproductive.
- **Norming.** In this phase, team members begin to work together and adjust their work habits and behaviors to support the team. The team members learn to trust one another.
- **Performing.** Teams that reach the performing stage function as a well-organized unit. They are interdependent and work through issues smoothly and effectively.
- **Adjourning.** In this phase, the team completes the work and moves on from the project. This typically occurs when staff is released from the project as deliverables are completed.

The duration of a particular stage depends upon team dynamics, team size, and team leadership. The project management team should have a good understanding of team dynamics to move the team members through all stages in an effective manner.

Value stream mapping. Value stream mapping is a display of the critical steps in a process and the time taken in each step to identify waste. Value stream mapping is a Lean technique used to document, analyze, and improve the flow of information or materials required to produce a product or service for a customer. A value stream begins, ends, and hopefully continues with a customer. A value stream is the set of activities that takes place to add value for customers, from the initial request through realization of value by the customers.

Variance analysis. Variance analysis is a technique for determining the cause and degree of difference between the baseline and actual performance. The technique uses mathematical models to forecast future outcomes based on historical results. Variance analysis reviews the differences (or variances) between planned and actual performance. This analysis can include duration estimates, cost estimates, resource utilization, resource rates, technical performance, and other metrics. Variance analysis reviews the variances from an integrated perspective considering cost, time, technical, and resource variances in relation to one another to get an overall view of variance on the project. This review allows for the appropriate preventive or corrective actions to be initiated.

Velocity. Velocity is a measure of a team's productivity rate at which the deliverables are produced, validated, and accepted within a predefined interval.

Virtual collaboration tools. Virtual collaboration tools are software applications and platforms designed to facilitate communication, coordination, and collaboration among project team members who may be geographically dispersed.

- **Example: Cloud-based collaboration platforms.** Cloud-based collaboration platforms or tools allow multiple project team members and other stakeholders to access, review, and edit various documents and information in real time as they are stored in the cloud.

Virtual reality (VR). Virtual reality is a computer modeling and simulation technique that allows project team members or other stakeholders to interact within an artificial, three-dimensional environment by using headsets, glasses, or other means of technology.

Virtual teams. Virtual teams are groups of people with a shared goal who fulfill their roles with little or no time spent meeting face to face. The use of virtual teams creates new possibilities when acquiring project team members. The availability of communication technologies such as email, audio conferencing, social media, web-based meetings, and videoconferencing has made virtual teams more feasible. The virtual team model makes it possible to do the following:

- Form teams of people from the same organization who live in widespread geographic areas;
- Add special expertise to a project team even though the expert is not in the same geographic area;
- Incorporate employees who work from home offices;
- Form teams of people who work different shifts, hours, or days;
- Include people with mobility limitations or disabilities;
- Move forward with projects that would have been held or canceled due to travel expenses; and
- Save the expense of offices and the physical equipment needed for employees.

The use of virtual teams can bring benefits such as the use of more skilled resources, reduced costs, less travel and relocation expenses, and the proximity of team members to suppliers, customers, or other key stakeholders. Virtual teams can use technology to create an online team environment where the team can store files, use conversation threads to discuss issues, and keep a team calendar.

Communication planning becomes increasingly important in a virtual team environment. Additional time may be needed to set clear expectations, facilitate communications, develop protocols for resolving conflicts, include people in decision-making, understand cultural differences, and share credit in successes.

Visual controls. In lean environments, information radiators are known as visual controls. Visual controls illustrate processes to easily compare actual against expected performance. Visual controls show a process using visual cues. Visual controls can be present for all levels of information from business value delivered to tasks that have started. They should be highly visible for anyone to see. Some examples include the following:

- **Task boards.** A task board is a visual representation of the planned work that allows everyone to see the status of the tasks. A task board can show work that is ready to be started (to do), work in progress, and work that is completed (see Figure 5-25). A task board allows anyone to see, at a glance, the status of a particular task or the number of tasks in each stage

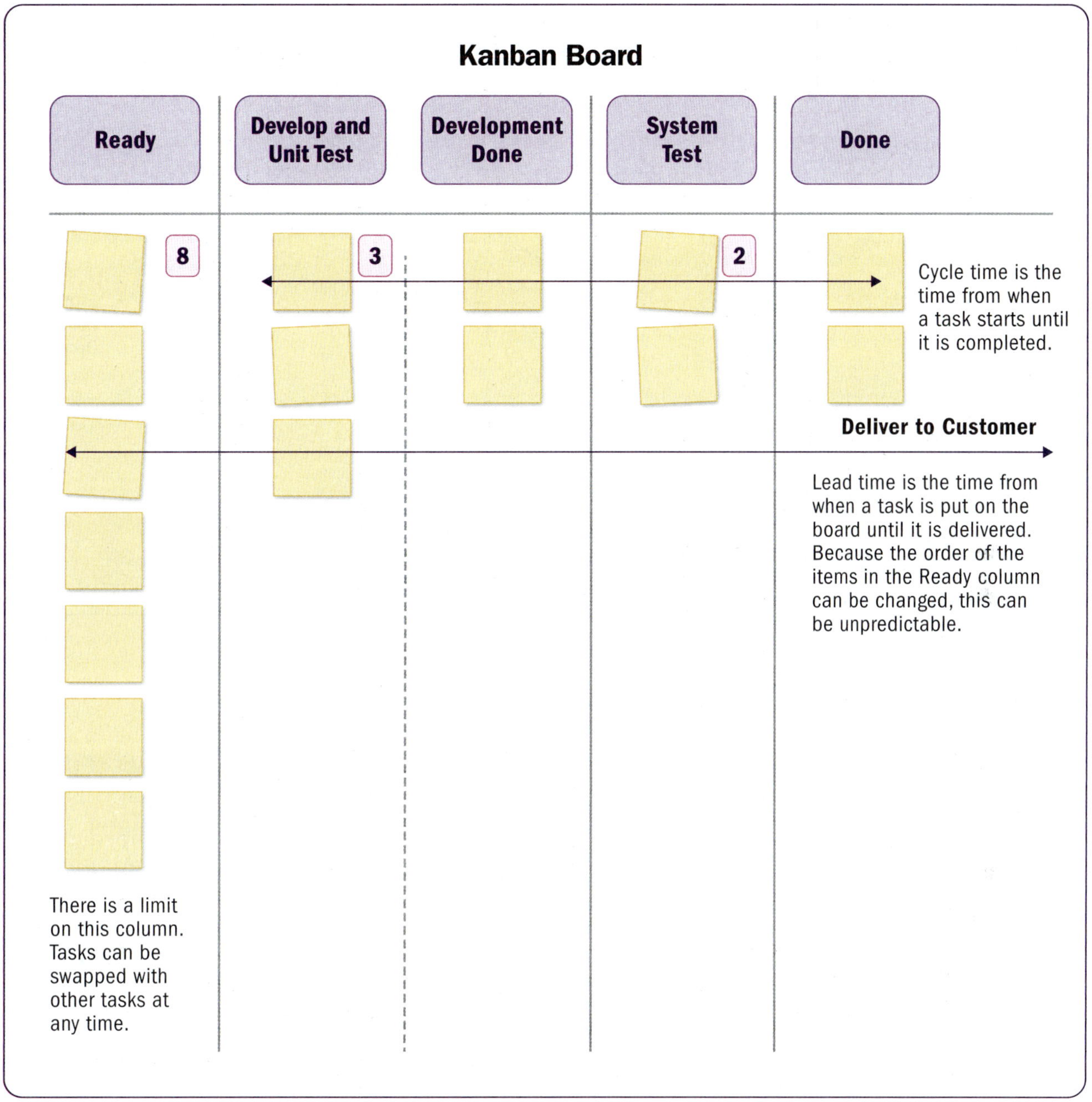

Figure 5-25. Task Board or Kanban Board

of work. Different color sticky notes can represent different types of work, and dots can be used to show how many days a task has been in its current position. Flow-based projects, such as those that use kanban boards, can use these charts to limit the amount of work in progress. If a column is approaching the work-in-progress limit, project team members can "swarm" around the current work to help those working on tasks that are slowing the flow.

- **Burn charts.** Burn charts, such as burnup or burndown charts, can show project team velocity. Velocity measures the productivity rate at which the deliverables are produced, validated, and accepted within a predefined interval. A burnup chart can track the amount of work done compared to the expected work that should be done (see Figure 5-26).

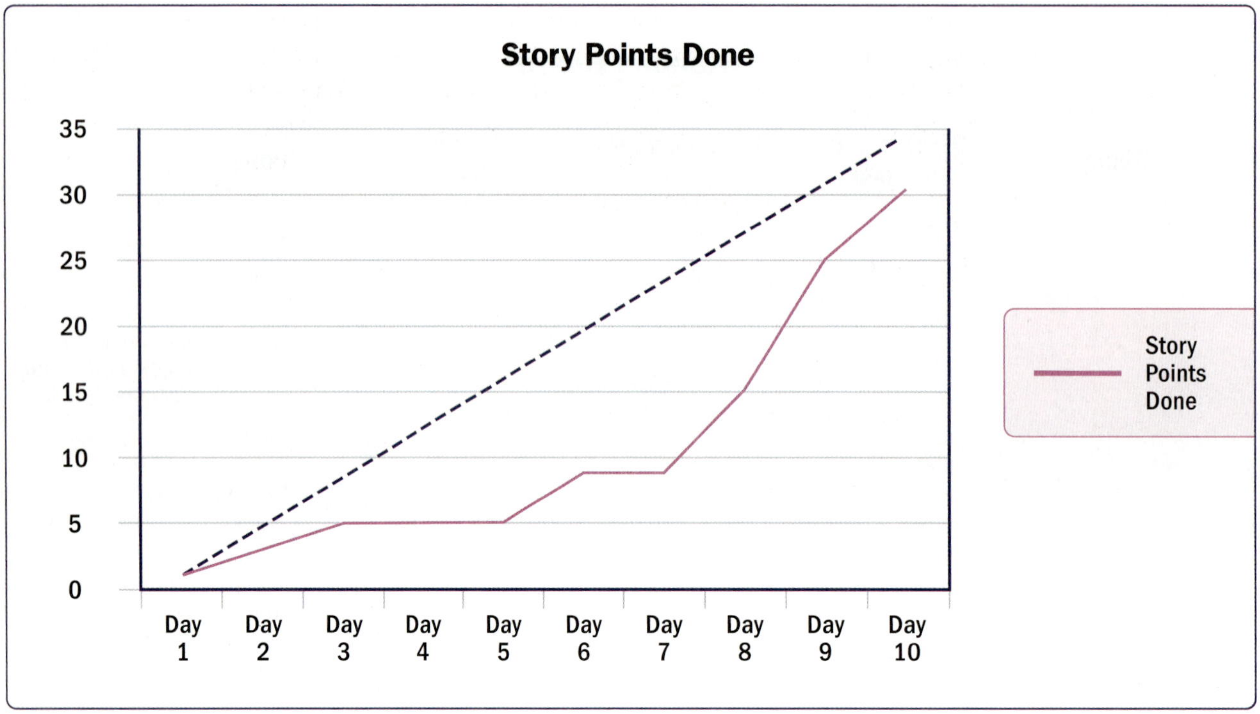

Figure 5-26. Burnup Chart

A burndown chart can show the number of story points remaining or the amount of risk exposure that has been reduced.

- **Other types of charts.** Visual charts can also include information such as an impediment list that shows a description of the impediment to getting work done, the severity, and the actions being taken to resolve the impediment.

Voting. Voting is a collective decision-making technique and assessment process having multiple alternatives with an expected outcome in the form of future actions. These techniques can be used to generate, classify, and prioritize product requirements. Examples of voting techniques include the following:

- **Unanimity.** A decision that is reached whereby everyone agrees on a single course of action.
- **Majority.** A decision that is reached with support obtained from more than 50% of the members of the group. Having a group size with an uneven number of participants can ensure that a decision will be reached rather than resulting in a tie.
- **Plurality.** A decision that is reached whereby the largest block in a group decides, even if a majority is not achieved. This method is generally used when the number of options nominated is more than two.

What-if analysis. What-if analysis is the process of evaluating scenarios in order to predict their effect (positive or negative) on project objectives. This process is an analysis of the question: "What if the situation represented by scenario X happens?" A schedule network analysis is performed using the schedule to compute the different scenarios, such as delaying a major component delivery, extending specific engineering durations, or introducing external factors such as a strike or a change in the permit process. The outcome of the what-if analysis can be used to assess the feasibility of the project schedule under different conditions, and in preparing schedule reserves and response plans to address the impact of unexpected situations.

Appendix X1
Contributors and Reviewers

The Project Management Institute is grateful to all of the contributors for their support and acknowledges their outstanding contributions to the project management profession.

X1.1 Contributors and Reviewers

The following list of contributors and reviewers had input into shaping the content of *The Standard for Project Management* and *A Guide to the Project Management Body of Knowledge (PMBOK® Guide)*—Eighth Edition. Individuals listed in bold served on the Eighth Edition Development Team and individuals listed in italics served on the Eighth Edition Review Team. Inclusion of an individual's name in this list does not represent their approval or endorsement of the final content in all its parts.

Jesse Fewell, MBA, PMI-ACP, PMP—Chair
Gabriele Bitine, PMI-RMP, PMP, PfMP
Edoardo Favari, PhD, PMI-ACP, PMP
Michael Hannan, Jonah, XSCALE, PMP
Alejandra Nazar Kafaty, CSM, Certified LEGO® SERIOUS PLAY® Facilitator, PMP
Rouzbeh Kotobzadeh, PMP, PgMP, PfMP
Amol Mansabdar, PDG:ACM, PMI-RMP, PMP
Laura Lazzerini Neuwirth, Agile PgM, PMI-PMOCP, PMP
Juarez Poletto Jr., MSc, PMP, PfMP
Arief Prasetyo, PhD, PMI-PMOCP, PMP
Emad Rahim, PhD, DM, PMP
Rich Rinaldi, MBA, PMP
Esteban Villegas L., PMI-ACP, PMP, PgMP
Heberth Campos, PMI-ACP, PMI-RMP, PMP
Long Q. Dam, PMP, PgMP, PfMP
Cynthia Snyder Dionisio, MBA, PMI-RMP, PMP
Sylvie Edwards, FPMAC, PMI-RMP, PMP
Subhajit Ghosh, PMI-ACP, PMP, PgMP
Shivani Gupta, PGDM, LPM, PMP
Daniel Hendling, MBA, PMI-ACP, PMP
Yingjin Liu, PMP, PgMP, PfMP
Cinzia Pellegrino, MBA, CSM, PMP
Kerri-Ann Williams, DBA, PMP
Dirk Withake, PMP, PgMP, PfMP
Stephan Wohlfahrt, PMI-ACP, DAVSC, PMP
Essowe Abalo
Allan Quintana Abarca, PMP
Yasser Abd Elaleem
Marwan Abdalla, PMI-RMP, PMI-PMOCP, PMP
Ramsey Abdallah, DHA, FACHE, PMP
Majed Abdeen, MSc, PMI-PMOCP, PMP
Ahmed Abdelbary, D.Eng
Abayzeed Elsmani Ahmed Abdelgadir, MBA, PMI-RMP, PMP
Ahmed Abdelghany
Farhad Abdollahyan, PMI-RMP, PMI-PMOCP, PMP
Mahmoud Abdu, Cons.PM, PRMG, PMP
Mustapha Abdul, CSP-SM, SPC, PMP
Habeeb Abdulla, PMP
Ali Hasan Abdullah Aidid
Bassem Abi Farah
Serwah Aboagye, MSc, PMP
Jose Abranches Goncalves, PMP
Ahmed S A Abuabdu
Anas Abu-Hamam
Mohammed Abuzaid, PMI-PBA, PMI-PMOCP, PgMP
Pavithra Acharya
Alejandro Arias Acosta
Manuel Acosta Ambrosio, Lic.
James M Adair
Bola Adesope, SAFe SPC, CBAP, PMP
Hamidur Rahman Adnan, PMP, PgMP, PfMP

Giovanni Adorni
Bahram Aghajanian
Kevin Aguanno, PMI-ACP, PMP
Kofi Agyekum, PE-IET, MghIS, PMP
Junaid Ahmad, PMI-RMP, PMI-PMOCP, PMP
Mohammad Ahmadzadeh Ghasemabadi, PhD, PMI-ACP, PMP
Mohammed Sameer Ahmed, MCA, CSM, PMP
Noran Ahmed
Mohammed Hadi Ahmed
Tanveer Ahmed, CAPM, PMP
Aatif Ahmed Ghouri
Vanita Ahuja, PhD, MRICS, PgMP
Saurabh Ahuja
Prescort Leslie Ahumuza, SPC, CAPM, PMP
Amirafshin Akhavan
Phill Akinwale, OPM3, PMI-RMP, PMP
Emi B. Akiode, BA, CBDA, PMP
Rizwan Akram, PMI-RMP, PMP
Iman Hilal Al Busaidi, PMI-ACP, PMI-PMOCP, PMP
Mohamad Al Hachoui
Tarik Al Hraki
Abdulkareem Al Ibrahim, PMP, PgMP, PfMP
Hamed Nasser Mubarak Al Khudhuri
Alexandre Alamino da Rocha
Osku Alanen, PMP
Sandrine Alaphilippe, MSc, PMP
Ali Al-Ashwal
Mohammed Dawood AlAssafi, PMI-PMOCP, PMP, PfMP
Mostafa Alattar
Sharaf Alattas, PMI-RMP, PMI-PBA, PMP
Francesco Albergo, PMP
Lori Alberstadt, MBA, CPMAI, PMP
José Rafael Alcalá Gómez, PMP
Wael Aldandashi, PMP
Mohamed Aldoubasi, MBA, PMI-RMP, PMP
Mohammed Alfaifi, PMP, PgMP, PfMP
Zyad Alhasan, PMP, PgMP, PfMP
Ahmed Ezeldin Mohammed Alhassan
Amer Ali
Ahmed Ali Eziza, MBA, PMO-CP, PMP
Mehdi Alibakhshi, PMI-PBA, PMP
Emre Aliç
Abbas Alimorad
Reza Alizadeh Foroutan
Hamed Nasser Mubarak ALKhudhuri, PhD
Hammam (Marshal) Alkouz
Leila Allahham
Oussama Allali
Amir Allam
Stephanie R. Allen, PMP
Riyad AlMallak, PMP, PgMP, PfMP
Muhannad Ali Almarzooq
Hanan Saad AlMaziad, PMP, PgMP, PfMP
Ayman Alminawi, EdD, CIA, PMP
Nizar Al-Moaid
Abdallah AlMousa
Ahmad Moh Al-Musallami, PMI-ACP, PMI-SP, PMP
Noura AlMusharraf, PhD, PgMP, PfMP
Amir K Al-Nizami, MBA, MPM, PMP
Aladdin Abu Alown, INSEAD MBA, PMP
Fadi AlQaisi, CBAP, PMI-RMP, PMP
Sayed Mohamed Alqassab, MSc, PMP
Saad Abdulkareem Mohammed Alqorosh, MSc
Raied Odeh Alreyahi
Hussain AlSalamin
Ahmed Alsenosy
Mohand Ali Alsikhan
Tamim A. Alsunidi
Abdulrahman Alulaiyan, MBA, PfMP
Ignacio Alva Rodriguez, PMI-ACP, DASSM, PMP
Emilio Alvarado Perez, MBA, BSc (Eng), PMP
Edgar Alvarez, MBA, PMP, PMO-CC
Hossam Al-Wazzan, MBA, MSP, PMP
Nahlah Alyamani, PMI-ACP, PMP, PgMP
Angelo Amaral
Barnabas Seth Amarteifio, PhD, MSc, BSc
Zeeshan Amjad, PMI-ACP, PMI-RMP, PMP
Serge Amon, MBA, PMP
Amirmasoud Amooee
Esteban Blazquez Amor
Wilson Anandaraj, MBA, PMP
Chevine Anderson, MBA, DAC, PMP
Sathya Sivaguruunathan Andivel, CSSBB, PMP, PgMP
Foivos-Konstantinos Angelakis, PMI-PBA, PMP
Venkataramiah Annapragada, B.Tech, PMI-RMP, PMP
Guillermo J Antón, MSc, PMP
Chijioke Stanley Anyanwu
Hamid Aougab, CSAT, PMP
Mohamed Taher Arafa, DBA, DAVSC, PMP
Viviane Arazi, DASSM, PMP, PgMP
Marco Arcuri
Yannick Arekion, MSc, CAPM, PMI-ACP
Kevin Furlong Arellano, PMP
Alfredo J. Arizaleta C.
Alfredo Armijos, PMI-RMP, PMO-CP, PMP
Alejandro Maceda Artiga, PMP
Rajendhiran Arulmani
Barbara Kuffour Asenso, PMP
Kalpesh Ashar, PMI-ACP, PMP
Catherine Asiimwe, MBA, CPA, PMP
Reza Atashfaraz, MSc, PMP
Ünsal Atasoy, MSc, DASM, PMP
Mohammed Azmy Ateia
Sivaram Athmakuri, PMI-ACP, PMI-PBA, PMP

Praveen Attada, PMP
Mohamed Attia
Abdul Habib Aulfat
Aung Kyaw Sint, PMI-CP, PMP, PgMP
Muniraju AV
Ashraf Mahmoud Awwad
Vahid Azadmanesh, DBA, PMP, PfMP
Charbel Azar
Emad E. Aziz, PMP, PgMP, PfMP
Hasan Azizieh, MBA, PMI-ACP, PMP
Akbar Azwir, PMP, PgMP, PfMP
Claudia M. Baca, OPM3
Andrew Bacchus
Vincent Bada, PMP
Charles Baggett, PMP
George Nicolaus Bagomwa, PMP
Amir Bahadorestani
Nasim Bahari, PhD, CSM, PMP
Rohit Bahl, PMI-RMP, PMP
Kenneth Bainey, MBA, BETI, PMP
Kristian Bainey
Supreet BainsSharma, SHRM-SCP, PMP
Hadis Bajelan
Jennifer Baker, PMO-CP, PgMP, PfMP
J. Balamurali, PMP
Fernand R. Baldonado, MBA, CAPM, PMP
Joel Bancroft-Connors
Clement Mwachande Banda, B.Eng, PMP
Saket Bansal, PMI-ACP, PMP, PgMP
Manuel Francisco Baquero Vanegas
Rui Luiz Barbosa Filho, DASM, PMI-PMOCP, PMP
Wellinghton Pereira Barboza, PMP
Angela Barrera
Primitivo Barrón Soria, PMI-ACP, PMI-SP, PMP
Jacinto Jorge Barroso, PMI-PMOCP, PMP
Adilbish Bat-Erdene, M.Eng, PMI-CP, PMP
Marcia Bates, P.Eng, PMP
Gabriela de Fatima Batista Castro, MSc, PMI-ACP, PMP
Bayar Batjargal
Rohit Bawa, PMP, PgMP, PfMP
William F. Baxter, PMP
Ali Bayati
Eduardo Bazo Safra, PMP
Yaman Bdaiwi, DBA, MCIArb, MCLDR
Pierre Beaudry, Jr., Adm.A
Nils O. Becht, PhD, C.Eng, PMP
Derek Beck, CPMAI+E, PMI-ACP, PMP
Edward Beck, EdD, PMP
Jochen Becker, PhD
Joshua Behl, PhD, PMP
Jamal A Beit Elmal, PhD, MSc, PMP
Nadjib Belkadi, PMP
Laurinda M. Bellinger, BSc, MS, PMP
Klao Bell-Lewis, PMP
Yan Bello Mendez, CDBA, PMP
Peter Bembir, BA, MPhil, PMP
Younes Ben Chigra, PMI-ACP, PMI-PBA, PMP
Lina Bencherif, MSc, MBA
Noura Bendakir, PMI-ACP, PMP
Ömür Benek, PhD, PMP
Fabio H. Benitez, BSc
Elwanda Bennett, PhD, MEDP, PMP
Neil Berenholz, LSSBB, PMP
Helene Bergeron
Michal Bernhard, PMP
Nico Beylemans, PMP
Nikhil Bharadwaj, B. Tech, MS, PMP
Bharathi Bhaskar, CSM, PMP
Harwinder Singh Bhatia, CSM, PMI-ACP, PMP
Deepa Bhide, DCH, MBBS, PMP
Jasbir Singh Bhogal
Sarika Bhowte
Ali Bidhendi
Apriel Biggs
Mohammed Bin Askar, PMP, PgMP, PfMP
Mohamad Abdul Rahman Bin Muzmar, Ir.
Rup Kumar BK, PMP
Nigel Blampied, PhD, PE, PMP
Patrice Blanchard
Greta Blash, PMO-CP, PMP, PgMP
Steve Blash, PMI-ACP, DASSM, PMP
Haydn Bleackley, BA, MAPM
Constanta Nicoleta Bodea
Cecilia Boggi
Kiron D. Bondale, PMI-RMP, DAC, PMP
Felipe Borges, PRINCE2, PMO-CP, PMP
David Augusto Borja Padilla, MSc, PMI-RMP, PMP
Elisabetta Borrini, PMI-RMP, DASSM, PMP
Michael Botyarov, PhD, PMP
Ramona Boulos, EMBA, PMI-ACP, PMP
Salma Bourebaa, MSc, PMP
João Carlos Boyadjian
Damiano Bragantini
Ellie Braham, SAFe, DASSM, PMP
Joshua D. Brandt, MSc
Wayne R. Brantley, MS Ed., PMI-ACP, PMP
Ralf Braune, Dr-Ing, PMP
Bernd Brier, PhD, PMP
Bart Briers
Idriss Brihoum
Jackie Briski, MA, PMP
David C. Broadbent, PMP
Ron T. Brown, PhD, CSM, PMP
Randel Brumm, MBA, BSc
Felix-Eduardo Bueno-Pascual, PhD,
Six Sigma Black Belt-ASQ, PMP

Syed Asad Hasnain Bukhari, AvMP, MBCS, PMP
Syed Qamar Abbas Bukhari, PMI-RMP, PMP, PgMP
Syed Raza Abbas Bukhari, MTE, PMP
Alexey Burdakov
James Burkholder, SPC, CSSBB, PMP
Gaetan Burm, MSc, PMP
Andrew William Burns
Luis Rene Bustos Tiburcio, MBA, PMP
Marco Cabrera Sandoval, MGP, IPMA B, PMP
Yiğit Çağlar, PhD, SPC, PMP
Shawna Calhoun, MBA, CSPO, PMP
Diego Calvetti
Joe Campa, PMI-RMP, PMO-CP, PMP
Carla M. Campion, B.Eng, PMI-RMP, PMP
Marco A. Cangiano, CAPM
Chiamba Canivete
Carmen Cano Masa
María Gabriela Cano Portocarrero, MBA, PMI-ACP, PMP
Paul Capello, CSM, PMP
Joel Carboni
Ismael Cardenas, MSc, PMP
Cheryl Carstens, CAPM, PMI-ACP, PMP
Deborah Carter, CISSP, PMP
José Cascante
Marine Castaneda Garcia, MSc, PMP
Alejandro Castellon
Alange Castelly
Emmanuel Castillo Miranda
Aitor Castro
Dominique Causse, PhD
Fabio Ceccarelli
Keen Soon Chan, PMP, PgMP
Vijay G. Chander
Vineet Chandra
Vineet Kumar Chandra
S. Chandramouli, PhD, PMI-ACP, PfMP
Oscar Danilo Chaparro, PMI-ACP, DASSM, PMP
Stéphane Chapelle, PMP
Panos Chatzipanos, PhD, Dr.Eur.Ing, F. ASCE
Rajiv Chauhan, PMP
Rosario Chavez, PMI-ACP, PMP, PfMP
Charles Chen
Xin Chen, MSc, PMP
Tarik Cherkaoui, ISO 9001 Lead Auditor, SPC, PMP
Chia Fah Choy
Washington Chimuzu, PMP
Williams Chirinos, MSc, LSSBB, PMP
Sudhansu Shekhar Choudhury, CDCP, PMI-CPMAI, PMP
Glenn J. Chundrlek, PMI-ACP, PMP
Diego da Silva Ciarrocchi
Devin Clinevell, MSPM, PMI-RMP, PMP
Austin Cochren, PMP
Femi Cocker, PhD
Raphael H. Cohen
Edward Coke, Jr., CAPM, PMP
Martin Collado Ramírez, MBA, PMP, PMO-CC
Raúl Collazos Castillo, PMI-ACP, DASSM, PMP
Sergio Luis Conte, PMI-ACP, PMI-PBA, PMP
Victor Corniel
Felipe Corrêa, PMI-PMOCP, PMP
Jose Alfredo Cortes Arellano
Ricardo Coutinho Mello, PhD, MSc, PMP
Harold G. Cristian, BSc, PGCert
Lei Cui
Joshua Cunio, DBA, NPPQ, PMP
Scott Cunningham
Joseph R. Czarnecki, SCPM, CSM, PMP
Larry Dalton, PMP, PgMP, PfMP
Graziella D'Amico, PMI-PBA, PMP
Anant Kant Dan, PMP
Gbenga Vincent Dania, MSIT, PMP
Habib Dan-kawu, B.Eng, CMRP, PMP
William H. Dannenmaier, MA, MBA, PMP
Peter Honest Dateme, FNIA, CFPM, PMP
Amedeo Dati, MBA, PMP
Tselmeg Davaajav, PMP
Shai Davidov, FAPM, PMP
Gina Davidovic, PMI-ACP, PMP, PgMP
William I. Dawe II
Para De
Leandro Barbeita de Carvalho, PMP
Antonio José Fernández de Castro Muñoz
Jose Bruno de Holanda da Silva, PMP
Jean Michel De Jaeger
Mario Alberto De la Cruz Hernandez, PMP
Joaquim V. De Lima
Fabricio de Souza Sales, MCP, PSM-I, PMP
Mustafa Degerli, PhD, PMI-RMP, PMP
Ebizi Deinkoru, PMI-ACP, DAVSC, PMP
Lars Del Campo, DASM
Guillermo Del Moral, PMI-ACP, PMI-RMP, PMP
Andrea Paola Delgado Castellanos
Sante Delle-Vergini, PhD, PMP
Endale Mekonnen Demissie, MSc, PMP, PfMP
Ronald Dempsey
Carmella M. Dennin, MBA, PMP
Jacqueline Dennis, ATP, PMP, PgMP
Amir Reza Derhami
Emmanuel Desdoigts, PMP
Jaheel Destine, BSc, CEH, PMP
Stephen A. Devaux, MSPM
Sridhar Chakravarthy Devulapally, MSc, MBA, PMP
Nivita Dhameja
Dayanidhi Dhandapany, M.Eng, FCIArb, PMP

Ginen Dharamshi, PMP, PfMP
Sachin Sadanand Dhaygude, SPC, PMI-ACP, PMP
Gaurav Dhooper, PAL-I, SAFe Agilist, PMI-ACP
Andrea di Biase, MBA, MSc, PMP
Jean-Philippe Di Maggio, MBA, CSM, PMP
George Diakonikolaou, PhD, PMP
Jorge Dias Veloso, PhD, PMP
Anand Dilip Nagarkatti, PMP
Dan Dilov, PMI-ACP, PMP, PgMP
Henrique Diniz, MSc, CPMAI+E, PMI-PMOCP
D. Dintsis, PMP, PgMP, PfMP
Louisa Dixon, MBA, PMP
Khaled Djelti
Doan Minh Hoa
Jordi Domingo Roquer, PMI-PMOCP, PMP
Marcio Jose dos Santos, MSc, PMI-ACP, PMP
Margareth Fabiola dos Santos Carneiro
Lassana Doumbia, MSc, PMP
William Dow
John D. Driessnack, CSM, PMP, PfMP
Sree Dudi, PMP
Nedal Dudin
Una Duggan, DASSM, PMP
Elisabet Duocastella Pla
Emiliano Durante, CPMAI, PMO-CP, PMP
Phumza Dyani
Wojciech Dymowski, SAFe LPM, SAFe Architect, PMP
Mehdi Ebrahimi
Haikal El Abed, Dipl.-Ing, PMI-ACP, PMP
Salwa El Mesbahi, PMP
Claude El Nakhl Khalil, PMO-CP, PMP
Tarek E. Elbehairi, PMP
Kimberly M. Elburn, MS, SFC, PMP
Abdulrahman Eldabak, PMI-ACP, PMP
Ahmed Mohamed Eldeep, PhD, PMI-RMP, PMP
Peter Elek, MBA, PMP
Abu Sabah Elfatieh Elnor, PhD, PMI-RMP, PMP
Mohamed Elfouly, PhD, PMP
Abuzar Ibrahim Ali Elgalib, BSc, MBA, PMP
Saleh Elgebaly, PMI-CP, PMP, PfMP
Mohammed Elmehdi Elguarni, MSc, PMP
Liliam Elhadem
Ahmed Elhakim, ITIL, PMI-RMP, PMP
Ahmed Elhassan, BSc, MSc, PMP
Osman Elhassan, MBA, PMI-ACP, PMP
Hussamedeen Hassan Elhaw
Ahmed Awad Ahmed Elhussein, MSc, PMI-SP, PMP
Gianluca Elia
Aileen Ellis, CHPC, PMP, PgMP
Lucie Ellis, SHRM-SCP, Prosci, PfMP
Hammam Elmahi, MBA, PMI-PBA, PMP
Wael Elmetwaly, PMI-ACP, PMP
Khaled El-Nakib, CB-PMO, PMI-ACP, PMP
Rami Elniem, PMP, PgMP, PfMP
Basel Mostafa Elsaady
Harri Emari, CQM, PMI-CP, PMP
Kemal Emre Ergül, PMP
Algin Erozan, MSc, PMI-ACP, PMP
Hadi Eskandar, MSc, PMP, PMI-PBA, PMP
Jose Daniel Esterkin, MBA, PMI-ACP, PMP
Didier B. Estibals, PMP
Clotilde Eteme
Mostafa Ettayeb, MSc, PMI-PMOCP, PMP
Mohaed Ezzat Abozied
Muhammad Faisal Faheem
Behnam Faizabadi, PhD, MP
Mohamed Fouad Fakhruldeen, MSc, PMP
Jamil Faraj, CBE, PMI-ACP, PMP
Fereydoun Fardad, PMI-PBA, PMI-RMP, PMP
Muhammad Zeeshan Fareed
Adel Farid, CAPM, PMI-RMP, PMP
Mohammad Hossein Farnoudkia, MSc, PMP
Leo Karam Fatayri
Jean-Luc Favrot, PMI-ACP, DASSM, PMP
Daniel Fay, PMI-PBA, PMO-CP, PMP
Abdul Fayad Majid
Amr Fayez, SFC, SSYB, PMP
Taras Fedoruk, PMO-CP, PMP, PgMP
Jean Ricardo Fernandes Ribeiro, MSc, PMP
Madhu Fernando, DBA, M.Eng, PMP
Bruno Otaviano Ferreira Araújo, MSc, PMO-CP, PMP
Ahmed Fikry
Christine Fiorentino, PMP
Achmad Firdaus, PMP
Luis Flores, PhD, PMI-RMP, PMP
Juan Carlos Flores López, PMI-ACP, PMP
Gustavo Flouret, GPM-b, PMP
Mitchell Fong, CDir, P.Eng, PMP
André Luis Fonseca Ricardi
Sandra Fonseca-Lind, DBA, EdD, USA
Davide Fontanel, BSc
Ali Forouzesh, PhD, OPM3cc, PfMP
Athanasios Fourtounas
Carlos Augusto Freitas, DAC, PMO-CP, PMP
Michael J. Frenette, PMO-CP, PMP
Robert S. Frey, DM, APMP Fellow
Linda Veronica Frias Gil, BSc, PMP
Dario Frimel
David Luigi Fuschi, PhD, PMP
Raja Sekhar G V D, MRICS, LSSGB, PMP
Nestor Gabarda Jr., ECE, PMI-ACP, PMP
Eng Marius Gaitan, PMI-PBA, PMP
Cruz Galdamez
Cristabel Galeana
Sara Gallagher, PMI-ACP, PMP
Chika Gana, ChPP, PMI-RMP, PMP

Amy Bretherick Gangl, MBA, CBAP, PMP
Juan Gabriel Gantiva, PMI-RMP, PMI-SP, PMP
Zhiheng Gao, PMI-ACP, PMP
Jaime Garcia Castro
Yadira Garcia Hernandez
Melody Gardner, DHSc, CCSM, CAPM
Hector Garduño
Ashutosh Garg, PMP, PgMP, PfMP
Abdulaziz Mohamed Gasim
Antonio Gaspar, PMP
Vimal Mathew Gasper, PMI-ACP, PMP
Moges Aregay Gebremariam, Eng, MSc
Andreas Georgiou
Parvez Ghadialy, B.Tech
Zahra Ghanbari, PMP
Mehdi A. Gharabaghi, PhD, PSPO I, PMP
Sanaz Ghazi, PhD, CSSBB, PMP
Elnaz Ghezelbash
Hadis Gholami, PhD, PMP, PfMP
Suman Ghosh, Litt.D (h.c.)
Marcos Giagnorio
Paul D. Giammalvo, PhD
Marco Giampaolo
Stavroula Giannakopoulou, MSc, PMP
Sherry P. Giles
Theofanis Giotis, MSc, PhD(c), PMP
Jiwan Giri, MS, MIS, PMP
Felipe Góes, MSc, MBA, PMP
Lise Goin, MSc
Thomas J. Goller, DASM, PMP
Luiz Henrique Gomes de Souza, MSc, HCMP, PMP
Herbert G. Gonder, PMI-ACP, PMP
Heberto Gonzalez
Ricardo Gonzalez Escandon, PMI-ACP, PMP
Marcos Eliut Gonzalez Fuentes, PhD, PMP
Gabriel A Gonzalez Garcia, MSc, PMP
Manuel Gonzalez Vazquez
Mohamed Mosaad Gouda, MSc, P3O, PMP
Silly Goudiaby, MSc, PMP
Koffi Goudjinou, PSM 1, PMP
Sumit Goyal, PhD, PgMP, PfMP
Scott M. Graffius, PMP
Aparna Grandhi
Melicia Grant, MSc, PMI-ACP, PMP
Aimee Green
Tabetha Gregory, PMO-CP, PMP
Mike Griffiths, PMI-ACP, PMP
Edoardo Grimaldi, IFPUG-CFPS, PMI-ACP, PMP
Denis Gritsiyenko, PhD, PMP
Tomasz Grochowski, PMP
Weibin Gu, PMI-ACP, PMP, PgMP
Elizabeth Güell, PMI-ACP, PMP
Magdalina Guenova, PhD, PMP
Julio Gabriel Guevara Rodriguez, B.Eng, PSPO, PMP
Pier Luigi Guida, Ing., PMP, PgMP
Gunawan, PSM-1, PMI-RMP, PMP
Ruchi Gupta, PMI-ACP, PMP, PgMP
Tushar Gupta, AEC, PRINCE2, PMP
Muhsin Anil Guvenatam, PMI-ACP, PMP
Ziad Antoine Haddad, MBA, ITIL, PMP
Nick Hadjinicolaou, PhD, MPM, PgMP
Anees Ahmed Haidary
Amanuel Mekonnen Hailemariam, PMI-PMOCP, PMP
Nerissa L. Haines
Mohamed Hamad, PSP, PMI-RMP, PMP
Yoshifumi Hamamichi, ITC, PMP
Nagy Hamamo, MB, PMO-CP, PMP
Jean-Christophe Hamani, MSc, PMI-PBA, PMP
Shahul Hameed, PMI-PBA, PMP, PgMP
David Hamilton, MBA, LSSBB, PMP
Ganie Hanifan, PMP, PgMP, PfMP
Mohammad Haque, PMI-ACP, PMI-PBA, PMP
Mohammed Majharul Haque, PMP, PgMP, PfMP
Sharif Adnan Haque
Keiko Hara, PMP
Sharad Harale, PMP
Sharyn E. Hardy, EdD, MBA, PMP
Jeff A. Harris, PMP
Ralph Hartenstein, PMP
Sherif Hashem, PhD, PMP
Gabrielle Bonin Haskins, PMP
Ahmed Hassan, DBA, PMI-ACP, PgMP
Ahmed Mohamed Hassan, LEED AP BD+C, PMP
Kiyokazu Hattori
Eckhard Hauenherm, PhD, PMI-ACP, PMP
Guangcheng He
Jiahao He
Siddhesh Hegde, PMP, PgMP
Mona Heidari
Khaled Heikal, PMP, PgMP, PfMP
Dmytro Heliuta
Frank Hendriks, MSc, PMI-ACP, PMP
Witold Hendrysiak, DASSM, PMP
Ian Hennem
Hector R. Hernandez
Sergio Herrera Apestigue, PMP
Abel Herrera Sillas, DM, PMP
Jaime Herreros Porras, PMP
Fabian Heuskin
Deborah Michelle Hill, CAPM, PMP
Yasser Magdy Hindawy, MBA, MSP, PMP
Shirley Hinton, PMP
Qudratullah Hiwadpal, MBA, PMP, PfMP
Hnin Nu Aye, PMP
Elliott Holder, PMI-SP
Viktoriia Honcharova, PMP

Hoo Chee Wai, PMI-ACP, PMI-RMP, PMP
Hiroto Horio, PMP
Cesar Jhonnatan Horna-Saldaña
Mahdi Hosseini
Maria Hrabikova, MBA
Zayar Htun, PMP, PgMP
Emily Jing Jing Hu
Jennifer Hubley
William Huddleston
Richard Hughes, PhD
Alexander Hundenborn, PMP, PgMP
Edward H P Hung, MBA, PMI-ACP, PMP
Debra A. Hunter, MS, PMP
Moe Huss, PhD
Ali Hussain Tawfiq Aghaykawn
Bassam Hussein, PhD, P.Eng
Yasir Mohamed Abdelrazig Hussien, PMI-RMP, PMI-PMOCP, PMP
Michael Huynh, CAL, CSP-SM, ICP-ACC
Peggy Hwu, PMP
Guillermo A. Ibañez, ITIL, Trainer PNL, PMP
Manuel Bernardo Ibáñez Ocampo
Hazem Ibrahim
Abanoub Ibrahim Tawfik
Lemya Musa Mohamed Idris
Shuichi Ikeda, CSM, CSPO, PMP
Dmitrii Ilenkov, PhD
Muhammad A. B. Ilyas, DASSM, PMP, PgMP
Muhammad Imran, DBA, MBA, PfMP
Raisyuli Indria, PMI-ACP, PMI-PMOCP, PMP
Dennis Esefolo Peter Inegbedion, Eur Ing, PMI-RMP, PMP
Tracey Inglimo
Andrea Innocenti, AHPP, SFC, PMP
Karin Inoue
Yanis Ioualitene, MSc, PMP
Javed Iqbal, PRINCE2, PMI-RMP, PMP
Álvaro Enrique Iriarte Aldana
Deema Islayem, PhD
Rony Iswanto, M.Eng, PMI-ACP, PMP
Maher Tarek Itani, COBIT, PMP
Kentaro Ito
Masaaki Iwane, PMP
Can Izgi, PMI-ACP, PMI-RMP
Sujitha J., CSM, PMP
Mitchell D. Jackett, MPPM, BBus
Rajesh Jadhav, PMP, PgMP, PfMP
Mahtab Jadidigili
Abolfazl Jafari Asl
Mohit Jain, PMP, PgMP
Jessika Jake, ITIL-SL, PMP, PfMP
Hasan Jalil, PMI-RMP, PMP
Muhammad Waleed Jamshed
Miroslav Jankovic, MBA, PSM I, PMP
Jill Jansen, PMP
Berndt Gustav Jansson, PMP
Bhuvana Jayaraman, PMP
Peng Jiang, PMP, PgMP, PfMP
Xiaohua (Sean) Jin
LaVirta Jones, CDFM, PMI-ACP, PMP
JinHun Joo, PMI-ACP, PMI-RMP, PMP
Yves Jordan
George Jucan, MBA, PMP
Pundlik Nanasaheb Jumbad, BE, M.Tech, PMP
Rami Kaibni, CBAP, PMP, PgMP
Lorelie M Kaid, MBA, CCMP, PMP
Younes Idrissi Kaitouni, MSc, PMP
Anjana Kaku, PMI-ACP, PMP
Keiichiro Kaneko
Miki Kaneko
Junpeng Kang
Col Harmeet Singh Kapoor
Athina Kapousouz
Aylin Kaptan
Alankar Karpe
Aras Kartouzian, PhD, PMI-PBA, PMP
Ramesh Kasthurirangan
Rohit Kathuria, P.Eng, PMP, PgMp
Yuichiro Kato
Andy Kaufman, PMI-ACP, PMP
Frieda Indileni Kavetuna
Serkan Kaya, PMI-ACP, PMP, PgMP
Aykut Deniz Kayalar
Amr Kaysar
Reyhane Kazemi
Amin Kebe
Pravin Kedia, PMP
Russell Keenan, MS, PMP
Ryan Kent
Deborah Ketai, CCMP, PMI-RMP, PMP
Ngo Tan Kha, MBA, PMP
Suhail Khaled, PMI-ACP, DAC, PMP
Muhammad Kamran Khalid, PhD, CSCP, PMP
Basher Elaqib Khalil, PSM, ITIL, PMP
Claude El Nakhel Khalil, PharmD, PMI-PMOCP, PMP
Azmathulla Khan, Hon. DB Counsel
Imtiaz Khan, SPC, CSM, PMP
Mudassar Khan, P.Eng, PMP
Muhammad Tahir Ali Khan, BSc, BE, PMP
Muhammad Waris Ali Khan, PhD, CAPM, PMP
Evgeny Khotulev, PMP
Peace Kikoni, DASSM, PMI-PMOCP, PMP
Brian Killeen, PMP
Harlan Kilmon, PMP
Olive Bume Ada Espe Kima-Oben
Toshifumi Kimura

Mert Kiranc, MSc, PMP
Konstantinos Kirytopoulos, PhD, DiplEng, PMP
Charles J. Kleinberg
Christopher D. Kline, MBA, PMP
Jerome Knysh, CMC, P.Eng, PMP
Sarv Kohli
Athens Kolias, MPM, PMI-ACP, PMP
Shiva Subramanyam Kondapalli, PMI-ACP, DASSM, PMP
Henry Kondo, PMP, PgMP, PfMP
Fred Koos, SPC, PMI-ACP, PMP
Amr Hamza Korayem
Aboozar Kordi, PMI-ACP, PMI-PBA, PMP
Martin Kostov, PMP
Ramakrishna Kosuri, MCA, M.Tech
Rajesh Kotak
Kevin E. Kovalic, PSM 1, MCP, PMP
Janelle Kowlessar, DASM, PMP
Keiichiro Koyama
Jiri Kratky, PMI-ACP, PMP
B Elaine Krazer, PMP
Mohsen Krichi, PRINCE2, PM2 Advanced, PMP
Srikanth Krishnamoorthy, BSc, PDGSA
Ramesh Krishnan
Andreja Kriznic
Miroslav Krupa, PhD, PMP, PgMP
Ravindrakumar Manikrao Kshirsagar, PhD, MBA, PMP
Ayodele Kuewumi, B.Tech, MBA, PMP
Emerson Luis Kuhl, MSc, MBA, KMP
Arturas Kuliesas
Anuj Kulkarni
Lalit Kumar
M Monoj Kumar, PMI-ACP, PMP
Rakesh Kumar, DBA, PMI-RMP, PMP
Sandeep Kumar, PMP
Sandeepan Kumar, PMI-ACP, PMP
Victoria S. Kumar, PMI-ACP, DASSM, PMP
Pacharo Kuntembwe, Eng, PMI-CP, PMP
Teppei Kuwano
Elton Kuzniewski, PMI-ACP, PMP
Dennis Kwan Kok Leong, CSP-SM, GDWPL, PMP
Patricia Kwasniak, MSc, MBA, PMP
Lt Col L Shri Harsha (Retd), DASSM, PMP, PgMP
Thierry Labriet, Prosci, FSEA-1, PMP
Marylene D. Lafon, PMP
Harisha Lakkavalli
Arun Lal
David Lal, BSc, CSM, PMP
Jorge Lamadrid, PMI-ACP, PMI-PBA, PMP
Soheil Lamei, PgMP, PfMP
Zethembiso Langa
Miriam Lanzetta, PMP
Philipp Larseille, PMP
Joe Lattouf, B.Eng, CET, PMP
Cristhian Laura Portugal
Quentin Laurent, PMI-ACP, PMI-SP, PMP
Tsun Yin Law, P.Eng, PMI-PBA, PMP
Patrick Lawrence, PMP
David Layden, B.Eng, MBA, PMP
Monette Vega Laylo, BSCS, MSIT, MCP
Jon M. Lazarus, MBA, PMP
Chris Le Roux, PhD, PMP
Sebastien Leclerc, MBA, CISM, PMP
Chia Kuang Lee, PhD, CQRM, PMP
Jonathan M. Lee, PMI-ACP, DAC, PMP
Olivier Lefebvre
Oliver F. Lehmann, MSc, ACE, PMP
Valerie Lehmann, PhD, MBA
Raman Lemtsiuhou, AKT, PMP
Julio Cesar Leon Mejia, MSc, PMP
Julien Leonard
Trent Leopold, MSc, PMI-PBA
Christian Myklebust Leten
Tshediso Letseleha
Marc Levingston, BCom, GCert Proj Mgmt, MBA
Ang Li
Mingyu Li
Nils Liliedahl, MSc, Eng, PMP
Keith Lilienfeld, CSM, SAFe 6 Agilist, PMP
Odair Oliveira Lima
Gabor Lipi, ATPI, PMP
Rebecca Lippert
William Neil Littell, PhD, PMP
Tong (James) Liu, PhD, PMP
Liu Zhanjun, PMP
Hector Llanos, PMI-RMP, PMP
Giorgio Locatelli, PhD
Roberto Lofaro
Sivakumar Loganathan
Anand Lokhande, PhD
Stefania Lombardi, PhD, PMP
Robert London, MSIE, PMI-RMP, PMP
Siaw Chuing Loo
Carlos López Javier, MBA, PMI-ACP, PMP
Fernando Lorefice, MBA, PMI-ACP, PMP
Hugo K. M. Lourenço, PMI-ACP, PMI-RMP, PMP
Sérgio Lourenço, PMI-RMP, PMP
Giuseppe Lovecchio, CPIM-F, CTSC, PMP
Edith Loza, CPO, Cia BASC, PMP
Rosa Savino Lozito, ITIL Mng, PMI-ACP, PMP
Antonino Lucantonio, PMP
Sergio Oswaldo Lugo, MBA, PMP
Kampamba Lukwesa, B.Eng, ACIArb, MEIZ
Daniel Luna Jeri, PMP, PgMP, PfMP
Jan Stephan Lundquist, PMI-ACP, PMI-RMP, PMP
Xian Luo, PMI-PBA, PMP

Alex Lyaschenko
Laura Gonzalez Lysaght, BSc, PMI-PMOCP, PMP
Jianfeng Ma, ITIL Expert, PMI-ACP, PMP
Xiaoli Ma, PMI-ACP, PMI-PBA, PMP
Bruno Macedo, PMI-SP
Daniel Magal
Ganesh Mahalingam, CSM, PMP
Tamilselvan Mahalingam, PhD, CSSBB, PMP
Mustafa Maher, PMI-RMP, PMI-PMOCP, PMP
Bob Mahler, PMI-RMP, PMP
Hazem Amin Ibrahim Mahmoud, MBA, PMI-PMOCP, PMP
Omar Mahmoud
Robert Maiale, PMI-CP, PMP
Shenila Makhani, MS, DASSM, PMP
Debra Malekia, MBA, PMP
Konstantinos Maliakas, BSMP, MSc, PMP
Joselito Mallari Jr., EMBA, PMI-ACP, PMP
Muhammad Asif Mallick, MBA, PMP
Rich Maltzman, PMP
Swarup Mandal, BE, Six Sigma Black Belt, PMP
Reza M. Mandara, PMP
Hussam Abdelmoniem Mandil, MBA, PMI-PMOCP, PMP
Sriram Manian, BE, MBA, PMP
Berliandi Manik
Philip D. Mann, PhD, PMI-RMP, PMP
Abdul Mansoor, PMP
Jorge Oscar Marchini, BSc
William Tell Marenco Olivares, PMP
Alessandro Margherta, PhD
Madhana Gopalan Marichamy, BE, CAPM, PMP
Antonio Marino, FranklinCovey Facilitator, PMI-ACP, PMP
Paolo Marino, MSc, SAFe SA, PMP
Nicolas Marion, MGP, PMI-ACP, PMP
Marisol Marion-Landais
Charlotte Marqueste
Bellec Martial, PMI-ACP, PMP, PgMP
Bradley Martin
Douglas Peyton Martin, PMP
Juan José Martín
Massimo Martinati, PMI-RMP, PMP
Fernando Martínez, PhD
German Martinez, PMI-ACP, DAC, PMP
Cesar R. Martinez G.
Rodolfo Martins Ribeiro, PMP
Javier Masias, MBA, PMP
Faraz Masood, MBA, PE, PMP
Mourad Mastour
Puian Masudi Far, PhD, CMC, PMP
Mayte Mata Sivera
K S Mathew, PMI-ACP, PMP
Mathivanan M, MBA, PMP, PfMP
Mohit Raj Mathur, PMP
Satoru Matsumoto, PMP
Taisei Matsumoto
Krystsina Mazhei
Leonardo Javier Mazur, CPA, PMP
Russ McCafferty, PMP
Andy McClary, PMP
Barbara McClellan-Tranchik, PMI
Jon McFadden, MBA, PMP
Jon McGlothian, PMI-ACP, DASSM, PMP
Shannon McGuffey, MS, PMP
Christopher Mckinney
Samuel McKnight
David McLachlan, CAPM, PMI-ACP, PMP
Alan McLoughlin, CSM, PMI-ACP, PMP
Ray Mead, PMP
Alain Patrick Medenou, MSc, ICF-PCC, PMP
Ramon Medero Concepcion, PMP, PgMP, PfMP
Veronica Medina Orellana, DASSM, PMP
Mohamed Samy Megahed
Emad L Megahied
Moez Mehdi
Justin Meier
Dora Luz Mejia Arango, PMI-ACP, PMP, PgMP
Luis Felix Mejia Tam
Marco Mello, DASSM, PMP
Andrea Menegus
Hilal Mengi, MBA, FCPA, PMP
Duane Mengo, PMI-ACP, PMI-PBA, PMP
Michael Mertens
Kentaro Midorikawa, PMP, PgMP, PfMP
Peter Botond Mihok
Gloria J. Miller, DBA
Manuel Minute, CGEIT, CCISO, PMP
Fereshteh Mirhosseini, PSPOI, PMI-ACP, PMP
Kunihiko Mishima
Smita Mishra, PMI-CP, PMI-RMP, PMP
Subrat Kumar Mishra, OPCSI, PMI-RMP, PMP
Kenyi Mitsuta, PMI-RMP, PMP
Tanuj Mittal, PMP
Amir Moawad
Ganesh Modi, PMP
Ata Modiri
Mahdi Moein, PMI-PBA, PMP, PfMP
Nkhumise Lentle Darius Moeletsi, Eng
Imadeldin Mohamed
Azam Mohammed, MSc, PMI-ACP, PMP
Habeeb Mohammed, PMP
Mannan Mohammed, P.Eng, PMI-ACP, PMP
Mansoor Mohammed, PMP, PgMP, PfMP
Safaa Adnan Mohammed, M.Eng
Venkatramvasi Mohanvasi

Elsayed Mohsen
Hoss Mohsenian
Elena Molina Reyes
Ala R. Momani
Dennis C. Monagle
Peter J. Monkhouse, MBA, PMP, PMI Fellow
Andrea Monroy, PMO-CP, PMP
Antonio Monteiro
Eduardo Montes, PMP
Reza Moradi, MBA, PSM, PMP
Jose S. Morales, DBA, PMP
Mauricio F. Morales R, M3.0, MCP, PMP
Masoud Moravej, MSc, PMP
Felipe Fernandes Moreira, PMP
Alexandre Morissette, BSc, PMP
Jose Moro Melon, CAPM, DASSM, PMP
Sherif Mostafa, PhD, CSM, FIEAust CPEng
Frederico Moura
Henrique Moura, PMI-ACP, PMI-RMP, PMP
Simón Moya Jimenez, MSc, IBM Data Science, PMP
Cephas Muchuchui
Nitin Mukesh
Dana Persada Mulyoto, MBA, eCBA, PMP
Muhammad Munib
Salman Munir, BE
Ingrid Lucia Muñoz Periñan, MSc, PMO-CP, PMP
Kristine Hayes Munson, PMP
Isaac Muonanu, MSc, EMBA
Vishnu Kiran Muppidi, MBA, PDM, PMP
Muktesh Murthy, MBA, PMP
Senkodi Murugesan, BE, CPMAI, PMP
Ata Ul Musawir, PhD, PMP
Faten Ali Mustafa
Hatim Sid Ahmed Mohamed Mustafa, PMI-ACP, PMI-RMP, PMP
Ahmed Ely Mustapha, PhD, CSP, PMP
Syed Ahsan Mustaqeem, PE, PMP
Victor S. Mutonga, PMP, PgMP, PfMP
Chamia Mutuku
Balakumaar MV
Anita Vijay Myana
Ruan Mynhardt, BSc, MBA, PMP
Myo Min Htoo, B.Eng, PMP, PgMP
Brijesh Nair, PMI-ACP, PMP, PgMP
Asaya Nakasone, PMP
Hiromi Nakatani, PRINCE2, CSP, PMP
Krishna Kumar Nanjundaprasad, DASM, PMI-ACP, PMP
Ovidiu Nanuti, MSc, PMI-RMP, PMP
Saima Naqvi, MBA, ITIL, PMP
Mohamed Naser Khalil
Jhenalyn Magat Natividad, CLSSYB, PMP
Asad Naveed, PMI-RMP, PMP
Sadık Nazik, MSc, MBA, PMP
Ahad Nazir, PMP
Jean Bosco Ndaruhutse, PMP
Trevor K. Nelson, PhD, MBA, PMP
Serge Rodrigue Nenkam, PhD, PMP, PfMP
Benjamin Netz, MBA, CSSBB, PMP
Adriano José da Silva Neves, PhD, CRISC, PMP
Gundo Nevhutalu, MSc, PMP
Willie Newson, PMI-ACP, PMP, PgMP
Ngô Vĩnh Hòa, PMI-ACP, PMP, PgMP
Esperant Ngongo Mbuli, ITIL V4, PSM I, PMP
Yao Yavo Basile N'Guessan
Albert Nguyen
(Eugene) Nguyen Xuan Binh
Khai Nguyen Nhu, PMP, PMI-PBA, ACP
Lâm Thu Nguyên, PMP, PgMP, PfMP
Maria V. Nguyen, MS, PMP
Nguyen Dang The, BSc, PMP
Nguyen Duc Hai
Nguyen Si Trieu Chau, PMP, PgMP, PfMP
Nguyen Tuan Le Giang, PMP, PgMP, PfMP
Nguyễn Xuân Bình
Andreas Nicklas, PMP
Aleksei Nikitin, PMI-ACP, PMI-RMP, PMP
G. A. Nikitin, PMP, PgMP
Esin (Esko) Nikolaev, PMP
Yuliia Nikolaieva
Yan Ning
Yamanta Raj Niroula, PMP
Nnogge Lovis Nkede, PMP, PgMP, PfMP
Udenwa Nnamdi, PMI-PBA, PMP
Jose Ignacio Noguera, CSSBB, PMI-ACP, PMP
Takamasa Nomura, PMI-ACP, PMP
Askar Nourzhanov, Dip IoD, EMBA, PMP
Nukala Lakshmana Ravi Kumar, FIE, MLE, PMP
Irony Nunes de Oliveira, KCP, KMP, PMP
Marco Antonio Núñez Estrada, BSc
Khalid Nurian, MS CS, MBA, PMP
Lisa Anne O'Connell
Michael O'Connor, PhD, PgMP, PfMP
Hiroyuki Ogura, PMP
Spencer Oklobdzija, PMP
Lola Okunrinboye, PMP
Daniel B. Oladejo, CEnv, MAPM, PMP
Jon G. Olazarri
Antonio Oliva Gonzalez
Cristian Olivares, PMP
Marcelo Oliveira Danza, MSc, PMP
Adedeji Oluwatosin Adeloro, Project+, FAAPM, PMP
Habeeb Omar, DASSM, PMO-CP, PfMP
Ifidon Omokhomion, PMP
Olanrewaju Ayobami Omoya, CPEng, MIEAust, PMP
Marian Oprea, PMI-ACP, PMP

Onyedika Godson Orakwue, CBAP, PMP
Littman Ordonez Parrilla, MBA, PMP
Jason R. Orloske
Luis Miguel Orozco Castro, MBA, PMI-ACP, PMP
Rosmel Ortiz Pimentel, PMP
Yuriy Oryeshkin, PMP
Mai Osama, MBA, PMP
Emilio Oteiza
Mahmoud Esameldin Othman
Cristiano Ottavian, ISIPM, P2P, PMP
Filippo Maria Ottaviani, PhD
Lixiong Ou
Chriss Oussama, PMP
Ouakour Oussama, PSM1, PMI-PMOCP, PMP
Frederick Baah Oware
Mohammad Mahmoud Owaydah, Eng
Thomas J. Owens
Edward Oyunga
Yoshihisa Ozaki, PMP, PgMP, PfMP
Takashi Ozawa
Ayhan Murat Özcan
Ayse Burcu Ozkaptan
S P Sreenivas Padala, PhD
Washington Fernando Padilla, PhD, PMP, PfMP
Ravindranath Palahalli, PMP
Raghul Palaniswamy, PMI-RMP, PMP, PgMP
Nikolaos Pallikaropoulos, MBA, M.Eng
Claude Palmarini
Jorge Palomino Garcia, MBA, PMI-ACP, PMP
Santosh Kumar Panda, Eng, PMI-CP, PMP
Dhananjay Kumar Pandey, PE,
Lean Six Sigma Black Belt, PMP
Rajeev R Pandey, EMBA, PhD(c), PMP
Hariyo D. Pangarso, MT, PMP
Vijayakrishnan Panikkar, B.Tech, PMP
Rakesh Pant, CSM, SAFe Analyst, PMP
Leonard Panta
Shiamala Paramasivam, PMP
Alessandro Paravano
Harsh Anilbhai Parikh, PMI-ACP, PMP
Chris Partridge
Ameen N Pasha, PMI-RMP, PMI-PMOCP, PMP
Patrícia Paula, PMI-ACP, PMI-PBA, PgMP
Gurumoorthy Paulraj
Marcus Paulus
Seenivasan Pavanasam
Leandro Slavec Pavani, PMP
Matthew Peet, MSc, PMP
Chrisanthi Peppa
Emma Perennes, MA, PMI-ACP, PMP
Tarcísio de Souza Peres
Hector Perez, PhD, MA, PMP
Maria Paula Perides, PhD, PMP
Andrey A. Petrov
Durga P Phuyal, PMI-ACP, DASSM, PMP
Pyae Phyo, BCSc, PMP
Les Pickersgill, PMP
Alina Piddubna
Donna Marie Pierre
Selvakumar M. Pillai, CRISIL-ESG Risk Analyst,
PMI-RMP, PMP
Thomas R. "Randy" Pilling, MPA,
DAWIA Advanced PM, PMP
Daniel Pimenta Guimaraes, PMP
Americo Pinto
Jose Ângelo Pinto, PMP
Monique Bonilauri Piou, MSG, PMP
Massimo Pirozzi, P3M
Shaligram Pokharel
Alejandro Polanco Carrasco, PMP
Hector J. Polo A.
Roberto Pons
Marco Porretta, PhD, PMP
Napoleon Posada Pajuelo, MBA, PMP
Mahyar Pourlak, PhD, QMS Lead Auditor, PE
Clifton Powell, MS, MEd, PMP
Girish Prabhakar, PMP, PgMP, PfMP
B K Subramanya Prasad, CSM, PMP
Adi Prasetyo, PhD, PMP
Dawson Preethi, BSc, MSc, PMP
Tony Prensa, DM, PMO-CP, PMP
Carl W. Pro, PMI-RMP, PMP
Edwin Alfred Provencal, PhD
Luigi Punzo, MBA, CISA, PMP
Alex Puppa, Prosci, CAPM, PMP
Zulfiqar Ali Qaimkhani, PMP, PgMP, PfMP
Sami Hakam Qasim
Qi Huan
Ronald Quartel, PMP
Otis Quinn, PMP
Shoaib Qureshi, MBA, CSM, PMP
SivaRaghavendra R
Stefan Radev, PhD
Hossein Radmehr, DBA, PMI-RMP, PMP
Gheorghe Radu
Abdul Raheem Samee, PMI-PBA, PgMP, PfMP
Noalur Rahim, BSc, PMP
Mohammad Rahimzadeh Khoee, PMP
Hossein Rahmatjou
Suthen Raja, ME, PMP
Sriramasundararajan Rajagopalan, PhD, PgMP, PfMP
Kingsley Porpatham Rajendran, ME
Ryoko Ralston, PMI-ACP, PMP, PgMP
Remya Ramakrishnan
Rakesh Ramasamy, MS, CSSBB, PMP
Manavasi K Ramesh

Ernesto Alexander Ramirez Guzman, BSc
Roderick Umandal Ramos, MIR, MTM, PMP
M V Rasamanikkam, MBA, PMP
Mahmoud Rashed, MBA, PMP, PMO-CC
Muhammad Asim Rashid
Muhammad Mohsin Rashid, PMI-RMP, PMI-PMOCP, PMP
Sagar Ashok Raut, PMI-PMOCP, PgMP, PfMP
P. Ravikumar, PMP, PgMP, PfMP
Samvit Rawal
Daniel Ray, PhD, CPO, PMP
Hema Rayalla
Alex Rebo
Venkata Ramana Murthy Reddi, PhD
Amarnath Boreddy Reddy
Krupakara Reddy, PRINCE2, CMMI, PMP
Maddireddy Vamsi Krishna Reddy
Djelloul Reguieg, PhD
Nabeel Ur Rehman, PMP, PgMP, PfMP
Eric Rehr, PMI-ACP, PMO-CP, PMP
Messias Reis, MSc, PMP
Laurent Renard
Vicky Restrepo
Carlos Alberto Restrepo Carvajal, PhD, PMI-RMP, PMP
Alexander V. Revin, PMP
Diego E. Reyes Beltran, PMP
Indira Reyes Oviedo, MSc, CSM, SAFe Agilist
Luis Eduardo Reyes Plasencia, MBA, PMI-PBA, PMP
Heba Rezk, BSc, PMI-ACP, PMP
Tashfeen Riaz, DAVSC, PMP, PgMP
Juan Carlos Ribero Gomez, MSc, PMP
Giuseppe Riccio, MSc
Crystal Richards
Gregg D. Richie, CNP, PMP
Fabio Rigamonti, MSc, PMP
Emilio G. Río, PMP
Syed Hasnain Rizvi, PhD, SPC, PMP
Bob Roark, MBA, PMP
John Robert, B. Tech, PGDBA
Hélio Rodrigues Costa, FHM, IPMA-A, PMP
Carlos Rodriguez
Christian Rodriguez
Ned Rodriguez
Francisco Javier Rodríguez Blanco, PMP
Joerg Roedle
David Rog, PSPO, CSM 2, PMP
Kathy Rogers, LSSBB, PMP
Pallav Rohatgi, PMI-ACP, PMI-RMP, PMP
Nicole Rohloff, CSM, PMP
Sergio Rojas A., Eng, MBA, PMP
Rizwan Roker, Lean Six Sigma Black Belt, PMI-ACP, PMP
Stelian Dan Roman, CSSBB, PMI-ACP, PMP
Rafael Romero
Sadegh Roozbehi
Nathalie Rosero Recalde, MPM, PMO-CP, PMP
Kristi Ross, MBA, CSM, PMP
Emanuele Rossetti
César Elías Rouillon Sixto
Bikram Keshari Routray, AgilePM Practitioner, Change Management Practitioner, PMP
Carlos Andres Rúa Machado
Richard Ruchhoeft, PE, PMP
Carlos Javier Ruiz Zapata, PMI-PMOCP, PMP
Ahmet Rumiye, DBA, PgMP, PfMP
Joseph Russell
Philip L. Russell, PMP
István Rusvai
Erica Ryan, MBA, PMP
Glenn Rypp, CPEng, MAppProjMgmt, CPSPM
Maged Saad, PhD, PMP, PfMP
Eyad Saadeh, PMP, PgMP, PfMP
Sachlani, PSMI, PMI-PMOCP, PMP
Ayman Sadek
Muhammad Safyan, CPM, SCE, PMP
Gopal Sahai, CTSC, PMI-PBA, PMP
Mary Saka
Hiroshi Sakurai
Mahmoud Salama, MBA, PMP
Nabil Salame, MSc
Xavier Salas Ceciliano, MSc, DASM, PMP
Luis Saldes Gómez, DASM, PMP
Ahmed Saleh Mokhtar, PMI-RMP, PMP
Nazih Salhab, PhD, PMI-PBA, PMP
Khamiss Salhi, Eng, PMP
Abdulai Salifu, SMC Certified, PRINCE2, PMP
Mario Salmona Petersen, PMI-SP, PMI-PBA, PMP
Omar A. Samaniego, NEC4, PMI-RMP, PMP
Abubaker Sami, PMP, PgMP, PfMP
Shantal San Juan Dzysiuk, Arq.
Pedro San Martin, MBA, CPA
Andrés Felipe Sánchez Sánchez
Julio Jesús Sánchez
Pilar Sanchez Albaladejo, PMI-ACP, PMP
Ramiro A. Sanchez Lopez, PhD, PMI-ACP, PMP
David Giner Sanchis, PMI-PMOCP, PMP
Yishai Sandak, MSc, PMI-ACP, PMP
Sunali Sandal, CSM, PMI-ACP, PMP
John Sanderson, PMP, PgMP, PfMP
Vasudha Sanghani, MBA, PSM, PMP
Ajay Sankaralingam
Edward Santavicca, MS, PMP
Nagalakshmi Santhanakrishnan, MSc, BSc
Alejandro Santiago Taylor
Luiz Santos, MBA, PMP
Ali Reza Sarhadi
Rajnish Sarin

Muhammad Azam Sarwar, MSc, PE, International BIM Certified
Harikrishnan Sasikumar, B.Tech, CFM, PMP
Takashi Sato, PMP
Anatolii Savin, MSPM, PMP, PfMP
Jean-Charles Savornin, PMP
Naota Sawabe
Karey J. Sayre, CSM, DASM, PMP
Gregor Schedlbauer, PMP, PfMP
Nicole Schelter, PMP
M. Scheurecker
Guy Schleffer, PhD, PMP, PgMP
Patrick Schmid, PSM1, PMP
Philippe Schulligen
Kathy Schwalbe, PhD, PMP
Bruce Schwickrath, PMP
Magda Scrobota, PMP
John Seay, PMI-ACP, PMP, PfMP
Toto Edrinal Sebayang
Goran Sečujski, MSc, PMP
Pavanasam Seenivasan
Roger Seip
G Lakshmi Sekhar, PMI-RMP, PMI-SP, PMP
Grégoire Semelet, ITIL, PMI-ACP, PMP
Danny Seow Wei Jie
Luis Sepulveda, PMI-ACP, PMI-PMOCP, PMP
Jorge David Serrano Pinilla, B.Eng, PMP
P. Seshan, PMI-ACP, PMP, PgMP
Suresh Sethuraman
Rachel Shadel, PMP
Faroug Abbas Shaheen
Mohammed Hadi Ahmed Shaikh
Mohamed Moustafa Abdelhamid Shalaby, DBA, MBA, PMP
Mohammad Shalan, CISA, CXO-GB, PMP
Mohamed Shaltout
Sumanth Shampur, BE, CSM, PMP
Mohamed Salah Sharaby, CCMP, PMI-RMP, PMP
Hushendra Sharma, MBA, PMP
Kavita Sharma, PMI-ACP, PMP, PgMP
Pankaj Sharma, PhD, PgMP, PfMP
Priya Sharma
Matthew Shaw, PE
Philip Sheikh
Bryan Shelby, PMP, PgMP, PfMP
Yufei Shen, PMP, PgMP, PfMP
Nitin Shende, SPC6, PMI-PBA, PMP
Georgi Shengelia, MSc, PMP
Dennis L. Sherman, PhD, DASM, PMP
William J. Shields, CCMP, PMI-ACP, PMP
Toshiki Shimoike, PhD, PMI-CP, PMP
Mukandi Herzel Shingirirai, MSc, PMP, PgMP
Farshad Shirazi, MSc, PMI-PBA, PMP
Akinsola Shokunbi
Faisal Adnan Siddiqui
Tajdar Ahmed Siddiqui, PMI-RMP, PMI-PMOCP, PMP
Bernhard Silesky, PMP
Wiverton Nunes Silva, PhD, BSc, MSc
Brenner Silva Ramirez
Rafael Beteli Silva Zanon, PMI-PBA, PMP
Christian Simonis, Dipl.-Ing, MBA, PMP
Carlos Singh, PMP, PgMP, PfMP
Gagandeep Singh, B.Tech, MBA
Jaskaran Singh
Shivam Singh
Sumit Kumar Sinha, PMP, PgMP, PfMP
Alex Sirni
Joseph Sisto, CSM, PMI-ACP, PMP
Arvind Sivaramakrishnan
Raji Sivaraman, MS, PMI-ACP, PMP
Gail Smith-McCarthy, PMP
Jeanette Snyder, PMP
Rafael Soares Ferreira
Behnam Sohrabiani, PMI-ACP, PMI-PBA, PMP
Islam Mohamed Soliman, PMI-ACP, PMP
Paul Solomon
Andreas Solomou, PMI-ACP, PMI-PBA, PMP
Edem Somevi, BSc, PMP
Xue Song, MPM, PMP
Christina Sookram
Mauro Sotille, PMI-RMP, PMI-PMOCP, PMP
Percy Soto Blas, MBA, PMP
Paulo Sousa
Fernando Souza, PMI-ACP, PMO-CP, PMP
Priya Sreeja, MS, PMP
Roopali Srivastava, PhD, AHPP, PMP
Marko Stakic, MBA, P.Eng, PMP
Julia Steel
Daria Stewart
Jim Stewart, PMP
Wendy M. Stinson, PMI-ACP, PMP
Mike Strachan, PMP
Maricarmen Suarez, PMI-ACP, PMP, PgMP
Sukumaran Subaramaniyan, P.Tech, PMP
Mokshagundam Sudhakar, MBA, PMI-RMP, PMP
Akihiro Sudo
Mohamed Ahmed Elhag Suliman, PMO-CP, PMP, PfMP
Alaa Sultan, PMP, PgMP, PfMP
Parkkavan Sundar, MBA
Masaru Sunohara
Langes Supramaniam, MSc, B.Eng, PMP
Suresh Supramaniam, CMBB, PMI-PBA, PMP
Bhavani Suresh, CISM, CGEIT, PMP
Oscar Gomez Svendsen
Lisa Sweeney, PMP
Nabiel Syed, PMP

Grzegorz Szalajko, CISA, DASSM, PMP
Piero Tagliapietra, MA, PMI-ACP, PMP
Ahmed Taha
Nooreddin M. Tahayneh, PMI-ACP, PMP, PfMP
Nilton Takagi, PhD
Martin D. Talbott, PMI-ACP, PMP
Mamoune Tall, MSc, LSSBB, PMP
Onalethata Tambula, DASM, CAPM, PMP
Tetsuya Tani, CBAP, PMP
Frank Tank
Awadalsaid Tara
Carsten Tautz, PhD, PMO-CP, PMP
Tarek Hassan Tawfik
Taruna Tayal, PMP
Thalita Rincon Martins Taylor, MBA, PMP
Oluwadara Tayo
Murat Tecimer
Benyamin Setiadi Tedjakusuma, MASc, PMP
Masoud Tehrani Majd
Jordi Teixido, PMP
Selim Tekin, BSc, PMI-ACP, PMP
Gokrem Tekir, PMP
Hector Teran
Atsufumi Teshima
Carlos Tessore
Riad Thalji, PMP
Gopinath Thekkeyil, M.Tech, PMP
Jigesh Thikkal Veetil, PMP
Brent J. Thompson, MBA, CPHIMS, PMP
Sal J. Thompson, MBA, CSM, PMP
Stuart Thorp, MIET, PgMP
Mohammed Thoufeeq, PhD, CLSSBB, PMP
Elizabeth Bice Tidwell, BA, CGEIT, PMP
Joseph Tierney, PMP
Jerad Tietz, PMP
Dmitry Timakov
Kevin Torres Barsallo, PMI-ACP, PMI-SP, PMP
Süleyman Tosun, PhD, PMP
Philippe Tournier, PMP
Biagio Tramontana
Pricilla Trassato, PMP
Christina Tsang-Reveche
John N. Tse, MBA, CSM, PMP
Christian Tshimbundu Tshakambowa
Despoina Tsirogianni
Ioannis Tsiroudis, BSc, M.Eng
Roksana Jahan Tumpa, PhD
Wing Ting Tung
Kellie Tyler
Alfredo Ugalde Maldonado
Terunori Umezawa
Tina Umino
Fatih Unal, MBA, ISTQB, CTFL
Madhusudhanan Penattu Unnikrishnan
Marcelo Filipe Rodrigues Urbano, BSc, MBA, DASSM
María José Urdaneta
Andrés Uribe, PMP
Ebenezer Uy, PMI-ACP, PMP
Ali Vahedi Diz, DBA, PMP, PgMP
Zahra Valavi
Jorge Valdés Garciatorres
Jose Felix Valdez, MSc, PMP
Valerii
Beatriz Vallina Acha
Shibu Valsalan, PhD, PMI-RMP, PMP
Tony Van Krieken, DASM, PMI-ACP, PMP
Tom Van Medegael, PMI-ACP, PMP
Steve VanArsdale, PMI-ACP, DASSM, PMP
Ravi Vanukuru, BE, PMP
Gopinath Konda Varadarajan
Harsh Vardhan, CSM, OSHA30, PMP
Cristian Vargas Andias
Enid T. Vargas Maldonado, PMI-ACP, PMI-PBA, PMP
Bhaskar R Varma, PMI-RMP, PMP
Haralambos Varvarigos, PMI-ACP, PMI-RMP, PMP
Paul C Charlesraj Vasantharaj, MS, MRICS, PMP
Tanika L. Vasquez, ACSM, CSPO, PMP
Sergio Vasquez Kaufmann, PMO-CP, PMP
Miguel Vasquez Kuong, GAIPC, SSPC, CAPM
Héctor Véjar Reyes, Eng
Jean Carlos Velasco Sanchez, MBA, PMP
Francisco Venegas, M. Arch, PMP
Riccardo Venturelli, CAPM
Juan Verastegui Maldonado, Eng, MBA, PMP
Alin Veronika, PMI-RMP, PMO-CP, PMP
Eddy Vertil, PhD, MPM, PMP
Ricardo Viana Vargas, PhD
Hugo Vidarte Basurco
J Miguel Vieira
Sivasankar Vijayasekaran, B.Eng, MBA, PMP
Roberto Villa, PMP
Tiziano Villa, PMI-ACP, DASSM, PMP
Javier Villegas Sierra
Dave Violette, MPM
Dennys Virhuez, Ing
Mangi Vishnoi, FIE BE, CSSGB, PMP
Andrea M. Vismara
Lislal Viswam, MSc, PMI-PMOCP, PMP
Emiliano Vitale
Ioannis Vithynos, PRINCE2P, PMI-ACP, PMP
Stephen W. Volz, DBA, PMP
Philip von Pander, PMI-ACP, PMP
Sameh Eldeeb Thabet Wahba, CPMC, PMC, PMP
Irshad Wani, PMP, PgMP, PfMP
Christopher Wanyoike, FIP, MSc, PMP
Aamir Waqas

Bunnojo Warashina
Muhammad Wasif, PMP
Oscar Wasilik, P.Eng, PMP
Tsunefumi Watanabe, PMP
Yuki Watanabe, PMP
Barb Waters, MBA, PMP
Chelsea Watson, MSOL, CAPM, PMP
Andrew Wealth, PMI-ACP, PMI-RMP, PMP
Wen Jing Yong, CAPM, PMP, PgMP
Lars Wendestam, MSc, PMP
Jodi Wert, MA, CCMP
Sean Whitaker
David Whitlock
Christopher W. Wiedel
Kristen V. Wiederhold, MBA, PMP, PgMP
Michal Wieteska, CSPO, PMP
Bronsen Wijaya
Brittany J. Wilkins
Christine Williams, MHA, ITIL, PMP
Elliot L Williams, ECBA, CBAP, PMP
Emmanuel Williams, PMP
Luke Williams, MSc, PMP
Randy A. Williams, PhD, PMI-ACP, PMP
T Lee WIlliams, PhD, Col (Ret.), PMP
Tasheka Wilson
Saman Wimaladasa, MBA, SAFe, PMP
Clark Yan Naing Soe Win, MBA, CSM, PMP
Ishan Wiratinga, BSc, MSc, PMP
Stephen D. Wise, PMI-ACP, PMP
Krzysztof Witkowski
Lars Wittek, PMI-ACP, PMI-RMP, PMP
Dorina Wofford, PMI, ITIL4, CSM
Paweł Remigiusz Wojtal
Wong Guan Boon, PMP
Juanita Woods, PhD, PMP, PgMP
Jack Wu, PMI-ACP, PMP
Wenyi Xiao, PMP
Bo Xu
Erick Silva Yagua, MSc, PMP
Masahito Yamamoto, MBA, CSM, PMP
Masaya Yamamoto
Gillian Yap
Ross Yates, PhD, ChPP, MPMI
Hasan Yavuz, MSc, PMP
Ming Yin Yeung, LLM, MBA, PMP
Fu Yongkang, DBA, PMI-ACP, PMP
Iliya Yordanov, PMP
Douglas Allen Young
Yu Xiu
Sisca Yuliharyani, MBA, PMP
Christopher P. Zack, PMI-ACP, PMP
Hany Zahran, PMP
Jean-Paul Zakhour, B.Eng, PMP
Daniel Alfredo Zamudio Lopez, CPMAI, PMI-RMP, DAVSC
Stefano Mario Zanantoni, PMP
Anton Zandhuis, PMP
Ricardo Luis Zanfelicce, PhD, CSM, PMP
Rula A Zanoona
Alessandri Zapata Rosas, PMP
Zhang Wei
Yuming Zhong
Zin Bo Aung, M.Eng, BE, PMP
Marcin Żmigrodzki
Alan Zucker, PMI-ACP, DAC, PMP

X1.2 PMI Team Members

Warren Duffie
Linda Garber
Kelly Heuer, PhD, CAPM
Pierre Le Manh, PMP
Christie McDevitt, APR
Joshua Parrott, MBI
Sarah Philbrick
Scott Shemo
Kim Shinners
Lisa Woo-Bloxberg

Appendix X2
Project Management Offices

X2.1 Introduction

The concept of the project management office (PMO) has evolved over the last few decades, moving from a process-focused entity that standardizes methodologies and tools for project management to a customer-oriented partner focused on delivering a value that is perceived by the customers and stakeholders within the organization. This transition can be seen as a shift from a process-centric to a customer-centric entity. As a result, the centralized activities provided by a PMO, whether related to portfolios, programs, or projects, are increasingly tailored to the unique needs and strategic direction of the organization.

In today's dynamic business environment, the PMO's role extends beyond merely executing projects; it involves aligning its services with strategic goals to maximize impact and relevance. While traditional benefits such as cost savings, efficiency gains, and improved stakeholder satisfaction remain important, modern PMOs are also expected to drive broader enterprise value. This effort includes establishing enterprise-wide good practices, fostering cross-team knowledge sharing, strengthening risk management capabilities, and developing project management competencies across the organization. By delivering both tangible and intangible benefits through these multifaceted contributions, PMOs can elevate their perceived value and ensure a sustainable, long-term impact on organizational performance.

X2.2 The PMO Value Proposition

The core value proposition of the PMO lies in its ability to enable strategic execution, enhance delivery performance, and strengthen organizational capabilities across portfolios, programs, and projects. A modern PMO does more than oversee processes; it acts as a business partner that helps the organization prioritize the right work, deliver it effectively, and continuously improve how value is realized.

This value is twofold: It includes both the actual value delivered, such as cost efficiencies, risk reduction, improved decision-making, and accelerated delivery, as well as the value perceived by its stakeholders, which is influenced by how well the PMO's services resonate with organizational needs and priorities.

While measurable outcomes like cost savings or efficiency gains are important, intangible benefits such as improved collaboration, enhanced transparency, and stakeholder confidence also significantly contribute to perceived value. Importantly, the perception of value is often shaped by the organization's project management maturity; more mature organizations tend to recognize and leverage PMO contributions more fully.

To sustain relevance, PMOs should ensure that their objectives translate into visible, day-to-day contributions that reflect what the business values most. This effort requires not only tracking delivery performance, but also continuously aligning PMO activities with evolving business needs, and ensuring that the PMO is seen not merely as a support function but as an essential enabler of enterprise success.

X2.3 Importance of Customer Centricity for a PMO

A customer-centric PMO focuses its services and operations on understanding and responding to stakeholder needs, ensuring that the value delivered is not only tangible, but also experienced as relevant and meaningful by its customers. In this context, the PMO evolves from a function that enforces standardized processes to one that serves as a flexible, responsive partner aligned with business outcomes.

Crucially, the concept of "customer" should be understood in its broadest sense. The PMO serves not only senior executives or external clients, but also internal stakeholders such as project managers, project teams, and delivery units. These groups rely on the PMO for practical support, timely guidance, and tools to help them succeed in delivering value. A truly customer-centric PMO recognizes this diversity and adjusts its services accordingly. Communication with customers should be tailored toward the customer's needs and the value that the customer expects, and not only the processes and methodologies required to achieve the value. The range of services that will be provided is then tailored by the PMO, based on what is needed and valued by the customer. The technical aspects—the tools and methodologies—are the means of how to deliver value to satisfy the customer's needs.

The success of the PMO depends on its ability to define a set of services that can bring added value to the customer and that will be positively perceived by the customer over time. The customer's perception and the identification of evolving customer needs are crucial elements of tailoring and also help to evolve the PMO over time. As business priorities shift, so should the PMO's offerings. Maintaining this relevance depends on the PMO's ability to translate strategic intent into operational support that resonates with different stakeholder groups. The success of the PMO is measured not only by how well it delivers its services, but by how well those services are aligned to the evolving context and priorities of the organization.

X2.4 PMO Type, Model, and Structure

The selection of a PMO type, model, and structure is a nuanced decision that requires careful consideration of the unique characteristics and needs of an organization. The wide range of available models can create a dilemma: determining which one is truly the "best" or "right" choice. This thinking often leads to the misguided belief that a single model is ideal, making others seem obsolete or irrelevant. Such a traditional approach, which seeks a perfect PMO model as a solution for organizational challenges, is fundamentally flawed because it encourages the adoption of a supposed "ideal" model and, if it fails, waits for the next model. This strategy overlooks a crucial aspect of PMOs, which is their inherent uniqueness.

PMOs are complex entities that defy universal consensus. There are no empirically proven, universally ideal, or consistently more effective PMO models. While various models, such as the directive PMO, supportive PMO, and agile PMO, offer valuable insights, they should not be viewed as mutually exclusive paths. Instead, these models should be seen as a palette of options that can be combined to meet specific organizational needs. The literature on PMOs presents a rich array of types, each offering unique perspectives on how these entities can function within organizations. This diversity reflects the complex and multifaceted nature of PMOs and the varied needs of the organizations they serve.

Recent approaches emphasize greater flexibility, moving away from rigid classifications and proposing more adaptable strategies grounded in the unique needs of each organization. While these approaches offer valuable insights into structuring and operating PMOs, it is crucial to understand that no single type should be seen as a universal solution. Instead, these models should inspire PMO professionals to develop tailored solutions that address their organizations' unique needs.

The evolution of PMOs highlights the growing understanding that flexibility and customization are key to their success. Empirical evidence consistently shows that the most valued PMOs are those that have customized structures to fit their unique organizational context, rather than rigidly adhering to a single, predefined model. The risk lies in the temptation to seek a "perfect" PMO model or to jump from one trendy type to another. Such approaches often lead to misalignment between the PMO and the organization's actual needs, resulting in decreased value perception and effectiveness. Instead of rigidly categorizing PMOs or adhering strictly to predefined types, successful PMOs often exhibit a blend of characteristics drawn from multiple types. This hybridization allows them to create a unique structure that best serves their specific context and stakeholder needs.

X2.5 PMO Maturity Models

PMO maturity models are essential tools for organizations aiming to enhance their project management capabilities. These models provide a structured framework that allows organizations to assess their current PMO maturity level, identify areas for improvement, and develop a roadmap for growth. By benchmarking against industry standards, organizations can set realistic goals and measure progress over time. This systematic approach not only optimizes project management practices but also ensures alignment with strategic objectives, ultimately leading to improved organizational performance.

A customer-centric PMO maturity model emphasizes the importance of aligning PMO services with the strategic goals of the organization. In this model, the PMO acts as a service provider, focusing on delivering value that meets the specific needs and expectations of its stakeholders. By placing the customer at the center, PMOs can tailor their services to maximize impact and relevance. This approach helps ensure that PMOs remain agile and responsive to changing business needs, thereby enhancing their perceived value within the organization and contributing to overall success.

The design of a PMO should consider industry-specific profiles and integrate seamlessly with the organizational structure. A mature PMO recognizes the unique challenges and requirements of its industry, adapting its practices and services accordingly. Additionally, the PMO should align with the existing organizational framework, fostering collaboration and communication across departments. This integration enables the PMO to leverage organizational resources effectively and promote a consistent project management approach throughout the enterprise, ensuring that the PMO's efforts are aligned with broader organizational goals.

The culture and mandate of a mature PMO should reflect and support the organization's culture, values, and strategic priorities. A well-developed PMO aligns its culture with that of the organization, facilitating smoother adoption of project management methodologies. Its mandate is to focus on delivering measurable value to the organization. By demonstrating a clear link between PMO activities and tangible business outcomes, the PMO gains recognition and support from key stakeholders. This recognition reinforces the PMO's role as a strategic asset, driving continuous improvement and maturity in project management practices across the organization.

X2.6 Learn More About PMOs

The following PMI standards and practice guides provide additional information about the role of a PMO from different perspectives. These resources may offer additional insights and useful information.

- Project Management Institute (PMI). (2025) *Project Management Offices: A Practice Guide*. PMI.
- Project Management Institute (PMI). (2024). *The Standard for Program Management—* Fifth edition. PMI.
- Project Management Institute (PMI). (2018). *The Standard for Organizational Project Management*. PMI.
- Project Management Institute (PMI). (2017). *The Standard for Portfolio Management—* Fourth edition. PMI.
- Project Management Institute (PMI). (2017). *The PMI Guide for Business Analysis*. PMI.
- Project Management Institute (PMI). (2017). *Agile Practice Guide*. PMI.
- Project Management Institute (PMI). (2015). *Governance of Portfolios, Programs, and Projects: A Practice Guide*. PMI.

Appendix X3 Artificial Intelligence

X3.1 Artificial Intelligence in the Project Context

Artificial intelligence (AI) describes a set of technologies that simulate human behavior on computers. This technology allows machines to perform tasks they were not directly programmed to do, learn from experiences, and adapt to new situations. AI has a broad range of applications, including pattern recognition, fraud detection, robotics, and the discovery of new drugs to combat diseases. The quick changes in the field of AI, and its rising potential, require great adaptability for staying current with new tools and in learning new ways of working.

Advances in the AI field, such as the development of large language models (LLMs), have expanded its applicability while simplifying its adoption, bringing the technology to the mainstream. What was once a tool only available to experts or companies with abundant resources is now accessible with minimal manual intervention. In that sense, the technology has become so pervasive that every professional, including project professionals, should obtain a better understanding of AI to remain productive.

Though AI's long-term impacts remain to be seen, it is already creating a major shift in most professions, increasing the productivity of the workforce and creating new job opportunities while possibly extinguishing others.

A common classification of AI systems is described as follows and is shown in Figure X3-1:

- **Artificial intelligence (AI).** AI is a broader term describing systems that can reason, learn, and act autonomously.
- **Machine learning (ML).** ML is a subfield of AI that uses data to train neural network models, which can predict outputs based on previous inputs.
- **Deep learning (DL).** DL is a more advanced ML type that relies on multilayered neural networks to extract features and make decisions. Deep learning often requires large data sets and significant computational resources.
- **Generative AI (GenAI).** GenAI is a subset of deep learning that applies large language models (LLMs) to create systems capable of generating new data such as text, speech, audio, pictures, and videos, among others.

For the sake of simplification, this appendix refers to the broader term "AI," even if some of the use cases are built using more specific techniques such as GenAI.

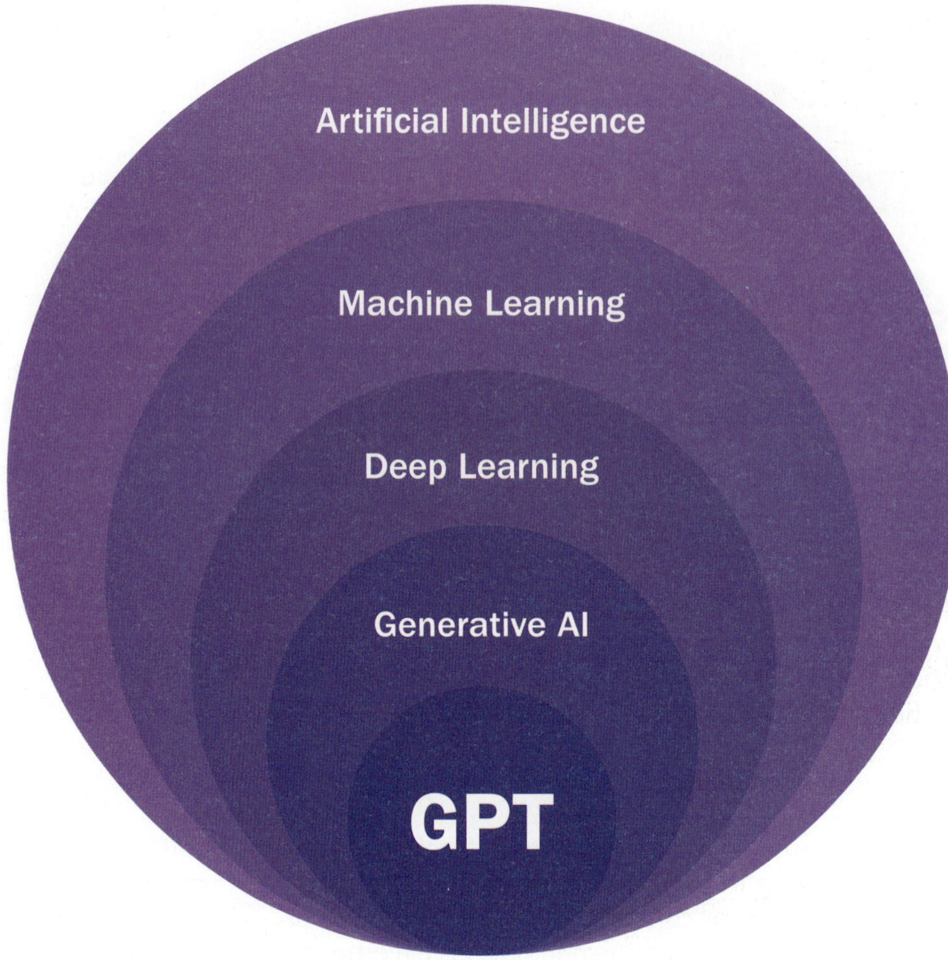

Figure X3-1. The Relationship Among the Technologies Needed to Make Generative Pretrained Transformers (GPTs) Work

X3.1.1 Strategies for AI Adoption

AI can support project management tasks in many ways. The more complex the task, the more human intervention is required to result in high-quality outcomes. In that sense, a good strategy is classifying tasks according to complexity and the need for human supervision. As a result of this classification, the opportunities to use AI fall into three categories:

- **Automation.** Tasks that are low complexity and require little human intervention in their final output can be automated. Common examples are report generation, document analysis, and conference call summarization. Standard prompts can be created and reutilized across different projects and teams. A good source of those prompts can be found in the PMI Prompt Library as part of the PMI Infinity™ tool.
- **Assistance.** At the assistance level, the tools complement analysis and iteratively build ideas toward an expected output. The result of the first iterations should not be considered complete without further analysis and refinement. Some examples are the creation of a risk

register or scheduling plan with buffers. A project professional is expected to review the results to ensure they are accurate and complete.

- **Augmentation.** Augmentation is the enhancement of existing capabilities and the exploration of new ones by professionals. Augmentation focuses on strategic and complex tasks such as balancing the options of a project portfolio to maximize the return of investment or performing risk forecasting based on external variables. Project professionals should use the tool as a brainstorming partner, exchanging ideas and refining the results through multiple iterations.

X3.1.2 State of the Market

There are many AI tools, both free and paid, available for public use. Typically, the free options restrict the number of questions (prompts) that can be submitted to the engine in a given interval of time. The other big difference is how the engine deals with user data. Paid versions allow the user to restrict the use of its data to retrain the models, ensuring privacy and protecting intellectual property.

X3.2 Common Use Cases

Table X3-1 demonstrates how AI can significantly enhance various aspects of project management, including planning, controlling, stakeholder engagement, risk management, and strategic decision-making.

Figure X3-2 presents some use cases classified by complexity and the need for human intervention.

X3.3 Responsible Use and Ethical Concerns

The use of AI in projects and organizations brings together associated benefits and risks that should be considered. On one hand, the use of AI may shift the daily work of project professionals from repetitive tasks to higher-level and more creative tasks. On the other hand, it is up to human beings to take the related risks into account and make appropriate decisions regarding AI's use and potential.

There are multiple ethical factors and risks that may play a critical role in the adoption of AI, particularly:

- **Bias.** AI systems can be subject to bias if they are trained with biased data or if the algorithms they are using introduce bias themselves. The risk of bias can be mitigated through different actions such as:
  - Diversification of the data sets on which the AI system is trained;
  - Periodic tests conducted on the AI system, with particular focus on bias; and
  - Involvement of different teams in the development of the AI system.
- **Privacy.** AI systems use large data sets that can be sensitive and regulated by privacy policies and laws. This use of sensitive information increases the need to properly secure the data and ensure that it is collected with a privacy policy in place. There is a risk that the data can be used in a way that violates privacy and ethical standards.
- **Accountability.** AI systems may be responsible for certain decisions, depending on the working arrangement. Ultimately, a human should be accountable for each decision, and this accountability should be clearly defined.

Table X3-1. Primary AI Use Cases in Project Management

Project Management Performance Domain	AI Strategy	Use Case
Governance	Augmentation	**Data-driven decision-making.** AI can analyze historical project data, market trends, and organizational priorities to help with the selection and prioritization of projects. AI can weigh elements such as potential ROI, strategic alignment, resource availability, and risk levels to recommend the best projects to take forward.
Governance	Assistance	**Multicriteria decision analysis.** AI can use sophisticated algorithms to evaluate multiple criteria all together, providing a balanced scorecard approach to prioritize projects based on their overall value and feasibility criteria. AI can also run resource-constrained scenarios to help choose projects with the highest impact use of available resources.
Governance	Augmentation	**Brainstorming/idea generation.** AI tools can generate ideas and suggestions based on a given set of parameters, keywords, or previous successful endeavors. These tools can also use machine learning to provide insights into emerging trends and technologies that can inspire new project ideas. Additionally, these tools can be used to generate ideas for documents such as business cases and project charters.
Governance	Assistance	**Collaborative platforms with AI.** Platforms enhanced with AI can facilitate brainstorming sessions by organizing and categorizing ideas in real time, ensuring all team contributions are considered and the best ideas surface.
Governance	Automation	**Automated reporting and representation.** AI can automatically generate comprehensive reports on project status, performance metrics, and compliance, reducing manual effort and increasing accuracy. AI can also be incorporated into visual tools, dashboards, and information radiators to improve the understanding of the project status for both the project team and stakeholders.
Governance	Automation	**Process automation.** Routine tasks such as project documentation, reports, compliance checks, lessons learned (at the portfolio level), and administrative approvals can be automated, allowing the PMO to focus on strategic activities.
Governance	Assistance	**Predictive analytics for planning.** AI can predict project timelines, resource needs, and potential bottlenecks by analyzing historical data and project specifics. This use of predictive analytics leads to more accurate and realistic project plans.

Table X3-1. *(Continued)*

Project Management Performance Domain	AI Strategy	Use Case
Governance	Automation	**Real-time monitoring.** AI tools can continuously monitor project progress against planned baselines, providing real-time updates and alerts for deviations, enabling timely corrective actions.
Governance	Assistance	**Early warning signaling.** Even when critical path analysis, burndown charts, or cumulative flow diagrams show that things appear to be progressing according to plan, AI tools can use pattern recognition from similar projects to indicate when things may be at risk of falling behind or going off track.
Governance	Augmentation	**Baseline optimization.** AI tools can augment trade-off analysis among scope, schedule, and cost factors to help determine the optimal baseline that maximizes a project's value proposition.
Governance	Automation	**AI chatbots.** Virtual assistants powered by AI can handle routine queries, provide project updates, and assist with task management, freeing up project managers to focus on more strategic activities.
Governance	Automation	**Task management.** AI assistants can track activities' progress, send reminders, or assign tasks based on team members' workloads and skill sets.
Governance	Automation	**Automated meeting minutes and summaries.** AI can schedule and transcribe meetings; identify key points, decisions, and action items; and generate detailed minutes automatically. AI can also provide concise summaries of meetings, pointing out important discussions and follow-up actions, helping ensure that all stakeholders are aligned.
Risk	Augmentation	**Risk identification and assessment.** AI algorithms can analyze historical project data and industry benchmarks to identify potential risks in new projects. By using predictive analytics, AI can assess the likelihood and impact of these risks, enabling project managers to develop comprehensive risk management plans early in the planning phase.
Risk	Automation	**Automated risk mitigation actions.** Once risks are detected, AI can suggest—and even automate—certain mitigation actions based on predefined rules on task assignment and historical data.

(continued)

Table X3-1. *(Continued)*

Project Management Performance Domain	AI Strategy	Use Case
Risk	Assistance	**Risk impact analysis.** AI can evaluate the impact of actual risks on project goals such as time, cost, and quality. By providing detailed impact assessments, AI helps project managers understand the gravity of risks and prioritize their responses accordingly.
Risk	Augmentation	**Risk-adjusted ROI analysis.** At the portfolio, program, or project level, AI can use pattern recognition to augment existing ROI analysis in factoring in risk adjustments to expected ROI assessments.
Stakeholders	Augmentation	**Stakeholder sentiment analysis.** AI-powered natural language processing (NLP) tools can analyze communication data (e.g., emails, chats, meeting notes, social media) to determine stakeholder feelings. By ethically understanding stakeholders' emotions and concerns, project managers can address issues proactively and improve engagement.
Stakeholders	Augmentation	**Personalized communication.** AI can investigate stakeholders' preferences and past interactions in order to tailor communication strategies. For example, AI can determine the most effective communication channels and frequencies for each stakeholder, ensuring timely and relevant communication that enhances engagement and satisfaction.
Schedule	Assistance	**Dynamic scheduling.** AI can optimize project schedules by considering project dependencies, resource availability, and milestone deadlines. AI can adjust schedules in response to internally and externally generated changes, ensuring optimal resource utilization.
Schedule	Assistance	**Schedule conflict resolution.** AI can identify potential scheduling conflicts (at the portfolio, program, or project level) and propose solutions to resolve them, minimizing delays and resource bottlenecks.
Schedule	Assistance	**Schedule risk impact analysis.** AI can apply pattern recognition to help assess schedule risks such as inherent risks associated with branching and merging paths.

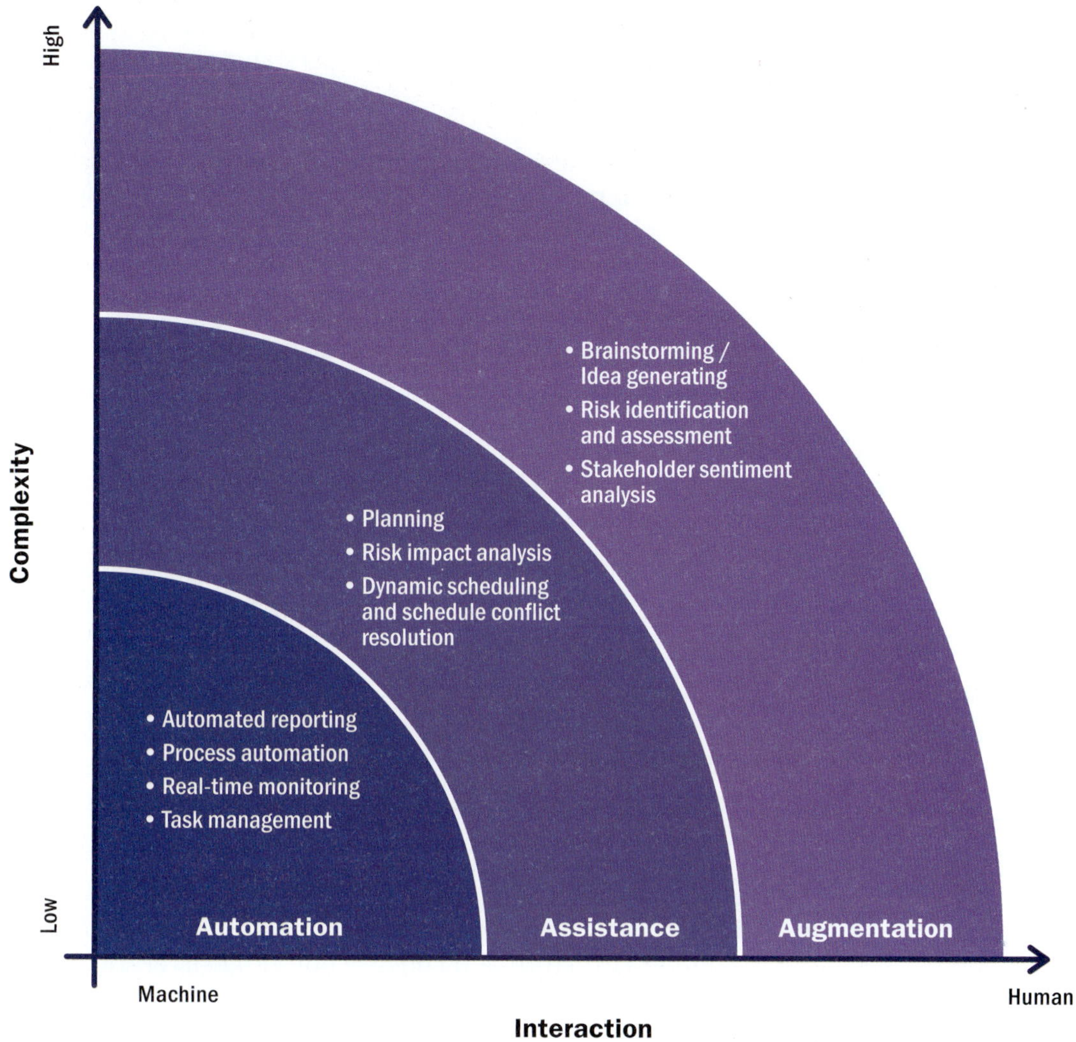

Figure X3-2. Use Cases Demonstrating Complexity and the Need for Human Intervention

- **Reliability.** The information obtained from AI should be checked and validated. It may be biased, incorrect, or irrelevant.
- **Safety.** The AI system should be properly designed, tested, and monitored to ensure the maximum required level of safety.
- **Transparency.** The information regarding the use of the data, how the data is handled, how the algorithms work, and how decision-making is conducted should be shared transparently with the end users and impacted parties.
- **Copyright.** A dilemma regarding the copyright ownership of information generated by AI may arise. It is important to be aware of the regulations and laws that apply to the data used by the AI systems. In certain cases, it is crucial to consider the level of human elaboration that has been involved in contributing to the output data generated by AI.
- **Sustainability.** Each request submitted to AI consumes electricity, water, and other resources. This factor should be considered when deciding to use AI in projects or for specific tasks.

Ethical guidelines in the performing organization, as well as AI policies, could represent a solid basis for building an organizational culture and establishing a common understanding of how AI should be used within the organization.

Project professionals should foster a culture of awareness and ethical use of AI, as well as contribute to increasing responsibility within the team for making ethical decisions related to AI adoption.

X3.4 Suggested Resources

- **PMI Infinity™**—An AI tool for project professionals from PMI: https://www.pmi.org/infinity
- **PMI Learning course**—"Generative AI Overview for Project Managers": https://www.pmi.org/shop/us/p-/elearning/generative-ai-overview-for-project-managers/el083
- **PMI Learning course**—"Data Landscape of GenAI for Project Managers": https://www.pmi.org/shop/us/p-/elearning/data-landscape-of-genai-for-project-managers/el106
- **PMI Learning course**—"Talking to AI: Prompt Engineering for Project Managers": https://www.pmi.org/shop/p-/elearning/talking-to-ai-prompt-engineering-for-project-managers/el128
- **PMI Learning course**—"Cognitive Project Management in AI (CPMAI)™ v7": https://www.pmi.org/shop/us/p-/digital-product/cognitive-project-management-in-ai-(cpmai)-v7---training-,-a-,-certification/cpmai-b-01
- **PMI Learning course**—"Practical Application of Generative AI for Project Managers": https://www.pmi.org/shop/us/p-/elearning/practical-application-of-generative-ai-for-project-managers/el173
- **PMI Learning course**—"AI in Infrastructure and Construction Projects": https://www.pmi.org/shop/us/p-/elearning/ai-in-infrastructure-and-construction-projects/el174
- **PMI Thought Leadership report**—*Shaping the Future of Project Management With AI*: https://www.pmi.org/learning/thought-leadership/ai-impact/shaping-the-future-of-project-management-with-ai
- **PMI Thought Leadership report**—*Talking to the Machine: Prompt Engineering Essentials for Project Professionals*: https://www.pmi.org/learning/thought-leadership/prompt-engineering
- **PMI guide**—*AI Essentials for Project Professionals*: https://www.pmi.org/standards/ai-essentials-for-project-professionals
- **PMI guide**—*Leading AI Transformation: Organizational Strategies for Project Professionals*: https://www.pmi.org/standards/leading-ai-transformation-organizational-strategies-for-project-professionals

**The links to courses and content referenced in this publication were accurate at the time of publication. Please visit PMI.org for the most current versions and newly available content.*

Appendix X4 Procurement

X4.1 Procurement Introduction

Procurement management plays a significant role in project management, involving the acquisition of goods, services, or results from external sources to meet project objectives. A buyer is an entity that purchases products or services, whereas the seller, vendor, contractor, or supplier is the entity that provides products or services. In a procurement and supply chain context, the buyer–seller relationship is characterized by information asymmetry and is a source of multiple relevant risks, as each party may possess different levels of information about the transaction. Procurement practices can influence project outcomes by impacting cost efficiency, quality standards, and timely delivery. In today's complex business environment, where projects often rely on specialized expertise and resources from external suppliers, understanding procurement management is essential for project managers.

Procurement is not classified as a separate performance domain in *A Guide to the Project Management Body of Knowledge (PMBOK® Guide)*. This decision reflects the unique position of procurement within organizational structures. Typically, project procurements are integrated into—or extend from—the larger organization's procurement department, leveraging established processes, policies, and vendor relationships, which ensures consistency across projects and allows for economies of scale. However, it is important to note that some large-scale or specialized projects may have dedicated procurement teams, operating with a degree of autonomy while still aligning with organizational standards.

This appendix provides a detailed understanding of procurement in projects. It covers the overall procurement flow, strategies for effective procurement management, make-or-buy analysis, source selection processes, and various contract types. Additionally, it addresses claim administration and alternative dispute-resolution methods. Throughout this appendix, good practices, such as establishing strong procurement policies, automating procurement processes, and implementing robust monitoring systems for key performance indicators (KPIs), are highlighted. Effective procurement practices significantly influence project success by ensuring cost efficiency, adherence to quality standards, risk mitigation, and timely delivery.

X4.2 Procurement Overview

Project procurement management encompasses the essential processes required to develop and administer agreements such as contracts, purchase orders, memoranda of agreements (MOAs), or service-level agreements (SLAs). These processes help ensure that the procurement of goods and services necessary for the project can be handled efficiently and effectively. The personnel authorized to procure these goods and services may include members of the project team, management, or members of the organization's purchasing department, depending on the organizational structure. Effective procurement management involves a series of activities designed to oversee and control procurement activities throughout the project life cycle.

The first stage in project procurement management is identifying the procurement needs and then planning for the same. During this phase, project managers or members of the purchasing department should involve key stakeholders early in the planning stage to ensure alignment on procurement objectives and constraints and document the decisions, as well as specify the procurement standards rules and regulations and identify potential sellers. This process involves conducting a thorough analysis of the project's needs, determining the resources required, and deciding whether to procure these resources internally or externally. The process also includes preparing procurement documents such as requests for proposals (RFPs) or invitations for bids (IFBs) (also called an invitation to tender [ITT]), which are then shared with potential sellers to solicit their responses. Proper planning ensures that all procurement activities align with the project's objectives and constraints.

The next stage is conducting the procurements. This step involves obtaining responses from potential sellers, evaluating these responses, selecting the most suitable seller, and awarding the contract. During this stage, it is crucial to ensure that the procurement process is transparent and fair, providing equal opportunities for all potential sellers to participate, as well as to ensure that the queries raised by bidders through requests for information (RFIs) are duly and adequately addressed. The selection of a seller should be based on predefined criteria such as cost, quality, and the seller's ability to meet the project requirements and timelines. Once a seller is selected, the contract is negotiated and finalized, outlining the terms and conditions under which the goods or services will be provided.

The final stage in the procurement process is monitoring and controlling procurements. This step involves managing procurement relationships, monitoring contract performance, and making necessary changes and corrections. Effective contract management can ensure that the seller meets their obligations and that the project receives the required goods and services on time and within budget. Any issues or discrepancies should be addressed promptly to avoid delays or additional costs. The process also includes closing out contracts once the procurement activities are completed, ensuring that all contractual obligations have been fulfilled and there are no outstanding issues. This stage is critical for ensuring the procurement process supports the overall success of the project.

X4.3 Make-or-Buy Analysis

A make-or-buy analysis is used to determine whether work or deliverables can best be accomplished by the project team or should be purchased from outside sources.

Factors to consider in the make-or-buy decision include the organization's current resource allocation, their skills and abilities, the need for specialized expertise, the desire to avoid expanding permanent employment obligations, and the need for independent expertise. This decision process also includes evaluating the risks involved with each make-or-buy decision.

Make-or-buy analysis may use payback period, return on investment (ROI), internal rate of return (IRR), discounted cash flow, net present value (NPV), cost-benefit analysis, or other techniques in order to decide whether to include something as part of the project or purchase it externally.

X4.4 Procurement Strategy

Once the make-or-buy analysis is complete and the decision is made to acquire from outside the project, a procurement strategy should be identified. The objective of the procurement strategy is to determine the project delivery method, the type of legally binding agreement(s), and how the procurement will advance through the procurement phases. The following factors should be considered:

- **Delivery methods.** Delivery methods are different for professional services versus construction projects.
- **For professional services**, delivery methods include buyer/services provider with no subcontracting, buyer/services provider with subcontracting allowed, joint venture between buyer and services provider, and buyer/services provider acts as the representative.
- **For industrial, integration, or build-out supply projects**, project delivery methods include turnkey, design-build (DB), design-bid-build (DBB), design-build-operate (DBO), build-own-operate-transfer (BOOT), and others.
- **Integrated project delivery** (IPD) contracts represent a more formalized and structured approach to collaborative project delivery. These contracts are typically used in complex construction projects where early involvement of all parties can significantly benefit the project outcome. Key characteristics of IPD contracts may include the following:
  - Multiparty agreement involving all key stakeholders (owner, designer, contractor);
  - Shared risks and rewards based on project outcomes;
  - Early involvement of key participants for better integration of expertise;
  - Collaborative decision-making leveraging the combined expertise of all parties; and
  - Open-book accounting for financial transparency.
- **Procurement phases.** The procurement strategy may also include information on procurement phases. Incorporating digital tools like procurement management software can streamline phase transitions and help ensure real-time tracking of milestones. Information on procurement phases may include the following:
  - Sequencing or phasing of the procurement, a description of each phase, and the specific objectives of each phase;
  - Procurement performance indicators and milestones to be used in monitoring;

- Criteria for moving from phase to phase;
- Monitoring and evaluation plan for tracking progress; and
- Process for knowledge transfer for use in subsequent phases.

X4.5 Bid Process and Documents

The bid process includes developing and publicizing bid documents, bidder conferences, and selecting a bidder. Bid documents may include the following:

- **Request for information (RFI).** An RFI is used to gather more information from the market prior to sending out bid documents to a set of selected vendors.
- **Request for proposal (RFP).** An RFP is used for projects with a complex or complicated scope where the buyer is looking for the vendor to provide a solution.
- **Request for quote (RFQ).** An RFQ is used when price is the main deciding factor and the proposed solution is readily available.

These three types of documents cover the majority of bidding needs. There are other bid documents; however, they tend to be industry specific.

Once the bid documents are distributed, the buyer generally has a bidder conference to respond to bidder questions and provide clarifying information. The bidders then develop their responses and deliver them to the buyer by the date specified in the bid documents.

Choosing the best vendor, sometimes known as source selection, is often based on a number of criteria, such as experience, references, price, and timely delivery. These variables may be weighted to reflect the relative importance of each. The buyer evaluates vendor bids against the criteria to select an appropriate vendor(s). The buyer and vendor then negotiate terms and conditions. Almost everything can be negotiated, from cost to delivery and payment dates, to location of work, ownership of intellectual property, and so forth. Figure X4-1 illustrates an example of how these steps might flow together.

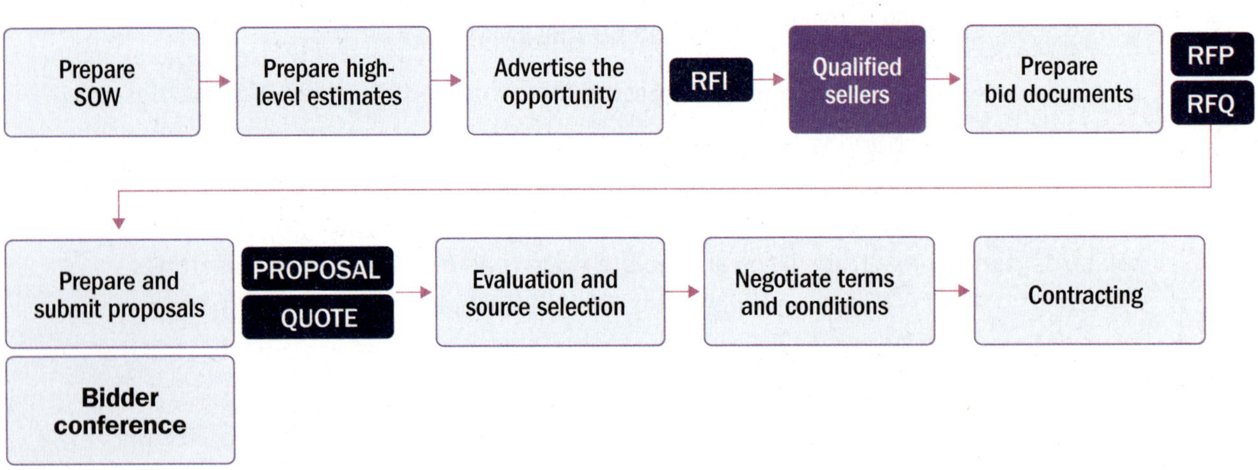

Figure X4-1. Example Procurement Process Flow

X4.6 Source Selection Analysis

It is necessary to review the prioritization of the competing demands for the project before deciding on the selection method. Since competitive selection methods may require sellers to invest a large amount of time and resources up front, it is a good practice to include the evaluation method in the tender documents so bidders know how they will be evaluated. This transparency helps infuse stakeholder trust in the selection method. Commonly used selection methods include the following:

- **Least cost.** The least cost method may be appropriate for procurements of a standard or routine nature where well-established practices and standards exist and from which a specific and well-defined outcome is expected that can be executed at different costs. In more complex procurements, least cost should be avoided as it may negatively impact quality.
- **Qualifications only.** The qualifications-only selection method applies when the time and cost of a full selection process would not make sense because the value of the procurement is relatively small. The buyer establishes a short list and selects the bidder with the strongest qualifications, expertise, and references.
- **Quality-based/highest technical proposal score.** The selected firm is asked to submit a proposal with both technical and cost details and is then invited to negotiate the contract if the technical proposal proves acceptable. Using this method, technical proposals are first evaluated based on the quality of the technical solution offered. The seller that submitted the highest ranked technical proposal is selected if their financial proposal can be negotiated and accepted.
- **Quality and cost based.** The quality-and-cost-based method allows cost to be included as a factor in the seller-selection process. In general, when risk and/or uncertainty are greater for the project, quality should be a key element when compared to cost.
- **Single source.** Single-source procurement is a formal process where only one supplier can satisfy the technical requirements due to unique technical competence and expertise. This method is used when there is only one source verified to possess patents or exclusive rights to manufacture and furnish the item or service. It is not an attempt to contract with a favored provider but is employed when no other options are available.
- **Fixed budget.** The fixed-budget method requires disclosing the available budget to invited sellers in the request and selecting the highest ranking technical proposal within the budget. Because sellers are subject to a cost constraint, they will adapt the scope and quality of their offer to that budget. The buyer should therefore ensure that the budget is compatible with the statement of work (SOW) and that the seller will be able to perform the tasks within the budget. This method is appropriate only when the SOW is precisely defined, no changes are anticipated, and the budget is fixed and cannot be exceeded.

X4.7 Source Selection Criteria

In choosing evaluation criteria, the buyer seeks to ensure that the proposal selected will offer the best quality for the services required. The source selection criteria may include but are not limited to the following:

- Capability and capacity;
- Product cost and life cycle cost;

- Delivery dates;
- Regulatory, compliance, or industry standards expertise or experience;
- Technical expertise and approach;
- Specific relevant experience;
- Adequacy of the proposed approach and work plan in responding to the SOW;
- Key team members' qualifications, availability, and competences;
- Financial stability of the firm;
- Management experience;
- Suitability of the knowledge transfer program, including training; and
- Sustainability credentials of the supplier.

For international projects, evaluation criteria may include "local content" requirements (e.g., participation by nationals among proposed key team members). This approach provides a more relevant cultural understanding.

The specific criteria may be a numerical score, color code, or a written description of how well the seller satisfies the buying organization's needs. The criteria will be part of a weighting system that can be used to select a single seller that will be asked to sign a contract and establish a negotiating sequence by ranking all the proposals by the weighted evaluation scores assigned to each proposal.

X4.8 Contract Type

Understanding various contract types is crucial for project managers, as it directly impacts project risk allocation, collaboration dynamics, and overall project success. Contract types define the terms and conditions under which goods, services, or results are acquired from external sources. Contract types establish the framework for financial arrangements, risk distribution, and the nature of relationships among project stakeholders.

Project managers should approach contract types from a dual perspective: as both a contractor and a client/customer. This dual viewpoint is essential because projects often involve both roles—contracting vendors as a customer and being contracted by clients. The project manager should consider both of these vantage points in order to successfully support effective procurement.

Each contract type has its advantages and disadvantages, and there are potential ways to exploit contractual terms. However, the goal should always be to structure contracts in a way that benefits all parties, creating a win-win scenario that fosters collaboration and project success.

In this appendix, we will explore two main categories of contract types: established contract models and collaborative contract models. By understanding these contract types and their implications, project managers can make informed decisions when selecting or negotiating contracts, balancing risk allocation, incentivizing performance, and creating collaborative environments that contribute to project success.

X4.8.1 Fundamental Contract Models

Some of the more common contract models and how they can be viewed from both the client and contractor perspectives are as follows (Please note that the types and names of contract types can vary in different industries and organizations.):

- **Fixed-price contract.** Fixed-price contracts are agreements that establish a predetermined fee against a clearly defined scope of work, transferring cost risk to the seller while offering budget predictability for the buyer. Fixed-price contracts are common in construction projects, product development, and service delivery where the work can be accurately estimated.
  - **Client perspective:** Provides budget certainty but may result in higher prices due to risk premiums.
  - **Contractor perspective:** Offers profit potential if managed efficiently but bears the risk of cost overruns.
- **Cost-reimbursable contract.** Cost-reimbursable contracts are a type of contract involving payment to the seller for the seller's actual costs, plus a fee typically representing the seller's profit. These contracts are used when the project scope is uncertain or when the project is high risk. Cost-reimbursable contracts are common in research and development projects, complex construction projects, and situations where flexibility is needed.
  - **Client perspective:** Allows for flexibility but carries the risk of cost escalation.
  - **Contractor perspective:** Reduces financial risk but may limit profit potential.
- **Time and materials (T&M) contract.** T&M contracts are a type of contract that is a hybrid contractual arrangement containing aspects of both cost-reimbursable and fixed-price contracts. The buyer typically pays for actual time and materials used plus a profit margin. These contracts are often used for smaller projects, maintenance work, or when the scope is not clearly defined at the outset. T&M contracts are common in technology services, consulting, and some construction projects.
  - **Client perspective:** Provides flexibility but requires close monitoring to control costs.
  - **Contractor perspective:** Ensures cost coverage but may lead to scrutiny of time and resource usage.
- **Target-cost contract.** Target-cost contracts set a target cost, with provisions for sharing cost savings or overruns between the buyer and seller. These contracts are used to encourage efficiency and cost control while maintaining flexibility. Target-cost contracts are often seen in large infrastructure projects or complex manufacturing projects.
  - **Client perspective:** Encourages cost control but requires clear definition of target costs and sharing mechanisms.
  - **Contractor perspective:** Offers incentives for efficiency but bears partial risk of cost overruns.

Moreover, there can be several hybrid contracts depending on the project requirements, which may incorporate elements of both fixed-price and cost-reimbursable models or other provisions for flexibility.

X4.8.2 Emerging Trends in Contract Management

While the fundamental contract types (fixed-price, cost-reimbursable, and T&M contracts) remain the foundation of project procurement, several emerging trends, driven by advancements in AI and automation, are reshaping how these contracts are structured, executed, and managed. AI-powered contract analysis tools now enable more accurate risk assessments, faster negotiation processes, and better compliance monitoring. Additionally, machine learning algorithms help predict cost overruns and optimize contract terms by analyzing historical project data. As AI continues to evolve, it is enhancing decision-making, improving contract performance tracking, and enabling more dynamic and adaptive contract management practices. Some of the emerging practices include the following:

- **Agile contracting.** Agile contracting is the application of agile principles to fundamental contract types, focusing on flexibility, iterative delivery, and continuous collaboration (e.g., a T&M contract with iteration-based deliverables).
- **Smart contracts.** Smart contracts consist of the integration of blockchain technology with traditional contract structures and the automated execution of contract items. Smart contracts enhance transparency and reduce intermediaries. This contract type is usually implemented in milestone-based payments.
- **Outcome-based contracts.** Outcome-based contracts are a shift from input-based pricing models. This contract type is applicable to fixed-price and cost-reimbursable contracts and focuses on measurable results rather than prescribed processes.
- **Sustainable contracting.** Sustainable contracting is the practice of embedding environmental, social, and governance (ESG) principles into contractual agreements to promote measurable sustainability outcomes, ensuring alignment with broader organizational goals and societal expectations.
- **Collaborative contracting.** Collaborative contracts use an enhanced risk-sharing or reward-sharing mechanism within fundamental contract types. This type of contract focuses on joint problem-solving and shared objectives (e.g., including a cap on a T&M contract, a reduced rate, or performance incentives).

As project environments continue to evolve, so should the approaches to contract management. These emerging trends demonstrate how traditional contracts are being adapted to meet the demands of modern projects, incorporating technological advancements, sustainability concerns, and collaborative methodologies. By understanding these emerging practices, project managers can enhance contract flexibility, improve risk management, and foster stronger collaborative relationships with vendors and stakeholders, ultimately contributing to successful project outcomes.

X4.9 Claims Administration

Claims and disputes are common in project management, occurring across various industries and project types with differing frequency and impact. In construction projects, disputes can significantly affect finances, with direct costs ranging from 0.5% to 5% of the total contract value. Time and cost overruns, often caused by variation orders, are among the primary factors leading to disputable claims.

As projects grow in complexity and involve more stakeholders, the likelihood of disputes increases. Therefore, it is essential for project managers to be proficient in claims administration and familiar with alternative dispute resolution (ADR) methods. Types of ADR include the following:

- **Negotiation.** Negotiation involves direct discussions between parties to resolve disputes without third-party intervention.
- **Mediation.** Mediation brings in a neutral third party to facilitate discussions between disputing parties to reach a mutually acceptable solution.
- **Arbitration.** Arbitration is a more formal process where an arbitrator or panel hears both sides and makes a binding decision.
- **Dispute review boards.** A dispute review board is a panel of neutral experts appointed at the start of a project to provide ongoing dispute avoidance and resolution.
- **Expert determination.** Expert determination is when an independent expert is appointed to make a decision on a specific technical or financial issue.
- **Litigation.** If all other means are exhausted but the disagreement between the stakeholders persists, litigation becomes the last option, where the dispute is referred to a court to be resolved.

X4.9.1 Relevance to Project Managers

Project managers play a crucial role in claims administration and dispute resolution. Project professionals should understand contract terms thoroughly to identify potential areas of dispute and manage risks proactively. Project managers should maintain detailed records of all project activities, changes, and communications to support potential claims. They should also foster open and clear communication among all stakeholders to help minimize misunderstandings that could lead to disputes. Recognizing potential conflicts early and addressing them promptly to prevent escalation are critical aspects of a project professional's job.

To effectively handle claims and disputes, project managers should seek to improve their negotiation and conflict-resolution skills, as this is likely to be the first engagement in a dispute or claim. In addition, some form of legal training or introduction to contract law and claims management during the early stages of a project is beneficial.

AI-powered tools can also play a crucial role by analyzing contract terms, identifying potential areas of dispute, and offering predictive insights into the likelihood of claims. Project managers can leverage AI to assess the risks associated with specific clauses and use data-driven insights to guide negotiations.

Establishing a strong working relationship with the organization's legal team for guidance and support is essential. Additionally, AI can enhance this collaboration by providing real-time contract analytics, tracking potential risks, and recommending proactive measures to resolve issues before they escalate.

X4.9.2 Sensitivity of Legal Actions and Upholding Ethics Codes

Project managers should be acutely aware of the sensitivity surrounding legal actions and the potential impact on project relationships. Key considerations include the following:

- **Nuanced communication.** Be mindful of the language used in all written communications, including emails, as these can be used as evidence in legal proceedings.
- **Escalation protocols.** Establish clear protocols for when and how to escalate disputes to legal action, considering the potential long-term consequences on stakeholder relationships.
- **Confidentiality.** Maintain strict confidentiality regarding dispute details to protect all parties involved and comply with legal requirements.
- **Impartiality.** Strive to remain objective and impartial when dealing with claims, focusing on facts rather than emotions or personal relationships.

By understanding the intricacies of claims administration and ADR, project managers can navigate these challenging aspects of project management more effectively, minimizing the negative impact on project outcomes and stakeholder relationships.

Appendix X5
Evolution of the *PMBOK® Guide*

Since its inception as the Project Management Body of Knowledge (PMBOK) in 1987, *A Guide to the Project Management Body of Knowledge (PMBOK® Guide)* has evolved while recognizing that fundamental elements of project management endure. Its evolution has captured significant and substantive changes in the nature of the content. A sampling of some of those key changes is reflected in Table X5-1.

X5.1 Evidence-Based

In preparation for development work of the eighth edition, PMI actively engaged in a multiphased research effort, engaging with stakeholders on a global level. PMI also partnered with a third-party consulting firm to guide research and ensure the study was free from organizational bias.

- **Phase 1—Qualitative.** This phase consisted of live, chat-based discussions over 2 days with a mix of project managers, including representatives from seven different countries. This phase enabled the discovery of themes and identified market needs for further validation. Participants were required to have familiarity with the seventh edition and at least one prior edition.
- **Phase 2—Quantitative.** In Phase 2, it was critical to validate and quantify hypotheses from Phase 1 on a global level. An online survey was sent to approximately 64,000 professionals who downloaded the seventh edition, with a response rate of just over 3,400 completions. Representation included a population across all PMI regions, a mix of early-, mid-, and late-career stages, with both Project Management Professional (PMP)® certification holders and non-PMP practitioners.
- **Phase 3—Draft feedback.** A team of 25 volunteers used the evidence from Phases 1 and 2 to iterate toward a full draft. PMI broadcast that draft to the community and yielded nearly 9,000 comments and suggestions. The feedback reinforced which elements were strong and which needed refinement.
- **Phase 4—ANSI review.** The core development team leveraged the feedback to refine a final draft, which was submitted to ANSI for formal review. That review resulted in approximately 3,900 additional practitioner comments, further validating the product.

Table X5-1. Evolutionary Changes of the *PMBOK® Guide*

***PMBOK®* *Guide* Edition**	**Key Evolutionary Changes**
1996	• Distinguished as "a guide to the body of knowledge," rather than the body of knowledge for project management. • Reflected the subset of the project management body of knowledge that is "generally accepted," meaning applicable to most projects most of the time, with widespread consensus that practices have value and usefulness. • Defined project management as "the application of knowledge, skills, tools, and techniques to project activities in order to meet or exceed stakeholder needs and expectations from a project." • Specific decision to shift to a process-based standard driven by a desire to show interactions among Knowledge Areas; create a robust and flexible structure; and recognize that International Organization for Standardization (ISO) and other standards organizations were establishing process-based standards.
Third (2004)	• First edition to incorporate the American National Standards Institute (ANSI) "ANSI standard" logo on the cover. • First edition to formally designate *The Standard for Project Management of a Project* separate and distinct from the Project Management Framework and Body of Knowledge. • Included material "generally recognized as good practice on most projects most of the time." • Defined project management as "the application of knowledge, skills, tools, and techniques to project activities to meet the project requirements."
Sixth (2017)	• First edition to make a distinct separation between the ANSI standard and the guide. • First time "agile" content is incorporated into the text, not just referenced in examples. • Expansion of Knowledge Area front material, including key concepts, trends and emerging practices, tailoring considerations, and considerations for agile/adaptive environments.
Seventh (2021)	• First edition in which project management is characterized as a "system for value delivery," with an attendant shift in focus toward a more holistic, value-oriented mindset, and less emphasis on project management mechanics. • First edition in which project management principles were elaborated. • Agile thinking and methods became more fully integrated compared to the sixth edition. • Shift from a process-based guide to a principles-based ANSI standard. • Shift from Knowledge Areas focused on processes to performance domains focused on results.

X5.2 Changes in the Eighth Edition

The results of market discovery offered clear and definitive findings that informed the content plan of the eighth edition. Key findings included the following:

- **Simplify the principles.** A significant number of respondents—88%—supported a principle-based standard, emphasizing the importance of project management principles. However, respondents also said principles should be more actionable and less confusing. Specifically, principles should have connection with performance domains while not overlapping. For example, a specific topic, such as engaging stakeholders, should not be formalized as both a principle and a performance domain.
- **Reintroduce Process Groups as Focus Areas.** A majority—80% of respondents—supported the reintroduction and refinement of Process Groups as foundational concepts within *The Standard for Project Management*. A full two-thirds of respondents also indicated these five historically accepted concepts are agnostic of development approach (e.g., adaptive, predictive, or hybrid). This edition reintroduces Initiating, Planning, Executing, Monitoring and Controlling, and Closing as Project Management Focus Areas, which can be performed via formal processes, informal practices, or policies. This approach was further validated by community feedback received through public exposure comment periods.
- **Reintroduce processes.** Again, 79% of respondents recommended that technical ways of working and processes should be directly integrated into the *PMBOK® Guide*. While noting that not all processes apply to every project all of the time, the market asserted process control theory to be considerably helpful in the practice of project management. Therefore, this edition offers 40 nonprescriptive processes that are fully embedded within the project management performance domains. When tailoring a project with a focus on delivering positive outcomes, these processes may be used as a reference as needed.

X5.3 Sources for the Eighth Edition

To implement the community direction for this eighth edition, the volunteer development team referenced a broad range of resources, ranging from academic literature to multiple PMI standards and practice guides.

Of all the sources, the *PMBOK® Guide*—Seventh Edition (2021) and *Process Groups: A Practice Guide* (2022) served as the primary reference points for historical project management concepts. Figure X5-1 illustrates the migration and synthesis of content from those primary sources to the *PMBOK® Guide*—Eighth Edition. A full list of the sources used in the creation of this edition can be found in the bibliography.

X5.4 Refinement of Project Management Principles

Market research and community input emphasized the importance of a principle-based standard for project management, as presented in the *PMBOK® Guide*—Seventh Edition. However, key improvements were recommended for consideration in this eighth edition, specifically the following:

- **Principles should be more actionable.** Although respondents overwhelmingly agreed that principles serve as universal drivers of project success, practitioners also requested more

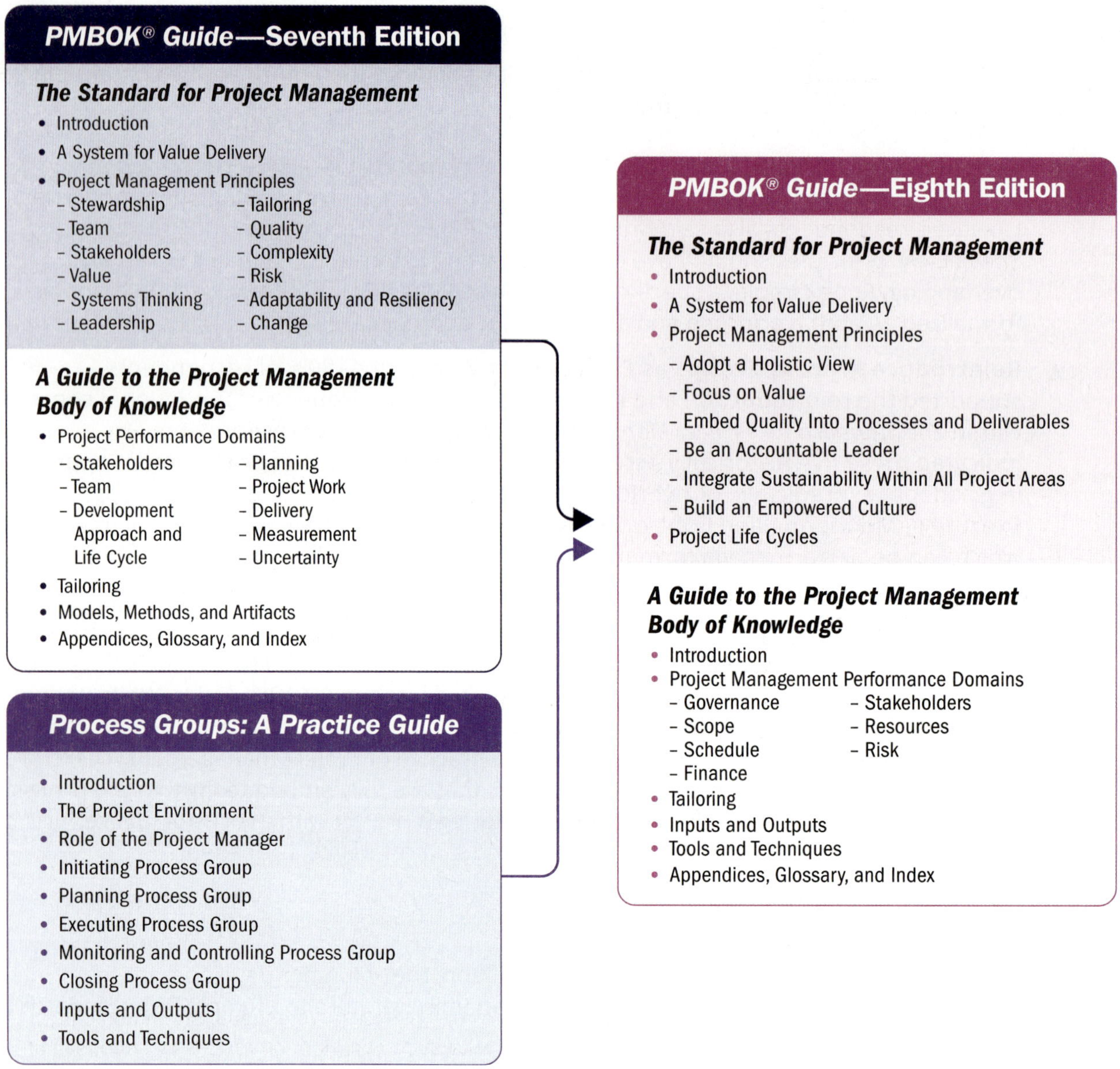

Figure X5-1. *PMBOK® Guide*—Eighth Edition Content Migration

guidance on how the principles should be manifested in practice. This edition includes both the implications for each project management performance domain, as well as multiple concrete examples showing "principles in action" for each of the principles.

- **Principles should be more focused.** The inaugural listing of principles covered concepts also presented in other sections of the seventh edition. For example, stakeholders were emphasized in both a principle and a performance domain, and tailoring was presented as both a principle and a dedicated section of the guide. This eighth edition undertook a systematic review of project management principles to minimize overlap. Table X5-2 lists the rationalization of the project management principles from the seventh edition to the eighth edition.

Table X5-2. Refinement of Project Management Principles

Seventh Edition Principles	Eighth Edition Location	Rationale
3.9 Navigate Complexity	Merged Principle: Adopt a Holistic View	The interactions of a project's organizations, stakeholders, and geographies represent a complex system. Success requires practitioners to "zoom out" to see the related constraints and changes.
3.5 Recognize, Evaluate, and Respond to System Interactions		
3.3 Effectively Engage With Stakeholders	Merged Principle: Focus on Value + Stakeholders Project Management Performance Domain	Value is the fundamental driver of projects. Value exists only when stakeholders are understood and then guided through the change the project experiences and fosters. Deeper discussion of stakeholder engagement is emphasized as a project management performance domain.
3.4 Focus on Value		
3.11 Embrace Adaptability and Resiliency		
3.12 Enable Change to Achieve the Envisioned Future State		
3.8 Build Quality Into Processes and Deliverables	Refined Principle: Embed Quality Into Processes and Deliverables	Quality is a dimension that spans both outputs described in performance domains and outcomes.
3.2 Create a Collaborative Project Team	Refined Principle: Build an Empowered Culture	Building an empowered culture involves the project team environment and effective collaboration with all stakeholders.
3.6 Demonstrate Leadership Behaviors	Merged Into Principle: Be an Accountable Leader	Clarify which leadership behaviors drive project success. Intentional stewardship is one such behavior and relates to professional accountability.
3.1 Be a Diligent, Respectful, and Caring Steward		
3.7 Tailor Based on Context	Migrated to Tailoring Section	While tailoring is a key concept for project success, practitioners prefer it to be discussed through concrete management mechanics and examples.
3.10 Optimize Risk Responses	Migrated to Risk Project Management Performance Domain	While managing potential threats and opportunities is core to project success, practitioners prefer it to be discussed through concrete mechanics, in relationship to other principles and performance domains.

References

[1] Project Management Institute (PMI). (2025). *The Standard for Project Management.* PMI.

[2] Project Management Institute (PMI). (2024). *Business Analysis for Practitioners: A Practice Guide*—Second edition. PMI.

[3] Project Management Institute (PMI). (2019). *The Standard for Earned Value Management.* PMI.

[4] Project Management Institute (PMI). (2019). *Practice Standard for Work Breakdown Structures*—Third edition. PMI.

[5] Project Management Institute (PMI). (2019). *Practice Standard for Scheduling*—Third edition. PMI.

Bibliography

Devaux, S. A. (2014). *Managing Projects as Investments: Earned Value to Business Value*. CRC Press.

Project Management Institute (PMI). (2014). *Navigating Complexity: A Practice Guide*. PMI.

Project Management Institute (PMI). (2017). *Agile Practice Guide*. PMI.

Project Management Institute (PMI). (2017). *The Standard for Portfolio Management*—Fourth edition. PMI.

Project Management Institute (PMI). (2018). *The PMI Guide to Business Analysis*. PMI.

Project Management Institute (PMI). (2020). *The Standard for Earned Value Management*. PMI.

Project Management Institute (PMI). (2022). *Process Groups: A Practice Guide*. PMI.

Project Management Institute (PMI). (2024). *AI Essentials for Project Professionals*. PMI.

Project Management Institute (PMI). (2024). *Business Analysis for Practitioners: A Practice Guide*—Second edition. PMI.

Project Management Institute (PMI). (2024). *The Standard for Program Management*—Fifth edition. PMI.

Project Management Institute (PMI). (2025). *Project Management Offices: A Practice Guide*. PMI.

Glossary

Many of the words defined here have broader, and in some cases, different dictionary definitions. In some cases, a single glossary term consists of multiple words (e.g., root cause analysis).

Note: Many terms are fully defined in Section 4, Inputs and Outputs, and Section 5, Tools and Techniques. This glossary is designed to provide definitions for additional terms that are not covered in those sections.

acceptance criteria. A set of conditions that are met before deliverables are accepted. See also *requirement*.

accuracy. Within the quality management system, accuracy is an assessment of correctness.

actual cost (AC). The realized cost incurred for the work performed on an activity during a specific time period. See also *budget at completion (BAC), earned value (EV), estimate at completion (EAC), estimate to complete (ETC),* and *planned value (PV)*.

adaptive approach. A development approach in which the requirements are subject to a high level of uncertainty and volatility and are likely to change throughout the project.

agile. A term used to describe a mindset of values and principles as set forth in the *Manifesto for Agile Software Development*.

ambiguity. A state of being unclear, having difficulty in identifying the cause of events, or having multiple options from which to choose.

artifact. A document or other item created during a portfolio, program, or project to help manage it and provide information to the project team, stakeholders, and management.

assumption. A factor in the planning process considered to be true, real, or certain, without proof or demonstration.

authority. The right to apply project resources, expend funds, make decisions, or give approvals.

baseline. The approved version of a work product that can be changed using formal change control procedures and is used as the basis for comparison to actual results.

benefit. A gain or asset realized by the organization and other stakeholders as the result of outcomes delivered.

bid documents. All documents used to solicit information, quotations, or proposals from prospective sellers.

bidder conference. Meetings with prospective sellers prior to the preparation of a bid or proposal to ensure all prospective vendors have a clear and common understanding of the procurement. Also known as contractor conferences, vendor conferences, or pre-bid conferences.

blocker. See *impediment*.

budget. The approved estimate for the portfolio, program, or project, or any work breakdown structure component or schedule activity.

budget at completion (BAC). The sum of all budgets established for the work to be performed. See also *actual cost (AC), earned value (EV), estimate at completion (EAC), estimate to complete (ETC),* and *planned value (PV)*.

burn chart. A graphical representation of the work remaining in a timebox or the work completed toward the release of a product or project deliverable.

business value. The net quantifiable benefit derived from a business endeavor that may be tangible, intangible, or both.

cadence. A rhythm of activities conducted throughout the project.

change. A modification to any formally controlled deliverable, project management plan component, or project document.

change control. A process whereby modifications to documents, deliverables, or baselines associated with the project are identified, documented, approved, or rejected. See also *change control board (CCB)*.

change control board (CCB). A formally chartered group responsible for reviewing, evaluating, approving, delaying, or rejecting changes to the project, and for recording and communicating such decisions. See also *change control*.

change management. A comprehensive, cyclic, and structured approach for transitioning individuals, groups, and organizations from a current state to a future state with intended business benefits.

Closing Focus Area. Processes performed to formally complete or close a project, phase, contract, or in some cases, to terminate a project before completion.

complexity. A characteristic of a program or project or its environment that is difficult to manage due to human behavior, system behavior, and ambiguity.

confirmation bias. A type of cognitive bias that confirms preexisting beliefs or hypotheses.

conformance. The degree to which the results meet the set quality requirements.

constraint. A limiting factor that affects the execution of a portfolio, program, project, or process.

contingency. An event or occurrence that could affect the execution of the project, which may be accounted for with a reserve.

contingency reserve. Time or money allocated in the schedule or cost baseline for known risks with active response strategies. See also *management reserve*.

continuous delivery. The practice of delivering feature increments immediately to customers, often through the use of small batches of work and automation technology.

contract. A mutually binding agreement that obligates the seller to provide the specified product, service, or result and obligates the buyer to pay for it.

control. The process of comparing actual performance with planned performance, analyzing variances, assessing trends to effect process improvements, evaluating possible alternatives, and recommending appropriate corrective action as needed.

cost performance index (CPI). A measure of the cost efficiency of budgeted resources expressed as the ratio of earned value to actual cost. See also *schedule performance index (SPI).*

cost-reimbursable contract. A type of contract involving payment to the seller for the seller's actual costs, plus a fee typically representing the seller's profit.

cost variance (CV). The amount of budget deficit or surplus at a given point in time, expressed as the difference between the earned value and the actual cost. See also *schedule variance (SV).*

crashing. A schedule compression technique used to shorten the schedule duration for the least incremental cost by adding resources. See also *fast tracking*.

criteria. Standards, rules, or tests on which a judgment or decision can be based or by which a product, service, result, or process can be evaluated.

critical path. The sequence of activities that represents the longest path through a project, which determines the shortest possible duration.

cumulative flow diagram. A chart indicating features completed over time, features in other states of development, and those in the backlog.

dashboard. A set of charts and graphs showing progress or performance against important measures of the project.

definition of done (DoD). A checklist of all the criteria required to be met so that a deliverable can be considered ready for customer use.

duration. The total number of work periods required to complete an activity or work breakdown structure component, expressed in hours, days, or weeks. See also *effort*.

earned value (EV). The measure of work performed expressed in terms of the budget authorized for that work. See also *actual cost (AC), budget at completion (BAC), estimate at completion (EAC), estimate to complete (ETC),* and *planned value (PV).*

effort. The number of labor units required to complete a schedule activity or work breakdown structure component, often expressed in hours, days, or weeks. See also *duration*.

epic. A large, related body of work intended to hierarchically organize a set of requirements and deliver specific business outcomes.

estimate. A quantitative assessment of the likely amount or outcome of a variable, such as project costs, resources, effort, or durations.

estimate at completion (EAC). The expected total cost of completing all work expressed as the sum of the actual cost to date and the estimate to complete. See also *actual cost (AC), budget at completion (BAC), earned value (EV), estimate to complete (ETC),* and *planned value (PV).*

estimate to complete (ETC). The expected cost to finish all the remaining project work. See also *actual cost (AC), budget at completion (BAC), earned value (EV), estimate at completion (EAC),* and *planned value (PV).*

Executing Focus Area. Consists of those processes performed to complete the work in a manner consistent with the integrated baseline, which can and should be changed whenever such a change would enhance the value proposition of the project.

expected monetary value (EMV). The estimated value of an outcome expressed in monetary terms.

explicit knowledge. Knowledge that can be codified using symbols such as words, numbers, and pictures.

external dependencies. Relationships between project activities and non-project activities.

fast tracking. A schedule compression technique in which activities or phases normally done in sequence are performed in parallel for at least a portion of their duration. See also *crashing*.

feature. A set of related requirements or functionalities that provides value to an organization.

fixed-price contract. An agreement that sets the fee that will be paid for a defined scope of work regardless of the cost or effort to deliver it.

flow. The measure of how efficiently work moves through a given process or framework.

forecast. An estimate or prediction of conditions and events in the project's future based on information and knowledge available at the time of the forecast.

function point. An estimate of the amount of business functionality in an information system, used to calculate the functional size measurement of a software system.

Gantt chart. A bar chart of schedule information where activities are listed on the vertical axis, dates are shown on the horizontal axis, and activity durations are shown as horizontal bars placed according to start and finish dates.

governance. The framework for directing and enabling an organization through its established policies, practices, and other relevant documentation.

histogram. A bar chart that shows the graphical representation of numerical data.

hybrid approach. A combination of elements from both adaptive and predictive approaches that is useful when there is uncertainty or risk around the requirements.

impediment. An obstacle that prevents the team from achieving its objectives. Also known as a *blocker*.

incremental approach. An adaptive development approach in which the deliverable is produced successively, adding functionality until the deliverable contains the necessary and sufficient capability to be considered complete.

Initiating Focus Area. Those processes performed to define a new project or new phase of an existing project by obtaining authorization to start the project or phase.

internal dependencies. Relationships between two or more project activities.

issue. A current condition or situation that may have an impact on one or more objectives. See also *opportunity, risk,* and *threat*.

iteration. A short cycle of development during which a product or deliverable is released or further matured. See also *sprint*.

iteration plan. A detailed plan for the current iteration.

iteration planning. A meeting to clarify the details of the backlog items, acceptance criteria, and work effort required to meet an upcoming iteration commitment.

iteration review. A meeting held at the end of an iteration to demonstrate the work that was accomplished during the iteration.

iterative approach. A development approach that focuses on an initial, simplified implementation then progressively elaborates, adding to the feature set until the final deliverable is complete.

kanban board. A visualization tool that shows work in progress to help identify bottlenecks and overcommitments, thereby allowing the team to optimize the workflow. See also *task board*.

knowledge. A mixture of experience, values and beliefs, contextual information, intuition, and insight that people use to make sense of new experiences and information.

lessons learned. The knowledge gained during a project that shows how project events were addressed or should be addressed in the future for the purpose of improving future performance.

life cycle. See *project life cycle*.

log. A document used to record and describe or denote selected items identified during execution of a process or activity. Usually used with a modifier, such as issue, change, or assumption.

management reserve. Time or money that management sets aside in addition to the schedule or cost baseline and releases for unforeseen work that is within the scope of the portfolio, program, or project. See also *contingency reserve*.

mandatory dependency. A relationship that is contractually required or inherent in the nature of the work.

method. A means for achieving an outcome, output, result, or project deliverable.

methodology. A system of practices, techniques, procedures, and rules used by those who work in a discipline.

metric. A description of a project or product attribute and how to measure it.

milestone. A significant point or event in a portfolio, program, or project.

milestone schedule. A type of schedule that presents milestones with planned dates.

minimum viable product (MVP). A concept used to define the scope of the first release of a solution to customers by identifying the fewest number of features or requirements that would deliver value.

modeling. Creating simplified representations of systems, solutions, or deliverables such as prototypes, diagrams, or storyboards.

monitoring. Collecting project performance data, producing performance measures, and reporting and disseminating performance information.

Monitoring and Controlling Focus Area. Those processes required to track, review, and regulate the progress and performance of the project; identify any areas in which changes to the plan are required; and initiate the corresponding changes.

Monte Carlo analysis/simulation. A method of identifying the potential impacts of risk and uncertainty using multiple iterations of a computer model to develop a probability distribution of a range of outcomes that could result from a decision or course of action.

Net Promoter Score℠.[1] An index that measures the willingness of customers to recommend an organization's products or services to others.

[1] Net Promoter®, NPS®, NPS Prism®, and the NPS-related emoticons are registered trademarks of Bain & Company, Inc., NICE Systems, Inc., and Fred Reichheld. Net Promoter Score℠ and Net Promoter System℠ are service marks of Bain & Company, Inc., NICE Systems, Inc., and Fred Reichheld.

network path. A sequence of activities connected by logical relationships in a project schedule network diagram.

objective. Something toward which work is to be directed—a strategic position to be attained, a purpose to be achieved, a result to be obtained, a product to be produced, or a service to be performed.

opportunity. A risk that would have a positive effect on one or more portfolio, program, or project objectives. See also *issue*, *risk,* and *threat*.

organizational breakdown structure. A hierarchical representation of the project organization that illustrates the relationship between project activities and the organizational units that will perform those activities.

outcome. An end result or consequence of a process or project.

performance measurement. Measures that characterize physical or functional attributes relating to system operation.

phase gate. A review at the end of a phase in which a decision is made to continue to the next phase, to continue with modification, or to end a program or project. See also *project phase*.

plan. A proposed means of accomplishing something.

planned value (PV). The authorized budget assigned to scheduled work. See also *actual cost (AC), budget at completion (BAC), earned value (EV), estimate at completion (EAC),* and *estimate to complete (ETC)*.

Planning Focus Area. Those processes that establish the total scope of the effort, define and refine the objectives, and develop the course of action required to attain those objectives.

portfolio. A collection of programs, projects, and operations managed as a group to maximize overall value delivery and achieve strategic objectives, meet mandatory obligations, or generate income streams. See also *program* and *project*.

portfolio management. The centralized management of one or more portfolios to achieve strategic objectives. See also *program management* and *project management*.

precision. Within the quality management system, precision is an assessment of exactness.

predictive approach. A development approach in which the project scope, time, and cost are determined in the early phases of the life cycle.

prioritization matrix. A scatter diagram that plots effort against value so as to classify items by priority.

product. An artifact that is produced, is quantifiable, and can be either an end item in itself or a component item.

product life cycle. A series of phases that represent the evolution of a product, from concept through delivery, growth, maturity, and to retirement. See also *project life cycle*.

product management. The integration of people, data, processes, and business systems to create, maintain, and evolve a product or service throughout its life cycle.

product owner. A person responsible for maximizing the value of the product and is accountable for the end product.

product scope. The features and functions that characterize a product, service, or result. See also *project scope* and *scope*.

program. A group of related projects and program activities managed in a coordinated manner to obtain benefits not available from managing them individually. See also *portfolio* and *project*.

program management. The application of knowledge, skills, and principles to a program to achieve the program objectives and to obtain benefits and control not available by managing program components individually. See also *portfolio management* and *project management*.

progressive elaboration. The iterative process of increasing the level of detail in a project management plan as greater amounts of information and more accurate estimates become available.

project. A temporary initiative in a unique context undertaken to create value. See also *portfolio* and *program*.

project calendar. A calendar that identifies working days and shifts that are available for scheduled activities.

project governance. The framework, functions, and processes that guide project management activities in order to meet or exceed target project objectives.

project lead. A person who helps the project team to achieve the project objectives, typically by orchestrating the work of the project. See also *project manager*.

project life cycle. The series of phases that a project passes through from its start to its completion. See also *product life cycle*.

project management. The application of knowledge, skills, tools, and techniques to project activities to meet or exceed the intended value. See also *portfolio management* and *program management*.

project management body of knowledge (PMBOK). A term that describes the knowledge within the profession of project management.

Project Management Focus Areas. A logical grouping of project management inputs, tools and techniques, and outputs. The Project Management Focus Areas include Initiating processes, Planning processes, Executing processes, Monitoring and Controlling processes, and Closing processes.

project management office (PMO). Organizational entities, typically established as departments or teams, primarily tasked with centralizing activities related to the management of portfolios, programs, and/or projects. The nature of these activities can vary according to the unique needs of each organization.

project management team. The members of the project team who are directly involved in project management activities.

project manager. The person assigned by the performing organization to lead the team that is responsible for achieving the project objectives. See also *project lead*.

project phase. A collection of logically related project activities that culminates in the completion of one or more deliverables. See also *phase gate*.

project review. An event at the end of a phase or project to assess the status, evaluate the value delivered, and determine if the project is ready to move to the next phase or transition to operations.

project scope. The work performed to deliver a product, service, or result with the specified features and functions. See also *product scope* and *scope*.

project sponsor. See *sponsor*.

project success. The consensus view across intended beneficiaries, other stakeholders, and project participants that a project was perceived to have delivered value that was worth the effort and expense.

project team. A set of individuals performing the work of the project to achieve its objectives.

prototype. A working model used to obtain early feedback on the expected product before actually building it.

quality. The degree to which a set of inherent characteristics of a project deliverable helps to meet or exceed the project's target objectives.

register. A written record of regular entries for evolving aspects of a project, such as risks, stakeholders, or defects.

regulations. Requirements imposed by a governmental body. These requirements can establish product, process, or service characteristics, including applicable administrative provisions that have government-mandated compliance.

release. One or more components of one or more products, which are intended to be put into production at the same time.

release planning. The process of identifying a high-level plan for releasing or transitioning a product, deliverable, or increment of value.

report. A formal record or summary of information.

requirement. A condition or capability that is necessary to be present in a product, service, or result to satisfy a business need.

reserve. A provision in the project management plan to mitigate cost and/or schedule risk, often used with a modifier (e.g., management reserve, contingency reserve) to provide further detail on what types of risk are meant to be mitigated.

responsibility. An assignment that can be delegated within a portfolio, program, or project management plan such that the assigned resource incurs a duty to perform the requirements of the assignment.

result. An output from performing project management processes and activities.

rework. Action taken to bring a defective or nonconforming component into compliance with requirements or specifications.

risk. An uncertain event or condition that, if it occurs, has a positive or negative effect on one or more portfolio, program, or project objectives. See also *issue*, *opportunity*, and *threat*.

risk acceptance. A risk response strategy that involves acknowledging the risk and taking no action unless it occurs. Acceptance of the risk's implication(s) usually means using schedule and/or cost reserves and accepting scope and/or quality reduction(s). See also *risk avoidance, risk enhancement, risk escalation, risk exploiting, risk mitigation, risk sharing,* and *risk transference*.

risk appetite. The degree of uncertainty an organization or individual is willing to accept in anticipation of a reward. See also *risk threshold*.

risk avoidance. A risk response strategy that involves eliminating the threat or protecting the portfolio, program, or project from its impact. See also *risk acceptance, risk enhancement, risk escalation, risk exploiting, risk mitigation, risk sharing,* and *risk transference*.

risk breakdown structure (RBS). A hierarchical representation of potential sources of risks.

risk enhancement. A risk response strategy that involves increasing the probability of occurrence or impact of an opportunity. See also *risk acceptance, risk avoidance, risk escalation, risk exploiting, risk mitigation, risk sharing,* and *risk transference*.

risk escalation. A risk response strategy that involves transferring the ownership of the risk to a relevant party in the organization because the risk is outside of scope or the team does not have sufficient authority to address it. See also *risk acceptance, risk avoidance, risk enhancement, risk exploiting, risk mitigation, risk sharing,* and *risk transference*.

risk exploiting. A risk response strategy whereby the project team acts to ensure that an opportunity occurs. See also *risk acceptance, risk avoidance, risk enhancement, risk escalation, risk mitigation, risk sharing,* and *risk transference*.

risk exposure. An aggregate measure of the potential impact of all risks at any given point in time in a portfolio, program, or project.

risk mitigation. A risk response strategy that involves decreasing the probability of occurrence or impact of a threat. See also *risk acceptance, risk avoidance, risk enhancement, risk escalation, risk exploiting, risk sharing,* and *risk transference*.

risk review. The process of analyzing the status of existing risks and identifying new risks. May also be known as a risk reassessment.

risk sharing. A risk response strategy that involves allocating ownership of an opportunity to a third party that is best able to capture the opportunity or absorb the impact of the threat. See also *risk acceptance, risk avoidance, risk enhancement, risk escalation, risk exploiting, risk mitigation,* and *risk transference*.

risk threshold. The measure of acceptable variation around an objective that reflects the risk appetite of the organization and stakeholders. See also *risk appetite*.

risk transference. A risk response strategy that involves shifting the impact of a threat to a third party, together with ownership of the response. See also *risk acceptance, risk avoidance, risk enhancement, risk escalation, risk exploiting, risk mitigation,* and *risk sharing*.

roadmap. A high-level timeline that depicts such things as milestones, significant events, reviews, and decision points.

role. A defined function to be performed by a project team member, such as testing, filing, inspecting, or coding.

S-curve diagram. A graph that displays cumulative costs over a specified period of time.

schedule model. A representation of the plan for executing the project's activities including durations, dependencies, and other planning information, used to produce a project schedule along with other scheduling artifacts.

schedule performance index (SPI). A measure of schedule efficiency expressed as the ratio of earned value to planned value. See also *cost performance index (CPI)*.

schedule variance (SV). A measure of schedule performance expressed as the difference between the earned value and the planned value. See also *cost variance (CV)*.

scope. The sum of the products, services, and results to be provided as a project. See also *product scope* and *project scope*.

scope creep. The uncontrolled expansion to product or project scope without adjustments to time, cost, and resources.

self-organizing team. A cross-functional team in which people assume leadership as needed to achieve the team's objectives.

specification. An attribute that is necessary to be present in a project deliverable to help meet or exceed a target business objective.

sponsor. An individual or a group that provides resources and support for the portfolio, program, or project, and is accountable for enabling success. See also *stakeholder*.

sprint. A timeboxed interval within a project during which a usable and potentially releasable increment of a product is created. See also *iteration*.

stakeholder. An individual, group, or organization that may affect, be affected by, or perceive itself to be affected by a decision, activity, or outcome of a portfolio, program, or project. See also *sponsor*.

standard. A document established by an authority, custom, or general consent as a model or example.

statement of work (SOW). A narrative description of products, services, or results to be delivered by the project.

status meeting. A regularly scheduled meeting to exchange and analyze information about the current progress of the project and its performance.

steering committee. An advisory body of senior stakeholders who provide direction and support for the portfolio, program, or project team and make decisions outside of the team's authority.

story point. A unit used to estimate the relative level of effort needed to implement a user story.

strategic plan. A high-level document that explains an organization's vision and mission plus the approach that will be adopted to achieve this mission and vision, including the specific goals and objectives to be achieved during the period covered by the document.

swarm. A method in which multiple team members focus collectively on resolving a specific problem or task.

tacit knowledge. Personal knowledge that can be difficult to articulate and share such as beliefs, experience, and insights.

tailoring. The deliberate adaptation of approach, governance, and processes to make them more suitable for the given environment and the work at hand.

task board. A visual representation of the progress of the planned work that allows everyone to see the status of the tasks. See also *kanban board*.

technical performance measures. Quantifiable measures of technical performance that are used to ensure system components meet the technical requirements.

template. A partially complete document in a predefined format that provides a defined structure for collecting, organizing, and presenting information and data.

threat. A risk that would have a negative effect on one or more portfolio, program, or project objectives. See also *issue, opportunity,* and *risk*.

threshold. A predetermined value of a measurable project variable that represents a limit that requires action to be taken if it is reached.

throughput. The number of items passing through a process.

time and materials (T&M) contract. A type of contract that is a hybrid contractual arrangement containing aspects of both cost-reimbursable and fixed-price contracts.

timebox. A short, fixed period of time in which work is to be completed.

tolerance. The quantified description of acceptable variation for a quality requirement.

triple bottom line. A framework for considering the full cost of doing business by evaluating a company's bottom line from the perspective of profit, people, and the planet.

uncertainty. A lack of understanding and awareness of issues, events, path to follow, or solutions to pursue.

use case. An artifact for describing and exploring how a user interacts with a system to achieve a specific goal.

validation. The assurance that a product, service, or result meets the needs of the customer and other identified stakeholders. See also *verification*.

value. The excess of monetary and nonmonetary benefits over investment that is gained from achieving the goals of a portfolio, program, or project.

value delivery system. A collection of strategic business activities aimed at building, sustaining, and/or advancing an organization.

value proposition. The value of a product or service that an organization communicates to its customers.

vanity metric. A measure that appears to show some result but does not provide useful information for making decisions.

variance. A quantifiable deviation, departure, or divergence away from a known baseline or expected value.

variance at completion (VAC). A projection of the amount of budget deficit or surplus, expressed as the difference between the budget at completion and the estimate at completion. See also *budget at completion (BAC), cost variance (CV),* and *estimate at completion (EAC)*.

verification. The evaluation of whether or not a product, service, or result complies with a regulation, requirement, specification, or imposed condition. See also *validation*.

vision statement. A summarized, high-level description about the expectations for a product such as target market, users, major benefits, and what differentiates the product from others in the market.

volatility. The possibility for rapid and unpredictable change.

waste. Activities that consume resources and/or time without adding value.

wideband Delphi. An estimating method in which subject matter experts go through multiple rounds of producing estimates individually, with a team discussion after each round, until a consensus is achieved.

work package. The work defined at the lowest level of the work breakdown structure for which cost, effort, duration, and resources are estimated and managed.

Index

D

E

F

G

H

I

J

K

L

M

N

O

P

Q

R

S

T

U

V

W

Y

production capabilities, enabling the organizations involved—and their stakeholders—to maximize value while balancing competing constraints. Additionally, value delivery in today's environment extends beyond organizational objectives to also include societal impact and sustainability goals.

Business value is a net quantifiable benefit in any form of tangible or intangible elements that may contribute to the overall health and well-being of the organization during a project, at the end of the project, or in the long term. Figure 2-1 offers examples of such tangible and intangible elements.

The following are some examples of ways that projects meet or exceed expected value thresholds. Note that such value thresholds should always be considered in their investment context; that is, the expected value should meet or exceed a target threshold of return on project investments, whether that value is financial or nonfinancial or tangible or intangible, such as:

- Creating a new product, service, or result that meets the needs of customers or end users;
- Delivering the project within the performance baseline when the project's constraints baseline represents a high-value outcome;
- Contributing to community development, environmental sustainability, and ethical responsibility;
- Improving efficiency, productivity, effectiveness, responsiveness, or employee well-being;
- Enabling the changes needed to facilitate an organizational transition to its desired future state; and
- Sustaining benefits enabled by previous programs, projects, or business operations, and ensuring continuity of operations.

Tangible	Intangible
Monetary assets	Goodwill
Productivity	Brand recognition and trademarks
Profitability	Public benefit
Stockholder equity	Acquired knowledge
Market share	Compliance
Infrastructure capabilities	Reputation
Utility	Employee well-being
Environmental improvements	Environmental awareness

Figure 2-1. Examples of Business Value

- **Lead the Team.** The process of guiding, developing, and managing the team to enhance performance and achieve project goals through feedback, collaboration, conflict resolution, or escalation.
- **Monitor and Control Resourcing.** The process of ensuring that the physical or virtual resources assigned and allocated to the project are available as planned. This process also monitors the planned versus actual use of resources and performs corrective actions as necessary.

2.6.2.1 Plan Resource Management

The key benefit of this process is that it establishes the approach and level of management effort needed to manage project resources based on the type and complexity of the project (see Figure 2-41).

This process is performed once or at predefined points in the project. Resource planning is used to determine and identify an approach to ensuring that sufficient resources are available for the successful completion of the project. Effective resource planning should consider and plan for the availability of—or competition for—scarce resources.

The specific tools and techniques for the Plan Resource Management process include the responsibility assignment matrix, organizational theory, green human resource management, resource-based view, and SWOT (strengths, weaknesses, opportunities, threats) analysis.

Plan Resource Management

Inputs

- Project charter
- Project management plan
  - Quality management plan
  - Scope baseline
- Project documents
  - Project schedule
  - Requirements documentation
  - Risk register
  - Stakeholder register
- Enterprise environmental factors
- Organizational process assets
- Etc.

Tools & Techniques

- Expert judgment
- Data gathering
  - Interviews
- Data analysis
  - SWOT analysis
- Data representation
  - Hierarchical charts
  - Responsibility assignment matrix
  - Text-oriented formats
- Organizational theory
- Meetings
- Green human resource management
- Resource-based view
- Etc.

Outputs

- Project management plan updates
  - Resource management plan
- Team charter
- Project document updates
  - Assumption log
  - Risk register
- Etc.

Figure 2-41. Plan Resource Management Inputs, Tools and Techniques, and Outputs

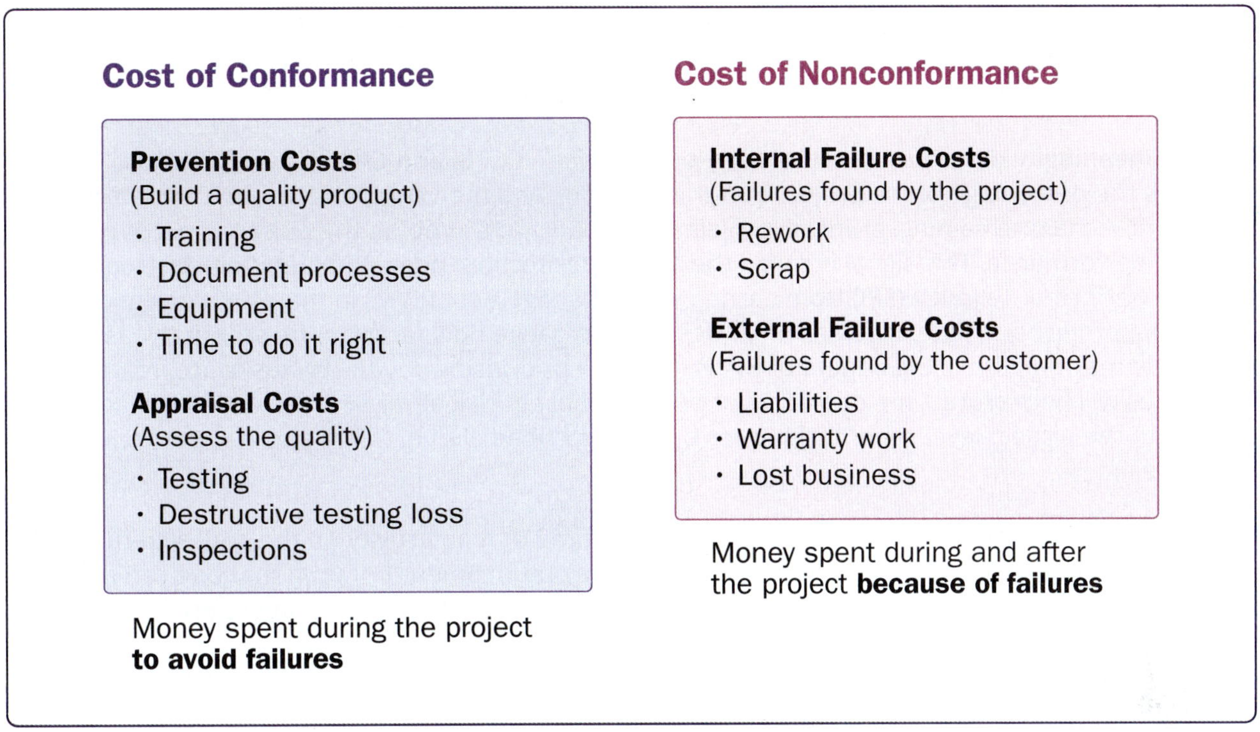

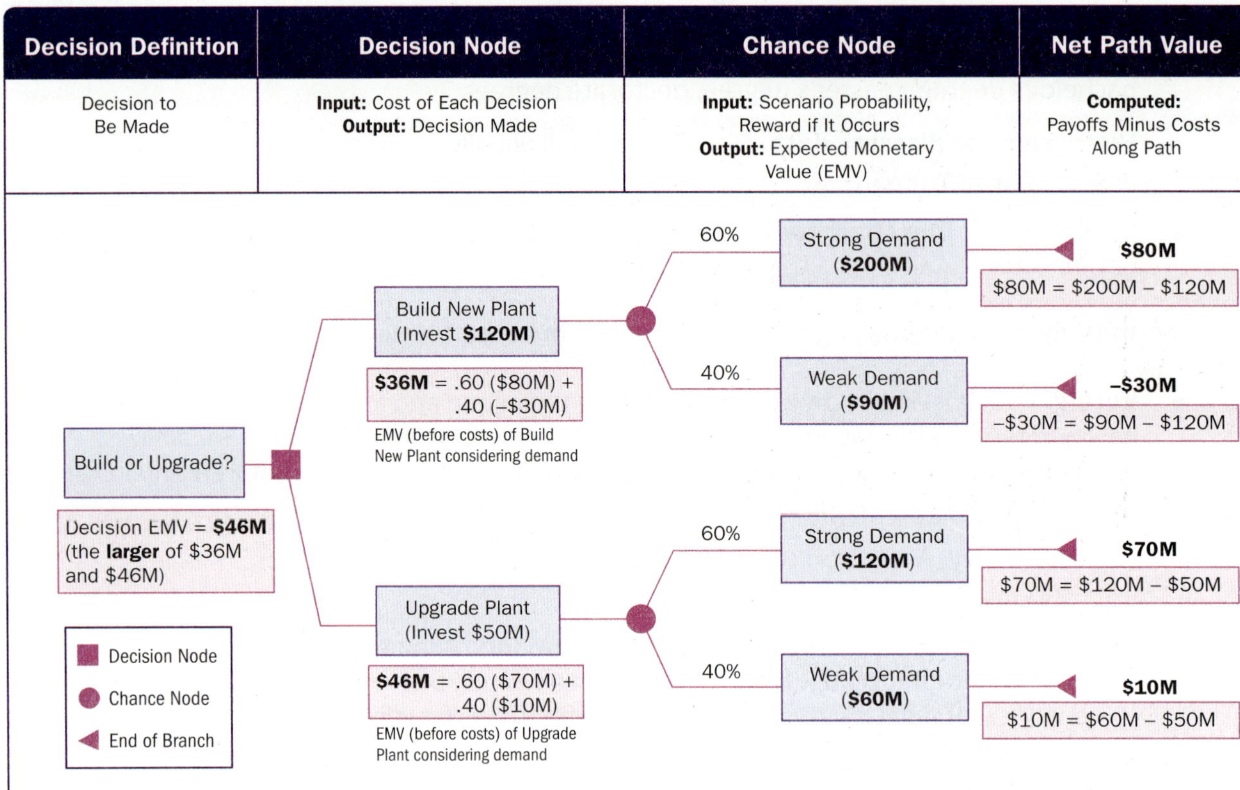

Note 1: All monetary values listed are in U.S. dollars.

Note 2: The decision tree shows how to make a decision between alternative capital strategies (represented as "decision nodes") when the environment contains uncertain elements (represented as "chance nodes").

Note 3: Here, a decision is being made whether to invest $120M to build a new plant or to instead invest only $50M to upgrade the existing plant. For each decision, the demand (which is uncertain, and therefore represents a "chance node") should be accounted for. For example, *strong* demand leads to $200M revenue with the new plant but only $120M for the upgraded plant, perhaps due to capacity limitations of the upgraded plant. The end of each branch shows the net effect of the payoffs minus costs. For each decision branch, all effects are added (see shaded areas) to determine the overall expected monetary value (EMV) of the decision. Remember to account for the investment costs. From the calculations in the shaded areas, the upgraded plant has a higher EMV of $46M—also the EMV of the overall decision. (This choice also represents the lowest risk, avoiding the worst-case possible outcome of a loss of $30M.)

Figure 5-5. Example Decision Tree

and complexity of the project. Decomposition of the total project work into work packages generally involves the following activities:

- Identifying and analyzing the deliverables and related work,
- Structuring and organizing the WBS,
- Decomposing the upper WBS levels into lower-level detailed components,
- Developing and assigning identification codes to the WBS components, and
- Verifying that the degree of decomposition of the deliverables is appropriate.

A portion of a WBS with some branches of the WBS decomposed down through the work package level is shown in Figure 5-6.

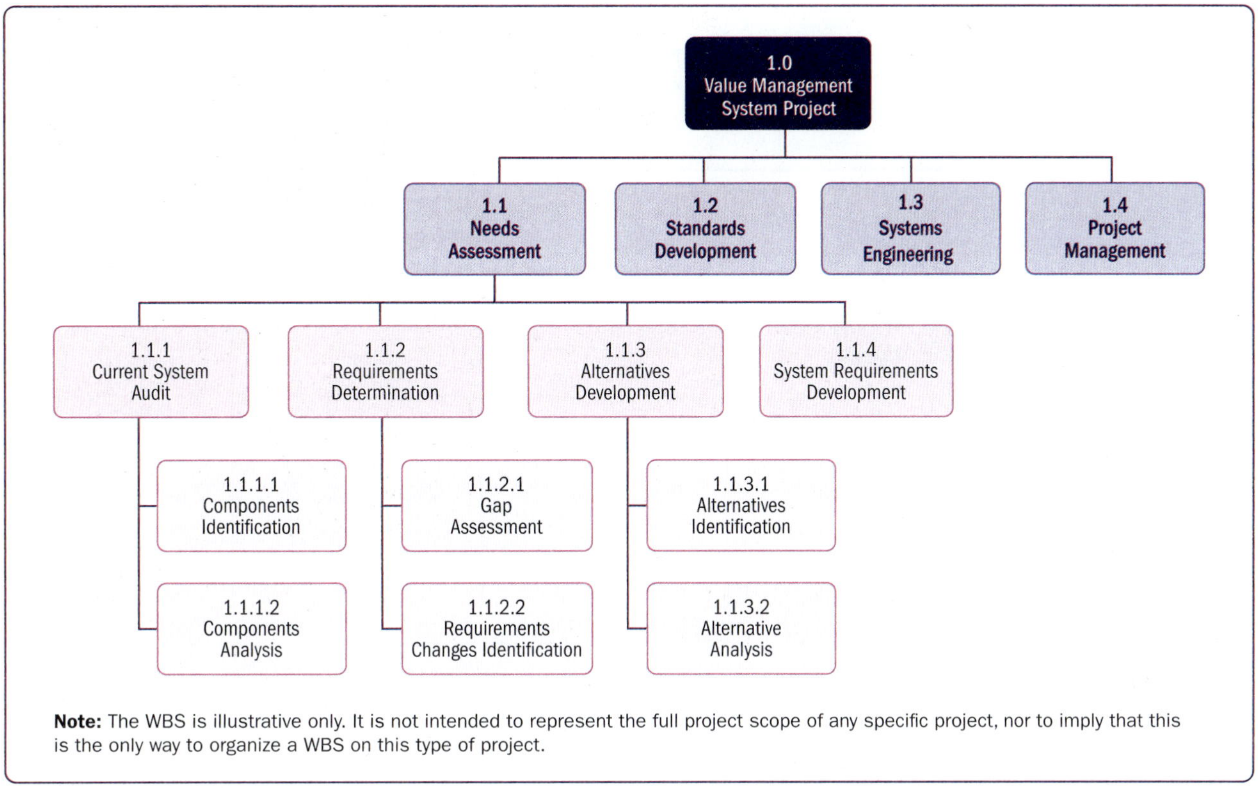

Index

A

B

C

D

E

F

G

H

J

K

L

M

N

O

P

Q

R

S

T

U

6.3 Connected Performance Domains

[illegible]

- Governance. [illegible]
- Schedule. [illegible]
- Schedule. [illegible]

[illegible]

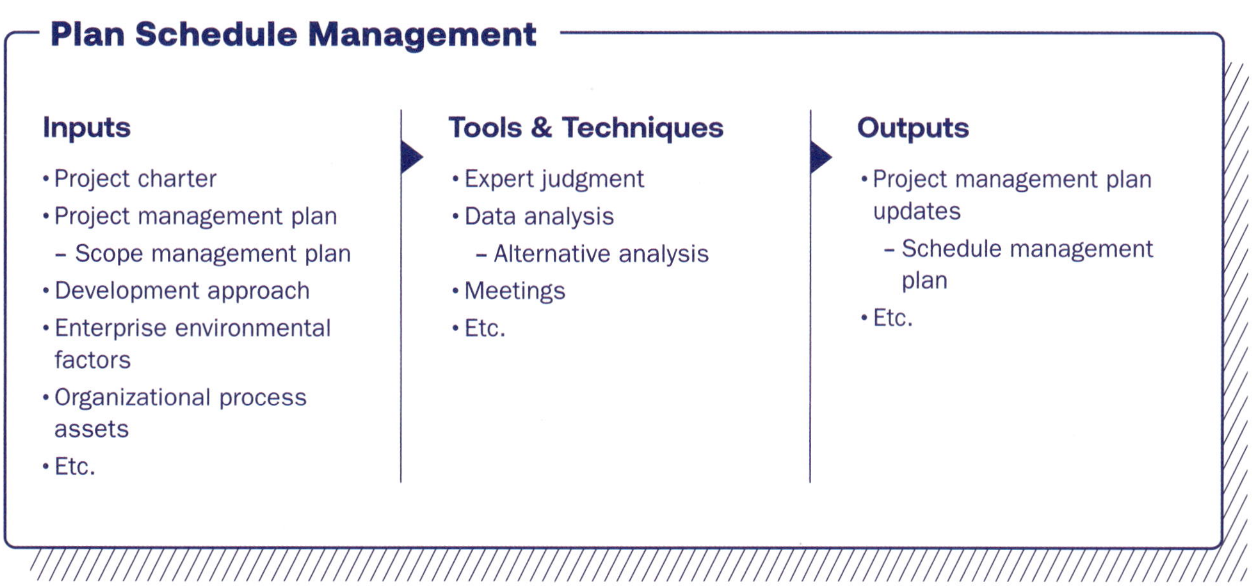

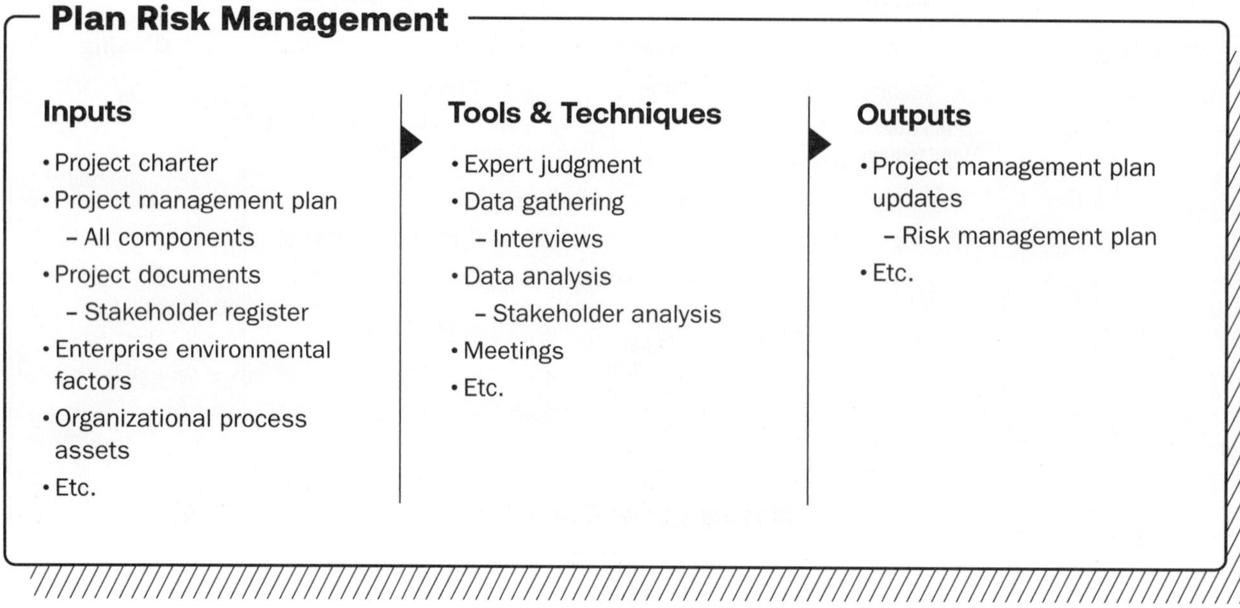

Project dashboards. A project dashboard is a set of charts and graphs showing progress or performance against important measures of the project. A common way of showing large quantities of information on metrics is a dashboard. Dashboards generally collect information electronically and generate charts that depict status. Often, dashboards offer high-level summaries of data and allow drill-down analysis into contributing data. Figure 5-16 and Figure 5-17 each provide examples of a dashboard.

Dashboards often include information displayed as stoplight charts (also known as red–amber–green [RAG] charts), bar charts, pie charts, and control charts. A text explanation can be used for any measures that are outside the established thresholds.

Organization Project Name					
Project Name and High-Level Description					
Exec Sponsor:			Project Manager:		
Start Date:		End Date:		Report Period:	
Status:	Schedule	Resources	Budget		

Key Activities	Recent Accomplishments	Upcoming Key Deliverables	Status
Activity #1			Concern
Activity #2			On Track
Activity #3			Issue

On Track	Complete	Concern	Issue	On Hold	Canceled	Not Started

Current Key Risks – Threats and opportunities; Mitigation	Current Key Issues – Description

Figure 5-16. Project Dashboard Example 1

B

C

D

E

F

G

H

I

J

K

L

M

N

O

P

S

T

U

V

W

Y

E

F

G

H

I

L

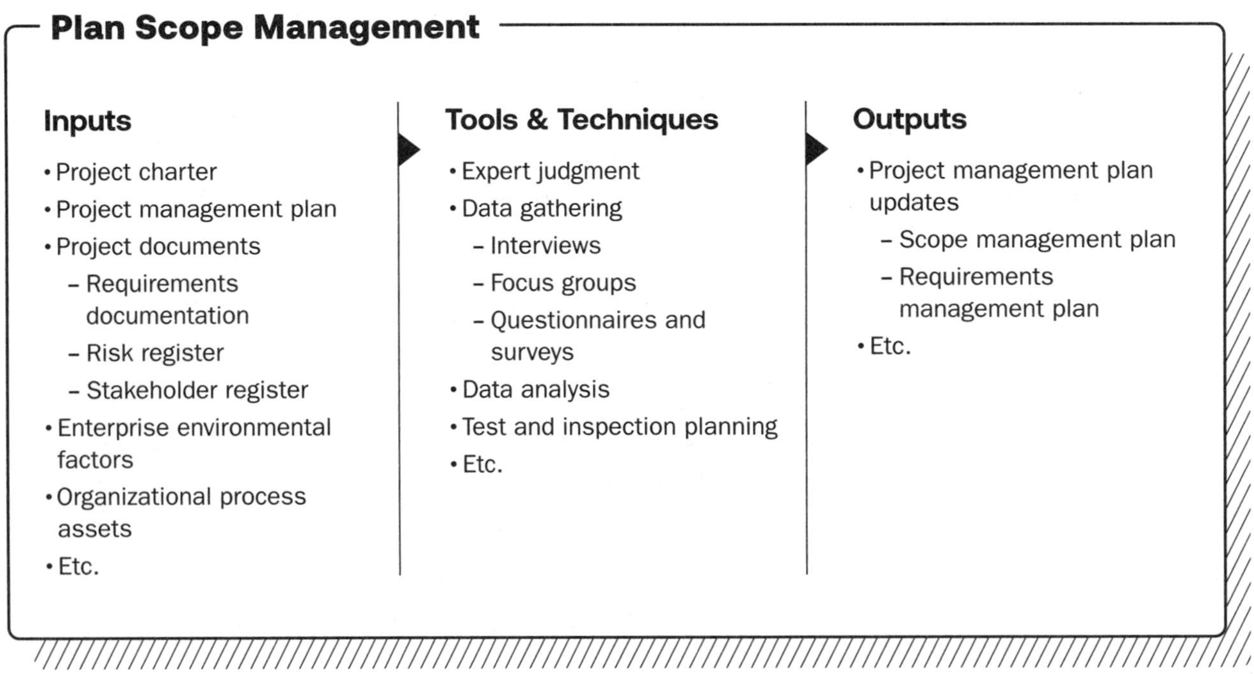

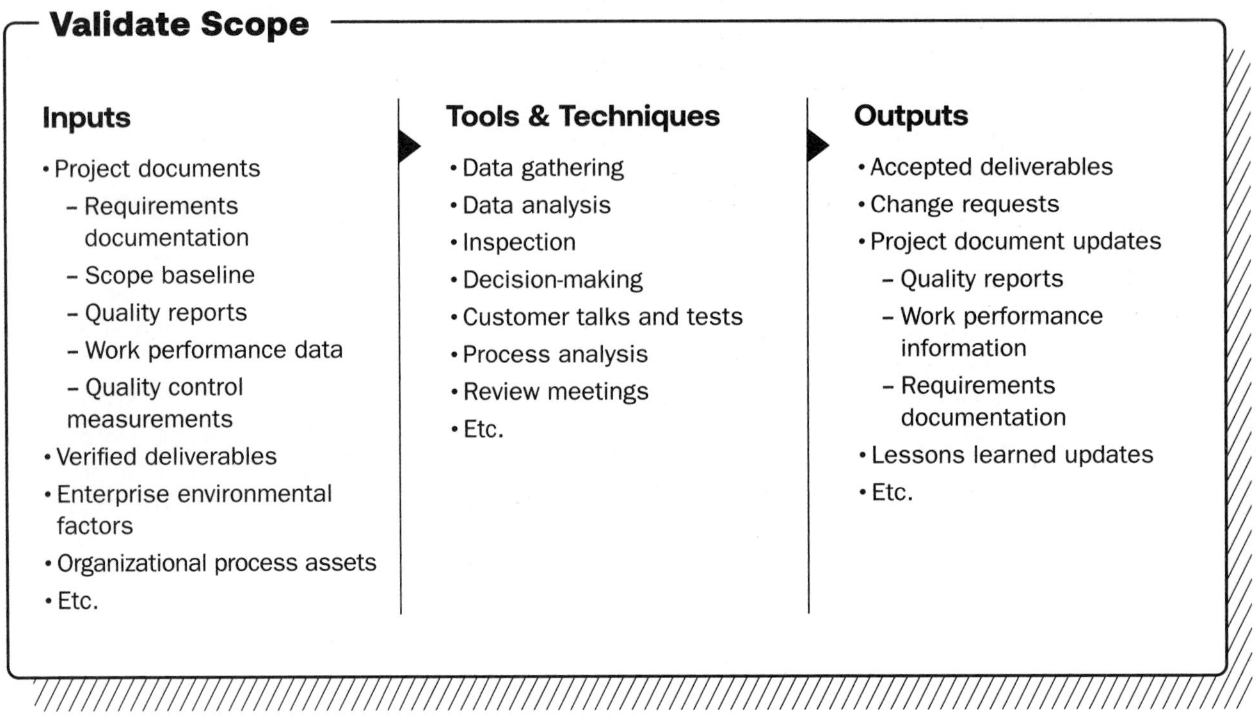

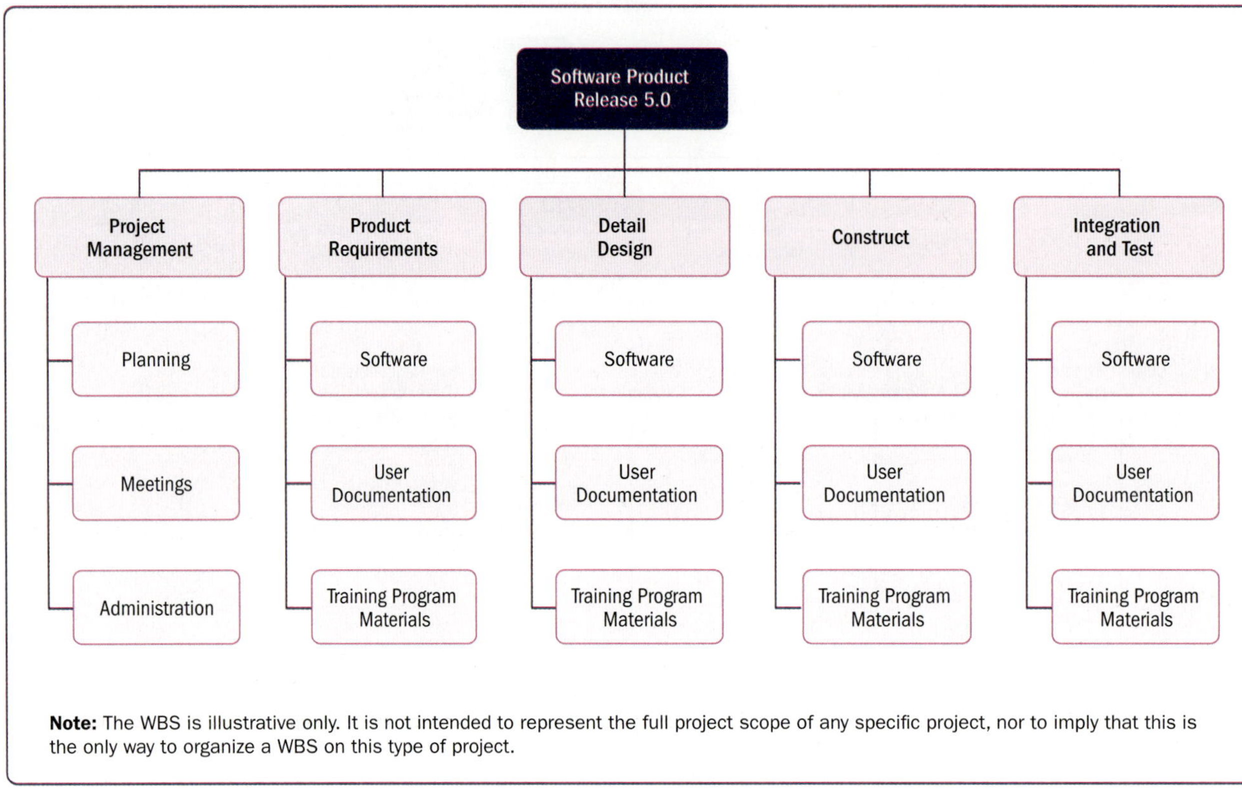

B

C

D

G

H

I

N

O

P

Q

R

S

T

U

V

W

Y

M

N

O

P

Decision Definition	Decision Node	Chance Node	Net Path Value
Decision to Be Made	**Input:** Cost of Each Decision **Output:** Decision Made	**Input:** Scenario Probability, Reward if It Occurs **Output:** Expected Monetary Value (EMV)	**Computed:** Payoffs Minus Costs Along Path

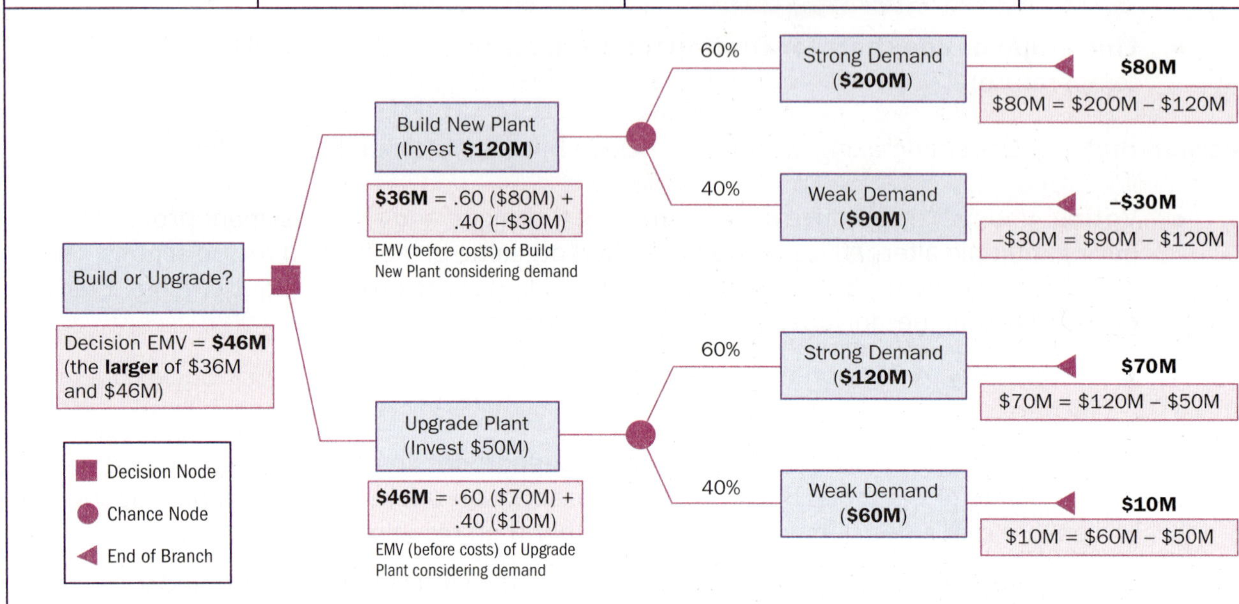

Note 1: All monetary values listed are in U.S. dollars.

Note 2: The decision tree shows how to make a decision between alternative capital strategies (represented as "decision nodes") when the environment contains uncertain elements (represented as "chance nodes").

Note 3: Here, a decision is being made whether to invest $120M to build a new plant or to instead invest only $50M to upgrade the existing plant. For each decision, the demand (which is uncertain, and therefore represents a "chance node") should be accounted for. For example, *strong* demand leads to $200M revenue with the new plant but only $120M for the upgraded plant, perhaps due to capacity limitations of the upgraded plant. The end of each branch shows the net effect of the payoffs minus costs. For each decision branch, all effects are added (see shaded areas) to determine the overall expected monetary value (EMV) of the decision. Remember to account for the investment costs. From the calculations in the shaded areas, the upgraded plant has a higher EMV of $46M—also the EMV of the overall decision. (This choice also represents the lowest risk, avoiding the worst-case possible outcome of a loss of $30M.)

Figure 5-5. Example Decision Tree

and complexity of the project. Decomposition of the total project work into work packages generally involves the following activities:

- Identifying and analyzing the deliverables and related work,
- Structuring and organizing the WBS,
- Decomposing the upper WBS levels into lower-level detailed components,
- Developing and assigning identification codes to the WBS components, and
- Verifying that the degree of decomposition of the deliverables is appropriate.

A portion of a WBS with some branches of the WBS decomposed down through the work package level is shown in Figure 5-6.

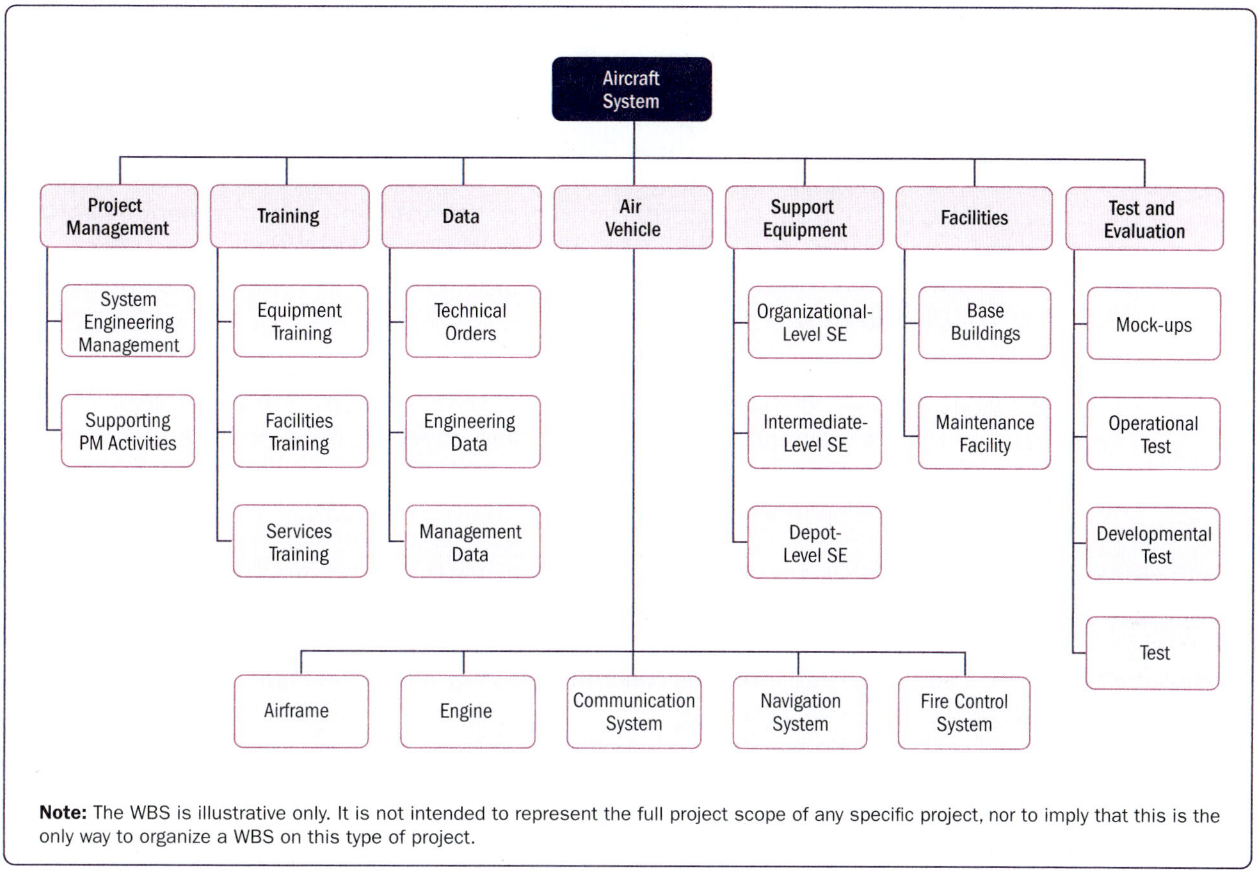

D

G

H

I

J

K

L

M

N

O

P

Q

R

S

T

U

V

W

Y

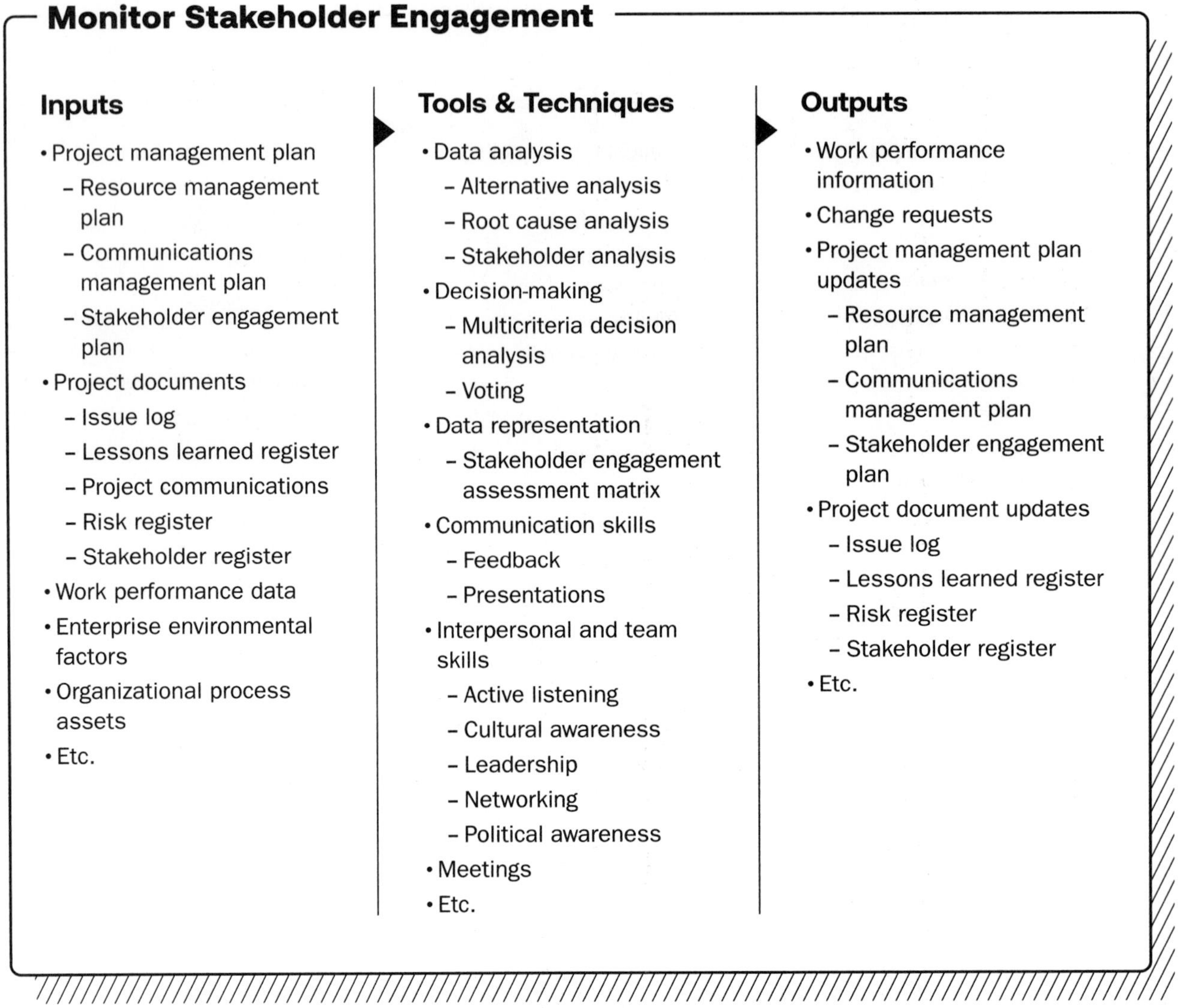

D

I

J

K

L

M

N

O

P

Q

R

S

T

U

V

W

Y

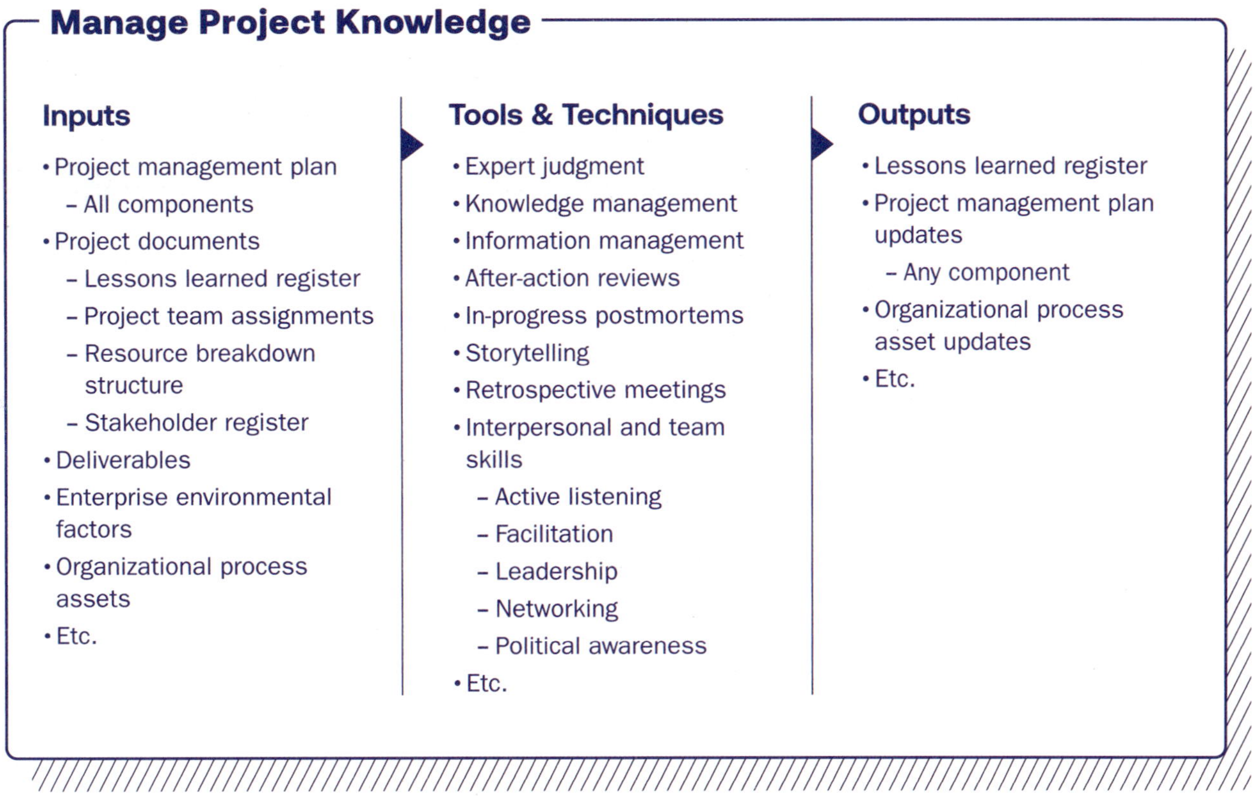

Theory of constraints (TOC). Theory of constraints is a body of knowledge focused on improving the system-level performance of an organization, end-to-end process, project portfolio, or project. The TOC application to a project or project portfolio is critical chain project management (CCPM). See also *critical chain project management* and *continuous improvement.*

To-complete performance index (TCPI). The to-complete performance index (TCPI) is a measure of the cost performance that should be achieved with the remaining resources in order to meet a specified management goal, expressed as the ratio of the cost to finish the outstanding work to the remaining budget. The TCPI is the calculated cost performance index that is achieved on the remaining work to meet a specified management goal such as the budget at completion (BAC) or estimate at completion (EAC). If it becomes obvious that the BAC is no longer viable, the project manager should consider the forecasted EAC. Once approved, the EAC may replace the BAC in the TCPI calculation. The equation for TCPI is: (BAC − EV) / (BAC − AC) where: BAC = budget at completion, EV = earned value, and AC = actual cost.

The TCPI is conceptually displayed in Figure 5-24. The equation for the TCPI is shown in the lower-left corner as the work remaining (defined as the BAC minus the EV) divided by the funds remaining (which can be either the BAC minus the AC, or the EAC minus the AC).

If the cumulative CPI falls below the baseline (as shown in Figure 5-24), all future work of the project should be performed immediately in the range of the TCPI (BAC) (as reflected in the top line of Figure 5-24) to stay within the authorized BAC. Whether this level of performance is achievable is a judgment call based on several considerations, including risk, time remaining in the project, and technical performance. Such a level of performance is displayed as the TCPI (EAC) line. The equation for the TCPI is based on the EAC: (BAC − EV) / (EAC − AC). The EVM formulas are provided in Table 5-1.

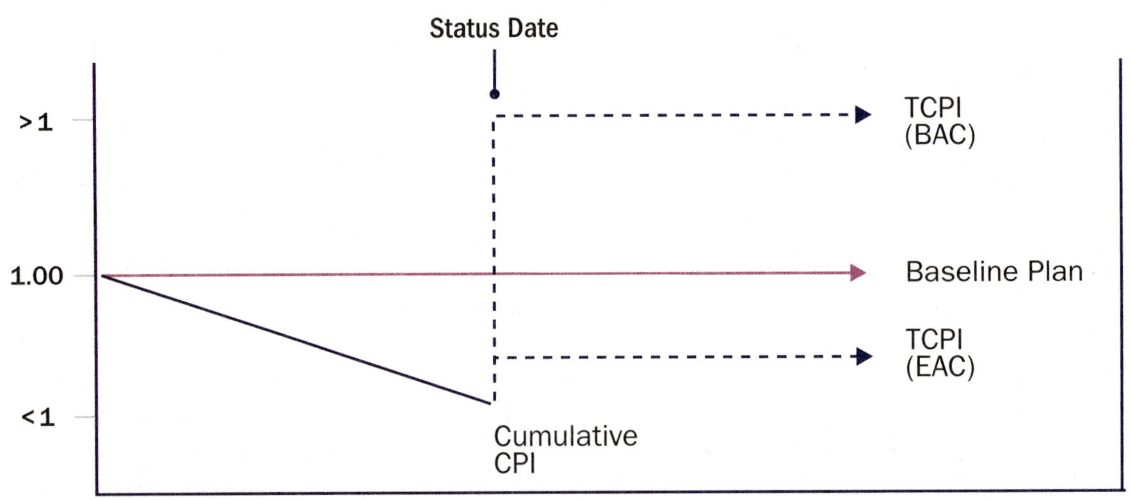

Formula:

$$\frac{\text{Work Remaining (BAC − EV)}}{\text{Funds Remaining (BAC − AC) or (EAC − AC)}} = \text{TCPI}$$

Figure 5-24. To-Complete Performance Index (TCPI)

B

C

D

E

F

G

H

I

J

K

L

M

N

O

P

Q

R

S

T

U

V

W

Y

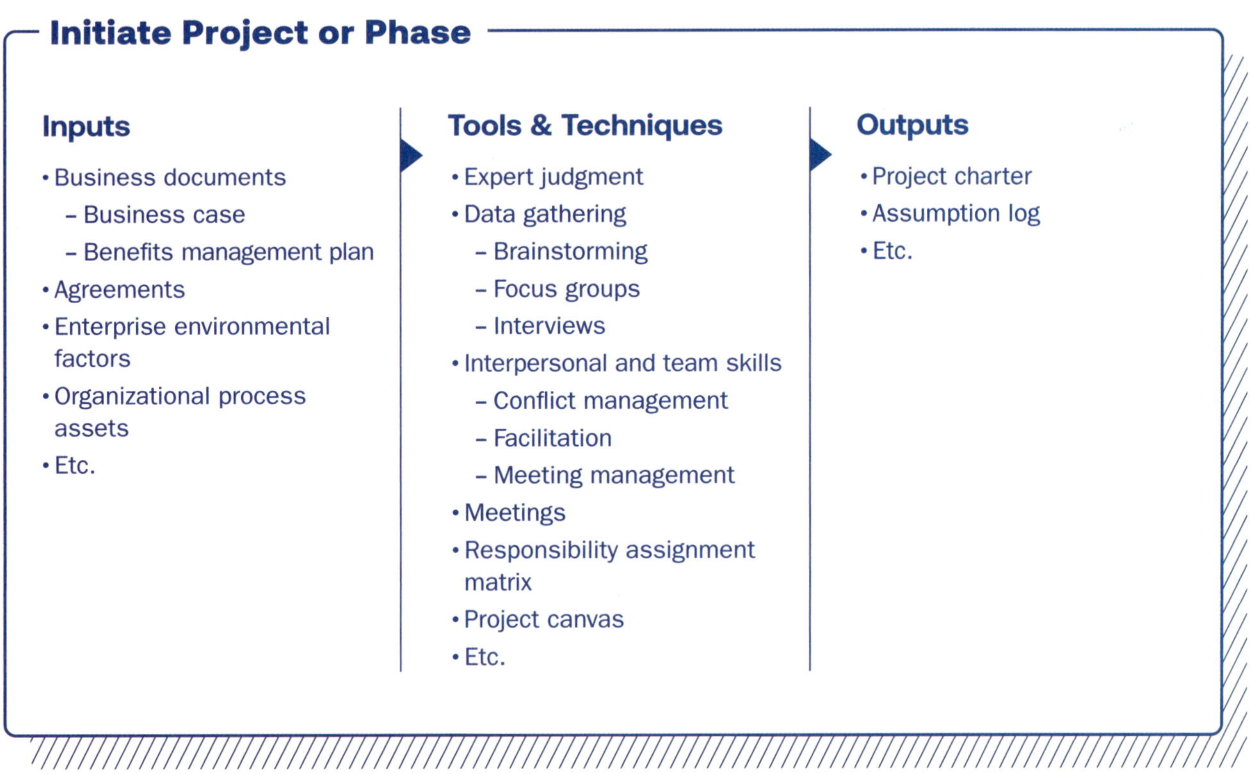

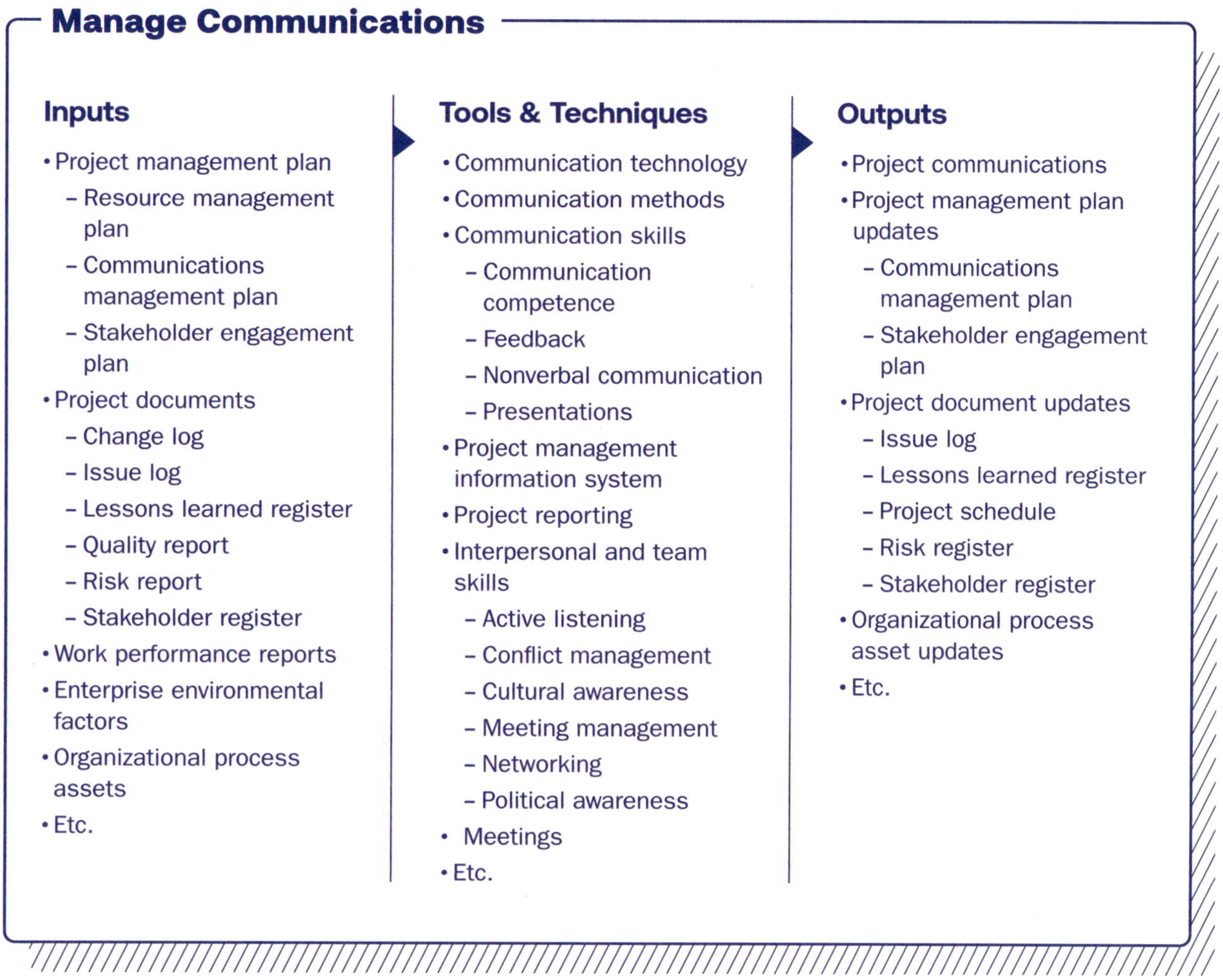

B

C

D

E

F

G

H

I

J

K

L

M

N

O

P

Q

R

S

T

U

V

W

Y

Burndown Chart

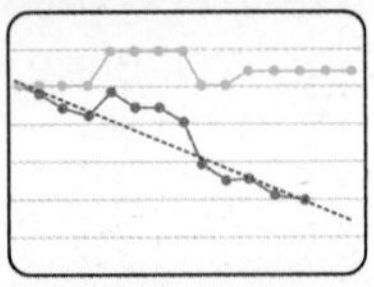

Shows how much work is yet to be completed

Burnup Chart

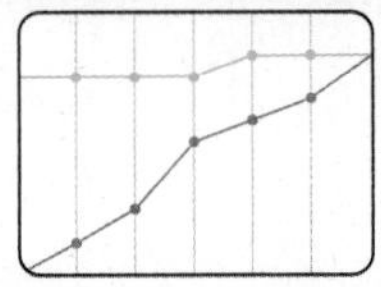

Shows how much work has been completed

Combined Burn Chart

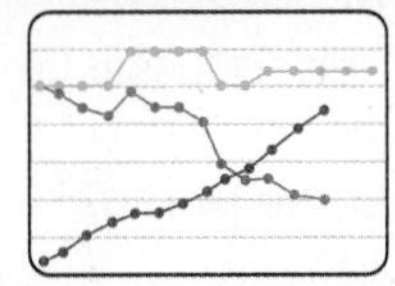

Shows how much work has been completed and how much remains

Reference	Risk Description	Date	Likelihood	Impact	Risk Rating	Response	Owner
1	The main supplier cannot deliver on time because of other commercial commitments	03/21	Likely	High	**High**	Include financial penalties in contract; build contingency into the schedule; monitor contractor performance	Annie
2	The lead time for the leased line exceeds 90 days	03/21	Unlikely	Medium	**Medium**	Order leased line earlier than necessary; incur additional rental fees	Jim
3	Release of the new system is delayed because user acceptance testing commences after the planned start	03/21	Very likely	High	**High**	Employ temporary staff to free up resources for testing; revise project schedule	Mark
4	There is insufficient capacity to create additional database instances for data migration and testing	04/18	Very unlikely	Medium	**Low**	Prioritize projects; temporarily remove alternative development instance	Jim

Risk Log

Figure 5-9. Information Radiator

In-progress postmortems. An in-progress postmortem is a structured process conducted at various stages of the project life cycle to analyze current performance, identify issues, and implement improvements. Unlike traditional postmortems held at the end of a project, these reviews are conducted periodically to ensure continuous improvement and timely problem-solving.

Inspections. An inspection is the examination of a work product to determine if it conforms to documented standards. The results of inspections generally include measurements and may be conducted at any level. The results of a single activity can be inspected or the final product of the project can be inspected. Inspections may be called reviews, peer reviews, audits, or walkthroughs. In some application areas, these terms have narrow and specific meanings. Inspections also are used to verify defect repairs.

Integrated change control. Integrated change control helps ensure that changes to the project are managed in a coordinated and controlled manner. By evaluating change requests, conducting impact analyses, making informed decisions, and documenting and communicating changes, the project can maintain alignment with its objectives and constraints, ultimately contributing to project success.

Interpersonal and team skills. Interpersonal skills that are used frequently in projects include emotional intelligence, decision-making, facilitation, and conflict management and resolution, among others. (See *emotional intelligence; decision-making; conflict management.*) As for team management, this effort entails applying knowledge, skills, tools, and techniques for management activities as well

D

G

H

I

J

K

L

M

N

O

P

Q

R

S

T

U

V

W

Y

M

N

O

P

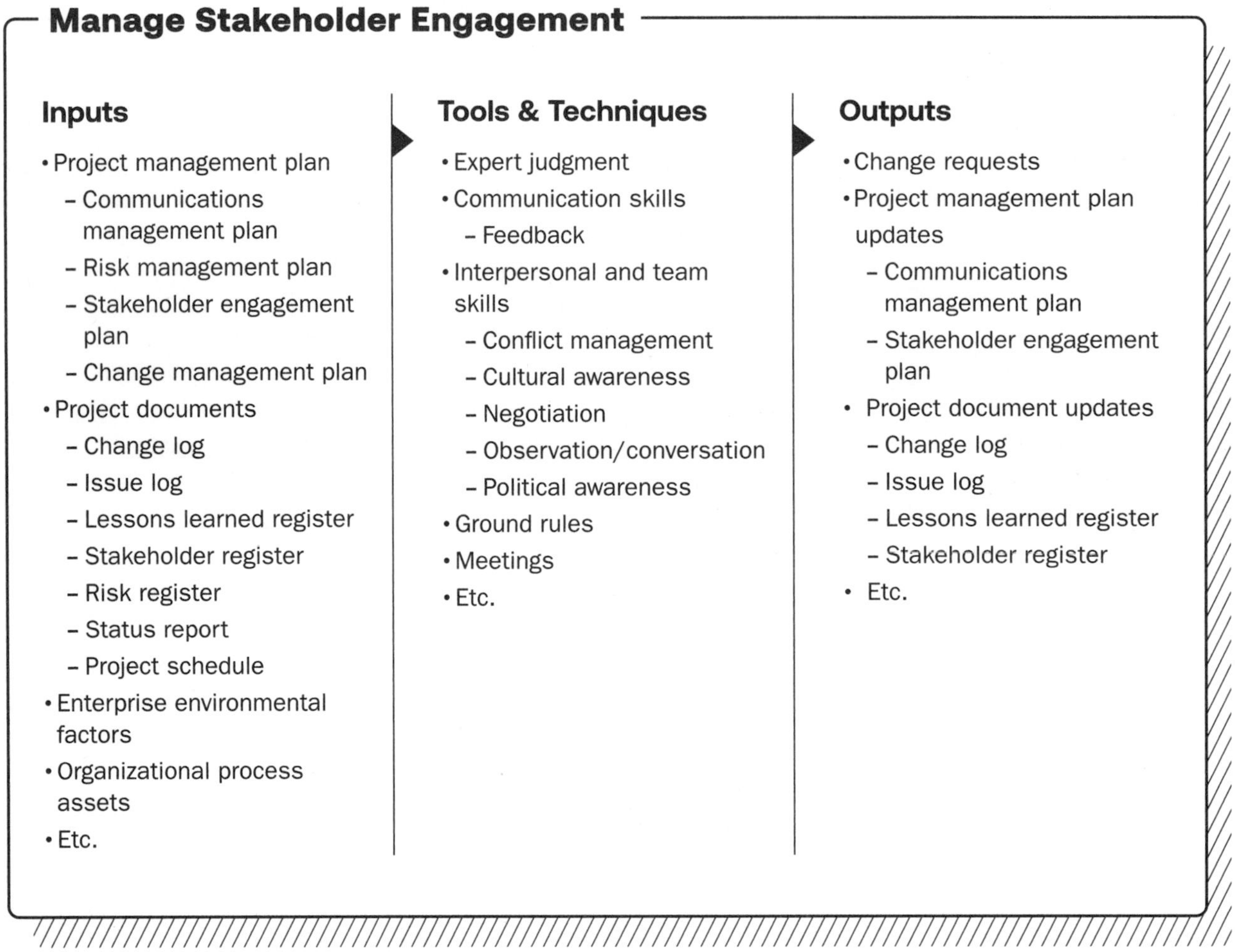

D

E

F

G

H

I

J

K

L

M

N

O

P

Q

R

S

T

U

V

W

Y